1 MONTH OF
FREE
READING

at

www.ForgottenBooks.com

By purchasing this book you are
eligible for one month membership to
ForgottenBooks.com, giving you
unlimited access to our entire
collection of over 1,000,000 titles via
our web site and mobile apps.

To claim your free month visit:

www.forgottenbooks.com/free917210

ISBN 978-0-266-96937-2
PIBN 10917210

Bryn Mawr College Calendar

Undergraduate Courses

Issue for the Session of 1976-77

August 1976, Volume LXIX, Number 3

Bryn Maur College Calendar. Published December, July, August, and September by Bryn Mawr College, Bryn Mawr, Pennsylvania 19010.

Second Class Postage paid at Bryn Maur, Pennsylvania.

Contents

PAGE

Academic Schedule 3
The Trustees, Directors, and Committees of the Board 5
The Faculty and Staff 6
Introduction 21
Admission 26
    Freshman Class 29
    Transfer and Foreign Students 29
    Readmission 31
    Leaves of Absence 31
Academic Facilities and Residence 33
Tuition and Residence Fees 38
General Information 41
    Student Advising 41
    Academic Standards and Regulations 41
    Health 42
Curriculum 44
    Premedical Preparation 48
    Preparation to Teach 49
    Coordination in the Sciences 49
    Credit for Creative Work in the Arts 50
    Language Houses 50
    Summer Institutes Abroad 50
    Junior Year Abroad 51
Employment and Vocational Counseling 53
Courses of Study 55
    Departmental Courses 56
    Interdepartmental Work 147
    Performing Arts 158
    Physical Education 158
Financial Aid 161
    Scholarship Funds 163
    Prizes and Academic Awards 180
    Scholarships for Medical Study 184
Loan Funds 185
Alumnae Representatives 188
Index 194

Visitors to the College are welcome and when the College is in session student guides are available to show visitors the campus. Appointments for interviews and for campus tours should be made in advance by letter or by telephone. The College offices are open Monday through Friday from nine until five and on Saturdays from nine until one when the College is in session.

Correspondence

The Post Office address is Bryn Mawr College, Bryn Mawr, Pennsylvania 19010. Telephone: 215 LA5-1000.

Correspondence about the following subjects should be addressed to:

The President
General interests of the College

The Dean
Academic work, personal welfare, and health of the students

The Director of Admissions
Admission to the Undergraduate College and entrance scholarships

The Dean of The Graduate School of Arts and Sciences
Admission and graduate scholarships

The Dean of The Graduate School of Social Work and Social Research
Admission and graduate scholarships

The Director of Halls
Rooms in the halls of residence

The Comptroller
Payment of bills

The Director of the Career Planning Office
Recommendations for positions and inquiries about students' self-help

The Alumnae Association
Regional scholarships and loan fund

Academic Schedule 1976-77

1976		*First Semester*
September	3	Halls of residence open to Freshman Week Committee
September	4	Halls of residence open to entering class at 8 a.m. Registration of entering undergraduate students
September	6-11	Deferred examinations
September	7	Halls of residence open to returning undergraduates at 8 a.m. Registration of returning students
September	9	Work of the 92nd academic year begins at 9 a.m.
September	13	French examinations for undergraduates
September	14	German examinations for undergraduates
September	15	Hebrew, Italian, and Spanish examinations for undergraduates
September	16	Greek, Latin, Mathematics, and Russian examinations for undergraduates
October	22	Fall vacation begins after last class
October	27	Fall vacation ends at 9 a.m.
November	24	Thanksgiving holiday begins after last class
November	29	Thanksgiving holiday ends at 9 a.m.
December	14	Last day of semester I classes
December	15-16	Review period
December	16	Written work due
December	17-22	College examinations for semester I
December	22	Winter vacation begins

1977		*Second Semester*
January	17	Work of the second semester begins at 9 a.m.
January	28-29	Deferred examinations
March	11	Spring vacation begins after last class
March	21	Spring vacation ends at 9 a.m.
March	26	Parents' Day
April	15-17	Geology field trip
April	18	French and German examinations for undergraduates
April	19	Greek, Hebrew, and Latin examinations for under-graduates
April	20	Italian and Spanish examinations for undergraduates
April	21	Mathematics and Russion examinations for under-graduates
April	29	Last day of semester II classes
April 30-May 3		Review period
May	3	Written work due
May	4-13	College examinations for semester II
May	16	Conferring of degrees and close of the 92nd academic year
May	20-22	Alumnae Weekend

Bryn Mawr College Faculty and Staff

For the Academic Year, 1976-77

Harris Llewellyn Wofford, Jr., A.B. (University of Chicago), J.D. (Howard University and Yale University), *President of the College*

Mary Patterson McPherson, PH.D. (Bryn Mawr College), LL.D. *Dean of the College*

Phyllis Pray Bober, PH.D. (New York University), *Dean of The Graduate School of Arts and Sciences*

Bernard Ross, PH.D. (University of Michigan), *Dean of The Graduate School of Social Work and Social Research*

Anne Lee Delano, M.A. (Columbia University), *Director of Physical Education*

James Tanis, TH.D. (University of Utrecht), *Director of Libraries* [1]

Elizabeth G. Vermey, M.A. (Wesleyan University), *Director of Admissions*

Frieda W. Woodruff, M.D. (University of Pennsylvania), *College Physician*

Emeriti

Eleanor A. Bliss, SC.D (Johns Hopkins University), *Dean Emeritus*

Rhys Carpenter, PH.D. (Columbia University), LITT.D., *Professor Emeritus of Classical Archaeology*

Rachel Dunaway Cox, PH.D. (University of Pennsylvania), *Professor Emeritus of Education and Psychology*

Frances de Graaff, PH.D. (University of Leyden), *Professor Emeritus of Russian*

Frederica de Laguna, PH.D. (Columbia University), *Professor Emeritus of Anthropology*

Grace Mead Andrus de Laguna, PH.D. (Cornell University), *Professor Emeritus of Philosophy*

Max Diez, PH.D. (University of Texas), *Professor Emeritus of German Literature*

Lincoln Dryden, PH.D. (Johns Hopkins University), *Professor Emeritus of Geology*

Grace Frank, A.B. (University of Chicago), *Professor Emeritus of Old French*

Mary Summerfield Gardiner, PH.D. (Bryn Mawr College), *Professor Emeritus of Biology*

Joshua C. Hubbard, PH.D. (Harvard University), *Professor Emeritus of Economics*

Myra Richards Jessen, PH.D. (Bryn Mawr College), *Professor Emeritus of German*

Richmond Lattimore, PH.D. (University of Illinois), LITT.D., *Professor Emeritus of Greek*

Marguerite Lehr, PH.D. (Bryn Mawr College), *Professor Emeritus of Mathematics*

Angeline H. Lograsso, PH.D. (Radcliffe College), *Professor Emeritus of Italian*

Katherine D. K. Lower, PH.D. (University of Wisconsin), *Professor Emeritus of Social Work and Social Research*

Helen Taft Manning, PH.D. (Yale University), *Professor Emeritus of History*

Fritz Mezger, PH.D. (University of Berlin), *Professor Emeritus of Germanic Philology*

Agnes Kirsopp Michels, PH.D. (Bryn Mawr College), *Professor Emeritus of Latin*

Milton Charles Nahm, B.LITT. (Oxford University), PH.D. (University of Pennsylvania), *Professor Emeritus of Philosophy*

Caroline Robbins, PH.D. (University of London), LL.D., LITT.D., *Professor Emeritus of History*

Arthur Colby Sprague, PH.D. (Harvard University), *Professor Emeritus of English Literature*

Roger Hewes Wells, PH.D. (Harvard University), *Professor Emeritus of Political Science*

Mary Katharine Woodworth, PH.D. (Bryn Mawr College), *Professor Emeritus of English*

Dorothy Wyckoff, PH.D. (Bryn Mawr College), *Professor Emeritus of Geology*

The notations through this section refer to the following:
[1]On sabbatical leave, 1976-77.
[2]On leave of absence, 1976-77.
[3]On sabbatical leave, semester I.
[4]On leave of absence, semester I.
[5]On sabbatical leave, semester II.
[6]On leave of absence, semester II.
[7]On leave of absence, with Junior Faculty Research Award, 1976-77.
[8]On leave of absence, semester I and on sabbatical leave, semester II.

Professors

Gertrude C. K. Leighton, A.B. (Bryn Mawr College), J.D. (Yale University), *Professor of Political Science* and *Secretary of the General Faculty*

Philip Lichtenberg, PH.D. (Western Reserve University), *Professor of Social Work and Social Research* and *Secretary of the Faculty of Social Work and Social Research*

Jay Martin Anderson, PH.D. (Harvard University), *Professor of Chemistry*

Hans Bänziger, PH.D. (University of Zürich), *Professor of German*

Ernst Berliner, PH.D. (Harvard University), *W. Alton Jones Professor of Chemistry*

Shirley Neilson Blum, PH.D. (University of California at Los Angeles) *Visiting Professor in History of Art*

Phillis Pray Bober, PH.D. (New York University), *Professor of Classical and Near Eastern Archaeology* and of *History of Art* and *Dean of The Graduate School of Arts and Sciences*

Charles M. Brand, PH.D. (Harvard University), *Professor of History*

Robert B. Burlin, PH.D. (Yale University), *Professor of English*

Robert H. Butman, M.A. (University of North Carolina), *Professor of English and the Performing Arts on the Theresa Helburn Fund* and *Director of the Theatre, on joint appointment with Haverford College*

Isabelle Cazeaux, PH.D. (Columbia University), *Professor of Music*

Robert L. Conner, PH.D. (Indiana University), *Professor of Biology*

Frederic Cunningham, Jr. PH.D. (Harvard University), *Professor of Mathematics*

Gérard Defaux, *D. ès L.* (Sorbonne), *Professor of French*

Charles G. Dempsey, M.F.A., PH.D. (Princeton University), *Professor of History of Art*

Richard B. Du Boff, PH.D. (University of Pennsylvania), *Professor of Economics*

Arthur P. Dudden, PH.D. (University of Michigan), *Professor of History*

Mary Maples Dunn, PH.D. (Bryn Mawr College), *Professor of History*

José María Ferrater Mora, *Licenciado en Filosofía* (University of Barcelona), *Professor of Philosophy* and *Fairbank Professor in the Humanities*[2]

Elizabeth Read Foster, PH.D. (Yale University), *Professor of History*

Richard C. Gonzalez, PH.D. (University of Maryland), *Professor of Psychology*

Joaquín González Muela, *D.en Fil.* (University of Madrid), *Professor of Spanish*

Jane C. Goodale, PH.D. (University of Pennsylvania), *Professor of Anthropology*

Robert L. Goodale, A.B., B.MUS. (Yale University), A.A.G.O. *Alice Carter Dickerman Professor of Music*

Michel Guggenheim, PH.D. (Yale University), *Professor of French*

Howard S. Hoffman, PH.D. (University of Connecticut), *Professor of Psychology*[5]

Janet L. Hoopes, PH.D. (Bryn Mawr College), *Professor of Education and Child Development* and *Director of the Child Study Institute*

Rosalie C. Hoyt, PH.D. (Bryn Mawr College), *Marion Reilly Professor of Physics*

Agi Jambor, M.A. (Royal Academy of Budapest), *Professor of Music*

Fritz Janschka, Akad. Maler (Akademie der Bildenden Kunste, Vienna), *Professor of Fine Art*[5]

Pauline Jones, PH.D. (Bryn Mawr College), *Professor of French*[5]

Howard C. Kee, PH.D. (Yale University), *Rufus Jones Professor of History of Religion*

Melville T. Kennedy, Jr., PH.D. (Harvard University), *Professor of Political Science*

Willard Fahrenkamp King, PH.D. (Brown University), *Dorothy Nepper Marshall Professor of Hispanic and Hispanic-American Studies*

George L. Kline, PH.D. (Columbia University), *Professor of Philosophy*

Barbara M. Lane, PH.D. (Harvard University), *Professor of History* and *Director of the interdepartmental major in The Growth and Structure of Cities*

Mabel Louise Lang, PH.D. (Bryn Mawr College), LITT.D., *Paul Shorey Professor of Greek*[8]

Frank B. Mallory, PH.D. (California Institute of Technology), *Professor of Chemistry*

Mario Maurin, PH.D. (Yale University), *Professor of French*

Ethel W. Maw, PH.D. (University of Pennsylvania), *Professor of Education and Child Development*

Machteld J. Mellink, PH.D. (University of Utrecht), *Leslie Clark Professor of Humanities* and *Professor of Classical and Near Eastern Archaeology*

Charles Mitchell, M.A., B.LITT. (Oxford University), LITT.D., *Professor of History of Art* and *Andrew W. Mellon Professor in the Humanities*

Jane M. Oppenheimer, PH.D. (Yale University), *William R. Kenan, Jr. Professor of History of Science*

John C. Oxtoby, M.A. (University of California), *Class of 1897 Professor of Mathematics*

Kyle M. Phillips, Jr., PH.D. (Princeton University), *Professor of Classical and Near Eastern Archaeology*[1]

Jean A. Potter, PH.D. (Yale University), *Professor of Philosophy*

John R. Pruett, PH.D. (Indiana University), *Professor of Physics*

Martin Rein, PH.D. (Brandeis University), *Visiting Professor of Social Work and Social Research*

Brunilde Sismondo Ridgway, PH.D. (Bryn Mawr College), *Professor of Classical and Near Eastern Archaeology*

Bernard Ross, PH.D. (University of Michigan), *Dean of The Graduate School of Social Work and Social Research* and *Professor of Social Work and Social Research*

J. H. M. Salmon, M.LITT. (Cambridge University), LIT.D. (Victoria University), *Marjorie Walter Goodhart Professor of History*

Eugene V. Schneider, PH.D. (Harvard University), *Professor of Sociology*

Alain Silvera, PH.D. (Harvard University), *Professor of History*

James E. Snyder, M.F.A., PH.D. (Princeton University), *Professor of History of Art*[5]

Milton D. Speizman, PH.D. (Tulane University), *Professor of Social Work and Social Research*[5]

K. Laurence Stapleton, A.B. (Smith College), *Mary E. Garrett Alumnae Professor of English Literature*

Isabel Scribner Stearns, PH.D. (Bryn Mawr College), *Professor of Philosophy*

James Tanis, TH.D. (University of Utrecht), *Director of Libraries* and *Professor of History*[1]

Myra L. Uhlfelder, PH.D. (Bryn Mawr College), *Professor of Latin*

Matthew Yarczower, PH.D. (University of Maryland), *Professor of Psychology*

George L. Zimmerman, PH.D. (University of Chicago), *Professor of Chemistry*

9

Associate Professors

Joseph Varimbi, PH.D. (University of Pennsylvania), *Associate Professor of Chemistry* and *Secretary of the Faculty of Arts and Sciences*

Carol L. Bernstein, PH.D. (Yale University), *Associate Professor of English*

Charles C. Bray, Jr. PH.D. (University of Pittsburgh), *Associate Professor of Social Work and Social Research*

Merle Broberg, PH.D. (The American University), *Associate Professor of Social Work and Social Research* and *Assistant Dean of The Graduate School of Social Work and Social Research*

Maria Luisa B. Crawford, PH.D. (University of California), *Associate Professor of Geology*

William A. Crawford, PH.D. (University of California), *Associate Professor of Geology*

Dan Davidson, PH.D. (Harvard University) *Associate Professor of Russian*

Gregory W. Dickerson, PH.D. (Princeton University), *Associate Professor of Greek*

Nancy C. Dorian, PH.D. (University of Michigan), *Associate Professor of German*

Richard S. Ellis, PH.D. (University of Chicago), *Associate Professor of Classical and Near Eastern Archaeology*

Noel J. J. Farley, PH.D. (Yale University), *Associate Professor of Economics*

Gloria Flaherty, PH.D. (Johns Hopkins University), *Associate Professor of German*

Charles E. Frye, PH.D. (Princeton University), *Associate Professor of Political Science*

Julia H. Gaisser, PH.D. (University of Edinburgh), *Associate Professor of Latin*

Jean Haring, D.S.W. (Western Reserve University), *Associate Professor of Social Work and Social Research*

Helen Manning Hunter, PH.D. (Radcliffe College), *Associate Professor of Economics*

Thomas H. Jackson, PH.D. (Yale University), *Associate Professor of English*

Stephen Jaeger, PH.D. (University of California at Berkeley), *Associate Professor of German*

Anthony R. Kaney, PH.D. (University of Illinois), *Associate Professor of Biology*[1]

Philip L. Kilbride, PH.D. (University of Missouri), *Associate Professor of Anthropology*[1]

Joseph E. Kramer, PH.D. (Princeton University), *Associate Professor of English*[3]

Michael Krausz, PH.D. (University of Toronto), *Associate Professor of Philosophy*

Jane C. Kronick, PH.D. (Yale University), *Associate Professor of Social Work and Social Research*[1]

Phillis S. Lachs, PH.D. (Bryn Mawr College), *Associate Dean of The Graduate School of Arts and Sciences* and *Associate Professor of History*

Samuel Tobias Lachs, PH.D. (Dropsie University), *Associate Professor of History of Religion*

Catharine Lafarge, PH.D. (Yale University), *Associate Professor of French*

Susan E. Maxfield, M.S. (Syracuse University), *Associate Professor of Education and Child Development* and *Director of the Phebe Anna Thorne School*

Clark McCauley, Jr. PH.D. (University of Pennsylvania), *Associate Professor of Psychology*[3]

Mary Patterson McPherson, PH.D. (Bryn Mawr College), LL.D., *Dean of the Undergraduate College* and *Associate Professor of Philosophy*

Dolores G. Norton, PH.D. (Bryn Mawr College), *Associate Professor of Social Work and Social Research*[2]

Carl Nylander, PH.D. (Uppsala University), *Associate Professor of Classical and Near Eastern Archaeology*

Eleanor Krane Paucker, PH.D. (University of Pennsylvania), *Associate Professor of Spanish*

Ruth L. Pearce, PH.D. (University of Pennsylvania), *Associate Professor of Russian*

Emmy A. Pepitone, PH.D. (University of Michigan), *Associate Professor of Education and Child Development*

Lucian B. Platt, PH.D. (Yale University), *Associate Professor of Geology*[1]

Judith R. Porter, PH.D. (Harvard University), *Associate Professor of Sociology*

Marc Howard Ross, PH.D. (Northwestern University), *Associate Professor of Political Science*

Stephen Salkever, PH.D. (University of Chicago), *Associate Professor of Political Science*

William Bruce Saunders, PH.D. (University of Iowa), *Associate Professor of Geology*

Russell T. Scott, PH.D. (Yale University), *Associate Professor of Latin*

Faye P. Soffen, ED.D. (University of Pennsylvania), *Associate Professor of Education and Child Development*[1]

Ruth O. Stallfort, M.S.S. (Simmons College School of Social Work), *Associate Professor of Social Work and Social Research*

Earl Thomas, PH.D. (Yale University), *Associate Professor of Psychology*

William W. Vosburgh, PH.D. (Yale University), *Associate Professor of Social Work and Social Research*

George E. Weaver, Jr. PH.D. (University of Pennsylvania), *Associate Professor of Philosophy*

Greta Zybon, D.S.W. (Western Reserve University), *Associate Professor of Social Work and Social Research*

Assistant Professors

Alfonso M. Albano, PH.D. (State University of New York at Stony Brook), *Assistant Professor of Physics*

Sandra M. Berwind, PH.D. (Bryn Mawr College), *Assistant Professor of English*

Robert A. Braun, PH.D. (University of Illinois at Urbana-Champaign), *Assistant Professor of Anthropology*

Peter M. Briggs, PH.D. (Yale University), *Assistant Professor of English*

Dennis Brunn, PH.D. (Washington University), *Assistant Professor of Social Work and Social Research*

Katrin Ristkok Burlin, PH.D. (Princeton University), *Assistant Professor of English*

Sandra S. Cornelius, PH.D. (Bryn Mawr College), *Part-time Assistant Professor of Social Work and Social Research*

11

Susan Dean, PH.D. (Bryn Mawr College), *Assistant Professor of English*

Nancy Dersofi, PH.D. (Harvard University), *Assistant Professor of Italian*[7]

Richard Gaskins, PH.D., J.D. (Yale University), *Assistant Professor of Social Work and Social Research* and of *Philosophy*

Stephen Goodwin, M.A. (University of Virginia), *Assistant Professor of English*

Richard Hamilton, PH.D. (University of Michigan), *Assistant Professor of Greek*

E. Jane Hedley, PH.D. (Bryn Mawr College), *Assistant Professor of English*

Stephen M. Holden, PH.D. (Bryn Mawr College), *Assistant Professor of Social Work and Social Research*[2]

Carole Elisabeth Joffe, PH.D. (University of California at Berkeley), *Assistant Professor of Social Work and Social Research*

Richard H. Jordan, PH.D. (University of Minnesota), *Assistant Professor of Anthropology*

Anne Kaier, PH.D. (Harvard University), *Assistant Professor of English*

Toba Kerson, PH.D. (University of Pennsylvania), *Assistant Professor of Social Work and Social Research*

Dale Kinney, PH.D. (New York University), *Assistant Professor of History of Art*

Sandra I. Kohler, PH.D. (Bryn Mawr College), *Assistant Professor of English*

Mary Jo Koroly, PH.D. (Bryn Mawr College), *Assistant Professor of Biology*

Kenneth N. Krigelman, PH.D. (University of Pennsylvania), *Assistant Professor of Mathematics*[7]

Li Way Lee, PH.D. (Columbia University), *Assistant Professor of Economics*

Steven Z. Levine, PH.D. (Harvard University), *Assistant Professor of History of Art on the Rosalyn R. Schwartz Lectureship*

Joyce Lewis, M.S.S. (Bryn Mawr College), *Assistant Professor of Social Work and Social Research*

Patricia J. Olds-Clarke, PH.D. (Washington University), *Assistant Professor of Biology*

George S. Pahomov, PH.D. (New York University), *Assistant Professor of Russian*

Nicholas Patruno, PH.D. (Rutgers University), *Assistant Professor of Italian*

William R. F. Phillips, PH.D. (University of Wisconsin), *Assistant Professor of Sociology*

Stephen Poppel, PH.D. (Harvard University), *Assistant Professor of History*

David J. Prescott, PH.D. (University of Pennsylvania), *Assistant Professor of Biology*

David Rabi, PH.D. (Dropsie University), *Assistant Professor of History of Religion on the Monte and Bertha Tyson Lectureship*

Fred C. Rothbaum, M.S. (Yale University), *Assistant Professor of Education and Child Development*

Grace Armstrong Savage, PH.D. (Princeton University), *Assistant Professor of French*

Carl B. Schmidt, PH.D. (Harvard University), *Assistant Professor of Music*[7]

Françoise Schremmer, PH.D. (University of Pennsylvania), *Assistant Professor of Mathematics*

Judith R. Shapiro, PH.D. (Columbia University), *Assistant Professor of Anthropology on the Rosalyn R. Schwartz Lectureship*

Stephen R. Smith, PH.D. (Massachusetts Institute of Technology), *Assistant Professor of Physics*

Samuel S. Snyder, PH.D. (Yale University), *Assistant Professor of Education and Child Development*

George C. Stephens, PH.D. (Lehigh University), *Assistant Professor of Geology*

Tracy Marie Taft, PH.D. (State University of New York at Buffalo), *Assistant Professor of Philosophy*

Steven N. Treistman, PH.D. (University of North Carolina), *Assistant Professor of Biology*

Lynn Visson, PH.D. (Harvard University), *Assistant Professor of Russian*[4]

Jill T. Wannemacher, PH.D. (Brown University), *Assistant Professor of Psychology on the Rosalyn R. Schwartz Lectureship*

Robert Earl Washington, PH.D. (University of Chicago), *Assistant Professor of Sociology*

Cathie J. Witty, PH.D. (University of California at Berkeley), *Assistant Professor of Social Work and Social Research*

J. Maitland Young, PH.D. (Yale University), *Assistant Professor of Chemistry*

Lecturers

Leslie Alexander, M.S.S. (Bryn Mawr College), *Part-time Lecturer in Social Work and Social Research*

Steven Alpern, PH.D. (New York University), *Lecturer in Mathematics*

Barbra Apfelbaum, A.B. (Smith College), *Lecturer in Italian*

Diane Balestri, PH.D. (Yale University), *Dean of the Class of 1978 and Part-time Lecturer in English*

Frances Bondhus Berliner, PH.D. (Bryn Mawr College), *Part-time Lecturer in Chemistry*

Stanley S. Clawar, PH.D. (Bryn Mawr College), *Visiting Lecturer in Sociology*

Donald Cooney, M.A. (Fordham University), *Part-time Lecturer in Social Work and Social Research*

Marck C. Fulcomer, PH.D. (Ohio State University), *Visiting Lecturer in Social Work and Social Research*

Hope K. Goodale, PH.D. (Bryn Mawr College), *Visiting Lecturer in Music*

Hiroko Sue Hara, PH.D. (Bryn Mawr College), *Elizabeth Gray Vining Visiting Lecturer in Anthropology*

Tadahiko Hara, PH.D. (Australian National University), *Elizabeth Gray Vining Visiting Lecturer in Anthropology*

Ruth B. Harvey, PH.D. (Bryn Mawr College), *Visiting Lecturer in Education and Child Development*

13

Patrick Henry, PH.D. (Yale University), *Visiting Lecturer in History of Religion*

Frances S. Hoekstra, PH.D. (Bryn Mawr College), *Part-time Lecturer in French*

Wendell P. Holbrook, A.B. (Morgan State College), *Lecturer in History*[4]

Isaac C. Hunt, LL.B. (University of Virginia), *Visiting Lecturer in Social Work and Social Research*

Arthur C. Huntley, M.D. (Thomas Jefferson University Medical College), *Visiting Lecturer in Social Work and Social Research*

James E. Irby, PH.D. (University of Michigan), *Visiting Lecturer in Spanish*

Eileen Tess Johnston, M.A. (University of Chicago), *Lecturer in English*

George D. Kelsey, PH.D. (Yale University), *Pitcairn-Crabbe Foundation Visiting Lecturer in History of Religion*

Aurelious Knighton, M.S.S. (University of Michigan), *Visiting Lecturer in Social Work and Social Research*

Paul Lehmann, TH.D. (Union Theological Seminary), *Roian Fleck Resident-in-Religion and Visiting Lecturer in History of Religion*

Phillis W. Lehmann, PH.D. (New York University), *Mary Flexner Lecturer in Classical and Near Eastern Archaeology* and in *History of Art* (on leave from Smith College)

Jay Leonard, B.A. (Boston University), *Lecturer in Geology*

Ramona T. Livingston, A.B. (William Jewell College), *Advisor to International Students* and *Lecturer in English*

Margaret S. Maurin, PH.D. (Bryn Mawr College), *Part-time Lecturer in French*

Ruth W. Mayden, M.S.S. (Bryn Mawr College), *Visiting Lecturer in Social Work and Social Research*

Elizabeth R. McKinsey, B.A. (Radcliffe College), *Lecturer in English*

Laurie McNally, M.S.S. (Bryn Mawr College), *Part-time Lecturer in Social Work and Social Research*

Braulio Montalvo, M.A. (Columbia University), *Caroline S. Rogers and Lucia Rogers Vorys Visiting Lecturer in Social Work and Social Research*

Kathryn G. Orkwiszewski, PH.D. (Bryn Mawr College), *Lecturer in Biology*

Patricia Onderdonk Pruett, PH.D. (Bryn Mawr College), *Associate Dean of the Undergraduate College* and *Lecturer in Biology*

Denise G. Ragona, PH.D. (Bryn Mawr College), *Part-time Lecturer in Biology*

Karen Meier Reeds, PH.D. (Harvard University), *Andrew W. Mellon Post-Doctoral Fellow* and *Lecturer in History of Science*

Patience B. Rockey, ED.D. (Harvard University), *Part-time Lecturer in Social Work and Social Research*

Masha Rozman, M.A. (Princeton University), *Lecturer in Russian*

Louis Schneiderman, M.S.S.W. (Columbia University), *Lecturer in Social Work and Social Research*

George A. Sheets, PH.D. (Duke University), *Andrew W. Mellon Post-Doctoral Fellow* and *Lecturer in Greek* and *in Latin*

Peter M. Smith, PH.D. (Harvard University), *Lecturer in Greek*

Djordje Soc, M.S.W. (University of California), *Lecturer in Social Work and Social Research*

Larry Stein, PH.D. (University of Iowa), *Visiting Lecturer in Psychology*
Eugene K. Wolf, PH.D. (New York University), *Visiting Lecturer in Music*

Instructors

Alexa Albert, M.A. (Bryn Mawr College), *Part-time Instructor in Sociology*
Mónica Estela Hollander, M.A. (University of Pennsylvania), *Instructor in Spanish*
Sheila Mall, A.B. (Temple University), *Part-time Instructor in French*
Esther Samuels, A.M. (University of Pennsylvania), *Part-time Instructor in Music*
Christine Savage, A.B. (Albright College), *Part-time Instructor in German*

Laboratory Coordinators

Erika Rossman Behrend, PH.D. (University of Pennsylvania), *Part-time Laboratory Coordinator*
Jane R. McConnell, PH.D. (Bryn Mawr College), *Part-time Laboratory Coordinator*
Alice S. Powers, PH.D. (Bryn Mawr College), *Part-time Laboratory Coordinator*

Tamara Brooks, M.S. (Julliard School of Music), *Director of Chorus and Orchestra*
Carol W. Campbell, M.A. (University of Pennsylvania), *Curator of Slides and Photographs*

Assistants

Elena C. Antonelli, A.B. (Immaculata College), *Assistant in Chemistry*
Gregory J. Arruda, A.B. (Bowdoin College), *Assistant in Biology*
Janer D. Belson, M.A. (Tufts University), *Assistant in Classical and Near Eastern Archaeology*
Stephen A. Biddle, B.A. (Villanova University), *Assistant in Philosophy*
Joan E. Carey, M.S. (Duquesne University), *Assistant in Biology*
Anna Rose Childress, M.A. (Bryn Mawr College), *Assistant in Psychology*
Floyd E. Demmon, B.S. (University of Notre Dame), *Assistant in Geology*
Louise DeWald, B.A. (Bryn Mawr College), *Assistant in Psychology*
Eugene DiSalvatore, B.A. (Temple University), *Assistant in Physics*
Mary A. Franz, B.A. (College of New Rochelle), *Assistant in French*
Christine Freme, B.A. (Bowdoin College), *Assistant in Biology*
Susan W. Groff, B.A. (Ursinus College), *Assistant in German*
Mark K. Hamilton, B.S. (St. Joseph's College), *Assistant in Chemistry*

15

Loraine G. Harpul, B.A. (Rosemont College), *Assistant in Biology*

Elizabeth Higdon, B.A. (University of California), *Assistant in History of Art*

Donald Hunderfund, B.A. (State University of New York at Genesee), *Assistant in Anthropology*

Esther Kasangaki, B.A. (Makerere University), *Assistant in Anthropology*

Sandra Klein, M.A. (Bryn Mawr College), *Assistant in Psychology*

Josephine Landrey, A.B. (Radcliffe College), *Assistant in Biology*

Sandra J. G. Linkletter, B.S. (University of Illinois), *Assistant in Chemistry*

Patricia Little, B.A. (Gettysburg College), *Assistant in Biology*

Lawrence E. Mark, B.A. (Gordan College), *Assistant in Geology*

Marsha L. Miller, B.A. (University of Delaware), *Assistant in Sociology*

Carol Moon, B.A. (Michigan State University), *Assistant in History of Art*

George J. Morrow, B.S. (Southampton College), *Assistant in Chemistry*

Vidhu S. Prasad, M.SC. (McGill University), *Assistant in Mathematics*

Robert M. Purcell, B.S. (Slippery Rock State College), *Assistant in Physics*

Michael Reinhart, B.S. (Millersville State College), *Assistant in Biology*

Janet Balshaw Rodney, B.A. (Elmira College), *Assistant in Music*

Cynthia H. Sarnoski, B.S. (Widener College), *Assistant in Chemistry*

David H. Schwamb, B.S. (Widener College), *Assistant in Physics*

Beverly Smith, B.A. (Chatham College), *Assistant in Psychology*

Roger Stoffregen, B.A. (Earlham College), *Assistant in Geology*

William Thomann, B.S. (Rider College), *Assistant in Geology*

Noreen T. Waldbauer, B.A. (Boston University), B.S. (Trinity College), *Assistant in Chemistry*

Patrick Gregory Warden, M.A. (Bryn Mawr College), *Assistant in Classical and Near Eastern Archaeology*

Howard Waxman, M.A. (University of Maine), *Assistant in Psychology*

Librarians

James Tanis, TH.D. (University of Utrecht), *Director of Libraries*[1]

Thomas Song, M.A., M.A.L.S. (University of Michigan), *Associate Director of Libraries*

Zoë M. Bemis, (Washington University, Yale University), *Reference Librarian*

Leo M. Dolenski, M.A. (Catholic University of America), M.L.S. (Drexel University), *Manuscripts Librarian*

John Dooley, M.L.S. (McGill University), *Bibliographer and Reference Librarian*

Florence D. Goff, M.A. (Villanova University), M.S.L.S. (Villanova University), *Cataloging Librarian*

John Jaffe, M.A., M.S.L.S. (Villanova University), *Acquisitions Librarian*

Mary S. Leahy, M.A. (Bryn Mawr College), *Rare Book Librarian*

Eileen Markson, M.A. (New York University), M.L.S. (Queens College of City University of New York), *Head, Art and Archaeology Library*

Yasuko Matsudo, M.L.S. (State University of New York, Albany), *Intercollege Librarian*

Charles McFadden, M.A. (Bryn Mawr College), M.S.L.S. (Drexel University), *Head, Gifts and Exchange Division*

Catherine E. Pabst, M.A. (University of Wisconsin), M.S.L.S. (Drexel University), *Head, Acquisitions Department*

Gertrude Reed, M.S.L.S. (Rutgers University), *Head, Reference Division* and *Archivist*

Ruth Reese, M.L.S. (Simmons College), *Intercollege Librarian*

Pamela G. Reilly, M.S.L.S. (Drexel University), *Head, Public Services Department*

Kathleen C. Seabe, M.S.L.S. (Simmons College), *Intercollege Librarian*

Penelope Schwind, M.S.L.S. (Drexel University), *Head, Cataloging Department*

Barbara F. Siegel, M.S.L.S. (Drexel University), *Serials Librarian*

Arleen Speizman, M.S.L.S. (Drexel University), *Cataloging Librarian*

Ethel W. Whetstone, A.B.L.S. (University of North Carolina), *Head, Sciences and Social Sciences Libraries*

Administrative Officers

Diane Balestri, PH.D. (Yale University), *Dean of the Class of 1978* and *Part-time Lecturer in English*

Judith Leopold Bardes, A.B. (Bryn Mawr College), *Director of Families and Friends*

Dolores E. Brien, PH.D. (Brown University), *Director of Career Planning*

Merle Broberg, PH.D. (The American University), *Assistant Dean of The Graduate School of Social Work and Social Research*

Lupe R. Gonzalez, *Financial Aid Officer of the Undergraduate College*

Rita C. Grass, A.B. (University of California), *Associate Director of Public Information*

Margaret M. Healy, PH.D. (Bryn Mawr College), *Executive Director of the Board of Trustees' Ad Hoc Committee on Financial Planning*

Deborah B. Hicks, A.B. (Bryn Mawr College), *Associate Director of Admissions*

Joseph S. Johnston, Jr., M.A. (University of Chicago), *Assistant to the President*

Patricia A. King, B.A. (Mills College), *Assistant Director of Resources*

Paul W. Klug, C.P.A., B.S. (Temple University), *Comptroller* and *Business Manager of the College*

Phyllis S. Lachs, PH.D. (Bryn Mawr College), *Associate Dean of The Graduate School of Arts and Sciences* and *Associate Professor of History*

Rebecca Fox Leach, A.B. (Bryn Mawr College), *Dean of the Class of 1979*

Ramona L. Livingston, A.B. (William Jewell College), *Advisor to International Students* and *Lecturer in English*

Margaret G. McKenna, A.B. (Bryn Mawr College), *Personnel Administrator*

Samuel J. McNamee, B.S. (Temple University), *Assistant Comptroller*

Charlotte A. Miller, A.B. (Bryn Mawr College), *Assistant Director of Admissions*

Kathleen K. Mooney, M.A. (Syracuse University), *Assistant Director of Career Planning*

Michelle Pynchon Osborn, A.B. (Smith College), *Director of Public Information*

Julie E. Painter, A.B. (Bryn Mawr College), *Administrator of Records and Financial Aid*

Martha Stokes Price, A.B. (Bryn Mawr College), *Director of Resources*

Patricia Onderdonk Pruett, PH.D. (Bryn Mawr College), *Associate Dean of the Undergraduate College* and *Dean of the Class of 1976* and *Lecturer in Biology*

Ellen Fernon Reisner, M.A. (Bryn Mawr College), *Assistant to the President* and *Alumna-in-Residence*

Robb N. Russell, M.S. (University of Illinois), *Director of Computer Services*

Thomas N. Trucks, B.S. (Villanova University), *Superintendent of Buildings and Grounds*

Jo-Anne Thomas Vanin, M.A.T. (Harvard University), *Dean of the Class of 1977*

Deborah Wolk, A.B. (Smith College), *Acting Financial Aid Officer of the Undergraduate College*

Sarah E. Wright, *Director of Halls*

Health

Frieda W. Woodruff, M.D. (University of Pennsylvania School of Medicine), *College Physician*

Martina M. Martin, M.D. (Thomas Jefferson University Medical College), *Assistant College Physician*

Anne Lee Delano, M.A. (Columbia University), *Director of Physical Education*

Eileen A. Bazelon, M.D. (Medical College of Pennsylvania), *Consulting Psychiatrist*

Dora Chizea, M.D. (Temple University School of Medicine), *Assistant College Physician*

Mary Geiger, M.D. (State University of New York at Albany), *Consulting Psychiatrist*

John F. Howkins, M.D. (Columbia University, College of Physicians and Surgeons), *Consulting Psychiatrist*

Howard B. Smith, M.D. (Thomas Jefferson University Medical College), *Consulting Psychiatrist*

Margaret Temeles, M.D. (Tufts University, School of Medicine), *Consulting Psychiatrist*

Physical Education

Anne Lee Delano, M.A. (Columbia University), *Director of Physical Education*

Linda Fritsche Castner, M.S. (Smith College), *Instructor in Physical Education*

Naomi L. Kocean, M.S. (Western Illinois University), *Instructor in Physical Education*

Barbara Lember, B.F.A. (Philadelphia College of Art), *Part-time Instructor in Dance*

Paula Carter Mason, B.S. (University of Wisconsin), *Part-time Instructor in Dance*

Jenepher Shillingford, M.ED. (Temple University), *Instructor in Physical Education*

Janet A. Yeager, *Instructor in Physical Education*

Halls of Residence

Catherine Asquier, M.A. (Sorbonne), *Warden of French House in Haffner Hall*

Jonita Carder, B.A. (Sweetbriar College), *Warden of Rockefeller*

Antoinette Flowers, M.A (Bryn Mawr College), *Warden of Pembroke East*

Jacqueline Guiton, M.A. (Bryn Mawr College), *Senior Resident of the Graduate Center*

Charles Heyduk, B.A. (La Salle College), *Warden of Radnor*

Judy Woods Koppitch, B.A. (Macalester College), *Warden of Rhoads*

Jane Lamb, M.A. (Case Western Reserve University), *Warden of Pembroke West*

Alice Pomponio Logan, M.A. (Bryn Mawr College), *Warden of Erdman*

Betsy Sandel, A.B. (Bucknell University), *Warden of Denbigh*

Doris Stump, *Lizentiat* (University of Zurich), *Warden of German House in Haffner Hall*

Luz M. Umpierre, M.A. (Bryn Mawr College), *Warden of Spanish House in Haffner Hall*

Wendy Weiss, B.A. (Kirkland College), *Warden of Merion*

Child Study Institute

Janet L. Hoopes, PH.D. (Bryn Mawr College), *Director*

Beatrice Schneider, M.S.S. (Bryn Mawr College), *Assistant to the Director*

Jean Ager, A.B. (Western College for Women), *Psychologist*

Shirley Alrich, M.A. (Bryn Mawr College), *Counselor*

Jean Astley, B.A. (University of Pennsylvania), *Reading Specialist*

Arlene Baggaley, M.A (Bryn Mawr College), *Part-time Counselor*

Eleanor Beatty, M.A. (George Washington University), *Psychologist*

Hannah Beiter, M.S. (University of Pennsylvania), *Reading Specialist*

Lynn Coren, M.S.S. (Bryn Mawr College), *Counselor*

Emma Dalsimer, B.S. (Ursinus College), *Part-time Counselor*

Charlotte Diamond, M.S.S. (Smith College), *Part-time Counselor*

Robert J. Dye, M.S. (University of Pennsylvania), *Reading Specialist*

Marjorie Edwards, M.S.S. (Bryn Mawr College), *Part-time Counselor*

Anne D. Emmons, M.S. (University of Pennsylvania), *Reading Specialist*

Kathleen Finnegan, M.A. (Temple University), *Psychologist*

Joel Goldstein, M.D. (Thomas Jefferson University Medical School), *Consulting Psychiatrist*

Anita Grinnell, M.S. (University of Pennsylvania), *Part-time Psychologist*

Ann Hamm, M.S.S. (Bryn Mawr College), *Social Caseworker*

Bernard Kanter, M.D. (Dalhousie University), *Consulting Psychiatrist*

Louella M. Kennedy, M.S.S. (Bryn Mawr College), *Part-time Social Caseworker*

Nina Korsh, B.A. (University of Pennsylvania), *Part-time Counselor*

Frederic J. Kwapien, M.D. (Tufts University School of Medicine), *Consulting Psychiatrist*

Barbara J. Lorry, M.S. (University of Pennsylvania), *Reading Specialist*

Ann S. McIlvain, M.ED. (Boston University), *Reading Specialist*

Herman Staples, M.D. (Hahnemann Medical College), *Consulting Psychiatrist*

Russell Sullivan, M.A. (Seton Hall University), *Counseling Psychologist*

Judith Vaden, M.S.S. (Bryn Mawr College), *Counselor*

Isabel Westfried, M.A. (Bryn Mawr College), *Chief Psychologist*

Mary Lee Young, M.S. (University of Pennsylvania), *Reading Specialist*

Phebe Anna Thorne School

Susan E. Maxfield, M.S. (Syracuse University), *Director*

Sandra P. Juliani, M.ED. (Tufts University), *Assistant Teacher*

Karen Pendleton, B.A. (William Smith College), *Assistant Teacher*

Tess L. Schutte, M.A (Bryn Mawr College), *Teacher*

Introduction

Bryn Mawr effectively combines a small undergraduate college with two graduate schools. In both The Graduate School of Arts and Sciences and the Undergraduate College the study of the liberal arts and sciences is pursued with members of the faculty who normally teach on both levels. They find that the teaching of undergraduates and the direction of graduate student research complement each other, so that the stimulation of investigation in the various fields of graduate study is reflected in all departments of undergraduate work. The undergraduate program emphasizes both depth and breadth of knowledge and understanding. No field is so broad that it cannot take advantage of the specialist's deep understanding; no specialty is so narrow that it may not profit from a breadth of perception.

Bryn Mawr College is convinced that intellectual discipline and enrichment provide a sound foundation for living. It believes in the rights of the individual and thinks óf the college community as a proving ground for the freedom of individuals to think and act as intelligent and responsible members of a democratic society.

In these beliefs Bryn Mawr has preserved the purpose and much of the tradition of its founders, a group of men and women belonging to the Society of Friends who were convinced that intelligent women deserve an education as rigorous and stimulating as that offered to men.

History of the College

This concern about the opportunity for women to study at the university level was felt strongly by Dr. Joseph Taylor, a New Jersey physician, who decided to give his estate to provide the land, the first buildings and the endowment for the new college. With much care Dr. Taylor chose the site, thirty-nine acres of land on a hill in Bryn Mawr, eleven miles west of Philadelphia. He supervised the erection of the first building and took part in formulating the plans that led to a new educational venture. This was the opening in 1885 of the first college for women with undergraduate instruction for the A.B. and graduate instruction for the M.A. and PH.D. degrees in all departments.

As he planned the College Dr. Taylor thought first of the education of young Friends. As Dr. Taylor's trustees in the early years considered the policies of the College they found themselves bound to allow freedom of conscience to all students. By 1893 it is clear from their studies and reports that they were determined to maintain a non-denominational college while strongly supporting the Friends' position of freedom of conscience and providing for continued opportunity within the College and through the College to encourage the student to develop and strengthen her own religious faith.

The first president of Bryn Mawr College was James E. Rhoads, a physician and one of the trustees responsible for the initial plans. The first dean was M. Carey Thomas, who devoted her life to securing for women the opportunity for higher education and the right to share in all the privileges and responsibilities of American citizenship. Miss Thomas succeeded to the presidency in 1893, after the resignation of Dr. Rhoads. In 1922 she was followed by Marion Edwards Park, already distinguished in the academic world for her scholarship in the classics and her ability as a teacher and administrator. From 1942 to 1970 Katharine Elizabeth McBride presided over the College in a time of great change and tremendous growth. The fifth president, Harris Llewellyn Wofford, Jr., was elected in 1969.

Since the early years of Bryn Mawr, the campus has grown from 39 to about 112 acres; new buildings have been added as required by additional students and by new undertakings in teaching and research.

The College As Community

Bryn Mawr College is committed to the principle of equal opportunity in education, as in employment.

Believing that a small college provides the most favorable opportunity for the students to participate in their own education, Bryn Mawr limits the number of undergraduates to approximately nine hundred. And since diversity in background and training serves not only to stimulate discussion but also to develop an intelligent understanding of such diversity, the undergraduate enrolment includes students from various types of schools, independent and public, foreign as well as American. The whole group, both graduate and undergraduate, is composed of students from all parts of the United States as well as from many foreign countries.

The resources of Bryn Mawr as a small residential college are augmented by its participation at the undergraduate level with Haverford College and Swarthmore College in an arrangement which coordinates the facilities of the three institutions while preserving the individual qualities and autonomy of each. Students may take courses at the other colleges, with credit and without additional fees. All three colleges share in some facilities and in various curricular and extra-curricular activities, but geographical proximity makes possible more regular and closer cooperation between Bryn Mawr .

and Haverford, which are only a mile apart. The calendars for the year are coordinated so that vacations and examination periods coincide. Bryn Mawr students regularly take courses at Haverford and may major in fields not represented in the Bryn Mawr curriculum. The cooperation greatly augments and enriches the academic offerings of both colleges. Collections in the two libraries are cross-listed, and students may study in either library.

The cooperation between Bryn Mawr and Haverford naturally extends beyond the classroom. Student organizations on the two campuses work closely together in matters concerned with student government and in the whole range of activities. Cooperation in living arrangements was initiated in 1969-70, and several residence halls on the two campuses are assigned to students of both colleges.

Bryn Mawr itself sponsors a broad cultural program which supplements the curriculum and enriches its community life. Various lectureships bring scholars and other leaders in world affairs to the campus not only for public lectures but also for classes and conferences with the students. Such opportunities are provided by the Mary Flexner Lecturer in the humanities and by the Anna Howard Shaw Lectures in the social sciences, the visiting professors on the Katharine E. McBride Fund for faculty appointments and by various individual lecturers in many of the departments of the College. The President's Office sponsors seminars on current issues which bring together distinguished leaders from the worlds of business, politics, finance and scholarship. Several of the student organizations also arrange conferences and lectures both on current national and international problems and within particular fields of social and cultural interest. The musical, dramatic and dance programs of the College are under the direction of the faculty and staff of Bryn Mawr and Haverford colleges and are arranged by the appropriate student organizations of the two colleges. The Arnecliffe Studio has facilities for painting and sculpture, where guidance and criticism are provided by the artist-in-residence. There is a dance studio in Rockefeller Hall.

Student organizations have complete responsibility for the many aspects of student activity, and student representatives join with members of the faculty and administration in making and carrying out plans for the college community as a whole. The Student Self-Government Association, to which every student belongs, provides a framework in which individuals and smaller groups function. The Association both legislates and mediates in matters of social and personal conduct. Through their Government

Association, the students share with the faculty the responsibility for the administration of the Academic Honor System. The Association also coordinates the activities of the many special interest clubs, open to all students; it serves as the liaison between students and College officers, faculty and alumnae. It has most recently been instrumental in perfecting a system of meal exchanges with Haverford, extending the shuttle bus service which the two colleges provide, and introducing college transportation between the two colleges and Swarthmore.

The Association is aided by the Committee on Student Life and the Board of Trustees and by the staff of the College to bring students in touch with their churches, to sponsor lectures or discussions on religious subjects, to plan services for worship and to take responsibility for giving students an opportunity to pursue and extend their religious interests.

Other major student organizations are concerned with political affairs, community service, the arts and athletics. Student organizations sponsor speakers, organize discussions and provide outlets for active participation in contemporary political issues.

The Bryn Mawr-Haverford Arts Council, independently or with other groups (College Theater, Orchestra, Chorus, Little Theater) sponsors work and performances or exhibitions in the arts. Under the aegis of the Athletic Association, the Dance Club choreographs its own productions. The Athletic Association also provides opportunities for all kinds of activities, from the Outing Club to organized intramural and varsity contests. *The Bryn Mawr-Haverford News,* published weekly, welcomes the participation of students interested in reporting and editing.

One of the most active of student organizations is the Curriculum Committee, which has worked out with the Faculty Curriculum Committee a system of self-scheduled examinations, currently in operation, as well as the possibility of receiving academic credit for "project" courses of a creative studio type or in social field work. Students participated in meetings of the Faculty Curriculum Committee for the first time in 1969-70 and continue to work with the faculty on an overall curriculum review which has to date resulted in a revision of the grading system, the initiation of five new interdepartmental majors and an interdepartmental area of concentration, and the opportunity to fulfill the divisional requirements at either Bryn Mawr or Haverford and to major in departments at Haverford College which have no counterpart department at Bryn Mawr.

Black students' organizations have also been active in arranging with members of the faculty and staff for visiting lecturers to teach new courses in the appropriate departments and in opening, in 1970-71, a Black Cultural Center which sponsors cultural programs open to the College community. It provides residence space for a few students. An active Women's Alliance has been working for several years with various departments on the establishment of appropriate courses on women. In 1971-72, in 1974-75 and again in 1975-76, a volunteer student group organized an all-College colloquium which involved discussion on the aims and direction of the College.

In 1970-71 for the first time the faculty voted to invite three seniors elected by the undergraduates to serve with faculty members on the College Admissions Committee. The Board of Directors requested the Undergraduate College and the student organizations from each of the graduate schools to elect representatives to sit with the Board in its stated meetings. Two undergraduate students began meeting with the Board in May 1971. Like the faculty representatives to the Board, the student members join in discussion but do not vote. In 1973 the faculty invited three students elected from the three upper classes to serve with alumnae and faculty on the Undergraduate Scholarship Committee.

Through their interest and participation in these many aspects of the College community the students exemplify the concern of Bryn Mawr's founders for intellectual development in a context of social commitment.

Admission

Bryn Mawr College is interested in candidates of character and ability who wish a liberal arts education and are prepared for college work by a sound education in school. The College has found highly successful candidates among students of varied interests and talents from a wide range of schools and regions in the United States and abroad.

In its consideration of candidates the College looks for evidence of ability in the student's high school record, her rank in class and her College Board tests, and asks her high school advisor and several teachers for an estimate of her character, maturity and readiness for college.

Program of Secondary School Studies

Candidates are expected to complete a four-year secondary school course. The program of studies providing the best background for college work includes English, languages and mathematics carried through most of the school years and, in addition, history and a laboratory science. A school program giving good preparation for study at Bryn Mawr would be as follows: English grammar, composition and literature throughout four years; at least three years of Mathematics, with emphasis on basic algebraic, geometric and trigonometric concepts and deductive reasoning; four years of one modern or ancient language, or a good foundation in two languages; some work in History and at least one course in laboratory science, preferably Biology, Chemistry or Physics. Elective subjects might be offered in, for example, History of Art, History of Music or biblical studies to make up the total of 16 or more credits recommended for admission to the College.

Since school curricula vary widely, the College is fully aware that many applicants for admission will offer programs that differ from the one described above. The College is glad to consider such applications provided students have maintained good records and continuity in the study of basic subjects.

Application for Admission

Students are advised to apply for admission to Bryn Mawr between the end of the junior year and January 15 of the senior year of high school. The College welcomes earlier consultation about school programs.

Only in exceptional circumstances will applications to the freshman class be accepted after January 15 of the student's senior year.

Application forms may be obtained from the Director of Admissions, Bryn Mawr College, Bryn Mawr, Pennsylvania 19010. A fee of $20 must accompany each application and is not refundable.

Candidates will be notified of the Committee on Admissions' action on their application in mid-April of the senior year.

Entrance Tests

The Scholastic Aptitude Test and three Achievement Tests of the College Entrance Examination Board are required of all candidates and should be taken by January of the senior year. If possible, Achievement Tests should be taken in current subjects. Students should offer three of the one-hour tests: one in English composition and two others. The College recommends but does not require that one of the three tests be taken in a foreign language, since a high score (received in the year prior to entrance) satisfies an A.B. degree requirement (see page 45, III B. I, C for details on language exemption). No special preparation, other than work well done in a good school, is required for successful performance on these tests.

Candidates are responsible for registering with the College Entrance Examination Board for the tests. Information about the tests, test centers, fees and dates may be obtained by writing to *College Entrance Examination Board, P.O. Box 592, Princeton, New Jersey 08540.*

Interviews

All candidates are expected to have an interview, before January 15, either at the College or with an alumna area-representative. Appointments for interviews and campus tours should be made in advance by writing or telephoning the Office of Admissions (215 LA5-1000). The Office of Admissions is open from nine to five on weekdays and, except during March, June, July and August, on Saturdays from nine to one. A student who is unable to visit the College should write to the Director of Admissions for the name and address of an alumna representative in her area.

Early Decision Plan

The Early Decision Plan is intended for promising students who have chosen Bryn Mawr as their first choice college by the fall of the senior year. Candidates under this plan may initiate applications at other colleges but they are expected to make only one Early Decision application. They agree, if admitted to Bryn Mawr under Early Decision, to accept admission and to *withdraw all other applications*.

Applications must be completed by November 15. Decisions on admission and financial aid will be mailed no later than December 15, and all other applications must be withdrawn by January 1.

A student who is applying for Early Decision should:

1. Complete the Scholastic Aptitude Test (SAT) and three Achievement Tests (ATs) of the College Entrance Examination Board no later than November.

2. File the Preliminary Application (a set of four cards), including the Early Decision Agreement Card, together with the twenty dollar application fee, between late spring of the junior year and November 1 of the senior year.

3. See that all other application forms (a personal history form, a secondary school report, two teacher recommendation forms) are returned by November 15. These forms will be mailed only after the Preliminary Application has been received by Bryn Mawr.

4. Arrange to have the required interview either at the College or with an alumna area-representative before November 15.

Each candidate who has completed the Early Decision Application by November 15 will be notified of the Committee on Admissions' decision no later than December 15. She will: (1) be informed that she has been admitted for the following academic year, or (2) be advised to transfer her application to the Regular Plan of admission, or (3) be refused admission.

A student who is admitted under Early Decision agrees to withdraw all other applications immediately, and she is asked to make a deposit of $100 by February 1, unless an extension is granted. The deposit will remain with the College while she is enrolled as an undergraduate and will be returned upon graduation or withdrawal from the College after one year of attendance.

Early Admission

Each year a few outstanding students are admitted after the junior year of high school. Students who wish to apply for Early Admission should plan to complete a senior English course before entrance to college and should write to the Director of Admissions about application procedures.

Deferred Entrance

A student admitted to the College may defer entrance to the freshman class for one year provided that she writes to the Director of Admissions requesting deferred entrance by May 1, the Candidate's Reply Date.

Advanced Placement

Students who have carried advanced work in school and who have honor grades (4 and 5) on the Advanced Placement Tests of the College Entrance Examination Board may, after consultation with the Dean and the departments concerned, be admitted to one or more advanced courses in the freshman year. Bryn Mawr accepts Advanced Placement Tests with honor grades in the relevant subjects as exempting the student from college requirements for the A.B. degree.[1] With the approval of the Dean and the departments concerned, one or more Advanced Placement Tests with honor grades may be presented for credit. Students who enter with three or more Advanced Placement Tests passed with honor grades may apply for sophomore standing.

The Advanced Placement Tests are given at College Board centers in May. Students may also consult the Dean or the Director of Admissions about the advisability of taking placement tests given by the College during Freshman Week.

Transfer Students

Each year a few students are admitted on transfer to the sophomore and junior classes. Successful transfer candidates have done excellent work at other colleges and universities and present strong high school records which compare favorably with those of entering Bryn Mawr freshmen.

Transfer candidates should file applications as early as possible and no later than March 15 for entrance in September, or no later than November 1 for the second semester of the year of entrance. Application forms and instructions may be requested from the Director of Admissions.

Transfer candidates will be asked to submit official test reports from the College Entrance Examination Board of the Scholastic Aptitude and Achievement Tests taken in high school. Those who have not previously taken these tests will be required to take only the Scholastic Aptitude Tests. Test registration information may be obtained from the College Entrance Examination Board, Box 592, Princeton, New Jersey 08540.

To qualify for the A.B. degree transfer students must have completed a minimum of two years of full-time study at Bryn Mawr. No credit will be

---

[1] The grade of 5 is required in English and in History.
See also pages 44-45, sections II and III.

given for work done elsewhere until the student has successfully completed a year's work at the College. Students who have failed to meet the prescribed standards of academic work or who have been put on probation, suspended or excluded from other colleges and universities, will under no circumstances be admitted.

Candidates for transfer will be notified of the action taken on their applications by early June or, for the second semester, in December.

Foreign Students

Bryn Mawr welcomes applications from foreign students between the ages of 17 and 21 who have outstanding secondary school records and who meet university entrance requirements in their native countries.

Application forms and instructions are available from the Director of Admissions. Foreign applications should be filed early in the year preceding entrance and must be complete by February 15. No application fee is required.

Foreign applicants will be asked to take the Scholastic Aptitude Test of the College Entrance Examination Board. Achievement Tests are recommended but not required. Test registration information may be obtained from the College Entrance Examination Board, Box 592, Princeton, New Jersey 08540 or the West Coast office of the Board at Box 1025, Berkeley, California 94701. Registration arrangements for students taking the tests abroad should be made at least two months prior to the scheduled testing date.

All foreign applicants whose native language is not English will be required to present credentials attesting to their proficiency in English. The Test of English as a Foreign Language (TOEFL) is recommended but not required for all non-native speakers of English unless they have a diploma from an institution in which English is the sole medium of instruction. TOEFL registration information can be obtained by writing to the Educational Testing Service, Princeton, New Jersey 08540.

Post-Baccalaureate Students in Premedical and Allied Health Fields

Men and women who hold an A.B. degree and need additional undergraduate training before making initial application to medical schools or graduate programs in allied health fields may apply as post-baccalaureate students. Applications are considered only for the fall semester. All forms and supporting credentials should be submitted as early as possible and no later than May 15. Application forms and instructions may be requested from the Director of Admissions.

Special Students

Highly qualified men and women who do not wish to undertake a full college program leading to a degree may apply for admission as special students to take courses on a per-course fee basis, space and resources permitting and subject to the approval of the Committee on Admissions and the department concerned. Application forms and instructions may be requested from the Director of Admissions. The number of special students admitted each semester is very limited.

Withdrawal and Readmission

A student who has withdrawn from College is not automatically readmitted. She must request readmission and should consult her Dean and the Director of Admissions concerning the procedure to be followed. Evidence of the student's ability to resume work at Bryn Mawr may be requested in the form of records from another university or medical approval. Applications for readmission will be reviewed twice during the year, in late February and in June. Students who file an application by February 15 will be notified of the Committee's decision in early March. Those who file by June 1 will be notified late in June.

Leaves of Absence

A student whose status at the College is not in question may apply to her Dean for a leave of absence. A leave may be requested for one semester or two consecutive semesters, and once approved, reinstatement will be granted. The estimated residential space available at the time a student wishes to return to the College will be a factor in the consideration of requests for leaves. Application must be made in writing by July 1 of the academic year preceding the requested leave (or November 1 for second semester leave). The deans and members of the student's major department will review any questions raised by the student or her Dean regarding the approval of the leave. In case of study at another institution, either foreign or domestic, the transfer of credits will be treated in the usual manner by the Committee on Transfer. A student should confirm her date of return, by letter to her Dean, by March 1 preceding return for the fall semester and by December 1 for return in the spring semester. (See page 38, Tuition.)

A student extending her leave beyond the approved period will have to apply for readmission.

Medical Leave of Absence

A student may, on the recommendation of the College Physician or her own doctor, at any time request a medical leave of absence for reasons of health (see page 38, Tuition). Re-entrance will be granted upon evidence of recovery.

Academic Facilities and Residence

Libraries

The new Mariam Coffin Canaday Library was officially opened in April 1970. As the center of the College's library system, it offers expanded facilities for study and research. The collections for the humanities and social sciences are largely in the Canaday Library, except for Art and Archaeology in the M. Carey Thomas Library, Music in Goodhart Hall and Psychology in Dalton Hall. In addition, there are libraries for the sciences and Mathematics in the Science Center. The collections of the Haverford College Library, which complement and augment those of Bryn Mawr, are equally accessible to the students.

Bryn Mawr's libraries operate on the open-stack system, allowing students free access to the collections, which comprise over 450,000 volumes. A union catalogue for all the libraries of Bryn Mawr and Haverford is located in the Canaday Library, as are the basic reference and other service facilities of the system. Students are urged to familiarize themselves with the various aids provided for study and research. A series of pamphlets on library use is available for handy reference, and the staff of librarians may be consulted for further assistance.

In addition to the books, periodicals and microfilms basic to a college library, the Canaday Library offers students a small but distinguished collection of research materials among its rare books and manuscripts. The Marjorie Walter Goodhart Medieval Library, for example, provides the basic texts for probing the mind of the late Middle Ages and the thought of the emerging Renaissance. These treasures are supplemented by a growing collection of sixteenth-century texts. Another noteworthy resource is the Louise Bulkley Dillingham Collection of Spanish-American books, which range from sixteenth-century exploration and settlement to contemporary Spanish-American life and culture.

The Rare Book Room houses the Marjorie Walter Goodhart Medieval Library of incunabula and medieval manuscripts. Important and extensive collections of early material on Latin America, Africa and Asia are to be found in the Dillingham, McBride and Plass collections. The Castle and Adelman collections expand the opportunities for the study of the graphic arts in books. In addition to these special collections are numerous other rare books and manuscripts.

The M. Carey Thomas Library still houses in the West Wing the books and other study materials of the Departments of Classical and Near Eastern Archaeology and History of Art. The study area in the stacks has been increased and the collections of slides and photographs have been made more accessible. Also in the West Wing is the Quita Woodward Memorial Room for recreational reading, with recent books in literature, art, religion and current affairs as well as many classics. The Record Club's collection is also housed and serviced there. The rest of the M. Carey Thomas Library provides offices for many of the faculty in the humanities and social sciences as well as the Great Hall, serving now as a Commons for the College community.

Haverford and Swarthmore Colleges and the libraries in Philadelphia are generous in making their resources available to students. The Union Library Catalogue of Philadelphia, situated at the University of Pennsylvania, enables students to locate easily the material in approximately one hundred seventy-five libraries in the Philadelphia metropolitan area.

Students wishing to use another library for material not available at Bryn Mawr must secure from the Head of the Public Services Department of the Library a letter of introduction stating the subject to be consulted.

Archaeology Collections

The Ella Riegel Museum of Classical Archaeology, housed on the third floor of the M. Carey Thomas Library, West Wing, contains a small study collection of Greek and Roman minor arts, especially vases, and a selection of pre-classical antiquities. The Museum was formed from private donations such as the Densmore Curtis Collection presented by Clarissa Dryden, the Elisabeth Washburn King Collection of classical Greek coins, and the Aline Abaecherli Boyce Collection of Roman Republican silver coins. The late Professor Hetty Goldman gave the Ella Riegel Museum an extensive series of pottery samples from the excavations at Tarsus in Cilicia. The collections are used for small research projects by undergraduate and graduate students.

Anthropology Museum and Laboratory

The Anthropology Laboratory in Dalton Hall houses several large collections of New World artifacts, including the W. S. Vaux Collection of archaeological and ethnological materials. This important collection, made during the last half of the nineteenth century, has as its main emphasis the artistic works of New World Indians. The Anne and George Vaux Collection represents a wide selection of American Indian basketry from the Southwest, California and the Pacific Northwest. The extensive Ward Canaday Collection contains outstanding examples of most of the ceramic and textile traditions for which Peru is known. Other comprehensive collections, given by faculty and friends of the College, represent the Old World Paleolithic and Neolithic, Paleo-Indian, Eastern Woodland, Southwestern, Middle Mississippian and Mexican antiquities. These collections have been enlarged by osteological materials and casts of fossil hominids. There is also a small but growing collection of ethnomusical recordings, representing the music of native peoples in all parts of the world. Students are expected to make use of these materials and laboratory facilities; there are limited display areas available for those interested in working on museum exhibits.

Laboratories

Laboratories, classrooms and libraries for Biology, Chemistry, Geology, Mathematics and Physics are located in the three buildings of the Science Center. Laboratories and classrooms for Psychology are in Dalton Hall.

In the Science Center the central building is the Marion Edwards Park Hall for Chemistry and Geology. Adjoining this building on the north is a building for Biology. South of Park Hall is the building for the physical sciences, which provides additional space for Chemistry and Geology, all the laboratories for Physics and classrooms and a library for Physics and Mathematics.

In all three buildings of the Science Center and in Dalton Hall there are large laboratories and lecture rooms for undergraduate students and smaller seminar rooms and laboratories for graduate students. In addition to the usual equipment, the science departments have special apparatus and instruments needed in particular research projects by faculty and graduate students and acquired, in part, through the Plan for the Coordination of the Sciences and through research grants from industry and other private sources and from government agencies.

In the Science Center there is an instrument shop with a staff of expert instrument makers to serve all the science departments, and several departments have smaller shops for the use of their own faculty and students. A glassblowing shop is manned by a part-time glassblower. There are rooms specially equipped for work with radioactive materials and for photographic work.

The Geology Department makes available for study and research several important collections. On deposit from the U. S. Geological Survey and the Defense Mapping Agency are 40,000 maps. The Department has extensive reference and working mineral collections, including the George Vaux, Jr., Collection and the Theodore D. Rand Collection, approximately 10,000 specimens each.

Through its membership in the Uni-Coll Corporation, a regional educational computer consortium, Bryn Mawr College has access to the resources and technical support of a major computing center. A high speed, remote batch terminal (printer at 600 lines per minute, card reader at 600 cards per minute) and nine teletypewriter terminals located on campus link the College with the Uni-Coll IBM 370, Model 168 computer. These facilities make available to faculty and students batch, remote job entry, and interactive computing supported by a large variety of programming systems.

Language Laboratory

The modern language departments jointly maintain a Language Laboratory. Its library of tapes contains recordings from the various literatures as well as material especially prepared for language drills. The simple but versatile equipment offers opportunities to improve both the speaking and comprehension proficiency of the student of foreign languages.

Halls of Residence

Nine halls of residence on campus each provide full living accommodations for from 50 to 142 students. Denbigh Hall, Merion Hall, Pembroke East, Pembroke West and Radnor Hall are named for counties in Wales, recalling the tradition of the early Welsh settlers of the area in which Bryn Mawr is situated. Rockefeller Hall is named for its donor John D. Rockefeller, and Rhoads North and South for the first president of the College, James E. Rhoads. Erdman Hall, first opened in 1965, was named in honor of Eleanor Donnelley Erdman, Class of 1921 and member of the Board of Directors. The Clarissa Donnelley Haffner Hall, which brings together into a "European village" three houses for students of French, German and Spanish, was opened in the fall of 1970.

In the year 1969-70 an experiment in coeducational living was tried: Radnor Hall housed students from both Bryn Mawr and Haverford; other

Bryn Mawr students occupied suites in a Haverford residence hall. The success of the experiment and increased interest in these arrangements have resulted in an extension of coeducational living to Rhoads and Erdman Halls at Bryn Mawr and to further units at Haverford.

College officers called wardens are in charge of the residence halls. They may be single women or married couples who are members of the Dean's staff but at the same time close to the undergraduates in age, and engaged either in teaching or in studying for an advanced degree. They are interested in all aspects of each student's welfare and they work, as well, with the student officers in each hall.

The College offers a variety of living accommodations including a few suites and a number of double rooms. However, many students occupy single rooms. The College provides basic furniture, but students supply linen, bed pillows, desk lamps, rugs, curtains, and any other accessories they may wish.

The maintenance of halls is the responsibility of the Director of Halls and a staff of managers. Food service is provided by a national food service organization. No special foods or diets can be obtained.

Rules for Residence

Residence in the college buildings is required of all undergraduates with these exceptions: those who live with their families in Philadelphia or the vicinity, and no more than fifty students who are permitted to live in houses or apartments of their own choosing after having received permission to do so from both the College and their parents. Married couples live off campus.

A student enrolled in the College who plans to be married must inform the Dean in advance and must make her own living arrangements.

The College maintains the halls of residence in order to provide simple, comfortable living for its students. It expects students to respect its property and the standards on which the halls are run. A printed statement of residence regulations is given each student. The College makes every effort to keep the residence charge low; the present rates are possible only because the students have agreed to assume the major responsibility for keeping their rooms clean and in order, thus permitting a reduction in service. Failure on the part of a student to meet the requisite standard in the care of her room may cause the College to refuse her residence the following year.

All the undergraduate halls are closed during the Christmas vacation. One hall is kept open during the spring vacation and here undergraduates may occupy rooms at $7.00 per day (including meals).

Non-Resident Students

For non-resident students, there is a suite of rooms in Erdman Hall containing study space, a kitchenette, dressing room and showers. College mail and campus notices will be sent there throughout the academic year. The warden of Erdman Hall is available for consultation.

Non-resident students are liable for all undergraduate fees except those for residence in a hall. A Dispensary fee of $50 entitles them to medical examination and consultation with the College Physician.

All foreign students will be automatically enrolled in the Student Health Service at a cost of $50 for non-residents.

Fees

Tuition

The tuition fee in 1976-77 for all undergraduate students, resident and non-resident, is $4225 a year.

The entire fee will be billed in July 1976 and due August 15, 1976. In the event of withdrawal from the College, refunds will be made according to the following schedule:

Withdrawals July 15 through September 8, 1976	100%
For new students only: withdrawals within the first two weeks of classes	100%
Withdrawals September 9 through October 31, 1976	75%
Withdrawals November 1 through January 16, 1977	50%
Withdrawals January 17, 1977 through March 11, 1977	25%
Withdrawals after March 11, 1977	0

The average cost of teaching each undergraduate is over $6300 a year. The difference over and above tuition must be met from private gifts and income from endowment. Contributions from parents able and willing to pay an additional sum are most welcome to help meet the expenses of instruction.

Residence

The charge for residence is $1790 a year and will be billed with tuition in full in July and be paid in two equal payments, that is, on August 15, 1976 and January 1, 1977. Refunds will be made according to the schedule above.

Students are permitted to reserve a room during the spring semester for the succeeding academic year, prior to payment of room and board fees, if they intend to be in residence during that year. Those students who have reserved a room, but decide later to withdraw from the College or take a leave of absence, will be charged a room change fee of $25.00. This charge will be deducted from the student's general deposit.

Procedure for Securing Refunds

Written notice must be received by the student's dean at least one week prior to the effective date of the withdrawal. Students who have received federally insured loans (loans guaranteed by state agencies-GSLP and National Direct Student loans-NDSL) to meet any educational expenses for the current academic year must make an appointment with the Comptroller of the College before leaving the campus to arrange for the appropriate refund of the loans in question.

General Deposit

All entering students are required to make a deposit of $100. This deposit will remain with the College while the student is enrolled as an undergraduate. After one year of attendance, the deposit will be returned thirty days after graduation or withdrawal from College. However, any unpaid bills and any expenses incurred as a result of destruction or negligence on the part of the student will be applied against the deposit.

Summary of Fees and Expenses for 1976-77

Tuition $4225
Residence 1790

Minor Fees

Laboratory fee per semester:
      One course of 2 hours or less a week $12.50
      One course of more than 2 hours a week 25.00
      Two or more courses of more than 2 hours a week 50.00

Health Insurance (Students' Health Care Plan) 59.50
                  (For foreign students) 67.20
Dispensary fee for non-resident students 50.00
Graduation fee (payable in the senior year) 25.00

Schedule of Payments

Tuition and residence fees will be billed in full and may be paid as follows:

For resident students

    $5120 due not later than August 15

    $ 895 due not later than January 1

For non-resident students

    $4225 due not later than August 15

No student will be permitted to attend classes or to enter residence until payment of the College charges has been made. No student will be registered at the beginning of a semester, or be graduated, or receive a transcript until all accounts, including a single activities fee of approximately $75.00, collected by the students, are paid. All resident students are required to participate in the College food plan.

An alternate payment plan is offered those who wish to pay tuition in two equal installments by August 15 and January 1. A service charge of $45.00 will be added to the second semester bill.

Faced with the rising costs affecting all parts of higher education, the College has had to raise tuition and other charges each of the last seven years, and further increases may be expected.

Monthly Payment Plan

For parents who wish to pay college fees on a monthly basis, the College offers the Education Plan in cooperation with the Provident National Bank. To finance a single year's cost it is necessary to sign an agreement by July 15. Contracts include the benefit of parent life, total and permanent disability insurance. For information, write to the Comptroller of the College.

General Information

Student Advising

The deans are responsible for the general welfare of undergraduates, and students are free to call upon them for help and advice on academic or more general problems. Each class has its own Class Dean. In addition to their class deans, students may work with the Financial Aid Officer who administers the financial aid program, including grants and loans, and with the Director of Career Planning. The wardens of residence halls, who are members of the Dean's staff, also are ready to advise and assist students. The College Physician, the consulting psychiatrists and counselors are also available to all students. The deans and wardens will give students information about appointments with these specialists.

For freshmen, the Student Freshman Week Committee and the College provide a special period of orientation. Freshman are asked to come into residence before the College is opened to upperclassman. The wardens of the various halls and a committee of upperclassmen welcome them and are available to answer questions and give advice. Freshmen with their parents may have interviews at that time with the President. In addition, freshmen have individual appointments with the deans to plan their academic program for the year. New students also take placement tests and a physical examination. To acquaint them with the many other aspects of college life, activities are sponsored by the undergraduate organizations.

Academic Standards and Regulations

Faculty rules governing academic work and the conduct of courses are stated in "Academic Rules for undergraduates," given to each freshman. All students are responsible for knowing the rules thoroughly. Rules concerning the Academic Honor System and student conduct are also stated in the Student Handbook.

Each student's academic work must be of sufficiently high quality to meet the academic standards set by the College. The Council of the Undergraduate College, composed of one faculty member from each department, reviews the records of those students whose work has fallen below the required standard. In such cases the Undergraduate Council may set specific requirements to be met by the student concerned and may also curtail privileges. In extreme cases the Undergraduate Council may exclude a student or require her to withdraw for a period of time from the College.

Integrity of all work is demanded of every student. Information about the Academic Honor System dealing with the conduct of examinations, written quizzes, and other written work is given to all entering students. Any infraction of these regulations or any action contrary to their spirit constitutes an offense. Infractions are dealt with by an Administrative Board composed of faculty and students.

Attendance at Classes

Regular attendance at classes is expected. Responsibility for attendance rests solely with each student. In general no attendance records are kept. Each instructor will make clear his view concerning absence from class.

Students should note that instructors are not notified of absences because of illness unless a student has missed three days of classes.

Absences for health or other urgent reasons are excused by the Dean, but any work missed must be made up. After a brief absence the student should consult her instructors about making up the work. In the case of a prolonged absence the Dean must be consulted as well as the instructors. If it seems probable to the Dean that a student's work may be seriously handicapped by the length of her absence, she may be required to drop one or more courses. Any student absent for more than twenty-five consecutive class days will generally be required to drop a course.

Health

Students receive clinic and hospital care in the College Dispensary and Infirmary, where a College Physician is in daily attendance. The 18-bed Infirmary is open when College is in session. Additional medical and surgical facilities are readily available at the Bryn Mawr Hospital and in nearby Philadelphia.

Students at Bryn Mawr and Haverford receive out-patient care in their respective College Dispensaries and in-patient care when necessary in the Bryn Mawr College Infirmary. Medical and psychiatric consultations with the College staff are available by appointment.

The Counseling Service is staffed by a clinical psychologist and consulting psychiatrists who are employed by the Health Service on a part-time basis. This service is available to all students eligible for Dispensary care and is limited to discussion of acute problems, diagnosis and recommendations for further care. A charge is made for visits in excess of four.

Certain health regulations must be met by all entering students. A medical examination blank provided by the College must be filed before

July 1. As part of this health report, certification of immunization against tetanus, diphtheria and poliomyelitis, an intradermal tuberculin test and ophthalmologist's certificate are required. If the intradermal tuberculin test is reported positive a chest x-ray is necessary. Students who have failed to hand in these reports will not be permitted to register until they have completed the necessary examinations and immunizations.

The residence fee paid by resident students entitles them to treatment in the College Dispensary and to care in the Infirmary for seven days, not necessarily consecutive, during the year, to attendance by the college physicians during this time and to general nursing. In cases requiring a special nurse, the expense incurred must be paid by the student. The fee for each day in the Infirmary after the seven-day period is $30. A nominal charge will be made for medicines and laboratory tests.

Non-resident students may pay a fee of $50, which entitles them to full use of the Student Health Service. Non-resident students need not pay the fee unless they desire Student Health Service privileges.

All communications from parents and guardians, outside physicians and others, concerning the health of a student should be addressed to the College Physician. Any student who becomes ill when absent from College must notify the Office of the Dean and present to the Infirmary when she returns a signed statement from her physician. If a student leaves the campus for reasons of health she should notify her Class Dean or the Infirmary.

The College reserves the right, if the parents or guardians of a student cannot be reached, to make decisions concerning operations or other matters of health.

Health insurance is required of all undergraduate students. If a student is not already covered, a student Health Care Insurance Plan is available through the Head Nurse at the Infirmary. The cost is $59.50 a year and includes coverage for one full calendar year. Foreign students must carry health insurance valid in the United States. The cost for such insurance taken out at Bryn Mawr is approximately $70 for a twelve-month period. Foreign students may obtain application forms for insurance from the Comptroller.

Insurance

The College is not responsible for loss due to fire, theft or any other cause. Students who wish to insure against these risks should do so individually or through their own family policies.

Curriculum

The present plan of study takes into account both the changes of recent years in secondary school education and the expectation of graduate school on the part of most students. It provides flexibility and makes it possible for students to include a wide range of fields of knowledge and to have great freedom to explore and elect. Some of the flexibility has been achieved by including all departments of the College in a divisional system, thus allowing both humanist and scientist a variety of ways in which to meet college requirements.

The Plan for the Curriculum

I. All candidates for the A.B. degree shall present 16 units[1] of work. In all cases one of these will be a unit of Senior Conference in the major subject.

II. Students must complete a unit of work in each of the four following disciplinary groups with courses that introduce students to these disciplines offered under departmental sponsorship at either Bryn Mawr or Haverford Colleges. A student with suitable preparation may, in consultation with the appropriate faculty members and her Class Dean, elect a course at the intermediate or advanced level.

Group I	*Group II*[5]	*Group III*[8]	*Group IV*
History	Biology	English	History
Philosophy	Chemistry	Literature	Philosophy
Anthropology[2]	Geology	Modern	Archaeology
Economics	Physics	Literatures	History of Art
Education	Psychology 101[6]	Classical	History of Religion[9]
Political Science	[Mathematics][7]	Literatures	Music[10]
Psychology[3]			
Sociology[4]			

---

1. A unit of work is the equivalent of eight semester hours and is either a year course or, when appropriate, two one-semester courses.
2. Anthropology 101, if at Bryn Mawr.
3. Two semester courses chosen from: 206, 207, 208, 305; any Haverford courses numbered 111 and above, with the exception of 240b.
4. At least one semester of work at the 100-level is required.
5. A unit of work in laboratory science to meet the *Group II* requirement must include a laboratory that meets a minimum of three hours a week.
6. Or in special cases Psychology 201a and 302b.
7. Mathematics alone may not be used to fill any *group* requirement. See page 45, II, a & c; III, B, 2.

The following directions and qualifications are to be noted:

A. A student (not majoring in subjects under Group II) may elect a second course under Group II, including Mathematics, as an alternative to any one of her other divisional requirements.

B. No course may satisfy more than one divisional requirement. Students majoring in History or Philosophy may count courses in their major as satisfying the requirement in either Group I or Group IV, but not both. Students majoring in Psychology may count courses in their major as satisfying either Group I or Group II, but not both. Students majoring in History of Religion may count courses in their major as satisfying either Group III or Group IV, but not both.

C. Courses taken to satisfy the requirements in English and Mathematics described below do not count as fulfilling divisional requirements.

III. In addition to the divisional requirements, each student must:

A. Include in her program two semesters of English composition (English 015) unless by a score of 5 on the Advanced Placement Test she has shown evidence that she has attained proficiency at this level.

B. Achieve a certain level of proficiency in languages or in one language and Mathematics, the level to be demonstrated in one of the three following ways:

1. She may demonstrate a knowledge of two foreign languages by

a. passing an examination offered by the College every spring and fall, or

b. passing with a grade of at least 2.0 a College course (one full unit) above the elementary level, or

---

8. Any combination of courses at Bryn Mawr listed below will satisfy the requirement:
   English 101 and all 200 courses under "Literature"
   French 201,202,203 and all 300 courses
   German 202 and all 300 courses
   Greek 101, 201, 202a, 203 and 301
   Italian 201, 202, 204, 301, 303 and 304
   Latin 101, 201, 202, 207, and all 300 courses
   Russian 203, 204, and all 300 courses with the exception of 305
   Spanish 201, 203 and all 300 courses
   History of Religion 103, 104, 201b, 207a, 208b, 209b, 301b, 305b.

   at Haverford:
   Classics 201a, 202b, 203a, 204b, 301a, 302b, 303a, 304b
   English 101 and all advanced courses with the exception of 190a
   French 200 level and above
   German 202a & b and all 300 courses
   Spanish 200 level and above.
9. Or Religion at Haverford.
10. Music 101 or 102, if at Bryn Mawr.

c. attaining a score of at least 650 (in one language) on a College Board Achievement Test or by passing with an honor grade an Advanced Placement Test.

2. She may offer one language to be tested as described above and demonstrate proficiency in Mathematics by

a. attaining a grade of 4 or 5 on the Advanced Placement Test, or

b. passing an examination offered by the Department of Mathematics each spring and fall, or

c. achieving a grade of at least 2.0 in a course in Mathematics (one full unit, to include at least one half-unit of calculus).

3. She may offer one language to an advanced level of proficiency to be demonstrated by passing with a grade of at least 2.0 one course or two semester courses at the 300 level.

IV. At the end of the sophomore year each student must choose a major subject and in consultation with the departmental advisor plan an appropriate sequence of major and allied courses. Usually a major is made up of four courses, two courses of allied work and one unit of Senior Conference in the major subject. No student will be required to offer more than six courses in the major subject. Students invited to participate in the Honors program count the Honors project as one of the major subject units.

In brief outline, each student's program will include:

1. a unit of work in English, unless she is exempt

2. work to achieve the required level of proficiency in

   one language, or

   two languages, or

   one language and mathematics

3. four units of work, one from each of the divisions I-IV

4. a major subject sequence of at least four units of work and two units of allied work and a Senior Conference

5. elective units of work to complete an undergraduate program of at least 16 units.

Each major department offers Honors work to a number of its senior students who have demonstrated unusual ability. Honors work is of more advanced character than that done in the regular courses and requires more initiative and power of organization than is usually expected of undergraduate students. Such work may be carried on in connection with an advanced course or may be planned especially for individual students. It usually includes independent work of a critical and analytical nature with source material, periodic reports and the preparation of an Honors paper.

A student with unusual interest or preparation in several areas could consider one of the interdepartmental majors, a double major, a major with a strong minor, or a special program involving work in several departments built around one major as a core. Such programs can be arranged by consulting the Dean and members of the departments concerned.

A student who wishes to pursue the study of a special area, figure or problem within a given discipline, may, if she finds a faculty member willing and able to supervise such work, substitute a supervised unit of independent study for one semester or year course.

In 1974 the faculty voted to change from a grading system employing only the letters A, B, C, D and F to a numerical system consisting of a scale of 4.0 to 0.

Each student must attain a grade of 2.0 or above in at least half of her graded courses and a grade of at least 1.0 in the remainder. In all courses in her major subject, she must attain grades of 2.0 or above. Should she receive a grade below 2.0 in a second-year or advanced course in the major subject, she may be required to change her major.

The degree of Bachelor of Arts is conferred upon students who have completed the course of study described above. The degree is awarded *cum laude, magna cum laude,* and *summa cum laude.* To students who have completed Honors work in their major subject the degree is awarded with Honors in that subject.

Credit for work taken elsewhere is given as follows:

1. Transfer credits (see page 29)
2. Cooperation with neighboring institutions

Under the Three-College Plan for Cooperation, full-time students at Bryn Mawr may register for courses at Haverford College and Swarthmore College without payment of additional fees. Such registration must be approved by the Dean and, in the case of required or major and allied work, by the departments concerned. Credit toward the Bryn Mawr degree will be granted for such courses.

Students may major in departments at Haverford College for which there are no corresponding departments at Bryn Mawr, e.g., Astronomy and Fine Arts (under the direction of Bryn Mawr's Professor of Fine Art).

3. Summer School Work

Students desirous of supplementing their work at Bryn Mawr by taking courses in summer school are encouraged to do so after their freshman year. Students who wish to present summer school work for credit should first obtain approval of their plan from their Class Dean and from the department concerned. No credit will be given for work in which a student has received a grade below 2.0. Credit given will be calculated on an hour-for-hour basis.

Supplementary requirements for the Degree:

1. Physical Education—All students must meet the requirement in Physical Education (see page 158).

2. Residence—Every candidate for the degree of Bachelor of Arts unless she is a transfer student or is permitted to accelerate her program or to take a junior year away will normally attend Bryn Mawr College for a period of four years. Students admitted on transfer from other colleges must complete sixteen units, eight of which must be taken while enrolled as a degree candidate at Bryn Mawr College. At least four of these units must be completed at Bryn Mawr during the junior or senior year.

3. Full Program of Work—With few exceptions, all students carry a complete program and do not spend more than the equivalent of the four undergraduate years in completing the work for the A.B. degree.

Student Health Lecture Series

A series of lectures and discussion is presented each year by the college Health Service. Such topics as drug addiction, sex counseling, adolescent mental health and basic health care are discussed. All freshmen must attend the program which is given in the fall.

Premedical Preparation

Bryn Mawr, through the curriculum in liberal arts and sciences, provides the opportunity of meeting requirements for admission to the leading medical schools of the country, and each year a number of its graduates enters these schools. The minimal requirements for most medical schools are met by the following courses: Biology 101, Chemistry 101, Chemistry 202, Mathematics 101, Physics 101. Some medical schools require Chemistry 203, and a second course in biology is required for all students who plan to attend medical school in the midwest, southwest or west.

The requirements may be fulfilled by a major in biology, with the election of Mathematics 101 and Physics 101, or by a major in chemistry, with the election of Biology 101. They can also be met by a major in other subjects, such as literature or history, with careful planning of the student's courses during her four years at Bryn Mawr and some work in the summer at an institution giving summer courses acceptable either to Bryn

Mawr in substitution for its regular course work or to the medical school of the student's choice. Students planning premedical work should consult early in their careers with the Associate Dean who is the premedical advisor for the College.

The College is able to award a number of scholarships for medical study from funds given for that purpose by friends interested in the advancement of women in medicine (see page 184). These may be applied for on admission to medical school and are awarded at the end of the senior year for use during the first year of medical study, with the prospect of renewal for later years if the student's need and her record in medical school warrant it.

Post-Baccalaureate Premedical Program

A post-baccalaureate premedical program is available to graduates of Bryn Mawr and other four-year accredited institutions. The program is designed to meet the needs of students who have not completed the premedical requirements during their undergraduate years and who have never applied for admission to a medical school. For details of the program, please write to the Premedical Advisor of the College, Taylor Hall, Bryn Mawr College, Bryn Mawr, Pennsylvania 19010.

Preparation to Teach

Students majoring in a liberal arts field which is taught in secondary school may, by appropriate planning early in the undergraduate career, prepare themselves to teach in the public junior and senior high schools of Pennsylvania. By reciprocal arrangement the Pennsylvania certificate is accepted by a number of other states. A student who wishes to teach should consult early in her college career with the chairman of the department concerned and of the Department of Education and Child Development so that appropriate curriculum plans may be made. (See page 73).

Coordination in the Sciences

In 1935, a grant from the Carnegie Corporation of New York enabled the College to put into operation a Plan for Coordination in the Sciences. Through the grant, the College is able to offer both undergraduate and graduate scholarships to students who wish to prepare themselves for future work in areas of interest to more than one natural science department.

The chairmen of the departments included in this plan (Biology, Chemistry, Geology, Mathematics, Physics, Psychology) will be glad to see students interested in this program and to advise them about their course of study. Such students should consult with the chairmen of the departments as early as possible.

Interdepartmental Work

Interdepartmental majors are offered in Classical Languages, Classical Studies, French Studies, The Growth and Structure of Cities, and Russian Studies; an interdepartmental area of concentration in Hispanic and Hispanic-American Studies (see page 153) is also offered.

In addition, each year certain courses are offered which cut across well-defined areas of knowledge and emphasize relationships among them. The interdepartmental courses are usually offered at the advanced level since the material considered requires some background in at least two disciplines.

Credit for Creative Work in the Arts

Students may major in Fine Arts at Haverford College under the direction of Bryn Mawr's Professor of Fine Art (see Fine Art under History of Art). Serious students of music, creative writing and the dance may receive elective academic credit for work in these fields. For details see the Performing Arts, the Department of Music and the Department of English.

Language Houses

Haffner Hall, which opened in the fall of 1970, comprises three separate units for qualified students of French, Italian, German and Spanish. In 1972-73 a small group of students wishing to speak Italian was included in a section of Haffner Hall. Students from Bryn Mawr and Haverford interested in the study of Russian occupy a section of Erdman Hall.

Sophomores, juniors or seniors who wish to live in a language house should apply to the head of the appropriate department. Adequate preparation in the language is a prerequisite and those who are accepted agree not to speak English at any time. Residence in a language house provides an excellent opportunity to gain fluency in speaking a foreign language, and is highly advisable for students planning to spend the junior year abroad.

Institut d'Etudes Françaises d'Avignon

Bryn Mawr College offers a summer program of intensive work in significant aspects of French culture. The program is open to men and women students from other colleges and from Bryn Mawr. Certain of the courses carry graduate credit. The *Institut* director and faculty members are French professors teaching in colleges and universities in the United States and France. Classes are held in the Palais du Roure and the facilities of the Bibliothèque Calvet are available to the group. Students live with families in Avignon. Applicants for admission must have strong academic records and have completed a course in French at the third-year college level or the equivalent. For detailed information concerning admission, curriculum, fees, academic credit and scholarships, students should consult Dr. Michel Guggenheim of the Department of French.

Centro de Estudios Hispánicos en Madrid

Bryn Mawr also offers a summer program of intensive work held in Madrid, Spain. The program, under the direction of a member of the Department of Spanish, is open to men and women students from other colleges and from Bryn Mawr. The instructors are members of college and university staffs familiar with teaching standards and practices in this country.

Courses are offered both for the student whose interest is Spain and for the student who wishes to specialize in Latin American affairs. Students live with Spanish families. All participate in study trips and attend an excellent series of carefully planned lectures and cultural events. Applicants must have strong academic records and must have completed the equivalent of three years of college-level Spanish. For information students should consult Dr. Eleanor Paucker of the Department of Spanish. A small number of scholarships is available each year. The *Centro* was made possible by a grant from the Henry L. and Grace Doherty Charitable Foundation of New York.

The Junior Year Abroad

Qualified students may apply for admission to certain groups which offer a junior year in Europe. Bryn Mawr students may study in Paris under the junior year plans sponsored by Barnard, Columbia, Sarah Lawrence, Smith and Sweet Briar colleges or at *L'Académie;* in Geneva, Florence or Hamburg with groups organized by Smith College or in Munich or Freiburg with the group sponsored by Wayne State University. Students may apply for admission to other Junior Year Abroad programs which have the approval of their major department and the Curriculum Committee.

Applicants must have excellent academic records and must give evidence of competence in the language of the country in which they plan to study. In general, two years of study at the college level are necessary to provide adequate language preparation. The junior year groups are not limited to language majors; they often include majors in, for example, History of Art, History or the social sciences. All students who plan to study abroad should consult the chairmen of their major departments to be certain that the work done in Europe may be coordinated with the general plan for the major subject.

Intercollegiate Center for Classical Studies in Rome

The Center is maintained by a cooperating group of colleges and universities, of which Bryn Mawr is a member. Students majoring in Latin, Greek or Archaeology who meet the Center's entrance requirements may apply for admission for one or both semesters of the junior year. The Center's curriculum includes courses in Greek and Latin literature, ancient history and archaeology, and provides for the study of Italian.

Guest Senior Year

A student, after consultation with her major department and her Dean, may apply for a guest senior year at another institution in the following circumstances: (a) if a program offered elsewhere will provide her with an opportunity of furthering her academic goals in a way not possible at Bryn Mawr (such cases to be submitted to the Curriculum Committee for approval); (b) for reasons of health or family emergency; (c) if she will be married and not remain in the Bryn Mawr area.

Scholarships and Other Student Aid

All students are, strictly speaking, on scholarship in the sense that their tuition fees cover only part of the costs of instruction. To those students well qualified for education in liberal arts and sciences but unable to meet the college fees, Bryn Mawr is able to offer further scholarship aid. Alumnae and friends of the College over many years have built up endowment for scholarships. Annual gifts from alumnae and alumnae clubs and from industrial and professional groups add to the amounts available each year. It is now possible to provide at least partial scholarships for approximately forty percent of the undergraduate students in the College. Full information about the scholarships available and other forms of help for meeting the expenses of college education will be found in the section, Financial Aid.

Child Care

Child care is available for Bryn Mawr and Haverford college families at the New Gulph Child Care Center, 911 New Gulph Road (215 LA5-7649) across from the Science buildings. Children three months through five years old are eligible. The Center is open five days a week, 9:00 a.m.-5:00 p.m., at an approximate cost of $1.25 per hour plus an additional charge for hot lunch if desired. Tuition for the semester is payable in advance.

The Center, conducted by a professional staff, incorporates age group developmental activities with high quality group care. Flexible schedules can be arranged to accommodate the programs of students, staff, faculty, and alumnae parents, based on the college calendar. A minimum of six hours' regular use per week is required. Following Commencement, a summer program is conducted for approximately two months.

Early registration for all programs is essential. For information contact the Director.

Career Planning

Students and alumnae are invited to make use of the services of the Career Planning Office which include: a) career and job counseling; b) group and private sessions on resume writing and job-hunting techniques; c) information on and referrals for on- and off-campus part-time jobs, and summer and permanent positions; d) maintaining and furnishing to employers, upon request, credentials files of alumnae containing biographical data and letters of recommendation.

During the academic year, the Office sponsors career conferences to provide students with a broader knowledge of career options. These conferences, made possible by a grant from the William C. Whitney Foundation in memory of Alexandra Colt Werkman '60' have focused within recent years on careers for women in law, medicine, the arts, and business and management.

In cooperation with the Alumnae Association, the Office provides students with access to a network of alumnae who make themselves available to students for personal consultation on career-related questions and who in practical ways assist students in determining their career fields. Students interested in exploring specific career fields may participate during the spring vacation in the Extern program, working as "shadow colleagues" with alumnae and other sponsors who are specialists in these fields. In addition, a number of competitive, paid, summer work-internships are

53

made available to Bryn Mawr students by grants from business corporations.

Bryn Mawr participates in the Federal College Work-Study Program established by the Economic Opportunity Act of 1964. This program provides funds for on- and off-campus jobs for students who meet the federal eligibility requirements. Students interested in this program should consult the Director of Financial Aid. (See page 162.)

Courses of Study 1976-77

Key to Course Numbers and Symbols

001-099   indicate elementary and intermediate courses.
With the exception of Greek 001 and Russian 001 these courses are not part of the major work.

100-199   indicate first-year courses in the major work.

200-299   indicate second-year courses in the major work.

300-398   indicate advanced courses in the major work; 399 is used for the Senior Conference.

400-499   indicate special categories of work (e.g., 401 for Honors, 403 for a supervised unit).

indicates elective courses, open to all students without prerequisite unless a special prerequisite is stated.

a   the letter "a," following a number, indicates a half-course given in the first semester.

b   the letter "b," following a number, indicates a half-course given in the second semester.

the letter "c," following a number, indicates a half-course given two hours a week throughout the year.

d   the letter "d," following a number, indicates a course of six-weeks' duration to be followed by an additional six weeks of independent supervised work.

[ ]   square brackets enclosing the title of a course indicate that the course is not given in the current year.

In general, courses listed as full-year courses must be carried through two semesters. In some cases one semester of such a course may be taken with credit, but only with permission of the student's Class Dean and the department concerned. One unit of work carried throughout the year is the equivalent of eight semester hours, or eleven quarter hours.

Selected Haverford and Swarthmore College courses are listed in this catalogue when applicable to Bryn Mawr programs. Consult the Haverford and Swarthmore College catalogues for full course descriptions.

Anthropology

Professor: Jane C. Goodale, PH.D., *Chairman*

Associate Professor: Philip L. Kilbride, PH.D.‡

Assistant Professors: Robert A. Braun, PH.D.
Richard H. Jordan, PH.D.
Judith R. Shapiro, PH.D.

Visiting Lecturers: Hiroko Sue Hara, PH.D.
Tadahiko Hara, PH.D.

Assistants: Donald Hunderfund, B.A.
Esther Kasangaki, B.A.

Professor of Music: Agi Jambor, M.A. (Ethnomusicology)

Associate Professor of German: Nancy C. Dorian, PH.D. (Linguistics)

The aim of the department is two-fold: (1) to introduce the liberal arts student to the discipline of anthropology: its aims, methods, theories and contributions to an understanding of the nature of human culture and society and (2) to provide for the major in anthropology, in addition to the above, a firm understanding of the basic concepts and history of the discipline through examination of theoretical works and intensive studies in the ethnography and prehistory of several world areas. Laboratory experience is provided in a number of courses.

Requirements in the Major Subject: 101, 203a, 320a and two additional half-units of intermediate (200) work chosen from 201a, 204a, 204b, 208a, 208b and 210a and one 300-level semester course in the area of ethnography, plus 399a and b (Senior Conferences). Two and one-half additional units of major or allied work are required, which may be taken at Bryn Mawr or Haverford.

Allied Subjects: Biology, The Growth and Structure of Cities Program, Classical and Near Eastern Archaeology, Economics, English Literature, Geology, History of Art, History of Religion, Linguistics, Philosophy, Political Science, Psychology, Sociology and interdepartmental "Culture

---

‡On leave for the year 1976-77.

and Civilization" courses (such as *"La Civilisation de France,"* "Hispanic Culture and Civilization," and "Introduction to Celtic Civilization").

. *Man, Culture and Society:* Members of the Department.

Man's place in nature, human evolution and the history of culture to the rise of early civilizations in the Old and New Worlds; forms of culture and society among contemporary peoples. Because the subject matter is extensive and the basic concepts unfamiliar, a full year is needed to gain an adequate understanding of the subject; therefore, both semesters are required for credit.

.* *Afro-American Heritage:* Mr. Kilbride.}

.* *American Indian Heritage.*}

. *Archaeological Methods of Analysis:* Mr. Jordan.

Lectures, laboratory and field experience will stress the methodological framework of archaeological investigation and interpretation. Prerequisites: 101, or equivalent introductory course in a related discipline, and permission of instructor.

. *Primitive Society:* Miss Goodale.

Social organization: an introduction to theory and methods and a study of significant contributions. Prerequisite: Anthropology 101.

. *South American Prehistory:* Mr. Braun.

The cultural history of the Andes and Amazonia up to the Spanish conquest. Interrelationships with Mesoamerica, Africa and Asia are explored. Cultural dynamics and stylistic and iconographic analysis of art
. are stressed. Prerequisite: Anthropology 101 or permission of instructor.

. *North American Prehistory:* Mr. Jordan.

A study of North American archaeology and cultural history. Introduction to methods and theory in archaeology and in the analysis of archaeological data. Prerequisite: Anthropology 101 or permission of instructor.

.* *Ethnomusicology:* Mme Jambor.

Gypsy, Hungarian, ancient and modern Israeli and East European folk music and American Indian music; ear training and practice in transcription.

. *Ethnomusicology:* Mme Jambor.

Native African music; preparation for museum curatorship of musical instruments; continued instruction in transcription. Prerequisite: Anthropology 205a or Music 111a (at Haverford).

[208a. *Old World Prehistory:* Mr. Jordan, Mr. Braun.]
& b.

[210a. *Human Evolution:* Mr. Jordan.]

218b. *Community Politics: A Cross-Cultural Approach:* Mrs. Ross, Mr. Ross.
(INT.)   See Political Science 218b.

[302b. *Africa: Sub-Saharan Ethnology:* Mr. Kilbride.]

303b. *Oceania: Topics in Melanesian Ethnography:* Miss Goodale.
An intensive study of selected Melanesian cultures and societies with emphasis on such topics as politics, law, economics, sex roles and identities, magic, religion, cultural dynamics and political development. Prerequisite: Anthropology 203a.

[304a. *The American Indian.*]

[305a. *Latin America: Native Cultures of South America:* Miss Shapiro.]

[306a. *Peasants:* Mr. Kilbride.]

306b. *Modern Latin American Communities:* Mr. Braun.
Selected problems in contemporary Latin American communities.

307a. *Topics in the Ethnography of South Asia:* Mr. Hara.

[308. *Language in the Social Context:* Miss Dorian.]
(INT.)

309b. *Topics in the Ethnography of Japan:* Mrs. Hara.

310a. *Introduction to Descriptive Linguistic Techniques:* Miss Dorian.
(INT.)   See Interdepartmental course 310a.

312b. *Field Methods in Linguistics:* Miss Dorian.
(INT.)   See Interdepartmental course 312b.

313b. *Linguistic Anthropology:* Miss Shapiro.
Examines language as a social and cultural phenomenon. Consideration will be given to theoretical and methodological relationships between linguistics and socio-cultural anthropology. Prerequisite: Anthropology 101, Interdepartmental 310a or equivalent preparation in anthropology and linguistics.

320a. *Cultural Theory:* Miss Shapiro.
The relationship of anthropology to other social sciences and an examination of the important anthropological contributions to cultural theory. Prerequisite: a half-unit of advanced (300) work.

. *Culture and Personality.*]

. *Physical Anthropology.*]

. *Cultural Ecology:* Mr. Braun.]

. *Woman, Culture and Society:* Miss Shapiro.]

. *Anthropology through Literature:* Mr. Hara.

. *Senior Conferences:*

. The topic of each seminar is determined in advance in discussion with students. Paper(s), report(s), quality of student's participation and examination will form the basis for evaluation. Seminars for 1976-77 are: 399a. *Symbolic Anthropology:* Miss Goodale and Miss Shapiro. 399b. Members of the Department.

. *Independent Work:*

. Independent work is offered to seniors of marked ability for one or two semesters. If undertaken successfully it may be credited as Honors work.

Interdepartmental Work: The Department of Anthropology participates in the interdepartmental major in The Growth and Structure of Cities and in the interdepartmental concentration in Hispanic and Hispanic-American Studies. See pages 150 and 153.

Biology

Professor: Robert L. Conner, PH.D., *Chairman*

Associate Professor: Anthony R. Kaney, PH.D.‡

Assistant Professors: Mary Jo Koroly, PH.D.
    Patricia J. Olds-Clarke, PH.D.
    David J. Prescott, PH.D.
    Steven N. Treistman, PH.D.

Lecturers: Kathryn G. Orkwiszewski, PH.D.
    Patricia Onderdonk Pruett, PH.D., *Associate Dean of the Undergraduate College*
    Denise M. Ragona, PH.D.

---

‡On leave for the year 1976-77.

Assistants: Gregory J. Arruda, A.B.
   Joan E. Carey, M.S.
   Christine Freme, B.A.
   Loraine G. Harpul, B.A.
   Josephine Landrey, A.B.
   Patricia Little, B.A.
   Michael Reinhart, B.S.

Laboratory Coordinator: Jane R. McConnell, PH.D.

Professor of History of Science: Jane M. Oppenheimer, PH.D.

Assistant Professor of Chemistry: J. Maitland Young, PH.D.

The courses offered are designed to present the principles underlying biological science to liberal arts students interested in understanding the biotic world in which man lives and his own position in it. Primary consideration is devoted, both in class and in the laboratory, to the interplay of development, structure and function in determining the unity and diversity which characterize the plant and animal kingdoms and to dynamic interrelationships of living organisms with each other and with their environment. Genetics, developmental biology and biochemistry are emphasized as unifying disciplines.

Requirements in the Major Subject: Biology 101 (unless either or both semesters are exempted), 201a, 362a, and any two of the following three courses—359b, 360b, 364b, and at least one other unit (two semester-courses) of advanced work, the Senior Conference, and Chemistry 101 and 202. Physics 101 and Mathematics 101 are strongly recommended as additional courses. Students should note that the ability to read French or German is essential for graduate work.

Allied Subjects: Chemistry, Physics, History of Science.

101. *General Biology:* Mrs. Olds-Clarke, Mr. Treistman, Mrs. Ragona, Mrs. Orkwiszewski.
Laboratory: Mrs. McConnell and assistants.
   A presentation of the fundamental principles of molecular, cellular and organismic biology. A selection of plants and animals is studied to illustrate problems and theories dealing with living systems and their interaction with the environment. Lecture three hours, laboratory three hours a week.

201a. *Genetics:* Mrs. Orkwiszewski.

A study of heredity and gene action. Lecture three hours, laboratory four hours a week. Prerequisite: Biology 101 or permission of instructor.

314. *History of Scientific Thought:* Miss Oppenheimer, Miss Reeds.
(INT.) See History 314.

350b. *Problems in Cellular Physiology:* Mr. Conner.

An inquiry into the recent literature about membrane phenomena, including the mechanisms for bulk transport, small molecule transport and chemical specificity. Lecture two hours a week. Prerequisites: Biology 362a and 364b or permission of instructor.

351b. *Problems in Genetics:* Mr. Kaney.}

352a. *Problems in Molecular Biology:* Mrs. Ragona.

A course dealing with current topics of interest in the field of molecular biology. Class meeting two hours a week. Prerequisites: Biology 362a and 364b.

353a. *Biochemistry: Macromolecular Structure and Function:* Mr. Prescott, Mr.
(INT.) Young.

The structure, chemistry and function of proteins, nucleic acids and polysaccharides are discussed with special emphasis on their roles in living systems. Lecture three hours, laboratory six hours a week. Prerequisites: Chemistry 202 and Biology 362a or permission of instructors. Physics 101 and Mathematics 101 are recommended.

353b. *Biochemistry: Intermediary Metabolism:* Mr. Conner, Mr. Prescott.
(INT.) Metabolic relationships of carbohydrates, lipids and amino acids are discussed with emphasis on the control of various pathways. Lecture three hours, laboratory six hours a week. Prerequisite: Biology 353a.

354a. *Recent Advances in Cell Biology:* Miss Koroly.

Emphasis on detailed analysis of the physiological and biochemical processes in one or two organelles which allow a specific cellular activity. Interdependence of structure and function will be examined. Two hours a week. Prerequisites: Biology 362a and 364b and Chemistry 202.

55b. *Problems in Neurophysiology:* Mr. Treistman.

A study of physiology of excitable cells and their interactions. Lecture two hours a week. Prerequisite: Biology 359b or permission of instructor.

61

[356. *Biophysics:* Miss Hoyt.]

357a. *Computer Usage in the Life Sciences:* Mrs. Pruett.
(INT.)   Experiments in the life sciences will be analyzed using computer techniques. The Fortran IV language will be developed and used throughout the course. Limited to advanced students with research experience; no previous training in the use of the computer required. Lecture two hours, laboratory two hours a week.

[358a. *Problems in Developmental Biology:* Mrs. Olds-Clarke.]

[359b. *Comparative and Systems Physiology:* Mr. Treistman.]

360b. *Developmental Biology:* Mrs. Olds-Clarke.
    Principles of developmental biology and vertebrate embryology. Lecture three hours, laboratory four hours a week. Prerequisite: Biology 201a.

362a. *Cellular Physiology:* Mr. Conner.
    A course devoted to a study of the activities of cells in terms of physical and chemical processes. Lecture three hours, laboratory four hours a week. Prerequisites: Biology 201a and Chemistry 202, which may be taken concurrently.

364b. *Cell Biology:* Miss Koroly.
    An examination of the ultra-structural organization, function and molecular development of selected eukaryotic organelles. Lecture three hours, laboratory four hours a week. Prerequisite: Biology 201a.

399. *Senior Conference:* All seniors write a comprehensive paper in a prescribed area of biology in conjunction with a faculty member. These papers serve as the basis for seminars intended to relate materials from various sub-disciplines of biology to each other, to examine subjects of current biological interest and to relate the field to the larger aspects of society. The method of evaluating the work will be determined in consultation between the seniors and the Department.

401. *Honors Work:* All qualified students are encouraged to do Honors work in one of the advanced fields. This entails one unit of laboratory work on an independent experimental research problem.

403. *Supervised Research in Biology:* Members of the Department.
    Laboratory research under the supervision of a member of the Department.

Teaching Certification: A sequence of work offered by the Department of Biology and the Department of Education of the College leads to a certificate to teach in the secondary schools of Pennsylvania.

COURSES AT HAVERFORD

Molecular Virology: Mr. Goff.

Fundamentals of Immunology: Mr. Finger.

Chemistry

Professors: Jay Martin Anderson, PH.D.
  Ernst Berliner, PH.D.
  Frank B. Mallory, PH.D.
  George L. Zimmerman, PH.D., *Chairman*

Associate Professor: Joseph Varimbi, PH.D.

Assistant Professor: J. Maitland Young, PH.D.

Lecturer: Frances Bondhus Berliner, PH.D.

Assistants: Elena C. Antonelli, A.B.
  Mark K. Hamilton, B.S.
  Sandra J. G. Linkletter, B.S.
  George J. Morrow, B.S.
  Cynthia H. Sarnoski, B.S.
  Noreen T. Waldbauer, B.S.

Assistant Professor of Biology: David J. Prescott, PH.D.

The major in chemistry is designed to give the student a sound background in the four major fields of chemistry: inorganic, analytical, organic and physical chemistry. The courses are arranged in such a sequence as to convey an insight into the development of chemical theories from basic scientific principles. In the advanced courses the student begins to be acquainted with current problems in special fields and with modern approaches to their solutions. The emphasis throughout is on the fundamental principles on which chemistry is based and which are exemplified and further clarified by laboratory work taken in conjunction with each course.

Requirements in the Major Subject: Chemistry 101, the three 200-level courses, one unit of advanced work and the Senior Conference. The required unit of advanced work shall consist of two semesters of courses selected from among 301b, 302a, 302b, 303a, 303b, 353, and 356b, with the provision that at least one of the semesters shall include laboratory work (i.e., 302a, 302b, 303b, 353). Physics 101 and Mathematics 101 are also required. Students are encouraged to take additional mathematics. A reading knowledge of German is valuable for work in chemistry beyond the undergraduate level.

Allied Subjects: Biology, Geology, Mathematics, Physics.

101a. *General Chemistry:* Mr. Anderson, Mrs. Berliner and assistants.

An introduction to the theories of chemistry and the study of the non-metals. Introductory quantitative techniques. No knowledge of chemistry is presupposed. Three lectures, three hours of laboratory a week.

101b. *General Chemistry:* Mr. Berliner, Mrs. Berliner and assistants.

Ionic equilibria and the systematic qualitative analysis of inorganic substances. A study of the metallic elements. Three lectures, three hours of laboratory a week.

201. *Inorganic Chemistry:* Mr. Varimbi.

Correlations of chemical and physical properties based on the periodic table; structures of inorganic compounds; equilibria in acid-base and complex-ion systems. Laboratory work includes analytical techniques, synthesis, purification, and characterization of a variety of compounds by chemical and instrumental methods. Three lectures, five hours of laboratory a week.

202. *Organic Chemistry:* Mr. Berliner, Mr. Mallory.

First semester: aliphatic chemistry; second semester: aromatic chemistry and natural products. Three lectures, five hours of laboratory a week.

203. *Physical Chemistry:* Mr. Anderson, Mr. Zimmerman.

Structure and kinetic-molecular theory of matter, elementary thermodynamics and chemical kinetics. Two lectures and one conference, laboratory five hours a week. Prerequisites: Mathematics 101 and Physics 101. (The latter may be taken concurrently with Chemistry 203.)

Advanced Inorganic Chemistry: Mr. Varimbi.

Group theory and some of its applications to structural and spectroscopic problems of ligand field theory. Elements of solid state chemistry: metals, semiconductors and surface reactions. Three lectures a week.

Advanced Organic Chemistry: Mr. Mallory, Mr. Berliner.

Lectures: theories and fundamental principles of organic chemistry. Laboratory: (first semester) organic qualitative analysis; (second semester) advanced synthesis and laboratory techniques. Two lectures, six hours of laboratory a week.

Quantum Mechanics of Atoms and Molecules: Mr. Zimmerman.

Prerequisites: Chemistry 203 and Mathematics 201 or its equivalent.

Atomic and Molecular Spectroscopy: Mr. Gavin (at Haverford 1976-77).

Topics include absorption and emission spectroscopy in the vacuum ultraviolet, the ultraviolet-visible and the infrared regions, nuclear magnetic resonance spectroscopy and raman spectroscopy. Two lecture-discussions, five hours of laboratory a week and regular use of a computer. Prerequisites: Chemistry 303a and some elementary knowledge of Fortran programming.

The Dynamics of Environmental Systems: Mr. Anderson.

Principles of the structure and function of ecosystems; techniques for the simulation of complex systems; the impact of man on the environment and man's management of resources. Three hours of lecture-discussion a week. Prerequisites: one year each of a natural and of a social science and some familiarity with digital computation.

Biochemistry: Macromolecular Structure and Function: Mr. Prescott, Mr. Young.

See Biology 353a.

Biochemistry: Intermediary Metabolism: Mr. Conner, Mr. Prescott.

See Biology 353b.

Biochemical Mechanisms: Mr. Lerman (at Haverford).

Prerequisite: Chemistry 202.

Senior Conference:

The Senior Conference consists of four half-semester special topic seminars. In each year, eight such seminars will be offered. Four of these will be given at Bryn Mawr and four at Haverford, and students are free to select the seminars at either institution according to their own interests and preparation. These special seminars will be in the broad areas of chemistry, for instance, biochemistry, inorganic, organic and physical chemistry, and will cover subject matter not usually taken up, or only briefly treated, in the regular courses. They will be on a level which has at least one semester of a 200-level course as a prerequisite. The topics will vary from year to year, and a list of topics will be made available to students towards the end of their junior year.

401. *Honors Work:* Honors work, consisting of individual research under the supervision of a member of the Department, may be undertaken in conjunction with any of the advanced courses by qualified students who are invited by the Department to participate in this program.

Teaching Certification: A sequence of work offered by the Department of Chemistry and the Department of Education of the College leads to a certificate to teach in the secondary schools of Pennsylvania.

Classical and Near Eastern Archaeology

Professors: Machteld J. Mellink, PH.D., *Chairman*
Kyle M. Phillips, Jr., PH.D.‡
Brunilde S. Ridgway, PH.D.

Professor of Classical and Near Eastern Archaeology and *of History of Art:*
Phyllis Pray Bober, PH.D., *Dean of The Graduate School of Arts and Sciences*

Mary Flexner Lecturer: Phyllis W. Lehmann, PH.D.

Associate Professors: Richard S. Ellis, PH.D.
Carl Nylander, PH.D.

Assistants: Janer D. Belson, M.A.
P. Gregory Warden, M.A.

The major courses provide an extensive survey of the ancient Mediterranean and Near Eastern civilizations, with emphasis on Greek art and archaeology.

---

‡On leave for the year 1976-77.

Requirements in the Major Subject: Archaeology 101, 201a or 204b or 208a; 203a and b, 205b, 301a and 302b and the Senior Conferences. All majors are urged to take Greek and ancient history and to acquire a reading knowledge of French and German.

Allied Subjects: Ancient History, Anthropology, History of Art, Greek, Latin, Akkadian, Hebrew.

101. *An Introduction to Ancient Art:* Mrs. Ridgway, Mr. Nylander.
       An historical survey of the art of the ancient Near East, Greece and Rome. Three hours of classes, one hour of informal discussion a week.

201a. *The Archaeology of Mesopotamia before 1600 B.C.:* Mr. Ellis.

202b. *Ancient Greek Cities and Sanctuaries:* Mr. Nylander.]
(INT.)

203a. *Roman Sculpture:* Mrs. Bober.
       Roman sculpture against the general background of Roman art.

203b. *Greek Sculpture:* Mrs. Ridgway.
       The development of Greek sculpture to the Hellenistic period.

204a. *The Ancient City:* Mr. Scott.
(INT.)   See INT. 204a in the interdepartmental major in The Growth and Structure of Cities.

204b. *Egypt and Mesopotamia from 1600-500 B.C.:* Mr. Ellis.]

205a. *The Ancient Near East:* Mr. Ellis.
       See History 205a.

205b. *Aegean Archaeology:* Miss Mellink.
       The pre-Greek and early Greek cultures of the Aegean area: Minoan Crete, Troy, the Aegean Islands, Mycenaean Greece and their overseas connections.

206b. *Ancient Near Eastern Architecture:* Mr. Ellis, Miss Mellink.
(INT.)   The development of architectural form and function in Western Asia. Reconstruction of historical sites on the basis of excavation and texts.

208a. *Medes and Persians:* Mr. Nylander.]

301a. *Greek Vase-Painting:* Mr. Phillips.]

302a. *Greek Architecture:* Mr. Nylander.
(INT.)   The Greek architectural tradition in its historical development, with a special study of the Greek temple.

[302b. *Roman Architecture:* Mr. Phillips.]

[303a. *Etruscan Archaeology:* Mr. Phillips.]

[304a. *Monumental Painting:* Mr. Phillips.]

305b. *The Bronze Age in Syria and Palestine:* Mr. Ellis.
The archaeology of the Levant and its relationships with surrounding cultures from the beginnings of urban civilization to the disturbances caused by the Sea Peoples c. 1200 B.C.

390b. *Studies in the Art of Greece in the Fourth Century B.C.:* Mrs. Lehmann.

399. *Senior Conference:* Weekly two-hour seminars with assigned readings and reports. Semester I: Mr. Ellis, Mr. Nylander; semester II: Miss Mellink, Mrs. Ridgway.

See also History 205a. *The Ancient Near East:* Mr. Ellis, Mr. Nylander.

401. *Honors Work:* A long written paper is submitted on a topic selected by the student and approved by the Department. In preparation, the student confers throughout the year with the member of the Department under whose direction the paper is prepared.

Interdepartmental Work: The Department of Classical and Near Eastern Archaeology participates in the interdepartmental majors in Classical Studies and The Growth and Structure of Cities. See pages 147 and 150.

Excavation: The Department has two excavation projects. The excavation of Karatash-Semayük in Lycia (Turkey) is conducted as a field seminar in the fall, with full credit for graduate students and seniors by invitation. The second project, the excavation of an Etruscan archaic site at Murlo near Siena, takes place during the summer on a non-credit basis for graduate and undergraduate students of archaeology.

Economics

Professor: Richard B. Du Boff, PH.D.

Associate Professors: Noel J. J. Farley, PH.D., *Chairman*
Helen Manning Hunter, PH.D.

Assistant Professor: Li Way Lee, PH.D.

At Haverford

President: John R. Coleman, PH.D.

Assistant Vice-President: Samuel Gubins, PH.D.

Professor: Holland Hunter, PH.D.

Associate Professor: Vernon J. Dixon, PH.D.

Instructor: Michael Weinstein, B.A.

The major in economics consists of courses given at Bryn Mawr and Haverford. It is designed to provide an understanding of economic processes and institutions and the interactions among the economic, political and social structures, to train students in the methods used to analyze those processes and institutions, and to enable them to make policy judgments.

Requirements in the Major Subject: Economics 111a and b and 112a and b, three units of intermediate and advanced work (including at least one unit of a 300-level course) and the Senior Conference. Courses 111a and b and 112a and b are designed to give the kind of informed perspective on economic principles and problems that is an integral part of a liberal education, as well as to provide a foundation for students to do further work in economics. The group of intermediate courses offers a full range of material on major topics in the discipline and is designed to meet a wide variety of student interests. The group of advanced courses supplies a methodological and theoretical foundation for those planning to make use of economics in their professional careers. In the selection of courses the student is urged to take three of the following courses: 203a or b, 303a, 304b, 310a. Students intending to do graduate work in economics should take 302b and Mathematics 101 and 201 and they should consult with members of the Department about their plans before selecting their courses.

Prospective majors in economics are advised to take Economics 111a and b and 112a and b by the end of the first semester of the sophomore year. As a general rule, the prerequisites for intermediate and advanced-level work are Economics 111a and b and Economics 112a and b or permission of instructor.

Allied Subjects: Mathematics, Political Science, History, Philosophy, Psychology, Sociology, Anthropology.

111a. *Introduction to Macroeconomics:* Members of the Department.
& b.   The analysis of national economic behavior including prosperity and depression. Theories of inflation and unemployment. The role of government in managing and mismanaging the economy by influencing total national expenditure and by regulating financial institutions. The international role of the United States. Focus is on Western mixed-capitalist economies.

112a. *Introduction to Microeconomics:* Members of the Department.
& b.   Techniques of analysis which apply to all economic systems in general and modern mixed-capitalism in particular. Topics include: determination of costs and prices for goods and services; the functioning of the marketplace; causes of wealth, poverty and income inequality; environmental protection; discrimination. The course is intended to provide a method of examining economic behavior which will continue to be useful in a changing economic world.

115b. *Economic Accounting:* Mr. Dixon (at Haverford).

201b. *American Economic Development:* Mr. Du Boff.
       Long-term trends in output, resources and technology; structure of consumption, production and distribution; foreign trade and investment, and the role of the state. Quantitative findings provide the points of departure, and the framework is one of imbalances and disequilibria in an expanding capitalist economy. Prerequisites: Economics 111a or b and Economics 112a or b.

[202b. *Latin American Economic Development.*]

203a. *Statistical Methods in Economics:* Members of the Department.
& b.   Frequency distributions, probability and sampling theory, simple correlation and multiple regression and an introduction to econometric terminology and reasoning. The computer programming and other techniques required are developed as part of the course. Prerequisites: Economics 111a or b and Economics 112a or b.

[204a. *Mathematics for Economists:* Mr. Weinstein (at Haverford).]

205a. *The Corporation and Public Policy:* Mr. Lee.
       The economic effects of anti-trust legislation on market structure in static and dynamic settings; corporate performance evaluated within the framework of theories of the firm; emphasis on individual industry studies; public utilities and government regulatory actions; pollution, discrimination and public policy. Prerequisite: Economics 112a or b.

International Economic Theory and Policy: Mr. Farley.

Current problems in international trade. The theory of trade. The balance of payments and theory of disturbances and adjustment in the international economy. Economic integration. The impact of growth in rich and poor countries on the development of the world economy. Prerequisite: Economics 111a or b and Economics 112a or b or permission of instructor.

Money and Banking: Mrs. Hunter.

The development and present organization of the money and banking system of the United States; domestic and international problems of monetary theory and policy. Prerequisites: Economics 111a or b and Economics 112a or b.

Economics of the Public Sector: Mr. Lee.]

Urban Economics: Mr. Dixon (at Haverford).

)

Developing Economies: Mr. Farley.

Analysis of the structural transformation and developing economies. Causes and roles of saving, investment, skills, technological change and trade in the development process; strategies and methods of economic planning. Prerequisites: Economics 111a or b and Economics 112a or b.

The Soviet System: Mr. Hunter (at Haverford).

)   An analysis of the structure and functioning of major Soviet economic, political and social institutions. Current conditions are studied as products of historical development. Prerequisite: two semester courses in economics, political science or history.

The Modern Corporation: Mr. Coleman (at Haverford).

Economic History and Growth, 1750-1970: Mr. Du Boff.

Topics include the underlying causes of economic growth and underdevelopment, the spread of industrialization and technological modernization to Western Europe and North America, resource allocation and political power, and "Is Economic Growth Worth It?" Prerequisites: Economics 111a or b and 112a or b or permission of instructor.

Topics in Cliometric History of the United States: Mr. Weinstein (at Haverford).

Seminar in Labor Resources: Mr. Coleman (at Haverford).

History of Economic Thought: Mr. Du Boff.]

225a. *Topics in Economics:* Members of the Department (at Haverford).
& b.

302b. *Introduction to Econometrics:* Mrs. Hunter.

    The econometric theory presented in Economics 203a and b is further developed and its most important empirical economic applications are considered. Each student will do a six-week empirical research project using multiple regression and other statistical techniques. Prerequisites: Economics 203a or b and permission of instructor.

303a. *Macroeconomic Analysis:* Mr. Dixon (at Haverford).

304b. *Microeconomic Analysis:* Mr. Lee.

    Systematic investigation of analytic relationships underlying consumer welfare, efficient resource allocation and ideal pricing. Introduction to operations research. Prerequisite: Economics 112a or b or permission of instructor.

310a. *Interindustry Economics:* Mr. Hunter (at Haverford).

[312a. *Economic Integration: Theory and Policy:* Mr. Farley.]

315b. *Advanced Economic Theory:* Mr. Weinstein (at Haverford).

321b. *Quantitative Analysis of Economic Change:* Mrs. Hunter.

    Business cycles and economic growth: theory, measurement and forecasting. Prerequisite: Economics 203a or b.

399. *Senior Conference:* Weekly two-hour seminars for which readings are assigned and reports are prepared. Semester I: economic theory; semester II: topic to be chosen by the students. Each student will have the option of writing a paper or taking an examination.

401. *Honors Work:* One unit of Honors work may be taken by students recommended by the Department.

Interdepartmental Work: The Department of Economics participates in the interdepartmental major in The Growth and Structure of Cities and in the interdepartmental concentration in Hispanic and Hispanic-American Studies. See pages 150 and 153.

Teaching Certification: A sequence of work offered by the Department of Economics and the Department of Education of the College leads to a certificate to teach in the secondary schools of Pennsylvania.

Education and Child Development

Professors: Janet L. Hoopes, PH.D., *Director, Child Study Institute*
Ethel W. Maw, PH.D., *Chairman*

Associate Professors: Susan E. Maxfield, M.S., *Director, Thorne School*
Emmy A. Pepitone, PH.D.
Faye P. Soffen, ED.D.‡

Assistant Professors: Fred Rothbaum, M.S.
Samuel S. Snyder, PH.D.

Lecturer: Ruth B. Harvey, PH.D.

The work in education is designed for students preparing for teaching or for work with children in a variety of fields. The curriculum treats the nature and development of the child, the psychology of teaching and learning and principles of measurement. It deals with the history, philosophy and objectives of the school as a social institution.

Although there is no major in education, a sequence of courses in the department enables the student to prepare for teaching in the secondary school. Students expecting to teach are urged to confer with the Department during the freshman year.

For students preparing for teaching, the first semester of the senior year is an extremely busy one. During student teaching, the student must be prepared to be in the school throughout the school day, five days a week.

The Thorne School is maintained by the Department as a laboratory for child study where undergraduates have experience with young children. The pre-kindergarten program, in which advanced students assist, provides training for those planning to teach.

The Department also operates the Child Study Institute. This is a mental health service supported by the College, by the Lower Merion Township Schools and by fees. Problems of learning and behavior are studied; psychological testing, psychiatric treatment, remedial teaching and a program of counseling for children and parents are carried on. Advanced students participate in the work, and undergraduate and graduate students observe in the schools and at the Institute.

---

‡On leave for the year 1976-77.

[101b. *The Social Foundations of Education:* Mrs. Pepitone.]

102b. *History and Philosophy of Education:* Mrs. Pepitone.

A study of the interrelation of education and culture from earliest times to the present day with particular consideration given to current educational issues as they are rooted in the historical process.

[201a. *Educational Psychology.*]

[206a. *Developmental Psychology:* Mr. Snyder. (In alternate years, Psychology 206a. *Developmental Psychology:* Miss Wannemacher.)]

206b. *Adolescent Development:* Mr. Rothbaum.

Patterns and problems of development—physical, cognitive, emotional, and social—as they relate to the adolescent period. Theory and research focusing on adolescents in home, school and society. Three hours a week with laboratory or other independent work required. Prerequisite: Education 206a or permission of instructor.

301a. *Principles of Teaching in the Secondary School:* Mrs. Maw.

The objectives, curriculum and organization of the secondary school. The nature of the learner and his relation to the school program and aims. Two-hour seminar a week; student teaching in the junior or senior high school. A full unit of work. Prerequisite: permission of instructor.

[302a. *Principles of Teaching in the Elementary School:* Mrs. Maw.]

See also Psychology 63b. Perception, Psycholinguistics and Reading: Mr. Travers (at Swarthmore).

Selected Graduate Seminars: For certain undergraduates who have taken developmental psychology or educational psychology the following graduate seminars are open upon the consent of the instructor with the permission of the student's Class Dean and the Dean of The Graduate School of Arts and Sciences:

Critical Issues in Human Development: Mr. Snyder.

Teaching Certification: Requirements for the state certificate to teach in the public secondary schools can be met by the appropriate selection of courses in this Department and in the major field or fields. Though each state has its own requirements, most follow the same pattern, namely the Bachelor of Arts degree with emphasis upon a content area offered in the secondary school plus professional preparation for teaching. At Bryn Mawr the suggested sequence includes Psychology 101 followed by Education 101b, 201a and 102b or 206a or 206b. Required of all is Education 301a.

English

Professors: Robert B. Burlin, PH.D., *Acting Chairman, Semester 1*
K. Laurence Stapleton, A.B.

Professor of English and Performing Arts: Robert H. Butman, M.A.

Associate Professors: Carol L. Bernstein, PH.D.
Thomas H. Jackson, PH.D.
Joseph E. Kramer, PH.D., *Chairman**

Assistant Professors: Sandra M. Berwind, PH.D.
Peter M. Briggs, PH.D.
Katrin Ristkok Burlin, PH.D.
Susan Dean, PH.D.
Stephen Goodwin, M.A.
E. Jane Hedley, PH.D.
Anne Kaier, PH.D.
Sandra I. Kohler, PH.D.

Lecturers: Diane Balestri, PH.D., *Dean of Class of 1978*
Eileen Tess Johnston, M.A.
Ramona T. Livingston, A.B.
Elizabeth R. McKinsey, B.A.

The Department offers an opportunity to explore all periods of English literature. Through comprehensive reading as well as close analysis, the major in English seeks to develop an historical perspective, critical and writing abilities and an understanding of the imaginative process.

Requirements in the Major Subject: Prerequisite: English 101a and b (Bryn Mawr or Haverford) or its equivalent. Four second-year or advanced units in English literature. At least one full unit must be at an advanced (300) level. At least one half-unit must be in the literature of the Middle Ages. Students may in consultation with their departmental advisors offer no more than one half-unit of advanced fiction writing or verse composition toward fulfillment of the four-unit requirement. Students may in consultation with their departmental advisors take a portion of their work at Haverford. The Senior Conference.

---

*On leave, semester I.

Allied Subjects: Majors are urged to build a strong ally in classical or modern literature, History, Philosophy or History of Art. Other courses in Music, History of Religion, Political Science, Sociology and Linguistics may also be counted. A second-year writing course may be substituted for one unit of allied work.

Students contemplating graduate work in English are reminded that most graduate schools require a reading knowledge of French and German, and frequently Latin as well, for the Ph.D.

015. *English Composition and Reading:* Members of the Department.

Training in writing discursive prose, with emphasis on the critical analysis of a few works by selected authors. There will be weekly papers, two class meetings a week and regular conferences. Brief descriptions of the topics and reading lists for 1976-77 will be sent to each student in May, to allow her to indicate her preference. (Note: there is one division of this course, called "Readings in English Literature," which may be substituted for the prerequisite to the English major. In this division there will be three class meetings a week, as well as more reading. The paper requirements are the same as for the other divisions.)

WRITING COURSES

Weekly papers are required in the following courses. Students who cannot meet this requirement should not elect any of these courses.

183a. *Art of Poetry:* Mr. Ransom (at Haverford).

190a. *Creative Writing:* Mrs. Walker (at Haverford).
& b.

191b. *Prose Writing:* Mr. Goodwin.

Class discussion, reading and writing assignments are designed to introduce students to a range of styles and techniques of prose writing other than fiction. Texts of several different kinds, including reviews and other forms of journalism, will be examined. Weekly papers are required.

192a. *Fiction Writing:* Mr. Goodwin.

Class discussion, reading and writing assignments are designed to introduce students to the techniques of prose fiction. Weekly papers are required.

193b. *Advanced Fiction Writing:* Mr. Goodwin.

The writing of at least two extended pieces of short fiction. Student writing and some assigned texts will be discussed in class. Prerequisites:

English 190a and b, 191b, or 192a. All students must submit a portfolio of writing for admission to this course.

* *Verse Composition:* Miss Stapleton.]

* *Playwriting and Production:* Mr. Butman.
    Writing of two original one-act plays.

* *Advanced Playwriting and Production:* Mr. Butman.
    Writing of a full-length play and preparation of its production-book. Prerequisite: permission of instructor.

Projects in Writing: Mr. Goodwin.]

LITERATURE

Major Works in English Literature: Members of the Bryn Mawr and Haverford departments.
    This prerequisite to the English major, taught jointly at Haverford and Bryn Mawr, is the critical study, in chronological sequence, of major works by major authors, including Chaucer, Spenser, Shakespeare, Milton, Pope and Wordsworth, and one other major work. The emphasis will be on close reading and on the continuity of traditions and modes in English and American literature.

Chaucer and His Contemporaries: Miss Malard (at Haverford), Mr. Burlin.
    The first semester will be devoted to a close reading of the *Canterbury Tales*. Emphasis will be given to Chaucer's exploitation and transcendence of medieval literary conventions, from the bawdy fabliau to the courtly romance to the saint's life. The second semester will concentrate upon Chaucer's early poems and the *Troilus*, with supplementary readings from the Middle English period.

Medieval Narrative: From Beowulf to Malory: Mr. Burlin.]

Sixteenth-Century Literature: Mrs. Hedley.
    A cross-section of the major literary genres in sixteenth-century England, with special emphasis on lyric poetry and the pastoral. Readings will include More's *Utopia*, Spenser's *Shepherd's Calendar*, Shakespeare's *As You Like It*; selected lyrics and satires by Wyatt, Gascoigne and others; Sidney's *Defense of Poetry*.

Renaissance Lyric Poetry: Mrs. Hedley.]

225a. *Shakespeare:* Mrs. Kohler; Miss Malard (at Haverford).
& b.   The first semester will be devoted primarily to the histories and comedies; the second semester to the tragedies and romances.

228b. *Modern Drama:* Mr. Kramer.

Major developments in the theater from Ibsen to the present will be explored. Close attention will be given to traditions and conventions associated with the specific theaters such as the Abbey, the Moscow Art and the Group and to schools of playwriting.

240a. *Restoration and Early Eighteenth-Century Literature:* Mr. Briggs.
& b.   Developments to be examined in the first semester include the rise of new literary genres and the contemporary effort to find new definitions of heroism and wit, good taste and good manners, sin and salvation. Principal readings will be drawn from Dryden, the Restoration dramatists, Swift and Pope.

In the second semester particular attention will be directed toward two developments: first, the cultural perspective and literary achievements of Johnson and his circle, and second, the experiments of a more heterogeneous group of writers whose diverse interests formed the basis of English Romanticism.

247b. *Eighteenth-Century English Novel:* Mrs. Burlin.

A study of selected novels in the context of relevant eighteenth-century intellectual trends and critical approaches: Defoe, Richardson, Fielding, Smollett, Sterne, Radcliffe, Burney, Edgeworth and Austen.

250a. *Nineteenth-Century English Poetry:* Mrs. Johnston.
& b.   A study of the major poets from Blake to Hardy, including some of their key theoretical writings. The development of several traditions, themes and forms will be emphasized.

[252a. *The Romantic Movement:* Miss Kaier.]
& b.

[253a. *The Lyric from 1750 to the Present:* Mrs. Johnston.]

254a. *Victorian Period:* Mr. Lester (at Haverford).

255b. *Clio in Nineteenth-Century British Literature:* Mrs. Hutchinson (at Haverford).

256a. *Hopkins and Swinburne:* Mr. Satterthwaite (at Haverford).

257a. *British Literature in Transition: 1880-1910:* Mrs. Hutchinson (at Haverford).

Development of the Novel: Mr. Lester (at Haverford).

Nineteenth-Century English Novel: Mrs. Burlin.]

American Literature to 1915: Miss McKinsey.

A study of the development of an American tradition in literature from the Puritans to the twentieth century with attention to major themes and techniques. Readings will center on major writers including Edwards, Franklin, Poe, Emerson, Thoreau, Hawthorne, Melville, Whitman, Twain, James and Adams.

Black American Literature: Mr. Miller (at Haverford).

Modern Literature of the American South: Miss McKinsey.]

American Literature from 1915 to the Present: Mr. Ransom (at Haverford).

American Studies: Mr. Ashmead (at Haverford).

Twain and Faulkner: Mr. Ashmead (at Haverford).

Modern Short Fiction: Mr. Goodwin.]

Twentieth-Century Literature: Mr. Jackson.

Twentieth-century literature in its relationship to earlier literary and intellectual traditions, principal themes and technical achievements, seen through extensive study of selected major twentieth-century writers.

Post-Colonial Fiction in English: Mr. Jackson.]

Tragedy: Miss Malard (at Haverford).

Comedy: Mr. Rose (at Haverford).

The Lyric: Mrs. Berwind.

Instruction in the techniques (tropological, rhetorical, formal and prosodic) by which poetry expresses its meaning. There will be some discussion of critical theory, but most of the time will be devoted to practical analysis of short poems from different periods.

The Language of Drama: Mr. Burlin.]

Urban Fiction.]

The following courses are open primarily to advanced students; enrollment will be restricted at the discretion of the instructor.

300. *Old English Literature:* Mr. Burlin.

After a brief introduction to the language and some reading of prose, the first semester will be devoted to short lyrics and questions of Old English poetic style; the second semester, to a careful study of the textual and critical problems of *Beowulf*. This is a full year course and the second semester cannot be taken unless the student has prior training in the language.

[301a. *Readings in Middle English Literature:* Mr. Burlin.]

302b. *Medieval Topics:* Miss Malard (at Haverford).

315b. *Sixteenth-Century Chivalric Romance:* Mrs. Hedley.

Sidney's *Arcadia* and Spenser's *Færie Queene* will be read. Special attention will be given to the conventions of chivalric romance.

{321a. *English Drama to 1642.*}
& b.

[323b. *Renaissance English Tragedy:* Mr. Kramer.]

325a. *Shakespeare:* Mr. Satterthwaite (at Haverford).

[326a. *Theatre of Ben Jonson:* Mr. Kramer.]

330a. *The Seventeenth Century:* Miss Stapleton.
& b.
The first semester will be devoted to the Metaphysical poets, especially Donne, and major prose writers such as Bacon and Sir Thomas Browne. An opportunity will be given for students who are interested to study some of the women writers of the period. The second term is devoted primarily to Milton.

355b. *Major Victorian Poets:* Mrs. Johnston.

The focus of the first half of the course will be on an intensive study of Tennyson's poetry. The second half will be devoted to the major poems of Browning and Arnold, as well as to some of Arnold's major prose writings.

[358a. *Jane Austen:* Mrs. Burlin.]

{358b. *Women Writers: Novels of the Mind:* Mrs. Burlin.}

361b. *American Literature of the New Republic:* Mr. Ransom (at Haverford).

{362b. *The Sublime in America:* Miss McKinsey.}

363b. *Melville:* Mr. Ashmead (at Haverford).

{364b. *William Faulkner.*}

Contemporary American Poetry: Mrs. Kohler.

A study of the major figures, beginning with the work of Robert Lowell.

Richard Wright: Mr. Miller (at Haverford).

The Development of Modern Poetry: Mr. Jackson.]

James Joyce: Mr. Lester (at Haverford).

William Butler Yeats: Mrs. Berwind.

An investigation of the relationships between the *Collected Poems* and selected prose of W. B. Yeats. *The Celtic Twilight, The Secret Rose* and *A Vision* will be among the prose works studied.

Virginia Woolf and E. M. Forster: Miss Kaier.

A study of the novels and literary criticism of Woolf and Forster. The works will be considered with regard to cultural perspective, novelistic form and technique and the premises of informal, impressionistic literary criticism.

The Sonnet: Mrs. Kohler.]

The Theory of Fiction: Mrs. Bernstein.

The study of several theories of fiction in historical, conceptual and systematic contexts. After an examination of ideas of fiction as they appear from the eighteenth century to the early modern period, there will be an intensive scrutiny of the meaning and function of such central conceptions as character, plot and style. The course will then focus on major theories ranging from the structural to the sociological. Three novels will be included in the readings.

Problems in Satire: Mr. Briggs.

A review of major developments in English satire since 1600 and simultaneously an exploration of traditional problem areas: the persona; social, moral and literary decorum; the limits of satiric metaphor and satire itself; form, mock-form and the tendency of satire to invade prevailing literary types. Major readings from Donne, Swift, Pope, Sterne, Blake, Byron and selected modern satirists.

Modern Poetic Theory: Mr. Jackson.]

Studies in Twentieth-Century Criticism: Mr. Jackson.]

Senior Conference: a: Mr. Jackson, Miss Kaier; b: Mrs. Burlin, Mr. Kramer.

The Senior Conference will continue for the entire year and will focus upon a core of reading, determined in advance by the two instructors for each semester. The reading will consist of substantial and significant works drawn from all periods of English and American literature, ranging from the late medieval period to the modern.

Majors in English will be expected to know the works in advance— either through course work or summer reading. The conferences will consider kinds of critical approaches to these works and will demand of the students further reading, as well as responsible participation. A work may be considered in its historical context (political, philosophical, occasional background); in the context of other works by the author (for both thematic and formal comparison); in the context of other works of the same period and, for structural and generic studies, in the context of the entire spectrum of English and American literature. Concurrently the student will become acquainted with examples of practical and theoretical criticism which exemplify these various approaches.

At the end of the year the students will be examined by a committee of four members of the Department who are not involved in supervision of the conference. The student may elect either a four-hour written examination or a fifty-minute oral. The examination will allow for many kinds of exemplification as well as intelligent use of supplementary and secondary reading. The grade for the year will be determined by the Examination Committee in consultation with the conference instructors.

401. *Honors Work:* In the senior year, Honors work, consisting of independent reading, reports and conferences, is offered to students of marked ability. Honors papers are due on the Friday two weeks before the end of classes.

Teaching Certification: A sequence of work offered by the Department of English and the Department of Education of the College leads to a certificate to teach in the secondary schools of Pennsylvania.

French

Professors: Gérard Defaux, D. ès L., *Acting Chairman, Semester II*
Michel Guggenheim, PH.D.
Pauline Jones, PH.D., *Chairman†*
Mario Maurin, PH.D.

———
†On leave, semester II.

Associate Professor: Catherine Lafarge, PH.D.

Assistant Professor: Grace Armstrong Savage, PH.D.

Lecturers: Frances Stokes Hoekstra, PH.D.
   Margaret S. Maurin, PH.D.

Instructor: Sheila Mall, A.B.

Assistant: Mary A. Franz, B.A.

The major in French includes work in both literature and language. In the first year students are introduced to the study of French literature, and special attention is given to the speaking and writing of French. Second-year courses treat French literature from the beginning to the present day. In these courses, students whose command of written French is inadequate will be expected to attend regular sessions devoted to special training in writing French. A second-year half-course is devoted to advanced language training, with practice in spoken as well as in written French.

Advanced courses offer detailed study of individual authors, genres and movements. Students are admitted to advanced courses after satisfactory completion of two semesters of 200-level courses in French literature or by placement test and permission of Department.

Students in all courses are encouraged to make use of the Language Laboratory. In French 001, 002 and 205c, the use of the Laboratory and intensive oral practice in small groups directed by a Department assistant form an integral part of the course. French majors find it valuable to supplement the work done at Bryn Mawr by study abroad either during the summer at the *Institut* in Avignon or by study abroad during the sophomore or junior year. Residence in French House for at least one year is advisable.

Requirements in the Major Subject: French 101, French 205c, four semesters of 200-level literature courses, two semesters of advanced literature courses and the Senior Conference. Students whose preparation for college has included advanced work in language and literature may, with consent of the Department, substitute a more advanced course for French 101. Occasionally, students may be admitted to seminars in the Graduate School. Such arrangements are made at the suggestion of the Department, with the approval of the Dean of The Graduate School of Arts and Sciences.

All French majors are expected to have acquired fluency in the French language, both written and oral. Unless specifically exempted by the Department, they are required to take French 205c.

Allied Subjects: Any other language or literature, European History, History of Art, Music, Philosophy.

001. *Elementary French:* Members of the Department.

The speaking and understanding of French are emphasized, particularly during the first semester. The work includes regular use of the Language Laboratory and is supplemented by intensive oral practice sessions three or four times a week. The course meets five times a week.

002. *Intermediate French:* Members of the Department.

The emphasis on speaking and understanding French is continued, texts from French literature are read and short papers are written in French. Students are expected to use the Language Laboratory regularly and to attend supplementary oral practice sessions twice a week.

101. *Introduction to Literary Analysis:* Members of the Department.

Presentation of essential problems in literary analysis by close reading of works selected from various periods and genres (drama, poetry, novels and short stories.) Participation in discussion and practice in written and oral expression are emphasized.

201a. *The Classical Age:* Mr. Cook (at Haverford).

Reading in the French seventeenth century, from Pascal's *Pensées* to La Bruyère's *Caractères*, with special attention to the flowering of the classical drama.

201b. *French Literature of the Eighteenth Century:* Miss Lafarge.

The course will include texts representative of the Enlightenment and the Pre-Romantic movement, with emphasis upon the development of liberal thought as illustrated in the *Encyclopédie* and the works of Montesquieu, Voltaire, Diderot and Rousseau.

202a. *French Literature of the Nineteenth Century:* Miss Jones, Mr. Maurin.

The poetry, drama and prose of Romanticism. A study of representative novelists such as Stendhal, Balzac and Flaubert. Poetry in the second half of the century: the aesthetics of the Parnasse, Baudelaire, the Symbolist movement.

202b. *French Literature of the Twentieth Century:* Mr. Guggenheim, Mr. Maurin.

A study of selected works illustrating the principal literary movements

84

from the turn of the century to the present. Gide, Proust, Valéry, Claudel, Surrealism, Existentialism, the Theater of the Absurd, the New Novel.

203a. *French Literature of the Middle Ages:* Mrs. Savage.}

204a. *French Literature of the Sixteenth Century:* Mr. Defaux.

A study of the development of Humanism, the concept of the Renaissance, and the Reformation. The course will focus on representative works, with special attention given to the prose of Rabelais and Montaigne, the *Conteurs*, the poetry of Marot, the Pléiade and d'Aubigné.

205c. *Stylistique et traduction:* Mr. Maurin, Mrs. Savage.

Intensive practice in speaking and writing. Conversation, discussion, advanced training in grammar and stylistics, translation of literary and non-literary texts and original composition. With the addition of a third hour each week, the course may be taken as either 205a or 205b.

[290. *La Civilisation de France:* Mr. Silvera; Mr. McCarthy (at Haverford).]
(INT.)

295a. *Paris in the Seventeenth and Eighteenth Centuries:* Miss Lafarge.
(INT.)   See INT. 295a in the interdepartmental major in The Growth and Structure of Cities.

295b. *Littérature, histoire et société de la Renaissance à la Révolution:*
(INT.) Mr. Guggenheim.
      See INT. 295b in the interdepartmental major in French Studies.

297a. *Le Seizième Siècle à travers le roman historique:* Mr. Salmon.
(INT.) .   See INT. 297a in the interdepartmental major in French Studies.

301. *French Lyric Poetry.*]

302. *French Novel.*}

303a. *La Vision de la femme dans la littérature française.*}

304a. *Ecrivains engagés de Montaigne à Sartre.*}

304b. *Le Théâtre de 1880 à 1939.*]

305a. *Baudelaire:* Miss Jones.

A study of the *Fleurs du mal* and the *Petits Poèmes en prose*, with emphasis upon the *modernité* of themes and techniques. Some attention will be given to the *Paradis artificiels* and a selection of Baudelaire's critical writings as primary sources of later definitions of the nature and function of the symbol in poetry and other arts.

85

306a. *Le Roman du vingtième siècle:* Mr. Guggenheim.
    A study of works representative of the twentieth-century French novel from *Le Grand Meaulnes* to the *Noveau Roman*, with particular attention given to thematic content and narrative techniques.

306b. *Molière et la comédie:* Mr. Defaux.
    A study of Molière's comedies placed in their socio-cultural context—with references to Corneille, Tristan l'Hermite, Scarron and other comic writers of the seventeenth century. Special attention will be given to the structural metamorphoses of Molière's plays and the evolution of his thought and comic vision.

311a. *Advanced Topics in French Literature:* Mr. Gutwirth (at Haverford).
    Topic for 1976-77: Views of the Self—from *La Chute* back to the *Essais*. A glance backward at major explorations of the self in French literature, from Albert Camus to Montaigne, by way of Gide's *Prométhée mal enchaîné*, Stendhal's *Le Rouge et le noir*, Diderot's *Neveu de Rameau*, La Rochefoucauld and Pascal.

311b. *Advanced Topics in French Literature:* Mr. Cook (at Haverford).
    Topic for 1976-77: To be announced.

399. *Senior Conference:* Mr. Defaux, Miss Lafarge.
    A weekly seminar on representative works of French literature followed at the end of the year by an oral explication of a French literary text and a three-hour written examination.

401. *Honors Work:* On the recommendation of the Department, students in their senior year will be admitted to Honors work consisting of independent reading, conferences and a long paper.

    Interdepartmental Work: The Department of French participates in the interdepartmental majors in French Studies and The Growth and Structure of Cities. See pages 148 and 150.

    Junior Year Abroad: Students majoring in French may, by a joint recommendation of the Dean of the College and the Department of French, be allowed to spend their junior year in France under one of the junior year plans, such as those organized by Barnard and Columbia, Hamilton, Hood, Sarah Lawrence, Smith, Swarthmore and Sweet Briar Colleges, New York University, Vanderbilt University, University of Vermont or L'Académie.

    Summer Study: Students wishing to enroll in a summer program may apply for admission to the *Institut d'Etudes françaises d'Avignon,* held under the auspices of Bryn Mawr. The *Institut* is designed for selected undergraduates and graduate students with a serious interest in French culture, most particularly for those who anticipate professional careers requiring a knowledge of the language and civilization of France. The curriculum includes general and advanced courses in French language, literature, social sciences, history and art. The program is open to students of high academic achievement who have completed a course in French at the third-year college level, or the equivalent.

Teaching Certification: A sequence of work offered by the Department of French and the Department of Education of the College leads to a certificate to teach in the secondary schools of Pennsylvania.

Geology

Associate Professors: Maria Luisa B. Crawford, PH.D, *Chairman*
    William A. Crawford, PH.D.
    Lucian B. Platt, PH.D.‡
    William Bruce Saunders, PH.D.

Assistant Professor: George C. Stephens, PH.D.

Lecturer: Jay Leonard, B.A.

Assistants: Floyd E. Demmon, B.S.
    Lawrence E. Mark, B.A.
    Roger Stoffregen, B.A.
    William Thomann, B.S.

The Department seeks to make students more aware of the physical world around them. The subject includes a study of the materials of which the world is made, of the physical processes which have formed the earth, especially near the surface, of the history of the earth and its organisms and of the various techniques necessary to investigate earth processes and history. Geology borrows widely from its sister sciences, combining many disciplines into an attack on the problem of the earth itself. An

---

‡On leave for the year 1976-77.

essential part of any geologic training lies outside the classroom, in field work.

Requirements in the Major Subject: Geology 101a andb, 201a and b, 202a, 204b, one advanced unit, the Senior Conference, and one full-year course in two of the following departments: Chemistry, Mathematics, Physics. Students may meet some of the major and allied requirements by advanced standing or placement examinations. A student who wishes to follow a career in geology should also plan to attend a summer field course, usually following the junior year.

Allied Subjects: Biology, Chemistry, Physics, Mathematics; Astronomy, Anthropology, Archaeology, Economics or Statistics are accepted in special cases.

101a. *Physical Geology:* Members of the Department.

A study of materials and structures of the earth; surface and near-surface processes such as the action of streams, glaciers and volcanoes and of the features to which they give rise. Three lectures, three hours of laboratory or field work a week, plus a one-day field trip on a Saturday.

101b. *Historical Geology:* Members of the Department.

The history of the earth from its beginning and the evolution of the living forms which have populated it. Three lectures, four hours of laboratory or field work a week. A three-day field trip is taken in the spring. Prerequisite: Geology 101a or its equivalent.

201a. *Crystallography and Mineralogy:* Mrs. Crawford, Mr. Stephens.

The study of geometrical crystallography and crystal chemistry; descriptive and determinative mineralogy. The emphasis is on the relation between the physical properties of crystalline substances and their structures and chemical constitution. Three lectures, four hours of laboratory a week. Prerequisite: Geology 101a and b or permission of instructor.

201b. *Optical Mineralogy and Mineral Paragenesis:* Mrs. Crawford.

Further work on determinative mineralogy, emphasizing the use of the petrographic microscope. The occurrence and typical associations of minerals. Three lectures, four hours of laboratory a week. Prerequisite: Geology 201a.

202a. *Invertebrate Paleontology:* Mr. Saunders.

A systematic survey of animal groups in geologic time, with emphasis on their morphology, ecology and evolution. Three lectures, three hours of laboratory a week. Prerequisite: Geology 101a and b or permission of instructor.

Geomorphology: Mr. Leonard.

A study of landforms and landscapes, erosion agents and processes.

Physiography: Mr. Crawford.]

Structural Geology: Mr. Stephens.

Recognition and description of deformed rocks; introduction to mechanics and patterns of deformation. Three lectures and three hours of laboratory or field work a week. Prerequisite: Geology 101a and b or permission of instructor.

Introduction to Geochemistry: Mr. Crawford.]

Stratigraphy: Mr. Platt, Mr. Saunders.]

Environmental Geology: Mr. Stephens.]

Marine Geology: Mr. Leonard.

Integrates modern concepts of fluid-sediment interactions and plate tectonics with the classical approach of marine sediment distribution and sea-floor topography. The major emphasis is on processes occurring on beaches and continental margins. Laboratory. Prerequisites: Physical and historical geology, paleontology or biology, one year of either physics or calculus, or permission of instructor.

Advanced Paleontology: Mr. Saunders.

Principles, theory and application of various aspects of paleontology such as evolution of interest. Three lectures, three hours of laboratory a week (with occasional augmentation by field work). Prerequisite: Geology 202a or permission of instructor.

Thermodynamics for Geologists: Mr. Crawford.

An elementary treatment of thermodynamics and phase diagrams as applied to geological systems. The laboratory consists of determination of thermodynamic properties, phase equilibria experiments and familiarization with basic electronics as applied to laboratory apparatus. Three lectures and three hours of laboratory a week. Prerequisites: Geology 101a and b, Geology 201a and b, Chemistry 101 or permission of instructor.

Geochemistry: Mr. Crawford.

A review of selected topics in geochemistry. Three lectures and four hours of laboratory a week. Prerequisite: Geology 303a or permission of instructor.

[304.   *Introduction to Petrology:* Mrs. Crawford, Mr. Crawford, Mr. Saunders.]

[305b.   *X-ray Crystallography:* Mrs. Crawford.]

307a.   *Principles of Economic Geology:* Mr. Stephens.
An introduction to the formation, localization and exploitation of metallic mineral deposits. Three lectures, three hours of laboratory a week. Prerequisite: Geology 101a and b, 201a or permission of instructor.

307b.   *Introduction to Geophysics:* Mr. Stephens.
A survey of geophysical principles and techniques including magnetic, gravity, seismic and electrical methods. Three lectures and three hours of laboratory a week. Prerequisite: Geology 101a and b or permission of instructor.

399.   *Senior Conference* shall consist of:
1. "Topics in Geology," led by members of the Department.
2. A written report on an independent project in the field, laboratory or library.

401.   *Honors Work:* Qualified students are admitted to Honors Work on the recommendation of the Department. This consists of one unit of field or laboratory work on a independent research problem.

Selected Graduate Courses: Certain graduate courses are open to properly trained undergraduates with the approval of the student's Class Dean and the Dean of The Graduate School of Arts and Sciences.

German

Professor: Hans Bänziger, PH.D.

Associate Professors: Nancy C. Dorian, PH.D.
Gloria Flaherty, PH.D., *Chairman*
Stephen Jaeger, PH.D.

Instructor: Christine Savage, A.B.

Assistant: Susan W. Groff, B.A.

The purpose of the major in German is to lay the foundation for an understanding and appreciation of German culture through its literature and language. Students may elect to concentrate on the German language or on German literature during their major program. The former program includes an introduction to applied German linguistics, Middle High German and Germanic philology. The latter program concentrates on important epochs and genres of literature in the German-speaking lands. A broad base for students in both options is attained through a common core of courses. All German majors are expected to acquire fluency in the German language both written and oral. They are encouraged to gain supplementary exposure to the German language through residence in the German House or by study abroad during the summer or the junior year or both.

The German departments of Bryn Mawr College and Haverford College cooperate to offer the widest possible range of courses to students of both colleges. Haverford German courses conducted in German are applicable to the Bryn Mawr German major.

Requirements in the Major Subject: The normal course sequence for the major is German 101, 201a or b, 202a and b and at least two other units at the 300-level. The Senior Conference is also required. Special consideration is given to students who have supplemented their linguistic training as outlined above.

Allied Subjects: Any language or literature, History, Political Science, Philosophy, Music, History of Art, History of Science.

01. *Elementary German:* Members of the Department.

The course offers the foundation of the language with emphasis on the four basic skills: reading, writing, listening and speaking. Increased importance is given to reading as the course progresses.

02. *Intermediate German:* Members of the Department.

Thorough review of grammar, exercises in composition, oral practice and specially selected readings for students who have had the equivalent of two years of high school German and for those who are not adequately prepared to take German 101.

01. *Readings in German Literature:* Members of the Department.

Thorough review of grammar with continued practice in speaking and writing. Reading and discussion of selected works of German literature, including poetry, *novellae* and drama.

201a.
& b.
Advanced Training in the German Language: Mr. Rosellini (at Haverford) and Mr. Bänziger.
First semester at Haverford. Advanced training in grammar, speaking and writing; stylistic exercises; reading of non-fictional material; oral reports and discussions; compositions.

202a.
Goethe and Schiller: Miss Flaherty.
Representative works will be read and examined closely. Special attention will be given to their historical and aesthetic backgrounds as well as to their position in the history of German literature.

202b.
Romanticism: Miss Flaherty.
A study of works by Novalis, Tieck, Kleist, Hoffman, Brentano and Eichendorff with emphasis on their relationship to the major artistic, intellectual and social trends of the time.

300b.
A Survey of German Literature: Mr. Bänziger.
Lecture course devoted to the literary and historical background (from the Middle Ages to the present) necessary for studies in German literature.

[301b.
History of the German Language: Miss Dorian.]

302a.
Vernacular Literature in Medieval Germany: Mr. Jaeger.
The appearance and development of literature in German will be studied with concentration on the heroic tradition, courtly romance, lyric poetry and the writings of the German mystics. Specific texts will be analyzed in detail and discussed within their cultural context.

303a.
Modern German Prose: Mr. Bänziger.
Some representative prose works of East and West Germany, Austria and Switzerland (Mann, Hesse, Frisch, Böll, etc.) in relation to their respective theoretical backgrounds (Nietzsche, Freud, Marx).

[304b.
The German "Novelle": Mr. Bänziger.]

[305a.
Modern German Drama: Mr. Bänziger.]

[306a.
German Poetry: Mr. Bänziger.]

[307b.
The Literature of Reformation: Mr. Jaeger.]

310b.
Lessing and the Enlightenment: Miss Flaherty.
A study of Lessing's major works and his relationship to contemporary literary, aesthetic, dramaturgical, historical and theological trends.

356a.
Advanced Topics in German Literature: Mr. Cary (at Haverford).
Kafka and Brecht. Prerequisite: permission of instructor.

99. *Senior Conference:* All senior majors are to participate in weekly conferences on selected works, topics and problems directly related to the study of German literature, language and culture. They will be required to submit papers or problem-sets to each of the instructors conducting each of the mini-mesters into which the two semesters will be divided. The material covered in Senior Conference will be tested either in individual units or with a comprehensive examination.

ɔɪ. *Honors Work:* On recommendation of the Department, students in the senior year will be admitted to Honors work consisting of independent reading, conferences and a substantial paper.

Teaching Certification: A sequence of work offered by the Department of German and the Department of Education of the College leads to a certificate to teach in the secondary schools of Pennsylvania.

Greek

Professor: Mabel Louise Lang, PH.D., *Chairman*‡

Associate Professor: Gregory W. Dickerson, PH.D. *Acting Chairman*

Assistant Professor: Richard Hamilton, PH.D.

Lecturers: George A. Sheets, PH.D.
   Peter M. Smith, PH.D.

The courses in language and literature are designed to acquaint the students with the various aspects of ancient Greek culture through a mastery of the Greek language and a comprehension of Greek mythology, religion and the other basic forms of expression through which that culture developed. The works of poets, philosophers and historians are studied both in their historical context and in relation to subsequent Western thought.

Requirements in the Major Subject: 001, 101a, 201a and b, 301a and b, one other half-unit course and the Senior Conference. Prospective majors in Greek are advised to take Greek 001 in the freshman year.

---

‡On leave for the year 1976-77.

Allied Subjects: Ancient History, Classical Archæology, History of Art, History of Religion, any language, Philosophy.

001. *Elementary Greek:* Mr. Dickerson.

Semester I: elements of grammar, prose composition, readings from ancient authors and the *New Testament.* Semester II: Plato's *Apology* and *Crito*; sight readings in class from Euripides' *Alcestis.*

101a. *Herodotus:* Mr. Dickerson.

After a review of Attic Greek with Lysias the reading is Book VI of Herodotus' *History*; prose composition is required.

101b. *Tragedy I:* Mr. Hamilton.

Sophocles' *Antigone* and Euripides' *Medea*; a critical literary paper is required.

201a. *Plato and Thucydides:* Mr. Hamilton.

The *Symposium* and an abridged version of the history of the Sicilian Expedition, with required prose composition.

201b. *Tragedy II:* Mr. Smith.

Euripides' *Bacchae* and Sophocles' *Oedipus Rex*; a critical literary essay is required.

202a. *Homer:* Mr. Smith.

Several books of the *Odyssey* are read and verse composition is attempted. A short essay is required.

203a.* *Greek Literature in Translation:* Mr. Hamilton.

Developmental theories of literary form and ethical values will be tested in a reading of Hesiod, Homer, Greek lyric poetry, Aeschylus, Herodotus and Sophocles. Consideration will be given to what scholars have done, should have done and should not have done with that material.

203b.* *Greek Literature in Translation:* Mr. Hamilton.

A reading of Euripides, Thucydides, Aristophanes, Menander, Plato, Aristotle, Theocritus, Apollonius and the *New Testament.*

[213a. *Myth in Practice and Theory:* Miss Lang.]
(INT.)

[214b.. *Development of Greek Tragedy:* Mr. Hamilton.}

301a. *Hesiod and the Lyric Poets:* Mr. Hamilton.

The Works and Days, and early elegiac and lyric poetry, including the odes of Pindar.

. *Aeschylus and Aristophanes:* Mr. Dickersòn.
   Aeschylus' *Agamemnon* and Aristophanes' *Frogs.*

. *Advanced Prose Reading:* Mr. Smith.]

. *Comparative Greek and Latin Grammar:* Mr. Sheets.

.) See Interdepartmental course 313a.

. *Greek Dialects:* Mr. Sheets.

.) See Interdepartmental course 313b.

. *Senior Conference:* Weekly meetings with the members of the Department
   to explore in depth two areas (such as Homer and Oral Poetry, the Lyric
   Age of Greece, Attic Tragedy, the Golden Age of Athens, Biography and
   Rhetoric in Early Greek History, Folklore and Mythology in Greece and
   History of Greek Literature). Oral reports will be scheduled throughout
   the year and at the end there will be a written examination in sight
   translation from Greek to English and whatever other evaluation of the
   conferences each group deems appropriate.

   For work in Greek History see History 205b.

. *Honors Work:* Honors may be taken by qualified seniors either in conjunction with the advanced course or after its completion.

   Interdepartmental Work: The Department of Greek participates in the
   interdepartmental majors in Classical Languages and in Classical Studies.
   See page 147.

History

Professors: Charles M. Brand, PH.D.
   Arthur P. Dudden, PH.D., *Chairman*
   Mary Maples Dunn, PH.D.
   Elizabeth Read Foster, PH.D.
   Barbara M. Lane, PH.D.
   Jane M. Oppenheimer, PH.D., *History of Science*
   J. H. M. Salmon, M.LITT., LIT.D.
   Alain Silvera, PH.D.
   James Tanis, TH.D., *Director of Libraries*‡

---

‡On leave for the year 1976-77.

Associate Professor: Phyllis S. Lachs, PH.D., *Associate Dean of The Graduate School of Arts and Sciences*

Assistant Professor: Stephen Poppel, PH.D.

Lecturers: Wendell P. Holbrook, A.B.*
    Karen Meier Reeds, PH.D.

Professor of Social Work and Social Research: Milton D. Speizman, PH.D.†

Associate Professor of Classical and Near Eastern Archaeology:
    Richard S. Ellis, PH.D.

Associate Professor of Greek: Gregory W. Dickerson, PH.D.

Associate Professor of Latin: Russell T. Scott, PH.D.

The history major is designed to enable the student to acquire historical perspective and historical method. Courses stress the development of ideas, cultures and institutions—political, social and economic—rather than the accumulation of data about particular events. Students study some topics and periods intensively in order to learn the use of documentary material and the evaluation of sources. Extensive reading is assigned in all courses to familiarize majors with varied kinds of historical writing and, in most courses, critical or narrative essays are required.

Requirements in the Major Subject: Students are expected to complete four units of history and two units of allied work meaningfully related to the discipline of history. The basic selection of courses is planned in the spring of the sophomore year and depends upon the special interests of each student together with the availability of courses. History 111 will ordinarily be required of all history majors, but it will not satisfy the departmental distribution requirements. A suitable distribution of work in history to be undertaken by history majors should include at least: (1) one European course, (2) one non-European course, (3) one ancient, medieval, or early modern course concentrated before 1789, (4) one modern course concentrated after 1789, (5) one and one-half 300-level courses with one half-unit at least to be taken during the senior year. A particular course may very well satisfy more than one of the above qualifications. History majors will, in addition to the foregoing requirements, participate in the History Senior Conference.

---

*On leave, semester I.
†On leave, semester II.

Allied Work: A wide choice is open to majors in history; in general those in modern fields will find courses in the social sciences most suitable, while those in earlier periods may select, with the permission of the department concerned, courses in classical studies, in philosophy and history of art. Intermediate or advanced courses in literature and in language may also serve to enrich the major offering.

Cooperation with Haverford College: The History departments of Haverford College and Bryn Mawr College have coordinated their course offerings. History 111 is offered jointly by members of both departments; several intermediate courses are given at one College or the other in alternate years. All courses offered by both departments are open to students of both colleges equally, subject only to the prerequisites stated by individual instructors. Both departments encourage students to avail themselves of the breadth of offerings this arrangement makes possible at both colleges.

Western Civilization: Members of the two departments.

A Bryn Mawr–Haverford combined course surveying Western European civilization from the fall of Rome to the present. The course deals with both institutional and intellectual currents in the Western tradition. Conferences, discussions and lectures deal with both primary materials and secondary historical accounts. The course is intended for freshmen and sophomores, but one section is designed for upperclassmen.

The Form of the City: Mrs. Lane.]

)

Urban Society: Mrs. Lane, Mr. Ross.

) See INT. 200b in the interdepartmental major in The Growth and Structure of Cities.

American History: Mr. Dudden.
American history from colonial times to the present.

Medieval European Civilization: Mr. Brand.}

Europe, 1789-1848: Mr. Silvera.

The French Revolution and the spread of revolutionary ideas and the idea of nationalism throughout the Napoleonic epoch will be covered in the first semester. Political and social history from the age of Metternich through the revolutions of 1848, including the effects of the Industrial Revolution, the growth of nationalism and the varieties of socialism will be covered in the second semester.

205a.   *The Ancient Near East:* Mr. Ellis.

An introduction to the history of the ancient Near East from the beginning of the third millennium B.C. to the rise of the Persian Empire. The sources and nature of the earliest history of Egypt and Mesopotamia; the international developments in Western Asia and Egypt during the second millennium B.C.; the Dark Ages and survival of traditions in the Near East at the beginning of Greek history.

205b.   *Ancient Greece:* Mr. Dickerson.

A study of Greece from the Trojan War to Alexander the Great, with particular attention to the constitutional changes from monarchy, through aristocracy and tyranny, to democracy in various parts of the Greek world. The stress will be on ancient sources, including historians, inscriptions, and archaeological and numismatic materials.

206a.   *Roman History:* Mr. Scott.

A study of Rome from the Iron Age to the end of the Republic with special attention to the rise of Rome in Italy, the Hellenistic world and the evolution of the Roman state. Ancient sources, literary and archaeological, are emphasised.

206b.   *The Roman Empire:* Mr. Scott.

Imperial history from the Principate of Augustus to the House of Constantine with particular attention to the evolution of Roman culture as presented in the surviving ancient evidence, literary and archaeological.

[207a.   *Latin America: Colonies and Revolutions:* Mrs. Dunn.]
(INT.)

208.   *Byzantine History:* Mr. Brand.

Political, institutional and cultural history of the Byzantine (Later Roman) Empire from the reforms of Diocletian and conversion of Constantine to the capture of Constantinople in 1453. Contacts with Arabic, Turkish, Armenian, Slavic and West European peoples will be stressed.

209.   *Early American History 1607-1789:* Mrs. Dunn

In the first semester, an investigation of the founding of the English colonies in North America and the West Indies and their development in the seventeenth and early eighteenth centuries. In the second semester, emphasis will be placed on the causes and interpretations of the Revolution, the writing and ratification of the Constitution.

The Near East: Mr. Silvera.

A survey of the Arab world and Turkey from the rise of Islam to the Arab-Israeli wars. Among the topics to be studied in the first semester are the legacy of Islam, the rise and decline of the Umayyad and Abbasid Caliphates and the development of the Muslim society and institutions under the Ottoman Empire. The second semester concentrates on the impact of the West and the growth of Arab nationalism.

Medieval Mediterranean World: Mr. Brand.]

Renaissance and Reformation: Mr. Salmon.]

American Economic History: Mr. Weinstein (at Haverford).

Europe since 1848: Mr. Spielman (at Haverford).

The Age of Absolutism: Mr. Spielman (at Haverford).]

A History of the Afro-American People: Mr. Holbrook.]

West African History: Mr. Holbrook.

A survey of West African history from the Iron Age to the present. Themes to be covered include: State-building in the Sudan and forest belt, the growth of Islam, the impact of Europe and the trans-Atlantic slave trade, responses to European penetration and decolonization.

History and Principles of Quakerism: Mr. Bronner (at Haverford).

Russian History: Mrs. Gerstein (at Haverford).

Russia in the Twentieth Century: Mrs. Gerstein (at Haverford).

History of China: Mrs. Mihelich (at Haverford).

Modern Jewish History: Mr. Poppel.]

La Civilisation de France: Mr. Silvera, Mr. McCarthy.]
)

Le Seizième Siècle à travers le roman historique: Mr. Salmon.
)   See INT. 297a in the interdepartmental major in French Studies.

The American City in the Twentieth Century: Mr. Speizman.]
)

Europe in the Twentieth Century: Mr. Poppel.

Selected topics and problems of recent European history.

France, 1559-1661: Mr. Salmon.]

Topics in the Recent History of the United States: Mr. Dudden.]

305a. *The Italian City-State in the Renaissance:* Mrs. Lane.
(INT.)   The evolution of the urban civilization of Northern Italy will be examined within its socio-economic as well as its cultural context. Florence and other major city-states will be investigated in detail.

307b. *Medieval Cities: Islamic, Byzantine, and Western:* Mr. Brand.
(INT.)   Introduction to the comparative study of economy, society, politics and culture of towns in the Islamic, Byzantine and Western European worlds from the seventh to thirteenth centuries. A reading knowledge of French or German or Italian is expected.

[308b. *The Jews in the Middle Ages:* Mr. Brand.]

[312b. *History of Women in Colonial America:* Mrs. Dunn.]

314. *History of Scientific Thought:* Miss Oppenheimer, Mrs. Reeds.
(INT.)   Changing relationships among developing scientific ideas and other intellectual, cultural and religious traditions.
Semester I: Classical and medieval natural history;
Semester II: The scientific renaissance and modern science..

[315a. *Topics in Modern British History:* Mrs. Lachs.]

317a. *Mexico: Independence to the Present:*. Mrs. Dunn.
(INT.)   Emphasis will be placed on cultural conflict; the historical development of institutions such as church, *hacienda* and *caciquismo,* and on the nature and dynamics of the protracted revolutionary movement from Hidalgo to Cardenas.

[320a. *Holland's Golden Age:* Mr. Tanis.]

◄ [321b. *Revolution within the Church:* Mr. Tanis.]

[322. *Religious Forces in Colonial America:* Mr. Tanis.]

328b. *Colonial Towns in North and South America:* Mrs. Dunn.
(INT.)   A comparative examination of origins of selected towns.

[330. *France since 1870:* Mr. Silvera.]

334b. *A History of Blacks in the American City:* Mr. Holbrook.
(INT.)   The early nineteenth-century experiences of slaves and freemen in American cities. A study of successive waves of black migrations which have contributed much to the contemporary American urban demographic pattern. Students will have the opportunity to do research and to write on the history of the black experience in Philadelphia.

[335b. *West African Leadership:* Mr. Holbrook.]

The Great Society: Mr. Dudden.

Topics in American History: Mr. Lane (at Haverford).]

American Diplomacy in the Twentieth Century: Mr. Gould (at Haverford).

Topics in Far Eastern History: Miss Mihelich (at Haverford).

Topics in Regional History: The Westward Movement: Mr. Bronner (at Haverford).]

Religious Utopian Movements in the United States: Mr. Bronner (at Haverford).

Topics in Early Modern European History: The French Revolution: Mr. Spielman (at Haverford).

Topics in Modern European History: The Russian Revolution: Mrs. Gerstein (at Haverford).

Topics in Medieval History: The Hundred Years' War: Mr. McKenna (at Haverford).

England under the Tudors and Stuarts: Mrs. Foster.]

The Great Powers and the Near East: Mr. Silvera.]

Topics in the Renaissance: Mr. Salmon.]

Topics in the Enlightenment: Miss Oppenheimer.
Scientific and philosophical ideas in the eighteenth century and their interplay with social and political thought. Each year a particular country (chosen by the students enrolled) will be treated in detail in reading and discussion; one long paper will be required.

Senior Conference: Mrs. Foster, Mr. Salmon.
A required seminar with alternative choices between Portrait of an Age: Elizabethan Society and Great Historians.

Honors Work: Honors work in any of the advanced fields is offered for the senior year to any history major who completes her third year with a record of distinction. An essay based on source material must be presented.

Supervised Study: Members of the Department.
Permission of instructor and Department chairman required.

Interdepartmental Work: The Department of History participates in the interdepartmental majors in French Studies and The Growth and Structure of Cities and the concentration in Hispanic and Hispanic-American Studies. See pages 148 and 150 and 153.

Teaching Certification: A sequence of work offered by the Department of History and the Department of Education of the College leads to a certificate to teach in the secondary schools of Pennsylvania. Current requirements call for two and one-half units of allied work in the social sciences.

History of Art

Professors: Charles G. Dempsey, M.F.A., PH.D., *Chairman*
    Charles Mitchell, M.A., B.LITT.
    James E. Snyder, M.F.A., PH.D.†

Professor of Fine Art: Fritz Janschka, *Akad. Maler†*

Mary Flexner Lecturer: Phyllis W. Lehmann, PH.D.

Assistant Professors: Dale Kinney, PH.D.
    Steven Z. Levine, PH.D.

Visiting Professor: Shirley Neilson Blum, PH.D.

Assistants: Elizabeth Higdon, B.A.
    Carol Moon, M.A

The Department regularly offers an introductory course (involving some studio work), a series of general intermediate courses and more concentrated advanced half-courses and instruction on special topics to majors in their senior year. The program is open also to undergraduates of Haverford College.

Requirements in the Major Subject: At least four units of course work in art history, normally including History of Art 101 and always one unit of advanced course work, together with the Senior Conference and two units of allied work. Intermediate courses with supplementary work may sometimes be counted as advanced at the discretion of the Department.

---

†On leave, semester II.

Students contemplating a major in History of Art are strongly advised to consult the Department as early as possible in their college careers, especially with regard to language preparation.

Allied Subjects: History, Latin, Greek, modern languages, Archaeology; others in consultation with the Department.

. *Introduction to Art History:* Members of the Department.
The course is designed as an introduction to the methods and scope of art history in the field of Western art from medieval to modern times. Studio work, two hours a week.

. *Early Medieval and Byzantine Art:* Mrs. Kinney.

. *Art of the Later Middle Ages:* Mr. Snyder.

. *Renaissance Art:* Mr. Mitchell.

. *Baroque Art:* Mr. Dempsey.

. *Modern Art:* Mr. Levine.

. *Santa Maria Maggiore:* Mrs. Kinney.

. *English Eighteenth-Century Art:* Mr. Mitchell.

. *Problems in Renaissance Iconography:* Mr. Dempsey.

. *Aesthetics of the Film:* Mr. Levine.

. *Studies in the Art of Greece in the Fourth Century B.C.:* Mrs. Lehmann.
See Archaeology 390b.

. *Problems in Early Netherlandish Painting, 1400-1470:* Mrs. Blum.

. *Senior Conference:* Members of the department hold regular conferences with senior majors on their special subjects. The evaluation is in three parts, each of three hours:
1. An examination to test knowledge of works of art,
2. A general examination on the history of art,
3. An examination on a special topic.

Honors Work: Offered to students on invitation of the department.

FINE ARTS MAJOR PROGRAM

Professor: Fritz Janschka, *Akad. Maler* (Vienna)†

At Haverford:

Professor of Fine Arts: Charles Stegeman, *Académie Royale des Beaux-Arts* (Brussels)

Associate Professor of Fine Arts: R. Christopher Cairns, A.B., M.F.A.

Assistant Professor of Fine Arts: Dru Shipman, B.A., M.F.A.

The major program in fine art is coordinated with, and complementary to, the fine arts major program at Haverford College, courses on either campus being offered to students of either College with the approval of the respective instructors.

The program is under the direction of the Bryn Mawr Professor of Fine Art, with whom intending fine art majors should plan their major curricula.

Requirements in the Major Subject: At least four units in fine art, which must include Haverford 101, one 300-level course (or an approved Haverford equivalent) and the Senior Conference. Fine art majors must also successfully take two units of allied work, of which a course in history of art must be one.

Allied Subjects: History of Art, History, classical and modern languages, Mathematics, Chemistry, Physics; others, by exception, in consultation with the Professor of Fine Art.

(For Haverford Fine Arts courses see the Haverford College Catalogue.)

225. *Graphic Arts:* Mr. Janschka.
Intaglio and relief printing; etching of liftground, aquatint and softground; drypoint; woodcutting and combined use of various methods. Prerequisite: Haverford Fine Arts 101 or proof of adequate previous training in drawing.

335. *Color Lithography:* Mr. Janschka.
An advanced graphic arts course with emphasis on color printing by lithographic processes. Making of editions. Prerequisites: Fine Art 225 or Haverford Fine Arts 231 or 241.

345. *Advanced Drawing:* Mr. Janschka.
Drawing as an independent art form. Line as a dominant composition factor over color. All drawing media and watercolor, tempera and acrylic paints. Prerequisite: Haverford Fine Arts 231 or 241 or Fine Art 225.

399. *Senior Conference:* Individual or joint approved projects pursued through the year under the direction of the Professor of Fine Art at Bryn Mawr.

401. *Honors Work:* Suitable fine art majors may be invited by the Professor of Fine Art to present an Honors project. Honors work requires (a) a major

project in fine art approved by the Professor of Fine Art, and (b) an extended paper discussing the theoretical, technical and other relevant problems involved in the achievement of the major project. Both the project and the paper will be evaluated by the Professor of Fine Art and a member of the History of Art Department, who may be joined, where it is judged appropriate, by a member of the Fine Arts faculty of Haverford College.

3. *Supervised Project:* Members of the Department.
 Permission of instructor and Department chairman required.

Final Examination in the Major Subject: This is in three parts—
  1. The presentation of one portfolio of work arising from courses taken in advanced drawing and a second portfolio resulting from work in advanced courses in painting or sculpture or graphics,
  2. The formal exhibition of a small selection of advanced works,
  3. The presentation of work done in the Senior Conference.
Work presented in the final examination will be judged and graded by a jury consisting of the Professor of Fine Art, members of the Haverford Fine Arts faculty and a member of the History of Art Department.

History of Religion

Professor: Howard C. Kee, PH.D., *Chairman*

Associate Professor: Samuel Tobias Lachs, PH.D.

Assistant Professor: David Rabi, PH.D.

Visiting Lecturers: Patrick Henry, PH.D.
 George D. Kelsey, PH.D.

Roian Fleck Resident-in-Religion: Paul Lehmann, TH.D.

Director of Libraries and *Professor of History:* James Tanis, TH.D.‡

Professor of Philosophy: Jean A. Potter, PH.D.

Associate Professor of Sociology: Judith R. Porter, PH.D.

---

‡On leave for the year 1976-77.

The history of religion major concentrates on the historical study of the religious traditions which have contributed most to shaping the culture of the West: the religion of Israel, Rabbinic Judaism and Christianity. The student is expected to achieve facility in critical analysis of the primary sources of these traditions and in tracing their development against the background of the cultural situations in which they arose and matured.

Requirements in the Major Subject: Four full courses in history of religion, of which at least one must be in a tradition other than that of the student's concentration. The Senior Conference is also required.

The normal pattern for the major consists of one introductory course (100 level), two intermediate courses (200 level) and two advanced half-courses or a full-year course (300 level). Students in advanced courses who are majoring in history of religion are required to demonstrate a working knowledge of the language appropriate to their field of concentration: Hebrew for the religion of Israel or Rabbinic Judaism, Greek for New Testament or Early Christianity, Latin for medieval Christianity, German for the Reformed period.

Allied Subjects: Latin and Greek, Philosophy, History, Archaeology, Anthropology.

LANGUAGE COURSES

001. *Elementary Hebrew:* Mr. Rabi.
Grammar, composition and conversation with primary emphasis on fluency in reading. Course designed for preparation in reading classical religious texts.

101. *Readings in the Hebrew Bible:* Mr. Rabi.
Readings in prose of Genesis. Course will include Hebrew composition, grammar, and conversation based on the Hebrew text.

[202b. *Readings in Rabbinic Literature:* Mr. Lachs.]

203. *Readings in the Hebrew Bible:* Mr. Rabi.
Narrative and historical writing. Samuel, Kings, Esther, Ruth.

212a. *Readings in the Greek New Testament:* Mr. Kee.

403. *Tutorial in Semitic Languages:* Mr. Rabi.

HISTORY OF RELIGION COURSES

History and Literature of the Bible: Mr. Kee.

a. A study of the history of Israel and its sacred literature against the background of the ancient Near East, the development of the legal, prophetic and wisdom traditions.

b. The beginnings of Christianity, tracing the influences of Judaism and of Hellenistic culture and religion on the life and thought of the New Testament community.

History and Literature of Judaism: Mr. Lachs.

a. Historical study of Judaism from the Exile through the Geonic period, with major focus on the literature.

b. Modern movements from the French Revolution to the present.

Introduction to Asian Religions: Mr. Swearer (at Swarthmore).]

Hinduism and Indian Culture.]

Topics in Biblical Literature: Mr. Lachs.

1976-1977: Wisdom Literature.

Jesus and the Gospel Tradition: Mr. Kee.

The social, cultural and conceptual background of the Gospel of Mark, its literary structure and genre.

Paul and the Rise of Gentile Christianity: Mr. Kee.

A study of the life and letters of Paul, of the cultural shift of Christianity into the Roman world and of the impact of Paul on the Early Church.

Sociology of Religion: Mrs. Porter.

See Sociology 209b.

Mahayana Buddhism: Mr. Song.]

Ethics and Society in Christian Perspective: Mr. Kelsey.

Explanation of the biblical and historical bases for dealing with such major ethical issues confronting contemporary society as abortion, medical ethics, forms of discrimination, personal rights and public security.

Shapers of Theology in the Twentieth Century: Mr. Lehmann.

A study of the major works and themes of contemporary religious thinkers: Karl Barth, Rudolph Bultmann, Paul Tillich and Reinhold Niebuhr.

Studies in Early Rabbinic and Medieval Judaism: Mr. Lachs.

Topics for 1976-77:

301b. *Christianity in the Johannine Tradition:* Mr. Kee.
Analysis of the content and background of the Gospel of John.

[305b. *Myth and History in the Gospel of John:* Mr. Kee.]

312a. *Studies in Early Christianity:* Mr. Henry.
Major trends in patristic thought: a study of the origin and development of the doctrines of the Trinity, Incarnation, Atonement and Original Sin as found in the writings of the Church Fathers.

315a. *Ethics and Public Policy:* Mr. Kelsey.
An interdisciplinary study of the relationship of ethical norms to
public policy, concentrating on the issues of racial and sexual discrimination, abortion and individual freedoms.

399. *Senior Conference:* Consists of a year-long seminar in which the students
will be introduced to the major literary materials, secondary sources,
reference works and critical issues in the literature of Judaism and Early
Christianity during the period approximately 200 B.C. to 200 A.D. In the
second semester the students will present to the seminar a report on some
theme or problem on which they will have conducted research, based on
their ability to handle one or many primary sources in the original
language.

COURSES AT SWARTHMORE

gion 28a. *Mysticism East and West:* Mr. Swearer.

ligion 41. *Religion and Ethics:* Mr. Urban.]

Honors Work: Qualified students are admitted to Honors work on the
recommendation of the Department.

Italian

Assistant Professors: Nancy Dersofi, PH.D.‡
Nicholas Patruno, PH.D., *Director*

Lecturer: Barbra Apfelbaum, A.B.

The aims of the major are to acquire a knowledge of the Italian language
and literature and an understanding of Italian culture and its contribution

---

‡On leave for the year 1976-77.

to Western civilization. Majors in Italian are urged to spend the junior year in Italy or to study in an approved summer school in Italy or in the United States, and they are also encouraged to take advantage of the facilities offered by Italian House.

Requirements in the Major Subject: Italian 102a, 201b, 301, 303a and b and at least one other advanced course. For students who enter the College with Italian, proper substitutions will be made. In all courses students are urged to use tapes available in the Language Laboratory.

Allied Subjects: Any other language or literature, History, History of Art, Philosophy, Music, Political Science; with departmental approval, any other field allied to the student's special interests.

. *Italian Language:* Mr. Patruno.

A practical knowledge of the language is acquired through hearing, speaking, writing and reading, going from concrete situations to the expression of abstract ideas and with a gradual introduction to the reading of Italian literature.

. *Intermediate Course in the Italian Language:* Miss Apfelbaum.

Intensive grammar review, readings from selected Italian authors and topics assigned for composition and discussion. Conducted entirely in Italian.

. *Advanced Course in the Italian Language:* Mr. Patruno.

Advanced work in composition and critical examination of literary texts. Prerequisite: permission of the Department, sometimes determined by a brief written examination. This course is recommended for students who wish to continue work in Italian literature.

. *Novel and Poetry of Modern Italy:* Mr. Patruno.

A study of the artistic and cultural developments of pre-Fascist, Fascist and post-Fascist Italy seen through the works of poets such as Ungaretti, Montale and Quasimodo and through the novels of Pirandello, Moravia, Silone, Vittorini, Pavese and others.

. *Foscolo, Leopardi and Manzoni:* Mr. Patruno.

A study of the Italian Romantic movement as reflected in these writers.

. *Literature of the Nineteenth Century.*]

. *Dante:* Miss Apfelbaum.

Principal emphasis on the *Divina Commedia.* Some attention given to Dante's minor works and to literary currents of the Middle Ages.

[303a. *Petrarca, Boccaccio and the Early Humanists.*]

[303b. *Literature of the Italian Renaissance.*]

[305a. *Arcadia and Enlightenment:* Miss Dersofi.]

[305b. *History of the Italian Theatre:* Miss Dersofi.]

399. *Senior Conference:* In the first semester weekly meetings devoted to the study of special topics in Italian literature chosen by the students, evaluated by an oral examination in January. In the second semester each senior will prepare under the direction of the instructor a paper on an author or a theme which she has chosen. At the end of the year students must demonstrate knowledge of the development of Italian literature by either an oral or written examination, according to their preference.

401. *Honors Work:* On the recommendation of the Department a student may undertake Honors work in Italian. Students work in a special field adapted to their interest under the direction of the Department.

Latin

Professor: Myra L. Uhlfelder, PH.D.

Associate Professors: Julia H. Gaisser, PH.D.
    Russell T. Scott, PH.D., *Chairman*

Lecturer: George A. Sheets, PH.D.

The major in Latin is planned to acquaint the student with the world of the Romans and their contribution to the modern world.

Requirements in the Major Subject: Latin 101a and b, 201a and b, 301a and b or 302a and b and the Senior Conference. 203b is a prerequisite for Honors work and required for those who plan to teach.

Courses taken at the Intercollegiate Center for Classical Studies in Rome (see page 52) are accepted as part of the major. For non-majors, Latin 201a and b are prerequisites for 300-level courses.

Allied Subjects: Greek, Hebrew, History, Classical and Near Eastern Archaeology, History of Art, History of Religion, Linguistics, Philosophy, Anthropology, any modern language or literature.

Elementary Latin: Miss Uhlfelder, Mr. Scott.

Basic grammar and composition, reading from prose authors and Vergil's *Aeneid.*

Intermediate Latin: Mr. Scott, Mrs. Gaisser.

Review of grammar with reading in prose and poetry for students who have had two years of Latin in school or do not feel adequately prepared to take Latin 101.

Latin Literature: Mrs. Gaisser.

Selections from Catullus' poems, Vergil's *Eclogues* and readings in prose. Prerequisite: more than two years of Latin in school, Latin 001 or Latin 002.

Latin Literature: Miss Uhlfelder.

Selections from Livy, Book I, and from Horace's *Odes.*

Horace and Satire: Mr. Sheets.

Selections from Horace's *Satires* and *Epistles,* the works of Petronius and Juvenal.

Latin Literature of the Silver Age: Mrs. Gaisser.

Readings from major authors of the first and second centuries A.D.

Medieval Latin Literature: Miss Uhlfelder.]

Latin Style: Members of the Department.

A study of Latin prose style, based on reading of prose authors and exercises in composition, and of Latin metrics with practice in reading aloud.

The Ancient City: Mr. Scott.

See INT. 204a in the interdepartmental major in The Growth and Structure of Cities.

Latin Literature of the High Middle Ages: Miss Uhlfelder.

Latin Authors and English Literature: Members of the Department.]

Vergil's Aeneid: Miss Uhlfelder.

Livy and Tacitus: Mr. Scott.

Cicero and Caesar: Mr. Scott.]

Lucretius: Mrs. Gaisser.]

313a. *Comparative Greek and Latin Grammer:* Mr. Sheets.
(INT.)   See Interdepartmental course 313a.

313b. *Greek Dialects:* Mr. Sheets.
(INT.)   See Interdepartmental course 313b.

For Roman history, see History 206a and b.

399. *Senior Conference:* Regular meetings with members of the Department to discuss reading in Latin literature are intended to supplement and synthesize work done in courses. The method of evaluating the work of the conference is determined each year. Majors must pass an examination in Latin sight translation which will be offered in September, February and May.

401. *Honors Work:* Honors work is offered to qualified students in classical or Medieval Latin literature or in Roman history. The results will be presented in a paper directed by a member of the Department.

Interdepartmental Work: The Department of Latin participates in the interdepartmental majors in Classical Languages, Classical Studies and The Growth and Structure of Cities. See pages 147 and 150.

Teaching Certification: A sequence of work offered by the Department of Latin and the Department of Education of the College leads to a certificate to teach in the secondary schools of Pennsylvania.

Mathematics

Professors: Frederic Cunningham, Jr., PH.D., *Chairman*
John C. Oxtoby, M.A.

Assistant Professors: Kenneth N. Krigelman, PH.D.‡
Françoise Schremmer, PH.D.

Lecturer: Steven Alpern, PH.D.

Assistant: Vidhu Prasad, M.SC.

‡On leave for the year 1976-77.

The major in mathematics is designed to provide a balanced introduction to the subject, emphasizing its nature both as a deductive and as an applied science, at the same time providing the technical foundation for more advanced study.

Requirements in the Major Subject: at least four and one-half units including Mathematics 101, 201a or b, 202b, 301, 303a, or the equivalent. The Senior Conference is also required.

Allied Subjects: Chemistry, Economics, Philosophy, Physics, Psychology.

Introduction to Automatic Computation: Mr. Krigelman.]

Calculus, with Analytic Geometry: Mr. Oxtoby, Mr. Cunningham, Mr. Alpern.

Differentiation and integration of algebraic and elementary transcendental functions, with the necessary elements of analytic geometry and trigonometry; the fundamental theorem, its role in theory and applications.

Methods and Models: Mr. Alpern.

Mathematical concepts, notations and methods commonly used in the social, behavioral and biological sciences, with emphasis on manipulative skills and real problem solving.

Calculus: Mrs. Schremmer.

Same material as in Mathematics 101, but covered in one semester. Open to students with some previous calculus, but not enough to place them in Mathematics 201a and b. Prerequisite: permission of instructor.

Intermediate Calculus and Linear Algebra: Mr. Cunningham.

Vectors, matrices and linear maps, functions of several variables, partial derivatives, multiple integrals.

Repeat of course 201a.

Intermediate Calculus and Linear Algebra: Mr. Cunningham.

Line integrals, vector analysis, infinite series, Taylor's theorem, differential equations.

Advanced Calculus: Mr. Oxtoby.

The classical theory of real functions, based on a construction of the real number system; elements of set theory and topology; analysis of Riemann integral, power series, Fourier series and other limit processes. Prerequisite: Mathematics 202b.

303a. *Introduction to Abstract Algebra:* Mr. Cunningham.

Groups, rings and fields and their morphisms. Prerequisite: Mathematics 201a or b.

303b. *Topics in Algebra:* Mr. Cunningham.

[304b. *Theory of Probability with Applications.*]

307a. *Game Theory:* Mr. Alpern.

The notion of a game in extended form; types of games; techniques for solving Nim-type games; problems in infinite games; matrix games, mixed strategies and von Neumann's Minimax Theorem; Kuhn's Theorem on games with perfect recall; non-zero sum games and n-person games.

308. *Introduction to Applied Mathematics:* Mrs. Schremmer.

Distributions, Fourier series and transforms, partial differential equations arising in physics, Green's function, eigenfunction expansions, calculus of variations. Prerequisite: Mathematics 301 or permission of instructor.

[309b. *Dynamical Systems:* Mrs. Schremmer.]

[310. *Theory of Functions of a Complex Variable:* Mr. Oxtoby.]

[311. *Differential Equations:* Mrs. Schremmer.]

[312a. *Topology:* Mr. Krigelman.]

[320. *Real Analysis:* Mr. Oxtoby.]

399. *Senior Conference:* Selected topics from various branches of mathematics are studied by means of oral presentations and the solution and discussion of problems.

401. *Honors Work:* Qualified students are admitted to Honors work on recommendation of the Department.

Teaching Certification: A sequence of work offered by the Department of Mathematics and the Department of Education of the College leads to a certificate to teach in the secondary schools of Pennsylvania.

Music

Professors: Isabelle Cazeaux, PH.D.
   Robert L. Goodale, A.B., B.MUS., A.A.G.O., *Chairman*
   Agi Jambor, M.A.

Assistant Professor: Carl B. Schmidt, PH.D.‡

Visiting Lecturers: Hope K. Goodale, PH.D.
   Eugene K. Wolf, PH.D.

Visiting Instructor: Esther Samuels, A.M.

Assistant: Janet Balshaw Rodney, B.A.

Director of Chorus and Orchestra: Tamara Brooks, M.S.

The purpose of the music major is to enable the student to appreciate the significance of music from an historical and sociological as well as from an aesthetic point of view and to develop a technique of intelligent listening, a faculty of critical judgment and the ability to use the materials of music as a means of expression for creative talent.

Students in the courses in history and appreciation of music must devote two hours or more a week to listening to recordings.

Students who are sufficiently advanced and who have completed at least one year of voice or music lessons while at the College may, with the approval of the Department, offer for one unit of academic credit a year of voice or instrument lessons. The unit of credit will include the lessons and also a recital or proficiency test arranged by the Department. The unit of credit will count as elective work and will not be counted toward the major.

Requirements in the Major Subject: Music 101 and 102 and at least two and one-half units of additional work, at least one of which must be advanced, the selection of courses depending upon the student's desire to specialize in the history and literature of music or the technique of composition. The Senior Conference is also required. A student intending to major in music must have sufficient knowledge of pianoforte or organ playing to enable her to play music of the technical difficulty of a Bach figured chorale. She is strongly urged to be a member of the Chorus or the

---

‡On leave for the year 1976-77.

Orchestra or an ensemble group. Equivalent courses at Haverford will not be accepted for the major.

Allied Subjects: History, History of Art, modern languages, English, Greek, Latin, Philosophy, History of Religion.

101. *An Introduction to the History and Appreciation of Music:* Members of the Department.

A comprehensive survey, with special emphasis on the technique of intelligent listening.

102. *Music Materials:* Mr. Goodale.

A course in the elements of theory. The study of harmony and counterpoint, simple formal analysis and an introduction to orchestration.

201. *Romantic Music:* Miss Cazeaux.

An historical treatment of the music of the age with particular attention to certain representative composers.

202. *Advanced Theory and Analysis:* Mr. Goodale.

A continuation of Music 102, with emphasis on analysis (harmonic, contrapuntal and formal) of larger forms. Prerequisite: Music 102 or its equivalent.

203a. *Bach:* Mme. Jambor.

Prerequisite: Music 101 or its equivalent.

203b. *The Classical Period:* Mme. Jambor.

Prerequisite: Music 101 or its equivalent.

205a. *Musical Criticism:* Miss Cazeaux.

Prerequisite: Music 101 or its equivalent.

[207b. *Studies in Vocal Music of the Nineteenth Century:* Mr. Schmidt.]

[209a. *The Symphonic Music of Bruckner, Mahler and R. Strauss:* Mr. Schmidt.]

[301. *Music of the Twentieth Century:* Mr. Goodale.]

[302a. *Medieval and Early Renaissance Music:* Miss Cazeaux.]

[302b. *Late Renaissance and Baroque Music:* Miss Cazeaux.]

303b. *Orchestration:* Mr. Goodale.

Prerequisites: Music 101, 102 and 202 or their equivalents. Music 202 may be taken concurrently with this course.

304b. *Interpretation of Music:* Mme. Jambor.

Interpretation of instrumental music of various ages. Members of the class will be invited to participate by performing. Prerequisites: Music 101 and 102 or their equivalents.

. *Free Composition:* Mr. Goodale.

This course is designed for those students whose chief interest lies in the field of composition. Prerequisite: permission of instructor.

. *Opera and Music Drama:* Miss Cazeaux.

. *The Influence of Spanish Literature on Music:* Mrs. Goodale.

Spanish drama and prose will be studied with empasis given to *El burlador de Sevilla (Don Giovanni), Don Alvaro (La Forza del Destino), Don Quijote (Don Quichotte* by Massenet, *El retablo de Maese Pedro)* and *El travador* (Il Trovatore). Students will be asked to investigate why such an overwhelming number of non-Spanish composers chose to write music on Spanish themes: Mozart, Bizet, Verdi, Massenet, Chabrier, Debussy, Strauss and others.

. *Music at the Court of Mannheim in the Eighteenth Century:* Mr. Wolf.

Emphasis will fall on the Mannheim symphony and its models, but with attention also given to the concerto, opera and church music as well as to the general historical, cultural, social and intellectual background of the Mannheim school.

. *Senior Conference:* Three conferences dealing with some aspects of the theory and history of music. Students may substitute for one of these a conference in an allied subject. Candidates' understanding of the material may be tested by written assignments, oral reports or other appropriate means.

. *Honors Work:* Honors work is offered for students recommended by the Department.

Interdepartmental Work: The Department of Music participates in the interdepartmental concentration in Hispanic and Hispanic-American Studies. See page 153.

[Sight-Singing and Dictation: Mr. Schmidt.]

The following organizations, carrying no academic credit, are sponsored by the Department:

The Bryn Mawr-Haverford Chorus. Director is Tamara Brooks. Several major choral works from different periods are offered in concerts during the course of the year.

The Renaissance Choir. Students (and faculty) who are confident sight-readers have the opportunity to perform a cappella music with one or two singers per voice part.

The Orchestra, whose Director is Tamara Brooks, is organized jointly with Haverford College. It plays concerts of its own and frequently joins the Chorus in the presentation of major works.

The ensemble groups are also organized jointly with Haverford College. Students in these groups are afforded the opportunity of studying chamber-music literature at first hand, as well as the experience of playing in public at student recitals.

Lessons in pianoforte, organ and voice may be taken at the student's expense. Lessons in other instruments may be arranged. The Department will be glad to assist in these arrangements.

Philosophy

Professors: José María Ferrater Mora, Lic Fil‡
    George L. Kline, PH.D.
    Jean A. Potter, PH.D., *Acting Chairman*
    Isabel Scribner Stearns, PH.D.

Associate Professors: Michael Krausz, PH.D.
    Mary Patterson McPherson, PH.D., *Dean of the College*
    George E. Weaver, Jr., PH.D.

Assistant Professors: Richard Gaskins, PH.D., J.D.
    Tracy Marie Taft, PH.D.

Lecturer: Thomas Song, M.A., M.A.L.S., *Associate Director of Libraries*

Assistant: Stephen A. Biddle, B.A.

The philosophy curriculum is organized into four divisions: Core, Metaphysics–Epistemology, Value Theory, and Persons–Periods. Courses in the Core Division are intended to provide students with a common background in philosophical problems, concepts and argumentation. Broadly, the Metaphysics–Epistemology Division is concerned

---

‡On leave of for the year 1976-77.

with what there is and the basis for our knowledge; the Value Theory Division is concerned with the nature of evaluative concepts such as Goodness and Beauty and the justification for claims involving these concepts; the Persons–Period Division is concerned with significant individual thinkers and traditions in the history of philosophy.

Intermediate-level courses in these divisions are intended to acquaint the student with the major areas of philosophical study both past and present and to provide a foundation for more advanced study. Advanced-level courses in these divisions are intended to provide the student with the means of integrating philosophy with her other studies and the opportunity for more intensive study in those areas of particular interest.

Both the division and level of a course can be determined from its three-digit course number. The first digit indicates level: 1 designates introductory; 2, intermediate and 3 advanced. The second digit indicates the division: 0 designates the Core Division; 1, the Metaphysics–Epistemology Division; 2, the Value Theory Division, and 3 the Persons–Periods Division.

Division 0: (Core): Greek philosophy, problems in philosophy, logic, modern philosophy.

Division 1: (Epistemology–Metaphysics): epistemology, metaphysics, intermediate logic, philosophy of science, philosophy of religion, philosophy of history, analytic philosophy, Existentialism, philosophy of time, history and philosophy of mathematics, philosophy of language, philosophy of social science, philosophy of creativity.

Division 2: (Value Theory): ethics, aesthetics, Western political philosophy.

Division 3: (Persons–Periods): Plato, Aristotle, medieval philosophy, Kant, Hegel, texts in medieval philosophy, Russian philosophy, Marx and Russian Marxism, British Idealism.

Prerequisites: No introductory-level course carries a prerequisite. However, all courses on both the intermediate and advanced levels carry prerequisites. Unless stated otherwise in the course description, any introductory course satisfies the prerequisite for an intermediate-level course and any intermediate course satisfies the prerequisite for an advanced-level course.

Requirements in the Major Subject: Each student majoring in philosophy must take a minimum of four units of course work and the Senior

Conference. The courses which the student must take are: (1) either Greek philosophy (101a or b) and modern philosophy (201b) or history of Western thought (100a and b); (2) logic (103a); (3) one half-unit of course work from each of divisions 1, 2 and 3; (4) one unit of advanced-level work. Any advanced-level course or courses may be taken to satisfy either requirement (3) or (4) above.

Courses in Philosophy at Haverford College: In any academic year, students may take for credit toward the major any course taught by members of the Haverford Philosophy Department not taught at Bryn Mawr in that year.

Allied Subjects: Biology, Chemistry, Economics, English, History, History of Art, Mathematics, Music, Physics, Political Science, Psychology, classical and modern literatures and certain courses in Anthropology, History of Religion and Sociology.

[100a. *Introduction to Philosophy: History of Western Thought:* Mr. Ferrater Mora.]

[100b. *Introduction to Philosophy: History of Western Thought:* Mr. Ferrater Mora.]

101a. *Introduction to Philosophy: Greek Philosophy:* Members of the department.
The origins and development of Greek philosophy, including the pre-Socratics, Plato, and Aristotle. .

101b. Repeat of course 101a.

102a. *Introduction to Philosophy:* Mr. Krausz.
A critical examination of such problems as the nature of knowledge, fact and value, freedom and determinism and the existence of God.

103a. *Logic:* Mr. Weaver.
An introduction to the fundamentals of deductive reasoning.

201b. *Introduction to Philosophy: Modern Philosophy:* Mr. Krausz.
The development of philosophic thought from Descartes to Kant.

[211a. *Epistemology:* Mr. Krausz.]

212a. *Metaphysics:* Miss Potter.
An examination of some critical problems of reality, with reference to important classical and modern theories.

213b. *Intermediate Logic:* Mr. Weaver.
The systematization of the semantic and combinatorial presuppositions of deductive reasoning and their interrelationships. Prerequisite: Philosophy 103a.

Ethics: Miss Potter.

A close study of important texts, with attention to such problems as responsibility, moral values, principles of moral decision and character.

Aesthetics: Mr. Krausz.]

Plato: Early and Middle Dialogues: Miss Taft.

An examination of several dialogues, including *Lysis, Charmides, Meno, Protagoras, Phaedrus, Symposium* and the *Republic.* Special attention will be given to structural and dramatic elements in the dialogues.

Aristotle: Miss Taft.]

History of Chinese Philosophy: Mr. Song.]

Medieval Philosophy: Miss Potter.

The history and development of medieval philosophy from its origins in classical and patristic thought through the fourteenth century.

Philosophy of Science: Mr. Krausz.]

Philosophy of Religion: Miss Potter.

The existence and nature of God and the character of religious language.

Philosophy of History: Mr. Krausz.]

Analytic Philosophy: Mr. Ferrater Mora.]

Existentialism: Mr. Ferrater Mora.]

Concepts of Time: Mr. Kline.]

History and Philosophy of Mathematics: Mr. Weaver.

The successive construction and development of the basic number systems of mathematics: positive integers, rational, real and complex numbers.

Philosophy of Creativity: Mr. Krausz.

A systematic examination of theories of creativity in the arts and sciences.

Philosophy of Language: Formal Grammars: Mr. Weaver.

A detailed examination of formal grammars with discussion of their relevance to linguistic theory and the philosophy of language.

Philosophy of the Social Sciences: Mr. Krausz.

A critical examination of various theories of human nature and human action.

[321b. *Philosophy of Anarchism:* Mr. Kline.]

[322b. *The Nature of Legal Reasoning:* Mr. Gaskins.]

[330a. *Kant:* Mr. Ferrater Mora.]

331a. *Hegel:* Mr. Gaskins.
A careful reading of the *Science of Logic* as the key to the dialectical method used by Hegel throughout his philosophical system.

[332b. *Texts in Medieval Philosophy:* Miss Potter.]

333a. *Russian Philosophy:* Mr. Kline.
A critical study of major trends in Russian thought from the eighteenth century to the present with special attention to ethics, social philosophy and the philosophy of history.

334b. *Marx and Russian Marxism:* Mr. Kline.
An intensive study of selected works of Marx, Engels, Plekhanov and Lenin and a critical survey of contemporary Soviet Marxism-Leninism.

[335b. *British Idealism:* Miss McPherson.]

336b. *Plato: Late Dialogues:* Miss Taft.
An examination of several dialogues, including *Theaetetus, Sophist, Statesman* and *Parmenides.* Special attention will be given to the structural and dramatic elements of the dialogues and to methods of interpretation. Prerequisite: Philosophy 231a.

399. *Senior Conference:* The Senior Conference is designed as a seminar combined with tutorial sessions. The Conference emphasizes critical thinking on a central philosophic issue. The work of the year is tested in part by a written examination of three hours in the spring.

401. *Honors Work:* Honors work consists of independent reading and conferences with the instructor, directed to the preparation of a paper on a subject dealing with the technical problems of philosophy or emphasizing the connection of philosophy with general literature, history, politics and science or with some special field in which the student is working.

Professors: Rosalie C. Hoyt, PH.D., *Chairman*
John R. Pruett, PH.D.

Assistant Professors: Alfonso M. Albano, PH.D.
Stephen R. Smith, PH.D.

Assistants: Eugene DiSalvatore, B.A.
. Robert M. Purcell, B.S.
˙ David H. Schwamb, B.S.

The plan for the physics major is based on the belief that an acquaintance with the methods used by professional workers in a field of intellectual activity is a necessary part of the general education of any student. The courses in physics emphasize the concepts and techniques that have led to our present state of understanding of the material universe; they are designed to relate the individual parts of physics to the whole rather than treat them as separate disciplines. In the advanced courses the student applies these concepts and techniques to increasingly independent studies of physical phenomena. Students are encouraged to supplement their courses in physics and mathematics with work in related sciences and by units of independent study or experimental work. Opportunities exist for interdisciplinary work, for participation by qualified majors in the research programs of the faculty and for training in machine shop, glass blowing, computer and electronic techniques. Special arrangements make advanced courses available to majors in other sciences.

Requirements in the Major Subject: Physics 101 or its equivalent, 201a, 202b, 306a, 307b and an additional half-unit of 300-level work in physics at Bryn Mawr or at Haverford, or in astronomy. (In special cases the Department will consider the substitution of other 300-level work for Physics 306a or 307b.) Two semesters of Senior Conferences, Chemistry 101, Mathematics 101 and 201, or their equivalent, a third unit of mathematics is strongly recommended. Students are encouraged to meet some of the major and allied requirements by advanced standing or placement examinations.

Allied Subjects: Astronomy (at Haverford), Biology, Chemistry, Geology, Mathematics, Philosophy, Psychology.

101. *Introduction to Modern Physics:* Miss Hoyt, Mr. Smith.

A study of the principal phenomena of classical and modern physics in the light of the developments of the past seventy years. Any mathematical methods needed beyond those of high school mathematics will be developed in the course. Three lectures and three hours of laboratory a week.

201a. *Electricity and Magnetism:* Mr. Pruett.

Direct and alternating current circuit theory, conduction in metals and semiconductors, semiconducting devices, magnetic effects of currents, electrostatics, Maxwell's equations. Three lectures and four hours of laboratory a week. Prerequisites: Physics 101 and Mathematics 201, which may be taken concurrently. Haverford Physics 111 and 112 and Mathematics 114b or 220b may be substituted.

202b. *Optics and Waves:* Mr. Pruett.

Application of Maxwell's equations and electromagnetic wave phenomena, superposition, interference and diffraction. Geometrical optics. Polarization. Dispersion and scattering of electromagnetic radiation. Introduction to the quantum nature of light. Selected topics in laser physics and modern optics. Three lectures and four hours of laboratory a week. Prerequisites: Physics 201a and Mathematics 201, which may be taken concurrently. Haverford Mathematics 114b or 220b may be substituted.

[207. *Physical Basis of Computer Science:* Mr. Pruett.]

305c. *Electronics:* Mr. Pruett.

Principles of solid state electronic devices and their applications to digital and analog computers and to other instruments. Four hours of laboratory a week. Prerequisite: Physics 201a, which may be taken concurrently.

306a. *Classical and Quantum Mechanics I:* Mr. Albano.

A unified treatment of the classical and quantum descriptions of physical phenomena. Intermediate classical mechanics through the Hamiltonian formulation. Coupled oscillations, normal modes and extension to continuous wave systems. Einstein and de Broglie relations, uncertainty and complementarity. Schrodinger's equation and elementary wave mechanics. Three lectures and four hours of laboratory a week. (With permission of the department, Haverford physics majors and majors in mathematics or chemistry may replace the laboratory by extra supervised work.) Prerequisites: Physics 202b and Mathematics 201. For

Haverford students, two years of physics and mathematics may be substituted.

Classical and Quantum Mechanics II: Miss Hoyt.

Quantum-mechanical measurement theory, state functions and transition probabilities. Classical and quantum descriptions of angular momentum. Central-force motion. The harmonic oscillator and the structure of the hydrogen and helium atoms. Three lectures and four hours of laboratory a week. (With permission of the Department, Haverford physics majors and majors in mathematics or chemistry may replace the laboratory by extra supervised work.) Prerequisite: Physics 306a.

Advanced Mechanics of Discrete and Continuous Systems: Mr. Albano.

Kinematics and dynamics of particles and macroscopic systems, including the use of configuration and phase space, normal mode analysis of oscillations, descriptions of the motions of rigid and elastic bodies. Mathematical methods, including aspects of the calculus of variations, linear algebra and differential equations, will be developed as needed. Four hours a week. Prerequisite: a 300-level physics course, which may be taken concurrently. (With permission of the instructor, advanced work in chemistry, astronomy or mathematics may be substituted.)

Advanced Electromagnetic Theory: Mr. Harrell (at Haverford).

Applications of Physics to Biology: Miss Hoyt.

In depth studies of such selected topics in biophysics as: nerve fiber transmission, muscle, retina and photoreceptors, primary processes in photosynthesis. Prerequisites: Physics 201a, 202b or the equivalent and Mathematics 201 or its equivalent. Chemistry 202 and Biology 101 are advisable.

Computer Usage in the Life Sciences: Mrs. Pruett.
) See Biology 357a.

Senior Conferences: The Senior Conferences consist of discussion meetings based on assigned readings and problem work. The students are examined at the end of each semester.

Thermodynamics and Statistical Mechanics: Mr. Smith.

Contemporary Physics (solids, nuclei, particles and other current research topics): Members of the Department.

Honors Work: Honors work may be taken by seniors recommended by the Department. It consists of reading and experimental work on some problem of physics.

403a. *Supervised Units in Special Topics:* Members of the Department.
& b.   Open to qualified juniors or seniors who wish to supplement their work
with independent study or laboratory work in a special area of physics,
subject to faculty time and interest. A written paper will be required at
the end of the semester or year.

Teaching Certification: A sequence of work offered by the Department of
Physics and the Department of Education of the College leads to a
certificate to teach in the secondary schools of Pennsylvania.

Political Science

The Caroline McCormick Slade Department of Political Science

President of the College: Harris L. Wofford, Jr., A.B., J.D.

Professors: Melville T. Kennedy, Jr. PH.D.
Gertrude C.K. Leighton, A.B., J.D.

Associate Professors: Charles E. Frye, PH.D.
Marc Howard Ross, PH.D., *Chairman*
Stephen Salkever, PH.D.

The major in political science is concerned with the study of normative
and empirical theories of government and with an analysis of the structures and processes of modern political communities.

Requirements in the Major Subject: Students majoring in political science
must take a minimum of four units of course work and the Senior
Conference in the major and two units in allied work. At least one unit of
major work must be taken in advanced courses. As a prerequisite to all
other courses offered, majors must complete one unit of work chosen from
among the following: 200a (INT.), 201a, 202, 203a, 204b, 205a, 206a,
207b, 208, 209, 210. Students who are not majors in the Department
may meet this prerequisite in the same way or alternatively by completing one half-unit of allied work and one half-unit in political science
chosen from the list of courses above.

The fields of the major, from which two must be selected for special
concentration, are: political philosophy and theory, politics and law in
American society, comparative politics, international politics and law.
At least three courses (one and one-half units of work), including a

minimum of one advanced course, must be taken in each of the fields selected. For courses arranged according to fields, see page 131. With the permission of the Department one of the fields may be taken in an allied subject.

Non-majors wishing to take a special field in political science must consult the chairman for approval of course plans in order to qualify for required Senior Conference program. See page 130.

With the permission of the Department, courses at Haverford, other than those listed below, may be taken for major or allied credit.

Allied Subjects: Anthropology, Economics, Education, History, Philosophy, Psychology and Sociology. With the permission of the department, certain courses offered by the modern language departments may be accepted as allied subjects.

Urban Society: Mrs. Lane, Mr. Ross.

) See INT. 200b in the interdepartmental major in The Growth and Structure of Cities.

American Politics: Mr. Ross.

An examination of the forces shaping political behavior and values in the United States, with particular attention to the processes of political socialization, public opinion formation, agenda building, decision making and policy implementation.

American Political Institutions and Their Dynamics: Mr. Waldman (at Haverford).

Government and Politics in East Asia: Mr. Kennedy.

An approach to modern Asian politics through a study of the major philosophic and institutional features of dynastic China and areas under Chinese cultural influence. India and Japan are considered for comparative purposes.

Twentieth-Century China and India: Mr. Kennedy.

A comparative examination of the politics of China and India in the twentieth century with special attention to the roles of nationalism and communism.

Government and Politics in Western Europe: Mr. Frye.

A comparative analysis of the contemporary political systems of Great Britain, France and Scandinavia, with special reference to factors making for stable and effective democracy.

Comparative Government and Politics: Mr. Glickman (at Haverford).

207b.   *Government and Politics in Western Europe:* Mr. Frye.

A comparative analysis of the contemporary political systems of Germany, Italy and the Soviet Union.

208a.   *International Politics:* Mr. Mortimer (at Haverford).
or b.

209a.   *Western Political Theory (Ancient and Early Modern):*
or b.   (a) Miss Shumer (at Haverford), (b) Mr. Salkever.

A study of fundamental problems of Western political thought. The course is designed to introduce the student both to the careful and critical reading of philosophic texts and to some of the important ways of formulating and answering central questions in political theory. Readings will be drawn from both ancient and early modern sources such as Plato, Aristotle, Machiavelli, Hobbes, Locke and Rousseau. (Limit 20 at Haverford).

210a.   *Western Political Theory (Modern):*
or b.   (a) Mr. Salkever, (b) Miss Shumer (at Haverford).

This course will focus on the same themes as Political Science 209, drawing on readings from a few of the following modern theorists: Rousseau, Burke, Kant, Hegel, Marx, Mill, Weber, Durkheim, Arendt, Marcuse. Prerequisite: Political Science 209a or b or permission of instructor. (Limit 20 at Haverford).

211a.   *The Soviet System:* Mr. Hunter (at Haverford).
(INT.)   See Economics 211a.

{212a.   *Western Political Thought: Ancient and Medieval.*}

{213b.   *Law and Civil Disobedience:* Mr. Wofford.}

218b.   *Community Politics: A Cross-Cultural Approach:* Mrs. Ross, Mr. Ross.
(INT.)   Examines political life at the local level in a cross-cultural context. Topics considered include authority and authority processes, socialization, legitimacy, decision making, community conflict, conflict resolution, law and political aggression and violence. Prerequisite: an introductory course in either political science, anthropology or sociology or permission of instructor.

219a.   *American Constitutional Law:* Mr. Williams.

221a.   *International Law:* Miss Leighton.

An examination of the doctrines and practices of international law. Traditional material is considered in the context of the contemporary political process, with some emphasis on methodological problems.

Political Behavior: Mr. Ross.]

Law and Education: Mr. Wofford.]

Law and Society: Miss Leighton.

An introduction to the nature of legal obligation and its relation to selected social institutions. Typical legal problems pertaining to the family, property and government are discussed.

Law, Policy and Personality: Miss Leighton.

Selected topics in the study of the relation between the legal process and personality development and structure. Attention is given, in the light of this perspective, to the policy implications of various legal doctrines pertaining to such subjects as divorce, child-rearing and criminal responsibility. Prerequisites: Political Science 219a, 301a, or 313b, or permission of instructor.

Problems in International Politics: Mr. Kennedy.

A rapid review of major approaches to the field, both analytic and substantive, followed by intensive consideration of particular operational concepts in international politics and of related concrete problems selected by the seminar.

European Fascism: Mr. Frye.]

Modern Germany: Mr. Frye.]

American Political Theory.]

Topics in Modern Political Thought: Mr. Frye.

Study of a medley of political problems (including alienation, freedom, political obedience) of modern societies from the perspective of different thinkers including Sartre, Marx and Marcuse.

Problems in Comparative Politics: Mr. Frye.]

Theory and Practice in Political Philosophy: Mr. Salkever.

A consideration of one of the central processes of political philosophy—the transition from Fact to Value. Typical alternative modes of linking theoretical and practical assertions will be studied through the works of ancient and modern philosophers. Prerequisites: Political Science 209b, or either Philosophy 101a or b or 201b.

China, Japan, India: Problems in Modernization: Mr. Kennedy.

Intensive review of established assessments and definitions of modernization and political development followed by a study of examples of recent political change in these societies. The seminar will participate in determining the countries and central questions on which the study focuses.

[313b. *Problems in Constitutional Law.*]

315a. *Ethics and Public Policy:* Mr. Kelsey.
See History of Religion 315a.

[315b. *American Bureaucracy.*]

[316b. *Ethnic Group Politics:* Mr. Ross.]
(INT.)

317a. *Political Culture and Political Leadership:* Mr. Frye.
A study of relations between political cultures and styles of political leadership in different Western countries.

[319a. *Problems in Legal Theory:* Mr. Salkever.]

[322b. *The Nature of Legal Reasoning:* Mr. Gaskins.]

399. *Senior Conference:* Each major is required to take at least one half-unit from the advanced research colloquia (399a at Bryn Mawr, 391-396 at Haverford) in the fall of her senior year and to write a senior research paper in the spring (399b). The colloquium will offer the student experience in conducting original research in political science. A student will normally take the colloquium in the fall of her senior year after having completed or while completing her other work in the appropriate area of concentration. The senior research paper will normally be in either of the student's two fields of concentration and will be supervised by a member of the Department whose specialty is in the same or related fields. The seniors will meet as a group towards the end of the second semester to share their research findings. A student may take more than one colloquium. Honors majors can fulfill their Senior Conference requirement in one of three ways: (1) they may take two colloquia in the first semester of their senior year, (2) they may take one colloquium in the fall and write their senior research project in the fall, or (3) they may take one colloquium in the fall and write their senior research paper in the spring.

Sections for 1976-77

1. *Freedom, Participation and Happiness:* Mr. Salkever.
A study of the consonance and opposition of freedom and political

participation. Readings will be drawn primarily, but not exclusively, from the tradition of American political thought.

2. *Political Socialization:* Mr. Frye.
A cross-cultural examination of how people acquire characteristic patterns of political orientation and behavior.

3. *Symbols and Politics:* Mr. Ross.
An examination of the role of symbols in shaping political demands and in mobilization and conflict. Topics considered will include the analysis of the symbolic orientations of the mass public, the creation of political symbols and their role in community formation.

4. *Topics in International Politics:* Mr. Kennedy.
A focus on current forces and directions in Asian politics.

[5. *Legal Research:* Miss Leighton.]

Senior Research: Members of the Department.
Students will conduct independent research under the direction of a member of the Department.

COURSES AT HAVERFORD

. *Constitutional Law:* Mr. Williams.

. *American Political Theory:* Miss Shumer.

. *Comparative Politics: Political Development.*

. *International Relations:* Mr. Mortimer.

.˙ *International Organization:* Mr. Mortimer.

. *Congress.*

. *Topics in Modern Political Theory:* Miss Shumer.

. *Research Seminar in American Foreign Policy:* Mr. Glickman.

. *Research Seminar: Political Theory:* Miss Shumer.

FIELDS OF CONCENTRATION

1. *Political Philosophy and Theory:* political analysis; Western political philosophy; recent political philosophy: sources and varieties; Western political thought: ancient and medieval; political behavior; theory and practice in political philosophy; selected topics in modern politi-

131

cal thought; American political theory (at Haverford); problems in contemporary American political theory (at Haverford).

2. *Politics and Law in American Society:* American national politics; community politics; ethnic group politics; political behavior; constitutional law; law and education; law and society; law, policy and personality; the American political process: parties and the Congress (at Haverford); problems in contemporary American political theory (at Haverford); public opinion, private interests and political system (at Haverford).

3. *Comparative Politics:* government and politics in East Asia; twentieth-Century China and India; government and politics in Western Europe; Western European integration; European Fascism; problems in comparative politics; China, Japan, and India: problems in modernization; the Soviet system (at Haverford); African civilization: tradition and transformations (at Haverford); comparative politics: political development (at Haverford); comparative political sociology (at Haverford); racial, ethnic and class politics (at Haverford).

4. *International Politics and Law:* international law; problems in international politics; courses on Asia and Europe; international relations (at Haverford); international organization (at Haverford); politics and international relations in the Middle East and North Africa (at Haverford); international politics of Communism (at Haverford).

401. *Honors Work:* Seniors admitted to Honors work prepare an independent research paper (one unit of credit) under the supervision of a member of the Department. Field work is encouraged.

Interdepartmental Work: The Department of Political Science participatēs in the interdepartmental major in The Growth and Structure of Cities and in the interdepartmental concentration in Hispanic and Hispanic-American Studies. See pages 150 and 153.

Teaching Certification: A sequence of work offered by the Department of Political Science and the Department of Education of the College leads to a certificate to teach in the secondary schools of Pennsylvania.

Psychology

Professors: Richard C. Gonzalez, PH.D., *Chairman*
Howard S. Hoffman, PH.D.†
Matthew Yarczower, PH.D.

Associate Professors: Clark McCauley Jr., PH.D.*
Earl Thomas, PH.D.

Assistant Professor: Jill T. Wannemacher, PH.D.

Lecturer: Larry Stein, PH.D.

Laboratory Coordinators: Erika Rossman Behrend, PH.D.
Alice S. Powers, PH.D.

Assistants: Anna Rose Childress, B.S.
Louise DeWald, B.A.
Sandra Klein, M.A.
Beverly Smith, B.A.
Howard Waxman, M.A.

The department offers to the major student a representative account of methods, theory and findings in comparative, developmental, experimental, physiological and social psychology. The program of work is coordinated with that at Haverford College (which offers training in experimental, personality and social psychology). It is planned to encourage the student, in the first two years of study, to sample widely from among the course offerings in these areas and to permit her, in the final two years, to focus attention (by course work and research) on the one or two areas of her principal interest.

Requirements in the Major Subject: Psychology 101 and two courses from each of the following groupings of courses: (a) Psychology 201a, 202b, 203a, 204b (or Haverford course 240b), (b) Psychology 206a, 207b, 208b (or Haverford course 208a), Haverford courses 200a, 209a (or 210b), (c) Psychology 301b, 302b, 305b, Haverford courses 309a, 344b; one unit of allied work in either biology, chemistry, physics, or mathematics. The Senior Conference is also required. Psychology 205a is strongly

---

*On leave, semester I.
†On leave, semester II.

recommended to students preparing for graduate work. Psychology is prerequisite to all other courses offered by the Department with the exception of Psychology 205a. Some second-semester courses at the 200 level, with permission of the Department, may be taken concurrently with Psychology 101.

Allied Subjects: Anthropology, Biology, Chemistry, Education, History of Science, Linguistics, Mathematics, Philosophy, Physics, Sociology. At least one unit must be taken from among Biology, Chemistry, Physics and Mathematics.

101. *Experimental Psychology:* Mr. Gonzalez, Mr. Thomas, Miss Wannemacher, Mr. Yarczower.

A survey of methods, facts and principles relating to basic psychological processes, their evolution, development and neurophysiology. Three hours of lecture and four hours of laboratory a week.

The following courses include individual laboratory research projects:

201a. *Learning Theory and Behavior:* Mr. Gonzalez.

Comparative studies of conditioning and instrumental learning; theories of learning; the evolution of intelligence.

202b. *Comparative Psychology:* Mr. Yarczower.

Evolution and behavior. The phylogeny of learning, perception, language, aggression and social behavior. Prerequisite: Psychology 201a.

203a. *Motivation:* Mr. Thomas.

The activation and regulation of goal-directed behavior: affectional processes, psychological drives, incentives, frustration, conflict, punishment and anxiety. Prerequisite: Psychology 201a which may be taken concurrently.

204b. *Sensory Processes:* Mr. Hoffman.

Peripheral and central mechanisms of sensory experience, with particular emphasis on analysis in the visual and auditory modalities. Classical psychophysics and modern signal detection theory.

205a. *Experimental Methods and Statistics:* Mr. Hoffman.

Measurement, descriptive statistics, probability, association, testing of hypotheses, the design of experiments and associated problems.

Developmental Psychology: Miss Wannemacher. (In alternate years, Education 206a. *Developmental Psychology:* Mr. Snyder.)

Development and behavior. The ontogeny of attention, perception, learning, language, intelligence and social interaction.

Language and Cognition: Miss Wannemacher.

Cognitive development and its relation to the development of language.

Social Psychology: Mr. McCauley.

Social influence and persuasion: audience and coaction effects; group dynamics; leadership, attitude change in relation to behavior change; stereotypes; social comparison theory; helping behavior.

Contemporary Issues in Behavior Theory: Mr. Yarczower.

Analysis of contemporary theory and research on: classical conditioning; attention, generalization and discrimination; punishment and avoidance; inhibition; biological constraints on learning. Prerequisite: Psychology 201a.

Physiological Psychology: Mr. Thomas.

The physiological and anatomical bases of experience and behavior: sensory processes and perception, emotion, motivation, learning and cognition. Prerequisite: Psychology 201a.

Psychological Measurement: Mr. McCauley.

Theory of testing and evaluation of representative psychological tests: reliability and validity; decisions using tests; IQ tests and the structure and inheritance of intelligence; selected aptitude and personality tests: SAT, GRE, MMPI, Rorschach.

Selected Problems in Comparative Psychology: Members of the Department.

Selected Problems in Physiological Psychology: Members of the Department.

Selected Problems in Experimental Psychology: Members of the Department.

Selected Problems in Social Psychology: Mr. McCauley.

Process and effects of mass media communications: pornography; television violence; commercial advertising; political advertising, including the psychology of voting; the agenda of public issues.

315a. *Selected Problems in Developmental Psychology:* Members of the Department.
& b.

357a. *Computer Usage in the Life Sciences:* Mrs. Pruett.
(INT.)   Experiments in the life sciences will be analyzed using computer techniques. The Fortran IV language will be developed and used throughout the course. Limited to advanced students with research experience; no previous training in the use of the computer is required. Lecture two hours, laboratory two hours a week.

399. *Senior Conference:* Seniors select four of the seven to ten mini-seminars offered by individual members of the faculty on topics announced late in the junior year. The topics vary from year to year, but each focuses on contemporary research in the faculty member's area of specialization. A paper is required in each seminar.

401. *Honors Work:* One unit of Honors work may be taken by students nominated by the Department.

403. *Supervised Research in Psychology:* Members of the Department.
      Laboratory or field research under the supervision of a member of the Department.

COURSES AT HAVERFORD

200a. *Human Learning and Memory:* Miss Naus.

208a. *Social Psychology:* Mr. Perloe.

209a. *Theories of Personality:* Mr. Heath.

215a. *Personality and Culture:* Mr. Davis.

{238a. *Psychology of Language:* Mr. D'Andrea.]

[240b. *Perception:* Miss Naus.}

306a. *Individual Differences:* Miss Naus.

309a. *Psychology of the Abnormal Personality:* Mr. Davis.

344a. *Development Through the Life Span:* Mr. Heath.

Russian

Associate Professors: Dan Davidson, PH.D.
　Ruth L. Pearce, PH.D., *Chairman*

Assistant Professors: George S. Pahomov, PH.D.
　Lynn Visson, PH.D.*

Lecturer: Masha Rozman, M.A.

Professor of Philosophy: George L. Kline, PH.D.

At Haverford:

Professor of Economics: Holland Hunter, PH.D.

Associate Professor of History: Linda G. Gerstein, PH.D.

The Russian major is designed to offer the student the opportunity to learn to both read and speak Russian and to achieve an understanding of the literature, thought and culture of both pre-revolutionary and contemporary Russia. The study of the Russian language is combined with a study in depth of one of the following areas of concentration: Russian literature, economics, Russian history or philosophy.

Students in all courses are encouraged to make use of tapes available in the Language Laboratory. Majors are encouraged to take advantage of various Russian language summer programs offered both here and in the Soviet Union and to compete for a place in the semester language program (senior year) at Leningrad State University. Residence in the Russian House for at least one year is advisable.

Requirements in the Major Subjects: Three years (or the equivalent) of work in the Russian language, two years of work in the area of concentration (Russian literature, economics, history or philosophy) of which one must be at the advanced level, one year of work outside the area of concentration and Senior Conference. A paper for which sources in Russian are used is required for an advanced course in the area of concentration. A comprehensive examination in the Russian language and in the area of concentration is given.

Allied Subjects: Any language or literature, Economics, History, History of Art, Music and Philosophy.

---

*On leave, semester I.

001. *Elementary Russian:* Members of the Department.
     The basic grammar is learned with enough vocabulary to enable the student to speak and understand simple Russian and to read simple texts. The course meets five times a week.

100. *Intensive Russian:* Members of the Department.
     A double course covering the work of Russian 001 and 101. Classes meet ten hours a week for two units of credit.

101. *Intermediate Russian:* Members of the Department.
     Continuing grammar study, conversation and vocabulary building. Readings in Russian classics and contemporary materials. The course meets five times a week.

200. *Advanced Training in the Russian Language:* Members of the Department.
     Intensive practice in oral and written expression based on literary and non-literary texts of Modern Standard Russian. Conducted in Russian.

201. *Readings in Russian:* Mrs. Pearce.
     Reading of literary and non-literary texts, selected in accordance with the needs and interests of the students. Emphasis is placed on vocabulary building and exposure to varying styles to enable the student to read advanced texts in her own or related fields.

203. *Russian Literature in Translation:* Mr. Davidson, Miss Visson.
     A study of Russian literature from its beginnings. Readings in representative works of various schools and genres with special emphasis on the nineteenth and twentieth centuries.

[204a. *Tolstoy.*]

[204b. *Dostoevsky.*]

[302. *Pushkin and His Time.*]

[303a. *Twentieth-Century Russian Literature of the Pre-Revolutionary Period.*]

[303b. *Twentieth-Century Russian Soviet Literature.*]

[305. *Advanced Russian Grammar.*]

306a. *Russian Prose and Poetry from Classicism to the Rise of Realism:* Mr. Davidson.
     A study of selected works of representative writers from Lomonosov to Gogol. Lectures and readings in Russian.

306b. *Russian Literature of the Second Half of the Nineteenth Century:* Mr. Pahomov.
     A study of selected prose writings of major Russian authors of the period. Lectures and readings in Russian.

Senior Conference: Members of the department.

The Senior Conference is intended to supplement course work. Format and topic vary from year to year according to the needs and interests of the students. The work of the conference will be evaluated by examination.

Honors Work: Honors work is offered to students recommended by the Department.

SEE ALSO

International Economic Theory and Policy: Mr. Farley.

Developing Economies: Mr. Farley.

Russian Philosophy: Mr. Kline.

Marx and Russian Marxism: Mr. Kline.

COURSES AT HAVERFORD

The Soviet System: Mr. Hunter.

Research Seminar: Mr. Dixon.

Russian History: Mrs. Gerstein.

Russia in the Twentieth Century.]

The Russian Revolution: Mrs. Gerstein.

Independent Study.

Sociology

Professor: Eugene V. Schneider, PH.D., *Chairman*

Associate Professor: Judith R. Porter, PH.D.

Assistant Professors: William R. F. Phillips, PH.D.
Robert Earl Washington, PH.D.

Visiting Lecturer: Stanley S. Clawar, PH.D.

Instructor: Alexa Albert, M.A.

Assistants: Marsha L. Miller, B.A.

Rita Buckley, B.A.

Associate Professor of Social Work and Social Research:

Dolores G. Norton, PH.D.‡

The aim of the major in sociology is to provide the student with a general understanding of the structure and functioning of modern society, its major institutions, groups and values, and of the interrelations of these with personality. Stress is also placed on the major strains and problems of modern society. Free elective work is offered to those who may be interested in applying their knowledge to the field of social work.

The work of this program is closely integrated with the work in sociology offered at Haverford College. Students should inquire about the possibilities of coordinated work with Haverford.

Requirements for the Major Subject: Sociology 102a and b, 302a and 305b and additional work to be chosen from courses offered at Bryn Mawr or courses above the introductory level at Haverford. A total of three and one-half units of course work is required in addition to the Senior Conference.

Allied Subjects: Anthropology, Economics, Social Psychology, Political Science, American and African History, Mathematics.

102a.   *Introduction to Sociology:* Mrs. Porter.

Analysis of the basic sociological perspectives, methods and concepts used in studying society. Emphasis is placed on culture, social system, personality and their interrelationships. Concrete applications of sociological analysis are examined.

102b.   *American Social Structure:* Mr. Schneider.

Analysis of the structure and dynamics of complex, industrial societies. Examples will be drawn from several societies, but major emphasis is on the United States.

[202a.   *Social Welfare and the Individual and His Environment:* Mrs. Norton.]

[202b.   *Social Problems and Social Work Practice.*]

[205b.   *Social Stratification:* Mr. Schneider.]

------

‡On leave for the year 1976-77.

Intergroup Relations: Mrs. Porter.

An examination of cultural, structural and personality change with a focus on minority groups. Emphasis is on black-white and minority relationships in the U.S.; there will be a cross-cultural comparison with race relationships in South Africa.

Sociology of Religion: Mrs. Porter.

Analysis of the interrelationship between religion and society, drawing upon the works of major social theorists. Emphasis is placed on the connection between religious systems and secular culture, social structure, social change, secular values and personality systems.

Sociology of Poverty: Mrs. Porter.

An analysis of the causes and effects of poverty in the United States. Issues covered will include the culture of poverty, the effects of poverty on institutions like the family, and the government poverty programs.

* *Field Work in Urban Studies:* Mr. Clawar.

An approach to the urban situation in the public school system. Field work and weekly seminars will be integrated. Topics to be covered, semester I: the tutorial relationship, social aspects of student development, the crisis literature, communications problems, ethnicity and educational values. Semester II: intellectualism in America, family influences on education, bureaucracy, desegregation and decentralization, schools and juvenile delinquency, sex roles and the schools.

Modernization: Mr. Washington.

Sociological problems of development confronting third world societies. The following topics will be covered: theories of modernization; the Western capitalist, the socialist and the Japanese patterns of modernization; the social problems created by colonialism, rapid population growth, social class exploitation, ethnic prejudice, urbanization, etc.; the problem of political priorities; democracy vs. political stabily.

Political Sociology: Mr. Phillips.}

Marginal Communities: the Sociology of the Outsider: Mr. Washington.}

Women, Sex Roles and Socialization: Miss Albert.

A critical analysis of the cultural, social, structural and personality theories of sex-role socialization. Students will have the opportunity to test the various theories in recent empirical data. Readings for the course will be selected from the areas of anthropology, sociology and child development, and an attempt will be made to construct a comprehensive interdisciplinary approach to sex-role socialization. The dynamics of social change with regard to the Women's Movement will also be investigated.

238b. *Women and the Social Structure:* Miss Albert.

The position of women in the economic, political and social systems of the United States. Emphasis will be placed on the economic system and the factors affecting women in the labor force. The aspirations and goals of various social categories of women will be investigated in depth in relation to the Women's Movement.

240a. *Urban Sociology:* Mr. Phillips.
(INT.) An analysis of urban social structures. Topics considered are: the urban polity, the psychology of urban life, the economic function of cities and contemporary urban problems.

245b. *Social Problems:* Mr. Washington.

A survey of major problems in American society as seen by sociologists and social critics. Topics considered: crime, education, drug addiction, the police, divorce, racial ghettos and violence.

255b. *The Sociology of Alienation:* Mr. Washington.

An examination of a variety of theoretical approaches to the phenomena of powerlessness, loss of meaning, estrangement and inauthenticity and an analysis of the social conditions giving rise to and resulting from alienation.

260a. *Social Control and Deviance:* Mr. Phillips.

An examination of the relationship between various types of "deviant" behavior (e.g. criminality, juvenile delinquency, drug and alcohol addiction, unconventional sexual behavior and mental illness) and the social institutions concerned with the "control" of such behavior (e.g. the police, the courts, prisons, rehabilitation clinics and groups, hospitals and mental institutions and the welfare system).

[280b. *Industrial Sociology:* Mr. Schneider.]

302a. *Social Theory:* Mr. Schneider.

An examination of the extent to which the writings of classical and modern theorists throw light on wide-ranging social, cultural and historical processes.

305b. *Sociological Methods:* Mr. Phillips.

An examination of various techniques for conducting empirical enquiry in research design, collection of data, methods of interviewing and analysis.

. *Senior Conference:* The form and evaluation of the conference will be determined in consultation with the senior majors.

. *Honors Work:* Honors work is offered to students who have demonstrated proficiency in their studies in the Department of Sociology and will consist of independent reading and research, conferences and the preparation of a written report.

Interdepartmental Work: The Department of Sociology participates in the interdepartmental major in The Growth and Structure of Cities and in the interdepartmental concentration in Hispanic and Hispanic-American Studies. See pages 150 and 153.

In general students may enroll for major credit in any course above the introductory level in the Department of Sociology at Haverford. Since alternative programs are possible, the student should consult the Department of Sociology at Bryn Mawr.

Spanish

Professors: Joaquín González Muela, *D. en Fil.*
   Willard Fahrenkamp King, PH.D., *Chairman*

Associate Professor: Eleanor Krane Paucker, PH.D.

Visiting Lecturer: James E. Irby, PH.D.

Instructor: Mónica Estela Hollander, M.A.

Professor of Philosophy: José María Ferrater Mora, *Lic. Fil.* ‡

The major in Spanish offers work in both language and the literature of all centuries, with emphasis on those periods when Spain and Spanish America have made their maximum contributions to Western culture.

   The introductory course treats a selection of the outstanding works of Spanish and Spanish-American literature in various periods ·and genres.

---

‡On leave for the year 1976-77.

Advanced courses deal more intensively with individual authors or periods of special interest. Students are admitted to advanced courses after satisfactory completion of two semesters of 200-level courses in Spanish literature or by placement test and permission of the instructor. Students may take an advanced course at Haverford if it contributes significantly to their special program. In certain cases, with the approval of the department and the Dean of The Graduate School of Arts and Sciences, advanced students may also take one graduate course.

One course is devoted to training in written and spoken Spanish. It is recommended that students supplement their course work by spending the junior year in Spain or Spanish America, studying in the summer at the *Centro* in Madrid or living in the Spanish House. It is strongly advised that all students make use of the tapes available in the Language Laboratory. In Spanish 001 the use of the Laboratory forms an integral part of the course.

Requirements in the Major Subject: The normal course sequence in the major is Spanish 101a and b, 201a or b, 202a or b, at least four semesters of advanced work and the Senior Conference. Students who spend the junior year in Spain may substitute an advanced literature course for Spanish 202a or 202b, and students whose pre-college training includes advanced work in literature may, with the permission of the Department, substitute a unit of more advanced work for 101a and b.

Allied Subjects: Any other language or literature, Anthropology, Economics, Hispanic Studies, History, History of Art, History of Religion, Linguistics, Music, Philosophy, Political Science, and Sociology.

001. *Elementary Spanish:* Miss Hollander, Mrs. Paucker.

Grammar, composition, oral and aural training, readings on the Spanish and Spanish-American background.

003. *Intermediate Spanish:* Mr. González Muela, Miss Hollander.

Intensive grammar reviews, exercises in composition and conversation, selected readings from modern Spanish texts.

101a. *Readings in Hispanic Literature:* Miss Hollander; Mr. García-Barrio (at
& b. Haverford).

A general view of Spanish history and culture as revealed in outstanding literary works of various periods and genres. Oral expression and practice in writing are emphasized.

Hispanic Literature of the Nineteenth Century: Mrs. Paucker.

Poetry and prose from the Romantic Revolt to Bourgeois Realism: Larra, Espronceda, Galdós, Clarín and others.

The Generation of 1898 and Modernismo: Mrs. Paucker.

The creation of new styles and new values by José Martí, Rubén Darío, Unamuno, Baroja and others.

Advanced Language Training and Composition: Mr. González Muela, Miss Hollander.

Training in phonetics and practice in conversation. Interpretation of texts, translation and original composition in Spanish. Assignments adapted to the needs and level of achievement of the individual student.

Contemporary Spanish American Poetry.}

Narrative Structure.}

The Mexican Novel since the Revolution of 1910: Mrs. Paucker.

Primary attention is given to novels by Mariano Azuela, Juan Rulfo, Carlos Fuentes and others whose work reflects the social and political upheavals of revolutionary Mexico.

Hispanic Culture and Civilization: Mrs. King.

)   See INT. 210a in the interdepartmental area of concentration in Hispanic and Hispanic-American Studies.

Medieval Spanish Literature: Mrs. Paucker.}

The Modern Novel in Spain: Mrs. King.}

Modern Poetry in Spain: Mr. González Muela.}

Cervantes: Mrs. King.

Primarily a study of *Don Quijote*—its structural innovations and its synthesis of the conflicting aesthetic and ideological currents of Cervantes's Spain.

Spanish Poetry and Drama of the Golden Age: Mrs. King.

Formal and thematic analysis of three lyric poets, Garcilaso, Góngora and Quevedo, and three major dramatists, Lope de Vega, Tirso and Calderón, of the Spanish national theater.

Senior Conference:

a. In the first semester a senior seminar is devoted to the study of a special topic in Spanish literature chosen by the students, to be evaluated by a written examination in January.

b. In the second semester individual conferences between each student and her instructor are designed to aid the student in the preparation of a paper on an author or theme as seen in the context of a whole period in Spanish literature and history. At the end of the semester each student has a brief oral examination in Spanish consisting of the explanation and interpretation of a Spanish text and serving, along with the papers, as the method of evaluation of this conference. (With the approval of the Department, the student may substitute the Hispanic Studies seminar for the second-semester Senior Conference, see page 153.)

401. *Honors Work:* Honors work is offered to students recommended by the Department. This work consists of independent reading, conferences and a long paper.

Interdepartmental Work: The Spanish Department participates in the interdepartmental area of concentration in Hispanic and Hispanic-American Studies. See page 153.

COURSES AT HAVERFORD

203b. *Spanish-American Literature:* Mr. García-Castro.

205a. *Studies in the Spanish-American Novel:* Mr. García-Castro.

209a. *Contemporary Spanish Theater:* Mr. García-Barrio.

305b. *Prose of the Sixteenth and Seventeenth Centuries:* Mr. García-Barrio.

Interdepartmental Work

As new fields of study open up and as old fields change, it becomes necessary for those interested in them to acquire the information and to learn the methods needed to understand them and to work in them, and these may sometimes be quite diverse. In order to provide an opportunity for students to work in these new areas, the faculty has approved the establishment of the following interdepartmental majors and interdepartmental area of concentration.

I. Interdepartmental Majors
Classical Languages

Major Advisors: Professor Dickerson (Greek)
   Professor Scott (Latin)

The major in classical languages is designed for the student who wishes to divide her time equally between the two languages and literatures.

Requirements: Six units of course work in Greek and Latin, normally three of each. At least one unit of advanced course work but no allied units. A special Senior Conference will be made up from the offerings of the two departments. See pages 93 and 110 for descriptions of courses and conferences.

Classical Studies

Major Advisors: Professor Dickerson (Greek)
   Professor Scott (Latin)
   Professor Ridgway (Classical and Near Eastern Archaeology)

The major in classical studies will provide a broad yet individually structured background for students whose interest in the ancient classical world is general, and who wish to lay the foundation for more specialized work in one particular area.

Requirements: Eight units of course work, at least one in each of the following: ancient history (History 205a and b; 206a and b), ancient philosophy (Philosophy 101a or b, 231a, 232b), classical archaeology

147

(Classical and Near Eastern Archaeology 101, 202b, 203a, 203b, 205b, 301a, 302a, 302b, 304a), Greek (all courses except 203a and b, 213a, 214b), Latin (all courses except 204a and 205a and b). At least one unit of advanced work is required, but no allied work. The Senior Conference will be in two parts: one in the field of the advanced unit and a special Classical Studies Conference on some topic to which all fields may contribute. (Two of the required eight units may be taken at Haverford College with the approval of the major advisors.)

French Studies

Major Advisors: Professors Salmon and Silvera (History)
Professor Guggenheim (French)

The major in French studies, offered jointly by the French and History departments, is intended for students who wish to acquire in depth an understanding of French life and culture. The major concentrates on a sequence of French and history courses so that literary themes and their historical context may be studied in parallel. In addition to the introductory course and the conference, courses specially designed for the program will be offered from time to time. Relevant courses in allied fields, such as political science, philosophy and history of art or music will be made available where possible. A junior year in France under one of the plans recommended by the French Department or summer study at the *Institut d'Etudes françaises d'Avignon* (held under the auspices of Bryn Mawr) forms an integral part of the program. Where students intend to take the junior year in France, early election of the major and the taking of the introductory course at sophomore level are recommended. Alternatively, special arrangements may be made to take an equivalent course in French civilization at a French university during the junior year in France. A good command of French, both written and spoken, is required. At least a year of residence in the French House in Haffner is advisable.

Requirements: Students whose interests are literary will normally elect three units of French and two of history, while those whose bent is historical will elect three units of history and two of French. At least one of these units from either department will be at the advanced level. Interdepartmental 290. *La Civilisation de France* serves as the introductory course. French 205c. *Stylistique et traduction,* or the equivalent, is a required course.

Allied Subjects: Economics, The Growth and Structure of Cities, History of Art, Music, Philosophy, Political Science, Sociology.

La Civilisation de France: Mr. Silvera, Mr. McCarthy (at Haverford).]
)   Conducted in French, this course studies the development of modern French life and culture in its historical context and explores the values and attitudes of French society as manifested in literature and the arts, politics, education and religion. Prerequisite: a good command of French. Serves as the introductory course for French Studies majors but is open to other qualified students.

Littérature, histoire et société de la Renaissance à la Révolution:
) Mr. Guggenheim.
   A study of French society from the Religious Wars to the Revolution as reflected in representative texts (letters, memoirs, plays, essays), with special emphasis on the historical background of two centuries of French literature. The course, conducted in French, is open to both French Studies majors and other qualified students.

Le Seizième Siècle à travers le roman historique: Mr. Salmon.
)   The course will explore the relationship between historical imagination and historical fact. It will show how historical novelists are influenced by the context of their own time and also how their interpretation may deepen an understanding of the period of which they write. Among the novels chosen is the Dumas trilogy on the Religious Wars.

Senior Conference: Mr. Salmon.
   A series of weekly seminars examining the relationship between literature, political theory and historiography within a selected period.

FRENCH LITERATURE

   See course listings under the French Department.

FRENCH HISTORY

   For description of courses offered at Bryn Mawr in the current year, see listings under the History Department.

Europe, 1789-1848: Mr. Silvera.

The Impressionist Era: Mr. McCarthy (at Haverford).]

[243b. *Contemporary France:* Mr. McCarthy (at Haverford).]

295a. *Paris in the Seventeenth and Eighteenth Centuries:* Miss Lafarge.
(INT.) See INT. 295a in the interdepartmental major in The Growth and
Structure of Cities.

[302. *France, 1559-1661:* Mr. Salmon.]

[330. *France since 1870:* Mr. Silvera.]

355a. *Topics in Early Modern European History: The French Revolution:* Mr. Spielman (at Haverford).

[375b. *Topics in the Renaissance:* Mr. Salmon.]

COURSES AT THE INSTITUT D'ETUDES FRANÇAISES D'AVIGNON

The following courses are given during the summer session:
Political Science s201. *La France d'aujourd'hui.*
Sociology s202. *La Vie quotidienne en France.*

401. *Honors Work:* On the recommendation of the Major Advisors, qualified
students in their senior year will be admitted to Honors work consisting
of independent reading and a long research paper.

The Growth and Structure of Cities

Major Advisor and Director of the Program: Professor Lane (History)

In this interdisciplinary major, the student will study the city from more
than one point of view. City planning, art and architecture, history,
political science, anthropology, archaeology, economics and sociology
will contribute toward her understanding of the growth and structure of
cities.

Requirements: All students must take Interdepartmental 190 and Interdepartmental 200b (one and one-half units). Each student should select,
in addition to these courses, three units from among the other major
courses listed below. Two additional units, above the introductory level,
must be chosen from any one department listed under Allied Subjects.
Each senior will prepare a paper or project embodying substantial research. The paper or project will be presented in written form to the
Committee on The Growth and Structure of Cities and in oral or visual

form to all seniors in the major, meeting as a group. These oral presentations and the resulting discussions will serve as the Senior Conference.

Allied Subjects: Anthropology, Fine Art, Classical and Near Eastern Archaeology, Economics, Greek, History, History of Art, Latin, Political Science, Sociology. Occasionally, with the permission of the Dean of the Graduate School, courses in Social Work and Social Research.

The Form of the City: Mrs. Lane.]
)

Urban Society: Mrs. Lane, Mr. Ross.
)   The techniques of the social sciences as tools for studying historic and contemporary cities.

Ancient Greek Cities and Sanctuaries: Mr. Nylander.]
)

The Ancient City: Mr. Scott.
)   The course will investigate the historical developments of the Greek and Roman cities of the Mediterranean from Alexander's conquest of Asia to the foundation of Constantinople. Particular attention will be paid to their organization and purpose, and an effort will be made to discern the theoretical and practical attitudes of the inhabitants towards their cities. Primary and secondary source material, where possible, will be in English.

Ancient Near Eastern Architecture: Mr. Ellis, Miss Mellink.
)   See Classical and Near Eastern Archaeology 206b.

Latin America: Colonies and Revolutions: Mrs. Dunn.]
)

Urban Economics: Mr. Dixon (at Haverford).
)

Community Politics: A Cross-Cultural Approach: Mrs. Ross, Mr. Ross.
)   See Political Science 218b.

Urban Sociology: Mr. Phillips.
)   See Sociology 240a.

Paris in the Seventeenth and Eighteenth Centuries: Miss Lafarge.
)   A study of the geography, architecture, economics, sociology and politics of Paris in these two periods. The course, conducted in English, is open to majors in The Growth and Structure of Cities and in French

Studies, as well as to other qualified students. A reading knowledge of French is required.

[300b. *The American City in the Twentieth Century:* Mr. Speizman.]
(INT.)

302a. *Greek Architecture:* Mr. Nylander.
(INT.)   See Classical and Near Eastern Archaeology 302a.

304b. *The Dynamics of Environmental Systems:* Mr. Anderson.
(INT.)   See Chemistry 304b.

305a. *The Italian City-State in the Renaissance:* Mrs. Lane.
(INT.)   See History 305a.

307b. *Medieval Cities: Islamic, Byzantine and Western:* Mr. Brand.
(INT.)   See History 307b.

[316b. *Ethnic Group Politics:* Mr. Ross.]
(INT.)

317a. *Mexico: Independence to the Present:* Mrs. Dunn.
(INT.)   See History 317a.

[328b. *Colonial Towns in North and South America:* Mrs. Dunn.]
(INT.)

334b. *A History of Blacks in the American City:* Mr. Holbrook.
(INT.)   See History 334b.

350a. *Topics in the History of Modern Architecture:* Mrs. Lane.
(INT.)   Selected aspects of the history of modern architecture such as housing, public buildings and industrial buildings will be studied in detail. The course will concentrate on actual building types, rather than on the design ideas of a few great architects. A reading knowledge of French or German is very desirable.

399. *Senior Conference:* Mrs. Lane and members of the Committee on The Growth and Structure of Cities.

Interdepartmental Area of Concentration
Hispanic and Hispanic-American Studies

Major Advisors: Professor Dunn (History)
   Professor King (Spanish)

The program is designed for students interested in a comprehensive study of the society and culture of Spanish America or Spain or both. Its aims are (1) to provide the student, through a formal major in anthropology, history, history of art, history of religion, economics, music, political science, sociology or Spanish, with a valid means for thorough study of one aspect of Hispanic or Hispanic-American culture, (2) to afford an introduction, through the study of allied courses dealing with Spain or Spanish America, to other aspects of the cultural complex, (3) to effect a synthesis of the student's studies through a Senior Conference, in which all students in the program participate, on a broad topic that cuts across all the major areas involved.

Requirements: Competence in Spanish; a major chosen from those listed above; Hispanic Studies 210a; at least two units of work chosen from courses listed below (or from approved courses taken in Spain or Spanish America); in the junior or senior year, a long paper or project dealing with Spain or Spanish America; the Senior Conference in Hispanic and Hispanic-American Studies. (In effect, the student supplements a major in one of the departments listed above with a concentration in Hispanic or Hispanic-American studies.)

Hispanic Culture and Civilization: Mrs. King.
)   A brief survey of the political, social and cultural history of Spain and Spanish America, concentrating on the emergence of specifically Hispanic values and modes of life. Major topics: spread of the Spanish Empire, Spanish-American Independence, racial and ethnic conflict, current social and economic problems, Spanish America's recent attempts to define its own identity.

Senior Conference: Major Advisors.

Courses: Anthropology 101, 204a, [305a], 306b, Economics [202b], History [207a], [211b], [212], INT. 317a, [H355a], History of Art 213, History of Religion 104a, 300b, 28 (at Swarthmore), Interdepartmental [308a and b], 310a, 312b, Philosophy [314b], Sociology 102a, Spanish:

any course (including those given at the Centro de Estudios Hispánicos in Madrid) except 001, 003 and 202a and b.

III. Interdepartmental Courses

Each year, certain courses are offered which cut across well-defined areas of knowledge and emphasize relationships among them. Such courses may be taught by two or more members of the faculty working in close cooperation. Since the material considered requires some background in at least two disciplines, the interdepartmental courses are usually offered at the advanced level. For students who have progressed to the more complex aspects of their major subjects, the interdepartmental courses provide an opportunity to apply their training to new and broader problems and to benefit from the experience of seeing their own subject from the points of view of several specialists. To facilitate free discussion, registration is generally restricted to a limited number of well-qualified students.

[190. *The Form of the City:* Mrs. Lane.]
(INT.)

200b. *Urban Society:* Mrs. Lane, Mr. Ross.
(INT.)   See INT. 200b in the interdepartmental major in The Growth and Structure of Cities.

[202b. *Ancient Greek Cities and Sanctuaries:* Mr. Nylander.]
(INT.)

204a. *The Ancient City:* Mr. Scott.
(INT.)   See INT. 204a in the interdepartmental major in The Growth and Structure of Cities.

206b. *Ancient Near Eastern Architecture:* Mr. Ellis, Miss Mellink.
(INT.)   See Classical and Near Eastern Archaeology 206b.

[207a. *Latin America: Colonies and Revolution:* Mrs. Dunn.]

[209a. *Urban Economics:* Mr. Dixon (at Haverford).]
(INT.)

210a. *Hispanic Culture and Civilization:* Mrs. King.
(INT.)   See INT. 210a in the interdepartmental area of concentration in Hispanic and Hispanic-American Studies.

The Soviet System: Mr. Hunter (at Haverford).
See Economics 211a.

Myth in Practice and Theory: Miss Lang.]

Community Politics: A Cross-Cultural Approach: Mrs. Ross, Mr. Ross.
See Political Science 218b.

Urban Sociology: Mr. Phillips.
See Sociology 240a.

La Civilisation de France: Mr. Silvera; Mr. McCarthy (at Haverford).]

Paris in the Seventeenth and Eighteenth Centuries: Miss Lafarge.
See INT. 295a in the interdepartmental major in The Growth and Structure of Cities.

Littérature, histoire et société de la Renaissance à la Révolution: Mr. Guggenheim.
See INT. 295b in the interdepartmental major in French Studies.

Le Seizième Siècle à travers le roman historique: Mr. Salmon.
See INT. 297a in the interdepartmental major in French Studies.

The American City in the Twentieth Century: Mr. Speizman.]

Europe in the Twentieth Century: Mr. Poppel.
See History 301b.

Greek Architecture: Mr. Nylander.
See Classical and Near Eastern Archaeology 302a.

The Dynamics of Environmental Systems: Mr. Anderson.
See Chemistry 304b.

The Italian City-State in the Renaissance: Mrs. Lane.
See History 305a.

Introduction to Celtic Civilization: Miss Dorian.]

Medieval Cities: Islamic, Byzantine and Western: Mr. Brand.
See History 307b.

Language in the Social Context: Miss Dorian.]

310a. *Introduction to Descriptive Linguisitic Techniques:* Miss Dorian.
(INT.)   .An introduction to techniques of synchronic linguistic analysis: typology, phonetics, phonemics, morphemics and syntax. A prerequisite for Interdepartmental 312b.

311b. *Diachronic Linguistics:* Miss Dorian.
(INT.)   An introduction to historical linguistics: the reconstruction of prehistoric linguistic stages, the establishment of language families and their interrelationships and the examination of processes of linguistic change. Pertinent materials will be drawn from a variety of languages, but the history of the English language, as the language common to all participants, will be central.

312b. *Field Methods in Linguistics:* Miss Dorian.
(INT.)   Practical experience in transcription and analysis of an unfamiliar language. There will be an informant, and students will be able to develop their own methodology for approaching a language with which they have no previous experience. Interdepartmental 310a is a prerequisite.

313a. *Comparative Greek and Latin Grammar:* Mr. Sheets.
(INT.)   The linguistic evolution of Greek and Latin from their Indo-European origins to the Christian era, with the primary focus on phonology and morphology; some fundamental concepts and methodologies of historical linguistics will be introduced.

313b. *Greek Dialects:* Mr. Sheets.
(INT.)   A descriptive examination of the dialects, a study of their evolution and implications for the pre-history of the Greeks and an analysis of literary dialects.

314. *History of Scientific Thought:* Miss Oppenheimer, Mrs. Reeds.
(INT.)   See History 314.

[316b. *Ethnic Group Politics:* Mr. Ross.]
(INT.)

317a. *Mexico: Independence to the Present:* Mrs. Dunn.
(INT.)   See History 317a.

328b. *Colonial Towns in North and South America:* Mrs. Dunn.
(INT.)   See History 328b.

334b. *A History of Blacks in the American City:* Mr. Holbrook.
(INT.)   See History 334b.

Topics in the History of Modern Architecture: Mrs. Lane.
See INT. 350a in the interdepartmental major in The Growth and Structure of Cities.

Biochemistry: Macromolecular Structure and Function: Mr. Prescott, Mr. Young.
See Biology 353a.

Biochemistry: Intermediary Metabolism: Mr. Conner, Mr. Prescott.
See Biology 353b.

Computer Usage in the Life Sciences: Mrs. Pruett.
See Biology 357a.

Performing Arts

101a. *Dance Composition:* Mrs. Mason, Mrs. Lember.
& b. Designed to teach modern dance technique in conjunction with choreographic theory. Assignments in composition are given to aid artistic awareness and the development of performing skills.

{201a. *Modern Dance: Advanced Techniques and Choreography:* Mrs. Mason, Mrs. Lember.}

403. *Voice* or *Instrument*
 Students who are sufficiently advanced and who have completed at least one year of voice or music lessons while at the College may with the approval of the Department of Music offer for one unit of academic credit a year of voice or instrument lessons. The unit will include the lessons and also a recital or proficiency test arranged by the Music Department.

Physical Education

Director: Anne Lee Delano, M.A.

Instructors: Linda Fritsche Castner, M.S.
 Naomi L. Kocean, M.S.
 Barbara Lember, B.F.A.
 Paula Carter Mason, B.S.
 Jenepher Shillingford, M.ED.
 Janet A. Yeager

The Department of Physical Education has developed a program to:
 1. Recognize the student with a high degree of neuromuscular coordination and physical stamina and encourage her to maintain this status.
 2. Provide incentive for all students to find some form of activity in which they may find pleasure and show improvement.
 3. Contribute to the total well-being of the student.

The program provides a Physical Education Profile Test optional for freshman and sophomores. Above-average performance releases the student from physical education for one year.

There is a two-year requirement to be completed preferably by the end of the sophomore year. In the freshman year each student will take three hours a week during the first semester: two hours in an activity of her choice and one hour in a specialized unit. The units are Dance Orientation, Relaxation and Sports Orientation. In the second semester and during the sophomore year each student will participate two hours a week in an activity of her choice. Each semester is divided into two terms in order that the student may participate in a variety of activities should she wish to do so.

All students must complete the freshman and sophomore requirements satisfactorily. Upperclassmen are invited to elect any of the activities offered. Transfer students will have their physical education requirement reviewed by the Director of Physical Education.

The Optional Test for Release

Areas contributing to a physical education profile to be determined by testing, using standardized tests and procedures adapted to college women:
1. Aptitude and Achievement Battery (performance skill)
   a. Standing long jump b. Sandbag throw c. Obstacle course
2. Fitness Battery (strength and endurance)
   a. Standing long jump c. Push-ups—modified
   b. Sit-ups   d. 12-minute run
3. Body weight control

The Swimming Test (for survival)

1. Jump into deep end of pool (feet first entry), demonstrate two strokes while swimming lengths of pool for ten minutes without stopping, resting or touching bottom or sides of pool, backfloat motionless for two minutes, tread water one minute.
2. The swimming test is administered to every new student at the beginning of the year unless she is excused by the College Physician.
3. Students unable to pass the test must register for beginning swimming.

Seasonal Offerings

Fall: archery, modern dance, golf, hockey, riding*, swimming, tennis, volleyball and American Red Cross Life Saving Course.

Winter: badminton, basketball, modern dance, ballroom dancing, exercise therapy, fencing, gymnastics, riding*, squash, swimming, volleyball and American Red Cross Water Safety Instructor Training Course.

Spring: archery, modern dance, ballroom dancing, golf, gymnastics, lacrosse, riding*, swimming, tennis, trampoline and American Red Cross Life Saving.

A Modern Dance Club and Varsity teams are open to students with special interests in those areas.

---

*with permission of the chairman of the Department

Financial Aid

The scholarships listed on the following pages have been made available to able and deserving students through the generosity of alumnae and friends of the College. Many of them represent the income on endowed funds which in some cases is supplemented by an additional grant, usually taken from expendable gifts from alumnae and parents. A student requesting aid does not apply to a particular fund but is considered for all awards administered by the College for which she is qualified.

The Alumnae Regional Scholarship Program is the largest single contributor to Bryn Mawr's Scholarship awards. Bryn Mawr is the only college with an alumnae-based scholarship program independent, yet coordinated with the College's own financial aid program. The Alumnae raise funds, interview candidates requesting and needing aid, and choose their scholars. An Alumnae Regional Scholarship carries with it special significance as an award for excellence, academic and personal.

An outstanding scholarship program has been established by the National Merit Scholarship Corporation, and several large corporations sponsor scholarship programs for children of employees. In addition to the generous awards made by these companies there are many others made by foundations and by individual and professional groups. Some of these are regional in designation. Students are urged to consult their schools and community agencies for information in regard to such opportunities.

Bryn Mawr College participates as a sponsor in the National Merit Scholarship Program and in the National Achievement Scholarship Program. As sponsor, the College awards several scholarships through the National Merit Corporation. National Merit Finalists who have indicated that Bryn Mawr is their first choice institution will be referred to the College for consideration for this award.

Financial aid is held each year by approximately forty percent of the undergraduate students. The value of the scholarships ranges widely, but the average grant is approximately $1800. Requests for financial aid are reviewed by the Scholarship Committee and judged on the basis of the student's academic promise and achievement on the one hand, and, on the other, her financial situation and that of her family. Bryn Mawr College, as a member of the College Scholarship Service of the College Entrance Examination Board, subscribes to the principle that the amount of aid granted a student should be based upon financial need. There are no funds in the award of the College which are awarded solely on merit. The Service assists colleges and other agencies in determining the student's need for financial assistance. All applicants must submit in support of application for financial aid the form entitled Parents' Confidential Statement which is prepared by the Service. When the total amount of aid needed has been determined, awards are made in the form of grants, loans and jobs.

Bryn Mawr College administers two kinds of loan programs. The first consists of funds established through the generosity of alumnae and friends of the College and the second is based on government funds made available through the National Direct Student Loan program. Full descriptions can be found on page 186.

Another federally funded program, the College Work-Study Program, enables the College to expand job opportunities for qualified students with on- and off-campus jobs, summer and winter, with eligible employers, either locally or near the student's home.

Applications for Financial Aid at Entrance

Application forms for financial aid are included in application materials sent to applicants who have submitted the preliminary application for admission. Each candidate for aid must also file with the College Scholarship Service a form entitled Parents' Confidential Statement in Support of Application for Financial Aid. These two forms must be filed with the College and with the College Scholarship Service *no later than January 1* of the student's final year in high school in the case of regular applicants, and *no later than October 1* in the case of applicants under the Early Decision Plan. Applications for financial aid for transfer students are due *no later than March 1.*

Since scholarship funds of the College are not sufficient to cover the needs of the many well-qualified applicants, students are urged to consult with their school counselors about national and local scholarships which may be available and to submit appropriate applications. Specific questions regarding aid at Bryn Mawr should be directed to the Financial Aid Officer.

Renewal of Undergraduate Financial Aid

Application for the renewal of financial aid must be made annually. The renewal of the award depends on the student's maintaining a good record and her continued need for assistance. Adjustments are made to reflect changes in the financial situation of the family. Marriage or reaching the age of 21, however, are not considered valid reasons for the withdrawal of parental support or for an increase in financial aid.

The necessary forms for renewal may be obtained in the Financial Aid Office and should be filed with the College Scholarship Service no later than January 31.

Scholarship Funds

The Mary L. Jobe Akeley Scholarship Fund was established by bequest of Mary L. Jobe Akeley. The income from this fund of $149,597 is to be used for undergraduate scholarships with preference being given to students from Ohio. (1968)

The Alumnae Bequest Scholarship Fund, now totaling $8,696, was established by bequests received for scholarships from alumnae of the College. (1965)

Alumnae Regional Scholarships are available to students in all parts of the United States and Canada. These scholarships, raised by alumnae, vary in amount but may cover full fees for four years. The awards are made by local alumnae committees and are announced to the candidates immediately after their notification of admission to the College. Holders of these scholarships who maintain a high standard of academic work and conduct, and who continue to need financial aid after the freshman year, are assured assistance either from alumnae committees in their districts or from the College. (1922)

The Marion Louise Ament Scholarship Fund, now totaling $81,989, was established by bequest of Berkley Neustadt in honor of his daughter Marion Louise Ament of the Class of 1944. The income is to be used for scholarships. (1967)

The Evangeline Walker Andrews May Day Scholarship was established by bequest of Evangeline Walker Andrews of the Class of 1893. The income from this fund of $10,000 is to be used for undergraduate scholarships in the Department of English. Mrs. Andrews originated the Bryn Mawr May Day which was first held in 1900. (1963)

The Edith Heyward Ashley and Mabel Pierce Ashley Scholarship Fund was founded by bequest of Mabel Pierce Ashley of the Class of 1910. In 1969,

---

Note: *The dates in parentheses in the listings on this and the following pages indicate the year the scholarship was established.*

the fund was increased by $25,000 by bequest of Edith Heyward Ashley of the Class of 1905. The fund now totals $50,000 and the income is to be awarded as a scholarship or scholarships to undergraduate students majoring in History or English. (1963)

The Elizabeth Congdon Barron Scholarship Fund. In 1960, by Mrs. Barron's bequest of $2,500, the Elizabeth Congdon Barron Fund was established "for the general purposes of the College." Through gifts from her husband Alexander J. Barron the fund was increased to $25,000 and the Elizabeth Congdon Barron Scholarship Fund was established. Through further gifts from Mr. Barron, the endowment has been raised to $55,000. (1964)

The Elizabeth P. Bigelow Memorial Scholarship Fund was established by gifts now amounting to $50,209 from Mrs. Henry B. Bigelow in memory of her daughter Elizabeth P. Bigelow, who was graduated *cum laude* in 1930. (1960)

The Star K. Bloom and Estan J. Bloom Scholarship Fund was established by a gift of $10,000 from Star K. Bloom of the Class of 1960 and her husband Estan J. Bloom. The income is to be awarded to academically superior students from the southern part of the United States with first preference given to residents of Alabama. (1976)

The Book Shop Scholarships are awarded annually from the income from the Book Shop Fund, which now amounts to $98,630. (1947)

The Bertha Norris Bowen and Mary Rachel Norris Memorial Scholarship Fund was established by bequest under the will of Mary Rachel Norris of the Class of 1905 in memory of Bertha Norris Bowen, who was for many years a teacher in Philadelphia. (1973)

The James W. Broughton and Emma Hendricks Broughton Scholarship Fund was established by a bequest from the estate of Mildred Hendricks Broughton of the Class of 1939 in honor of her parents. The income from this fund shall be used for the purpose of paying tuition and other necessary expenses of students attending Bryn Mawr College. The students selected for such financial aid shall be from the midwestern part of the United States. (1972)

The Hannah Brusstar Memorial Scholarship Fund was established by a bequest from the estate of Margaret E. Brusstar of the Class of 1903. The income from this fund is to be awarded annually to an undergraduate student who shows unusual ability in Mathematics. (1976)

The Bryn Mawr Alumnae Physicians Fund for Premedical Students was established under the sponsorship of two alumnae directors of the College. The income from this fund is to provide a flexible source of financial help to women at Bryn Mawr who have decided to enter medicine, whether or not they choose to major in physical sciences. (1976)

Bryn Mawr at the Tenth Decade—Undergraduate Student Aid. A pooled fund was established in the course of the Tenth Decade Campaign for those who wish to contribute to endowment for undergraduate student aid but who do not wish to designate their gift to a specific named fund.

The Mariam Coffin Canaday Scholarship Fund was established by a gift of $18,866 from the Ward M. and Mariam C. Canaday Educational and Charitable Trust. The income from this fund was capitalized until in 1969 the fund reached the amount of $25,000. The income henceforth is to provide scholarships with preference given to students from Toledo, Ohio, or from District VI of the Alumnae Association. (1962)

The Antoinette Cannon Memorial Scholarship Fund was established by a gift of $30,400 by Janet Thornton of the Class of 1905 in memory of her friend Antoinette Cannon of the Class of 1907. (1963)

The Jeannette Peabody Cannon Memorial Scholarship Fund, now totalling $13,441, was established in memory of Jeannette Peabody Cannon, Class of 1919, through the efforts of the New England Alumnae Regional Scholarship Committee, of which she was a member for twenty years. The scholarship is awarded every three years on the nomination of the Alumnae Scholarship Committee to a promising member of the freshman class, residing in New England, who needs financial assistance. The scholarship may be held during the remaining three years of her college course provided a high standard is maintained. In 1962, the fund was increased from $7,405 to $13,441 by a generous gift from Mrs. Donald Wing of New Haven. (1949)

The Susan Shober Carey Award was founded in memory of Susan Shober Carey by gifts now totalling $3,300 from the Class of 1925 and is awarded annually by the President. (1931)

The Florence and Dorothy Child Memorial Scholarship of Bryn Mawr College was founded by bequest of Florence C. Child of the Class of 1905. The income from this fund of $115,494 is to be used for the residence fees of students who without such assistance would be unable to live in the halls. Preference is to be given to graduates of the Agnes Irwin School and to members of the Society of Friends. If no suitable applicants are available in these two groups, the scholarship aid will then be assigned by the College to students who could not live in residence halls without such assistance and who are not holding other scholarships. (1957)

The Augusta D. Childs Scholarship Fund was established by bequest of $45,000 from the estate of Augusta D. Childs. The income is to be used for undergraduate scholarships. (1970)

The Jacob Orie and Elizabeth S. M. Clarke Memorial Scholarship was established by bequest of $5,000 from the estate of Elizabeth Clarke and is awarded annually to a student born in the United States or any of its territories. (1948)

The Class of 1903 Scholarship Fund was established by gift of $12,295 on the occasion of the fiftieth reunion of the Class. The income from this fund is to be awarded annually to a member of the freshman, sophomore or junior class for use in the sophomore, junior or senior years. (1953)

The Class of 1922 Memorial Scholarship Fund was established at the suggestion of members of the Class of 1922 as a perpetual class fund to which members of the class can contribute during the Tenth Decade Campaign and beyond. (1973)

The Class of 1943 Scholarship Fund was established by gifts of $34,937 from the James H. and Alice I. Goulder Foundation Inc. of which Alice Ireman Goulder of the Class of 1943 and her husband are officers. Members of the Class of 1943 and others add to the fund which continues to grow, and it is hoped that eventually the yearly income will provide full scholarship aid for one or more students at Bryn Mawr. (1974)

The 1967 College Bowl Scholarship Fund of $16,000 was established by the Bryn Mawr College team from its winnings on the General Electric College Bowl Television Program. The scholarship grants were donated by the General Electric Company and by Seventeen Magazine and supplemented by gifts from the Directors of the College. The members of the team were Ashley Doherty (1971), Ruth Gais (1968), Robin Johnson (1969) and Diane Ostheim (1969). Income from this fund will be awarded to an entering freshman in need of assistance. (1967)

The Julia Cope Collins Scholarship was established by bequest of $10,000 from the estate of Julia Cope Collins, Class of 1889. (1959)

The Alice Perkins Coville Scholarship Fund, now totalling $76,587, was established by Agnes Frances Perkins of the Class of 1898 in honor of her sister Alice Perkins Coville. The income from this scholarship fund is used to aid a deserving student in need of financial assistance. (1948)

The Regina Katharine Crandall Scholarship was established by a group of her students as a tribute to Regina Katharine Crandall, Margaret Kingsland Haskell Professor of English Composition from 1918 to 1933. The income from this fund, which now amounts to $10,225, is awarded to a sophomore, junior or senior who in her written English has shown ability and promise and who needs assistance to continue her college work. (1950)

The Annie Lawrie Fabens Crozier Scholarship Fund was established by a gift of $31,656 from Mr. and Mrs. Abbott P. Usher in memory of Mrs. Usher's daughter, Annie Lawrie Fabens Crozier of the Class of 1951. The scholarship, in varying amounts up to full tuition, is to be awarded to a junior or senior of distinction who is majoring in English. (1960)

The Rebecca Taylor Mattson Darlington Memorial Scholarship Fund was established by members of her family in memory of Rebecca Taylor Mattson Darlington, Class of 1896. The income is to be used for undergraduate scholarships. (1967)

The Pacific Northwest Student Aid Endowment Fund was established by a gift from Natalie Bell Brown of the Class of 1943 for Bryn Mawr at the Tenth Decade. The fund is to be used for students needing financial aid, with preference given to students from the Pacific Northwest. (1976)

The E. Merrick Dodd and Winifred H. Dodd Scholarship Fund of $2,000 was established by bequest of Dr. and Mrs. Dodd. (1953)

The Abby Slade Brayton Durfee Scholarship Fund, which now amounts to $13,000, was founded in honor of his wife by bequest of Randall N. Durfee, Jr. and Mrs. Charles Bennett Brown of the Class of 1930. Preference is given to candidates of English or American descent and to descendants of the Class of 1894. (1924)

The Susan Grimes Walker Fitzgerald Fund was established by a gift from Susan Fitzgerald of the Class of 1929 in honor of her mother Susan Grimes Walker Fitzgerald of the Class of 1893. It is to be used for foreign graduate and undergraduate students studying at Bryn Mawr or Bryn Mawr students doing research abroad in the summer or during the academic year. (1976).

The Anne Long Flanagan Scholarship was established by a gift of $29,687 from Anne Long Flanagan of the Class of 1906 on the occasion of the 55th reunion of the class. The income is to be used to provide scholarships for Protestant students. (1961)

The Cora B. Fohs and F. Julius Fohs Perpetual Scholarship Fund was established by a gift of $75,000 from the Fohs Foundation. The income only is to be used. (1965)

The Folly Ranch Fund was established by an anonymous gift of $100,000, the income from which is to be used for graduate and undergraduate scholarships in honor of Eleanor Donnelley Erdman, Class of 1921, Clarissa Donnelley Haffner, Class of 1921, Elizabeth P. Taylor, Class of 1921 and Jean T. Palmer, Class of 1924. (1974)

The Foundation Scholarships, varying in amount up to full tuition and tenable for four years, are made available by the Trustees of Bryn Mawr College. They are awarded to members of the Society of Friends who cannot meet the full expenses of tuition and residence. (1894)

The William Franklin Scholarship Fund was established by a bequest of $35,985 from Susan B. Franklin of the Class of 1889. The income from this fund is to be used for scholarships for deserving girls, preference being given whenever possible to girls from the Rogers High School, Newport, Rhode Island. (1957)

The Edgar M. Funkhouser Memorial Scholarship Fund of $30,000 was established from his estate by Anne Funkhouser Francis of the Class of 1933. Awards may vary in amount up to full tuition and be tenable for four years. Income from this fund may be awarded annually, first preference being given to residents of southwest Virginia; thereafter to students from District IV eligible for aid in any undergraduate year. (1964)

The Helen Hartman Gemmill Scholarship, value $500, first given for the year 1970-71, is awarded annually to a student majoring in English from funds provided by the Warwick Foundation. (1967)

The Anna Hallowell Memorial Scholarship was founded in memory of Anna Hallowell by her family. The income on a fund of $2,585 is awarded annually to the junior in need of aid who has the highest academic record. (1912)

The Katharine Hepburn Scholarship, value $1,000, first given for the year 1969-70, is awarded annually in honor of Katharine Hepburn to a student interested in the study of drama and motion picture and in the cultivation of English diction and of literary appreciation. (1952)

The Katharine Houghton Hepburn Memorial Scholarship was given in memory of Katharine Houghton Hepburn of the Class of 1900. The income on this fund, now totalling $41,010, is awarded for the junior or senior year to a student or students who have demonstrated both ability in her or their chosen field and independence of mind and spirit. (1957)

The Jeanne Crawford Hislop Memorial Scholarship Fund of $5,000 was given in memory of Jeanne Crawford Hislop of the Class of 1940 by Mr. and Mrs. John H. Hislop and Mrs. Frederic W. Crawford. The income from this fund has been supplemented by gifts from Mrs. John H. Hislop. This scholarship, awarded to a junior, may be renewed for the senior year. (1939)

The George Bates Hopkins Memorial Scholarships were founded by a gift of $10,056 from Mrs. Elizabeth Hopkins Johnson in memory of her father. Preference is given to students of Music and, in default of these, to students majoring in History, and thereafter to students in other departments. (1921)

The Maria Hopper Scholarships, two in number, were founded by bequest under the will of Maria Hopper of Philadelphia and are awarded annually. The income from this fund of $10,224 is used for aid to a sophomore. (1901)

The Leila Houghteling Memorial Scholarship Fund in the amount of $10,180 was founded in memory of Leila Houghteling of the Class of 1911 by members of her family and a group of her contemporaries. It is awarded every three years on the nomination of the Alumnae Scholarships and Loan Fund Committee to a member of the freshman class in need of financial assistance and is held during the remaining three years of her college course. (1929)

Huguenot Society of America Grant. On the recommendation of the College a student of Huguenot ancestry may be nominated for a grant up to $1,000 to be used for college expenses. (1962)

The Shippen Huidekoper Scholarship Fund of $5,000 was established by an anonymous gift. The income is awarded annually on the nomination of the President. (1936)

The Evelyn Hunt Scholarships, two in number, were founded in memory of Evelyn Hunt by bequest of $10,000 under the will of Evelyn Ramsey Hunt of the Class of 1898. (1931)

The Lillia Babbitt Hyde Scholarship Fund was established by gifts of $25,600 from the Lillia Babbitt Hyde Foundation to establish the Lillia Babbitt Hyde Scholarship for award in so far as possible to students whose major subject will lead to a medical education or a scientific education in chemistry. (1963)

The Jane Lilley Ireson Scholarship was established by a bequest of $246,776 under the will of Jennie E. Ireson, her daughter. The income on each $5,000 of this fund is to be awarded as a scholarship to a worthy student who may require financial assistance. (1959)

The Alice Day Jackson Scholarship Fund of $10,195 was given by the late Percy Jackson in memory of his wife Alice Day Jackson. The income from this fund is awarded annually to an entering student. (1930)

The Elizabeth Bethune Higginson Jackson Scholarship Fund was established by gifts in memory of Elizabeth Bethune Higginson Jackson of the Class of 1897 by members of her family and friends. The income from the fund is to be used for scholarships for undergraduate students as determined by the College Scholarship Committee. (1974)

The Sue Mead Kaiser Scholarship Fund was established by the alumnae of the Bryn Mawr Club of Northern California and other individuals in memory of Sue Mead Kaiser of the Class of 1931. (1974)

The Kathryn M. Kalbfleisch and George C. Kalbfleisch Scholarship Fund was established under the will of Kathryn M. Kalbfleisch of the Class of 1924; the income from the fund of $220,833 is to be used for scholarships. (1972)

The Alice Lovell Kellogg Fund was founded by a bequest of $5,000 by Alice Lovell Kellogg of the Class of 1903. The income is to be used for undergraduate scholarships. (1967)

The Minnie Murdoch Kendrick Memorial Scholarship, tenable for four years, was founded by bequest under the will of George W. Kendrick, Jr., in memory of his wife. The income on this fund of $5,362 is awarded every four years to a candidate nominated by the Alumnae Association of the Philadelphia High School for Girls. (1916)

The Misses Kirk Scholarship Fund, now amounting to $1,401, was founded in honor of the Misses Kirk by the Alumnae Association of the Kirk School in Bryn Mawr. (1929)

The Elizabeth B. Kirkbride Scholarship Fund was established by a gift of $1,150 from Elizabeth B. Kirkbride of the Class of 1896. The income is to be used for undergraduate scholarships. (1964)

The Clara Bertram Little Memorial Scholarship was founded by Eleanor Little Aldrich, in memory of her mother. The income from a fund now totalling $11,000 is awarded to an entering student from New England on the basis of merit and financial need. (1947)

The Mary Anna Longstreth Memorial Scholarship, established by a gift of $5,000 and carrying free tuition, was given in memory of Mary Anna Longstreth by alumnae and children of alumnae of the Mary Anna Longstreth School and by a few of her friends. (1913)

The Lorenz-Showers Scholarship Fund now amounting to $5,000 was established by Justina Lorenz Showers of Dayton, Ohio, of the Class of 1907, in honor of her parents Edmund S. Lorenz and Florence K. Lorenz and of her husband John Balmer Showers. (1943)

The Alice Low Lowry Memorial Scholarship Fund was established by gifts in memory of Alice Low Lowry of the Class of 1938 by members of her family and friends. The income from a fund now totaling $29,101 is to be used for scholarships for undergraduate and graduate students. (1968)

The Katharine E. McBride Undergraduate Scholarship Fund was established by a gift of $5,000 made by Gwenn Davis Mitchell, Class of 1954. This fund now amounts to $5,600. The income is to be used for scholarships. (1969)

The Gertrude Howard McCormick Scholarship Fund was established by gift of $25,000 by the late Gertrude Howard McCormick. The scholarship, value $1,000, is awarded to a student of excellent standing, preferably for her freshman year. If she maintains excellent work in college, she may continue to receive scholarship aid through her sophomore, junior and senior years. (1950)

The Mary McLean and Ellen A. Murter Memorial Fund, now amounting to $14,320, was founded in memory of her two aunts by bequest of Mary E. Stevens of Germantown, Philadelphia. By vote of the Board of Directors the income is used for an annual scholarship. (1933)

The Midwest Scholarship Endowment Fund was established by the Alumnae of District VII in order "to enlarge the benefits which can be provided for able students from the midwest." The income from this fund is to be awarded in the same manner as regional scholarships. (1974)

The Beatrice Miller Memorial Scholarship Fund was established by a bequest of $83,966 from the estate of Beatrice Miller Ullrich of the Class of 1913. The income only is to be used for scholarships. (1969)

The Constance Lewis and Martha Rockwell Moorhouse 1904 Memorial Scholarship Fund, now amounting to $17,930, was established by the Class of 1904 in memory of their classmates Constance Lewis and Martha Rockwell Moorhouse. (1920)

The Evelyn Flower Morris Cope and Jacqueline Pascal Morris Evans Scholarship Fund, amounting to $13,000, was established by members of their families in memory of Evelyn Flower Morris of the Class of 1903 and Jacqueline Pascal Morris of the Class of 1908. (1959)

The Jean Brunn Mungall 1944 Memorial Scholarship Fund, now amounting to $39,766, was established by the Class of 1944. The class on its 25th anniversary in May 1969 increased the fund by $16,600. The income is to be used for scholarships. (1955)

The Frank L. Neall and Mina W. Neall Scholarship Fund was established by a legacy of $25,000 from the estate of Adelaide W. Neall of the Class of 1906 in memory of her parents. The income is to be used for scholarship purposes at the discretion of the Trustees of the College. (1957)

The New Hampshire Scholarship Fund of $15,000 was established in 1965 by the Spaulding-Potter Charitable Trust. A matching fund was raised by contributions from New Hampshire alumnae. Income from the two funds will be awarded each year to an undergraduate from New Hampshire on the recommendation of the New England Regional Scholarship Committee. (1965)

The Alice F. Newkirk Scholarship Fund was founded by a bequest of $2,500 by Alice F. Newkirk. The income is for scholarships. (1965)

The Mary Frances Nunns Scholarship was established by a bequest of $25,275 under the will of Mary Frances Nunns. The income only is to be used. (1960)

The Florence Morse Palmer Scholarship was founded in memory of Florence Morse Palmer by her daughter, Jean T. Palmer of the Class of 1924, by gifts now totalling $10,000. (1954)

The Margaret Tyler Paul Scholarship was established by a 40th reunion gift of $30,000 from the Class of 1922. (1963)

The Fanny R. S. Peabody Scholarship Fund was established by bequest of $177,927 in the will of Fanny R. S. Peabody. The income from the Peabody Fund is awarded to students from the western states. (1943)

The Delia Avery Perkins Scholarship was established by bequest of $58,474 from Delia Avery Perkins of the Class of 1900. Mrs. Perkins was Chairman of the New Jersey Scholarship Committee for a number of years. The income on this fund is to be awarded to students entering from Northern New Jersey. (1965)

The Ethel C. Pfaff Scholarship Fund was established by a bequest of $295,616 from Ethel C. Pfaff of the Class of 1904. The income from this fund is to be awarded to entering freshmen. (1967)

The Philadelphia Board of Public Education Scholarships, tenable for four years, are awarded to graduates of Philadelphia high schools nominated by the Board of Public Education of Philadelphia. (1898)

The Louise Hyman Pollak Scholarship was founded by the Board of Trustees from a bequest of $5,061 by Louise Hyman Pollak of the Class of 1908. The income from this fund, now totalling $6,681, which has been supplemented by gifts from the late Julian A. Pollak and his son David Pollak is awarded annually to an entering student from one of the central states, east of the Mississippi River. Preference is given to residents of Cincinnati. (1932)

·*The Anna M. Powers Memorial Scholarship* was founded in memory of Anna M. Powers by a gift from her daughter Mrs. J. Campbell Harris. The income on this fund of $5,542 is awarded annually to a senior. (1902)

The Anna and Ethel Powers Memorial Scholarship was established by a gift of $1,000 in memory of Anna Powers of the Class of 1890 by her sister Mrs. Charles Merrill Hough. The fund is now re-established at $13,634 in memory of both Anna Powers and her sister Mrs. Hough (Ethel Powers), by Nancy Hough Smith of the Class of 1925. (1919)

The Thomas H. Powers Memorial Scholarship was founded in memory of Thomas H. Powers by bequest under the will of his daughter Mrs. J. Campbell Harris. The income on this fund of $4,598 is awarded annually to a senior. (1902)

The Princeton Book Sale Scholarship was established by the Alumnae of the Bryn Mawr Club of Princeton. The income from the fund is to be used for scholarships for students chosen by the College Scholarship Committee. (1974)

The James E. Rhoads Memorial Scholarships were founded in memory of the first President of the College Dr. James E. Rhoads by the Alumnae Association of Bryn Mawr College. In 1958 and 1959, the Alumnae Association increased the fund to $27,010, the income from which is awarded annually to two students. The James E. Rhoads Memorial Junior Scholarship is awarded to a student who has attended Bryn Mawr College for at least three semesters, has done excellent work and expresses her intention of fulfilling the requirements for the degree of Bachelor of Arts at Bryn Mawr College. The James E. Rhoads Memorial Sophomore Scholarship is awarded to a student who has attended Bryn Mawr College for at least one semester and who also meets the above conditions. (1898)

The Amelia Richards Scholarship was founded in memory of Amelia Richards of the Class of 1918 by bequest of $11,033 under the will of her mother Mrs. Frank P. Wilson. It is awarded annually by the Trustees on the nomination of the President. (1921)

The Ida E. Richardson, Alice H. Richardson and Edward P. Langley Scholarship Fund was established by bequest of $81,065 under the will of Edward P. Langley. The income is to be used for scholarships. (1970)

The Maximilian and Reba E. Richter Scholarship Fund was established by a bequest of $50,000 in the will of Max Richter, father of Helen Richter Elser of the Class of 1913. The income from this fund is to be used to provide assistance for one or more students in the obtaining of either an academic or professional degree. The fund shall be administered on a non-sectarian basis to such applicants as are deemed worthy by habits of character and scholarship. No promises of repayment shall be exacted but it is hoped that students so benefited will desire when possible to contribute to the fund in order that similar aid may be extended to others. Such students shall be selected from among the graduates of public high schools or public colleges in the City of New York. (1961)

The Nancy Perry Robinson Memorial Scholarship Fund was established by a gift of $15,000 from Mrs. Huston B. Almond, of Philadelphia, in memory of her godchild Nancy Perry Robinson of the Class of 1945. The income of the fund is to be awarded annually to an undergraduate student, with preference given to a student majoring in the French language. (1973)

The Serena Hand Savage Memorial Scholarship was established in memory of Serena Hand Savage of the Class of 1922 by her friends. The income from a fund of $24,552 is awarded to a member of the junior class who shows great distinction of scholarship and character and who needs financial assistance. This scholarship may be renewed in the senior year. (1951)

The J. Henry Scattergood Scholarship Fund was established by a gift of $15,000 from the Friends' Freedmen's Association to be used for undergraduate scholarships for black students. (1975)

The Constance Schaar Scholarship Fund, now totalling $4,866, was established in 1964 by her parents and friends in memory of Constance Schaar of the Class of 1963. The Class of 1963 added their reunion gift in 1964 to this fund. (1964)

The Scholarship Endowment Fund was established by a gift of $4,300 from Constance E. Flint. The income only is to be used for scholarships. (1970)

The Judith Harris Selig Scholarship Fund was established in memory of Judith Harris Selig of the Class of 1957 by members of her family, classmates and friends. In 1970, the fund was increased by a further gift of $18,000 from her parents Dr. and Mrs. Herman S. Harris. The income from the fund, now totalling $40,078, is to be used for undergraduate scholarships. (1968)

The Mary Williams Sherman Memorial Scholarship Fund, now amounting to $4,150, was established by bequest of Bertha Williams of Princeton, New Jersey. (1942)

The Frances Marion Simpson Scholarships, carrying up to full tuition and tenable for four years, were founded in memory of Frances Simpson Pfahler of the Class of 1906 by Justice Alexander Simpson, Jr., by gifts amounting to $20,682. One scholarship is awarded each year to a member of the entering freshman class who cannot meet in full the fees of the College. In awarding these scholarships first preference is given to residents of Philadelphia and Montgomery Counties who have been prepared in the public schools of these counties; thereafter, under the same conditions, to residents of other counties of Pennsylvania, and, in special cases, to candidates from other localities. Holders of these scholarships are expected to repay the sums advanced to them. If they become able during their college course to pay the tuition fees in whole or in part, they are required to do so. (1912)

The Gertrude Slaughter Scholarship Fund was established by bequest of $19,909 by Gertrude Taylor Slaughter of the Class of 1893. The income on this fund is to be used for undergraduate scholarships, preferably to students of Greek or Latin. (1964)

The Anna Margaret Sloan and Mary Sloan Scholarships were founded by bequest of Mary Sloan of Pittsburgh. The income from this fund of $16,858 is awarded annually to students majoring in Philosophy or Psychology. (1942)

The Cordelia Clark Sowden Scholarship Fund was established by a bequest of $15,000 from the estate of Helen C. Sowden. The income from this fund is used for scholarships to be awarded by Bryn Mawr College under the rules in effect at the time of the award. (1957)

The Amy Sussman Steinhart Scholarship, carrying full tuition, was founded in memory of Amy Sussman Steinhart of the Class of 1902 by her family and friends. The income from gifts now totalling $33,652 is awarded annually to an entering student from one of the states on the west coast. (1932)

The Mary E. Stevens Scholarship Fund was given in memory of Mary E. Stevens by former pupils of The Stevens School in Germantown. The income on this fund of $3,188 is awarded annually to a junior. (1897)

The Anna Lord Strauss Scholarship and Fellowship Fund was established by a gift from Anna Lord Strauss to support graduate and undergraduate students in need of financial assistance who are interested in fields leading to public service or which involve education in the process of government. (1976)

The Summerfield Foundation Scholarship was established by a gift from the Solon E. Summerfield Foundation. The income from this fund, which now totals $18,000, is to be used to assist able students who need financial help to continue their studies. (1958)

The Mary Hamilton Swindler Scholarship was established in honor of Mary Hamilton Swindler, Professor of Classical Archaeology from 1931 to 1949, by a group of friends and former students, by gifts totalling $8,493. The income from this fund is used for a scholarship for the study of Archaeology. (1950)

The Elizabeth P. Taylor Scholarship Fund, now amounting to $20,771, was established by a bequest from Elizabeth P. Taylor of the Class of 1921. (1961)

The Ethel Vick Wallace Townsend Memorial Fund was established by Elbert S. Townsend in memory of his wife Ethel Vick Wallace Townsend of the Class of 1908. The income on this fund, held by the Buffalo Foundation, is to be used for undergraduate scholarships. (1967)

The Trustees' Scholarships, varying in amount up to full tuition, and tenable for four years, are made available by the Trustees of Bryn Mawr College for students prepared in the high schools of Philadelphia and its suburbs. Two of these scholarships are awarded annually to candidates who have received all their preparation for entrance in Philadelphia high schools and are recommended by the Board of Public Education of Philadelphia; two are awarded annually to candidates who have received all their preparation for entrance in public schools in the suburbs of Philadelphia and are awarded by the College after consultation with the principals of the schools presenting candidates. The amount of the award varies according to the need of the applicant. (1895)

Two or sometimes three of these scholarships are supported by the income from *The Jacob Fussell Byrnes and Mary Byrnes Fund,* which was established in memory of her mother and father by a bequest of $51,513 under the will of Esther Fussell Byrnes. (1948)

The Mildred Clarke Pressinger von Kienbusch Scholarship Fund was established by C. Otto von Kienbusch in memory of his wife Mildred Clarke Pressinger von Kienbusch of the Class of 1909. The income from this fund of $30,000 will be awarded each year to a student in need of assistance. (1968)

The Mary E. G. Waddell Scholarship Fund was established by a bequest from the Estate of Mary E. G. Waddell. The income from this fund is to be used for scholarships for undergraduates and graduate students, interested in the study of Mathematics, who are daughters of American citizens of Canadian descent. (1971)

The Julia Ward Scholarship Fund was established by a gift of $7,075 for a scholarship in memory of Julia Ward of the Class of 1923 by one of her friends and by additional gifts from others. The income on this fund which now amounts to $34,146 is to be used for undergraduate scholarships. (1962)

The Eliza Jane Watson Scholarship Fund was established by gifts of $25,000 from the John Jay and Eliza Jane Watson Foundation. The income from this fund is to be used to assist one or more students as selected by the College to meet the cost of tuition. (1964)

The Elizabeth Wilson White Memorial Scholarship was founded in memory of Elizabeth Wilson White by a gift of $7,513 by Thomas Raeburn White. It is awarded annually by the President. (1923)

The Thomas Raeburn White Scholarships, established by a gift of $25,000, made by Amos and Dorothy Peaslee on April 6, 1964 in honor of Thomas Raeburn White, Trustee of the College from 1907 until his death in 1959, Counsel to the College throughout these years and President of the Trustees from 1956 to 1959. The income from this fund is to be used for prizes to undergraduate students who plan to study foreign languages abroad during the summer under the auspices of an approved program. (1964)

The Mary R. G. Williams Scholarship Fund was established from the Fund for Promoting College Education for Women established by bequest of Mary R. G. Williams. The income from this fund of $5,694 will be used for emergency grants for students who are paying their own way through college. (1957)

The Mary Peabody Williamson Scholarship was founded by bequest of $1,000 by Mary Peabody Williamson of the Class of 1903. (1939)

The Marion H. Curtin Winsor Memorial Scholarship was established by a bequest of $10,000 in the will of Mary Winsor, in memory of her mother. The income on this fund is to be awarded to a resident black student. (1960)

The Mary Winsor Scholarship in Archaeology was established by a bequest of $3,000 under the will of Mary Winsor. The income only is to be used. (1960)

The Ellen Winsor and Rebecca Winsor Evans Memorial Scholarship Fund was established by a bequest of $5,230 in the will of Rebecca Winsor Evans. The scholarship is to be awarded to a resident black student. (1962)

The Rebecca Winsor Evans and Ellen Winsor Memorial Scholarship Fund was established by a bequest of $5,230 in the will of Ellen Winsor. The scholarship is to be awarded to a resident black student. (1962)

The Gertrude Miller Wright Scholarships were established under the will of Dorothy M. Wright of the Class of 1931, for needy students of Bryn Mawr College. (1973)

The Lila M. Wright Memorial Scholarship was founded in memory of Lila M. Wright by gifts totalling $2,987 from the alumnae of Miss Wright's School of Bryn Mawr. (1934)

The Georgie W. Yeatman Scholarship was founded by bequest of $1,000 under the will of Georgie W. Yeatman of Philadelphia. (1941)

Scholarships for Foreign Students

The Bryn Mawr Canadian Scholarship will be raised and awarded each year by Bryn Mawr alumnae living in Canada. The scholarship, varying in amount, will be awarded to a Canadian student entering either the undergraduate or graduate school. (1965)

The Chinese Scholarship comes in part from the annual income of a fund now totalling $50,185 established by a group of alumnae and friends of the College in order to meet all or part of the expenses of a Chinese student during her four undergraduate years at Bryn Mawr College. (1917)

The Marguerite N. Farley Scholarships for foreign students were established by bequest of Marguerite N. Farley. The income from a fund of $331,425 will be used for scholarships for foreign graduate and undergraduate students covering part or all of their expenses for tuition and residence. (1956)

The Margaret Y. Kent Scholarship Fund, Class of 1908 was established by bequest of Margaret Y. Kent of the Class of 1908. The income from the fund of $7,000 is to be used to provide scholarship assistance to foreign students. (1967)

The Middle East Scholarship Fund was established by a gift from Elizabeth Cope Harrison of the Class of 1958. The purpose of the fund is to enable the College "to make scholarship awards to able students from a number of Middle Eastern Countries." (1975)

The Special Trustees' Scholarship is awarded every four years to a foreign student. It carries free tuition and is tenable for four years. The scholarship for students from foreign countries was first offered by the Trustees in 1940.

The Undergraduate Scholarship, raised by the Undergraduate Association and awarded by the Association in consultation with the Director of Admissions, is awarded each year to a foreign student entering Bryn Mawr. (1938)

Prizes and Academic Awards

The following awards, fellowships, scholarships and prizes are in the award of the faculty and are given solely on the basis of academic distinction and achievement.

The Bryn Mawr European Fellowship has been awarded each year, since the first class was graduated in 1889. It is given for merit to a member of the graduating class, to be applied toward the expenses of one year's study at some foreign university. The holder of this fellowship receives in addition an *Elizebeth S. Shippen Scholarship for Foreign Study.*

The Maria L. Eastman Brooke Hall Memorial Scholarship was founded in memory of Maria L. Eastman, Principal of Brooke Hall School for Girls, Media, Pennsylvania, by gifts totaling $3,310 from the alumnae and former pupils of the school. It is awarded annually to the member of the junior class with the highest general average and is held during the senior year. Transfer students who enter Bryn Mawr as members of the junior class are not eligible for this award. (1901)

The Elizabeth Duane Gillespie Fund for Scholarships in American History was founded by a gift from the National Society of Colonial Dames of America in the Commonwealth of Pennsylvania in memory of Elizabeth Duane Gillespie. Two prizes are awarded annually on nomination by the Department of History, one to a member of the sophomore or junior class for work of distinction in American History, a second to a student doing advanced work in American History for an essay written in connection with that work. The income from this fund of $1,970 has been supplemented since 1955 by annual gifts from the Society. (1903)

The Elizabeth G. Shippen Scholarships were founded by two bequests of $5,000 each under the will of Elizabeth S. Shippen of Philadelphia. Three scholarships are awarded annually, one to the member of the senior class who receives The Bryn Mawr European Fellowship, and two to members of the junior class, as follows: 1. *The Shippen Scholarship in Science* to a student whose major subject is Biology, Chemistry, Geology or Physics; 2. *The Shippen Scholarship in Foreign Languages* to one whose major subject is French, German, Greek, Italian, Latin, Russian or Spanish. To be eligible for either of these two scholarships a student must have completed at least one semester of the second-year course in her major subject. Neither may be held by the winner of the Charles S. Hinchman Memorial Scholarship. Work in elementary courses will not be considered in awarding the scholarship in foreign languages; 3. *The Shippen Scholarship for Foreign Study* (See The Bryn Mawr European Fellowship, page 180). (1915)

The Charles S. Hinchman Memorial Scholarship was founded in the memory of the late Charles S. Hinchman of Philadelphia by a gift of $12,000 made by his family. It is awarded annually to a member of the junior class for work of special excellence in her major subjects and is held during the senior year. (1917)

The Sheelah Kilroy Memorial Scholarships in English were founded in memory of their daughter Sheelah, by Dr. and Mrs. Phillip Kilroy by a gift of $5,000. These scholarships are awarded annually on the recommendation of the Department of English as follows: to a student for excellence of work in second-year or advanced courses in English, and to the student in the first-year course in English Composition who writes the best essay during the year. (1919)

The Jeanne Quistgaard Memorial Prize was given by the Class of 1938 in memory of their classmate Jeanne Quistgaard. The income on this fund of $690 may be awarded every two years to a student in Economics. (1938)

The Esther Walker Award was founded by the bequest of $1,000 from William John Walker in memory of his sister Esther Walker of the Class of 1910. It may be given annually to a member of the senior class who in the judgment of the faculty shall have displayed the greatest proficiency in the study of living conditions of northern blacks. (1940)

The M. Carey Thomas Essay Prize is awarded annually to a member of the senior class for distinction in writing. The award is made by the Department of English for either creative or critical writing. It was established in memory of Miss Thomas by her niece Millicent Carey McIntosh of the Class of 1920. (1943)

The Katherine Fullerton Gerould Memorial Prize was founded in 1946 by a gift of $1,300 from a group of alumnae, many of whom were students of Mrs. Gerould when she taught at Bryn Mawr from 1901 to 1910. The fund was increased by a bequest of $2,400 by one of her former students.

It is awarded by a special committee to a student who shows evidence of creative ability in the fields of informal essay, short story, longer narrative or verse. (1946)

The Hester Ann Corner Prize for distinction in literature was established in memory of Hester Ann Corner of the Class of 1942 by gifts totalling $2,625 from her classmates and friends. The award is made annually to a junior or senior on the recommendation of a committee composed of the chairmen of the departments of English and of classical and modern foreign languages. (1950)

The Academy of American Poets Prize of $100 has been recently awarded each year to the student who submits to the Department of English the best poem or group of poems. The award, given by the Academy of American Poets, was first made in 1957.

The Helen Taft Manning Essay Prize in History was established in honor of Helen Taft Manning, in the year of her retirement, by her class (1915). The income on a fund of $2,600 is to be awarded as the Department of History may determine. (1957)

The Bain-Swiggett Poetry Prize was established by a gift of $1,000 from Mr. and Mrs. Glen Levin Swiggett. This prize is to be awarded by a committee of the faculty on the basis of the work submitted. The income only is to be used. (1958)

The Charlotte Angas Scott Prize in Mathematics. A prize to be awarded annually to an undergraduate on the recommendation of the Department of Mathematics was established by an anonymous gift in memory of Charlotte Angas Scott, Professor of Mathematics and a member of the faculty of Bryn Mawr College from 1885 to 1924. The income only from this gift is to be used. (1961)

The Anna Pell Wheeler Prize in Mathematics. A prize to be awarded annually to an undergraduate on the recommendation of the Department of Mathematics was established by an anonymous gift in honor of Anna Pell Wheeler, Professor Emeritus of Mathematics and a member of the faculty of Bryn Mawr College until her death in 1966. The income only from this gift is to be used. (1961)

The Emma Osborn Thompson Prize in Geology was founded by bequest of Emma Osborn Thompson of the Class of 1904. From the income on the bequest of $500 a prize is to be awarded from time to time to a student in Geology. (1963)

The Gertrude Slaughter Fellowship was established by a bequest of $50,000 in the will of Gertrude Taylor Slaughter of the Class of 1893. The Fellowship is to be awarded to a member of the graduating class for excellence in scholarship to be used for a year's study in the United States or abroad. (1964)

The Commonwealth Africa Scholarship was established by a grant of $50,000 from the Thorncroft Fund Inc. at the request of Helen and Geoffrey de Freitas. The income from this fund will be used to send, for at least six months, a graduate to a university or college in Commonwealth Africa, or former British colony in Africa, to teach or to study, with a view to contributing to mutual understanding and the furtherance of scholarship. (1965)

The Alexandra Peschka Prize was established in memory of Alexandra Peschka of the Class of 1964 by gifts from her family and friends. The prize of $100 is awarded annually to a member of the freshman or sophomore class for the best piece of imaginative writing in prose. The award will be made by a committee of the Department of English who will consult the terms stated in the deed of gift. (1968)

The Katherine Stains Prize Fund in Classical Literature was established by Katherine G. Stains in memory of her parents Arthur and Katheryn Stains, and in honor of two excellent twentieth-century scholars of Classical Literature, Richmond Lattimore and Moses Hadas. The income on the fund of $1,000 is to be awarded annually as a prize to an undergraduate student for excellence in Greek Literature, either in the original or in translation. (1969)

The Horace Alwyne Prize was established by the Friends of Music of Bryn Mawr College in honor of Horace Alwyne, Professor Emeritus of Music. The award is presented annually to the student who has contributed the most to the musical life of the college. (1970)

The Hope Wearn Troxell Memorial Prize is awarded annually by the alumnae of Southern California to a student from alumnae District IX, with first consideration to a student from Southern California. The prize is awarded in recognition of the student's responsible contribution to the life of the College community. (1973)

The Berle Memorial Prize Fund in German Literature was established by Lillian Berle Dare in memory of her parents Adam and Katharina Berle. The income on the fund ($1,000) is awarded annually to an undergraduate for excellence in German literature. Preference is given to a senior who is majoring in German and who does not come from a German background. (1975)

Scholarships for Medical Study

The following scholarships may be awarded to seniors intending to study medicine, after their acceptance by a medical school, or to graduates of Bryn Mawr intending or continuing to pursue a medical education. Applications for the scholarships should be made to the Premedical Advisor before March 15 preceding the academic year in which the scholarship is to be held. Applications for renewal of scholarships must be accompanied by letters of recommendation from instructors in the medical school.

The Linda B. Lange Fund was founded by bequest of $30,000 under the will of Linda B. Lange of the Class of 1903. The income from this fund will provide the Anna Howard Shaw Scholarship in Medicine and Public Health, awarded on recommendation of the President and faculty to a member of the graduating class or a graduate of the College for the pursuit, during an uninterrupted succession of years, of studies leading to the degrees of M.D. and Doctor of Public Health. The award may be continued until the degrees are obtained. (1948)

The Hannah E. Longshore Memorial Medical Scholarship was founded by Mrs. Rudolf Blankenburg in memory of her mother by a gift of $10,000. The scholarship is awarded by a committee of the faculty to a student who has been accepted by a medical school. It may be renewed for each year of medical study. (1921)

The Jane V. Myers Medical Scholarship Fund of $10,000 was established by Mrs. Rudolf Blankenburg in memory of her aunt. The scholarship is awarded by a committee of the faculty to a student who has been accepted by a medical school. It may be renewed for each year of medical study. (1921)

The Harriet Judd Sartain Memorial Scholarship Fund was founded by bequest of $21,033 under the will of Paul J. Sartain. The income from this fund is to establish a scholarship which is awarded to a member of the graduating class who in the judgment of the faculty needs and is deserving of assistance for the study of medicine. This scholarship may be continued for the duration of her medical course. (1948)

Loan Funds

Bryn Mawr College administers two kinds of loan programs. The first consists of four funds established through the generosity of alumnae and friends of the College. Applications for loans must be accompanied by the Parents' Confidential Statement prepared by the College Scholarship Service of the College Entrance Examination Board.

The Students' Loan Fund of the Alumnae Association of Bryn Mawr College was founded by the Class of 1890 for the use of students who need to borrow money in order to continue their college work. The fund is managed by the Alumnae Scholarships and Loan Fund Committee.

Loans may be used for any purpose approved by the committee, but not more than $500 may be borrowed by a student in any one year. The total for four years must not exceed $1,500. Students who wish loans may obtain from the Financial Aid Office or the Alumnae Office the necessary blanks which must be accompanied by a letter of recommendation from the Financial Aid Officer. As a rule, money is not lent to freshmen or to students in their first semester of graduate work.

While the student is in college no interest is charged, but she may reduce the principal of the loan if she so desires. The interest rate is three percent, to be paid after the student leaves the College. The entire principal must be paid within five years from the time the student leaves college at the rate of twenty percent each year.

Contributions to the Loan Fund may be sent to the Chairman of Scholarships and Loan Fund, Bryn Mawr College Alumnae Association, Bryn Mawr, Pennsylvania 19010.

The Mary Hill Swope Loan Fund was established June 1, 1945 by a gift of the late Mrs. Gerard Swope (Mary Hill, A.B. 1896) under the following conditions:

To assist in the education of young women irrespective of race, color or creed attending Bryn Mawr College, the income of the fund to be lent to students in the following manner:

a. The following order of preference shall be followed in awarding such loans—to students coming from New Jersey, to students coming from Missouri, to students coming from any other location who have had not less than one year of residence at the College.

b. The loans in the above order of preference, and in the following manner, shall be awarded by the President of Bryn Mawr College, or by a committee appointed by him from time to time.

c. Applicants for loans shall be considered not only from the standpoint of academic attainment and financial need, but also from the standpoint of character and personal qualifications for deriving the greatest good from a continuation of their studies.

d. These loans shall be used primarily to enable the exceptional student to continue her studies, which otherwise would be prevented through lack of means.

e. Except under extraordinary circumstances, the maximum amount which may be borrowed annually is $500. No interest is charged while the student is in college. The interest rate is three percent, to be paid after the student leaves college. The principal is to is to be repaid within five years from the time the student graduates or leaves Bryn Mawr at the rate of twenty percent each year.

The Gerard and Mary Hill Swope Loan Fund was established in 1962 under the following conditions:

a. Non-scholarship students and graduate students are also eligible to apply for loans from this fund.

b. The maximum amount which can be borrowed for any given academic year is $500.

c. While the student is in college or graduate school no interest is charged, but she may reduce the principal of the loan if she so desires. The interest rate is three percent, to be paid after the student leaves college. The entire principal must be repaid within five years from the time the student leaves college at the rate of twenty percent each year.

d. Loans are awarded by the Scholarship Committees of the Undergraduate School, The Graduate School of Arts and Sciences and The Graduate School of Social Work and Social Research.

The Clareth Fund was established in 1971 by a bequest to the College from the Estate of Ethel S. Weil. The income only is to be used for students "specializing in economics or business." There is no interest due but the student must begin to repay the loan within six years after graduation.

The second kind of loan program, administered by the College, is based on government funds made available through *The National Direct Student Loan Program*. Applications for loans must be accompanied by the

Parents' Confidential Statement prepared by the College Entrance Examination Board. The three percent interest and repayment begin one year after the student has completed her education.

Students who, upon graduation, teach on a full-time basis in public or private non-profit elementary and secondary schools and in institutions of higher education are allowed cancellation of their debts at the rate of ten percent for each year of teaching up to a maximum cancellation of fifty percent of the total loan.

International Initiatives Loan Fund makes loan funds available to currently enrolled undergraduate and graduate students through a special donation for the purpose of supporting independent study or research projects abroad. It is not normally available to students in a regular junior year abroad program. Full information and applications are available in the Office of the Associate Dean.

The Government Insured Student Loan Program is a government subsidized program which was instituted to enable students to meet educational expenses. Application is made through the students' home banks. Each year the student may borrow from $1,000 to $2,500 depending on the State regulations in effect in her State. Repayment begins nine months after the student is no longer enrolled, at least half-time, at an accredited institution. The interest is seven percent. The government will pay this interest until the repayment period begins provided the financial situation of the family warrants it. The Parents' Confidential Statement must be submitted to the institution in order to determine whether or not the family qualifies for this interest subsidy. If the family does not wish to submit financial information, the student is still eligible for the loan but she is responsible for the interest payments while she is in school.

Alumnae Representatives

Officers of the Alumnae Association

President, Mrs. William S. Cashel, Jr. 1144 Norsam Road,
Gladwyne, Pennsylvania 19035

First Vice President, Mrs. David S. Cooper, 225 Kelburne Avenue,
N. Tarrytown, New York 10591

Second Vice President, Mrs. Matthew R. Gordon-Clark, 218 Cornell Avenue,
Swarthmore, Pennsylvania 19081

Third Vice President, Mrs. John L. Kemmerer, 638 Jeffrey Lane,
Wayne, Pennsylvania 19087

Recording Secretary, Ms. Barbara Schieffelin Powell, 46 Sacramento Street,
Cambridge, Massachusetts 02138

Corresponding Secretary, Mrs. Josephine E. Case, 80 North Moore Street, Apt.
34J, New York, New York 10013

Treasurer, Mrs. Charles R. Wood, 125 Orchard Lane,
Haverford, Pennsylvania 19041

Chairman, Alumnae Fund, Mrs. Richard E. Fisher, 425 Glyn Wynne,
Haverford, Pennsylvania 19041

Chairman, Selection Committee, Mrs. Robert Cavanaugh,
912 W. Northern Parkway, Baltimore, Maryland 21210

Chairman, Scholarship & Loan Fund Committee, Mrs. Richard W. Day,
36 Lloyd Road, Montclair, New Jersey 07042

Chairman, Wyndham Committee, Mrs. Fred Alexander, 1400 Youngsford Road,
Gladwyne, Pennyslvania 19035

Executive Director, Mrs. Betsy F. Havens

Executive Secretary, Alumnae Fund, Mrs. Charles P. Dethier

Coordinator for Graduate Alumnaeli, Mrs. Charles A. MacIntosh

The Editors, The Alumnae Bulletin, Mrs. Samuel Mason and
Mrs. James A. Rittenhouse, Wyndham, Bryn Mawr College 19010

Alumnae Trustees of Bryn Mawr College

Mrs. Thomas Bates, 1312 Middle Road, Bettendorf, Iowa 52722

Mrs. W. Donner Denckla, 91 Knickerbocker Road,
Tenafly, New Jersey 07670

Mrs. John G. Laylin, 438 River Bend Road, Great Falls, Virginia 22066

Mrs. John E. Lippmann, 90 Riverside Drive, New York, New York 10024

Miss Georgia L. McMurray, 784 Columbus Avenue, Apt. 14E,
New York, New York 10025

Mrs. J. Peter Schmitz, 6401 Wydown Boulevard, Saint Loüis, Missouri 63105

Mrs. William H. Taft III, 3101 35th Street, N.W.,
Washington, D. C. 20016

Officers of Alumnae Groups and College Representatives

District I: Maine, New Hampshire, Vermont, Massachusetts, Rhode Island, Connecticut (except Fairfield County)

Councillor, Mrs. James H. Jackson, 356 Walnut Street, Brookline, Massachusetts 02146

District Admissions Coordinator, Mrs. Martin A. Hitchcock, 29 Wildwood Street, Winchester, Massachusetts 01890

Club Presidents:

Boston...........	Mrs. William H. Harris, 665 Concord Avenue, Belmont, Massachusetts 02178
Hartford	Mrs. Worth Loomis, 70 Terry Road, Hartford, Connecticut 06105
New Haven.......	Miss Linda L. Chang, 235 Lawrence Street, New Haven, Connecticut 06511
Rhode Island......	Mrs. Nicholas Retsinas, 64 Blaisdell Avenue, Pawtucket Rhode Island 02860

District II: New York, Fairfield County (Connecticut), Northern New Jersey

Councillor, Mrs. Joseph M. Schack, 127 West 12th Street, New York, New York 10011

District Admissions Coordinator, Mrs. George L. Curran, R. D. 2, Box 308A, Red Hook, New York 12571

Club Presidents:

Fairfield County ...	Mrs. Stanley B. Garrell, 310 Hillbrook Lane, Fairfield, Connecticut 06430
New York........	Julia L. Kagan, 377 Bleecker Street, 4-B, New York, New York 10014
Long Island.......	Miss Natalie Naylor, 496 Clarendon Road, Uniondale, New York 11553
Westchester	Mrs. Richard J. Miller, 119 Alder Drive, Briarcliff Manor, New York 10510
Albany, Troy, Schenectady.....	Mrs. Arthur W. Wright, 642 Western Avenue, Albany, New York 12203
Buffalo	Mrs. Marcella Brett, 20 Colonial Drive, Buffalo, New York 14226
Rochester	Mrs. Thomas F. Griswold, Huntington Hills, Rochester, New York 14622
Princeton	Miss Diana D. Lucas, 105 Mercer Street, Princeton, New Jersey 08540
Northern New Jersey	Mrs. John F. Parell, 6 Jerome Place, Upper Montclair, New Jersey 07043

*Candidates for admission who wish to talk with an alumna are invited
to write to the District Admissions Coordinator in their area*

District III: Pennsylvania, Southern New Jersey, Delaware

Councillor, Mrs. Frank M. Masters, Jr., R. D. 4, Box 848,
Harrisburg, Pennsylvania 17112

District Admissions Coordinator: Mrs. Samuel Diamond, 2021 Pine Street,
Philadelphia, Pennsylvania 19103

Club Presidents:

Philadelphia ...... Mrs. Charles H. Greenbaum, 1237 Imperial Road,
Rydal, Pennsylvania 19046

Central Pennsylvania Mrs. Duryea Cameron, 1952 High Street,
Camp Hill, Pennsylvania 17011

Western
Pennsylvania .... Mrs. Simeon A. Friedberg, 1220 S. Negley Avenue,
Pittsburgh, Pennsylvania 15217

Delaware .... Mrs. Ernest H. Beck, 48 Paschall Road,
Wilmington, Delaware 19803

District IV: Maryland, Virginia, West Virginia, District of Columbia

Councillor, Mrs. R. Lewis Wright, 3505 Old Gun Road,
Midlothian, Virginia 23113

District Admissions Coordinator: Miss Doris Dewton, 3551-A2 S. Stafford Street,
Arlington, Virginia 22206

Club Presidents:

Washington ...... Mrs. Norman Grossblatt, 6711 Georgia Street,
Chevy Chase, Maryland 20015

Baltimore .... Mrs. William R. Richardson, 1003 Wagner Road,
Ruxton, Maryland 21204

Richmond .... Mrs. Jacob Haun, Jr., 1408 Wilmington Avenue,
Richmond, Virginia 23227

Norfolk .... Mrs. Ralph W. Miner, Jr., 1006 Hanover Avenue,
Norfolk, Virginia 23508

District V: North Carolina, South Carolina, Georgia, Florida, Alabama,
Mississippi, Louisiana, Arkansas, Tennessee

Councillor, Mrs. David C. Aschman, 20 S. Prospect Drive,
Coral Gables, Florida 33133

District Admissions Coordinator: Mrs. Henry M. Farrell, 208 Park Shore East,
Columbia, South Carolina 29204

Club Presidents:

Piedmont .... Miss Mary J. Wilson, 1413 Watts Street,
Durham, North Carolina 27701

Florida .... Mrs. David C. Aschman, 20 S. Prospect Drive,
Coral Gables, Florida 33133

Louisiana .... Mrs. Bernard Lemann, 7703 Burthe Street,
New Orleans, Louisiana 70118

Georgia .... Gail McK. Beckman, 1270 W. Peachtree Street, N.W.
Apt. 16C, Atlanta, Georgia 30309

District VI: Ohio, Indiana, Kentucky, Michigan

Councillor, Mrs. Robert E. Mangum, 57 Riverview Park Drive,
Columbus, Ohio 43214

District Admissions Coordinator: Mrs. J. R. Taylor Bassett III,
3356 Chalfant Road, Shaker Heights, Ohio 44120

Club Presidents:

Indiana .... Ms. Victoria Munn, 5830 N. Haverford, Indianapolis,
Indiana 46220

Detroit .... Mrs. Bruce Steinhauer, 1304 Bishop Road,
Grosse Pointe, Michigan 48230

Ann Arbor .... Ms. Suzanne Fedunok, 1120 Granger Avenue,
Ann Arbor, Michigan 48104

Cincinnati .... Mrs. Philip Walters, 4 Hedgerow Lane,
Cincinnati, Ohio 45220

Cleveland .... Mrs. Edward J. Stevens III, 16106 Chadbourne Road,
Cleveland, Ohio 44120

Columbus .... Mrs. Harold E. Coon, 1901 Coventry Road,
Columbus, Ohio 43212

District VII: Illinois, Iowa, Wisconsin, Minnesota, North Dakota, South Dakota,
Nebraska, Kansas, Missouri

Councillor, Mrs. Terence Lilly, 627 S. Oak Street, Hinsdale, Illinios 60521

District Admissions Coordinator: Mrs. John H. Morrison, 2717 Lincoln Street,
Evanston, Illinois 60201

Club Presidents:

Chicago .... Mrs. John H. Morrison, 2717 Lincoln Street,
Evanston, Illinois 60201

St. Louis .... Mrs. Richard Zacher, 6605 Waterman,
St. Louis, Missouri 63130

Kansas City .... Mrs. Walter M. Dickey, 8133 Sagamore Road,
Leawood, Kansas 66206

District VIII: Colorado, Arizona, New Mexico, Texas, Oklahoma

Councillor, Mrs. Donald H. Nelson, 4131 Oak Road, Tulsa, Oklahoma 74105

District Admissions Coordinator: Mrs. William S. Masland,
9020 E. Eagle Feather, Tucson, Arizona 85715

Club Presidents:

Colorado .... Mrs. George A. Lincoln, 32854 Upper Bear Creek Road,
Evergreen, Colorado 80439

Tucson .... Mrs. Thacher Loring, 10858 East Tanque Verde Road,
Tucson, Arizona 85715

Dallas .... Mrs. Robert L. Lichten, 6338 Aberdeen Avenue,
Dallas, Texas 75230

Houston .... Mrs. Stephen L. Klineberg, 2109 Goldsmith,
Houston, Texas 77025

Austin .... Mrs. Benjamin D. Meritt 712 West 16th Street,
Austin, Texas 78701

Greater Phoenix ... Lynn Badler, 8221 E. Garfield L-17,
Scottsdale, Arizona 85257

District IX: California, Nevada, Utah, Hawaii

Councillor, Mrs. Pauline A. Adams, 1020 San Mateo Drive, Menlo Park,
California 94025

District Admissions Coordinator: Mrs. Richard C. Walker, 927 Candlelight Place,
La Jolla, California 92037

Club Presidents:

Northern California .. Mrs. Tom Talamini 2 Shell Court, Mill Valley,
California 94141

Southern California .. Mrs. Dave Watson, 627 Seventh Street, Santa Monica,
California 90402

San Diego .... Mrs. Richard C. Walker, 927 Candlelight Place,
La Jolla, California 92037

District X: Washington, Oregon, Idaho, Montana, Wyoming, Alaska

Councillor, Mrs. Samuel H. Brown, 11604 Interlaaken Drive S.W. Tacoma,
Washington 98498

District Admissions Coordinator: Mrs. Robert Mazo, 2460 Charnelton Street,
Eugene, Oregon 97405

Club President:

Portland .... To be elected

Seattle .... Mrs. John L. Eddy, Jr., 2628 82nd Avenue N.E.,
Bellevue, Washington 98004

Foreign

Argentina: Miss Ana Maria Barrenechea, Coronel Diaz 1815,
80 "A", Buenos Aires

Canada: Mrs. I. Bernard Schacter, 411 Richview Avenue, Toronto, Ontario
Mrs. Helen H. Nixon, 150 McLeod Street, Ottawa, Ont. K2P, 0Z7
Mrs. David G. Carter, 49 Rosemount Avenue, Westmount 217,
Montreal, P.Q.

Denmark: Mrs. Harald Vestergaard, Hambros Alle 19, 2900 Hellerup

England: Mrs. Cuthbert Orde, Flat 3, 5 Cadogan Square, London
SWIX OHT, England

France: Mme. Jean Maheu, 1 Rue Clovis, Paris V
Mme. Michel Worms de Romilly, 63, rue Notre-Dame-des-Champs 75006,
Paris

Germany: Mrs. Hans Loening, 2802 Fischerhude,
In der Bredenau 81, West Germany

Greece: Miss Elizabeth Douli, Korae 18, Nea Smyrne, Athens

India: Miss Harsimran Malik, 7 Palam Marg, Vasant Vihar, New Delhi 57

Italy: Mrs. Enrico Berra, Piazzale Biancamano, 20121, Milano

Japan: Miss Taki Fujita, 20-4, 2-chome, Higashi-Nakana, Nakano-ku, Tokyo

Libya: Mrs. E. A. Eriksen, Esso Standard Libya Inc. Essofield P. O. Box 385,
Tripoli

Mexico: Mrs. Arturo Gomez, Liverpool 149-102, Mexico 6, D.F.

Norway: Mrs. Harald Sommerfeldt, Hoff Terace 4, Skoyen, pr Oslo

Philippine Islands: Mrs. Ofelia Torres Reyes, 14 Ilagan Street,
San Francisco del Monte, Quezon City

Turkey: Miss Suna Kili, Bogazici Universitesi, P.K. 2, Bebek-Istanbul

Venezuela: Mrs. Oscar deSchnell, Apartado 69, Caracas

Index

Absence
  from Classes, 42
  from College, 31
Academic Awards, 180
Academic Honors, 47
Academic Honor System, 41
Academic Schedule, 3-4
Academic Standards, 41
Administration, Officers of, 6, 17
Admission, 26
Advanced Placement, 29
Advising, 41
Alumnae Officers, 188
Alumnae Representatives, 188
Anthropology, 56
Anthropology Museum and
  Laboratory, 34
Application for Admission, 26
Archaeology, Classical and
  Near Eastern, 66
Archaeology Collections, 34
Arts Council, 24
Athletic Association, 24
Attendance at Classes, 42
Auxiliary Libraries, 33
Avignon, Summer Institute, 50, 86

Bachelor of Arts Degree,
  Requirements for, 44-48
Biology, 59
Biochemistry, 61
Black Cultural Center, 24
Board of Trustees, 5
Boyce Collection, 34

Canaday, Mariam Coffin,
  Library, 33
Canaday, Ward, Collection, 35
Career Planning Office, 53
Charges, Minor Fees, 39
Charges, Reduction of for
  Absence, 38
Chemistry, 63
Child Study Institute, 19, 73
Classical and Near Eastern
  Archaeology, 66
Classical Languages, 147
Classical Studies, 147
College Entrance·
  Examination Board, 28
College History, 21
Computer Center, 36
Conduct, 41
Cooperation with Neighboring
  Institutions, 23, 34, 47

Coordination in the Sciences,
  Plan for, 49
Correspondence, Names for, 2
Council of the Undergraduate
  College, 41
Course Numbers, Key to, 55
Creative Work in the Arts, 50
Credit for Work at Other
  Institutions, 29, 47
Curriculum, 44-54
Curriculum Committee, 24
Curtis Collection, 34

Deans, 41
District Councilors, 188-193

Early Admission, 28
Early Decision Plan, 27
Economics, 68
Education, Department of, 73
Employment and Vocational
  Counseling, 53
English, 75
Entrance Requirements, 26
Entrance Tests, 27
European Fellowship, 180
Excavations, 68
Expenses, 38-40

Faculty, 6-15
Fee, Residence and Tuition, 38
Financial Aid, 161
Fine Art, 103
Flexner Lectures, 23
Foreign Students, 30, 179
French, 82
French House, 50
French Studies, 148
Freshmen, Arrival of, 41

General Deposit, 39
Geology, 87
German, 90
German House, 50
Goldman, Hetty, Collection, 34
Goodhart, Medieval Library, 33
Government, Student, 23
Grades, 47
Graduate School, 21
Greek, 93
Growth and Structure of Cities, 150
Guidance
  Academic, 41
  Vocational, 53

Haverford College, Cooperation
  with, 22-25, 34, 47
Health, 42

Hebrew, 106
Hispanic and Hispanic-American
    Studies, 153
History, Department of, 95
History of Art, 102
History of Religion, 105
History of Science, 100
Honors, Degree with, 47
Honors Work, 46
Hygiene, 48

Infirmary, 42
Insurance
    Health, 43
    Personal Property, 43
Interdepartmental
    Courses, 50, 154
    Work, 147
Intercollegiate Center for
    Classical Studies in Rome, 52
Italian, 108

Junior Year Abroad, 51

King Collection, 34

Laboratories, 35
Language Examinations, 45
Language Houses, 50
Language Laboratory, 36
Language Requirement, 45
Latin, 110
Leaves of Absence, 31
Libraries, 33
Loan Funds, 185

Madrid, Summer Institute, 51
Major and Allied Work, 47
Mathematics, 112
Medical School Scholarships, 184
Music, 115

National Direct Student Loan
    Program, 186
Non-resident Students, 38

Officers
    Administration, 6, 17
    Alumnae Association, 188
    Board of Trustees, 5
Performing Arts, 158
Phebe Anna Thorne School, 20, 73
Philosophy, 118
Physical Education, 158
Physical Examination, 159
Physics, 123
Placement Tests, 29-30
Political Science, 126
Premedical Preparation, 30, 48

Presidents of the College, 22
Prizes, 180
Psychology, 133

Readmission, 31
Requirements for Admission, 27
Requirements for the
    A.B. Degree, 44-48
Residence, 36
    During Vacations, 38
    Halls, 36
    Rules for, 37
Riegel Museum, 34
Russian, 137

Scholarships, 163
Science Center, 35
Sciences, Plan for
    Coordination in, 49
Secondary School Studies,
    Program of, 26
Senior Conference, 46
Shaw Lectures, 23
Sociology, 139
Spanish, 143
Spanish House, 50
Staff, 16-20
Student Organizations, 23-25
Students' Association for
    Self-Government, 23
Students' Loan Fund, 185
Summer Institutes Abroad, 50
Summer School Work, 47
Supplementary Requirements for
    the Degree, 48
Swarthmore College,
    Cooperation with, 23, 34, 47

Teaching, Preparation for, 49
Thomas, M. Carey, Library, 34
Transfer Students, 29
Trustees, 5
Tuition, 38

Undergraduate Association, 23
Union Library Catalogue, 34
U. S. Geological Survey
    Map Collection, 35

Vacations, Residence during, 36
Vaux Collections, 34
Vocational Guidance, 53

Werkman Fund, 53
Withdrawal from College, 31
Woodward, Quita,
    Memorial Library, 34
Work-Study Program, 54

Directions to Bryn Mawr College

By automobile from the East or South-East take the Walt Whitman Bridge to I-676/Schuylkill Expressway and follow this north until it meets with I-76; *or* take the Benjamin Franklin Bridge to I-76/Vine Street until it meets with I-676. In either case, continue north on I-76 to Exit 41, "City Ave.—U.S. 1 South." Proceed south on City Ave./U.S. 1 for 1.1 miles from the exit ramp and then turn right on Conshohocken State Road (PA 23). (There is a shopping center on the right shortly before this turn.) After three-tenths of a mile, Conshohocken State Road makes a sharp turn to the left over a railroad overpass and comes to a traffic light. Continue straight through this intersection; you are now on Montgomery Avenue, which you follow for about five miles (bearing right at a fork at about the three mile point), to Morris Avenue in the town of Bryn Mawr. Harcum Junior College will be on the left shortly before Morris Avenue. Turn right onto Morris Avenue, proceed to the next traffic light and then turn left onto New Gulph Road for approximately 1½ blocks. Visitors may use the College parking lot, entering at Merion Gate, which is directly opposite 815 New Gulph Road. The parking lot on Morris Avenue also may be used by visitors.

By automobile from the South take I-95 through Wilmington, Delaware, to Chester, Pennsylvania, then take the exit marked "PA 352—Edgemont Ave." (It is also marked with a sign for "Chester Business District.") Immediately look for, and follow, signs for PA 320 North. Continue north on PA 320 for approximately 10.5 miles from the I-95 exit, until you come to Bryn Mawr Avenue. (This is about two miles after you cross PA 3, and has a traffic light.) Turn right, and follow Bryn Mawr Avenue for approximately two miles until you come to a traffic light at Haverford Road. Continue on Bryn Mawr Avenue, which bears slightly to the left, until you come to Lancaster Avenue in the town of Bryn Mawr. (This is the second traffic light after Haverford Road.) Turn right on Lancaster Avenue for one block, and then left at the first traffic light onto Morris Avenue. Follow the road, which will curve under the railroad tracks, until you come to the traffic light at Montgomery Avenue. Proceed across Montgomery Avenue to the next traffic light. Turn left on to New Gulph Road for approximately 1½ blocks. Visitors may use the College parking lot, entering at Merion Gate, which is directly opposite 815 New Gulph Road. The parking lot on Morris Avenue also may be used by visitors.

By automobile from the West, North or Northeast take the Pennsylvania Turnpike to the Valley Forge Exit (24). From the Valley Forge Exit of the Turnpike, take the Schuylkill Expressway (I-76) east, turning off at Exit 36, "PA 320, Gulph Mills," which is 3.5 miles from the toll gate. Follow PA 320 south for approximately four-tenths of a mile and turn left at the first traffic light onto Old Gulph Road. Proceed on this for approximately three miles, and the College will be on your right. The College parking lot is the third entrance on the right after Roberts Road.

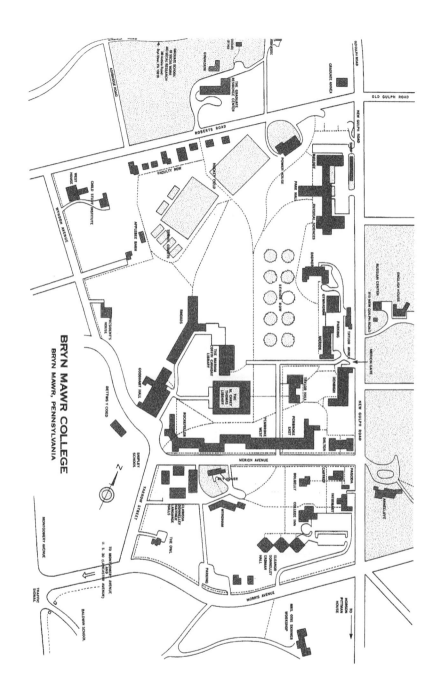

BRYN MAWR COLLEGE
BRYN MAWR, PENNSYLVANIA

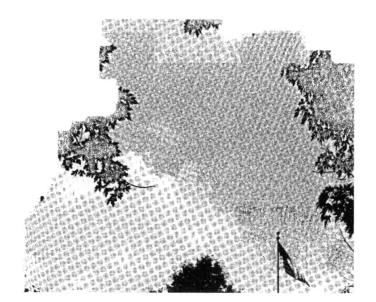

Issue for the
September

Bryn Mawr College Calendar
The Graduate School
of Social Work and Social Research

Issue for the Session 1976-77
September 1976 *Volume LXIX Number 4*

The Graduate School of Social Work and Social Research of Bryn Mawr College offers a basic two-year program leading to the degree of Master of Social Service and an advanced program leading to the degree of Doctor of Philosophy.

The Master's degree program is based upon the premise that preparation for social work practice and research requires a core of knowledge as well as skill in the application of this knowledge. A curriculum of concurrent course work and practicum is provided.

The Doctor of Philosophy program is planned to broaden the student's knowledge of social welfare in general and, through intensive research, to deepen his or her knowledge in one field in particular. The curriculum is intended for full-time study; however, students who have been admitted to the doctoral program may arrange to begin on a part-time basis.

CORRESPONDENCE regarding admission to The Graduate School of Social Work an Social Research should be addressed to:

Office of Admissions
The Graduate School of Social Work and Social Research
Bryn Mawr College
300 Airdale Road
Bryn Mawr, Pennsylvania 19010

BRYN MAWR COLLEGE CALENDAR published December, July, August an September by Bryn Mawr College, Bryn Mawr, Pennsylvania 19010. *Second clas postage paid at Bryn Mawr, Pennsylvania.*

Contents

Academic Calendar 7

Admission to The Graduate School of Social Work
    and Social Research 9
    Foreign Applicants 9
    Financial Aid 10
    Truth in Lending Law 10
    Endowed Funds 10
    Prizes 11
    Transfer Credit 12
    Registration 13
    Mutual Accountability 14
    The Master's Student Adviser 15
    The Doctoral Student Adviser 15

Programs and Degrees 17
    Master of Social Service 17
    Special Part-Time Program 19
    Master of Law and Social Policy 20
    Doctor of Philosophy 22

Graduate Program for the Master of Social Service 25
    Practicum 38

Graduate Program for the Master of Law and Social Policy .. 44

Graduate Program for the Doctor of Philosophy 48

Fees 58

Resources for Graduate Work at the College 61

History of the School 62

Graduate Student Housing 65

Health 66
    Medical Services 66
    Medical Requirements 66
    Insurance 67

Child Care Center 67

Career Planning Office 67

Student and Alumni Associations 69
    Recruitment of Minority Group Students 69

College Facilities 70

Trustees of Bryn Mawr College 71

Officers of the College 72

Officers of Administration of the College 72

Advisory Board of the School 74

Faculty of the School 75

Administration of the School 76

Standing Committees of the Faculty 77

Frontispiece–
The Graduate School of Social Work and Social Research

Ethnic Minority Content in the Curriculum

Because racism constitutes a profound problem in this country, The Graduate School of Social Work and Social Research seeks to mitigate the effects of racism among its students and faculty through its educational program. In addition, the School hopes to develop and make available reports and curriculum material which will combat racism among administrators, alumni, and all social welfare professionals.

The School accepts the responsibility for educating social workers prepared to serve all persons within the social welfare system and will strive to change those economic, political and social structures which constrain the opportunities and potential of minority groups.

The School is undertaking to incorporate appropriate content on ethnic minority groups in courses throughout the curriculum. By accepting this task as a central and continuing concern the School intends to foster self-awareness, clearer perspectives and more sensitivity toward all people on the part of both minority and non-minority students and faculty.

Academic Calendar 1976-77
The Graduate School of
Social Work and Social Research

First Semester—1976

Sept. 7   *Graduate residences open.*

Sept. 8   *Registration of all social work students.*

Sept. 9   *Convocation. First semester seminars begin.*

Oct. 22   *Fall vacation begins at 5:00 p.m. (Practicum continues on regularly scheduled days.)*

Oct. 27   *Fall vacation ends at 9:00 a.m.*

Nov. 22-24   *Registration for second semester.*

Nov. 24   *Thanksgiving holiday begins after last seminar. (No practicum.)*

Nov. 29   *Thanksgiving holiday ends at 9:00 a.m.*

Dec. 14   *Last day of seminars for first semester; practicum continues on regularly scheduled days.*

Dec. 20-22   *Examinations.*

Dec. 22   *Winter vacation begins at 6:00 p.m.*

1977

Jan. 6   *Practicum resumes on regularly scheduled days.*

Jan. 14   *Last day of practicum in first semester.*

Second Semester—1977

Jan. 17   *Convocation. Second semester seminars and practicum resume on regularly scheduled days.*

Feb.   1   *Ph.D. dissertations must be submitted to the Office of
The Graduate School of Social Work and Social Re-
search for Oral Examination prior to April 1. (See
March 30 below for Oral Examination after April 30.)*

Mar. 11   *Spring vacation begins at 5:00 p.m. (Practicum continues on regularly scheduled days.)*

Mar. 21   *Spring vacation ends at 9:00 a.m.*

Mar. 30   *Final Date for submission of Ph.D. dissertations to the
Office of The Graduate School of Social Work and
Social Research for Commencement, 1977. (Oral
examination will be scheduled after April 30.)*

Apr. 28   *Last day of seminars and practicum.*

May   2   *Master's Papers due.*

May 4-6   *Examinations.*

May 16   *Conferring of degrees and close of 92nd academic year
of the College and the 61st year of the School.
Graduate residences close.*

The information in this Calendar is the best available at the time of
publication. The contents are subject to change and are not binding
on the College.

8

Admission to The Graduate School of Social Work and Social Research

The Graduate School of Social Work and Social Research is open to qualified graduates from colleges or universities of recognized standing. Both men and women are admitted to the School and are accepted as candidates for the degrees of Master of Social Service, Master of Law and Social Policy, and Doctor of Philosophy.

Application for admission, to be made to the Office of Admissions of the School, must be supported by official transcripts of the applicant's academic record, both graduate and undergraduate. The Miller Analogies Test is required. (Instructions concerning this test will be given after the application has been received.) A letter from the dean of each college or university attended and letters from two or more professors with whom the applicant did his or her preparation are required.

An application fee of $20 must accompany the application. This fee is not refunded or credited toward tuition. The closing date of applications is February 1.

A personal interview is usually arranged with a member of the faculty of the School. If the applicant lives a considerable distance from Bryn Mawr, an interview can usually be arranged with an appropriate person in the area.

Within ten days after official notice of admission to The Graduate School of Social Work and Social Research, an enrollment fee of $100 is to be paid to the Comptroller of Bryn Mawr College. This fee is credited to the tuition for the first semester. It is not refunded if the student fails to register.

Foreign Applicants

The closing date for applications is February 1 for admission the following September. Applications must include the scores of the Test of English as a Foreign Language (TOEFL). For information concerning the TOEFL write to: TOEFL, Educational Testing Service, Princeton, New Jersey 08540.

A very limited amount of financial support is available for foreign students.

Financial Aid

A limited amount of financial aid is available for full-time students in The Graduate School of Social Work and Social Research. Some fellowships and scholarships are provided from the general funds of the College, the Alumnae Association, from the gifts of alumni and other generous donors, and from government agencies and private foundations.

Bryn Mawr also participates in the National Direct Student Loan Program and the College Work-Study Program.

The terms of the various awards and loans differ and will be discussed with the applicant at the time of the admission interview. Both merit and need are factors to which consideration is given in making certain awards. Requests for financial assistance are considered after the application process is completed and applicants have been admitted into The Graduate School of Social Work and Social Research. *The School requires that students seeking financial aid file an application for financial aid with the Graduate and Professional School Financial Aid Service.* This form will be sent upon request after a student is admitted.

Students are urged to explore loans which are made available through the state in which they have established residence, such as the Pennsylvania Higher Education Assistance Authority loan in Pennsylvania.

Truth in Lending Law

The following information refers to 1975 Master of Social Service degree graduates:

Option	Total	Seeking Work in U.S.	Reporting	Salary Range	Median
Clinical Social Work	29	24	17	$10,000-12,000	$10,700
Social Service Management	11	10	7	9,700-12,600	10,600
Community Planning and Development	9	7	5	12,000-14,500	13,400
Social Planning	20	19	15	10,000-16,500	12,500

Endowed Funds

Emily Greene Balch Lecture Fund for Social Work and Social Research. Inspired by the alumna niece of Emily Greene Balch, A.B. '89, this permanent lecture fund honors one of the two American women ever to receive the Nobel Peace Prize.

Agnes M.H. Byrnes Memorial for Social Work and Social Research. Established for The Graduate School of Social Work and Social Research by the bequest of Miss Byrne, who received her Ph.D. in Social Work in 1920.

The Fanny Travis Cochran Scholarship Fund. Established in 1936 on the occasion of the 50th Anniversary of the College. Miss Cochran is a member of the Class of 1902.

Alfred and Mary Doughty Student Loan Fund. A gift from the Alfred and Mary Doughty Foundation established this self-perpetuating student loan fund.

Marguerite N. Farley Scholarship Fund. Established in 1956 to provide scholarships for foreign students.

Margaret Friend Low Fund for General Purposes–School of Social Work and Social Research. Established by an alumna of the Class of 1911 impressed by the work of graduate students in Social Work and Social Research.

Lillian and Jack Poses Scholarship Fund. Established by Lillian Shapiro Poses, a former student in Social Work and Social Research, and her husband, for student aid in The Graduate School of Social Work and Social Research.

Joan Sall Rivitz Memorial Scholarship Fund for Social Work and Social Research. This scholarship fund was established as a memorial by the father of an alumna of the Bryn Mawr Graduate School of Social Work and Social Research. Mrs. Rivitz received her M.S.S. in 1963 and her Ph.D. in 1972.

J. Henry Scattergood Scholarship. Established by a grant of the Friends Freedmen's Association to scholarship endowment for the support of black students at Bryn Mawr. The fund is named in memory of a former Trustee who served as Treasurer of the College for 26 years.

Leila Woodruff Stokes Fund for Faculty Support in The Graduate School of Social Work and Social Research. This fund was created by an alumna of the Class of 1907 shortly before her death. Leila Woodruff Stokes was a friend and classmate of Carola Woerishoffer, whose legacy was the impetus for establishing The Graduate School of Social Work and Social Research.

Chair in Social Work and Social Research Fund. A $10,000 gift from an anonymous donor established this fund as a nucleus to attract further donations.

Prizes

The Susan B. Anthony Memorial Prize, value $500, commemorating the great work of Susan B. Anthony for women, was founded

11

by her friend Anna Howard Shaw and her niece Lucy E. Anthony. It is offered every two years to a graduate student at Bryn Mawr College who has published or submitted in final form for publication the best study dealing with the industrial, social, economic or political position of women. The award is made by a committee of which the President of the College is chairman.

The Susan M. Kingsbury Grant in Social Research, value $300, is awarded every third year on the recommendation of the Dean of The Graduate School of Social Work and Social Research to advanced students, men and women, preferably candidates for the degree of Doctor of Philosophy.

Transfer Credit

Transfer credit in an amount up to the equivalent of one year of the program for the M.S.S. may be allowed for work done at other accredited schools of social work. Such transfer credit will not be given until the candidate has completed a semester's work at Bryn Mawr. In each case transfer credit must be recommended by the Dean.

Residence Requirements

For both the Ph.D. and M.S.S. degrees one year in full-time residence is required. Two sequential semesters in one academic year meet this requirement.

Persons registering for full-time programs should consult with advisers before undertaking employment concurrent with a full-time academic program because of the demands upon time for the expected high-quality performance of students. It is expected that full-time students will give priority to academic commitments.

Persons registered as full-time students who are provided fellowship or scholarship support through Bryn Mawr College may be employed up to eight hours per week during the academic year as long as satisfactory academic performance is maintained. In principle, this amount of time for employment beyond the full-time curriculum is reasonable.

University of Pennsylvania Reciprocal Plan

Under the Reciprocal Plan, courses at the University of Pennsyl vania Graduate School of Arts and Sciences are available to Bry Mawr graduate students. All full-time students and such part-tim students as intend to become candidates for degrees are eligible The number of courses which may be taken at the University i limited to one per semester. The procedure for registration an payment of tuition fees is the same as for students enrolled wholly at Bryn Mawr, with the exception that the student will present a letter of introduction to the Dean of The Graduate School of Arts and Sciences of the University of Pennsylvania when registering there. The University charges a small general fee for the use of the library, a library deposit, which is refundable, and fees for late registration. Ordinarily students are not advised to undertake such work during their first year at Bryn Mawr.

Degree Candidacy

Students become candidates for advanced degrees only after they have met the School's requirements and, in the case of the Ph.D. degree, made formal application which has been approved by the members of the faculty on the Doctoral Committee of The Graduate School of Social Work and Social Research.

Continuing Enrollment

Students who have completed the required course work for the Ph.D. degree and are continuing independent work on their dissertations must retain their enrollment and degree candidacy by registering for one or more seminars each semester or must register under the Continuing Enrollment Plan. Such students will be billed under the Continuing Enrollment Plan unless they have asked for a leave of absence in writing and a leave has been granted.

In addition, students who are not planning to register for academic seminars but who are planning (1) to present themselves for College examinations, (2) to use the College libraries, or (3) to consult members of the Faculty must register under the Continuing Enrollment Plan. Such enrollment does not carry academic credit.

Summer Work

Arrangements can be made for doctoral students to continue research during the summer or to enroll for tutorials and independent study. Students should register for such work with the Dean at The Graduate School of Social Work and Social Research early in May.

Registration

Every student in The Graduate School of Social Work and Social Research must register for courses during the registration period listed in the School Calendar. Permission to make any change in registration must be received from the Dean of the School. Students who do not complete their registration during the registration period or who change their selections after the close of the registration period are subject to the Late Registration Fee, and after a specified date, the Add-Drop Fee.

Only courses given in The Graduate School of Social Work and Social Research are described in this Calendar. Unless otherwise noted, these are for one semester. Descriptions of other graduate courses given at Bryn Mawr may be found in the Calendar of The Graduate School of Arts and Sciences.

Grading

Two grades are given for graduate work, *Satisfactory* and *Unsatisfactory*. Ph.D. students may be given extensions to November 1 if there are extenuating circumstances. However, there will be no extension beyond November 1 of the academic year following that in which the work was due. After November 1 the work will be graded *Unsatisfactory* or the term *Incomplete* will remain permanently on the record.

First-year Master's students must complete all work by July 31 in order to move into the second year. Extensions beyond the date the Grade Sheets are due in the Dean's Office are only given when there are extenuating circumstances.

Mutual Accountability

The essential educational relationships in the School are based upon the principle that members of the faculty and students are accountable to each other on an equitable basis. Procedures to implement this principle which have been developed through joint effort of members of the faculty and members of the Student Association are given below.

It is the instructor's responsibility to provide the student with an evaluation (i.e., Satisfactory, Unsatisfactory, or Incomplete grade) for the course or seminar. A qualitative analysis of oral or written presentations, examinations, or other educational performances, as well as a written analysis of the student's semester performance at the end of the semester are optional.

The student's responsibility, as a condition of receiving a grade, is to (a) participate in either an oral or written mid-term analysis of the quality of the course or seminar, and (b) prepare for the Dean and the instructor a signed evaluation of the instructor's work. Such written evaluations make systematic the student contribution to the development of the School, particularly with regard to questions of faculty reappointment, promotion, and tenure. An end-of-semester signed written analysis of the instructor's performance to be shared only with the instructor is optional.

The Master's Student Adviser

At the beginning of each academic year a member of the faculty is assigned to serve as adviser to each student. Responsibilities of the adviser include: providing educational guidance in selection of a student's course of study; registering the student; orienting the student to the School, its curriculum, and its policies; identifying and consulting with the student on problems which may be interfering with the student's educational progress; informing the Dean when a student's performance places him or her in academic jeopardy and presenting to the Committee on the Evaluation of the Educational Performance of Master's Students a summary of the student's performance in each course; and representing the student's interests when necessary.

The faculty adviser is expected to schedule three conferences each semester, one of which may be the course registration conference. Additional conferences may be initiated by the student or scheduled by the adviser.

In the M.S.S. program the adviser consults with first-year students about choice of second-year practice options and the option of the Master's Paper.

The Doctoral Student Adviser

The primary role of the adviser is to serve as: an educational counselor; an interpreter of procedure and policy; a source of information on such matters as courses available in other settings, and research and funding opportunities; and as a consultant on course selection. The adviser also has an educational and evaluative role in recommending the student for candidacy.

Exclusion

The College reserves the right to exclude at any time any student whose academic standing is unsatisfactory or whose conduct renders him or her an undesirable member of the college community. In such cases fees will not be remitted or refunded in whole or in part; fellowships and scholarships will be cancelled.

Withdrawal and Readmission

A student who has withdrawn from the School is not automatically readmitted. After a year's absence he or she may request readmission and should consult the Dean and the Chairman of Admissions concerning the procedure to be followed.

Leaves of Absence

A student whose academic work is in good standing may apply to the Dean for a leave of absence. A leave is generally requested for an academic year. If the student wishes to return to the program at the end of that year, he or she should write to the Dean requesting reinstatement. Available space in the program and length of time the student has been away from the School will be factors affecting reinstatement. A student extending leave beyond the approved period will need to reapply for admission to the School.

Medical Leave of Absence

The student may, on the recommendation of a physician, request a medical leave of absence for reasons of health at any time. Readmission may be granted upon recommendation of the Dean based upon evidence of the student's capacity to meet the demands of his or her program.

Membership in Professional Organizations

We strongly recommend that students join one or more related professional organizations, such as the National Association of Social Workers, the Council on Social Work Education, American Public Welfare Association, Child Welfare League of America, the Association for Clinical Social Work. These organizations offer reduced rates for students and provide a number of benefits, including publications and insurance programs. The National Association of Social Workers, particularly through its state chapters and local divisions, gives students an immediate opportunity to participate in professional activities with leaders in the field.

Cancellation of Courses

The School reserves the right to cancel scheduled courses on the basis of size of enrollment or availability of instructors.

16

Programs and Degrees

Bryn Mawr College awards the degrees of Master of Social Service, Master of Law and Social Policy, and Doctor of Philosophy in The Graduate School of Social Work and Social Research.

The Degree of Master of Social Service

The program for the M.S.S. degree is designed to prepare graduates for Clinical Social Work, Social Service Management, Community Organizing, Policy Research and Development, or Program Planning and Administration. Two academic years of full-time study are required. The degree represents the completion of a concurrent program of course work and practicum. Provision is made for field instruction in a range of public and voluntary agencies and organizations with programs in such fields and settings as: aging, child welfare, community mental health, consumer organizations, corrections, day care, drug and alcohol dependency and abuse, family services, housing, intergroup relations, legal services, legislative offices, maternal and child health, mental retardation, neighborhood organization, physical rehabilitation, psychiatric services, public assistance, public education, public health, public welfare administration, school social work, social planning, social welfare research, teaching undergraduate programs, women's issues, and youth services.

Prerequisites. The prerequisite for the M.S.S. degree is a Bachelor's degree or its equivalent from a college or university of recognized standing in the United States, or a degree or certificate of the same standard from a foreign university.

PROGRAM OF WORK

The first-year program is similar for all students except for the selection of either Social Casework or Community Social Work as the principal focus in social work practice. The first-year required courses are:

> Social Casework I and II *or*
> Community Social Work I and II
> > and the following:
> Personality Theory *or* Normal Growth and Behavior
> Social Theory and Social Work
> Social Welfare Policy and Services: Historical Perspectives, *or* Social Welfare Policy and Services: Social Policy Analysis

Introduction to Research and Statistics and a second required
research course

Field Instruction I and II

In addition the student is expected to select one elective during
the first year of study.

The courses required in the second year are in part determined by
the student's area of practice concentration. These include a choice
of Clinical Social Work, Social Service Management, Community
Organizing, Policy Research and Development, or Program Planning and Administration. In addition, each student also takes a
practicum.

SECOND-YEAR OPTIONS

Clinical Social Work

Clinical Social Work is concerned with the alleviation of problems
in the social functioning of individuals, families, and small groups.
Direct and indirect methods of intervention, such as individual,
family, and group treatment, advocacy, collaboration, and consultation are used to accomplish this purpose. A related responsibility
is improvement in the structure and functioning of the various
systems which affect social functioning and social services.

Social Service Management

Social Service Management has as its central goal the improvement
of the structure and quality of social services. Social Service Management prepares students to assume the responsibility for organizing and marshalling the delivery of services; identifying and translating client needs into appropriate agency programs; training and
supervision of other categories of social welfare personnel; manpower development and examination and evaluation of policies;
and developing the monitoring of organizational structure and procedures in relation to delivery of services.

Policy Research and Development

This practice concentration provides knowledge and skills required
for the analysis of problems in given areas of social welfare; the
determination of consequences of existing policies; the projection
of consequences of new, alternative policies; the political feasibility
of alternative policies; and the drafting of new policies and regulations. The student is expected to develop in-depth knowledge and
skills in at least one substantive field in addition to generally applicable knowledge and practice skills.

Program Planning and Administration

This practice concentration provides knowledge and skills required
for administering, planning, implementing, and evaluating human

service programs. Areas of consideration include planning and control, community analysis, program and budget development, consumer participation, social policy intervention, leadership, staff relations, and a range of issues in administration. Knowledge in depth of at least one substantive field of human services is encouraged.

Community Organizing

Community Organizing stresses the strategies, tactics, and value-issues involved in direct work with groups mobilizing against major social problems, such as poverty and racism. In addition, direct community and workplace organizing within the social service sector is emphasized. Urban community development, neighborhood and workplace-based social action, and social movement organizing are three types of organizing explored in the two-semester sequence.

REQUIREMENTS FOR THE MSS DEGREE

Candidates for the M.S.S. degree must complete a minimum of eighteen semester courses, including a practicum. Each student's program of study consists of a combination of required and elective courses. One course credit may be an acceptable Master's Paper in an area of social work or social welfare.

ELECTIVES

Electives are offered in this School and in The Graduate School of Arts and Sciences at Bryn Mawr. With permission of the Dean of The Graduate School of Social Work and Social Research, students in the School may elect courses in The Graduate School of Arts and Sciences of the University of Pennsylvania under the Reciprocal Plan.

The reduction of required courses and the increase in electives is one principle which has guided the development of the curriculum. Another principle provides the opportunity for each student who demonstrates competence in a required course, including the practicum, to request a waiver of this required course in favor of an additional elective.

SPECIAL PART-TIME PROGRAM

It is possible for a small number of students for the Master's degree to extend the two-year program to three years. The pattern is to complete the first graduate year's requirements over a period of two years on a part-time basis, and to complete the second year's requirements during the third year on a full-time basis.

Except for the Law and Social Policy Program, Bryn Mawr only enrolls students registered for degree programs.

CERTIFICATION FOR SOCIAL WORK IN THE SCHOOLS

If a student is interested in social work in the schools in Pennsylvania, certification may be acquired through the Department of Education and Child Development.

The choice of certain electives both in The School of Social Work and Social Research and in the Department of Education, and a practicum in a school setting will prepare a student for such certification as part of the MSS program. Students interested in such an option should confer with the appropriate faculty person in the Department of Education and Child Development.

NON-CREDIT SEMINAR

Supervision in Social Work

This seminar relates basic learning theory to learning in social work. Emphasis is placed on identifying learning patterns of the student or staff member, the appropriate use of the supervisory method, and selection of educational experiences related to varying patterns. It is given on an audit basis for those with limited field instruction or supervisory experience. There is no fee for persons who are serving as field instructors for students in the practicum.

The Degree of Master of Law and Social Policy

The Law and Social Policy program is a new curriculum designed for students of social service. It offers a full year of instruction in basic legal processes and legal problems, with a special effort to relate legal perspectives to major problems in social work practice. The program makes no pretense of surveying all fields of law as one finds them in law school, nor does it try to teach legal doctrine or paralegal skills. The aims rather are to prepare social service professionals to analyze legal problems relevant to their work, to enable them to work productively and critically with lawyers, and to help them become effective agents for social change through law.

The program is open to students who are enrolled concurrently for the M.S.S. degree at Bryn Mawr. Such students may begin the sequence of law courses in their second year and will continue in full-time study for a third year, during which they will complete all requirements for the M.S.S. and the M.L.S.P. Both degrees will be conferred at the end of the third year.

In addition, beginning in 1977-78, persons who already hold the M.S.S. or its equivalent will be able to enroll for the entire program of law courses in a single year of full-time study. They will receive the M.L.S.P. degree at the end of that year.

The courses in this program are also available on an individual basis to students in the regular M.S.S. program, students in the Ph.D. program, holders of the M.S.S. or its equivalent, and other interested persons. Students who are enrolled for the M.S.S. degree may count up to four of these courses as electives. However, classes will be kept small, and first priority for enrollment will go to students who choose the program as a whole.

Part-time study in this program may be allowed under special circumstances.

The curriculum has been carefully planned to provide a thorough grounding in legal methods, a balanced treatment of the entire legal system, and an integration of the legal perspective with the problems of social service and social policy. The courses to be offered are as follows:

Foundation Courses:

*Judicial Process
*Legislative and Administrative Processes
*Legal Research and Reform

Seminars:

*The Adjudicatory Mode of Dispute Resolution
*Equality and the Law
The Right of Individual Self-Determination
Law and Social Policy (a course with varying themes, for 1977-78 the topic will be Income Maintenance)
Practice Skills: Advocacy and Negotiation

Practicum

Courses marked with an asterisk will be offered in 1976-77; thereafter all courses will be offered each academic year. All are required for students who expect to receive the M.L.S.P. degree.

Candidates for this new degree will be strongly urged to take the three foundation courses in the same semester. These courses are designed to give an intensive orientation in basic skills of legal analysis as well as an introduction to the legal problems dealt with in later courses. The seminars will provide varied settings for the integration of law and social service concerns. Some will concentrate on policy analysis and reform, others will emphasize personal interactions with lawyers and social welfare clients. All of them, it is hoped, will offer insights into substantive rights and normative judgments in areas of urgent social problems.

Every effort will be made to design field instruction in settings where legal and social service interests converge. Individual placements will depend on particular interests and backgrounds.

The Law and Social Policy program is an entirely new type of program with unique possibilities. It differs from a number of joint-degree programs with law schools in that it does not require students to complete a conventional J.D. program alongside course work in another professional school. The concepts and materials of legal study have here been entirely reorganized for the benefit of professionals who do not intend to become practicing members of the bar. While the program has been planned and will be staffed by lawyers, a significant effort has been made to create new courses which analyze law as part of a larger social process and which draw on social science and normative methods to supplement legal analysis.

As the program grows, these goals may lead to the sponsoring of special summer institutes devoted to specific issues in law and social policy.

The Degree of Doctor of Philosophy

The curriculum for the Ph.D. provides a program of study from which a person may enter one of many careers, depending upon the changing needs and opportunities in social welfare and the interests and capabilities of the individual. Preparation for research and teaching are central to the goals of the program. Development of a variety of research competencies is encouraged; preparation for teaching in all areas of the social work curriculum, graduate and undergraduate, is also provided. The study of social work practice emphasizes theoretical work. Social policy development and analysis is given special attention.

The Ph.D. program in social work and social research prepares the student for understanding the nature and interdependence of individual and societal needs, and developing and promoting means by which these needs can be met most fully. Successful completion of the Ph.D. degree presumes demonstration of the scholarly pursuit of knowledge characterized by abstract logical thinking, critical evaluation, ability to reach new integration, and capacity to disseminate appropriately what one knows.

The candidate for the Ph.D. degree should have ability of a high order, intellectual curiosity, critical judgment, independence, a broad general education, and a Master's degree, usually in social work. Some experience in social welfare is desirable.

The program is planned to broaden the student's knowledge of social welfare in general and, through intensive study and research, to deepen his or her knowledge in one field in particular. The curriculum includes the following areas:

Social Work and Social Welfare: Past and Present

Social and Behavioral Sciences

Social Research

Social Work Practice: Theories, Research, and Issues

    1. Societal Focus

    2. Community/Institutional Focus

    3. Individual/Family/Group Focus

A student's course of study and Preliminary Examination are organized around a Major Area. The Major Area may be either Social Work and Social Welfare: Past and Present, or Social and Behavioral Sciences.

Minimum requirements include four courses in the Major Area, and two courses in each of the other areas. In Social Work and Social Welfare at least one course shall be taken in the Social Policy area and one in the History area. In Social Work Practice the two required courses must be taken in the same practice area. In the Social and Behavioral Sciences at least one course should be taken in the Social area and one in the Behavioral area.

In general, a minimum of twelve semester seminars plus two courses focusing on the dissertation is completed in preparation for the Ph.D. degree. Beyond the required seminars, doctoral students may elect courses in this School, The Graduate School of Arts and Sciences at Bryn Mawr, or The Graduate School of Arts and Sciences at the University of Pennsylvania under the Reciprocal Plan.

The requirements for the Ph.D. degree in The Graduate School of Social Work and Social Research are listed below.

1. An acceptable baccalaureate degree and undergraduate preparation satisfactory to the School.

2. In general, a Master's degree from an accredited school of social work or social welfare and preparation satisfactory to the School. Exceptions may be made for a student who has completed a Master's degree and satisfactory preparation in an allied field and presents significant experience in social work or social welfare or for a student in the M.S.S. program whose competence and qualifications as demonstrated in performance in this program promise that he or she can meet the demands of the Ph.D. program without first completing the M.S.S. degree.

3. Completion of a minimum of one academic year in full-time residence in The Graduate School of Social Work and Social Research. The residence requirement is met by two consecutive semesters of study from September through May; three or four courses are to be taken in each of these semesters.

4.   Satisfactory completion of a course of study consisting of a minimum of twelve semester courses or seminars, including both those which are required and those which are elective. In addition, two tutorials in supervised work on the dissertation are required.

5.   A reading knowledge of a modern foreign language tested by a written examination. In certain circumstances students whose native language is not English may offer English as a foreign language.

6.   The acceptance of the student into candidacy for the Ph.D. degree. Application for candidacy may be made only after successful completion of the residence requirement and the foreign language requirement.

7.   Satisfactory completion of the Preliminary Examination consisting of written examinations in four areas and an oral examination by the candidate's Supervising Committee. The examinations are intended to test the candidate's general knowledge in his or her areas and fields rather than familiarity with particular courses. They are organized around the student's Major Area and based on a reading list to be developed by the student and the supervising committee. One of the written examinations may be a take-home examination arranged between the student and the supervising committee. Preliminary Examinations are scheduled in October, mid-January and late March.

8.   The preparation of a dissertation judged to be worthy of publication. The dissertation must represent independent investigation and writing and must contain new material, results, or interpretations.

9.   A satisfactory Final Oral Examination in the special area in which the dissertation has been written.

10.   The publication of the dissertation in whole or in part. Microfilming is accepted as a method of publication.

Graduate Program for the Master of Social Service

Candidates for the M.S.S. degree must complete a minimum of eighteen semester courses or seminars, including a practicum. Each student's program of study consists of a combination of required and elective courses.

The basic first-year program is similar for all students except that the student selects either Social Casework or Community Social Work as his or her principal focus in social work practice. The first-year required courses are:

Social Casework *or* Community Social Work (two semesters)

Field Instruction—coordinated with one of the above (two semesters)

Introduction to Research and Statistics and a second required research course

Personality Theory *or* Normal Growth and Behavior

Social Theory and Social Work

Social Welfare Policy and Services: Historical Perspectives, *or* Social Welfare Policy and Services: Social Policy Analysis

In addition, the student is expected to select one elective during the first year. Thus, the usual first-year program is composed of ten semester courses.

It is possible for students to waive by way of written examination during the first week of the fall semester any required course with the exception of the practicum and practice seminars. It is understood that in the event of a waiver the student must select another course in the same area as that of the course waived.

The courses required in the second year are determined by the student's area of concentration in social work practice. The second-year options are: Community Organizing, Policy Research and Development, Program Planning and Administration, Clinical Social Work, or Social Service Management. Field Instruction is coordinated with one of these choices. Normally, the first-year preparation for Community Organizing, Policy Research and Development, and Program Planning and Administration is Community Social Work; the preparation for Clinical Social Work or Social Service Management is Social Casework. In addition, the student is expected to enroll in four electives, two each semester. A Master's Paper in an area of social work or social welfare may be undertaken for credit as one elective. Thus, the usual second-year program is comprised of eight semester courses or seven semester courses plus

25

a Master's Paper. Students in Clinical Social Work are required to take: Personality Theory, Normal Growth and Behavior, and Psychopathology.

M.S.S. degree students are required to take at least one course designated as particularly relevant to minority concerns. Courses which meet this requirement vary from semester to semester and are designated prior to pre-registration by the Curriculum Committee Task Force on Incorporating Content on Minorities into the Curriculum. Examples of such courses include: Race, Poverty and Human Development; Social Work and Ethnic Minorities; and the Black Family Structure, the Black Community and Social Work.

REQUIRED COURSES

First Year of the MSS Program

The student selects either Social Casework or Community Social Work as his or her principal focus in social work practice. Other required first-year courses are Field Instruction I and II, Introduction to Research and Statistics and a second required research course, Personality Theory or Normal Growth and Behavior, Social Theory and Social Work, Social Welfare Policy and Services: Historical Perspectives or Social Welfare Policy and Services: Soci Policy Analysis.

Any student may petition for a waiver of a required course i favor of an elective. The petition is directed to the Dean afte consultation with the student's adviser and recommendation fro the instructor of the course to be waived. A student's record ar background of preparation are reviewed. In addition, success completion of an examination in the area is required.

Community Social Work I

Community Social Work is based on the assumption that man crucial human problems, such as poverty, racism, and the oppre sion of groups because of age, class, and sex, derive largely from th structure of institutions, communities, and from the larger socia economic order. Consequently, philosophies and strategies f change at the institutional, community, and societal level have be developed. The aim of this course is to introduce students to a bro range of community social work philosophies and strategies, and assist each student in clarifying his or her own approach. Speci emphasis is placed on increasing skills in the analysis of co munities, organizations, and social policies and on increasing skil in deriving strategies from such analyses.

26

Community Social Work II

Emphasis of the seminar is on increasing practical skills and understanding of three types of community social work: Community Organizing, Program Planning and Administration, and Policy Research and Development. In introducing students to each type of community practice, consideration is given to value issues, techniques of problem solving, selection of strategies, and to the roles and tasks of the community social worker.

Social Casework I

The function of social casework in social work as related to the problems of individuals and primary groups is considered. Theory and application of the technical processes of psychosocial study, diagnosis and casework services are examined. Attention is given to understanding the person and the dynamic relationship with his or her social-cultural environment and to the conflicts and issues in social work practice.

Social Casework II

Understanding the basic processes applied to casework practice in varying age groups, areas of problem and agency settings is deepened. Increasing use is made of students' case materials. The seminar studies the relationships among purpose, skill, social resources, social systems and human needs.

Field Instruction I and II

A practicum in basic social work principles and concepts in a field setting is provided. Field instructors carry responsibility for facilitating students' learning in relation to all areas of the curriculum. Field Instruction I and II are taken collaterally with Social Casework I and II or Community Social Work I and II.

Personality Theory

Fundamental ideas in personality theory are presented which are considered to be especially pertinent to the various practices of social workers. Presentation leans heavily upon psychoanalytic theory, but students are encouraged to study in several theories of personality of their own choosing. Emphasis is upon general principles connected with the determination of the shape and content of an individual's personal-social functioning.

Normal Growth and Behavior

This seminar considers major biological, psychological, social, and cultural determinants of normal human growth and behavior

27

throughout the life cycle. Cross-cultural perspectives are emphasized. Stress is placed on the individual's continuing adaptation to change within himself or herself and in the world. Discussion includes optimal life experiences which promote healthy growth.

Social Theory and Social Work

Starting with a general consideration of theory and its relevance to social practice, this seminar provides a working acquaintance with major contemporary sociological models which have special bearing upon social work. The applicability of these models to the analyses of family, community, social deviance, power, and social conflict is also examined.

Social Welfare Policy and Services: Historical Perspectives

The organization and growth of social welfare and social work as major social institutions are examined from historical and philosophical viewpoints. The evolution of social welfare attitudes and services in Great Britain and the United States is studied with attention given to the philosophical systems within which developments have taken place. Particular attention is given to the establishment of the current social welfare system in the United States and proposals to reform or change it. The role of social work within that system is described, and its future role discussed.

Social Welfare Policy and Services: Social Policy Analysis

This course begins with a discussion of some of the leading theoretical statements on contemporary social policy and social services, then moves to a case study approach in different policy areas. Child care and health care services receive special emphases.

SOCIAL RESEARCH AND STATISTICS AREA

Introduction to Research and Statistics and a second research course are required of all students. If students pass the written waiver examination, they may waive the course, Introduction to Research and Statistics, and select an alternate course. Additional offerings are intended to support specialized interests and are coordinated with practice areas of the curriculum.

Introduction to Social Research and Statistics

This seminar is designed to provide the student with a range of basic concepts, decisions, and techniques involved in the conduct of social research. Emphasis is placed upon the development of research design relevant to social work practice. Special attention is given to elementary statistical methods and procedures for data collection, data analysis, and reporting of findings.

Clinical Research

This seminar focuses on intensive research as an adjunct to clinical treatment in social casework, mental health, and such other fields as probation and parole. Bodies of technique, such as the case study, use of personal documents, participant observation, and content analysis of interviews are considered. Current clinical research in social work is reviewed and attention is also given to professional and ethical issues.

Evaluative Research

Various modes of evaluation—process, goal achievement, impact—are viewed in the context of public and agency programming. Related matters, such as responses to requests for proposals, design of evaluation, administration of evaluative components as well as the relationship of evaluation to budgeting, cost/benefit analysis, policy formation, and information system development are considered.

Institutional and Community Research

Bodies of technique for analyzing larger social units, such as organizations, communities, urban areas, are stressed. The relationship of this mode of analysis to policy formation, social planning, and the legislative process is reviewed. Utilization of existing data series as well as gathering primary data is a keynote.

Statistics and Computing

The practical application of statistical methods to answer research questions is the central focus of this seminar. Computing is taught as a body of skills and as a means of overcoming computational hurdles. Use of SPSS is taught.

Second Year of the MSS Program

The second-year options are Community Organizing, Policy Research and Development, Program Planning and Administration, Clinical Social Work, and Social Service Management. Field Instruction III and IV are coordinated with these choices.

Normally, the first-year preparation for Community Organizing, Policy Research and Development, and Program Planning and Administration is Community Social Work; for Clinical Social Work or Social Service Management the preparation is Social Casework.

Clinical Social Work (two semesters)

Throughout the two semesters students are expected to develop ever deepening knowledge and skill in clinical social work practice. This includes differential psycho-social diagnosis and methods of intervention, e.g., individual, family and group treatment; the systems approach; and crisis intervention as practiced in a variety of settings. In addition, there is critical analysis of various theories of practice and theoretical positions and the interventions arising from these. Current issues in clinical social work and their relationships to issues in social welfare are explored. The particular issues examined are determined, in part, by the interests of the members of the seminar.

Social Service Management (two semesters)

Social Service Management involves the marshalling of social policy concerns, diagnostic and treatment skills, and knowledge of human behavior to provide appropriate social services and bring about organizational change within social institutions. Social Service Management builds upon direct service experience and prepares students to plan with other persons to provide services by personnel other than the Master's degree social worker, to train and supervise the variety of persons providing direct service, to provide staff development and in-service training, to provide consultation and education, to work with community resources around coordination of existing services as well as toward developing new resources, to participate in the team delivery of social services, and to monitor and evaluate the quality of those services. While a student might carry a case or two in direct service, the purpose would be directed toward the larger goal of better understanding and thereby improving service delivery and accountability to clients rather than limited to the narrower goal of improving direct service skills.

Community Organizing (two semesters)

The focus of this two-semester seminar is on direct work as an organizer with people experiencing injustices on a neighborhood, institutional, community, or city-wide level. Specific problems and opportunities offered by organizing among blacks, women, welfare recipients, white working people, the aging, and human service workers, are explored in depth. Three types of organizing (community development, social action, and social movement organizing) are critically examined. Emphasis throughout the year is placed on clarifying the values of the organizer and on increasing practical skills in direct work with people organizing for social change.

Policy Research and Development (two semesters)

During the two semesters significant literature from a combination of academic disciplines is examined for the purpose of providing students with understanding and analytic skills in the following areas: policy definition, specifically in social welfare issues; an understanding of the policy-making process and the identification of key elements in policy formulation; the construction of analytic frameworks for policy analysis and policy research; an examination of the processes of policy implementation; identification of the administrative issues implicit in policy formulation and implementation; examination of the issues and techniques for policy research and evaluation; and the formulation of research designs for the analysis of policy development, implementation, and evaluation in specific social problem areas. The course is conducted in seminar style, with shared faculty-student responsibility for the learning process.

Program Planning and Administration (two semesters)

This seminar engages theories and concepts of organizations, administration and management, decision-making, program planning and community structures. The basic objective is development of abilities in administering service programs, establishing a concrete planning-administrative process, mobilizing community resources, developing proposals and funding, evaluating agency impact, coordinating human services, and establishing specific policies and procedures within the human service agency.

Field Instruction III and IV

A practicum is taken collaterally with Clinical Social Work, Social Service Management, Community Organizing, Policy Research and Development, and Program Planning and Administration. For all second-year students the practicum consists of three days per week for each of the two semesters. Students in the Community area may elect two days per week in the field but will be required to carry an additional course.

ELECTIVES

Administration in Human Services

This seminar is concerned with the structure, operation, and change of human service agencies. Subjects discussed include: varieties and uses of organizational structure; policy formulation; decision-making; organizational change; management functions; the role of the staff in administration; principles of personnel management, including Affirmative Action programs; social workers' unions; and origins, flows and uses of resources and information.

Adolescence, Juvenile Delinquency and Intervention

The focus of this seminar is on the normal aspects of adolescence in its physical, psychological, and social dimensions within the climate of current living. Special consideration is given to juvenile delinquency: theories; the juvenile justice system; and goals, strategies, and methods of social work intervention.

American City in the Twentieth Century

This course deals primarily with social transformations in the cities under the impact of rapid urbanization. It also considers political, aesthetic, and cultural changes in American cities. (Offered in conjunction with the inter-departmental program, The Growth and Structure of Cities.)

Black Family Structure, the Black Community, and Social Work

The black family is examined in terms of its own history and family interaction, not as a deviation from a norm. The course examines the history of the black family, family interaction on different socio-economic levels, and some aspects of the black community.

Change and Resistance to Change in Social Work

This course examines social work in general as the expression of liberalism and the consequent problems that attend it. The welfare state, modes of treatment, professionalism, and social change perspectives in the light of a liberal-radical differentiation are analyzed. Some alternate expressions of social work are developed. Students are expected to participate in the development and management of the seminar within the constraints of the topic.

Community Mental Health

This seminar emphasizes the nature of mental health services and the concepts of comprehensiveness, prevention, community participation and continuity of care. Professional opportunities available in community mental health and skills and knowledge most necessary for today's mental health practitioner are considered. The work of the Community Mental Health Center is the main focus of the seminar. Students design a comprehensive Community Mental Health Center and discuss the elements involved.

Comparative Personality Theory

This seminar systematically examines and compares some of the major personality theories as well as newer theories. There is an attempt to apply the theories critically to a range of social work situations and concerns, and evaluate their use to social workers.

Criminal Justice System: Current Issues and Practices in Adult Corrections—Prison, Parole, and Probation

Issues and diverse treatment practices in the delivery of human services within adult probation, parole, institutions, and ancillary agencies are examined against society's dual aims of rehabilitation and self-protection. The current and potential roles of social work in these areas of the criminal justice system are evaluated. Visits to selected institutions and agencies in this field, for direct exposure to such settings and discussions with their staffs, may be planned.

Criminal Justice System: Issues and Practices in Juvenile Delinquency—Intervention in the Legal System

Issues and practices in the delivery of human services to the juvenile and his family, the community, and the justice system and ancillary agencies are examined in the areas of prevention and treatment of delinquency. Developing roles for social work in keeping pace with emerging patterns in prevention, programs, and treatment practices, including de-institutionalization, are studied. Visits to selected institutions and agencies in this field, for direct exposure to such settings and discussion with their staffs, may be planned.

Family Therapy

The purpose of this seminar is to provide a framework within which students can understand the field of family therapy. The focus is on family systems and the changes which can be made within these systems. Healthy and maladaptive family interaction patterns from the current and intergenerational view are examined, as are problem areas and basic principles. Various schools of thought on working with couples and families are considered. Attention is given to areas of student interest.

Gerontology: Current Policies and Issues

Focused readings and discussions by students alternate with guest lectures by specialists in gerontology. Policies and issues in legislation, health, mental health, income maintenance, social service programs, research, housing, and nursing home care are considered. (Not offered in 1976-77.)

Gerontology: Theory and Research

The origins and boundaries of gerontology are examined. Roles and role-expectations of the elderly in different cultures are compared. The demographic characteristics of the elderly and the physiological and psychological changes associated with aging are identified. Changes in the nature of human productivity in later life and the potential of the elderly as a political bloc are considered. Readings and discussion focus on findings and problems of research in each area.

Group Process

This seminar undertakes to study characteristics of the group process and content of understanding individual and group behavior. Typical problems include basic issues in working with groups; interaction patterns; practical applications of group theory; effective ways of working with committees, citizen-community groups, therapy groups, agency personnel, boards, clients; tools and techniques in working with groups; moving toward problem-solving and change through groups.

Group Therapy

This seminar is designed to give the student a foundation in the field of group psychotherapy. It is structured so that the student participates in group interaction similar to that occurring in therapy groups and correlates this experience with group theory. Videotapes of clinical groups are available as is video playback of a seminar meeting.

Introduction to Health and Health Care

The purpose of this course is to provide basic understanding of normal human body development and common physical disorders. A brief overview of planning in preventive and remedial health care, as well as community systems of resources and how to use them effectively, will be included. More specifically, attention will be given to areas of information essential for understanding common acute and chronic diseases and health issues, and their associated social and psychic problems. The possible roles of the social worker as contributing agent for change will be examined. Specific content may include information re: normal body functions and changes, birth control and obstetrics, childhood diseases, common diseases (e.g., circulatory, gastrointestinal, venereal, arthritic, sensory, neurological); doctor, patient, and social worker relations; epidemiology; systems of health care delivery, as well as when and how to use them; and economics and medical care.

Introduction to Human Sexuality

This course will start with a survey of materials from each of five categories: bio-physical; psycho-emotional; socio-cultural; politico-legal; and ethical, moral and religious. A more intensive examination will then be made of the bio-physiological and the psycho-emotional aspects of human sexuality. Focus will be placed on a variety of topics bearing on social work practice. These include: homosexuality, auto-eroticism, sex and the aging, sex and the mentally retarded and the physically handicapped, family planning and birth control, sex education, and sex therapy and counselling.

Issues in Child Welfare

Current issues and questions in the field of child welfare and their meaning for practitioners are considered. Content is drawn from areas such as child abuse and neglect (both institutional and parental), child care, health, adoptions, placement, and advocacy. Attention is paid to programs currently existing, their rationale and impact, and the gaps that persist.

Law as an Instrument of Social Change

This course uses cases, statutes, and other materials to examine the successes and failures of the legal system, particularly the judicial branch, in fashioning new rights and remedies for persons heretofore disadvantaged in American society. The concepts of due process of law and equal protection of the law are given particular emphasis as are the implications of these developments for social workers and their relationships with clients and client groups. It is also a goal of this course to expand the student's knowledge of the legal system under which Americans live--its strengths, its weaknesses, and how as a citizen one can help make it more effective.

Marriage Counseling

This seminar examines theories of marital interaction, theories of therapy, and value systems of the marital counselor. Specific topics are chosen by participants who carry responsibility for presentation of materials and class discussion.

Master's Paper

A Master's Paper may be undertaken with the permission of two faculty persons who would serve as Readers, or as the result of a research project in a particular interest area with one instructor and a second Reader. Whether students are enrolled in such research projects or whether students are developing a Master's Paper independently with first and second Readers, one course credit will be given after satisfactory completion of the Master's Paper.

The Ombudsman and Other Advocacy Systems

Institutional arrangements for communication, redress, and advocacy for citizens in their dealings with various levels of government are reviewed. Emphasis is given to the development and application of a classification scheme for such organizations and to the consideration of such models as the classical ombudsman and the decentralized agency. Comparative material is used from various American schemes and such foreign experience as that in Scandinavia, Great Britain and New Zealand.

Organizations and Social Welfare

Major theoretical developments in the field of formal organizations are considered with special emphasis on their application to social welfare, including such matters as the structure and processes of public welfare bureaucracies, organizations as instruments of policy, relationships with professions and the role of informal organization.

Problems and Treatment of Alcoholism and Drug Abuse

Issues inherent in alcohol and drugs and their abuse are examined. Focus includes epidemiology, myths, causation theories, effects of abuse, legislative considerations and enforcement, changing treatment approaches and their effectiveness, prevention and public education, and the growing role of social work in this field. Treatment and planning agencies may be visited for observation and staff discussion.

Psychopathology

The symptomatic pictures seen in adults in the major clinical diagnoses of the psychoses, psychosomatic disorders, character disorders, addictions and the neuroses are covered. Genetic, dynamic, and structural aspects of these illnesses are examined with discussion of implications for prevention and treatment.

Race, Poverty, and Human Development

The effect of varying socio-economic and racial environments on human development is examined in all areas, physical, emotional, cognitive, and social. The definition and effect of poverty and racism is specifically explored in relation to the larger socio-economic system. The course has a dual orientation in which theoretical material is applied to actual situations.

Selected Concepts in Personality Theory

This seminar is built upon concepts that are thought to be fundamental to clinical practice and social action at the same time. Critical analysis is made of recent interpretations of such concepts developed by the instructor. Related writings from a variety of authors in personality theory are also studied.

Social Work and Ethnic Minorities

This course considers some of the special social welfare problems of blacks, Puerto Ricans, Chicanos and other Spanish-speaking groups, Asian-Americans, native Americans, Appalachian whites, and other ethnic minorities in American society. The course undertakes to help students cope realistically with these problems and with ethnic differences. Special attention is given to increasing awareness and understanding of the underlying causes of prejudice and stereotyping, and to developing ways of dealing with these problems.

Staff Supervision in Social Service

This seminar is designed for those Master's students who will be expected to assume supervisory and/or staff development responsibilities. The seminar takes its direction from the function of supervision which is seen as primarily twofold: 1) the provision of more effective delivery of service to the consumer; and 2) the education and professional development of staff.

Treatment of Children in Families

An overview of treatment of children from a range of social and economic backgrounds. The seminar examines approaches to the understanding and modification of problems by intervention through the family. Emphasis is placed on careful examination of interactional patterns rather than systematic study of the total treatment process. The development of theory very closely related to the happenings in the family is attempted. Video tapes are used, along with readings and other sources of information.

Urban Economics

The purpose of the course is to introduce the student to the tools of economic analysis that apply to urban problems and the techniques of benefit-cost analysis as applied to social welfare programs. (Not offered 1976-77.)

Women and Social Issues

This course explores various aspects of the situation of women in contemporary American society. Social policies with particular relevance for women are examined, and women are discussed as both consumers and providers of social services. Among the specific areas covered in the course are AFDC and other income maintenance strategies, the women's health movement, family planning policies, child care and other policies affecting working women. Particular attention is paid in this course to the situation of minority women.

Students may also elect courses from the new program in Law and Social Policy. See course descriptions on pages 44-47.

PRACTICUM

The practicum is an integral part of the curriculum for the Master of Social Service degree. A placement is arranged for each student: in both semesters of the first year in Social Casework and in Community Social Work; in the second year in Clinical Social Work, Social Service Management, Community Organizing, Policy Research and Development, and Program Planning and Administration. The purpose of the practicum is to provide the opportunity for the student to apply theory in order to deepen knowledge and develop skill in its use. Students' assignments are goal-oriented and are planned to give content, sequence, and progression in learning. Practicum experience in an agency or in a field laboratory runs concurrently with the practice seminar in order to maximize opportunity for the student to integrate the content of the two. Each student's practicum is usually arranged in a different setting for each year of the program. Most practicums are in the five-county Philadelphia metropolitan area. Placements are made regularly, however, in Harrisburg, in the State of Delaware, and in the national capital area. The practicum for M.S.S. students has been provided in field placements concerned with the following topics, among others:

Aging
Child welfare
Community mental health
Consumer organizations
Corrections
Day care
Drug and alcohol dependency and abuse
Family services
Health services
Housing
Intergroup relations
Legal services
Legislative offices
Maternal and child health
Mental retardation
Neighborhood organization
Physical rehabilitation
Psychiatric services
Public assistance
Public education
Public health
Public welfare administration
School social work
Social planning
Social welfare research
Teaching—undergraduate programs
Women's issues
Youth services

FIELD INSTRUCTION SETTINGS

Students were placed during 1975-76 in the following agencies and organizations:

Albert Einstein Medical Center, Community Mental Health/Mental Retardation Center

Albert Einstein Medical Center, Daroff Division

American Foundation, Institute of Corrections

American Oncologic Hospital

Bryn Mawr Youth Psychotherapy Center

Bucks County Department of Adult Services

Central Montgomery Mental Health/Mental Retardation Center

Child Care Service of Delaware County
    Media Office
    Eastern Community Office, Upper Darby

Child Study Institute of Bryn Mawr College

Children's Aid Society of Pennsylvania

CHOICE (Concern for Health Options: Information, Care and Education)

CO-MHAR (Community Organization for Mental Health and Mental Retardation)

Community College of Philadelphia, Division of Social and Behavioral Sciences and Human Service Careers

Community Life Services, Inc., of Delaware County

Correlative Therapy Educational Center

Crozer-Chester Medical Center, Community Mental Health/Mental Retardation Clinic

Delaware Council to Reduce Crime, Wilmington, Delaware

Delaware County Aging Service, Media

Delaware County Juvenile Court, Probation Department, Media

Delaware County Mental Health/Mental Retardation Board, Media

Delaware Technical and Community College, Department of Human Service Technology, Wilmington, Delaware

Family Court of Delaware, New Castle County, Wilmington, Delaware

Family Service of Philadelphia
  North District Office
  Northeast District Office

Family Service, Mental Health Centers of Chester County

Family Service of Montgomery County, Plymouth Meeting

Germantown Settlement House

Girls' Clubs of Philadelphia

Hahnemann Medical College and Hospital
  Community Mental Health/Mental Retardation Services
  Child Clinic
  Department of Social Work Services, Maternal and Child
    Health Unit
  Poplar Guidance and Counseling Center

Housing Association of Delaware Valley

Irving Schwartz Institute for Children and Youth

Jewish Family Service of Philadelphia

Law, Education, and Participation (LEAP), Temple University,
  School of Law

Legal Aid of Delaware County, Chester

Life Guidance Services, Inc., Broomall

Lower Merion Community Mental Health and Mental Retardation
  Center, Ardmore

Maryland State Government: Community Corrections Task Force

Mental Health Association of Southeastern Pennsylvania

Montgomery County Board of Public Assistance, Norristown

Montgomery County Mental Health/Mental Retardation
  Drug and Alcohol Program
  Mental Retardation Department

Montgomery County Office on Older Adults, Norristown

Moss Rehabilitation Hospital

Northwest Interfaith Movement

Northwest Tenants' Organization, Inc.

Olde Kensington Redevelopment Corporation, Senior Wheels East

Commonwealth of Pennsylvania
  Commission for Women
  Department of Public Welfare, Deputy Secretary for Social
    Services, Harrisburg
  Eastern Pennsylvania Psychiatric Institute, Adult Unit

Governor's Office, Office of Human Resources, Child Development Committee

Haverford State Hospital

Health Advocacy Program

Norristown State Hospital

Office of the Governor, Harrisburg

State Representative, Thomas J. Stapleton, Jr.

Pennsylvania Committee for Criminal Justice Standards and Goals, Harrisburg

Pennsylvania Hospital
Community Mental Health and Mental Retardation Center
Social Service Department

Pennsylvania Prison Society

City of Philadelphia
Councilman Beatrice Chernock
Department of Public Health, Office of Mental Health and Mental Retardation

Philadelphia Child Guidance Clinic, Institute of Family Counseling

Philadelphia Geriatric Center

Philadelphia Party

Philadelphia Psychiatric Center
Social Service Department
Community Mental Health, Adult Day Treatment Unit

Philadelphia Welfare Rights Organization

Saint Christopher's Hospital for Children, Psychiatric Clinic

Saint Phillips Get Set Program of Philadelphia Psychiatric Center and Philadelphia Board of Education

School District of Philadelphia

Sojourner Foundation

Thomas Jefferson University Medical Center, Community Mental Health/Mental Retardation Center

United Communities of South Philadelphia, Southwark House

United Farmworkers

United States Department of Health, Education, and Welfare
Public Health Service, Region III
Social and Rehabilitation Service, Region III
Office of the Regional Director, Region III

United States Congressman, Robert Edgar, Upper Darby

University City Science Center

Veterans Administration Hospital, Coatesville

SOCIAL WORK AND SOCIAL RESEARCH

munity Mental Health Consortium

patient Program

nst Rape

an Association

Graduate Program for the
Master of Law and Social Policy

The general goals of this new program and the requirements for the degree of Master of Law and Social Policy are described on pages 20-22. The courses described below are the required courses for the M.L.S.P. degree. They are also available as electives to students in the M.S.S. and Ph.D. programs, as well as to other qualified applicants.

Students who are working concurrently for the M.S.S. will normally begin this sequence in their second year, completing all requirements for both degrees in a third year of study. Persons who already hold the M.S.S. degree may take the entire program in one year. All eight courses will be offered in a single year during 1977-78 and thereafter.

Foundation Courses

Judicial Process

This is a study of how courts interpret, apply, and, in an important sense, make the law. It probes the judicial method of argument—mastery of which is sometimes called "thinking like a lawyer"—as it is used by judges and advocates. Students will learn how to read a court opinion and how to frame an argument in legal terms. Consideration will be given to variations on the method as it occurs in common law, statutory interpretation, and constitutional law. In each area judicial action will be analyzed not only in logical terms but also from behavioral and political perspectives. Such study poses the question of the competence of courts to deal with complex social problems, such as the enforcement of school desegregation orders or the supervision of public institutions.

Legislative and Administrative Processes

In contrast to the preceding course, this one will concentrate on the more consciously political, less formal and legalistic branches of the legal system: the legislative process with its broad scope for deliberation over the ends of public policy, and administrative bodies, whose role in modern society has increased enormously. This course will be built around a series of problems or case studies designed to illustrate the variety of influences on legislative and administrative action, influences in addition to the formal and legal restraints which are built into each process. Specific case studies will explore the varieties of legislative regulatory devices, delegation of authority and oversight, the scope of administrative discretion, and at least one complex problem involving the interaction of state and federal agencies, courts, and legislatures.

Legal Research and Reform

This course introduces students to the basic techniques of legal research and asks them to apply those techniques in formulating proposals for legal reform. Lectures and library exercises will be used to communicate essential research skills, including use of court opinions, statutes, regulations, legal scholarship, and the wealth of legal finding aids. Short individual research problems will then be assigned, and midway through the semester students will cooperate in a common research effort in a selected area of statutory activity, such as Freedom of Information laws. Working either individually or in small groups, students will prepare a research report on a particular part but will also become familiar with the whole of the overall effort. These reports will then be used as the basis for drafting model statutes or for proposing changes in existing laws.

Seminars

The Adjudicatory Mode of Dispute Resolution

This course will examine the trial process as a method of resolving disputes and will compare this process to such alternative forms as administrative hearings, arbitration, and informal tribunals. The effectiveness of these processes in a variety of contexts will be assessed—custody disputes, welfare hearings, criminal cases. A central purpose will be to define the procedures necessary for a fair hearing in these different settings. An attempt will be made to relate the structure of a case—its procedural context—to the justice of the outcome. In this connection rules of evidence will be discussed, the role of judge and jury, and the techniques of judicial enforcement.

Equality and the Law

Equality is central to the legal process as a public policy goal, as a constitutional value, and as the formal ideal of all adjudication. There is, however, an important tension between the material or substantive notions of equality found in policy planning and the more formalistic sense of equality developed in the judicial process. This conflict will be explored in depth in at least four areas: racial segregation, public education, poverty, and sex discrimination. An examination will be made of some of the landmark constitutional

45

cases which have led the law toward more substantive interpretations of equality. The seminar will also see how the abstractness of the standards and imperfections of legal enforcement with respect to the Constitution have shifted the conflict between substance and formalism more into the legislative arena. Recent sociological and economic literature on race, education, and poverty will also be discussed.

The Right of Individual Self-Determination

This course will explore the legal and social consequences of marking off a private sphere of action free from public control. At least two distinct traditions have encouraged this concern for individual rights: the classical liberal objections to state interference in autonomous social and economic areas, and more recent arguments for protecting the individual personality from encroachments by either the state or civil society. Both of these trends will be assessed in a variety of substantive areas: sexual privacy and abortion, the right to treatment, the right to refuse treatment, and family law. A search will be made for the legal substance behind these and other purported rights—in recent constitutional theory, in the state action doctrine extending the powers of the federal government, and in the procedural safeguards that have accompanied governmental power in its modern expansion. (To be offered 1977-78.)

Law and Social Policy: Income Maintenance

This course will look at the major cash programs—old-age insurance, unemployment insurance, and public assistance—as well as related "in-kind" assistance programs which together constitute public law of income maintenance. The social policies and values behind these programs will be discussed in the context of their historical development, their contemporary legislative and administrative support, and their judicial clarification in court challenges to welfare administration. The effect of judicial review on state compliance with federal law and on evolving standards of fair procedure will be examined in detail. In addition to its central importance for social service, this field of social policy also raises important issues of federal-state interaction, public administration, public finance, and fiscal policy—all of which need to be accounted for in planning a policy of income maintenance.

This is the first course to be offered under the general title of Law and Social Policy. Other topics may be examined as the program develops. (To be offered 1977-78.)

Practice Skills: Advocacy and Negotiation

This course will emphasize the informal techniques and interpersonal skills of successful practice in the border areas between law

46

and social service. A series of problems will be presented which encourage role-playing and critical analysis in various settings: client interviews, negotiating sessions, administrative hearings, formal testimony of experts in court. Themes will be selected from family law, mental health, corrections and rehabilitation, community action, and contacts with bureaucracy. The course will be taught by a team of lawyers and social workers, and the workshop format is designed to encourage students to see and sense the reactions of both professions to the same set of problems. Social work students will experience some of the conflicts of working alongside lawyers, but they will also discover the rich possibilities in successful collaboration. (To be offered 1977-78.)

PRACTICUM

The Law and Social Policy program continues the tradition of the School that classroom instruction should be supplemented by work in the field. Students in this program will be assigned placements that emphasize the interaction of law and social service. (To be offered 1977-78.)

Graduate Program for the Doctor of Philosophy

Consistent with the School's philosophy with respect to advanced study, the program is planned to broaden the student's knowledge of social welfare in general and, through intensive study and research, to deepen his or her knowledge in one area in particular. The curriculum includes seminars, tutorials, and independent study in the following areas:

Social Work and Social Welfare: Past and Present

Social and Behavioral Sciences

Social Research

Social Work Practice: Theories, Research and Issues
1. Societal Focus
2. Community/Institutional Focus
3. Individual/Family/Group Focus

A student's course of study, and Preliminary Examination, are organized around a Major Area. The Major Area may be *either* Social Work and Social Welfare: Past and Present, *or* Social and Behavioral Sciences.

Requirements include four courses in the Major Area, and two courses in each of the other areas. In Social Work and Social Welfare, at least one course shall be taken in the Social Policy area and one in the History area. In Social Work Practice, the two required courses must be taken in the same practice area. In the Social and Behavioral Sciences at least one course should be taken in the Social area and one in the Behavioral area.

When area requirements consist of specifically designated courses, a student may seek a waiver, by examination, of such a course. Such a waiver will not reduce the total number of courses required in the area nor the overall total of courses required for the degree, i.e., twelve semester courses plus two dissertation tutorials.

Beyond the required seminars doctoral students may elect courses in this School, The Graduate School of Arts and Sciences at Bryn Mawr, or The Graduate School of Arts and Sciences at the University of Pennsylvania under the Reciprocal Plan.

Social Work and Social Welfare: Past and Present

American Postwar Social Thought

This course is a careful examination of the books, chiefly outside of social work, which have been instrumental in the development of social and political movements since World War II. Selections range through philosophy, theology, psychiatry, economics, and sociology. They are works which have been widely read by the educated public and policy makers. Some of the authors represented in past terms are Reinhold Niebuhr, Robert Nisbet, John Dewey, Milton Friedman, Daniel Bell, David Riesman, J.K. Galbraith, and Victor Frankl. The list changes every time the course is offered.

Comparative Social Welfare: Issues of Distribution and Redistribution

This seminar considers issues of income distribution and redistribution in the United States and selected Western European countries. Utilizing a cross-cultural frame of reference and data from empirical studies, the seminar gives attention to both social policy concerns with respect to redistribution and as methodological problems. (Not offered 1976-77.)

Comparative Social Welfare: Social Service Programs

Social welfare and social security programs in various societies other than the United States are studied. Among those to be examined are the systems in Sweden and the United Kingdom. (Not offered 1976-77.)

The Contribution of Social Science to Social Policy and Practice

This seminar examines how policy-related social science is organized and financed in the United States, then questions usefulness of such research and strategies which might make such research more purposeful for social policy and social practice.

Introduction to English and American Social Welfare History and Thought

Social welfare is examined as an historical institution. The development of a succession of philosophical systems within which this institution evolved is considered, and the influence upon both philosophy and welfare of social and economic changes is studied. Stress is placed upon historical and contemporary literature, which is examined for the light it casts upon the field of study. Anglo-American experience until 1930 is emphasized in this course. (Not offered 1976-77.)

49

Introduction to Social Policy

Different concepts of social policy are examined with special attention to issues in a number of different fields, such as: income transfers, medical care, social services, manpower training, education and housing. An attempt at an overall assessment of social policy is made based on empirical studies in the United States and selected advanced industrial societies in Western Europe. Attention is given to problems of citizen participation, coordination, evaluation, and social change. The course concludes with an interpretation of the limits and the future of social policy. (Not offered 1976-77.)

Issues in Social Work Education

Selected issues in current social work education are examined in historical perspective. (Not offered 1976-77.)

New Deal, Fair Deal, New Frontier, and Great Society: American Social Welfare 1930-69

The past half-century is studied intensively as the seminal period for contemporary social welfare programs. The collapse of traditional relief measures before the onslaught of the Great Depression, the ameliorative and reform measures of the Roosevelt administrations, and efforts to expand and correct these and other programs in the ensuing twenty-five years are examined, all with a view to understanding the weight of the past upon the present, and to judge the directions in which further change is most likely. (Not offered 1976-77.)

Personality Issues in Social Policies and Programs

This seminar is concerned with personality and policy; the assumptions about personality functioning in social policies; the impact of public social policy on personality; the impact of personality factors on policies; personalities in policy-making positions; personality theories as origins for the development of social policy; and social equality and personality. (Not offered 1976-77.)

Policy Analysis of Specific Service Systems: Community Mental Health

This seminar examines the theoretical roots of the present community mental health system. Community mental health concepts of comprehensiveness, prevention, community participation, and continuity of care are analyzed in relation to policies governing the design and operation of Community Mental Health Centers. Students participate in the criticism and design of mental health service delivery policies.

Policy Analysis of Specific Service Systems: Health Care

This course deals with a range of issues in the delivery of health care services. Among the topics discussed are national health insurance, community mental health, the division of labor among health professionals, and movements of health consumers. (Not offered 1976-77.)

Social Policy and the Family

The main theme of this course is the relationship between the state and the family. Various social policies regulating family life are examined from a historical and contemporary perspective. Among the specific issues discussed are the recent rise of single-parent families, child care policies, juvenile justice policies, and current developments in marriage and divorce laws. (Not offered 1976-77.)

Social Policy and Social Services

This course begins with a consideration of leading theoretical statements on social policy by British and American writers. It proceeds to a more concrete discussion of dilemmas in the organization of human services. Among these are public sector vs. private sector, accountability of service professionals, and the emergent roles of service consumers.

Social and Behavioral Sciences

Comparative Personality Theories

Some of the more well known dynamics of personality theories are examined in relation to the development of the human personality. An attempt is made to understand the similarities and differences of the theories and to relate the theories to the development of the total person. (Not offered 1976-77.)

Freud's Psychoanalytic Theory

Examination is made of psychoanalysis as a personality theory. Special attention is paid to metapsychology in psychoanalytic theory and to psychoanalysis as social theory. Intensive analysis of basic writings by Freud and his collaborators forms the focus of the seminar.

Formal Organizations

This seminar considers structure and process in large-scale organizations. Starting from major theories of social organization, the course focuses upon those organizations which are planned to coordinate the efforts of large numbers of persons to accomplish specific goals. Leadership, organizational pathologies and the role of the individual are considered. (Not offered 1976-77.)

Group Theory

This seminar undertakes an investigation of group process characteristics. Individual and group behavior are studied, using significant group theorists, such as Homans, Lewin, Festinger, Goffman, Yalom, Blau, Kelman, and Bales. Theory will be related to the basic issues involved in research on interaction and leadership patterns in a variety of work-oriented and therapy groups. (Not offered 1976-77.)

Human Development in the First Third of Life

This course examines human development as a total system physically, socially, emotionally, and cognitively, from prenatal development through young adulthood. Major human development theorists, such as Erikson, Piaget, and others are reviewed. Implications for social policies that will contribute to maximum potential human development are explored. (Not offered 1976-77.)

Occupations and Professions

This course reviews classic and contemporary sociological approaches to the study of occupations and professions. The focus is on the dynamics of professionalization, the bureaucratization of professional work, professional/client relations, and related issues. Particular attention is paid to human service professions.

Psychoanalysis after Freud

Psychoanalytic writings from the 1930's to the present are studied. Emphasis varies with class selection among the array of theorists and directions that have developed in psychoanalytic theory.

Race and Ethnic Relations

This seminar critically examines the theoretical concepts of prejudice, institutional racism, and cultural racism. Concepts of ethnicity, and ethnic movements and relations are also reviewed. Problems of social policy, social services, and social work practice are then studied in the light of ethnic and race relations concepts.

Social and Cultural Aspects of Health, Illness and Treatment

Starting with the assumption that social and cultural influences shape definitions and expectations concerning health, illness, and treatment, this seminar identifies instances and implications of such influences. Coverage includes a range of sociocultural environments and methods of treatment, and pertinent literature from the fields of anthropology and sociology. (Not offered 1976-77.)

Social Change

This seminar engages in an active search for an adequate abstract model of social change. Special attention is directed to modern systems theory. Major social theories are examined for relevant contributions to an understanding of social change; contemporary patterns of change in society are documented; and limitations in attempts to guide change at different levels of social organization are noted. (Not offered 1976-77.)

Social Philosophy and the Problem of Ideology

The problem of ideology consists of clarifying the standpoint of the observer (or agent) who wishes to understand (or change) society. It forces us to ask what kind of value structure we impose on our social environment and what the consequences are for social theory and public policy planning. The course begins with a careful reading of two classic sources on the nature of ideology (Marx and Mannheim) and then turns to consider the positivistic challenge to ideological thinking posed by natural scientific method. Particular attention will be given to modern critiques of science and technology which find elements of relativism and ideology hidden behind the pretense of objectivity (Kuhn, members of the Frankfurt School). Finally, the problem of ideology in the area of public policy will be discussed, particularly as it affects the choice between legal and political methods of social control.

Women in Society

This course provides a cross-cultural examination of the position of women in society today. Components of social structure and cultural values which extend or constrain options open to women are identified. Special attention is given to the problems of specific groups of women, such as, the poor, the single parent, the professional woman. (Not offered 1976-77.)

Social Research

Data Analysis I

Data analysis is seen as one step in the research process. Statistical methods of analysis include descriptive and inferential statistics with major emphasis on partial and multiple correlation and regression, and analysis of variance and co-variance. Knowledge of the assumptions and conditions under which statistical methods are valid, and discrimination in the selection, application and interpretation of statistical tests is developed. Use of the computer in analysis is also taught.

Data Analysis II

Special attention is given to recent innovations, persistent problems and current issues in multivariate data analysis. Among the topics covered in this seminar are multiple factor analysis, step-wise regression analysis, path analysis, problems of handling cross-cultural data, and techniques for developing data to test social policy.

Formulation of Social Research

A seminar-workshop approach gives attention to the process of research development through various stages from idea to an operational project. Use of theory and use of methodology are included. Each student develops his or her own research idea throughout the course culminating in a research proposal. (Not offered 1976-77.)

Historical Methodology in Social Welfare

The use of historical research in social welfare is studied and applied. Selection of possible topics for study, uncovering of sources, methods of research are among the topics covered. The literature of historical methodology is examined and its lessons applied to social welfare. Development of skills in preparation and writing of research papers is stressed. (Not offered 1976-77.)

Participant Observation: Institutional Setting

This course introduces students to the basic techniques of participant observation through involvement in a group research project in an institutional setting. The class also reads and discusses major works in the participant observation tradition.

Research Methodology

In this seminar a study is made of contemporary methodological approaches to problems in social and behavioral research with application for social welfare. There is intensive coverage of survey research design, case study and clinical method, design of social experiments, and evaluation of social work programs.

Social Demography

Demographic characteristics of the United States and appropriate techniques of analysis are studied with principal attention to the components of demographic change and their implications for social welfare. Students present original analyses of trends in contemporary population characteristics and their distribution in the United States. (Not offered 1976-77.)

Urban Ethnography

This practicum, based in urban working-class neighborhoods, provides experience in participant observation, interviewing, taking life histories, and other techniques for the study of workplace and family life, incipient social movements, working women's issues, and the relation of neighborhoods to social policy change.

Social Work Practice: Theories, Research, and Issues

SOCIETAL FOCUS

Intervention in Governmental Processes

This course cuts across the several levels of American Government in identifying those points in the legislative process and the implementation of government programs where influence by professionals or client and citizen groups may be applied. Mechanisms, organizational vehicles, and strategies for exerting such influence are inventoried. (Not offered 1976-77.)

Program Development

This seminar examines the process of developing programs in response to federal and state legislation, regulations, and guidelines. Students participate in developing a framework for the comparative analysis of practice in this process.

Social Policy Fiscal Planning

This seminar highlights aspects of economic analysis related to the growing role of governments in the economy. Special emphasis is given to the area of social welfare. Factors affecting economic development of urban areas, the fiscal problems of subnational governments, prospects for the development of impoverished areas, and current issues of urban fiscal planning are considered. Attention is also given to economic aspects of the development of social policy, especially movement towards cost-benefit analysis.

COMMUNITY/INSTITUTIONAL FOCUS

Community Organization and Community Development

This seminar focuses on several distinct philosophies and theories of community organization in the advanced industrial nations, and of community development in developing nations. Issues of social change vs. social service, participation vs. cooptation, ideology and values, and the role of the community worker are examined in the light of current theory and research. The experiences of international social agencies in community development are also explored. (Not offered 1967-77.)

Program and Agency Evaluation

This seminar focuses on appropriate processes and systems for evaluating human service organizations and their individual programs. Various approaches to evaluating effectiveness and efficiency are carefully examined. Practical problems of implementation are discussed. Students create an evaluation design, have it criticized, and criticize other designs. Skills in evaluative research are sharpened.

Program Development and Agency Administration

This seminar engages a series of alternative theories and concepts of organizations, administration, decision-making, program planning and community structures. Theoretical material is related to specific administrative issues, such as establishing a concrete planning process, establishing policies and procedures, evaluating agency efficiency and impact, and mobilizing community resources. (Not offered 1976-77.)

Social Movements

This seminar examines major theories of social movements with an emphasis on movements for social and economic change in the advanced industrial nations. Such theories are then applied to problems of social work practice and social policy. Specific emphasis is given to research on the role of the organizer within social movements.

INDIVIDUAL/FAMILY/GROUP FOCUS

Critical Appraisal of Strategies of Intervention

The essence of this seminar is the linking of practice research to practice. While the emphasis is on effectiveness of intervention strategies, other related areas are also examined, such as characteristics of the problem population and those of the helpers.

Practice in Clinical Social Work: Critical Analysis

A broad range of interventive strategies on the individual and small group level is studied. Emphasis is placed upon comparative

56

examination of many perspectives. Choice of particular strategies is worked out with the class. (Not offered 1976-77.)

Problem Definition, Practices, Strategies and Related Issues

This seminar focuses on social casework (individual, group, and family treatment) in the perspective of social problems, strategies, issues of practice, education, and professional leadership. These areas are examined in the light of history of clinical social work and the developing trends within the context of societal factors. (Not offered 1976-77.)

Specific Intervention Strategies: Family Therapies

This seminar analyzes various approaches in family therapy in relation to theory, research, population needs, and issues of training.

Law and Social Policy

Doctoral students may also enroll in courses from the new program in Law and Social Policy. See course descriptions on pages 44-47.

Other Courses

Courses in the Bryn Mawr Graduate School of Arts and Sciences may be elected as part of the student's program with the permission of the Dean of The Graduate School of Social Work and Social Research and the instructor of the course to be taken.

Graduate courses in The Graduate School of Arts and Sciences of the University of Pennsylvania are also available for doctoral students of Bryn Mawr College. For information regarding the reciprocal arrangement with the University, see the section under Admissions (page 12).

Fees

Application: $20 (non-refundable).

Tuition

Full-time Students: $3,600 a year (1976-77).*

Part-time Students: $600 a semester for each course or seminar.

Auditors: Fees for auditors are the same as those for students registered in courses for credit.

All students enrolled in courses are charged a general materials fee of $10 per semester.

Students enrolled in the practicum are charged a practicum mate-rials fee of $30 a semester. In addition, students are required to meet traveling and other expenses incurred in relation to the practicum.

Continuing enrollment for Ph.D. candidates: Candidates who have completed the required academic courses including two tutorials in dissertation research and who are continuing independent work on their dissertations either in the vicinity of Bryn Mawr or in other places must retain their enrollment and degree candidacy by registering for one or more courses each semester or by paying a continuing enrollment fee of $150 each semester.

Students who wish to present themselves for examinations must be enrolled.

Doctoral students who are not working on dissertations and not consulting with the faculty or using the library may apply to the Dean of The Graduate School of Social Work and Social Research for a leave of absence for one or more semesters. No fee is required while on leave of absence. Students will be expected to be enrolled in courses or on the Continuing Enrollment Program unless granted a leave of absence.

---

*Faced with the rising costs of higher education, the College has had to raise tuition each of the last six years. Further increases may be expected.

Payment of Fees

The tuition fee will be billed by semester. In the event of withdrawal from The Graduate School of Social Work and Social Research, refunds will be made according to the following schedule.

For Semester I
    Withdrawals prior to September 9   100%
    Withdrawals September 9 through October 31   50%
    Withdrawals November 1 to end of semester   0%
For Semester II
    Withdrawals prior to January 17   100%
    Withdrawals January 17 through March 11   50%
    Withdrawals March 12 to end of semester   0%

For those students living at the Graduate Residence Center, the charge for residence is $1790 in 1976-77. In accordance with the above schedule, if a student withdraws from graduate study a refund will be made of that portion of the fee which represents room, with the proviso that the College is able to reassign the student's space to some other student not previously in residence. The student is not entitled to dispose of the room he or she leaves vacant.

Appropriate reduction or remission will also be made for that portion of the residence fee which represents the cost of food.

Procedure for securing refunds: Written notice must be received by the Dean of The Graduate School of Social Work and Social Research at least one week prior to the effective date of the withdrawal. Students who have received federally insured loans (loans guaranteed by state agencies—Guaranteed Student Loan Program - GSLP and National Direct Student Loans - NDSL) to meet any educational expenses for the current academic year must make an appointment with the Comptroller of the College before leaving the School to arrange for the appropriate refund of the loans in question.

Students whose fees are not paid within 10 days of receipt of bill in each semester will not be permitted to continue in residence or to attend classes. Degrees will not be awarded to any student owing money to the College or any College facility, nor will any transcripts be issued.

Summary of Expenses for the Academic Year 1976-1977

Regular

Tuition Fee $3,600

One Semester Course or Seminar 600

Residence in graduate student housing 1,790

Contingent

Application Fee .... $ 20

Charge for microfilming Ph.D. Dissertation 40

Continuing Enrollment Fee 300

Dispensary Fee 40

Graduation Fee for all Graduate Degrees 25

Health Insurance (United States citizens) 60

Health Insurance (foreign students) 70

Late Registration Fee[1] 10

General Materials Fee 20

Practicum Materials Fee (Master's Students only) 60

Add-Drop Fee[2] 10

---

[1]Effective after September 14, semester I, and January 25, semester II.

[2]The period for adding and dropping courses or seminars without fee will end September 28, semester I, and February 8, semester II.

Resources for Graduate Work at Bryn Mawr

Library

The Mariam Coffin Canaday Library, and the eight auxiliary libraries of Bryn Mawr College, including the Art and Archaeology collection in the M. Carey Thomas Library, contain over 450,000 books and regularly receive more than 2000 periodicals as well as many scholarly series. The Library is open throughout the year with a liberal schedule of hours. Books are readily accessible on open stacks and in study rooms; individual carrels are available for advanced students.

The John D. Gordan Reference Center provides a focus for reference books and services in the new library. In its card catalog, the main entry cards of the Haverford College Library join those of the Bryn Mawr Library, thus bringing more than 685,000 entries into one file. In addition, the Library is a member of the Union Catalogue of Pennsylvania, which locates approximately 7,200,000 volumes in the Philadelphia area and throughout the state, including the libraries of the American Philosophical Society, the Library Company of Philadelphia, the Historical Society of Pennsylvania, the Academy of Natural Sciences, the Free Library of Philadelphia, the Franklin Institute, the College of Physicians, the Rosenbach Foundation, the University of Pennsylvania and Temple University.

Computer Center

Through its membership in the Uni-Coll Corporation, a regional educational computer consortium, Bryn Mawr College has access to the resources and technical support of a major computing center. A high speed, remote batch terminal (printer at 600 lines per minute, card reader at 600 cards per minute) and nine teletypewriter terminals located on campus link the College with the Uni-Coll IBM 370, Model 168 computer. These facilities make available to faculty and students batch, remote job entry, and interactive computing supported by a large variety of programming systems.

History of the School

The Graduate School of Social Work and Social Research was opened at Bryn Mawr College in the fall of 1915 as the Carola Woerishoffer Graduate Department of Social Economy and Social Research. It was established as a tribute to Carola Woerishoffer, a Bryn Mawr graduate of the class of 1907, and was the first graduate program of social work education to be offered by a college or university. Subsequently the name was modified from Social Economy and Social Research to Social Work and Social Research. In August 1970, it became one of the three Schools which comprise Bryn Mawr College.

The School opened with eight graduate students; no undergraduates were admitted. Under the initial plan, two-thirds of the student's time was given to the study of theory and statistics, the remaining third to "practical investigation," with a half year spent in "field work" in a social service institution or a social welfare organization in Philadelphia or New York.

The course of study was planned for one, two, or three years, with three years required for the Ph.D. degree and one and two years for a certificate. The Master of Social Service degree replaced the two-year certificate in 1947. Its plan of "field work" and its inclusion of work in labor and industrial relations and in community organization made it somewhat different from the other early schools of social work. Under its first director, Dr. Susan M. Kingsbury, four fields of study were offered: Community Organization, Social Casework, Industrial Relations, and Social and Industrial Investigation. Included among the organizations offering field work for students in these early days were: The Family Society of Philadelphia, The Children's Aid Society, the White Williams Foundation, the Big Sister Association, the Young Women's Christian Association, the Criminal Division of the Municipal Court of Philadelphia, the Social Services Department of the University of Pennsylvania Hospital, and various social settlements.

In 1919, Bryn Mawr became one of the six charter members of the American Association of Schools of Social Work. In this period following World War I, social work education was rapidly changing in response to the continuous expansion of social work into new settings. The curricula of the schools responded to these changes in a variety of ways. At Bryn Mawr, preparation for social casework was expanded and additional courses in public welfare and social

62

legislation were offered. However, the emphasis on research and social investigation which was central to the early curriculum of the School continued.

Bryn Mawr had the first doctoral program in social work education and awarded the first Ph.D. in 1920. The doctoral program at the School of Social Service Administration at the University of Chicago followed later in the 1920s. Today thirty-one schools in the United States offer doctoral programs.

By 1935 Bryn Mawr was one of twenty-nine schools belonging to the American Association of Schools of Social Work. Twenty-five were in colleges or universities and only four were independent schools. Bryn Mawr is currently a member of the Council on Social Work Education, successor to the American Association of Schools of Social Work and the accrediting body for social work education.

The Graduate School of Social Work and Social Research currently has approximately one hundred sixty-five full-time students. A number of factors have contributed to this expansion: the acquisition in 1958 of a separate building at 815 New Gulph Road and increased Federal support for education for social work, especially scholarship aid in the form of traineeships.

There are more than eighty graduate schools of social work accredited by the Council on Social Work Education in the United States and Canada. Although many changes have taken place both at Bryn Mawr and in social work education, the vision of those responsible for the design of the School at its founding has been proven by experience to have been remarkably correct.

The School now has approximately 1,000 living graduates. Since its inception it has granted awards to more than 1,175 persons; this includes awards of professional certificates and M.A. degrees, neither of which has been offered since 1947. The School has granted 68 Ph.D. degrees and, since 1947, more than 950 M.S.S. degrees.

At the time of its founding, the School admitted only women; since the late 1930s both men and women have been admitted and during the last ten years men have constituted about one third of the student body.

Graduates of the School are located in all regions of the United States and many foreign countries. Their present positions range within a wide spectrum of governmental and voluntary organizations and agencies. They are widely represented in child and family welfare, community mental health, corrections, gerontology, health, housing, intergroup relations, legal services, mental retardation, prevention and treatment of alcohol addiction and drug abuse, neighborhood organization, public education, public welfare administration, social planning, social rehabilitation, and social welfare research. Approximately half are executives, supervisors or administrators, or consultants. Recipients of the doctoral degree are chiefly in teaching and research positions.

In the fall of 1975 the School celebrated its sixtieth anniversary. At the same time it moved to a new building at 300 Airdale Road. Over the course of its sixty-one years, the School's graduates have contributed substantially to leadership in both public and voluntary social welfare.

Graduate Student Housing

Housing on campus is provided for about sixty-five graduate students in the Graduate Residence Center, Batten House, and the Annex. There is a separate bedroom for each student. No housing on campus is available for married students. Rooms are furnished except for rugs and curtains. Students should bring towels and bed linen. (Local rental services will supply sheets and pillowcases for a modest fee. Arrangements can be made on arrival.) Because of College fire regulations, smoking is not permitted in the bedrooms. There are smokers on certain floors. The dining room, available to all resident students, is located in the Center.

Application for a room should be made as early as possible. A room contract, which will be sent upon request, must be signed and returned to the Office of The Graduate School of Arts and Sciences with a deposit of ten dollars. The deposit will be deducted from the residence fee; it will be refunded only if the student cannot be accommodated.

A student who has reserved a room will be held responsible for the residence charge unless notice of withdrawal is sent in writing to the Dean of The Graduate School of Arts and Sciences before August 15.

The regular charge for residence (room, board and health service) for graduate students is $1,790 a year, payable one half early in the first semester and the other half early in the second. Although one or more housing units may be closed during Christmas and spring vacations, when food and health services are not provided, residence on campus covers the period from the opening of College in the fall until Commencement Day.

Baggage will be accepted at the College after August 20. It should be sent prepaid, addressed to the Graduate Center and marked with the owner's name.

Health

Medical Services

The College maintains an 18-bed infirmary with a staff of physicians and nurses. The infirmary is open when College is in session. The college physicians may be consulted without charge by students residing in campus housing and by students living off campus who have paid the dispensary fee. Specialists practicing in Bryn Mawr and Philadelphia serve as consulting physicians to the College. If consultation is necessary, the student must meet the expense.

The residence charge paid by graduate students living in campus housing entitles them to treatment in the College dispensary, and to care in the Infirmary for seven days (not necessarily consecutive) during the year, and to attendance by the college physicians during this time. After the seven-day period, the fee is $30.00 for each day in the Infirmary.

Graduate students who do not live in campus housing may pay a $40.00 fee which entitles them to full use of the Student Health Service. The fee is not billed automatically and is not covered by scholarship or other grants. The dispensary fee is to be paid in the Comptroller's Office where a dispensary card is issued.

The College maintains a counseling and diagnostic service staffed by clinical social workers and consulting psychiatrists. They are at the Infirmary on a part-time basis. All students eligible for dispensary care may use this service. The counseling service offers confidential consultation and discussion of personal and emotional problems. Definitive and long-range psychotherapy is not available. A charge is made for visits in excess of four.

Medical Requirements

All graduate students, after admission but before registration, must file a medical history and health evaluation form with the Infirmary. There are no exceptions to this rule.

In addition to a statement of health, signed by a physician, the following are required: tetanus and polio immunizations; proof of freedom from active tuberculosis based on either a negative skin test to tuberculosis or, in the presence of a positive test, a normal chest x-ray within six months of admission.

Insurance

All graduate students are urged to carry health insurance. Students up to age twenty-five are entitled to the Bryn Mawr College Student Health care insurance at a cost of about $59.50 per year. Those wishing more complete coverage may purchase Blue Cross and Blue Shield insurance on an individual basis, subject to screening by the insurance company. Application for College health insurance should be made through the Head Nurse in the Infirmary.

Foreign Students. The College also makes available a policy which provides fuller coverage of medical, surgical, and hospital costs. This insurance is required of all students whose permanent residence is not in the United States unless they have equally complete protection of another kind effective in the United States. The cost for students under age thirty is about $70.00 for a twelve-month period, starting in September.

Child Care Center

Child care is available for Bryn Mawr-Haverford families at the New Gulph Child Care Center, 911 New Gulph Road (215 LA5-7649). The Center, conducted by a professional staff, incorporates age group developmental activities with high quality group care. Children, three months through five years old, are eligible. The Center is open five days a week, 9-5, at an approximate cost of $1.25 per hour plus an additional charge for hot lunch if desired. A minimum of six hours' regular use per week is required. Following Commencement, a summer program is conducted for approximately two months. Early registration for all programs is essential. For information contact the Director. Tuition for the semester is payable in advance. Limited scholarship help is available.

Career Planning Office

Graduate students are invited to make use of the services of the Career Planning Office. These services include counseling on career interests and concerns; information on specific openings for summer, temporary and permanent, full- and part-time positions; consultation on job-hunting methods. Upon request the Career Planning Office also collects, maintains and makes available to prospective employers the credentials of graduate students and alumnae/i. The credentials include biographical data and faculty and employer references.

Equality of Opportunity

Bryn Mawr College admits students of any race, color, national and ethnic origin to all the rights, privileges, programs and activites generally accorded or made available to students at the College. It does not discriminate on the basis of race, color, or national or ethnic origin in administration of its educational policies, admissions policies, scholarship and loan programs, and athletic and other College-administered programs.

Student and Alumni Associations

Student Associations of The Graduate School of Social Work and Social Research

All Master's students in The Graduate School of Social Work and Social Research are eligible for membership in the Student Association. The Student Association, faculty and administration work together to promote the objectives of the School.

The Doctoral Student Association is open to all full- and part-time doctoral students. It provides an open forum for discussion of common concerns with reference to the advanced program as well as broader professional interests.

Alumni Association of The Graduate School of Social Work and Social Research

The Alumni Association of the School was organized to further the interests of the School and its alumni. This Association is part of the larger Alumnae Association of Bryn Mawr College. The Steering Committee of the Alumni Association is comprised of the following:

Jacob Armstrong	Chair
Elizabeth McDaid	Vice Chair
Malin Van Antwerp	Secretary
Alice Boardman	Treasurer

Recruitment of Minority Group Students

A Student-Faculty-Alumni Committee is active in recruitment of interested and qualified minority group students.

The Graduate School of Social Work and Social Research is especially interested in having minority group students explore graduate social work education at Bryn Mawr. Inquiries may be directed to the Office of Admissions, 300 Airdale Road, Bryn Mawr, Pa. 19010.

College Facilities

Student-Faculty Lounge

There is a Student-Faculty Lounge at The Graduate School of Social Work and Social Research for the use of Social Work faculty and students.

Parking

Parking for Social Work students is available at The Graduate School of Social Work and Social Research. Regular bus service is available from The Graduate School of Social Work and Social Research to Canaday Library.

Mailboxes

There are student mailboxes at The Graduate School of Social Work and Social Research. Mail addressed to students in the School should include 300 Airdale Road, Bryn Mawr, Pennsylvania 19010.

Wyndham

Wyndham is the College Alumnae House where the headquarters of the Bryn Mawr College Alumnae Association is located. Graduate students are invited to use the dining and other facilities.

The Board of Trustees of Bryn Mawr College

Officers of the College

Harris Llewellyn Wofford, Jr., AB (University of Chicago) JD (Howard University and Yale University) *President of the College*

Bernard Ross PH D (University of Michigan) *Dean of The Graduate School of Social Work and Social Research*

Merle Broberg PH D (The American University) *Associate Dean of The Graduate School of Social Work and Social Research*

Phyllis Pray Bober PH D (New York University) *Dean of The Graduate School of Arts and Sciences*

Mary Patterson McPherson PH D (Bryn Mawr College) *Dean of the Undergraduate College*

Gertrude C. K. Leighton AB (Bryn Mawr College) JD (Yale University) *Secretary of the General Faculty*

Milton D. Speizman PH D (Tulane University) *Secretary of the Faculty of The Graduate School of Social Work and Social Research†*

James Tanis TH D (University of Utrecht) *Director of Libraries‡*

Frieda W. Woodruff MD (University of Pennsylvania) *College Physician*

Officers of Administration of the College

Dolores E. Brien PH D (Brown University) *Director of Career Planning*

Margaret M. Healy PH D (Bryn Mawr College) *Executive Director of the Board of Trustees' Ad Hoc Committee on Financial Planning*

Joseph S. Johnston, Jr. MA (University of Chicago) *Assistant to the President*

Paul W. Klug CPA BS (Temple University) *Comptroller and Business Manager of the College*

Phyllis S. Lachs PH D (Bryn Mawr College) *Associate Dean of The Graduate School of Arts and Sciences*

Ramona L. Livingston AB (William Jewell College) *Advisor to Foreign Students* and *Lecturer in English*

Margaret G. McKenna AB (Bryn Mawr College) *Personnel Administrator*

Samuel J. McNamee BS (Temple University) *Assistant Comptroller*

---

†On leave semester II.
‡On leave 1976-77.

Michelle Pynchon Osborn AB (Smith College) *Director of Public Information*

Julie E. Painter AB (Bryn Mawr College) *Administrator of Records and Financial Aid*

Martha Stokes Price AB (Bryn Mawr College) *Director of Resources*

Patricia Onderdonk Pruett PH D (Bryn Mawr College) *Associate Dean of the Undergraduate College*

Ellen Fernon Reisner MA (Bryn Mawr College) *Assistant to the President and Alumna-in-Residence*

Thomas N. Trucks B S (Villanova University) *Superintendent of Buildings and Grounds*

Sarah E. Wright *Director of Halls*

Faculty of The Graduate School of Social Work and Social Research for the Academic Year 1976-77

M. Leslie Alexander MSS (Bryn Mawr College) *Lecturer*

Charles C. Bray PHD (University of Pittsburgh)*Associate Professor*

Merle Broberg PHD (The American University)*Associate Dean of The Graduate School of Social Work and Social Research and Associate Professor*

Dennis Brunn PHD (Washington University) *Assistant Professor*

Donald F. Cooney MA (Fordham University) Lecturer

Sandra S. Cornelius PHD (Bryn Mawr College)*Assistant Professor, Coordinator of Admissions, and Coordinator of Field Instruction* (Semester I)

Mark C. Fulcomer PHD (Ohio State University) *Visiting Lecturer*

Richard H. Gaskins JD (Yale Law School) PHD (Yale University) *Assistant Professor* and *Coordinator of the Law and Social Policy Program*

Samuel Gubins PHD (The Johns Hopkins University) *Visiting Lecturer*

Jean Haring DSW (Western Reserve University) *Associate Professor*

Stephen Holden PHD (Bryn Mawr College) *Assistant Professor*‡

Isaac C. Hunt JD (University of Virginia) *Visiting Lecturer*

Arthur C. Huntley MD (Jefferson Medical College) *Visiting Lecturer*

Carole Joffe PHD (University of California, Berkeley) *Assistant Professor*

Toba S. Kerson DSW (University of Pennsylvania) *Assistant Professor*

Arelious Knighton MSW (University of Michigan) *Visiting Lecturer*

Jane C. Kronick PHD (Yale University) *Associate Professor*‡

Howard Lesnick LLB (Columbia Law School) *Visiting Lecturer in the Law and Social Policy Program*

Joyce Lewis MSS (Bryn Mawr College) *Assistant Professor* and *Coordinator of Field Instruction* (Semester II)*

Philip Lichtenberg PHD (Western Reserve University) *Professor*

‡On leave 1976-77.
*On leave semester I, 1976-77.
†On leave semester II, 1976-77.

Katherine D.K. Lower PH D (University of Wisconsin) *Professor Emeritus*

Ruth W. Mayden MSS (Bryn Mawr College) *Visiting Lecturer*

Laurie N. McNally MSS (Bryn Mawr College) *Lecturer*

Braulio Montalvo MA (Columbia University) *Visiting Lecturer*

Dolores Norton PH D (Bryn Mawr College) *Associate Professor*‡

Leslie R. Price JD (University of Pennsylvania) *Visiting Lecturer in the Law and Social Policy Program*

Martin Rein PH D (Brandeis University) *Visiting Professor*

Patience B. Rockey ED D (Harvard University) *Visiting Lecturer*

Bernard Ross PH D (University of Michigan) *Dean of The Graduate School of Social Work and Social Research* and *Professor*

Louis Schneiderman MSSW (Columbia University) *Lecturer*

Djordje Soc MSW (University of California, Berkeley) *Lecturer*

Milton D. Speizman PH D (Tulane University) *Professor* and *Secretary of the Faculty of The Graduate School of Social Work and Social Research*†

Ruth O. Stallfort MSS (Simmons College), Third-Year Certificate (Columbia University) *Associate Professor*

James Tanis THD (University of Utrecht) *Director of Libraries*‡

William W. Vosburgh PH D (Yale University) *Associate Professor*†

Tawana Ford Whaley MSS (Bryn Mawr College) *Field Instruction Consultant*

Cathie J. Witty PH D (University of California, Berkeley) MPA (Harvard University) *Assistant Professor*

Harris Llewellyn Wofford, Jr., JD (Howard University and Yale University)
President of the College

Greta Zybon DSW (Western Reserve University)
Associate Professor

Administration of The Graduate School of Social Work and Social Research

Bernard Ross PH D (University of Michigan) *Dean*

Merle Broberg PHD (The American University) *Associate Dean*

Milton D. Speizman PH D (Tulane University) *Secretary of the Faculty*

Sandra S. Cornelius PH D (Bryn Mawr College) *Coordinator of Admissions* and *Coordinator of Field Instruction* (Semester I)

Joyce Lewis MSS (Bryn Mawr College) *Coordinator of Field Instruction* (Semester II)*

Grace M. Irish AB (Vassar College) *Administrative Assistant*

Standing Committees of the Faculty of The Graduate School of Social Work and Social Research for 1976-77

Secretary of the Faculty
Mr. Speizman 1976-79†

Committee on Nominations
Miss Zybon 1974-77
Mr. Soc 1975-78
Ms. Joffe 1976-79

Committee on Policy
Dean Ross *Chair*
Mr. Speizman *ex officio*†
Mr. Vosburgh 1974-77†
Miss Zybon 1975-78
Mr. Gaskins 1976-79

*Committee on Admissions and
Financial Awards*
Mr. Broberg *Chair*
Dean Ross *ex officio*
Mrs. Cornelius *ex officio*
Mr. Soc 1976-78
Mr. Bray 1976-78

Committee on Master's Curriculum
Dean Ross *ex officio*
Mr. Brunn 1975-77
Miss Haring 1975-77
Mr. Vosburgh 1976-78†
Mrs. Cornelius 1976-78

*Committee on Evaluation of
Educational Performance of
Master's Students*
Dean Ross *Chair*
Mrs. Cornelius *ex officio*
Mr. Lichtenberg 1976-77
Mr. Bray 1976-77

---

‡On leave 1976-77.
†On leave semester II, 1976-77.

*Committee on Field Instruction
and Placement*
Mrs. Cornelius *Chair*
Mr. Broberg *Vice Chair*
Dean Ross *ex officio*
Mr. Bray 1976-77
Miss Haring 1976-78

*Committee on Initial Appointments
to the Faculty*
Dean Ross *Chair*
Mr. Vosburgh 1976-77†
Ms. Joffe 1976-77
Miss Zybon 1976-77

Doctoral Committee
Mr. Broberg *Chair*
Dean Ross *ex officio*
Mr. Bray
Mr. Brunn
Mrs. Cornelius
Mr. Gaskins
Miss Haring
Mr. Holden‡
Ms. Joffe
Mrs. Kerson
Mrs. Kronick‡
Mr. Lichtenberg
Mrs. Norton‡
Mr. Speizman†
Mr. Vosburgh†
Ms. Witty
Miss Zybon
and
All students enrolled in the
Doctoral Program

Representatives to the Advisory Board

Mr. Lichtenberg 1976-77
Mr. Bray 1976-77

Representatives to Committee on Computer Facilitiees

Mr. Brunn 1976-78
Mr. Broberg 1976-78

Representative to the Committee to Supervise the Degree of Doctor of Philosophy

Mr. Bray 1975-78

Directions to Bryn Mawr

Bryn Mawr College is located approximately eleven miles west of Philadelphia and nine miles east of Paoli.

By air: From the Philadelphia International Airport take the airport limousine or SEPTA bus to 30th Street Station in Philadelphia and from there the Paoli Local to Bryn Mawr, or take a taxi or the Bennett Limousine Service directly to 300 Airdale Road from the airport, a distance of 14 miles.

By automobile: From the east or west take U.S. 30 or the Pennsylvania Turnpike. From the Valley Forge Exit of the Turnpike, take the Schuylkill Expressway (Pa. #43—Interstate #76), turning right at exit number 36, Pa. #320, Gulph Mills, which is 3.5 miles east of the toll gate; continue into Montgomery Avenue to the town of Bryn Mawr, a distance of 4 miles from the Expressway. Turn left at the traffic light at the intersection of Airdale Road and Montgomery Avenues. School is located at 300 Airdale Road.

Parking is available at The Graduate School of Social Work and Social Research.

By bus: All Greyhound buses arrive at the Philadelphia terminal at 17th and Market Streets, adjoining Suburban Station. Trailways buses arrive at 13th and Arch Streets, three blocks from Suburban Station. Take the Paoli Local from Suburban Station to Rosemont Station.

By railroad: Connections from the east, north and south are best made from 30th Street Station, Philadelphia, on the Paoli Local of the Penn Central Railroad, which leaves the station every thirty minutes. Those coming by rail from the west are advised to leave the train at Paoli (rather than North Philadelphia) and take the Local from Paoli to Rosemont Station.

To walk to the main campus from the Bryn Mawr Station, go one block to the traffic light at the intersection of Morris and Montgomery Avenues, cross Montgomery onto Morris and take the next left onto Yarrow Street, which leads directly to the campus.

To walk to The Graduate School of Social Work and Social Research, use the Rosemont Station, one stop beyond Bryn Mawr coming from the East and one stop beyond Villanova coming from the West. Cross Montgomery Avenue and continue on Airdale Road. School is on the left.

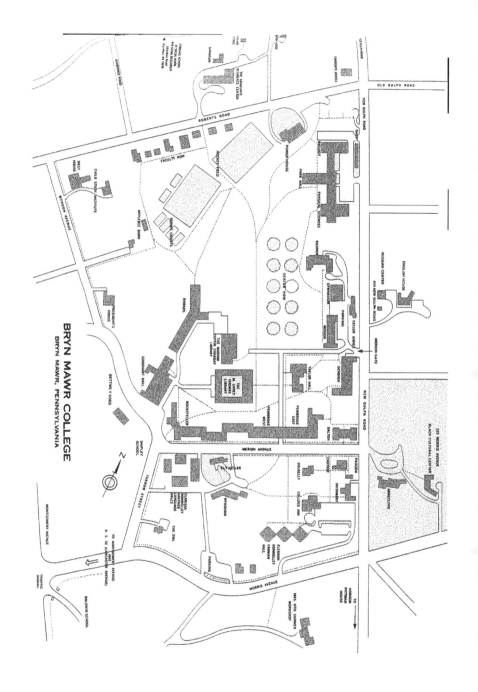

BRYN MAWR COLLEGE
BRYN MAWR, PENNSYLVANIA

College Calendar

Bryn Maw
The Gradu
of Arts an

Bryn Mawr College Calendar
The Graduate School
of Arts and Sciences

Issue for the Session of 1976-77

July 1976 *Volume LXIX Number 2*

BRYN MAWR COLLEGE CALENDAR published December, July, August, and September by Bryn Mawr College, Bryn Mawr, Pennsylvania 19010. *Second class postage paid at Bryn Mawr, Pennsylvania.*

Graduate Work at Bryn Mawr

Graduate education at Bryn Mawr is built upon a close working relationship between students and mature scholars. Each student begins training on the level appropriate for his individual experience and pursues a flexible program designed for his special requirements. Small seminars provide an opportunity to share research projects and to work under the direct supervision of the faculty.

Founded in 1885, the Bryn Mawr Graduate School was the first graduate school for women in the United States. Since 1931 both men and women have been admitted, but only after 1965 were adequate funds obtained to offer support for men comparable to that offered to women. Always small in relation to other graduate schools, Bryn Mawr has expanded gradually in response to the need for men and women well prepared for teaching and research. In 1970 The Graduate School of Arts and Sciences and The Graduate School of Social Work and Social Research were organized as two distinct schools. Today, the student enrollment in The Graduate School of Arts and Sciences is about four hundred seventy.

Graduate work leading to the degrees of Master of Arts and Doctor of Philosophy is available in:

Anthropology

Biochemistry

Biology

Chemistry

Classical and Near Eastern Archaeology

Economics

Education and Child Development

English

French

Geology

German

Greek

History

History and Philosophy of Science

History of Art

Latin

Mathematics

Mediaeval Studies

Music

Philosophy

Physics

Political Science

Psychology

Russian

Sociology

Spanish

Work leading to the degrees of Master of Social Service and Doctor of Philosophy is available in The Graduate School of Social Work and Social Research.

College Calendar 1976-77
The Graduate School
of Arts and Sciences

First Semester—1976

Aug. 1   *Applications for loans due*

Aug. 20   *Final date for filing completed applications for admission for 1976-77*

Sept. 2, 3, 7-10, 13, 14   *Registration period for semester I*

Sept. 7   *Graduate residences open*

Sept. 9   *Convocation*
Work of the 92nd academic year begins at 9 A.M.

Oct. 9   *French examinations for M.A. and Ph.D. candidates*

Oct. 22   *Fall vacation begins after last seminar*

Oct. 27   *Fall vacation ends at 9 A.M.*

Oct. 30   *Spanish, Italian, Russian, Latin, statistics examinations for M.A. and Ph.D. candidates*

Nov. 6   *German examinations for M.A. and Ph.D. candidates*

Nov. 24   *Thanksgiving holiday begins after last seminar*

Nov. 29   *Thanksgiving holiday ends at 9 A.M.*

Dec. 1   *Final date for filing completed applications for admission for semester II*

Dec. 6-15   *Registration period for semester II*

Dec. 22   *Winter vacation begins*

Second Semester—1977

Jan. 17   *Convocation*
           Work of semester II begins at 9 A.M.

Jan. 19   *Applications for M.A. candidacy due in the Office of*
           The Graduate School of Arts and Sciences

Jan. 25   *Final date for filing completed applications for scholar-*
           ships (foreign students) for 1977-78

Feb. 1   *Final date for filing completed applications for fellow-*
           ships, scholarships, and grants (citizens of the United
           States and Canada) for 1977-78

Feb. 19   *German examinations for M.A. and Ph.D. candidates*

Feb. 26   *Spanish, Italian, Russian, Latin, statistics examina-*
           tions for M.A. and Ph.D. candidates

Mar. 5   *French examinations for M.A. and Ph.D. candidates*

Mar. 11   *Spring vacation begins after last seminar*

Mar. 21   *Spring vacation ends at 9 A.M.*

Mar. 30   *Ph.D. dissertations in all fields except natural sciences*
           and Mathematics must be submitted to the Office of The
           Graduate School of Arts and Sciences

Apr. 6-8   *Spring registration period for semester I, 1977-78*

Apr. 11   *M.A. papers due for candidates away from Bryn Mawr*

Apr. 20   *Ph.D. dissertations in the natural sciences and Mathe-*
           matics must be submitted to the Office of The Graduate
           School of Arts and Sciences

Apr. 29   *Last day of seminars*

May 16   *Conferring of degrees and close of 92nd academic year*
           Graduate residences close

Admission to The Graduate School of Arts and Sciences

Requirements

Students must be graduates of colleges or universities of acknowledged standing. For special requirements set by individual departments, see the departmental listings beginning on page 16.

Procedure

The applicant should write to the Dean of The Graduate School of Arts and Sciences, Bryn Mawr College, Bryn Mawr, Pennsylvania 19010, for application forms, indicating the field of special interest. The application must be supported by official transcripts of the student's complete academic record and by letters from the dean and two or more professors with whom he has done his major work. Although an interview is not required, candidates who wish to come in person to discuss their plans or the Bryn Mawr program are welcome. The applicant should write directly to the chairman of the department to arrange a meeting. No application will be considered until all the necessary documents have been received. Students are accepted for either full-time or part-time work. For citizens of the United States and Canada and for foreign students living in the United States, there is an application fee of $20.00 which is not refundable.

Graduate Record Examinations and Graduate School Foreign Language Tests

Applicants are advised to take the Graduate Record Examination Aptitude Test as well as the Advanced Tests in their fields of special interest. In certain departments these examinations are required, as indicated in the departmental listings. Inquiries concerning the Graduate Record Examinations should be addressed to Graduate Record Examination, Educational Testing Service, Box 955, Princeton, New Jersey 08540 or to Graduate Record Examination, Educational Testing Service, 1947 Center Street, Berkeley, California 94704.

Satisfactory scores in the Graduate School Foreign Language Test are accepted by some departments in fulfillment of the language requirement for higher degrees. Students should consult the departmental listings and make arrangements to take these tests at any Test Center. Applicants are encouraged to take the test within one year prior to the date they wish to enter. Interested students should write to Graduate School Foreign Language Test, Educational Testing Service, at the address listed above.

Dates

1. *Citizens of the United States and Canada:*
Applications for admission in all departments except Education and Child Development must be complete by August 20. Applications for admission to the Department of Education and Child Development must be complete by February 1. Graduate Record Examinations: October 16, December 11, 1976; January 8, February 26, April 23, and June 11, 1977. Graduate School Foreign Language Tests: October 9, 1976; February 5, April 9, and June 25, 1977.

2. *Foreign applicants:*
The closing date for admission is August 20, except for the Department of Education and Child Development, for which the closing date is February 1. Applications must include the scores of the Test of English as a Foreign Language (TOEFL), the Examination of the English Language Institute of the University of Michigan, or another approved language test. Since applications from students who desire financial aid must be completed by January 25, applicants must arrange to take language tests well before that date. Candidates offering scores of the TOEFL must register for it in September and take the test not later than October of the year preceding the year in which they wish to enter.

For information concerning the TOEFL write to: TOEFL, Educational Testing Service, Princeton, New Jersey 08540. Tests are given on September 18 and November 20, 1976; February 26 and May 21, 1977.

Students in departments requiring the Graduate Record Examination should also arrange to take these tests not later than October.

3. *Applicants for financial aid:*
Students wishing to apply for fellowships, scholarships, assistantships, tuition grants, or other forms of financial aid must present complete applications by the following dates:

For United States and Canadian citizens:
Applicants for fellowships, scholarships, assistantships, full-time and part-time tuition grants .... February 1
Applicants for loans .... August 1

For foreign citizens:
Applicants for scholarships .... January 25

GAPSFAS forms must be submitted to the Educational Testing Service, Princeton, New Jersey 08540 by January 20 (see page 82).

Admission to Graduate Seminars and Courses

Admission to graduate seminars and courses is under the jurisdiction of the various departments. Students whose preparation is inadequate may be required to complete appropriate undergraduate courses before being enrolled in a full graduate program.

Registration

All graduate students, after consultation with the chairmen of their departments, must register at the Office of The Graduate School of Arts and Sciences in the M. Carey Thomas Library each semester during the registration period listed in the College Calendar. Changes in registration require the approval of the department chairman and the Dean.

Personal registration is an important obligation of the graduate student. Those who fail to register in the stated period will be charged a late registration fee.

Students wishing certification to outside agencies must complete a form to be signed also by the department chairman and deposited in the Office of The Graduate School of Arts and Sciences.

Continuing enrollment

Students who have completed the required academic units for the Ph.D. degree and are continuing independent work on their dissertations must retain their enrollment and degree candidacy by registering for one or more units each semester or under the continuing enrollment plan.

In addition, students who are not planning to register for academic units but who are planning (1) to present themselves for College examinations, (2) to use the College libraries or laboratories, or (3) to consult members of the faculty must register under the continuing enrollment plan. Such enrollment does not carry academic credit.

Degree Candidacy

Students become candidates for advanced degrees only after they have met departmental requirements and made formal application which has been approved by the Council of The Graduate School of Arts and Sciences.

Resources for Graduate Work at Bryn Mawr

The Mariam Coffin Canaday Library and the eight auxiliary libraries of Bryn Mawr College, including the Art and Archaeology Library in the M. Carey Thomas Library, contain over 450,000 books and regularly receive more than 2000 periodicals as well as many scholarly series. The Library is open throughout the year with a liberal schedule of hours. Books are readily accessible on open stacks and in study rooms; individual carrels are available for advanced students.

The John D. Gordan Reference Center provides a focus for reference books and services in the library. In its card catalog, the main entry cards of the Haverford College Library join those of the Bryn Mawr Library, thus bringing more than 685,000 entries into one file. In addition, the Library is a member of the Union Catalogue of Pennsylvania, which locates approximately 7,200,000 volumes in the Philadelphia area and throughout the state, including the libraries of the American Philosophical Society, the Library Company of Philadelphia, the Historical Society of Pennsylvania, the Academy of Natural Sciences, the Free Library of Philadelphia, the Franklin Institute, the College of Physicians, the Rosenbach Foundation, the University of Pennsylvania, and Temple University.

The Rare Book Room houses the Marjorie Walter Goodhart Mediaeval Library of incunabula and mediaeval manuscripts. Important and extensive collections of early material on Latin America, Africa, and Asia are to be found in the Dillingham, McBride, and Plass collections. The Castle and Adelman collections expand the opportunities for the study of the graphic book-arts. The Adelman Collection also substantially increases the Library's holdings of literary and related manuscripts. In addition to these special collections are numerous other rare books and manuscripts.

Bryn Mawr has a study collection of archaeological and ethnological materials which is used for research by graduate and undergraduate students. The Ella Riegel Museum of Classical Archaeology contains examples of the Greek and Roman arts, especially vases, and a small group of pre-classical antiquities. It includes the classical Greek coins assembled by Elisabeth Washburn King and the Aline Abaecherli Boyce Collection of Roman Republican silver coins, as well as the Densmore Curtis Collection presented by Clarissa Dryden. Professor Hetty Goldman donated an extensive series of pottery samples from the excavations at Tarsus in Cilicia. Old World Paleolithic, Neolithic, Paleo-Indian, Eastern Woodland, Southwestern, Middle Mississip-

9

pian, and Mexican antiquities are also represented at Bryn Mawr in addition to the Ward Canaday Collection of outstanding examples of most of the known ceramic and textile traditions of Peru.

The Geology Department has valuable materials for research, including the extensive working and reference mineral collections of Theodore D. Rand and George Vaux, Jr. The Department is also a map repository for the U.S. Geological Survey and the Defense Mapping Agency.

In addition, students use the resources of the Philadelphia area: the Philadelphia Museum of Art, the Pennsylvania Academy of the Fine Arts, the Barnes Foundation, the Rodin Museum, the Rosenbach Museum, and the University Museum of the University of Pennsylvania. They take advantage of the musical life of the city by attending the Philadelphia Orchestra and by playing or singing with local groups.

Laboratories, classrooms, and libraries for Biochemistry, Biology, Chemistry, Geology, Mathematics, and Physics are located in the three buildings of the Science Center. At the Center are rooms designed for work with radioactive materials, for photomicrography and for glassblowing; there is a machine shop with expert instrument makers in charge and a workshop available to graduate students. Laboratories and classrooms for Anthropology and Psychology are in Dalton Hall. In addition to the usual equipment, apparatus and instruments for particular research projects by faculty and graduate students have been acquired, in part, through the Plan for the Coordination of the Sciences (see page 85), through research grants from industry and other private sources, and from government agencies.

Through its membership in the Uni-Coll Corporation, a regional educational computer consortium, Bryn Mawr College has access to the resources and technical support of a major computing center. A high speed, remote batch terminal (printer at 600 lines per minute, card reader at 600 cards per minute) and nine teletypewriter terminals located on campus link the College with the Uni-Coll IBM 370, Model 168 computer. These facilities make available to faculty and students batch, remote job entry, and interactive computing supported by a large variety of programming systems.

Program of Study

The program of study consists of selected seminars, courses, or individual work under the close direction of members of the faculty. For the sake of convenience, this program is divided into academic units which are to be completed at Bryn Mawr College. Three academic units constitute a full year's program. An academic unit may be a year's seminar or two semester seminars, one or more undergraduate courses for graduate credit, independent study in preparation for the Preliminary Examinations, or supervised units of work.

A minimum of three academic units at Bryn Mawr is required for the degree of Master of Arts. Candidates for the degree of Doctor of Philosophy generally complete three full years of graduate work which must, with certain exceptions, include a minimum of six academic units at Bryn Mawr. Of these units at least one must be a unit of supervised work on the dissertation. The dissertation units, undertaken after a student has been admitted to candidacy, may be part of the residence requirement or in addition to it.

The number of units required for the Doctor of Philosophy may be reduced to no less than four for those who have held academic appointments at Bryn Mawr College for two or more years. Students holding the A.B. degree from Bryn Mawr College shall offer a minimum of three units. The Council of The Graduate School of Arts and Sciences may, on recommendation of the departments, reduce the requirements for other students.

For the list of advanced undergraduate courses which with additional work may be accepted as graduate units subject to the approval of department chairmen and the Dean of The Graduate School of Arts and Sciences, see the departmental offerings beginning on page 16.

In many departments, members of the faculty and graduate students meet from time to time in Journal Clubs or Colloquia to discuss current research or to review recent publications in their field of study.

Under the Reciprocal Plan, courses at the University of Pennsylvania Graduate School of Arts and Sciences are available to Bryn Mawr graduate students. All full-time students and such part-time students as intend to become candidates for degrees are eligible. The number of courses which may be taken at the University is limited to the equivalent of one unit per year. The procedure for registration and payment of tuition fees is the same as for students enrolled wholly at Bryn Mawr, with the exception that the student must present a letter of introduction to the Dean of The Graduate School of Arts and Sciences of the University of Pennsyl-

11

vania when registering there. The University charges a small general fee for the use of the library, a library deposit, which is refundable, and fees for late registration. Ordinarily students are not advised to undertake such work during their first year at Bryn Mawr.

Students enrolled in the program in the History and Philosophy of Science attend seminars at the American Philosophical Society and at the University of Pennsylvania and register for these seminars at Bryn Mawr.

Equality of Opportunity

Bryn Mawr College is commited to the principle of equal opportunity in education, as in employment, without discrimination.

Summer Work

Bryn Mawr has no regular summer session on campus. Occasionally, at the invitation of members of the faculty, arrangements can be made for graduate students to continue research during the summer. The amount of credit for the work and the tuition fee to be charged depend upon the particular circumstances. Students should register for such work at the Office of the Dean of The Graduate School of Arts and Sciences early in June.

Summer Institutes in France and Spain

Bryn Mawr College offers a summer program of intensive work in significant aspects of French culture at the *Institut d'Etudes Françaises d'Avignon*. Certain courses carry graduate credit. For information write to Dr. Michel Guggenheim, Department of French, Bryn Mawr College.

For a similar summer program in aspects of Hispanic culture at the *Centro de Estudios Hispánicos* in Madrid, write to Dr. Eleanor K. Paucker, Department of Spanish, Bryn Mawr College.

Degree Requirements

The Graduate School of Arts and Sciences offers programs leading to the degrees of Doctor of Philosophy and Master of Arts.

The Degree of Doctor of Philosophy

The course of study is designed to prepare students for professional careers as scholars and teachers. Candidates should have ability of high order, intellectual curiosity, critical judgment, independence, a broad general education, fundamental training in the major and allied fields, and the determination needed to carry through an exacting program.

The general requirements, to which should be added those of the various departments, are as follows:

1. Undergraduate preparation in major and allied fields which is satisfactory to the departments concerned and to the Council of The Graduate School of Arts and Sciences.

2. A minimum of three full years of work beyond the A.B. degree in major and allied fields. Graduates of other colleges must complete at least six academic units at The Graduate School of Arts and Sciences of Bryn Mawr College. Of these units, at least one must be a unit of supervised work on the dissertation. The dissertation units may be part of the residence requirement or in addition to it. The residence requirement may be reduced by the Council of The Graduate School of Arts and Sciences for candidates who have held academic appointments for two or more years at Bryn Mawr College and occasionally for others. Students who hold the A.B. degree from Bryn Mawr College must complete a minimum of three academic units at Bryn Mawr.

3. The recommendation of the student as a candidate by the director of the dissertation and the major department and the acceptance of the recommendation by the Council of The Graduate School of Arts and Sciences. Application for candidacy, on a form to be obtained at the Office of the Dean of The Graduate School of Arts and Sciences, may be made as early as the spring of the student's first year, provided that the student has been registered for two units of graduate work at Bryn Mawr.

4. Knowledge of the foreign languages, computer languages (such as FORTRAN, ALGOL, PL/I, etc.), and special techniques (such as statistics) required by the individual departments. In certain circumstances, students whose native language is not English may offer English for one of the languages. These requirements must be fulfilled before the student takes the Preliminary Examinations.

5. Satisfactory Preliminary Examinations in the fields established for the candidate. These examinations are intended to test the candidate's knowledge of the principles of the subject, exemplified by the command of several fields or areas, the ability to apply knowledge to new problems, and power of organization.

6. The preparation of a dissertation worthy of publication, which presents the results of independent investigation in the fields of the major subject and contains original material, results, or interpretations.

7. A satisfactory Final Oral Examination in the special fields in which the dissertation has been written.

8. The publication of the dissertation in whole or in part. Microfilming is accepted as a method of publication.

A special pamphlet describing regulations for the Ph.D. degree will be issued to students applying for candidacy.

The Degree of Master of Arts

The general requirements for the M.A. degree are as follows:

1. Undergraduate preparation in major and allied fields which is satisfactory to the departments concerned.

2. A knowledge of one modern foreign language and such additional foreign languages or special techniques as the individual departments may require. Students whose native language is not English, except for those majoring in the language and literature of their native tongue, are not required to present an additional language.

3. The completion of a satisfactory program of work endorsed by the department and accepted by the Council of The Graduate School of Arts and Sciences. Application for such endorsement must be submitted on appropriate forms to the Dean of The Graduate School of Arts and Sciences not later than one week after the beginning of the second semester of the academic year in which the candidate wishes to take the degree. The program of study must include three units of work: (1) one seminar or graduate course, (2) a second seminar or supervised unit of graduate work, (3) a third seminar or an undergraduate course recommended by the major department. If undergraduate courses are included in this last unit, they must be supplemented by additional individual work. Only one such course may be offered for the M.A. degree. Under certain circumstances advanced undergraduate courses in science can be counted as seminars, subject to the approval of the department and the Dean of The Graduate School of Arts and Sciences. Candidates whose major department conducts a Journal Club or Colloquium are expected to include it in their program.

4. The preparation of a paper in a special field normally related to one of the seminars or units of graduate work in the candidate's program. Candidates currently at Bryn Mawr College shall submit this paper by the date set by the department. Candidates not currently on campus must submit the paper 30 days before Commencement of the academic year of the degree.

5. Each candidate, after all other requirements have been completed, must pass a Final Examination.

6. Work for the degree may be spread over several years which need not be in succession but must be included in a five-year period (60 months).

Graduate Program in Arts and Sciences 1976-77

Graduate Seminars and Courses

Graduate seminars and courses vary from year to year. Parentheses designate courses or seminars not given in the current year. Undergraduate courses which may with additional work be offered for graduate credit are listed by number. The letter "a" following a number indicates a half-course given in the first semester; the letter "b" following a number indicates a half-course given in the second semester; the letter "c" following a number indicates a half-course given two hours a week throughout the year.

Special graduate requirements are listed under each department. For the general degree requirements for the M.A. and the Ph.D., see pages 13-15.

Anthropology

Professor: Jane C. Goodale PHD *Chairman*

Associate Professor: Philip L. Kilbride PHD‡

Assistant Professors: Robert A. Braun PHD
Richard H. Jordan PHD
Judith R. Shapiro PHD

Visiting Lecturers: Hiroko Hara PHD
Tadahiko Hara PHD

Associate Professor of German (Linguistics): Nancy C. Dorian PHD

Prerequisites. A good undergraduate preparation in Anthropology or a closely related discipline is desirable. Students whose undergraduate training is not entirely adequate will be required to take such undergraduate courses as may seem necessary.

Language Requirements. Candidates for the M.A. or Ph.D. must offer one of the following two options: (1) two modern languages (French, German, Russian, Spanish) or (2) one modern language (French, German, Russian, Spanish) and statistics or computer science. Language skills may be tested by either the Graduate

---

‡On leave 1976-77

School Foreign Language Test (GSFLT) of the Educational Testing Service or examinations administered by Bryn Mawr College. Entering students may offer scores of the GSFLT taken within twelve months of the date on which they begin graduate work at Bryn Mawr. Competency in statistics and computer science will be acknowledged when the student satisfactorily passes an appropriate graduate course in statistics or computer science at Bryn Mawr College.

Program and Examination for the M.A. For students with an excellent undergraduate preparation, the program may consist of a minimum of three units of work in seminars or advanced undergraduate courses arranged for graduate credit, one of which may be in an allied subject. The program usually takes two years. The M.A. paper may be based on an essay offered in a seminar. The Final Examination consists of one four-hour written examination, but the Ph.D. Preliminary Examinations may be substituted for the M.A. Examination. All graduate students are expected to take the M.A. before proceeding to the Ph.D., except, of course, those who enter Bryn Mawr College with an M.A.

Program and Examinations for the Ph.D. The Department emphasizes the holistic nature of the anthropological discipline and will expect each student to become familiar with various cultural, social, and archaeological approaches and the anthropology of at least two geographical regions, in addition to areas and topics of professional specialization.

The Preliminary Examinations for candidates for the Ph.D. (usually taken near the end of the third year of graduate work) will consist of four three-hour written examinations and an oral examination of one hour. One of these examinations may be in an allied field.

Since the dissertation is usually based upon field work, it is difficult for a student to obtain the degree in less than five years.

General Degree Requirements for the M.A. and the Ph.D. See pages 13-15.

SEMINARS AND GRADUATE COURSES

Four or five seminars are offered each semester. Rarely is the same seminar offered in consecutive years in order to allow the greatest possible choice and variety to each student over a two to three-year period. For advanced students units of supervised readings are sometimes substituted for seminars. Topics of the seminars are chosen from those listed below; those being offered in 1976-77 are designated by the name of the instructor and the semester in which they will meet.

General

(Basic Principles of Anthropology)
(Cultural Theory)
(History of Anthropology)

Ethnology

(Africa)
(Australia)
(Circumpolar Peoples)
Europe: Miss Shapiro—semester I
(Latin America)
(Melanesia)
(North America)
Polynesia: Miss Goodale—semester II
(South America)

Special Topics

Child-Rearing and Socialization: Mrs. Hara—semester I
Comparative Perspectives on the Family: Mr. Hara, Mrs. Hara—
   semester II
(Complex Societies)
(Cultural Dynamics)
(Cultural Ecology)
(Environmental Archaeology)
Ethnographic Methods: Miss Goodale—semester I
(Linguistic Anthropology)
(Peasant Cultures)
(Population Dynamics)
(Psychological Anthropology)
(Religion and World View)
(Social Organization)
Topics in Methods of Archaeological Analysis: Mr. Jordan—
   semester II
(Topics in Methods of Ethnographic Analysis)

Prehistory

(Africa)
(Arctic Archaeology)
(Human Evolution and Old World Prehistory)
(Middle America)
The Neolithic Period and the Rise of Civilization: Mr. Braun—
   semester I
(Rise of Old World Civilizations)
(North America)
(South America)

306b *Modern Latin American Communities*: Mr. Braun
307a *Topics in Ethnography of South Asia*: Mr. Hara
309b *The Ethnography of Japan*: Mrs. Hara
313b *Linguistic Anthropology*: Miss Shapiro
320a *Cultural Theory*: Miss Shapiro
326a *Anthropology through Literature*: Mr. Hara
(Int. 308 *Introduction to Linguistics*)
Int. 310a *Linguistic Techniques*: Miss Dorian
Int. 312b *Field Methods in Linguistics*: Miss Dorian

In addition, courses at the University of Pennsylvania are available under the terms of the Reciprocal Plan (see page 11).

Biochemistry

Committee on Biochemistry:

Professor of Biology: Robert L. Conner PH D

Professors of Chemistry: Ernst Berliner PH D
                          Frank B. Mallory PH D *Chairman*

Assistant Professors of Biology: Mary Jo Koroly PH D
                                   David J. Prescott PH D

Assistant Professor of Chemistry: J. Maitland Young PHD

This interdisciplinary program offers work within the Departments of Biology and Chemistry and leads to the M.A. or Ph.D. degree. It is administered by the Committee on Biochemistry, which consists of members of the two departments. Depending on their backgrounds and interests, students may enter the program either through the Department of Biology or the Department of Chemistry.

Prerequisites. Undergraduate training consisting of a major or its equivalent in either Biology or Chemistry and one-year courses or their equivalents in physiology, organic chemistry, and physical chemistry. Students lacking any one of these specific courses should make up this deficiency during their first year in the Biochemistry program.

Major and Allied Subjects. Students will receive their advanced degrees in either Biology or Chemistry with a major in Biochemistry. The allied field will usually be a branch of Biology or Chemistry different from Biochemistry. It may also be selected from fields in Biophysics, Physics, Mathematics, or Psychology. Other combina-

19

tions may be accepted with the approval of the Committee and the Council of The Graduate School of Arts and Sciences.

Language Requirements. See the requirements set by each department.

Program and Examination for the M.A. Students who are candidates for the M.A. will usually offer one graduate course or seminar in Biochemistry, another seminar or advanced undergraduate course arranged for seminar credit, and a unit of research. This unit consists of an experimental investigation carried out under the direction of a member of either department. The results of this unit must be made the subject of a written paper. The Final Examination consists of a four-hour written examination or a three-hour written and one-hour oral examination.

Program and Examinations for the Ph.D. All students must take the core curriculum in Biochemistry, which includes Biochemistry 353, or its equivalent if taken elsewhere, and a series of graduate courses and seminars in Biochemistry. In addition, students will usually take other graduate courses or seminars, depending on their interests, in either department in order to acquire a broad general background for research or teaching in Biochemistry. They will usually devote a large portion of their time to research carried out under the direction of one member of either department. The Preliminary and Final Examinations are taken in accordance with the regulations set by the department in which the student is enrolled.

General Degree Requirements for the M.A. and Ph.D. See pages 13-15.

SEMINARS AND GRADUATE COURSES

See listings under the Departments of Biology and Chemistry.

SELECTED UNDERGRADUATE COURSES

See listings under the Departments of Biology and Chemistry.

Biology

Professor: Robert L. Conner PHD *Chairman*
Associate Professor: Anthony R. Kaney PHD‡

---

‡On leave 1976-77

Assistant Professors: Mary Jo Koroly PHD
                   Patricia J. Olds-Clarke PHD
                   David J. Prescott PHD
                   Steven N. Treistman PHD

Lecturers: Kathryn Z. Orkwiszewski PHD
           Patricia Onderdonk Pruett PHD *Associate Dean
           of the Undergraduate College*
           Denise M. Ragona PHD

Professor of History of Science: Jane M. Oppenheimer PHD

Assistant Professor of Chemistry: J. Maitland Young PHD

Prerequisites. An undergraduate major in Biology, Zoology, or Botany, including courses in general and organic chemistry. Some college-level preparation in Mathematics and Physics is desirable. Students with majors in other subjects may be admitted but will be required to make up any deficiencies in their preparation in Biology before being admitted to graduate courses. All applicants should submit scores from the Graduate Record Examination Aptitude Test and the Advanced Test in Biology.

Major and Allied Subjects. Candidates for the M.A. and Ph.D. degrees may specialize in Biochemistry, cell biology, cellular physiology, developmental biology, genetics, molecular biology, microbiology, or neurophysiology, but must take work also from areas not chosen for specialization. Allied subjects may be selected from fields in Chemistry, Physics, and Psychology, and in special cases from other related fields, with the approval of the Council of The Graduate School of Arts and Sciences.

Language Requirements. Candidates for the M.A. degree should offer French, German, or statistics. Candidates for the Ph.D. degree must offer two foreign languages: French and German (or some other language by special permission of the Department and the Council of The Graduate School of Arts and Sciences), or one foreign language and statistics. The statistics requirement may be satisfied by passing a graduate course in statistics at Bryn Mawr or by examination administered by the Biology Department. Language skills will be tested by the examinations administered by Bryn Mawr College.

Program and Examination for the M.A. One full year, or its equivalent, of course work in seminars and advanced undergraduate courses arranged for seminar credit and a written report on a piece of experimental work carried out under the direction of a member of the Department. Qualified students may substitute a unit of supervised research for formal course work. The Final Examination consists of a three-hour written examination covering the areas of study and a one-hour oral examination concentrating particularly on

21

the interpretation and significance of the experimental problem and its relation to Biology more generally.

Program and Examinations for the Ph.D. The Preliminary Examinations for the Ph.D. consist of three written examinations, each of four hours' duration, and an oral examination of one to two hours. These examinations will cover the areas included in the course work in the major and allied fields. After the subject of the dissertation has been decided, the student will meet with the faculty of the Department to outline and discuss the subject and the proposed plan of research. The Final Examination is oral, covering the subject of the dissertation in relation to the general field of Biology.

General Degree Requirements for the M.A. and Ph.D. See pages 13-15.

GRADUATE COURSES

Mr. Prescott

Advanced Biochemistry—semesters I and II

A course emphasizing the biophysical and bio-organic aspects of Biochemistry. A detailed treatment of protein chemistry and catalysis will be included. Two hours' lecture. No laboratory. Prerequisites: Biology 353, Chemistry 203.

For Statistics: See offerings in The Graduate School of Social Work and Social Research and the Department of Psychology.

Journal Club: All faculty members and graduate students meet each week for presentation of current research in Biology. Graduate students, faculty, and outside speakers will participate.

SEMINARS

All seminars and advanced undergraduate courses arranged for seminar credit are offered for one semester each year. Four seminars are offered each year, with each area being offered in alternate years. The topics considered in any semester are selected in accordance with the needs and desires of the students enrolled. A list of seminar topics offered by each instructor in recent years is given below:

Mr. Conner

Cellular Physiology

Membrane Structure and Function

Regulation of Lipid Metabolism

Molecular Endocrinology

Mr. Kaney

Genetics

Somatic Cell Genetics

Genetics of Ciliated Protozoans

Structure and Function of the Chromosome

Miss Koroly
Cell Biology
Cell Communication
Structure/Function Relationships in Selected Organelles
Mechanisms of Intracellular Motion

Mrs. Olds-Clarke
Developmental Biology
Gametogenesis and Development
Fertilization
Sex Differentiation

Mr. Prescott
Biochemistry
Neurochemistry
Protein Structure and Chemistry
Peptide Hormones

SELECTED UNDERGRADUATE COURSES

The following advanced undergraduate courses with supplemental
work may be taken for graduate credit:

350b *Problems in Cell Physiology*: Mr. Conner
(352a *Problems in Molecular Biology*: Mrs. Ragona)
353 *Biochemistry*: Mr. Conner, Mr. Prescott
354a *Problems in Cell Biology*: Miss Koroly
355b *Problems in Neurophysiology*: Mr. Treistman
(356 *Biophysics*: Miss Hoyt)
(358a *Analysis of Development*: Mrs. Olds-Clarke)
362a *Cellular Physiology*: Mr. Conner
364b *Cell Biology*: Miss Koroly
Int. 357a *Computer Use in the Life Sciences*: Mrs. Pruett

Chemistry

Professors: Jay Martin Anderson PHD
Ernst Berliner PHD
Frank B. Mallory PHD
George L. Zimmerman PHD *Chairman*

Associate Professor: Joseph Varimbi PHD

Assistant Professor: J. Maitland Young PHD

Lecturer: Frances Bondhus Berliner PHD

Assistant Professor of Biology: David J. Prescott PHD

Fields of Study and Research. The primary aim of the instruction of graduate students in the Department of Chemistry is to provide a sound background in modern chemistry and to prepare men and women for a professional career in productive scholarship, research, and teaching in chemistry. Courses and seminars are offered to enable the students to acquire a command of their chosen fields, in addition to a sufficiently broad general background so that they will be prepared for the variety of assignments in chemistry teaching or research which they may later encounter. Thesis research is the major part of the training. Research training is centered on a variety of investigations carried out by the members of the faculty. Currently there are active research programs involving both faculty and students in the following areas of organic, inorganic, physical, and theoretical chemistry, and of Biochemistry: kinetics of electrophilic substitution and addition, relative reactivities of polynuclear aromatic systems, isotope effects, organic photochemistry, nuclear magnetic resonance as applied to substituent effects and through-space nuclear coupling, reactions in liquid ammonia and other non-aqueous solvents, photochemical cis-trans isomerizations, ultraviolet and vacuum ultraviolet absorption studies of hydrated transition metal ions, nuclear magnetic resonance as applied to nuclear relaxation, molecular collision dynamics, and enzyme mechanisms.

Under the Plan for the Coordination of the Sciences there are special opportunities for research and training in such interrelated areas as geochemistry, chemical physics, etc. See page 85.

Prerequisites. An undergraduate preparation in Chemistry including courses in inorganic, analytical, organic, and physical chemistry, college Physics, and Mathematics (calculus). All applicants should submit scores on the Aptitude Test and the Advanced Test in Chemistry of the Graduate Record Examinations. Applicants lacking some of these prerequisites may be considered for admission under special circumstances in consultation with the Department.

Major and Allied Subjects. Students may specialize in Biochemistry, organic, inorganic, or physical chemistry. The allied subject for the Ph.D. may be chosen from the fields of Mathematics, Physics, inorganic geology, Biology and a branch of Chemistry different from that of the major subject. Other combinations may be accepted with the approval of the Council of The Graduate School of Arts and Sciences and on the recommendation of the Department. The typical work for the allied subject would be a year's course or seminar on an approved level.

Language Requirements. Candidates for the M.A. must offer German, French, or Russian. Candidates for the Ph.D. may offer German and either French, Russian, or demonstrated skill in digital computation, numerical analysis, and the theory of error. This skill may be demonstrated by an examination consisting of two parts, a

24

practical part requiring the successful execution of a FORTRAN (or other equivalent language) program and a written examination on numerical analysis and error theory, or by a satisfactory grade in an appropriate course.

Language skills may be tested by either the Graduate School Foreign Language Test (GSFLT) of the Educational Testing Service or the examinations administered by Bryn Mawr College. Entering students may offer scores of the GSFLT taken within twelve months of the date on which they begin graduate work at Bryn Mawr.

Program and Examination for the M.A. Students who are candidates for the M.A. will usually offer one seminar in their special field, another seminar or advanced undergraduate course in Chemistry or an allied field, and one unit of research. This unit consists of an experimental investigation carried out under the direction of a member of the Department. The Final Examination consists of a four-hour written examination or a three-hour written and one-hour oral examination.

Program and Examinations for the Ph.D. Ph.D. students will normally be expected to devote a large portion of their time to experimental or theoretical research carried out under the direction of a member of the Department. They will usually take all seminars offered in their special fields during their stay at Bryn Mawr, in addition to such courses as will give them a broad background in Chemistry. The Preliminary Examinations will normally be taken in the student's third year of graduate study. They consist of two four-hour written examinations and two oral examinations, each one or two hours in duration. The two written examinations will be from the candidate's major field. One will be a broad examination in the general aspects of that field. The second will be in the special field of the candidate's research and will include questions designed to test familiarity with, and ability to interpret, material from the recent chemical literature. One of the oral examinations will be held soon after the written examinations have been completed and will be for the purpose of clarifying and augmenting the candidate's responses on the two written examinations. The three examinations described so far must be completed within a period of five weeks. The other oral examination will involve the defense of two original chemical research proposals previously submitted by the candidate. No more than one of these proposals may deal with work related to the special field of the student's research. All four of the examinations must be completed within a period of one year. The Final Examination is oral and is devoted to the subject matter of the student's dissertation.

General Degree Requirements for the M.A. and the Ph.D. See pages 13-15.

Colloquium. All members of the Department and the graduate students meet every week for a presentation of current research in Chemistry, usually by outside speakers.

SEMINARS AND GRADUATE COURSES

In order to meet the needs of the students and to offer them as wide a selection of topics as possible, the seminars are arranged in such a way that each one is usually given at least once within a three-year period. The topics listed below are given in one-semester seminars, counting one-half unit of credit each. Ordinarily four seminars are offered each year. Individual programs are flexible, and the contents of the seminars are likely to vary with the research interests of the students and the current research activities of the faculty.

The seminars listed below are illustrative of those that have been offered in recent years.

Mr. Anderson
Intermediate Quantum Mechanics
Introduction to Molecular Spectroscopy
Nuclear Magnetic Resonance

Mr. Berliner
Physical Organic Aspects of Aromatic Chemistry
Physical Organic Chemistry
Structure and Physical Properties of Organic Compounds

Mrs. Berliner
Natural Products
Chemistry of Heterocyclic Compounds

Mr. Mallory
Organic Photochemistry
Recent Methods in Organic Synthesis
Spectral Applications in Current Organic Chemistry

Mr. Varimbi
Inorganic Chemistry
Statistical Thermodynamics
Theory of Electrolytic Solutions

Mr. Young
Chemistry of Coenzymes
Mechanism of Enzymatic Reactions
Physical Chemistry of Proteins and Nucleic Acids

Mr. Zimmerman
Applications of Group Theory in Quantum Mechanics
Introduction to Chemical Physics
Photochemistry

For additional seminars in Biochemistry, see the Department of Biology.

The following advanced undergraduate courses may be taken for graduate credit:

301b *Advanced Inorganic Chemistry*: Mr. Varimbi
302 *Advanced Organic Chemistry*: Mr. Berliner, Mr. Mallory
303a *Quantum Mechanics of Atoms and Molecules*:
     Mr. Zimmerman
303b *Atomic and Molecular Spectroscopy*: Mr. Gavin
     (at Haverford—1976-77)
353 *Biochemistry*: Mr. Conner, Mr. Prescott, Mr. Young

Classical
and Near Eastern Archaeology

Professors: Phyllis Pray Bober PHD *Dean*
          The Graduate School of Arts and Sciences
          Machteld J. Mellink PHD *Chairman*
          Kyle M. Phillips, Jr. PHD‡
          Brunilde S. Ridgway PHD

Mary Flexner Lecturer: Phyllis W. Lehmann PHD

Associate Professors: Richard S. Ellis PHD
                  Carl Nylander PHD

Prerequisites: An undergraduate major in Archaeology or at least two courses in Archaeology combined with a major in Greek, Latin, ancient history, or History of Art. It is expected that students of Classical and Near Eastern Archaeology will have a basic knowledge of Greek, Latin, and ancient history. Students with incomplete preparation in Archaeology will be advised to take selected undergraduate courses during their first year in graduate school.

Allied Subjects. Greek, Linear B, Latin, Akkadian, Hebrew, Hittite, Egyptian, History of Art, ancient history, Anthropology, a science related to the archaeological program of the candidate.

Language Requirements: For the M.A. and Ph.D., a good reading knowledge of German and French. For the Ph.D., a reading knowledge of Greek or a Near Eastern ancient language. Language skills may be tested by either the Graduate School Foreign Language Test

‡On leave 1976-77

(GSFLT) of the Educational Testing Service or the examinations administered by Bryn Mawr College.

Program and Examination for the M.A. Three units of work in Archaeology or in Archaeology and an allied field. The Final Examination is written (three hours) and oral (one hour).

Program and Examinations for the Ph.D. The students spend the first two years in residence, participating in seminars and preparing for the Preliminary Examinations. The third year is usually spent at the American School of Classical Studies in Athens or at another archaeological research center abroad. Museums in Europe and the Near East are visited during this year, and participation in excavations is arranged when possible (see below).

The Preliminary Examinations, normally taken at the end of three years of graduate work, consist of four four-hour papers in selected fields such as Greek and Roman sculpture, architecture, monumental painting, Greek vase-painting, numismatics, Aegean prehistory, prehistory of Western Asia, Mesopotamian art and archaeology, or the archaeology of Anatolia, Syria, Palestine, or Cyprus. One of the papers may be written in an allied field. The Final Examination covers the field of the dissertation.

General Degree Requirements for the M.A. and the Ph.D. See pages 13-15.

Excavations. The Department currently sponsors two excavation projects:

I. An investigation of the Bronze Age habitation of ancient Lycia in progress since 1963 at the third millennium B.C. site of Karatash near Elmali.[1] Advanced graduate students participate in this excavation which is organized as a field seminar during the fall term with full graduate credit. The program provides instruction in excavation and field techniques and gives an opportunity to visit other sites, excavations, and museums in Turkey, with discussion of the problems of the Bronze Age in the Aegean and Anatolia. The final publication will be prepared on the basis of the joint field reports of the participants.

II. The Etruscan project, started in 1966, is the excavation of the archaic site of Murlo near Siena, organized in cooperation with the Archaeological Museum in Florence. The work takes place during the summer and offers qualified graduate and undergraduate students training in excavation techniques while participating in the study of a townsite and necropolis of the sixth century B.C.[2]

---

[1]cf. *American Journal of Archaeology* 68 (1964) 269-278; 69 (1965) 241-251; 70 (1966) 245-257; 71 (1967) 251-267; 72 (1968) 243-263; 73 (1969) 319-331; 74 (1970) 245-259; 75 (1971) 257-261; 76 (1972) 257-269; 77 (1973) 293-307; 78 (1974) 351-360; 79 (1975) 349-355.

Cooperation with the University of Pennsylvania. Attention is drawn to the courses offered by the Departments of Classical Archaeology, Anthropology, History of Art, Oriental Studies, and Biblical Archaeology at the University of Pennsylvania. Under the Reciprocal Plan, (see page 11), students may register for a unit of work at the University or pursue research at the University Museum.

SEMINARS AND GRADUATE COURSES

The following seminars are offered in 1976-77:

Mr. Ellis
The Royal Cemetery of Ur—semester I
Mesopotamian and Syrian Sculpture of the Second Millennium B.C.—semester II

Miss Mellink
Field Seminar in Anatolia—semester I
The Early Bronze Age in Anatolia—semester II

Mr. Nylander
Troy—semester I
The Alexander Mosaic or *Aspects of Achaemenian Art and Architecture*—semester II

Mrs. Ridgway
Hellenistic Sculpture—semester I
Greek Funerary Monuments—semester II

SELECTED UNDERGRADUATE COURSES

201a *The Archaeology of Mesopotamia before 1600 B.C.*:
   Mr. Ellis
203a *Roman Sculpture*: Mrs. Bober
203b *Greek Sculpture*: Mrs. Ridgway
205b *Aegean Archaeology*: Miss Mellink
206b *Ancient Near Eastern Architecture*: Mr. Ellis, Mr. Nylander
302a *Greek Architecture*: Mr. Nylander
305b *The Bronze Age in Syria and Palestine*: Mr. Ellis
390b *Studies in the Art of Greece in the Fourth Century B.C.*:
   Mrs. Lehmann
History 204a *The Ancient City*: Mr. Scott
History 205a *The Ancient Near East*: Mr. Ellis

---

[2]cf. *American Journal of Archaeology* 71 (1967) 133-139; 72 (1968) 121-124; 73 (1969) 333-339; 74 (1970) 241-244; 75 (1971) 245-255; 76 (1972) 249-255; 77 (1973) 319-326; 78 (1974) 265-278; 79 (1975) 357-366.

29

Economics

Professor: Richard B. Du Boff PHD

Associate Professors: Noel J. J. Farley PHD *Chairman*
Helen Manning Hunter PHD

Assistant Professor: Li Way Lee PHD

Prerequisites. An undergraduate major in Economics, with work in such related fields as History and Political Science. Superior applicants with majors in other disciplines may be admitted. Applicants must submit scores on the Aptitude Test and Advanced Tests of the Graduate Record Examinations. Students whose undergraduate training in Economics is incomplete may be required to take such undergraduate courses as the Department thinks necessary.

Allied Subjects. Most subjects in the other social sciences and in History and Philosophy are acceptable. Mathematics and statistics are necessary to advanced work in Economics.

Language Requirements. Candidates for the M.A. and Ph.D. must show reading proficiency in one modern foreign language. Candidates for the Ph.D. must in addition show either reading proficiency in a second modern foreign language or proficiency in Mathematics beyond the level required for admission to graduate seminars in Economics (i.e., beyond the level of first-year college calculus and basic linear algebra). Mathematical skills will be tested by an examination to be set by the Department. The topics to be covered will be agreed upon in advance and may vary according to the student's particular field of interest in Economics.

Language skills will be tested by the Graduate School Foreign Language Test (GSFLT) of the Educational Testing Service. Entering students may offer scores of the GSFLT taken within twelve months of the date on which they begin graduate work at Bryn Mawr.

Program and Examination for the M.A. It is expected that the work for the M.A. degree will require not less than one calendar year of graduate study. All candidates for the M.A. degree must complete three units of formal course work (seminars, courses, and supervised units) prior to submitting the M.A. research paper. One of these units must be in economic theory, one in statistics and econometrics, and one in the student's special field of interest. Course examinations in each of these three fields must be passed before the candidate presents the research paper. After acceptance of the paper a Final Examination must be passed.

Program and Examinations for the Ph.D. Candidates for the Ph.D. will take as much formal course work as is necessary to prepare them for the Ph.D. examinations. The Preliminary Examinations will consist of four three-hour written papers and an oral examination; one of the written papers will be in microeconomic analysis and one in macroeconomic analysis; the other two papers will be in fields related to the candidate's major interest. The Final Oral, taken after the dissertation has been accepted, will be devoted to the subject matter of the dissertation.

General Degree Requirements for the M.A. and the Ph.D. See pages 13-15.

SEMINARS

Seminars are chosen each year from the following topics:

Mr. Du Boff
  American Economic Development
  Economic History and Growth 1750-1970

Mr. Farley
  International Economic Development
  International Trade Policy
  International Trade Theory

Mrs. Hunter
  Econometrics
  Macroeconomic Analysis
  Monetary Theory and Institutions

Mr. Lee
  Corporate Financial Theory
  Industrial Organization
  Microeconomic Analysis
  Public Finance

SELECTED UNDERGRADUATE COURSES

203a *Statistical Methods in Economics*: Mrs. Hunter
222b *History of Economic Thought*: Mr. Du Boff
302b *Introduction to Econometrics*: Mrs. Hunter
303a *Macroeconomic Analysis*: Mrs. Hunter
304b *Microeconomic Analysis*: Mr. Lee

Education and Child Development

Professors: Janet L. Hoopes PHD *Director*
  Child Study Institute
  Ethel W. Maw PHD *Chairman*

Associate Professors: Susan E. Maxfield MS *Director*
  Phebe Anna Thorne School
  Emmy A. Pepitone PHD
  Faye P. Soffen ED D‡

Assistant Professors: Fred Rothbaum MS
  Samuel S. Snyder PHD

The program prepares students for college teaching and research in educational psychology and child development, for child guidance, for school psychology, school counseling, for teaching in the schools and for early childhood education. The training is carried on in a setting of service to public and laboratory schools and to the community at large. Classes, seminars, and staff conferences provide opportunity for students from several related disciplines to develop competence in the team approach to the children's specialties in education, psychology, and guidance agencies. Trends in physical, intellectual, and emotional growth from infancy to maturity are stressed.

Bryn Mawr has program approval from the Pennsylvania Department of Education for several curriculum sequences which prepare candidates for public school professions. These courses of study include teacher education in ten liberal arts fields, school psychology, and school counseling, both elementary and secondary. Students who satisfactorily complete an approved program will, on the recommendation of this Department, receive the state certificate in the appropriate field.

Prerequisites: An undergraduate preparation in the liberal arts which must include work in general Psychology and statistics. Students whose undergraduate training in Psychology is not adequate will be required to take such undergraduate courses as seem necessary. Applicants for admission are asked to submit scores of the Graduate Record Examination Aptitude Test and a statement of their academic plans and goals. Undergraduate grades of at least B level are necessary.

Major and Allied Subjects: Candidates for advanced degrees are

---

‡On leave 1976-77

expected to become competent in several different areas: child development, clinical evaluation, counseling and guidance, history and philosophy of education, learning, the school as a social institution, secondary education, elementary education, early childhood education, and childhood psychopathology. For the M.A., two fields are required. For the Ph.D., four fields must be presented. One field may be an allied field and is individually arranged. Field examinations are given once each semester.

Language and Statistics Requirements: For the M.A., students are required to pass an examination in one modern foreign language and demonstrate a working knowledge of descriptive and inferential statistics. For the Ph.D., students are required to pass an examination demonstrating reading knowledge of one modern foreign language and competence in statistics. The statistics requirement for both degrees may be satisfied by passing the course *Foundations of Research* at a satisfactory level or by demonstrating equivalent competencies. Language skills may be tested by either the Graduate School Foreign Language Test (GSFLT) of the Educational Testing Service or the examinations administered by Bryn Mawr College. Entering students may offer scores of the GSFLT taken within twelve months of the date on which they begin graduate work at Bryn Mawr.

Program and Examination for the M.A. Candidates will normally offer three units of graduate work in Education, although one of the three may be taken in an allied field. A paper embodying the results of independent research is required. The Final Examination consists of two three-hour written examinations, one in each field offered, and a one-hour oral examination on the M.A. paper.

Examinations for the Ph.D. The Preliminary Examinations consist of four-hour written examinations in each of the fields offered and an oral examination. The Final Examination is an oral examination in the field of the Ph.D. dissertation.

General Degree Requirements for the M.A. and the Ph.D. See pages 13-15.

The Phebe Anna Thorne School and the Child Study Institute. The Phebe Anna Thorne School is maintained by the Department as a laboratory nursery school for normal children where students may observe and assist in the program for three- and four-year-olds. For those preparing for teaching, medical work with children, child welfare or guidance, the school provides opportunity for direct experience with early childhood development. Students preparing for early childhood education spend substantial blocks of time in the Thorne School.

The Department also operates at the College the Child Study Institute, a mental health center where problems of learning and behavior are studied and remedial measures planned and carried out with parents and children. The service is given by a staff of qualified specialists in child psychiatry, psychology, school counseling, and remedial teaching. Advanced students participate at various levels of responsibility. Referrals from the schools, from physicians, social agencies, and families give students the opportunity for acquaintance with a diversity of clinical material.

A separate building on the college grounds houses the Department, the Thorne School, and the Institute, with rooms equipped for nursery school teaching and for individual examination of pupils, remedial teaching, individual and group therapy, and student observation.

SEMINARS

The seminars offered are selected from the following. (In most cases, laboratory practice is required.) All seminars run throughout the academic year unless otherwise indicated. Some seminars are offered in alternate years.

Miss Hoopes
  Clinical Evaluation
  Advanced Theory and Practice in Clinical Evaluation

Mrs. Maw
  Educational Psychology
  Curriculum of the Elementary School—semester II

Miss Maxfield
  Developmental Psychology
  Early Childhood Educaton
  Theory and Practice in Early Childhood Education

Mrs. Pepitone
  History and Philosophy of Education—semester I
  The Social Psychology of the School
  Analysis of Social Structure and Interaction in the Classroom
  The American School—semester II

Mr. Rothbaum
  The Psychology of Exceptional Children—semester I
  The Diagnosis and Remediation of Learning Disabilities—
    semester II
  Childhood Psychopathology—semester II

Mr. Snyder
  Critical Issues in Human Development
  Selected Topics in Developmental Psychology—semester II

34

Mrs. Soffen
Principles and Organization of the Guidance Program
The Counseling Process: Theory and Practice
The Group Process in Counseling and Guidance
The Psychology of Occupations
Advanced Theory and Practice in Counseling and Guidance

Members of the Department
Foundations of Research

SELECTED UNDERGRADUATE COURSES

206a *Developmental Psychology*: Mr. Snyder
206b *Adolescent Development*: Mr. Rothbaum
301a *Principles of Teaching in the Secondary School*:
    Mrs. Maw
(302a *Principles of Teaching in the Elementary School*:
    Mrs. Maw)

Courses 301a and 302a satisfy the student-teaching requirement of most states. Plans for registration should be made with Mrs. Maw in the spring before the student expects to take the course in the fall.

English

Professors: Robert B. Burlin PHD *Acting Chairman, Semester I*
    K. Laurence Stapleton AB

Associate Professors: Carol L. Bernstein PHD
    Thomas H. Jackson PHD
    Joseph E. Kramer PHD *Chairman**

Assistant Professors: Sandra M. Berwind PHD
    Peter M. Briggs PHD
    Katrin Ristkok Burlin PHD
    E. Jane Hedley PHD
    Anne Kaier PHD
    Sandra I. Kohler PHD

Lecturers: Eileen T. Johnston MA
    Elizabeth R. McKinsey AB

Prerequisites. An undergraduate major in English or its equivalent.

---

*On leave semester I

35

Students should have had some training in at least one other field of the humanities: a classical or a modern foreign literature, History, the History of Art, or Philosophy. All applicants should submit scores in the Aptitude Test of the Graduate Record Examination.

Language Requirements. For the M.A. degree, a knowledge of either French or German adequate to the reading of basic scholarly and literary texts. For the Ph.D., the student must either pass examinations in both French and German or demonstrate superior competence in one by satisfactorily completing one unit of graduate work in that language or its literature at Bryn Mawr. (In special cases, with the approval of the appropriate language department and of the Department of English, equivalent work at another university may be accepted.) With the approval of the Department, another modern language may be substituted for French or German when it can be shown to be particularly pertinent to a projected dissertation. Students working toward the doctorate are also required to show evidence of an adequate knowledge of Latin or Greek. It is expected that the doctoral candidate will satisfy these requirements at the beginning of the second year of graduate study; they must be completely satisfied before the doctoral candidate takes the Preliminary Examinations.

Language skills may be tested by either the Graduate School Foreign Language Test (GSFLT) of the Educational Testing Service or the examinations administered by Bryn Mawr College. Entering students may offer scores of the GSFLT taken within twelve months of the date on which they begin graduate work at Bryn Mawr.

Program and Examination for the M.A. Three units of work in English or two in English and one in an allied field. The M.A. paper is due on April 23. The Final Examination is written, four hours in length, and on the general field of the M.A. paper. (If the M.A. courses are completed in one year, the paper and the Final Examination are frequently deferred through the following summer.)

Program and Examinations for the Ph.D. Work of the Department is carried on through small seminars and supervised units of independent study. Six units of graduate work are required, one of which may be in an allied field. Candidates will be expected to spend at least one year in full-time graduate work. The program must include some training in Old or Middle English or in the history of the English language.

After being accepted for doctoral candidacy, the student will take Preliminary Examinations in five parts: four written (four hours each) and one oral (one or two hours). One written examination may be in an allied field. The choice of the four fields will be determined by the student in consultation with the graduate advisor and the departmental examiners who will form the Supervising Committee. The candidate is expected to demonstrate a balanced knowledge of different periods.

Before proceeding with the dissertation, it is expected that the doctoral candidate will submit a prospectus to be discussed with the departmental members of the Supervising Committee. The Final Examination is in the field of the dissertation.

General Degree Requirements for the M.A. and the Ph.D. See pages 13-15.

SEMINARS

Since many seminars run through the year, students must begin work in the first semester.

Mrs. Bernstein
(Nineteenth Century English Novel)
Victorian Poetry and Prose

Mr. Burlin
(Chaucer)
Mediaeval Drama—semester I

Mrs. Burlin
Jane Austen, the Brontës, and George Eliot—semester II

Mr. Jackson
Twentieth Century Literature

Miss Kaier
Wordsworth and Keats—semester II

Mr. Kramer
Renaissance Drama—semester II
(Shakespeare)

Miss Stapleton
(Milton)
Studies in Poetry

SELECTED UNDERGRADUATE COURSES

300   *Old English*: Mr. Burlin
315b *Sidney's* Arcadia *and Spenser's* Færie Queene: Mrs. Hedley
330   *Seventeenth Century Literature*: Miss Stapleton
355b *Major Victorian Poets*: Mrs. Johnston
366b *Hawthorne and James*: Miss McKinsey
367a *Contemporary American Poetry*: Mrs. Kohler
375a *W. B. Yeats*: Mrs. Berwind
376a *Virginia Woolf and E. M. Forster*: Miss Kaier
384b *Theory of Fiction*: Mrs. Bernstein
385a *Problems in Satire*: Mr. Briggs

French

Professors: Gérard Defaux *D ès L, Acting Chairman, Semester II*
  Michel Guggenheim PHD
  Pauline Jones PHD *Chairman*†
  Mario Maurin PHD

Associate Professor: Catherine Lafarge PHD

Assistant Professor: Grace Armstrong Savage PHD

Prerequisites. An undergraduate major in French, based on study in school and at least three years of college French, including some advanced work in literature, with evidence of ability to present reports and carry on discussion in French. Training in Latin corresponding to at least two years' study in school is advisable.

Applicants should submit scores in the Aptitude Test and Advanced Test of the Graduate Record Examinations taken within two years of the date on which they wish to begin graduate studies at Bryn Mawr. Candidates are required to support their application by at least one essay written in French for an advanced undergraduate course or graduate seminar previously taken, as well as by an essay written in English. They are strongly urged to arrange for a personal interview with a member of the Department.

Major and Allied Subjects. Students specialize in French literature from the Middle Ages to the present. Successful completion of a course in Old French philology and Mediaeval French literature is required of Ph.D. candidates. In special cases and with the consent of the Department, one of the following may be accepted as an allied subject: any literature, ancient or modern; comparative philology; European history; Philosophy; History of Art.

Language Requirements. For the M.A. degree, one Romance language other than French, *or* German, *or* evidence of extensive training in Mediaeval or advanced Latin. For the Ph.D. degree, *either* a reading knowledge of two modern languages (including one Romance language other than French) *or* superior competence in one. Students may satisfy the latter requirement by completing satisfactorily at least one unit of graduate work at Bryn Mawr in a Romance literature other than French, or in German literature. Language requirements must be fulfilled before the doctoral candidate takes the Preliminary Examinations.

Language skills may be tested by either the Graduate School Foreign Language Test (GSFLT) of the Educational Testing Service or the examinations administered by Bryn Mawr College. Entering

---

†On leave semester II

students may offer scores of the GSFLT taken within twelve months of the date on which they begin graduate work at Bryn Mawr.

Program and Examination for the M.A. Candidates will offer two units of graduate work in French and a third unit in either French or an allied field. An M.A. paper on a topic related to the work in one of the seminars is required. The Final Examination consists of a three-hour written examination and a one-hour oral examination, both in French.

Admission to Candidacy for the Ph.D. After completing three full units of graduate work at Bryn Mawr, students are required to pass a qualifying examination before admission to doctoral candidacy. The paper and Final Examination required for the completion of the Bryn Mawr M.A. program may be substituted for the qualifying examination.

Program and Examinations for the Ph.D. Candidates will offer six units of graduate work, one of which may be in an allied field. Suitable related fields should be discussed with the department concerned and with the Department of French.

Students are encouraged to study and do research abroad whenever appropriate and feasible. Opportunities for summer study are provided by the graduate courses given at the Bryn Mawr *Institut d'Etudes Françaises d'Avignon.* Under the terms of an exchange agreement between Bryn Mawr College and *L'Ecole Normale Supérieure de Fontenay-aux-Roses,* a *poste de répétitrice* is available at Fontenay each year for an advanced doctoral candidate recommended by the Bryn Mawr Department of French.

The Preliminary Examinations consist of four papers written in French and an oral examination. The Final Examination is oral and covers the field in which the dissertation has been written.

General Degree Requirements for the M.A and the Ph. D. See pages 13-15.

SEMINARS AND GRADUATE COURSES

An introductory course in Old French philology and Mediaeval French literature is offered every two years. Students wishing further work in this field may register for a unit of supervised work at Bryn Mawr or attend graduate courses at the University of Pennsylvania. Graduate seminars in selected fields of French literature are given each year, so arranged that the same one will not be given in successive years. The seminars, conducted in French, are selected from the following:

Mr. Defaux
> *(Rabelais, Montaigne)*
> *(Villon, Charles d'Orléans, Marot)*
> *(Les Conteurs au XVIe siècle)*
> *Poètes du XVIe siècle*—semester II

Mr. Guggenheim
(Rousseau et le préromantisme)
(Précieux, mondains et moralistes du XVIIe siècle)
Voltaire—semester I

Miss Jones
(Verlaine et Rimbaud)
(Baudelaire, Mallarmé, Laforgue)
(Vigny et Camus)

Miss Lafarge
Stendhal et Flaubert—semester II
(Le Thème de la prison au XIXe siècle)
(Diderot, Marivaux, Giraudoux)
(Le Thème de Paris dans la littérature du XVIIIe·siècle)

Mr. Maurin
Essayistes du XXe siècle—semester I
(Le Théâtre de 1940 à 1960)
(L'Autobiographie de Chateaubriand à Sartre)
(Réalisme et naturalisme)
(Romancières des XIXe et XXe siècles)
(Valéry, Claudel, Proust, Gide)
(Travaux pratiques sur la littérature moderne)

Mrs. Savage
(L'Art du conte et de la nouvelle des Cent Nouvelles Nouvelles
à Flaubert)
Philologie et littérature médiévales—semesters I and II

SELECTED UNDERGRADUATE COURSES

(301   *French Lyric Poetry*)
(303a *French Novel*)
(303b *La Vision de la femme dans la littérature française*)
(304a *Ecrivains engagés de Montaigne à Sartre*)
(304b *Le Théâtre de 1880 à 1939*)
 305a *Baudelaire*: Miss Jones
 306a *Le Roman du XXe siècle*: Mr. Guggenheim
 306b *Molière et la comédie*: Mr. Defaux

Courses offered at the *Institut d'Etudes Françaises d'Avignon:*
Molière or *Racine*
Les Fleurs du Mal or *Rimbaud*
Le Surréalisme
Travaux de traduction et de stylistique

Preparatory course for degree candidates in other departments:
Reading French. This course, which does not carry academic
credit, is designed to assist students in meeting the language

requirements for advanced degrees in fields other than French. An extra charge will be made. Specific information may be obtained from The Graduate School of Arts and Sciences during registration.

Geology

Associate Professors: Maria Luisa B. Crawford PHD *Chairman*
William A. Crawford PHD
Lucian B. Platt PHD‡
W. Bruce Saunders PHD

Assistant Professor: George C. Stephens PHD

Lecturer: J. Edward Leonard PHD

Prerequisites. A bachelor's degree in a natural science or Mathematics. Students who have not majored in Geology will be expected to make up deficiencies in their preparation during their first years of graduate study.

Major and Allied Subjects. Students may specialize in economic geology, geochemistry, mineralogy–petrology, paleontology–stratigraphy, or regional and structural geology. The allied subject for the Ph.D. may be either another field of Geology or any one of the other natural sciences or Mathematics; other subjects may be accepted in special cases.

Language Requirements. For the M.A. degree, one of the following: Russian, German, or French. Candidates for the Ph.D. degree may offer two foreign languages from the following: Russian, German, or French; or one language from this list and proficiency in digital computation or statistics. This proficiency will be tested by the Department or may be demonstrated by the satisfactory completion of an appropriate course.

Language skills may be tested by either the Graduate School Foreign Language Test (GSFLT) of the Educational Testing Service or the examinations administered by Bryn Mawr College. Entering students may offer scores of the GSFLT taken within twelve months of the date on which they begin graduate work at Bryn Mawr.

Program and Examination for the M.A. At least three units of work are required, one of which will consist of a field or laboratory research project under the direction of a member of the faculty. The

‡On leave 1976-77

results of the research project must be reported in a Master's thesis. The student must also pass a Final Examination consisting of a four-hour written and a one-hour oral test.

Program and Examinations for the Ph.D. Candidates will spend a major portion of their time on a research problem; ordinarily, this will involve field mapping and collecting, together with laboratory study. The number of units of course work to be taken will depend on the student's preparation. A set of Preliminary Examinations which test general knowledge in Geology, knowledge in the candidate's special field, and either an allied subject or an additional field in Geology must be passed before the student becomes deeply involved in the research project. A Final Examination follows the completion of the Ph.D. dissertation. This examination covers the field of the dissertation

Every graduate student in the Department is expected to assist in the ongoing work of the Department.

General Degree Requirements for the M.A. and the Ph.D. See pages 13-15.

General Degree Requirements for the M.A. and the Ph.D. See pages 13-15.

SEMINARS AND GRADUATE COURSES

Two or three courses or seminars are offered each semester. These are usually chosen so that each is offered once every other year. The specific content of the seminars is determined by the current interests of faculty and students. Students wishing to do so may also attend graduate courses at the University of Pennsylvania under the Reciprocal Plan (see page 11).

attend graduate courses at the University of Pennsylvania under the Reciprocal Plan (see page 11).

Mr. Crawford
  Geochemistry and Analytical Techniques
  Selected topics in the geochemistry of the earth combined with instruction in wet chemical and instrumental means of silicate analysis. Mechanical separations and experimental petrology.
  Igneous Petrology
  Selected subjects in the structure, physical chemistry, and origin of igneous rocks. Prerequisite: Geology 303a, *Thermodynamics for Geologists*, or its equivalent.

Mrs. Crawford
  Metamorphism
  The physical and chemical processes of metamorphism, accompanied by regional studies. Prerequisite: Geology 303a, *Thermodynamics for Geologists*, or its equivalent.
  Advanced Mineralogy
  The study of selected rock-forming mineral groups accompanied by instruction in optical, chemical, and x-ray techniques.

Mr. Platt
Structural Geology
Modern concepts in structural geology and theories of deformation.

Tectonics
Stratigraphic and structural relations of mountain ranges leading to analysis of their origin.

Mr. Saunders
Paleontology
Study of selected animal groups in geologic time.

Sedimentary Petrology
The constitution and the origin of sedimentary rocks; .their source, transportation, and deposition.

Mr. Stephens
Ore Deposits
Nature and occurence of metallic ores and their depositing solutions. Introduction to ore microscopy.

Exploration Geophysics
Gravity and magnetics in the regional and local search for mineral deposits.

SELECTED UNDERGRADUATE COURSES

302a *Advanced Paleontology:* Mr. Saunders
303a *Thermodynamics for Geologists*: Mr. Crawford
(304 *Petrology*: Mr. Crawford, Mrs. Crawford, Mr. Saunders)
305b *X-Ray Crystallography*: Mrs. Crawford
306b *Stratigraphy*: Mr. Saunders

German

Professor: Hans Bänziger PHD

Associate Professors: Nancy C. Dorian PHD
Gloria Flaherty PHD *Chairman*
C. Stephen Jaeger PHD

Prerequisites. An undergraduate major or minor in German or an equivalent preparation. All applicants are requested to submit scores in the Aptitude Test and Advanced German Test of the Graduate Record Examinations.

Major and Allied Subjects. Students may specialize in either German literature or German philology. One of these two fields or an area in the humanities, especially the literatures, may serve as the allied subject. Graduate students are encouraged to acquaint themselves with the theory and practice of teaching German.

Language Requirements. Normally French for the M.A.; French and another language, preferably Latin, for the Ph.D. With the approval of the Department, the satisfactory completion of a graduate seminar at Bryn Mawr in a foreign literature other than German may be offered for one language requirement. In special cases, with the approval of the appropriate language department and of the Department of German, equivalent work at another university may be accepted.

Language skills are tested by the Graduate School Foreign Language Test (GSFLT) of the Educational Testing Service; should there be no GSFLT for a student's specialty, she or he should apply to the Department for examinations administered by Bryn Mawr College. Entering students may offer scores of the GSFLT taken within twelve months of the date on which they begin graduate work at Bryn Mawr.

All graduate students are required to complete the Bryn Mawr M.A. Should a student have an M.A. in German from another institution, she or he will be expected to take a four-hour qualifying examination in German literature or Germanic philology or both after one full year of study and before proceeding to do the remaining units in preparation for the Ph.D. Preliminary Examinations.

Program and Examination for the M.A. The program consists of three units in German literature or in German literature and an allied field. In addition to acquainting the student with the field in general, the M.A. program introduces various methods of literary criticism. Every candidate must present a paper which represents satisfactory evidence of independent research. The Final Examination consists of a three-hour written examination and an oral examination of one hour.

Program and Examinations for the Ph.D. Every candidate must fulfill certain requirements in German literature and Germanic philology. Those majoring in Germanic philology take a minimum of one unit in German literature and will select the following courses: history of the German language, Gothic, Old High German, Middle High German, structural linguistics, and either Old English or Old Norse. Those majoring in German literature will take a minimum of one unit in Germanic philology and will normally take one unit each in the mediaeval, classical, and modern periods, as well as at least one genre course. The German Department encourages its students to participate in seminars given by other departments. It also encourages its students to study abroad and draws attention to the

Anna Ottendorfer Memorial Research Fellowship for study at a German university. The Preliminary Examinations consist of four written tests, one of which must be taken in an allied field, and an oral examination. The Final Examination covers the field of the dissertation.

General Degree Requirements for the M.A. and the Ph.D. See pages 13-15.

SEMINARS

Mr. Bänziger
   Brecht and Dürrenmatt—semester I
   (Franz Kafka)
   (Gottfried Keller and German Realism)
   (Hofmannsthal and Rilke)
   (Thomas Mann and Max Frisch)

Miss Dorian
   (Comparative Germanic Grammar)
   (Old High German)
   The Structure of German—semester I

Miss Flaherty
   (Bibliography and Methods in Criticism)
   (German Baroque Literature)
   (Goethe and Schiller)
   (Romanticism)

Mr. Jaeger
   German Renaissance Literature—semester II
   (Middle High German Literature)

SELECTED UNDERGRADUATE COURSES

300b *A Survey of German Literature*: Mr. Bänziger
(301b *History of the German Language*: Miss Dorian)
302a *Vernacular Literature in Mediaeval Germany*: Mr. Jaeger
303a *Modern German Prose*: Mr. Bänziger
(305a *The Modern German Drama*: Mr. Bänziger)
310b *Lessing and the Enlightenment*: Miss Flaherty

Preparatory courses for degree candidates in other departments:
   Reading German. This course, which does not carry academic credit, is designed to assist students in meeting the language requirements for advanced degrees in fields other than German. An extra charge will be made. Specific information may be obtained from The Graduate School of Arts and Sciences during registration.

45

Greek

Professor: Mabel L. Lang PHD *Chairman‡*

Associate Professor: Gregory W. Dickerson PHD *Acting Chairman*

Assistant Professor: Richard Hamilton PHD

Lecturer: Peter M. Smith PHD

Andrew W. Mellon Post-Doctoral Fellow: George A. Sheets PHD

Prerequisites. An undergraduate major or minor in Greek, based on at least four years of college Greek, or the equivalent, with representative reading from Greek literature and history which, in the opinion of the Department, provides an adequate basis for graduate work. It is expected that all graduate students in Greek will have some knowledge of Latin.

Allied Subjects. Any literature, ancient or modern, ancient history, ancient philosophy, Classical Archaeology, linguistics.

Language Requirements. French and German for both the M.A. and the Ph.D. Language skills may be tested by either examinations administered by Bryn Mawr College or the Graduate School Foreign Language Test (GSFLT) of the Educational Testing Service. Entering students may offer scores of the GSFLT taken within twelve months of the date on which they begin graduate work at Bryn Mawr.

Program and Examination for the M.A. The program consists of two units of graduate work in Greek and a third unit in an allied field. Before admission to the Final Examination candidates must pass an examination in Greek sight translation. The Final Examination consists of a three-hour written examination and an oral examination of one hour.

Program and Examinations for the Ph.D. Before admission to the Preliminary Examinations candidates must pass a rigorous examination in Greek sight translation. The Preliminary Examinations consist of four written papers, one of which shall be in an allied subject, and an oral examination. The fields from which the three major papers may be selected include: epic poetry (with emphasis on Homer), lyric poetry (with emphasis on Pindar), tragedy, comedy, the Orators, the Historians, the Pre-Socratics, Plato, Hellenistic poetry, and various periods of Greek history. The Final Examination covers the field of the dissertation.

General Degree Requirements for the M.A. and the Ph.D. See pages 13-15.

---

‡On leave 1976-77

Mr. Dickerson
Aeschylus' Oresteia—semester I

Mr. Hamilton
Euripides—semester II

Mr. Smith
Herodotus—semester I
Hesiod and His Influence—semester II

101 *Herodotus and Tragedy*: Mr. Dickerson, Mr. Hamilton
201 *Plato and Thucydides; Tragedy*: Mr. Hamilton, Mr. Smith
202a *Homer*: Mr. Smith
301 *Lyric Poetry; Aeschylus and Aristophanes*:
     Mr. Dickerson, Mr. Hamilton
Int. 313a *Comparative Greek and Latin Grammar*: Mr. Sheets
Int. 313b *Greek Dialects*: Mr. Sheets

History

Professors: Charles M. Brand PHD
     Arthur P. Dudden PHD *Chairman*
     Mary Maples Dunn PHD
     Elizabeth Read Foster PHD
     Barbara M. Lane PHD
     Jane M. Oppenheimer PHD
     J.H.M. Salmon LITD
     Alain Silvera PHD
     James Tanis THD *Director of Libraries*‡

Associate Professor: Phyllis S. Lachs PHD *Associate Dean*
     The Graduate School of Arts and Sciences

Assistant Professor: Stephen Poppel PHD

Lecturer: Wendell P. Holbrook AB*

Fields of Study. Master's and doctoral programs should be developed from seminars and courses available. Research for these

---

‡On leave 1976-77
*On leave semester I

and dissertations should grow out of seminars and units offered by the History Department and those allied with it.

Prerequisites. A thorough undergraduate preparation in History, the humanities, and the social sciences. Students who wish to work in ancient or mediæval fields must be able to read the essential ancient languages. Those planning work in modern European history or American history must have a reading knowledge of one modern language, preferably French or German, upon entrance. Those planning doctoral programs should have two languages upon entrance or acquire the second language at once. Applicants are urged to take the Graduate School Foreign Language Test (GSFLT) of the Educational Testing Service before beginning their graduate studies.

Language Requirements. Entering students may offer scores of the GSFLT taken within twelve months of the date on which they begin graduate work at Bryn Mawr.

At least one modern foreign language, to be approved by the Department, is required of M.A. degree candidates. Either the College language examination or the GSFLT must be attempted before the end of the first semester's work; the examination must be passed before the end of the following summer or before candidacy for the degree is requested, whichever is earlier.

At least two modern foreign languages, the choice of which must be approved by the Department during the student's first academic year, are required of the Ph.D. candidates. Students entering with an A.B. must attempt either a College language examination or the GSFLT before the end of the first semester's work and must pass the examination in one language before they may enter upon a third semester of work. They must attempt an examination in the second language no later than their third semester of work and must pass an examination on this second language before they may enter upon a fifth semester of work. Students entering with an M.A. must attempt examinations in both languages before the end of their first semester and must pass examinations in both before they may enter upon a third semester of work. The time limit for part-time students is determined by the academic year, not by the number of units completed. Candidates for the Ph.D. in ancient or mediaeval history must also demonstrate ability to read one classical language. Directors of research may also require demonstration of ability in special techniques.

In practice, since not all languages are tested by GSFLT and since the College language examinations are scheduled toward the beginning of the second semester, proof of language facility must often be established early in the second semester of work to enable the student to enter upon a third semester of work. In addition, since financial aid decisions are made early in semester II, often before semester II language examinations are completed, students applying for financial aid for the succeeding academic year should demonstrate language competence before the end of semester I.

Program and Examination for the M.A. The program consists of three units of work in History or in History and an allied field, together with a paper and a final examination. The Final Examination is written and is usually four hours in length.

Program and Examinations for the Ph.D. All students are expected at some time to take a seminar or course in which some aspects of historiography and historical method are studied. The Preliminary Examinations test the student's competence in four fields of History or in three fields of History and one field in an allied subject. For example, allied work in mediaeval literature, art, or philosophy is usually recommended to students of mediaeval history, and one of these may be offered in the Preliminary Examinations. Students whose dissertations are in American history will be required to take at least two fields in modern European history. Students specializing in English history must offer at least two fields of mediaeval or modern European history for examination. The field of the projected dissertation will be included in the Preliminary Examinations.

The purpose of the Final Examination is to test the candidate's knowledge of the special field or fields in which the dissertation has been written and to evaluate plans for publication.

General Degree Requirements for the M.A. and the Ph.D. See pages 13-15.

See pages 13-15.

SEMINARS AND GRADUATE COURSES

The seminars are arranged to allow the fullest possible choice for students over a two- or three-year period of study. Normally the same seminar will not meet two years in succession. Topics listed below indicate the area in which seminars will be offered according to the needs of students.

Ancient History

Students should consult pages 46 and 56 where the offerings of the Departments of Greek and Latin are listed.

Mediaeval and Renaissance History

Mr. Brand
  (Topics in Mediaeval History)
  (The Fifth and Sixth Centuries)
  (The Twelfth Century)
  Venice from the Tenth through the Thirteenth Centuries—
    semester I

49

Early Modern European History

Mr. Salmon
  French Political Ideas from the Wars of Religion to the
  Enlightenment

Mr. Tanis
  (The Reformed Reformation in Northern Europe)
  (Selected Topics in Sixteenth Century Religious Turmoil)

Modern European History

Mrs. Lane
  (Modern Germany: National Socialism, Bauhaus)
  (Topics in the History of Twentieth Century Europe)

Mr. Poppel
  Topics in the History of Nineteenth and Twentieth Century
  Europe

Mr. Silvera
  (The French Third Republic)
  (Europe and the Near East)

American and British History

Mr. Dudden
  (The Progressive Era)
  (The New Deal)
  (The United States in the Second World War)
  Topics in Recent American History

Mrs. Dunn
  (Seventeenth Century America)
  (Eighteenth Century America)
  Social History of Colonial America

Mrs. Foster
  Parliament in the Early Stuart Period
  (Social and Economic History of the Early Stuart Period)

Mr. Tanis
  (Puritanism and the Great Awakening)

Methodology and Historiography

Mr. Krausz
  (Philosophy of History—offered in the Department of
  Philosophy*)*

Mr. Salmon
  (Readings in Eighteenth Century Historiography)

Mr. Tanis
  (Historiography of the Reformation)

African and Afro-American History

Topic to be announced.

History of Science

Miss Oppenheimer
  Embryology and Evolution

SELECTED UNDERGRADUATE COURSES

300-level courses may, with additional work, be offered for graduate credit.

301b *Topics in Modern European History: Germany*: Mr. Poppel
305a *Italian City States*: Mrs. Lane
307b *Mediaeval Cities*: Mr. Brand
314 *History of Scientific Thought*: Miss Oppenheimer
317a *Mexico*: Mrs. Dunn
335b *Blacks in the American City*: Mr. Holbrook
350a *Topics in the History of Modern Architecture*: Mrs. Lane
380a *Topics in the Enlightenment*: Miss Oppenheimer

History and Philosophy of Science

Committee on History and Philosophy of Science:

Professor of Chemistry: Ernst Berliner PHD

Professor of History: Mary Maples Dunn PHD *Director*

Professor of History of Science: Jane M. Oppenheimer PHD

Professors of Philosophy: José María Ferrater Mora *Lic Fil*‡
                Michael Krausz PHD

Andrew W. Mellon Post-Doctoral Fellow: Karen Meier Reeds PHD

At the University of Pennsylvania:

Professors: John E. Brainerd SCD
      Thomas Park Hughes PHD
      Arnold W. Thackray PHD *Chairman*

Assistant Professor: Robert E. Kohler, Jr. PHD

---

‡On leave 1976-77

At the American Philosophical Society:
Whitfield J. Bell, Jr. PH D

This program within the Department of History has been developed in collaboration with the American Philosophical Society and the Department of the History and Sociology of Science at the University of Pennsylvania. Courses taken at any of the participating institutions may be credited toward an advanced degree.

Prerequisites. Undergraduate preparation in science, Philosophy, and History.

Major and Allied Subjects. The student's major subject will be History of Science, to be supported by intensive work in the field of History related to his special area of interest. Allied subjects may be Philosophy and other areas in science and History.

Language Requirements. Students must offer at least one modern foreign language, to be determined by the Department, for the Master's degree. Students who wish to continue work toward the Ph.D. must have completed the examinations in two modern foreign languages, to be determined by the Department, before taking the Preliminary Examinations.

Language skills may be tested by either the Graduate School Foreign Language Test (GSFLT) of the Educational Testing Service or the examinations administered by Bryn Mawr College. Entering students may offer scores of the GSFLT taken within twelve months of the date on which they begin graduate work at Bryn Mawr.

Program and Examination for the M.A. The program consists of at least two units of work in the History of Science and one unit of work in a related field of History or Philosophy. The Final Examination is written and is usually four hours in length.

Program and Examinations for the Ph.D. The Preliminary Examinations test the student's competence in four general fields, three in the History of Science and one in a related field of History or Philosophy. The Final Examination covers the field of the dissertation which must be in History of Science.

General Degree Requirements for the M.A. and the Ph.D. See pages 13-15.

SEMINARS AND GRADUATE COURSES

Miss Oppenheimer
Embryology and Evolution

Mrs. Reeds
Printing, Science, and Culture in the Renaissance—semester II

At the University of Pennsylvania:

Mr. Bell
Bibliography and Sources for the History of Science—semester II

Mr. Hughes
Seminar in the Social History of Technology—semester I
Technology in Industrial America, 1880-1950—semester II

Mr. Kohler
Seminar in American Science—semester I
History of the Bio-Medical Sciences—semester II

Mr. Thackray
Seminar in the Social History of Science—semester I
Science and the Industrial Revolution—semester II

History of Art

Professors: Phyllis Pray Bober PHD *Dean*
The Graduate School of Arts and Sciences
Charles G. Dempsey MFA PHD *Chairman*
Charles Mitchell B LITT LITTD
James E. Snyder MFA PHD†

Mary Flexner Lecturer: Phyllis W. Lehmann PHD

Assistant Professors: Dale Kinney PHD
Steven Z. Levine PHD

Visiting Professor: Shirley N. Blum PHD

Museum Assistant: Ian J. Lochhead MA

Field of Study. The history of Western art from early Christian to modern times.

Prerequisites. The normal prerequisite for admission is undergraduate training in art history, but students with special abilities or sound training in cognate disciplines are occasionally admitted.

Allied Subjects. History, Archaeology, classics, modern languages; others, exceptionally, by arrangement.

Language Requirements. Students are expected to read or to be learning the languages necessary for their special fields of study and not to delay their research by lack of linguistic competence. Advanced study of Western art history normally involves a working

---

†On leave semester II

knowledge of Latin, French, German, and Italian. Both M.A. and Ph.D. candidates are required to prove by examination their knowledge of two languages other than their own, to be approved by the Department.

Language skills will be tested by the examinations administered by Bryn Mawr College. Entering students may offer scores of the Graduate School Foreign Language Test (GSFLT) of the Educational Testing Service taken within twelve months of the date on which they begin graduate work at Bryn Mawr.

Program and Examination for the M.A. (a) Three units of graduate work, one of which may be in an allied field, (b) an extended paper on an approved topic, (c) a written (or written and oral) examination to test the candidate's ability to place this topic in its art-historical context.

Program and Examinations for the Ph.D. Prime emphasis is placed on a program of study and research leading to the dissertation, and students normally begin to work under a personal supervisor soon after entry. The Preliminary Examinations consist of four written papers and an oral examination on four areas of art history (or on three of these and one allied subject). After two or three years at Bryn Mawr, students normally go abroad for a period of research on their dissertations.

General Degree Requirements for the M.A. and the Ph.D. See pages 13-15.

Kress Program. The Department participates in the Samuel H. Kress Foundation Fellowship Program.

SEMINARS AND GRADUATE COURSES

Five one-term seminars on widely spaced topics that change from year to year are given annually, in addition to individial units of supervised work. Graduate students are sometimes advised to take selected intermediate or advanced undergraduate courses. Topics for 1976-77:

Mr. Dempsey
Problems in the Reform of Italian Art, 1550-1600—semester II

Mrs. Kinney
Early Christian and Byzantine Syria—semester I

Mr. Levine
French Eighteenth Century Painting—semester II

Mr. Mitchell
The Patronage of Julius II—semester II

Mr. Snyder
Carel van Mander's Het Schilder-boeck—semester I

310b *Santa Maria Maggiore*: Mrs. Kinney
312a *English Eighteenth Century Art*: Mr. Mitchell
313a *Problems in Renaissance Iconography*: Mr. Dempsey
314a *Aesthetics of the Film*: Mr. Levine
391b *Problems in Early Netherlandish Painting, 1400-1470*:
    Mrs. Blum
Archaeology 390b *Studies in the Art of Greece in the Fourth Cen-*
    tury B.C.: Mrs. Lehmann

History of Religion

Professor: Howard C. Kee PHD *Chairman*

Associate Professor: Samuel Tobias Lachs PHD

Professor of History: James Tanis THD *Director of Libraries*‡

Roïän Fleck Resident in Religion: Paul Lehmann THD

Visiting Lecturer: Patrick Henry PHD

A degree program at the graduate level is not offered in History of Religion. For work in this area, students should consult the offerings of the Department of History. The courses listed below are open to graduate students and may be taken for graduate credit with permission of the major department.

212a *Readings in the Greek New Testament*: Mr. Kee
300 *Studies in Early Rabbinic and Mediaeval Judaism*:
    Mr. Lachs
(301 *Studies in Early Christianity—Christian Ethics*: Mr. Kee)
(302a *Jewish Antecedents of Early Christianity*)
(303b *Myth and History*: Mr. Kee)
(305a *Myth and History in the Gospel of John*: Mr. Kee)
312b *Studies in Patristic Christianity*: Mr. Henry

---

‡On leave 1976-77

Italian

Assistant Professors: Nancy Dersofi PHD‡
Nicholas Patruno PHD *Director*

Lecturer: Barbra Apfelbaum AB

No graduate program is offered in Italian. The courses listed below are open to graduate students and may be taken for graduate credit with the permission of the major department.

 301   *Dante*: Miss Apfelbaum
(303a *Petrarch, Boccaccio, and the Early Humanists*)
(303b *Literature of the Italian Renaissance*)
(305a *Arcadia and Enlightenment*: Miss Dersofi)
(305b *History of the Italian Theater*: Miss Dersofi)

Latin

Professor: Myra L. Uhlfelder PHD

Associate Professors: Julia H. Gaisser PHD
Russell T. Scott PHD *Chairman*

Andrew W. Mellon Post-Doctoral Fellow: George A. Sheets PHD

Prerequisites. An undergraduate major or minor consisting of at least three years of Latin in college. All graduate students in Latin are expected to have begun the study of Greek. Scores in the Aptitude Test of the Graduate Record Examination should be submitted.

Allied Subjects. The Department recommends as allied subjects: Greek, Classical Archaeology, ancient history, linguistics, or, for students whose special interest is in the mediaeval period, mediaeval history or a vernacular literature.

Language Requirements. French and German are required for both the M.A. and Ph.D. Language skills may be tested by either the Graduate School Foreign Language Test (GSFLT) of the Educational Testing Service or the examinations administered by Bryn Mawr College.

---

‡On leave 1976-77

Program and Examination for the M.A. Candidates will normally offer two units of work in Latin and one unit in an allied field. Students will normally complete the work for the degree in one year, but, in cases in which it seems advisable to supplement the student's undergraduate preparation, a second year may be necessary. Candidates must pass a test in Latin sight translation before being admitted to the Final Examination, which consists of a three-hour written and a one-hour oral examination.

Program and Examinations for the Ph.D. Candidates will normally complete a two-year program of four units of work in Latin and two in an allied field. Three of these units may be those offered for the M.A. degree, which usually forms part of the doctoral program. Candidates should then undertake a program of independent reading planned to enable them to pass the Preliminary Examinations as soon as possible, after which they will concentrate on the dissertation. In some cases it may be advisable to carry one or two more units of work in the third year. The Preliminary Examinations consist of two four-hour written papers on Latin literature; one four-hour written paper on a special field such as a particular period of Roman history, the works of a special author, Mediaeval Latin literature, epigraphy, palaeography, or the history of classical scholarship; one four-hour written paper in the field of the allied subject, and a general oral examination. Students whose major interest is in the mediaeval period will take the two examinations in Latin literature, one in Mediaeval Latin literature, and a fourth in a field related to the Middle Ages or to the transmission of the classics. Before admission to the Preliminary Examinations, all students must pass tests in sight translation of Latin and Greek. The Final Examination will be oral and on the field of the dissertation.

General Degree Requirements for the M.A. and the Ph.D. See pages 13-15.

SEMINARS AND GRADUATE COURSES

Over a period of a few years, seminars will afford the student opportunity to work in specific areas of classical (Republican and Imperial) and mediaeval literature and civilization. Authors, genres, periods, or special topics dealt with in the seminars will vary according to the needs and desires of graduate students. A balance of prose and poetry, of literature and history, and of earlier and later periods is kept in mind in the establishment of the program.

The following seminars are offered in 1976-77:

Mrs. Gaisser
The Alexandrian Tradition—semester II

Mr. Scott
Roman Politics of the First Century B.C.—semester I

Miss Uhlfelder
Classical Rhetoric—semesters I and II

SELECTED UNDERGRADUATE COURSES

205a,b *Latin Literature of the High Middle Ages*: Miss Uhlfelder
301a *Livy and Tacitus*: Mr. Scott
301b *Vergil's* Aeneid: Mrs. Gaisser
(302a *Cicero and Caesar*: Mr. Scott)
(302b *Lucretius*: Miss Uhlfelder)
Int. 313a *Comparative Greek and Latin Grammar*: Mr. Sheets
Int. 313b *Greek Dialects*: Mr. Sheets

Mathematics

Professors: Frederic Cunningham, Jr. PHD *Chairman*
John C. Oxtoby MA

Assistant Professors: Kenneth Krigelman PHD‡
Françoise Schremmer PHD

Lecturer: Steven Alpern PHD

Prerequisites. A good undergraduate preparation in Mathematics or in Mathematics and Physics.

Major and Allied Subjects. Students may specialize in any of the broad divisions of Mathematics: algebra, analysis, geometry, or applied mathematics but are expected also to acquire a well-rounded knowledge of the subject as a whole. Certain courses in Physics, Chemistry, or Philosophy (logic) are accepted as allied work.

Language Requirements. Candidates for the M.A. must have a reading knowledge of French, German, or Russian. Candidates for the Ph.D. must pass examinations in two of the three: French, German, Russian.

Language skills will be tested by either the Graduate School Foreign Language Test (GSFLT) of the Educational Testing Service or the examinations administered by Bryn Mawr College. Entering students may offer scores of the GSFLT taken within twenty-four months of the date on which they begin graduate work at Bryn Mawr.

---

‡On leave 1976-77

Program and Examination for the M.A. The program consists of three units of work in Mathematics, or in Mathematics and an allied field, and an M.A. paper. Advanced undergraduate courses which supplement the student's preparation may under certain conditions be taken for graduate credit. The Final Examination is usually oral and one hour in length.

Program and Examinations for the Ph.D. Candidates will take such courses and seminars as are needed to provide a sufficiently broad foundation. As they progress they will devote an increasing portion of their time to individual study and research under the direction of a member of the Department. The Preliminary Examinations are taken after the student is well advanced and usually consist of three or four written examinations intended to test the candidate's breadth of knowledge and understanding of the structure of Mathematics as a whole. An oral examination is usually included. The Final Examination is oral and is devoted to the candidate's special field and the subject of the dissertation.

General Degree Requirements for the M.A. and Ph.D. See pages 13-15.

Journal Club. A Mathematical Colloquium at the University of Pennsylvania meets approximately every two weeks. Lectures by visiting mathematicians are also frequently presented at Haverford and Swarthmore Colleges.

SEMINARS AND GRADUATE COURSES

At least three graduate courses or seminars are offered each year. Additional courses or directed reading and research can be arranged. The seminars offered in any year are selected to meet the needs of the individual students. Some may be offered for one semester only.

Mr. Alpern
  Differential Games

Mr. Alpern, Mr. Oxtoby
  Ergodic Theory

Mr. Cunningham
  Functional Analysis
  General Topology
  Linear Spaces
  Theory of Functions

Mr. Krigelman
  Geometry of Manifolds
  Algebraic Topology
  Differential Topology

59

Mr. Oxtoby
  Measure Theory
  Point Set Topology
  Theory of Functions

Mrs. Schremmer
  Partial Differential Equations
  Applied Mathematics
  Fluid Mechanics

SELECTED UNDERGRADUATE COURSES

301 *Advanced Calculus*: Mr. Oxtoby
303a *Introduction to Abstract Algebra*: Mr. Cunningham
303b *Topics in Algebra*: Mr. Cunningham
308 *Introduction to Applied Mathematics*: Mrs. Schremmer
(309b *Dynamical Systems*: Mrs. Schremmer)
(310a *Theory of Functions of a Complex Variable*:
      Mr. Oxtoby)
(311 *Differential Equations*: Mrs. Schremmer)
(312a *Topology*: Mr. Krigelman)
(320 *Real Analysis*: Mr. Oxtoby)

Mediaeval Studies

Committee on Mediaeval Studies:

Professor of English: Robert B. Burlin PHD

Professor of History: Charles M. Brand PHD *Chairman*

Professors of History of Art: Charles Mitchell B LITT LITT D
                                James E. Snyder MFA PHD†

Professor of Latin: Myra L. Uhlfelder PHD

Professor of Music: Isabelle Cazeaux PHD

Professor of Philosophy: Jean A. Potter PHD

Professor of Spanish: Joaquín González Muela D en Fil

Associate Professor of German: C. Stephen Jaeger PHD

Assistant Professor of French: Grace Armstrong Savage PHD

Assistant Professor of History of Art: Dale Kinney PHD

---

†On leave semester II

Graduate work for the M.A. in the mediaeval field may be done either under a particular department or under the Mediaeval Studies Committee. Doctoral studies in the mediaeval period will usually come under the supervision of a particular department; in exceptional cases students with outstanding preparation will be permitted to take the Ph.D. in Mediaeval Studies.

Students applying for admission to the Mediaeval Studies program must submit: (1) a statement of their purpose in undertaking a degree in Mediaeval Studies, their plan of study, and their previous preparation in relevant fields; (2) a sample of their written work.

Mediaeval work in a particular department will fall under the regulations of that department. For work under the Mediaeval Studies Committee the regulations are as follows:

Prerequisites. The Committee must be satisfied that all candidates for admission have done sufficient undergraduate work to undertake graduate studies in the mediaeval field and have a reading knowledge of Latin and two modern languages.

Major and Allied Subjects. Any literature, ancient, mediaeval or modern, History, Philosophy, Classical Archaeology, History of Art, and History of Music.

Language Requirements. For the M.A. and Ph.D., Latin and two modern languages. Other languages may be substituted by permission of the Committee according to the candidate's special program. Language skills may be tested by either the Graduate School Foreign Language Test (GSFLT) of the Educational Testing Service or the examinations administered by Bryn Mawr College. Entering students may offer scores of the GSFLT taken within twelve months of the date on which they begin graduate work at Bryn Mawr.

Program and Examination for the M.A. Candidates will normally work in two departments and will offer at least two units of graduate work in any of the mediaeval fields and a third unit in any of the fields listed as allied. An extended paper, usually growing out of the work of one of the seminars, will be required in addition to an examination. The Final Examination may either be written (four hours) or written and oral (three hours—one hour).

Program and Examinations for the Ph.D. The course of study will normally be under the guidance of one professor. Prime emphasis will be placed on a program of research leading to a dissertation. Satisfactory Preliminary Examinations in two mediaeval fields and one allied field, written and oral, will be required. The Final Examination will cover the field of the dissertation.

General Degree Requirements for the M.A. and the Ph.D. See pages 13-15.

61

See listings under the various departments.

See listings under the various departments.

Music

Professors: Isabelle Cazeaux PHD
Robert L. Goodale ABBMUS AAGO *Chairman*
Agi Jambor MA

Assistant Professor: Carl B. Schmidt ‡

Visiting Lecturers: Hope K. Goodale PHD
Eugene K. Wolf PHD

Prerequisites. Two years of harmony, counterpoint, and analysis, three years of history and appreciation of music, of which at least one should be in an advanced course, and a reading knowledge of one modern language, preferably German. Candidates must have a sufficient knowledge of pianoforte or organ playing to be able to play music of the technical difficulty of a Bach figured chorale.

Allied Subjects. Any modern language or literature, History, History of Art, History of Religion, Philosophy.

Language Requirements. Two modern languages are required for the M.A. degree, preference being given to German and French. For candidates for the Ph.D. degree two languages are required, one of which must be German. Language skills will be tested by the examinations administered by Bryn Mawr College.

Program and Examination for the M.A. The program consists of three units of work in Music or in Music and an allied field. The Final Examination is written and four hours in length.

Examinations for the Ph.D. The Preliminary Examinations consist of four papers in the major field or three papers in the major field and one in an allied field, and an oral examination. The Final Examination covers the subject matter of the dissertation.

General Degree Requirements for the M.A. and the Ph.D. See pages 13-15.

---

‡On leave 1976-77

Practice rooms with pianos will be available for a fee of $10 per semester. Students permitted to play the organ in the Music Room will be charged $20 per semester.

SEMINARS AND GRADUATE COURSES

Miss Cazeaux
Musicology

Mr. Goodale
Studies in Music of the Twentieth Century

Mme. Jambor
The Interpretation of Music

SELECTED UNDERGRADUATE COURSES

Undergraduate courses taken for graduate credit require additional work.

202 *Advanced Theory and Analysis*: Mr. Goodale
205a *Music Criticism*: Miss Cazeaux
305 *Free Composition*: Mr. Goodale
306b *Opera and Music Drama*: Miss Cazeaux
310a *The Influence of Spanish Literature on Music*: Mrs. Goodale
310b *Music of the Mannheim School*: Mr. Wolf

Philosophy

Professors: José María Ferrater Mora *Lic Fil*‡
George L. Kline PHD
Jean A. Potter PHD *Acting Chairman*
Isabel Scribner Stearns PHD

Associate Professors: Michael Krausz PHD
Mary Patterson McPherson PHD *Dean The Undergraduate College*
George E. Weaver, Jr. PHD

Assistant Professors: Richard H. Gaskins PHD JD
Tracy M. Taft PHD

Lecturer: Thomas Song MA MALS *Associate Director of Libraries*

‡On leave 1976-77

Prerequisites. In general, an undergraduate major in Philosophy. Students whose undergraduate training does not include a major in Philosophy may be required to take such undergraduate courses as the Department considers necessary.

Allied Subjects. Subjects in most fields of the humanities, Mathematics, and natural and social sciences.

Language Requirements. One modern language for the M.A., French and German for the Ph.D. At the discretion of the Department, another language may be substituted for French or German when the student's research requires it.

Language proficiency will be tested by either the Graduate School Foreign Language Test (GSFLT) of the Educational Testing Service or examinations administered by Bryn Mawr College. Entering students may offer scores of the GSFLT taken within twelve months of the date on which they begin graduate work at Bryn Mawr.

Program and Examination for the M.A. Three units of work in Philosophy or in Philosophy and an allied field. The Final Examination is usually written and four hours in length.

Program and Examinations for the Ph.D. All students must demonstrate competence in logic before receiving the Ph.D. This requirement may be met in several ways: by successful completion, before admission to candidacy, of an intermediate course or graduate seminar in logic; or by special examination before admission to candidacy; or by passing a preliminary examination in the systematic field of logic. The Preliminary Examination will consist of four written papers, two of which are to be in systematic fields and two in authors or periods.

General Degree Requirements for the M.A. and the Ph.D. See pages 13-15.

Graduate Philosophy Colloquium: Graduate students are encouraged to participate in the monthly meetings of the Graduate Philosophy Colloquium. Papers are read by faculty and students of Bryn Mawr as well as visiting lecturers. In addition, both the Fullerton Club and the Philadelphia Logic Colloquium hold their monthly meetings at Bryn Mawr and the graduate students are invited to attend.

SEMINARS

Mr. Ferrater Mora
   (Methods of Research in the History of Philosophy)
   (History of Philosophic Concepts)
   (Kant: Epistemology and Metaphysics)
   (Phenomenology: Husserl and Heidegger)

Mr. Kline
Ethics
A close examination of classical texts in ethical theory, with some attention to twentieth century authors.
(Hegel)
(Whitehead)

Mr. Krausz
Aesthetics
A systematic examination of major theories of art and aesthetics.
(Philosophy of Science)
(Theory of Inquiry)

Miss Potter
(Mediaeval Philosophy)
(Continental Rationalism)
(Philosophy of Religion)

Miss Stearns
Epistemology
(Metaphysics)
(American Philosophy)

Miss Taft
Aristotle
A thorough study of Aristotle's *Metaphysics* and *De Anima*. When important, digressions will be made into other works, including *Categories* and *Physics*. Then, in the light of the *Metaphysics* and *De Anima*, Aristotle's ethical and political works will be examined.
(Plato)

Mr. Weaver
Logic: The Expressive Power of First Order Sentences
Examination of the problems concerning what sentences and sets of sentences in first order languages can express, how the grammatical features of these languages contribute to their expressive power, and what, if any, limitation can be placed on their expressive power.
(Completeness and Decidability)
(Introduction to Set Theory and Logic)

SELECTED UNDERGRADUATE COURSES

213b *Intermediate Logic*: Mr. Weaver
318a *Philosophy of Language: Formal Grammars*: Mr. Weaver
319a *Philosophy of the Social Sciences*: Mr. Krausz
331a *Hegel*: Mr. Gaskins
333a *Russian Philosophy*: Mr. Kline
334b *Marx and Russian Marxism*: Mr. Kline

65

YSICS

Professors: Rosalie C. Hoyt PHD *Chairman*
John R. Pruett PHD

Assistant Professors: Alfonso M. Albano PHD
Stephen R. Smith PHD

Prerequisites. An undergraduate major in Physics or in a field of study closely allied to Physics (e.g., Mathematics, Chemistry, Engineering). Students who have not majored in Physics will usually find it necessary to take some undergraduate courses before entering graduate seminars. All applicants for admission to graduate work in Physics are requested to submit scores in the Aptitude Test and Advanced Test of the Graduate Record Examinations.

Allied Subjects. With permission of the Department, candidates for the Ph.D. degree may offer as an allied subject Mathematics, Biology, Chemistry, or Geology, provided they have taken advanced work in one of these fields.

Language Requirements. For the M.A. and the Ph.D. degrees, two languages are required; one, French, German, or Russian; the second, a computer language approved by the Department. Language skills will be tested by the examinations administered by Bryn Mawr College.

Program and Examination for the M.A. An oral qualifying examination must be passed before the student is admitted to candidacy. The subject matter of the examination will include only material ordinarily covered in undergraduate college Physics courses, but the student will be expected to handle this material on a reasonably mature level. Each candidate is expected to have completed Physics 308-309, or its equivalent, and to have a mathematical preparation acceptable as adequate for the M.A. degree. The three units of work offered for the degree will ordinarily include one unit of experimental physics and at least one graduate seminar in theoretical physics. The paper will usually consist of a report on a special field related to one of the seminars or units of graduate work offered for the M.A. The M.A. Examination is a one-hour oral examination.

Program and Examinations for the Ph.D. Each candidate must have completed Physics 308-309 or its equivalent, have a mathematical preparation acceptable as adequate for the Ph.D. degree, and have passed the oral qualifying examination described above before being recommended for candidacy.

The Preliminary Examinations are intended to test the candidate's general background and to determine whether it is broad and deep enough to serve as a preparation for original research work in a specialized field. In general, two years of full- or part-time graduate work should prepare the student for these examinations, and candidates for the Ph.D. are urged to submit themselves for examination at this stage of their work. The examinations will consist of three four-hour written examinations, one problem set, and an oral examination lasting approximately one hour. Each of the three four-hour examinations will cover one of the following fields of Physics, to be chosen by the Department: (1) classical mechanics, including relativity theory, vibrations, and wave motion; (2) electricity and magnetism, including field problems and electromagnetic waves, the latter with particular reference to optical phenomena; (3) quantum mechanics, with applications to atomic and nuclear structure; (4) thermodynamics and statistical mechanics, including both classical and quantum statistics. The student devotes approximately twelve hours to direct work on the problem set over a three-day period. Any books, periodicals, notes, etc. may be used in connection with the problem set. The oral examination is devoted to general Physics.

Unless the candidate has demonstrated adequate acquaintance with experimental physics in other ways, either the research leading to the dissertation must be, at least in part, experimental or the candidate must take a seminar in experimental physics. The Final Examination will cover the field of the dissertation.

General Degree Requirements for the M.A. and Ph.D. See pages 13-15.

Colloquium. All members of the Department and all graduate students meet weekly for the discussion of current problems.

SEMINARS

Three or more graduate seminars in theoretical physics are offered each year. In addition, a seminar in experimental physics is arranged individually for students desiring it and generally serves as an introduction to a research problem.

Experimental Physics

Miss Hoyt, Mr. Pruett, Mr. Smith

Theoretical Physics

Mr. Pruett
  Quantum Mechanics
  Necessity for the quantum hypothesis. The Schroedinger and Heisenberg formulations with applications to atomic structure. The Dirac approach with applications to relativistic electron

theory and the quantum theory of radiation. Prerequisite: an advanced undergraduate course in mechanics or in theoretical physics.

Mr. Smith

Electromagnetic Theory

Potential theory, Maxwell's Equations, applications to waves subject to various boundary conditions, transmission lines, wave guides, radiating systems. Prerequisite: an advanced undergraduate course in electricity and magnetism or in theoretical physics.

At least one of the following advanced seminars is given each year:

Mr. Albano

Elementary Particles

Characteristics of elementary particles, symmetries and invariance principles, scattering theory, weak and strong interactions. Prerequisite: *Quantum Mechanics*.

Non-Equilibrium Thermodynamics

Phenomenological theories of irreversible processes. Statistical foundations of non-equilibrium thermodynamics. Onsager-Casimir relations. The fluctuation-dissipation theorem. Interfaces and the non-equilibrium thermodynamics of boundary conditions. Prerequisite: *Statistical Mechanics* or consent of the instructor.

Statistical Mechanics

Classical kinetic theory and transport phenomena. Ensembles in classical and quantum statistical mechanics. Selected applications. Prerequisite: *Quantum Mechanics*.

Miss Hoyt

Chemical Physics and Biophysics

Interatomic and intermolecular forces, vibrational and rotational states of molecules. Dynamical properties of biological membranes, the biophysics of photosynthesis and photo-sensitive receptors. Prerequisite: *Quantum Mechanics*.

Mr. Pruett

Nuclear Physics

An introductory study of classical nuclear physics followed by applications of quantum mechanics to nuclear problems and associated high-energy phenomena. Some quantum electrodynamics and meson theory will be included. Prerequisite: *Quantum Mechanics* or its equivalent.

Mr. Smith

Physics of the Solid State

Classification and characteristics of solids, theory of mechanical, electrical, thermal, and magnetic properties. Prerequisite: *Quan-*

tum Mechanics and *Electromagnetic Theory*. Either may be taken concurrently.

Quantum Optics
Interaction of the radiation field with quantum-mechanical systems. Quantization of radiation. Spontaneous and stimulated emission. Semi-classical and quantum theories of lasers and laser amplifiers. Operating characteristics of gas lasers. Optical coherence and statistical characteristics of various radiation fields. Prerequisites: *Quantum Mechanics* and *Electromagnetic Theory*.

SELECTED UNDERGRADUATE COURSES

306a *Classical and Quantum Mechanics*: Mr. Albano
307b *Classical and Quantum Mechanics*: Miss Hoyt
308b *Advanced Mechanics of Discrete and Continuous Systems*: Mr. Albano
309a *Advanced Electromagnetic Theory*

Political Science

The Caroline McCormick Slade Department of Political Science

President of the College: Harris L. Wofford, Jr. AB JD

Professors: Melville T. Kennedy, Jr. PHD
Gertrude C. K. Leighton AB JD

Associate Professors: Charles E. Frye PHD
Marc H. Ross PHD *Chairman*
Stephen Salkever PHD

Prerequisites. A good undergraduate training in Political Science and related subjects. Scores of the Graduate Record Examination Aptitude Test and Advanced Test are required in applications for admission.

Major and Allied Subjects. The major fields offered in Political Science are political philosophy and theory, Western comparative politics, non-Western comparative politics, American political process, political behavior, American constitutional law, and international politics and law. Allied fields may be chosen in the other social sciences, in History and Philosophy, and, with the special permission of the Department, in certain subjects in literature. Candidates for the Ph.D. are expected to prepare themselves in four fields, one of which may be allied.

69

Language Requirements. One modern foreign language for the M.A. Two foreign languages (only one need be modern) or one modern language and statistics for the Ph.D. Language skills may be tested by either the Graduate School Foreign Language Test (GSFLT) of the Educational Testing Service or the examinations administered by Bryn Mawr College. The statistics requirement may be satisfied by passing an approved course in statistics.

Program and Examination for the M.A. The program consists of three units of work in Political Science, but a unit from an allied field may be substituted for one of these. The Final Examination will be written or oral or both.

Program and Examinations for the Ph.D. Candidates are expected to offer four fields, one of them being the field in which the dissertation is written. These fields are tested by written and oral Preliminary Examinations. An oral Final Examination will cover fields related to the dissertation.

General Degree Requirements for the M.A. and the Ph.D. See pages 13-15.

SEMESTER SEMINARS

Mr. Frye
  European Comparative Politics
  Intellectuals in Comparative Perspective

Mr. Kennedy
  International Politics
  Topics in Politics of China, Japan, India

Miss Leighton
  Aspects of Political Behavior
  International Law
  Jurisprudence

Mr. Ross
  American Politics: Political Behavior
  Community Politics

Mr. Salkever
  Aristotle
  Constitutional Law

SELECTED UNDERGRADUATE COURSES

218b *Community Politics*: Mr. Ross
230b *Political Behavior*: Mr. Ross
301b *Law and Society*: Miss Leighton
302b *Law, Policy, and Personality*: Miss Leighton
303a *Problems in International Politics*: Mr. Kennedy

305b *European Fascism*: Mr. Frye
311b *Theory and Practice in Political Philosophy*: Mr. Salkever
313b *Problems in Constitutional Law*: Mr. Salkever
316b *Ethnic Group Politics: Concepts and Process*: Mr. Ross
317a *Political Culture and Political Leadership*: Mr. Frye
319a *Problems in Legal Theory*: Mr. Salkever

Psychology

Professors: Richard C. Gonzalez PHD *Chairman*
Howard S. Hoffman PHD†
Matthew Yarczower PHD

Associate Professors: Clark McCauley, Jr. PHD*
Earl Thomas PHD

Assistant Professor: Jill T. Wannemacher PHD

Lecturers: Alice S. Powers PHD
Larry Stein PHD

Prerequisites. Undergraduate training in Psychology is recommended, but outstanding applicants with training only in related fields may be accepted. Students who have not majored in Psychology as undergraduates may find it necessary to devote a substantial portion of the first year to undergraduate courses. All applicants residing in the United States at the time of the application must submit scores on the Aptitude Test and Advanced Test of the Graduate Record Examinations.

Major and Allied Subjects. The orientation in the various fields is experimental, and there are no facilities for clinical training. Work in Psychology may be coordinated with work in one of the following allied areas: Anthropology, Biology, Chemistry, Mathematics, Philosophy, and Physics.

Language Requirements. Candidates for the M.A. must pass an examination in one of the following languages: French, German, Russian. Candidates for the Ph.D. must offer two foreign languages: French and German (or some other foreign language with permission of the Department) or one foreign language and statistics. The statistics requirement will be tested by the Department. Language

*On leave semester I
†On leave semester II

skills will be tested by the examinations administered by Bryn Mawr College.

Program and Examination for the M.A. The program of work must include three units (six one-semester seminars or courses) which usually will be chosen from the group of seminars and courses listed below. Before final approval of the Master's paper, each candidate must pass a written examination in statistics. The Final Oral Examination, one hour in length, deals with the Master's paper and related topics.

Program and Examinations for the Ph.D. Ph.D. candidates are expected to devote a large portion of their time to supervised research. In the first year, the research is done under the close supervision of the candidate's faculty advisor; a written report of the year's research activities (the form and content of which are determined by the candidate and his advisor) is submitted to the Department, and an oral presentation based on the report is made to the faculty and graduate student members of the Department. In addition to research, candidates, in their first two years of residence, take the six one-semester graduate courses listed below (or, if they elect to do so, a written examination in the subject matter instead of any one or all of the courses). The Preliminary Examinations, which should be taken early in the third year, consist of three written examinations of four hours each and an oral examination of one to two hours. The written examinations are in the following areas: learning and motivation, physiological psychology, social psychology, developmental psychology, or, with approval of the Department, in two of these areas and in one of the allied subjects listed above. (The area of comparative psychology as such is not represented in a separate examination; comparative issues are treated in each of the other area-examinations.) The oral examination deals with the areas of the written examinations. Work beyond the Preliminary Examinations consists of seminars in selected topics and of dissertation research. The Final Oral Examination deals with the dissertation and the field in which it was written.

General Degree Requirements for the M.A. and the Ph.D. See pages 13-15.

GRADUATE COURSES

Mr. Gonzalez
Learning Theory

Mr. Hoffman
Statistics

Mr. McCauley
Experimental-Social Psychology

Mr. Thomas
Physiological Psychology

Miss Wannemacher
Developmental Psychology

Mr. Yarczower
Comparative Psychology

SEMINARS

Seminars are offered on specialized topics in the areas of experimental, comparative, developmental, physiological, and social psychology. Among those offered most recently are the following: *Communication Theory, Experimental Design, Parameters of Reinforcement, Physiological Techniques and Instrumentation, Psychopharmacology, Stimulus Control of Behavior, Aversive Control, Neurophysiology of Reward and Punishment, Comparative Neuroanatomy.*

SELECTED UNDERGRADUATE COURSES

201a *Learning Theory and Behavior*: Mr. Gonzalez
202b *Comparative Psychology*: Mr. Yarczower
203a *Motivation*: Mr. Thomas
204a *Sensory Processes*: Mr. Hoffman
207b *Language and Cognition*: Miss Wannemacher
302b *Physiological Psychology*: Mr. Thomas

Russian

Associate Professors: Dan E. Davidson PHD
Ruth L. Pearce PHD *Chairman*

Assistant Professors: George S. Pahomov PHD
Lynn Visson PHD*

Professor of Philosophy: George L. Kline PHD

Prerequisites. An undergraduate major or minor in Russian or an equivalent preparation with some work in literature. Applicants should submit scores in the Aptitude Test of the Graduate Record Examination, a brief biography written in Russian, and at least one

---

*On leave semester I

essay written in English on a literary topic. The English essay may have been written for an advanced undergraduate course or graduate seminar previously taken.

Allied Subjects. Any language or literature, European history, Political Science, Russian philosophy.

Language Requirements. For the M.A., French or German. For the Ph.D., French, German, and one Slavic language other than Russian. Language skills may be tested by either the Graduate School Foreign Language Test (GSFLT) of the Educational Testing Service or the examinations administered by Bryn Mawr College. Entering students may offer scores of the GSFLT taken within twelve months of the date on which they begin graduate work at Bryn Mawr.

Program and Examination for the M.A. Three units of work in Russian or in Russian and an allied field. The Final Examination consists of a three-hour written examination and an oral examination of one hour.

Examinations for the Ph.D. The Preliminary Examinations consist of four written papers, one of which must be taken in an allied field, and an oral examination. The Final Examination will cover the field of the dissertation.

General Degree Requirements for the M.A. and the Ph.D. See pages 13-15.

SEMINARS AND GRADUATE COURSES

Seminars offered each year are selected in accordance with the needs and interests of the students enrolled. Normally the same seminar is not given in two successive years. In cooperation with the Department of Slavic Languages of the University of Pennsylvania, the student may also register at that institution under the Reciprocal Plan (see page 11) for a unit of work chosen from the graduate courses offered in Slavic. Undergraduate 300-level courses, with additional work, may also be offered for graduate credit.

Mr. Davidson
  Karamzin and Early Romanticism—semester II

Mr. Pahomov
  (Chekhov)
  (Classics of Russian Drama from Fonvizin to Chekhov)
  (Russian Romanticism)
  (The Russian Short Story)
  Turgenev and Goncharov—semester I

Mrs. Pearce
(History of the Development of the Russian Literary Language)
History of the Russian Language: Phonology and Morphology
—semester I
(Old Church Slavic: Phonology and Morphology)
(Readings in Old Church Slavic)
(Studies in Russian Grammar)

SELECTED UNDERGRADUATE COURSES

306a *Russian Prose and Poetry from Classicism to the Rise of Realism*: Mr. Davidson
306b *Russian Prose Literature of the Second Half of the Nineteenth Century*: Mr. Pahomov
Philosophy 333a *Russian Philosophy*: Mr. Kline
Philosophy 333b *Marx and Russian Marxism*: Mr. Kline

At the University of Pennsylvania

Russian 631 *Old Church Slavic*: Mr. Plewer: semester I
Russian 632 *Readings in Old Church Slavic*: Mrs. Brooks: semester I
Russian 649 *Tolstoy*: Staff: semester II
Russian 653 *Selected Topics in Nineteenth Century Prose*: Mr. Morson: semester I

Sociology

Professor: Eugene V. Schneider PHD *Chairman*

Associate Professor: Judith R. Porter PHD

Assistant Professors: William R. F. Phillips PHD
Robert E. Washington PHD

Prerequisites. An undergraduate preparation in Sociology or some closely related social science is desirable. Students whose undergraduate training is not entirely adequate may be required to take certain undergraduate courses.

Major and Allied Subjects. Students may wish to take some work in related fields: Anthropology, Economics, Psychology, Political Science, History, and statistics. In addition, courses in Sociology and allied subjects may be taken at the University of Pennsylvania under the terms of the Reciprocal Plan (see pages 11-12).

75

Language and Statistics Requirements. Candidates for the M.A. must offer one modern foreign language and statistics. Candidates for the Ph.D. degree must offer two modern foreign languages (usually French and German) or one modern foreign language and statistics. The statistics requirement will be tested by the Department or may be met by passing a graduate course in statistics.

Language skills will be tested by the examinations administered by Bryn Mawr College. Entering students may offer scores of the Graduate School Foreign Language Test (GSFLT) of the Educational Testing Service taken within twelve months of the date on which they begin graduate work at Bryn Mawr College.

Program and Examination for the M.A. The program consists of three units of work. The Final Examination may consist of one four-hour written paper, or one three-hour written paper and an oral examination of one hour.

Program and Examinations for the Ph.D. The Preliminary Examinations for candidates for the Ph.D. will consist of four three-hour written papers and an oral examination of one hour. These examinations will be in general sociology, sociological theory, and two special fields, one of which may be an allied field. The Final Examination will cover the field of the dissertation.

General Degree Requirements for the M.A. and the Ph.D. See pages 13-15.

See pages 13-15.

SEMINARS

Seminars will be given in special branches of Sociology, such as:

Sociological Theory	*Industrial Sociology*
Social Stratification	*Race Relations*
Sociology of Religion	*Sociology of Poverty*
Personality and	*Political Sociology*
Social Structure	*Sociology of Developing*
Sociology of Knowledge	*Countries*
Sociological Methods	*Comparative Societies*

UNDERGRADUATE COURSES

Under exceptional circumstances a student may be registered for an advanced undergraduate course which with additional work may be accepted for graduate credit.

Spanish

Professors: Joaquín González Muela *D en Fil*
Willard F. King PHD *Chairman*

Associate Professor: Eleanor K. Paucker PHD

Visiting Lecturer: James E. Irby PHD

Professor of Philosophy: José María Ferrater Mora *Lic Fil‡*

Prerequisites. An undergraduate major in Spanish; representative reading from Spanish literature of the Middle Ages, Golden Age, and contemporary period. Spanish-American literature may be offered in addition. Applicants for admission in Spanish are asked to submit scores on the Aptitude Test and Advanced Test of the Graduate Record Examinations. Candidates are urged to arrange for a personal interview with a member of the Department whenever possible.

Allied Subjects. Any. literature, ancient or modern, including Mediaeval Latin literature; European or Spanish-American history; classical or romance philology; Spanish-American literature.

Language Requirements. For the M.A., either German or one Romance language other than Spanish. For the Ph.D., German and French; in special cases the Department may accept other languages. The Ph.D. candidate's preparation must give evidence of adequate knowledge of Latin; if it does not, Latin must be included in the graduate program.

Language skills may be tested by either the Graduate School Foreign Language Test (GSFLT) of the Educational Testing Service or the examinations administered by Bryn Mawr College. Entering students may offer scores of the GSFLT taken within twelve months of the date on which they begin graduate work at Bryn Mawr.

Program and Examination for the M.A. The program consists of three units of graduate work in Spanish or two units of graduate work in Spanish and one other in an allied field. An M.A. paper on a topic related to the work in one of the seminars is required. The Final Examination consists of a three-hour written section and an oral of one hour, both in Spanish.

Examinations for the Ph.D. The Preliminary Examinations consist of four written papers, one of which must be taken in an allied field, and an oral examination. Suitable related fields should be discussed with the member of the Department with whom the candidate plans

---

‡On leave 1976-77

to work on the dissertation. The Final Examination will cover the field of the dissertation.

General Degree Requirements for the M.A. and the Ph.D. See pages 13-15.

SEMINARS

The seminars are arranged to allow the widest possible choice for students over a two- or three-year period of study. Normally the same seminar will not be given two years in succession.

Members of the Department
  (The History of the Spanish Language)
  (The Mediaeval Castilian Epic and Lyric)
  Mediaeval Prose from Alfonso el Sabio to the Corbacho— semester II
  Ideological Currents in Renaissance Spain—semester I
  Cervantes: Drama, Poetry, and Novel (with the exception of Don Quijote)—semester II
  (Prose Fiction of the Golden Age)
  (Imperial Spain: History, Literature, Thought)
  (Theater of the Golden Age)
  Poetry of the Golden Age
    Topic for 1976-77: Popular and Elite Styles—semester I
  (Studies in Nineteenth Century Spanish Literature)
  Studies in Spanish American Literature
    Topics for 1976-77: The Modern Argentine Narrative— semester I
    Aspects of *Modernista* Poetry—semester II
  (Studies in Twentieth Century Spanish Literature)

SELECTED UNDERGRADUATE COURSES

(302a *Mediaeval Spanish Literature*: Mrs. Paucker)
(303a *The Modern Novel in Spain*: Mrs. King)
(303b *Modern Poetry in Spain*: Mr. González Muela)
304a *Cervantes*: Mrs. King
304b *Poetry and Drama of the Golden Age*: Mrs. King

Fees

Application (payable by citizens of the United States and Canada and foreign students living in the United States): $20.

Tuition
Full-time students:
$3450 a year (or $1725 for a semester)
Part-time students:
2 academic units $2250 a year (or $1125 a semester)
1 academic unit $1400 a year (or $700 a semester)
Auditors:
Fees for auditors are the same as those for students registered in courses for credit.

Continuing enrollment (see page 8): $150 a semester, except for students using Bryn Mawr College laboratories for dissertation research. In these cases fees will be determined in consultation with the major department.

Payment of Fees

Both tuition and residence fees will be billed by semester. The Education Plan of monthly payment in cooperation with the Bryn Mawr Trust Company is available for those who prefer to pay fees in monthly installments. Direct correspondence to the Comptroller of the College.

Students whose fees are not paid within ten days of receipt of bill in each semester will not be permitted to continue in residence or to attend classes. Degrees will not be awarded to any student owing money to any College facility, nor will any transcripts be issued.

Refund Policy

In the event of withdrawal from The Graduate School of Arts and Sciences, refunds will be made according to the following schedule:

For Semester I
Withdrawals prior to Sept. 9   100%
Withdrawals Sept. 9 through Oct. 31   50%
Withdrawals Nov. 1 through Jan. 16   0%

For Semester II
Withdrawals prior to Jan. 17   100%
Withdrawals Jan. 17 through March 11   50%
Withdrawals March 12 to end of semester   0%

For those students living at the Graduate Residence Center, the charge for residence is $1790 in 1976-77. In accordance with the above schedule, if a student withdraws from graduate study a refund will be made of that portion of the fee which represents room, with the proviso that the College is able to reassign the student's space to some other student not previously in residence. The student is not entitled to dispose of the room he or she leaves vacant.

Appropriate reduction or remission will also be made for that portion of the residence fee which represents the cost of food.

Medical Leave

In case of absence from the College extending six weeks or more because of illness, there will be a proportionate reduction or remission in the charge for the cost of food.

Procedure for Securing Refunds

Written notice must be received by the Dean at least one week prior to the effective date of withdrawal. Students who have received loans under NDSL or GSL to meet any educational expenses for the current academic year must make an appointment with the Associate Dean before leaving the campus to arrange for appropriate repayment of the loans in question.

Summary of Expenses for the Academic Year

Regular

Tuition Fee (full time)	$3450
Residence in graduate student housing	1790

Contingent

Application Fee	$ 20
Continuing Enrollment Fee	300
Course in Reading German or French	100
(flat fee from September to February)	
Dispensary Fee	40
Health Insurance (United States citizens)	60
Health Insurance (foreign students)	70
Graduation Fee for all Graduate Degrees	25
Charge for Microfilming Ph.D. Dissertation	37
Late Registration Fee	10
Add and Drop Fee	10
(after the first week of a new semester)	

Faced with the rising costs of higher education, the College has had to raise tuition each of the last six years. Further increases may be expected.

Exclusion

The College reserves the right to exclude at any time students whose academic standing is unsatisfactory or whose conduct renders them undesirable members of the college community. In such cases fees will not be refunded or remitted in whole or in part; fellowships and scholarships will be cancelled.

Fellowships and Graduate Scholarships

Fellowships and graduate scholarships are provided from the general funds of the College, from the gifts of alumnae and other generous donors, and from government agencies and private foundations. The majority of these awards are made on the basis of an annual competition. Fellowships carry a stipend of $2300 in addition to tuition and are available only to students who have completed one full year of graduate work. Graduate scholarships have a value of $1800 in addition to tuition and may be held by citizens and noncitizens and by students at all levels of graduate work leading to the M.A. or Ph.D. degree. Other awards vary in value.

Application

Application from citizens of the United States and Canada should be made to the Dean of The Graduate School of Arts aand Sciences and must be filed complete not later than February 1. In writing for forms applicants should state their fields of concentration. Applications from foreign students must be received not later than January 25. Scores of the Test of English as a Foreign Language (TOEFL) or the examination of the English Language Institute of the University of Michigan must be included. Therefore the TOEFL must be taken by the previous November (see page 7).

Graduate and Professional School Financial Aid Service

The Graduate School of Arts and Sciences is a participant in the Graduate and Professional School Financial Aid Service (GAPSFAS), Educational Testing Service, Princeton, New Jersey 08540. All applicants for financial aid must file a GAPSFAS form entitled "Application for Financial Aid for the Academic Year 1977-78." Copies of the form are available locally in most colleges and universities; they may also be obtained by writing directly to Princeton. The completed form must be returned to the Graduate and Professional School Financial Aid Service by January 20.

The GAPSFAS form contains three sections: Part I for the applicant, Part II for the applicant's spouse or spouse to be, and Part III for the applicant's parents. Part I and, when applicable, Part II, must be completed as part of the application for financial aid at Bryn Mawr. Part III is not required for Bryn Mawr College aid. (See page 89 for loan requirements.)

Fellowships in the Award or Nomination of the College

Bryn Mawr College Fellowships of $2300 in addition to tuition are offered annually in Anthropology, Biochemistry, Biology, Chemistry, Classical and Near Eastern Archaeology, Economics, Education and Child Development, English, French, Geology, German, Greek, History, History and Philosophy of Science, History of Art, Latin, Mathematics, Music, Philosophy, Physics, Political Science, Psychology, Russian, Sociology, and Spanish.

Alumnae Association Fellowships are provided from the contributions of former graduate students to the Alumnae Fund; from the Alumnae Regional Scholarship Committees of Eastern Pennsylvania, Southern New Jersey, and Delaware and of New York and Southern Connecticut, and from the Alumnae Association of New Haven.

Marion Louise Ament Fellowship. Graduate fellowships in Spanish are occasionally awarded from the fund established in 1966 in honor of Marion Neustadt, Class of 1944.

The Henry Joel Cadbury Fellowship Fund in the Humanities was established in 1973 by the Board of Bryn Mawr College in honor of Henry Joel Cadbury, Trustee Emeritus. The fund was made possible by donations from current and former trustees and directors of the College and friends of Dr. Cadbury in order to provide annual support for graduate students in the Humanities who have reached an advanced stage of their graduate work.

The Theodore N. Ely Fund. A fellowship or scholarship in Art or Archaeology is awarded to a graduate student from the interest on this fund, which was established in 1959 by bequest of Katrina Ely Tiffany, Class of 1897.

The Folly Ranch Fund was established by an anonymous gift in 1974. The income is used for graduate and undergraduate scholarships in honor of Eleanor Donnelley Erdman, Clarissa Donnelley Haffner, and Elizabeth P. Taylor, Class of 1921, and Jean T. Palmer, Class of 1924.

The Margaret Gilman Fund. A fellowship or scholarship in French is awarded from the interest on this fund, which was established in 1958 by bequest of the late Margaret Gilman, Professor of French at Bryn Mawr College.

The Howard Lehman Goodhart Fellowship is awarded to an advanced student in Mediaeval Studies.

The Helen Schaeffer Huff Memorial Research Fellowship is awarded for a year of research work in Physics or Chemistry at Bryn Mawr College. Candidates must be students who have demonstrated their ability for research. If other qualifications are equal among a number of candidates, preference will be given to a student whose field of research overlaps the fields of Chemistry and Physics. This fellowship is normally awarded to a post-doctoral candidate to enable her to continue her research program. In such cases the stipend will be $6500. In exceptional cases, candidates engaged in important research who have not completed the work for the doctorate will be considered. For such students the stipend will be less, the amount to be determined on the basis of the candidate's qualifications.

The Helen Schaeffer Huff Memorial Research Fellow has no duties except those connected with her own research, but she may arrange with the department in which she is working to do a small amount of teaching if she so desires.

The S. Maude Kaemmerling Scholarship was established in 1959 by the estate of S. Maude Kaemmerling and increased by a gift in 1965. The income on the fund is to be used for graduate scholarships and fellowships.

The Melodee Siegel Kornacker Fellowship in Science was established in 1976 by Melodee Siegel Kornacker, Class of 1960. The income is used for a graduate fellowship in Biology, Chemistry, Geology, Physics, or Psychology.

The Samuel H. Kress Foundation Fellowships in varying amounts are awarded to advanced graduate students in History of Art.

The Katharine Elizabeth McBride Fellowship. In the 75th Anniversary Year a fund for a graduate fellowship in honor of Katharine McBride was established by certain alumnae. The endowment of this fellowship was increased by a gift from the Class of 1925 on its 40th reunion. The fellowship is awarded in any department to a candidate for the Ph.D. degree who is about to complete two years or more of graduate work.

The Emmy Noether Fellowship was founded by gifts from many donors in memory of Emmy Noether who came to Bryn Mawr College from Germany in 1933 and who died April 14, 1935. It is open to students in the United States and in foreign countries who are advanced graduate students of Mathematics. It is awarded by the Department of Mathematics of Bryn Mawr College and may be used, subject to the approval of the Department, at any institution in the United States or in a foreign country.

The Ida H. Ogilvie Fellowships in Geology are awarded each year from part of the income of the Ida H. Ogilvie Fund, which was established in 1965 through the bequest of Dr. Ogilvie, a member of the Class of 1896.

The Max Richter Fellowship Fund was established in 1962 and increased in 1965 by gifts from the Trustees of the Richter Memorial

Foundation. Income from the endowment provides fellowships to advanced students interested in public affairs.

The Mildred Clarke Pressinger von Kienbusch Fellowship was established in 1964 by a gift in honor of Mildred Clarke Pressinger von Kienbusch of the Class of 1909. The income on this fund is to be used for a graduate student working toward the doctorate. This award may be made to a beginning graduate student.

Scholarships and Fellowships under the Plan for the Coordination of the Sciences. The departments of the natural sciences and Mathematics administer a fund for the Coordination of the Sciences, given to the College in 1935 by the Carnegie Corporation of New York. Its purpose is to encourage and facilitate teaching and research in fields such as biochemistry, biophysics, geochemistry, geophysics, and psychophysics.

From this fund, the Committee for the Coordination of the Sciences awards fellowships, scholarships, assistantships, postdoctoral research fellowships, or other grants as seem appropriate.

The Mary Waddell Fellowship Fund provides grants of $1000 each for the study of Mathematics to daughters of American citizens of Canadian descent.

Whiting Fellowships in the Humanities are awarded to students in their final dissertation year. Each fellowship carries a stipend of $400 per month, plus tuition, together with a modest allowance for research expenses and a family allowance if needed. These fellowships are available in the Departments of Classical and Near Eastern Archaeology, English, French, German, Greek, History, History of Art, Latin, Mediaeval Studies, Music, Philosophy, Russian, and Spanish.

Fellows by Courtesy. Fellows who continue their studies at the College after the expiration of their fellowships may, by a vote of the Directors, receive the rank of Fellow by Courtesy.

Travelling Fellowships

The Fanny Bullock Workman Travelling Fellowship for a year of study or research abroad was established in 1927 by bequest of Fanny Bullock Workman and by gift of her husband, Dr. W. Hunter Workman. It is awarded to a candidate for the degree of Doctor of Philosophy at Bryn Mawr College who could not have the advantages of such a year without assistance. At the discretion of the faculty, the fellowship for any one year may be divided between two students, or the same student may hold the fellowship for more than one year.

The Anna Ottendorfer Memorial Research Fellowship in Teutonic philology and German language and literature, founded in 1907 by

85

Mrs. Anna Woerishoffer in memory of her mother, is to be applied to the expense of study and residence for one year at a German university. It is awarded to a student who has completed at least one year of graduate study at Bryn Mawr College and who shows ability to conduct independent investigations in the fields of Teutonic philology or German literature. The choice of a university is determined by the holder's preference, subject to the approval of the faculty.

The Ella Riegel Fellowship or *Scholarship* in Classical Archaeology was founded in 1937 by bequest of Ella Riegel. It is awarded on the recommendation of the Department of Classical and Near Eastern Archaeology to advanced students in this subject. It is given for study abroad but may, at the discretion of the Department, be used at Bryn Mawr College.

Graduate Scholarships

Bryn Mawr College Graduate Scholarships of $1800 each in addition to tuition are offered annually to students for work in any department of The Graduate School of Arts and Sciences.

Scholarships for Foreign Students. These scholarships are designated for foreign students who have excelled in their university studies. Applicants must have had three or four years of university training. Each scholarship carries a stipend which covers full tuition and residence in graduate student housing during the academic year. (Meals during vacations are not included and students will need to provide their own funds for these and other expenses.) Scholarship holders are expected to carry a full program of graduate work and to attend regularly the courses for which they are registered. Work is given in seminars or small discussion groups in which the students, as well as the instructor, actively participate. It is essential, therefore, that the student be able not only to read and write English, but to understand it and speak it fluently.

The Marguerite N. Farley Scholarships for Foreign Students, which provide tuition and a stipend to cover room and board on campus, are offered to students from any country outside the United States and Canada. Occasionally a fellowship is awarded from this fund to a foreign student who has completed at least one year at Bryn Mawr.

A special British Scholarship, which provides tuition and a stipend to cover room and board on campus, is awarded to students from the United Kingdom who are sponsored by The English-Speaking Union.

Special Foreign Scholarships for French, German, Hebrew, Italian, and Spanish, which provide tuition and a stipend to cover room and board on campus plus $200, have been established for students whose languages form a part of the Bryn Mawr curriculum. Holders of these scholarships are asked to devote four or five hours a week to supervised teaching or other assistance in the appropriate language department. The Special Scholarship for French has been named in memory of Marcelle Pardé who was a member of the French Department of Bryn Mawr College between 1919 and 1929. The Special Scholarship for Spanish has been named in memory of Miguel Catalan, distinguished Spanish physicist and friend of Bryn Mawr.

Duties of Fellows and Scholars

Fellows and Graduate Scholars are required to carry a full academic program at Bryn Mawr College. They are expected to attend official functions. Fellows are not permitted to accept other appointments. Scholars, with the permission of the Dean of The Graduate School of Arts and Sciences, may undertake a limited amount of paid work. Each Travelling Fellow is asked to present a written report of the work done during the fellowship year. This report should be sent about the first of March to the Dean of The Graduate School of Arts and Sciences for transmittal to the student's department.

Assistantships

Teaching Assistantships are available in some departments. These positions carry salaries of $2900-3100 for half-time work, $1950-2050 for one-third-time work, and include tuition without fee. The duties differ with departments. In departments of science, assistantships provide teaching and laboratory experience.

Graduate Assistantships are available in some departments. These positions provide full-time tuition and wages according to the hours of work given to the department.

Research Assistantships are available in the Departments of Biology, Chemistry, Geology, Physics, and Psychology.

Internships and Field Work Placements. The Department of Education and Child Development offers each year one internship, with stipend, in school psychology. The intern is placed in the Child Study Institute and receives individual supervision there. Supervised practicum experience at the Institute is also available, usually without stipend.

Supervised field work placements, with stipend, are available in school counseling. These are open to advanced, highly qualified candidates in the school counseling program sequence. Supervised practicum experience in counseling is also available, usually without stipend.

Tuition Grants

Tuition grants are available for full-time and part-time students. Gifts from the Alumnae Fund have increased the number of these grants.

Graduate Prize

The Susan B. Anthony Memorial Prize, commemorating the great work of Susan B. Anthony for women, was founded by her friend, Anna Howard Shaw, and her niece, Lucy E. Anthony. It is offered from time to time to a graduate student at Bryn Mawr College who has published or submitted in final form for publication the best study dealing with the industrial, social, economic, or political position of women. The award is made by a committee of which the President of the College is chairman.

Loan Funds

National Direct Student Loan Program. These loans are available to qualified students who are registered for at least two units of graduate work. Application is made on a special form which is obtained from the Office of Admissions and Awards after a student has been admitted to The Graduate School of Arts and Sciences. The application and a GAPSFAS form (see page 82) must be filed by August 1. Allocation of loan funds is made early in September.

Guaranteed State Loan Program. Students are encouraged to apply for Guaranteed State Loans through their local banks. Part of the application is completed by The Graduate School of Arts and Sciences. A GAPSFAS form is required.

All students who are applying for National Direct Student Loans and Guaranteed State Loans are advised that GAPSFAS Part III is required from those who do not meet the governmental definition of independent student. Therefore, if you expect to apply for either a federal or state loan, complete Part III if, during the last twelve months, you a) resided with, or b) have been claimed as a federal income tax deduction by, or c) been the recipient of an amount in excess of $600 by one (or both) of your parents.

The Students' Loan Fund of the Alumnae Association of Bryn Mawr College was established by the Class of 1890 for the use of students who need to borrow money in order to continue their college work and for the purpose of receiving contributions, no matter how small, from those who are interested in helping students obtain an education. The fund is managed by the Alumnae Scholarships and Loan Fund Committee.

Loans may be used for purposes approved by the Committee, who try to provide small loans to relieve undue financial pressure or to meet special emergencies. As a rule, money is not lent students in their first semester of graduate work nor are these loans intended to meet the expenses of tuition. Not more than $500 may be borrowed by a student in any one year, except under extraordinary circumstances. The total for four years must not exceed $1500.

While the student is in college no interest is charged; after the student leaves college the interest rate is three percent. The entire principal must be repaid within five years from the time the student leaves college at the rate of twenty percent each year. Students who wish to borrow from the Loan Fund may obtain application blanks for this purpose from the Office of Admissions and Awards of The Graduate School of Arts and Sciences.

Career Planning Office

Graduate students are invited to make use of the services of the Career Planning Office. These services include counseling on career interests and concerns; information on specific openings for summer, temporary and permanent, full- and part-time positions; consultation on job-hunting methods. Upon request the Career Planning Office also collects, maintains, and makes available to prospective employers the credentials of graduate students and alumnae. The credentials include biographical data and faculty and employer references.

Graduate Student Council

The Graduate Student Council, composed of one representative elected annually from each department offering a graduate program, serves as a vehicle through which graduate students may voice their concerns and needs to the faculty and administration. When appropriate, the Council also initiates and carries out specific programs to meet these needs.

Graduate students work primarily in one department, so that the Council provides a means of communicating with students in all departments. Council meetings are held at least once a month in the Graduate Lounge located in the M. Carey Thomas Library. Graduate student opinion is sometimes solicited through questionnaires, so that the Council may best represent various opinions.

Representatives of the Council sit on various College committees such as those concerned with the Library and computer services. In addition, the Council is represented at meetings of the Board of Directors.

The Council also plays a major role in devising policies and procedures for on-campus graduate housing and supports a Housing Service to coordinate summer and off-campus housing opportunities.

Graduate Student Housing

Housing on campus is provided for about sixty-five graduate students in the Graduate Residence Center, Batten House, and the Annex. There is a separate bedroom for each student. Rooms are furnished except for rugs and curtains. Students should bring towels and bed linen. (Local rental services will supply sheets, blankets, and pillowcases for a modest fee. Arrangements may be made on arrival.) Because of college fire regulations, smoking is not permitted in the bedrooms. There are smokers on certain floors. The dining room, available to all resident students, is located in the Center.

Application for a room should be made as early as possible. A room contract, which will be sent upon request, must be signed and returned to the Office of The Graduate School of Arts and Sciences with a deposit of ten dollars. The deposit will be deducted from the residence fee; it will be refunded only if the student cannot be accommodated.

A student who has reserved a room will be held responsible for the residence charge unless notice of withdrawal is sent in writing to the Dean of The Graduate School of Arts and Sciences by August 15.

The regular charge for residence (room and board) for graduate students is $1790 a year, payable one half early in the first semester and the other half early in the second. Although one or more housing units may be closed during Christmas and spring vacations, when food and health service are not provided, residence on campus covers the period from the opening of College in the fall until Commencement Day. Baggage will be accepted at the College after August 20. It should be sent prepaid, addressed to the proper residence hall, and marked with the owner's name.

Health

Medical Services

The College maintains an 18-bed Infirmary with a staff of physicians and nurses. The Infirmary is open when College is in session. The college physicians may be consulted without charge by students residing in campus housing and by students living off campus who have paid the dispensary fee. Specialists practicing in Bryn Mawr and Philadelphia serve as consulting physicians to the College. If consultation is necessary, the student must meet the expense.

The residence charge paid by graduate students living in campus housing entitles them to treatment in the College dispensary, to care in the Infirmary for seven days (not necessarily consecutive) during the year, and to attendance by the college physicians during this time. After the seven-day period, the fee is $30.00 for each day in the Infirmary.

Graduate students who do not live in campus housing may pay a $40.00 fee which entitles them to full use of the Student Health Service. The fee is not billed automatically and is not covered by scholarship or other grants. The dispensary fee is to be paid in the Comptroller's Office where a dispensary card is issued.

The College maintains a counseling and diagnostic service staffed by clinical social workers and consulting psychiatrists. They are at the Infirmary on a part-time basis. All students eligible for dispensary care may use this service. The counseling service offers confidential consultation and discussion of personal and emotional problems. Definitive and long-range psychotherapy is not available. A charge is made for visits in excess of four.

Medical Requirements

All graduate students, after admission but before registration, must file a medical history and health evaluation form with the Infirmary. There are no exceptions to this rule.

In addition to a statement of health, signed by a physician, the following are required: tetanus and polio immunizations; proof of freedom from active tuberculosis based on either a negative skin test, or in the presence of a positive test, a normal chest x-ray within six months of admission.

Insurance

All graduate students are urged to carry health insurance. Students are entitled to the Bryn Mawr College Student Health care insurance at a cost of about $59.50 per year. Those wishing more complete coverage may purchase Blue Cross and Blue Shield insurance on an individual basis, subject to screening by the insurance company. Application for College health insurance should be made through the Head Nurse in the Infirmary.

Foreign Students. The College makes available a policy which provides fuller coverage of medical, surgical, and hospital costs. This insurance is required of all students whose permanent residence is not in the United States unless they have equally complete protection of another kind effective in the United States. The cost for students under age thirty is about $70.00 for a twelve-month period, starting in September.

All foreign students will be automatically enrolled in the Student Health Service at a cost of $40 for non-residents.

Child Care Center

Child care is available for Bryn Mawr-Haverford families at the New Gulph Child Care Center, 911 New Gulph Road (215 LA5-7649). The Center, conducted by a professional staff, incorporates age group developmental activities with quality group care. Children three months through five years old are eligible. The Center is open five days a week, 9 to 5, at an approximate cost of $1.25 per hour plus an additional charge for hot lunch, if desired. A minimum of six hours' regular use per week is required. Following Commencement, a summer program is conducted for approximately two months. Early registration for all programs is essential. For information contact the Director. The tuition for the semester must be paid in advance. Limited scholarship help is available.

Faculty and Staff of The Graduate School of Arts and Sciences
for the Academic Year 1976-77

Harris L. Wofford, Jr., AB (University of Chicago) JD (Howard University and Yale University) *President of the College*

Phyllis Pray Bober PHD (New York University) *Dean of The Graduate School of Arts and Sciences*

Mary Patterson McPherson PHD (Bryn Mawr College) *Dean of the Undergraduate College*

Bernard Ross PHD (University of Michigan) *Dean of The Graduate School of Social Work and Social Research*

Phyllis S. Lachs PHD (Bryn Mawr College) *Associate Dean of The Graduate School of Arts and Sciences*

Gertrude C. K. Leighton AB (Bryn Mawr College) JD (Yale University) *Secretary of the General Faculty*

Joseph Varimbi PHD (University of Pennsylvania) *Secretary of the Faculty of Arts and Sciences*

Alfonso M. Albano PHD (State University of New York at Stony Brook) *Assistant Professor of Physics*

Steven Alpern PHD (New York University) *Lecturer in Mathematics*

Jay Martin Anderson PHD (Harvard University) *Professor of Chemistry*

Barbra Apfelbaum AB (Smith College) *Lecturer in Italian*

Hans Bänziger PHD (University of Zürich) *Professor of German*

Ernst Berliner PHD (Harvard University) *W. Alton Jones Professor of Chemistry*

Frances Bondhus Berliner PHD (Bryn Mawr College) *Lecturer in Chemistry*

Carol L. Bernstein PHD (Yale University) *Associate Professor of English*

Sandra M. Berwind PHD (Bryn Mawr College) *Assistant Professor of English*

The notations throughout this section
refer to the following footnotes:
†On leave semester II
‡On leave 1976-77
*On leave semester I

Eleanor A. Bliss SCD (Johns Hopkins University) *Dean Emeritus*

Shirley Neilson Blum PH D (University of California) *Visiting Professor of History of Art.*

Phyllis Pray Bober PH D (New York University) *Dean of The Graduate School of Arts and Sciences* and *Professor of Classical and Near Eastern Archaeology* and *of History of Art*

Charles M. Brand PH D (Harvard University) *Professor of History*

Robert A. Braun PH D (University of Illinois) *Assistant Professor of Anthropology*

Peter M. Briggs PH D (Yale University) *Assistant Professor of English*

Katrin Ristkok Burlin PH D (Cornell University) *Assistant Professor of English*

Robert B. Burlin PH D (Yale University) *Professor of English*

Rhys Carpenter PH D (Columbia University) LITT D *Professor Emeritus of Classical Archaeology*

Isabelle Cazeaux PH D (Columbia University) *Professor of Music*

Robert L. Conner PH D (Indiana University) *Professor of Biology*

Rachel Dunaway Cox PH D (University of Pennsylvania) *Professor Emeritus of Education and Child Development* and *of Psychology*

Maria Luisa B. Crawford PH D (University of California) *Associate Professor of Geology*

William A. Crawford PH D (University of California) *Associate Professor of Geology*

Frederic Cunningham, Jr. PH D (Harvard University) *Professor of Mathematics*

Dan E. Davidson PH D (Harvard University) *Associate Professor of Russian*

Gérard Defaux D ès L (Sorbonne) *Professor of French*

Frances de Graaff PH D (University of Leyden) *Professor Emeritus of Russian*

Frederica de Laguna PH D (Columbia University) *Professor Emeritus of Anthropology*

Grace Mead Andrus de Laguna PH D (Cornell University) *Professor Emeritus of Philosophy*

Charles G. Dempsey MFA PH D (Princeton University) *Professor of History of Art*

Nancy Dersofi PHD (Harvard University) *Assistant Professor of Italian*‡

Gregory W. Dickerson PH D (Princeton University) *Associate Professor of Greek*

Max Diez PH D (University of Texas) *Professor Emeritus of German Literature*

Nancy C. Dorian PH D (University of Michigan) *Associate Professor of German*

Lincoln Dryden PH D (Johns Hopkins University) *Professor Emeritus of Geology*

Richard B. Du Boff PH D (University of Pennsylvania) *Professor of Economics*

Arthur P. Dudden PH D (University of Michigan) *Professor of History*

Mary Maples Dunn PH D (Bryn Mawr College) *Professor of History*

Richard S. Ellis PH D (University of Chicago) *Associate Professor of Classical and Near Eastern Archaeology* .

Noel J. J. Farley PH D (Yale University) *Associate Professor of Economics*

José María Ferrater Mora *Licenciado en Filosofía* (University of Barcelona) *Professor of Philosophy* and *Fairbank Professor in the Humanities*‡

Gloria Flaherty PH D (Johns Hopkins University) *Associate Professor of German*

Elizabeth Read Foster PH D (Yale University) *Professor of History*

Grace Frank AB (University of Chicago) *Professor Emeritus of Old French*

Charles E. Frye PH D (Princeton University) *Associate Professor of Political Science*

Julia H. Gaisser PH D (University of Edinburgh) *Associate Professor of Latin*

Mary Summerfield Gardiner PH D (Bryn Mawr College) *Professor Emeritus of Biology*

Richard H. Gaskins PH D JD (Yale University) *Assistant Professor of Philosophy*

Richard C. Gonzalez PH D (University of Maryland) *Professor of Psychology*

Joaquín González Muela *Den Fil* (University of Madrid) *Professor of Spanish*

Hope K. Goodale PH D (Bryn Mawr College) *Visiting Lecturer in Music*

Jane C. Goodale PH D (University of Pennsylvania) *Professor of Anthropology*

Robert L. Goodale AB BMUS (Yale University) A AG O *Alice Carter Dickerman Professor of Music*

Michel Guggenheim PH D (Yale University) *Professor of French*

Richard Hamilton PH D (University of Michigan) *Assistant Professor of Greek* and *of Latin*

Hiroko Hara PH D (Bryn Mawr College) *Lecturer in Anthropology*

Tadahiko Hara PH D (Australian National University) *Lecturer in Anthropology*

E. Jane Hedley PHD *(Bryn Mawr College) Assistant Professor of English*

Howard S. Hoffman PH D (University of Connecticut) *Professor of Psychology*†

Wendell P. Holbrook AB (Morgan State College) *Lecturer in History**

Janet L. Hoopes PH D (Bryn Mawr College) *Professor of Education and Child Development* and *Director of the Child Study Institute*

Rosalie C. Hoyt PH D (Bryn Mawr College) *Marion Reilly Professor of Physics*

Joshua C. Hubbard PH D (Harvard University) *Professor Emeritus of Economics*

Helen Manning Hunter PH D (Radcliffe College) *Associate Professor of Economics*

James E. Irby PH D (University of Michigan) *Visiting Lecturer in Spanish*

Thomas H. Jackson PH D (Yale University) *Associate Professor of English*

C. Stephen Jaeger PH D (University of California) *Associate Professor of German*

Agi Jambor MA (Royal Academy of Budapest) *Professor of Music*

Myra Richards Jessen PH D (Bryn Mawr College) *Professor Emeritus of German*

Eileen T. Johnston MA (University of Chicago) *Lecturer in English*

Pauline Jones PH D (Bryn Mawr College) *Professor of French*†

Richard H. Jordan PH D (University of Minnesota) *Assistant Professor of Anthropology*

Anne Kaier PH D (Harvard University) *Assistant Professor of English*

Anthony R. Kaney PH D (University of Illinois) *Associate Professor of Biology*‡

Howard C. Kee PH D (Yale University) *Rufus Jones Professor of History of Religion*

Melville T. Kennedy, Jr. PH D (Harvard University) *Professor of Political Science*

Philip L. Kilbride PH D (University of Missouri) *Associate Professor of Anthropology*‡

Willard F. King PH D (Brown University) *Dorothy Nepper Marshall Professor of Spanish*

Dale Kinney PH D (New York University) *Assistant Professor of History of Art*

George L. Kline PH D (Columbia University) *Professor of Philosophy*

Sandra I. Kohler PH D (Bryn Mawr College) *Assistant Professor of English*

Mary Jo Koroly PH D (Bryn Mawr College) *Assistant Professor of Biology*

Joseph E. Kramer PH D (Princeton University) *Associate Professor of English**

Michael Krausz PH D (University of Toronto) *Associate Professor of Philosophy*

Kenneth Krigelman PH D (University of Pennsylvania) *Assistant Professor of Mathematics‡*

Phyllis S. Lachs PH D (Bryn Mawr College) *Associate Dean of The Graduate School of Arts and Sciences* and *Associate Professor of History*

Samuel Tobias Lachs PH D (Dropsie University) *Associate Professor of History of Religion*

Catherine Lafarge PH D (Yale University) *Associate Professor of French*

Barbara M. Lane PH D (Harvard University) *Professor of History*

Mabel L. Lang PH D (Bryn Mawr College) *Paul Shorey Professor of Greek‡*

Richmond Lattimore PH D (University of Illinois) LITT D *Professor Emeritus of Greek*

Li Way Lee PH D (Columbia University) *Assistant Professor of Economics*

Paul Lehmann TH D (Union Theological Seminary) *Roian Fleck Resident in Religion* and *Visiting Lecturer in History of Religion*

Phyllis W. Lehmann PH D *Mary Flexner Lecturer in Classical and Near Eastern Archaeology and in History of Art*

Marguerite Lehr PH D (Bryn Mawr College) *Professor Emeritus of Mathematics*

Gertrude C. K. Leighton AB (Bryn Mawr College) J D (Yale University) *Secretary of the General Faculty* and *Professor of Political Science*

J. Edward Leonard PH D (Boston University) *Lecturer in Geology*

Steven Z. Levine PH D (Harvard University) *Assistant Professor of History of Art*

Angeline H. Lograsso PH D (Radcliffe College) *Professor Emeritus of Italian*

Frank B. Mallory PH D (California Institute of Technology) *Professor of Chemistry*

Helen Taft Manning PH D (Yale University) *Professor Emeritus of History*

Mario Maurin PH D (Yale University) *Professor of French*

Ethel W. Maw PH D (University of Pennsylvania) *Professor of Education and Child Development*

Susan E. Maxfield MS (Syracuse University) *Associate Professor of Education and Child Development* and *Director of the Phebe Anna Thorne School*

Clark McCauley, Jr. PH D (University of Pennsylvania) *Associate Professor of Psychology**

Elizabeth R. McKinsey AB (Radcliffe College) *Lecturer in English*

Mary Patterson McPherson PH D (Bryn Mawr College) *Dean of the Undergraduate College* and *Associate Professor of Philosophy*

Machteld J. Mellink PH D (University of Utrecht) *Leslie Clark Professor of Classical and Near Eastern Archaeology*

Fritz Mezger PH D (University of Berlin) *Professor Emeritus of Germanic Philology*

Agnes Kirsopp Michels PH D (Bryn Mawr College) *Professor Emeritus of Latin*

Charles Mitchell B LITT (Oxford University) LITT D *Professor of History of Art* and *Andrew W. Mellon Professor of Humanities*

Milton Charles Nahm B LITT (Oxford University) PH D (University of Pennsylvania) *Professor Emeritus of Philosophy*

Carl Nylander PH D (Uppsala University) *Associate Professor of Classical and Near Eastern Archaeology*

Patricia J. Olds-Clarke PH D (Washington University) *Assistant Professor of Biology*

Jane M. Oppenheimer PH D (Yale University) *William R. Kenan, Jr. Professor of History of Science*

Kathryn Z. Orkwiszewski PH D (Bryn Mawr College) *Lecturer in Biology*

John C. Oxtoby M A (University of California) *Class of 1897 Professor of Mathematics*

George S. Pahomov PH D (New York University) *Assistant Professor of Russian*

Nicholas Patruno PH D (Rutgers University) *Assistant Professor of Italian*

Eleanor K. Paucker PH D (University of Pennsylvania) *Associate Professor of Spanish*

Ruth L. Pearce PH D (University of Pennsylvania) *Associate Professor of Russian*

Emmy A. Pepitone PH D (University of Michigan) *Associate Professor of Education and Child Development*

Kyle M. Phillips, Jr. PH D (Princeton University) *Professor of Classical and Near Eastern Archaeology* ‡

William R. F. Phillips PH D (University of Wisconsin) *Assistant Professor of Sociology*

Lucian B. Platt PH D (Yale University) *Associate Professor of Geology* ‡

Stephen Poppel PH D (Harvard University) *Assistant Professor of History*

Judith R. Porter PH D (Harvard University) *Associate Professor of Sociology*

Jean A. Potter PH D (Yale University) *Professor of Philosophy*

Alice S. Powers PH D (Bryn Mawr College) *Lecturer in Psychology*

David J. Prescott PH D (University of Pennsylvania) *Assistant Professor of Biology*

John R. Pruett PH D (Indiana University) *Professor of Physics*

Patricia Onderdonk Pruett PH D (Bryn Mawr College) *Associate Dean of the Undergraduate College* and *Lecturer in Biology*

Denise M. Ragona PH D (Bryn Mawr College) *Lecturer in Biology*

Karen Meier Reeds PH D (Harvard University) *Andrew W. Mellon Post-Doctoral Fellow* and *Lecturer in the History of Science*

Brunilde S. Ridgway PH D (Bryn Mawr College) *Professor of Classical and Near Eastern Archaeology*

Caroline Robbins PH D (University of London) LITT D LLD *Professor Emeritus of History*

Marc H. Ross PH D (Northwestern University) *Associate Professor of Political Science*

Fred Rothbaum MS (Yale University) *Assistant Professor of Education and Child Development*

Stephen Salkever PH D (University of Chicago) *Associate Professor of Political Science*

J. H. M. Salmon LITT D (Victoria University) *Marjorie Walter Goodhart Professor of History*

W. Bruce Saunders PH D (University of Iowa) *Associate Professor of Geology*

Grace Armstrong Savage PH D (Princeton University) *Assistant Professor of French*

Carl B. Schmidt PH D (Harvard University) *Assistant Professor of Music* ‡

Eugene V. Schneider PH D (Harvard University) *Professor of Sociology*

Françoise Schremmer PH D (University of Pennsylvania) *Assistant Professor of Mathematics*

Russell T. Scott PH D (Yale University) *Associate Professor of Latin*

Judith R. Shapiro PH D (Columbia University) *Assistant Professor of Anthropology*

George A. Sheets PH D *Andrew W. Mellon Post-Doctoral Fellow* and *Lecturer in Greek* and *in Latin*

Alain Silvera PH D (Harvard University) *Professor of History*

Peter M. Smith PH D (Harvard University) *Lecturer in Greek*

Stephen R. Smith PH D (Massachusetts Institute of Technology) *Assistant Professor of Physics*

James E. Snyder MFA PH D (Princeton University) *Professor of History of Art*[†]

Samuel S. Snyder PH D (Yale University) *Assistant Professor of Education and Child Development*

Faye P. Soffen ED D (University of Pennsylvania) *Associate Professor of Education and Child Development*[‡]

Thomas Song MA MALS (University of Michigan) *Associate Director of Libraries* and *Lecturer in Philosophy*

Arthur Colby Sprague PH D (Harvard University) *Professor Emeritus of English Literature*

K. Laurence Stapleton AB (Smith College) *Mary E. Garrett Alumnae Professor of English Literature*

Isabel Scribner Stearns PH D (Bryn Mawr College) *Professor of Philosophy*

Larry Stein PH D (University of Iowa) *Lecturer in Psychology*

George C. Stephens PH D (Lehigh University) *Assistant Professor of Geology*

Tracy M. Taft PH D (State University of New York at Buffalo) *Assistant Professor of Philosophy*

James Tanis TH D (University of Utrecht) *Director of Libraries* and *Professor of History* and *History of Religion*[‡]

Earl Thomas PH D (Yale University) *Associate Professor of Psychology*

Steven N. Treistman PH D (University of North Carolina) *Assistant Professor of Biology*

Myra L. Uhlfelder PH D (Bryn Mawr College) *Professor of Latin*

Joseph Varimbi PH D (University of Pennsylvania) *Secretary of the Faculty of Arts and Sciences* and *Associate Professor of Chemistry*

Lynn Visson PH D (Harvard University) *Assistant Professor of Russian**

Jill T. Wannemacher PH D (Brown University) *Assistant Professor of Psychology on the Rosalyn R. Schwartz Lectureship*

Robert E. Washington PH D (University of Chicago) *Assistant Professor of Sociology*

George E. Weaver, Jr. PH D (University of Pennsylvania) *Associate Professor of Philosophy*

Roger Hewes Wells PH D (Harvard University) *Professor Emeritus of Political Science*

Harris L. Wofford, Jr. AB (University of Chicago) J D (Howard University and Yale University) *President of the College*

Eugene Wolf PH D (New York University) *Visiting Lecturer in Music*

Mary Katharine Woodworth PH D (Bryn Mawr College) *Professor Emeritus of English*

Dorothy Wyckoff PH D (Bryn Mawr College) *Professor Emeritus of Geology*

Matthew Yarczower PH D (University of Maryland) *Professor of Psychology*

J. Maitland Young PH D (Yale University) *Assistant Professor of Chemistry*

George L. Zimmerman PH D (University of Chicago) *Professor of Chemistry*

Officers of Administration

Dolores E. Brien PH D (Brown University) *Director of Career Planning*

Merle Broberg PH D (The American University) *Assistant Dean of The Graduate School of Social Work and Social Research*

Margaret M. Healy PHD (Bryn Mawr College) *Director of the Ad Hoc Committee of the Board on the Financing of the College*

Joseph S. Johnston, Jr. MA (University of Chicago) *Assistant to the President*

Paul W. Klug CPA BS (Temple University) *Comptroller and Business Manager of the College*

Ramona L. Livingston AB (William Jewell College) *Advisor to Foreign Students* and *Lecturer in English*

Margaret G. McKenna AB (Bryn Mawr College) *Personnel Administrator*

Samuel J. McNamee BS (Temple University) *Assistant Comptroller*

Michelle Pynchon Osborn AB (Smith College) *Director of Public Information*

Julie E. Painter AB (Bryn Mawr College) *Administrator of Records and Financial Aid*

Martha Stokes Price AB (Bryn Mawr College) *Director of Resources*

Patricia Onderdonk Pruett PH D (Bryn Mawr College) *Associate Dean of the Undergraduate College*

Ellen Fernon Reisner MA (Bryn Mawr College) *Assistant to the President* and *Alumna-in-Residence*

Thomas N. Trucks BS (Villanova University) *Superintendent of Buildings and Grounds*

Sarah E. Wright *Director of Halls*

Health

Frieda W. Woodruff M D (University of Pennsylvania) *College Physician*

Eileen A. Bazelon MD (Medical College of Pennsylvania) *Consulting Psychiatrist*

Anne Lee Delano MA (Columbia University) *Director of Physical Education*

Mary Geiger MD (State University of New York at Albany) *Consulting Psychiatrist*

John F. Howkins MD (Columbia University, College of Physicians and Surgeons) *Consulting Psychiatrist*

Howard B. Smith MD (Jefferson Medical College) *Consulting Psychiatrist*

Margaret S. Temeles MD (Tufts University School of Medicine) *Consulting Psychiatrist*

Librarians

James Tanis THD (University of Utrecht) *Director of Libraries*‡

Thomas Song MA MALS (University of Michigan) *Associate Director of Libraries*

Zoe M. Bemis (Washington University, Yale University) *Reference Librarian*

Leo M. Dolenski MA (Catholic University of America) MLS (Drexel University) *Manuscripts Librarian*

John Dooley MLS (McGill University) *Bibliographer and Reference Librarian*

Florence D. Goff MA MSLS (Villanova University) *Cataloging Librarian*

John Jaffe MA MSLS (Villanova University) *Acquisitions Librarian*

Mary S. Leahy MA (Bryn Mawr College) *Rare Book Librarian*

Eileen Markson MA (New York University) MLS (Queens College of City University of New York) *Head, Art and Archaeology Library*

Yasuko Matsudo MLS (State University of New York, Albany) *Intercollege Librarian*

Charles McFadden MA (Bryn Mawr College) MSLS (Drexel University) *Head, Gifts and Exchange Division*

Catherine E. Pabst MA (University of Wisconsin) MSLS (Drexel University) *Head, Acquisitions Department*

Gertrude Reed MSLS (Rutgers University) *Head, Reference Division and Archivist*

Ruth Reese MLS (Simmons College) *Intercollege Librarian*

Pamela G. Reilly MSLS (Drexel University) *Head, Public Services Department*

Penelope Schwind MSLS (Drexel University) *Head, Cataloging Department*

Kathleen C. Seabe MLSL (Simmons College) *Intercollege Librarian*

Barbara F. Siegel MSLS (Drexel University) *Serials Librarian*

Arleen Speizman MSLS (Drexel University) *Cataloging Librarian*

Ethel W. Whetstone ABLS (University of North Carolina) *Head, Sciences and Social Sciences Libraries*

Child Study Institute

Janet L. Hoopes PH D (Bryn Mawr College) *Director*

Anne D. Emmons MS (University of Pennsylvania) *Director, Remedial Reading Service*

Beatrice Schneider MSW (Western Reserve University) *Administrative Assistant*

Isabel Westfried MA (Bryn Mawr College) *Chief Psychologist*

Phebe Anna Thorne School

Susan E. Maxfield MS (Syracuse University) *Director*

The Council of The Graduate School of Arts and Sciences

Dean Bober, *Chairman*
President Wofford *ex officio*
Mr. Berliner
Mr. Burlin
Mr. Dempsey
Mrs. Foster
Mr. Guggenheim
Miss Hoopes
Miss Hoyt
Mr. Kennedy
Mrs. King
Dean Lachs

Committee on Graduate Awards

Dean Lachs, *Chairman*
President Wofford *ex officio*
Dean Bober
Miss Hoyt
Mr. Kramer (sem. II)
Miss Lafarge
Mr. Weaver (sem. I)

Excavations	28
Exclusion from the College	81
Expenses	80
Faculty	95
Fees	79
Fellowships	82
Financial Aid	82
Foreign Students, Application	7
Financial Aid	7
Scholarships	86
French	38
Geology	41
German	43
Goldman Collection, Hetty	9
Goodhart, Marjorie Walter, Mediaeval Library	9
Gordan, John D., Reference Center	9
Graduate Prizes	88
Graduate Record Examinations	6
Graduate Residence Center	91
Graduate Student Council	90
Greek	46
Health	92
Health Staff	104
History	47
History and Philosophy of Science	51
History of Art	53
History of Religion	55
Housing	91
Infirmary	92
Institut d'Etudes Françaises *d'Avignon*	12
Insurance, Health	92
Italian	56
King Collection, Elisabeth W.	9
Laboratories	10
Language Requirements	6
Latin	56
Libraries	9
Library Staff	105
Loan Funds	89
Madrid, Summer Institute	12
Master of Arts, Degree	14-15
Mathematics	58
Mediaeval Studies	60
Music	62
Officers	
Administrative	104
Board of Trustees	94
Opportunity, Equality of	12

Phebe Anna Thorne School	33
Philosophy	63
Philosophy of Science	51
Physical Examination	92
Physics	66
Plan for Coordination in the Sciences	10, 85
Political Science	69
Program of Study	11, 16
Psychology	71
Rand Collection, Theodore	10
Rare Book Room	9
Reciprocal Plan, University of Pennsylvania	11
Registration	8
Riegel Museum, Ella	9
Religion, History of	55
Requirements for Admission	6
for Degrees	13-15
Residence Center	91
Resources for Graduate Work	9
Russian	73
Scholarships	82, 86
Science Center	10

Sciences, Plan for Coordination in	10, 85
Seminars and Courses	16
Social Work and Social Research, Graduate School of	3, 22
Sociology	75
Spanish	77
Staff, Academic and Administrative	95
Student Employment	90
Summer Work	12
Teaching Certification	32
Trustees	94
Tuition	79
Tuition Grants	88
Tuition Scholarships	82, 86
University of Pennsylvania, Reciprocal Plan	11
U.S. Geological Survey Maps	10
Vaux Collection, George Jr.	10

Directions to Bryn Mawr College

By automobile from the East or South-East take the Walt Whitman Bridge to I-676/Schuylkill Expressway and follow this north until it meets with I-76; *or* take the Benjamin Franklin Bridge to I-76/Vine Street until it meets with I-676. In either case, continue north on I-76 to Exit 41, "City Ave.—U.S. 1 South." Proceed south on City Ave./U.S. 1 for 1.1 miles from the exit ramp and then turn right on Conshohocken State Road (PA 23). (There is a shopping center on the right shortly before this turn.) After three-tenths of a mile, Conshohocken State Road makes a sharp turn to the left over a railroad overpass and comes to a traffic light. Continue straight through this intersection; you are now on Montgomery Avenue, which you follow for about five miles (bearing right at a fork at about the three mile point), to Morris Avenue in the town of Bryn Mawr. Harcum Junior College will be on the left shortly before Morris Avenue. Turn right onto Morris Avenue, proceed to the next traffic light and then turn left onto New Gulph Road for approximately 1½ blocks. Visitors may use the College parking lot, entering at Merion Gate, which is directly opposite 815 New Gulph Road. The parking lot on Morris Avenue also may be used by visitors.

By automobile from the South take I-95 through Wilmington, Delaware, to Chester, Pennsylvania, then take the exit marked "PA 352—Edgemont Ave." (It is also marked with a sign for "Chester Business District.") Immediately look for, and follow, signs for PA 320 North. Continue north on PA 320 for approximately 10.5 miles from the I-95 exit, until you come to Bryn Mawr Avenue. (This is about two miles after you cross PA 3, and has a traffic light.) Turn right, and follow Bryn Mawr Avenue for approximately two miles until you come to a traffic light at Haverford Road. Continue on Bryn Mawr Avenue, which bears slightly to the left, until you come to Lancaster Avenue in the town of Bryn Mawr. (This is the second traffic light after Haverford Road.) Turn right on Lancaster Avenue for one block, and then left at the first traffic light onto Morris Avenue. Follow the road, which will curve under the railroad tracks, until you come to the traffic light at Montgomery Avenue. Proceed across Montgomery Avenue to the next traffic light. Turn left on to New Gulph Road for approximately 1½ blocks. Visitors may use the College parking lot, entering at Merion Gate, which is directly opposite 815 New Gulph Road. The parking lot on Morris Avenue also may be used by visitors.

By automobile from the West, North or Northeast take the Pennsylvania Turnpike to the Valley Forge Exit (24). From the Valley Forge Exit of the Turnpike, take the Schuylkill Expressway (I-76) east, turning off at Exit 36, "PA 320, Gulph Mills," which is 3.5 miles from the toll gate. Follow PA 320 south for approximately four-tenths of a mile and turn left at the first traffic light onto Old Gulph Road. Proceed on this for approximately three miles, and the College will be on your right. The College parking lot is the third entrance on the right after Roberts Road.

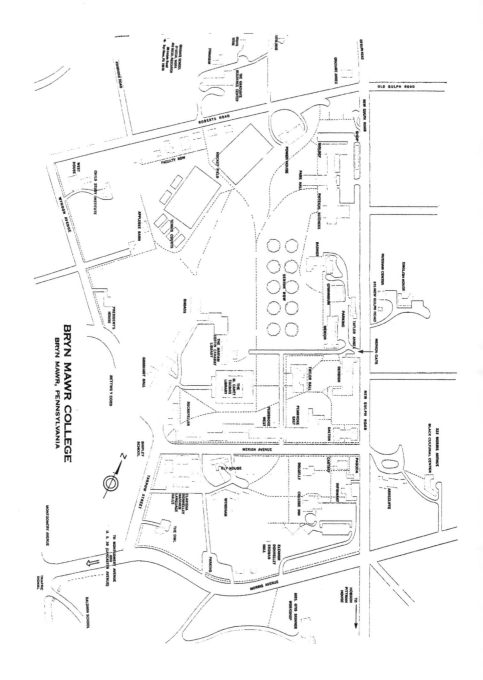

BRYN MAWR COLLEGE
BRYN MAWR, PENNSYLVANIA

Bryn Mawr College Calendar

Undergraduate Courses

Issue for the Session of 1977-78

August 1977, Volume LXX, Number 3

Bryn Maur College Calendar. Published December, July, August, and September by Bryn Mawr College, Bryn Mawr, Pennsylvania 19010.

Second Class Postage paid at Bryn Mawr, Pennsylvania.

Contents

PAGE

Academic Schedule 3
The Trustees, Directors, and Committees of the Board 5, 6
The Faculty and Staff 7
Introduction 22
Admission 27
    Freshman Class 30
    Transfer and Foreign Students 30
    Readmission 32
    Leaves of Absence 32
Academic Facilities and Residence 34
Tuition and Residence Fees 39
General Information 42
    Student Advising 42
    Academic Standards and Regulations 42
    Family Educational Rights and Privacy Act 43
    Health 44
Curriculum 47
    Premedical Preparation 51
    Preparation to Teach 52
    Coordination in the Sciences 52
    Credit for Creative Work in the Arts 53
    Language Houses 53
    Summer Institutes Abroad 53
    Junior Year Abroad 54
Employment and Vocational Counseling 56
Courses of Study 57
    Departmental Courses 58
    Interdepartmental Work 152
    Performing Arts 163
    Physical Education 163
Financial Aid 166
    Scholarship Funds 168
    Prizes and Academic Awards 185
    Scholarships for Medical Study 189
Loan Funds 191
Alumnae Representatives 194
Index 200

Visitors to the College are welcome and when the College is in session student guides are available to show visitors the campus. Appointment for interviews and for campus tours should be made in advance by letter or by telephone. The College offices are open Monday through Friday from nine until five and on Saturdays from nine until one when the College is in session.

Correspondence

The Post Office address is Bryn Mawr College, Bryn Mawr, Pennsylvania 19010. Telephone: 215 LA5-1000.

Correspondence about the following subjects should be addressed to:

The President
General interest of the College

The Dean
Academic work, personal welfare, and health of the students

The Director of Admissions
Admission to the Undergraduate College and entrance scholarships

The Dean of The Graduate School of Arts and Sciences
Admission and graduate scholarships

The Dean of The Graduate School of Social Work and Social Research
Admission and graduate scholarships

The Director of Halls
Rooms in the halls of residence

The Comptroller
Payment of bills

The Director of the Career Planning Office
Recommendations for positions and inquiries about students' self-help

The Alumnae Association
Regional scholarships and loan fund

Academic Schedule 1977-78

1977		*First Semester*
September	2	Halls of residence open to Freshman Week Committee
September	3	Halls of residence open to entering class at 8 a.m. Registration of entering undergraduate students
September	6	Halls of residence open to returning undergraduates at 8 a.m.
September	7	Registration of returning students
September	8	Work of the 93rd academic year begins at 9 a.m.
September	9-10	Deferred examinations
September	15	French examinations for undergraduates (evening)
September	16	Greek, Latin, Mathematics, and Russian examinations for undergraduates (afternoon)
September	19	German examinations for undergraduates
September	20	Hebrew, Italian, and Spanish examinations for under-graduates
October	21	Fall vacation begins after last class
October	26	Fall vacation ends at 9 a.m.
November	23	Thanksgiving holiday begins after last class
November	28	Thanksgiving holiday ends at 9 a.m.
December	13	Last day of semester I classes
December	14-15	Review period
December	15	Written work due
December	16-21	College examinations for semester I
December	21	Winter vacation begins

1978		*Second Semester*
January	16	Work of the second semester begins at 9 a.m.
January	27-28	Deferred examinations
March	10	Spring vacation begins after last class
March	20	Spring vacation ends at 9 a.m.
April	14-16	Geology field trip
April	17	French and German examinations for undergraduates
April	18	Greek, Hebrew, and Latin examinations for under-graduates
April	19	Italian and Spanish examinations for undergraduates
April	20	Mathematics and Russian examinations for under-graduates
April	28	Last day of semester II classes
April 29-*May* 2		Review period
May	2	Written work due
May	3-12	College examinations for semester II
May	15	Conferring of degrees and close of the 93rd academic year
May	19-21	Alumnae Weekend

Standing Committees of the Board of Trustees

Bryn Mawr College Faculty and Staff

For the Academic Year, 1977-78

Harris L. Wofford, Jr., A.B. (University of Chicago), J.D. (Howard University and Yale University), *President of the College*

Mary Patterson McPherson, PH.D. (Bryn Mawr College), LL.D. *Dean of the College*

Phyllis Pray Bober, PH.D. (New York University), *Dean of The Graduate School of Arts and Sciences*

Bernard Ross, PH.D. (University of Michigan), *Dean of The Graduate School of Social Work and Social Research for Semester I, 1977-78*

Anne Lee Delano, M.A. (Columbia University), *Director of Physical Education*

James Tanis, TH.D. (University of Utrecht), *Director of Libraries*

Elizabeth G. Vermey, M.A. (Wesleyan University), *Director of Admissions*

Frieda W. Woodruff, M.D. (University of Pennsylvania), *College Physician*

Emeriti

Eleanor A. Bliss, SC.D (Johns Hopkins University), *Dean Emeritus*

Rhys Carpenter, PH.D. (Columbia University), LITT.D., *Professor Emeritus of Classical Archaeology*

Rachel Dunaway Cox, PH.D. (University of Pennsylvania), *Professor Emeritus of Education and Psychology*

Frances de Graaff, PH.D. (University of Leyden), *Professor Emeritus of Russian*

Frederica de Laguna, PH.D. (Columbia University), *Professor Emeritus of Anthropology*

Grace Mead Andrus de Laguna, PH.D. (Cornell University), *Professor Emeritus of Philosophy*

Max Diez, PH.D. (University of Texas), *Professor Emeritus of German Literature*

Grace Frank, A.B. (University of Chicago), *Professor Emeritus of Old French*

Mary Summerfield Gardiner, PH.D. (Bryn Mawr College), *Professor Emeritus of Biology*

Joshua C. Hubbard, PH.D. (Harvard University), *Professor Emeritus of Economics*

Agi Jambor, M.A. (Royal Academy of Budapest), *Professor Emeritus of Music*

Myra Richards Jessen, PH.D. (Bryn Mawr College), *Professor Emeritus of German*

Richmond Lattimore, PH.D. (University of Illinois), LITT.D., *Professor Emeritus of Greek*

Marguerite Lehr, PH.D. (Bryn Mawr College), *Professor Emeritus of Mathematics*

Angeline H. Lograsso, PH.D. (Radcliffe College), *Professor Emeritus of Italian*

Katherine D. K. Lower, PH.D. (University of Wisconsin), *Professor Emeritus of Social Work and Social Research*

Helen Taft Manning, PH.D. (Yale University), *Professor Emeritus of History*

Fritz Mezger, PH.D. (University of Berlin), *Professor Emeritus of Germanic Philology*

Agnes Kirsopp Michels, PH.D. (Bryn Mawr College), *Professor Emeritus of Latin*

Milton Charles Nahm, B.LITT. (Oxford University), PH.D. (University of Pennsylvania), *Professor Emeritus of Philosophy*

Caroline Robbins, PH.D. (University of London), LL.D., LITT.D., *Professor Emeritus of History*

Arthur Colby Sprague, PH.D. (Harvard University), *Professor Emeritus of English Literature*

Roger Hewes Wells, PH.D. (Harvard University), *Professor Emeritus of Political Science*

Mary Katharine Woodworth, PH.D. (Bryn Mawr College), *Professor Emeritus of English*

Dorothy Wyckoff, PH.D. (Bryn Mawr College), *Professor Emeritus of Geology*

The notations through this section refer to the following:
[1] On sabbatical leave, 1977-78.
[2] On leave of absence, semester I.
[3] On leave of absence, semester II.
[4] On sabbatical leave, semester I.
[5] On leave of absence, 1977-78.
[6] On sabbatical leave, semester II.
[7] On leave of absence, with Junior Faculty Research Award.

Professors

Gertrude C. K. Leighton, A.B. (Bryn Mawr College), J.D. (Yale University), *Professor of Political Science* and *Secretary of the General Faculty*[1]

Willard Fahrenkamp King, PH.D. (Brown University), *Dorothy Nepper Marshall Professor of Hispanic and Hispanic-American Studies* and *Secretary of the General Faculty for 1977-78*

Milton D. Speizman, PH.D. (Tulane University), *Professor of Social Work and Social Research* and *Secretary of the Faculty of Social Work and Social Research*

Jay Martin Anderson, PH.D. (Harvard University), *Professor of Chemistry*

Hans Bänziger, PH.D. (University of Zürich), *Professor of German*[2]

Ernst Berliner, PH.D. (Harvard University), *W. Alton Jones Professor of Chemistry*

Phyllis Pray Bober, PH.D. (New York University), *Professor of Classical and Near Eastern Archaeology* and *of History of Art* and *Dean of The Graduate School of Arts and Sciences*

Charles M. Brand, PH.D. (Harvard University), *Professor of History*

Robert B. Burlin, PH.D. (Yale University), *Professor of English*

Robert H. Butman, M.A. (University of North Carolina), *Professor of English and the Performing Arts on the Theresa Helburn Fund* and *Director of the Theatre, on joint appointment with Haverford College*

Isabelle Cazeaux, PH.D. (Columbia University), *Professor of Music*

Robert L. Conner, PH.D. (Indiana University), *Professor of Biology*

Frederic Cunningham, Jr. PH.D. (Harvard University), *Professor of Mathematics*

Gérard Defaux, D. ès L. (Sorbonne), *Professor of French*

Charles G. Dempsey, M.F.A., PH.D. (Princeton University), *Professor of History of Art*

Richard B. Du Boff, PH.D. (University of Pennsylvania), *Professor of Economics*

Arthur P. Dudden, PH.D. (University of Michigan), *Professor of History*

Mary Maples Dunn, PH.D. (Bryn Mawr College), *Professor of History*[3]

José María Ferrater Mora, *Licenciado en Filosofía* (University of Barcelona), *Professor of Philosophy* and *Fairbank Professor in the Humanities*

Elizabeth Read Foster, PH.D. (Yale University), *Professor of History*

Richard C. Gonzalez, PH.D. (University of Maryland), *Professor of Psychology*

Joaquín González Muela, D.en Fil. (University of Madrid), *Professor of Spanish*

Jane C. Goodale, PH.D. (University of Pennsylvania), *Professor of Anthropology*

Robert L. Goodale, A.B., B.MUS. (Yale University), A.A.G.O. *Alice Carter Dickerman Professor of Music*

Norman K. Gottwald, PH.D. (Columbia University), *Visiting Professor of History of Religion*

Michel Guggenheim, PH.D. (Yale University), *Professor of French*

Madelyn K. Gutwirth, PH.D. (Bryn Mawr College), *Visiting Professor of French*

Marcel M. Gutwirth, PH.D. (Columbia University), *Visiting Professor of French*

Howard S. Hoffman, PH.D. (University of Connecticut), *Professor of Psychology*[4]

Janet L. Hoopes, PH.D. (Bryn Mawr College), *Professor of Education and Child Development* and *Director of the Child Study Institute*[4]

Rosalie C. Hoyt, PH.D. (Bryn Mawr College), *Marion Reilly Professor of Physics*[5]

9

Fritz Janschka, Akad. Maler (Akademie der Bildenden Kunste, Vienna), *Professor of Fine Art*

Pauline Jones, PH.D. (Bryn Mawr College), *Professor of French*

Melville T. Kennedy, Jr., PH.D. (Harvard University), *Professor of Political Science*

George L. Kline, PH.D. (Columbia University), *Professor of Philosophy*

Samuel T. Lachs, PH.D. (Dropsie University), *Professor of History of Religion*

Barbara M. Lane, PH.D. (Harvard University), *Professor of History* and *Director of the interdepartmental major in The Growth and Structure of Cities*[1]

Mabel Louise Lang, PH.D. (Bryn Mawr College), LITT.D., *Paul Shorey Professor of Greek*

Howard Lesnick, LL.B. (Columbia University), *Visiting Professor of Social Work and Social Research*

Nicholas J. Mackintosh, D.PHIL (Oxford University), *Katharine E. McBride Visiting Professor of Psychology*

Frank B. Mallory, PH.D. (California Institute of Technology), *Professor of Chemistry*[1]

Dorothy N. Marshall, PH.D. (Bryn Mawr College), *Visiting Professor on the IBM Hispanic Studies Fund*

Mario Maurin, PH.D. (Yale University), *Professor of French*

Ethel W. Maw, PH.D. (University of Pennsylvania), *Professor of Education and Child Development*

Machteld J. Mellink, PH.D. (University of Utrecht), *Leslie Clark Professor of Humanities* and *Professor of Classical and Near Eastern Archaeology*

Charles Mitchell, M.A., B.LITT. (Oxford University), LITT.D., *Professor of History of Art* and *Andrew W. Mellon Professor in the Humanities*

Jane M. Oppenheimer, PH.D. (Yale University), SC.D. *William R. Kenan, Jr. Professor of History of Science*

John C. Oxtoby, M.A. (University of California), *Class of 1897 Professor of Mathematics*

Kyle M. Phillips, Jr., PH.D. (Princeton University), *Professor of Classical and Near Eastern Archaeology* and *Director of Massenzia, Rome*

Jean A. Potter, PH.D. (Yale University), *Professor of Philosophy*

John R. Pruett, PH.D. (Indiana University), *Professor of Physics*

Martin Rein, PH.D. (Brandeis University), *Visiting Professor of Social Work and Social Research*

Brunilde Sismondo Ridgway, PH.D. (Bryn Mawr College), *Rhys Carpenter Professor of Classical and Near Eastern Archaeology*[3]

Bernard Ross, PH.D. (University of Michigan), *Dean of The Graduate School of Social Work and Social Research for Semester I, 1977-78* and *Professor of Social Work and Social Research*

J. H. M. Salmon, M.LITT. (Cambridge University), LIT.D. (Victoria University), *Marjorie Walter Goodhart Professor of History*

Eugene V. Schneider, PH.D. (Harvard University), *Professor of Sociology*

Alain Silvera, PH.D. (Harvard University), *Professor of History*[5]

James E. Snyder, M.F.A., PH.D. (Princeton University), *Professor of History of Art*

K. Laurence Stapleton, A.B. (Smith College), *Mary E. Garrett Alumnae Professor of English Literature*[4]

Isabel Scribner Stearns, PH.D. (Bryn Mawr College), *Professor of Philosophy*

James Tanis, TH.D. (University of Utrecht), *Director of Libraries* and *Professor of History*

Myra L. Uhlfelder, PH.D. (Bryn Mawr College), *Professor of Latin*

Matthew Yarczower, PH.D. (University of Maryland), *Professor of Psychology*

George L. Zimmerman, PH.D. (University of Chicago), *Professor of Chemistry*

Associate Professors

Joseph Varimbi, PH.D. (University of Pennsylvania), *Associate Professor of Chemistry* and *Secretary of the Faculty of Arts and Sciences*

Alfonso M. Albano, PH.D. (State University of New York at Stony Brook), *Associate Professor of Physics*

Carol L. Bernstein, PH.D. (Yale University), *Associate Professor of English*

Charles C. Bray, Jr. PH.D. (University of Pittsburgh), *Associate Professor of Social Work and Social Research*

Merle Broberg, PH.D. (The American University), *Associate Professor of Social Work and Social Research* and *Associate Dean of The Graduate School of Social Work and Social Research*

Georgia B. Christopher, PH.D (Yale University), *Katharine E. McBride Visiting Associate Professor of English*

Maria Luisa B. Crawford, PH.D. (University of California), *Associate Professor of Geology*

William A. Crawford, PH.D. (University of California), *Associate Professor of Geology*

Dan Davidson, PH.D. (Harvard University) *Associate Professor of Russian*

Gregory W. Dickerson, PH.D. (Princeton University), *Associate Professor of Greek*

Nancy C. Dorian, PH.D. (University of Michigan), *Associate Professor of Linguistics in German and Anthropology*

Richard S. Ellis, PH.D. (University of Chicago), *Associate Professor of Classical and Near Eastern Archaeology*[5]

Noel J. J. Farley, PH.D. (Yale University), *Associate Professor of Economics*[6]

Gloria Flaherty, PH.D. (Johns Hopkins University), *Associate Professor of German*[1]

Charles E. Frye, PH.D. (Princeton University), *Associate Professor of Political Science*

Julia H. Gaisser, PH.D. (University of Edinburgh), *Associate Professor of Latin*

Richard Hamilton, PH.D. (University of Michigan), *Associate Professor of Greek*

Helen Manning Hunter, PH.D. (Radcliffe College), *Associate Professor of Economics*

Thomas H. Jackson, PH.D. (Yale University), *Associate Professor of English*

Stephen Jaeger, PH.D. (University of California at Berkeley), *Associate Professor of German*

Anthony R. Kaney, PH.D. (University of Illinois), *Associate Professor of Biology*

Philip L. Kilbride, PH.D. (University of Missouri), *Associate Professor of Anthropology*

Joseph E. Kramer, PH.D. (Princeton University), *Associate Professor of English*

Michael Krausz, PH.D. (University of Toronto), *Associate Professor of Philosophy*[1]

Jane C. Kronick, PH.D. (Yale University), *Associate Professor of Social Work and Social Research*

Phyllis S. Lachs, PH.D. (Bryn Mawr College), *Associate Dean of The Graduate School of Arts and Sciences* and *Associate Professor of History*[1]

Catharine Lafarge, PH.D. (Yale University), *Associate Professor of French*

Susan E. Maxfield, M.S. (Syracuse University), *Associate Professor of Education and Child Development* and *Director of the Phoebe Anna Thorne School*

Clark McCauley, Jr. PH.D. (University of Pennsylvania), *Associate Professor of Psychology*

Mary Patterson McPherson, PH.D. (Bryn Mawr College), LL.D., *Dean of the Undergraduate College* and *Associate Professor of Philosophy*

Eleanor Krane Paucker, PH.D. (University of Pennsylvania), *Associate Professor of Spanish*

Ruth L. Pearce, PH.D. (University of Pennsylvania), *Associate Professor of Russian*

Emmy A. Pepitone, PH.D. (University of Michigan), *Associate Professor of Education and Child Development*

Lucian B. Platt, PH.D. (Yale University), *Associate Professor of Geology*

Judith R. Porter, PH.D. (Harvard University), *Associate Professor of Sociology*

David J. Prescott, PH.D. (University of Pennsylvania), *Associate Professor of Biology*

Marc Howard Ross, PH.D. (Northwestern University), *Associate Professor of Political Science*[1]

Stephen Salkever, PH.D. (University of Chicago), *Associate Professor of Political Science*[4]

William Bruce Saunders, PH.D. (University of Iowa), *Associate Professor of Geology*[4]

Russell T. Scott, PH.D. (Yale University), *Associate Professor of Latin*

Faye P. Soffen, ED.D. (University of Pennsylvania), *Associate Professor of Education and Child Development*

Ruth O. Stallfort, M.S.S. (Simmons College School of Social Work), *Associate Professor of Social Work and Social Research*

Earl Thomas, PH.D. (Yale University), *Associate Professor of Psychology*

William W. Vosburgh, PH.D. (Yale University), *Associate Professor of Social Work and Social Research*

Assistant Professors

Leslie Alexander, PH.D. (Bryn Mawr College), *Part-time Assistant Professor of Social Work and Social Research*

Peter Beckmann, PH.D. (University of British Columbia), *Assistant Professor of Physics*

Sheila K. Bennett, PH.D. (University of North Carolina), *Assistant Professor of Sociology*

Sandra M. Berwind, PH.D. (Bryn Mawr College), *Assistant Professor of English*[7]

Robert A. Braun, PH.D. (University of Illinois at Champaign-Urbana), *Assistant Professor of Anthropology*

Peter M. Briggs, PH.D. (Yale University), *Assistant Professor of English*

Dennis Brunn, PH.D. (Washington University), *Assistant Professor of Social Work and Social Research*

Katrin Ristkok Burlin, PH.D. (Princeton University), *Assistant Professor of English*

Sandra S. Cornelius, PH.D. (Bryn Mawr College), *Part-time Assistant Professor of Social Work and Social Research*

Susan Dean, PH.D. (Bryn Mawr College), *Part-time Assistant Professor of English*

Nancy Dersofi, PH.D. (Harvard University), *Assistant Professor of Italian*

Richard Gaskins, PH.D., J.D. (Yale University), *Assistant Professor of Social Work and Social Research* and *of Philosophy*

Stephen Goodwin, M.A. (University of Virginia), *Assistant Professor of English*[7]

E. Jane Hedley, PH.D. (Bryn Mawr College), *Assistant Professor of English*

Stephen M. Holden, PH.D. (Bryn Mawr College), *Assistant Professor of Social Work and Social Research*

Carole Elisabeth Joffe, PH.D. (University of California at Berkeley), *Assistant Professor of Social Work and Social Research*[7]

Eileen Tess Johnston, PH.D. (University of Chicago), *Assistant Professor of English*

Richard H. Jordan, PH.D. (University of Minnesota), *Assistant Professor of Anthropology*

Anne Kaier, PH.D. (Harvard University), *Assistant Professor of English*

Toba Kerson, PH.D. (University of Pennsylvania), *Assistant Professor of Social Work and Social Research*

Dale Kinney, PH.D. (New York University), *Assistant Professor of History of Art*[7]

Li Way Lee, PH.D. (Columbia University), *Assistant Professor of Economics*

Steven Z. Levine, PH.D. (Harvard University), *Assistant Professor of History of Art on the Rosalyn R. Schwartz Lectureship*

Joyce Lewis, M.S.S. (Bryn Mawr College), *Assistant Professor of Social Work and Social Research*

Margaret S. Maurin, PH.D. (Bryn Mawr College) *Part-time Assistant Professor of French*

Annette Niemtzow, PH.D. (Harvard University), *Assistant Professor of English*

Patricia J. Olds-Clarke, PH.D. (Washington University), *Assistant Professor of Biology*[7]

George S. Pahomov, PH.D. (New York University), *Assistant Professor of Russian*[7]

Nicholas Patruno, PH.D. (Rutgers University), *Assistant Professor of Italian*

Stephen Poppel, PH.D. (Harvard University), *Assistant Professor of History*

David Rabi, PH.D. (Dropsie University), *Assistant Professor of History of Religion on the Monte and Bertha Tyson Lectureship*

Fred C. Rothbaum, PH.D. (Yale University), *Assistant Professor of Education and Child Development*

Grace Armstrong Savage, PH.D. (Princeton University), *Assistant Professor of French*[7]

Carl B. Schmidt, PH.D. (Harvard University), *Assistant Professor of Music*

Françoise Schremmer, PH.D. (University of Pennsylvania), *Assistant Professor of Mathematics*[7]

Judith R. Shapiro, PH.D. (Columbia University), *Assistant Professor of Anthropology on the Rosalyn R. Schwartz Lectureship*

Stephen R. Smith, PH.D. (Massachusetts Institute of Technology), *Assistant Professor of Physics*

Samuel S. Snyder, PH.D. (Yale University), *Assistant Professor of Education and Child Development*

George C. Stephens, PH.D. (Lehigh University), *Assistant Professor of Geology*

Kenneth G. Strothkamp, PH.D. (Columbia University), *Assistant Professor of Chemistry*

Tracy Marie Taft, PH.D. (State University of New York at Buffalo), *Assistant Professor of Philosophy*

Steven N. Treistman, PH.D. (University of North Carolina), *Assistant Professor of Biology*

Lynn Visson, PH.D. (Harvard University), *Assistant Professor of Russian*

Jill T. Wannemacher, PH.D. (Brown University), *Assistant Professor of Psychology on the Rosalyn R. Schwartz Lectureship*[7]

Robert Earl Washington, PH.D. (University of Chicago), *Assistant Professor of Sociology*

Robert J. Wicks, PSY.D. (Hahnemann Medical College), *Assistant Professor of Social Work and Social Research*

Cathie J. Witty, PH.D. (University of California at Berkeley), *Assistant Professor of Social Work and Social Research*

Lecturers

Courtney Adams, PH.D. (University of Pennsylvania), *Lecturer in Music*

John Archibald, M.S.S. (Bryn Mawr College), *Part-time Lecturer in Social Work and Social Research*

Diane Balestri, PH.D. (Yale University), *Dean of the Class of 1981 and Part-time Lecturer in English*

Nancy Bancroft, M.A. (Columbia University), *Pitcairn Crabbe Foundation Visiting Lecturer in History of Religion*

Frances B. Berliner, PH.D. (Bryn Mawr College), *Part-time Lecturer in Chemistry*

Diana Cassell, PH.D. (Bryn Mawr College), *Lecturer in Biology*

Victory V. Chase, M.A. (University of California at Berkeley), *Part-time Lecturer in English*

Stanley S. Clawar PH.D. (Bryn Mawr College), *Visiting Lecturer in Sociology*

Cecile K. Dalton, PH.D. (University of California at Los Angeles), *Lecturer in Chemistry*

Christopher Davis, A.B. (University of Pennsylvania), *Visiting Lecturer in English*

John Drury, M.A. (Cambridge University), *Roian Fleck Resident-in-Religion* and *Visiting Lecturer in History of Religion*

Harrison Eiteljorg II, PH.D (University of Pennsylvania), *Lecturer in Classical and Near Eastern Archaeology*

Maria deJ. Ellis, PH.D. (Yale University), *Part-time Lecturer in Classical and Near Eastern Archaeology*

Alan C. Emdin, PH.D. (University of Chicago), *Lecturer in Political Science*

Susan J. Erickson, M.A. (Yale University), *Lecturer in German*

Neil Forsyth, PH.D. (University of California at Berkeley), *Andrew W. Mellon Post-doctoral Fellow and Lecturer in Greek*

Elaine A. Friedrich, M.A. (University of Michigan), *Part-time Lecturer in Political Science*

Christina Gillis, PH.D. (Bryn Mawr College), *Part-time Lecturer in English*

Nancy L. Hagelgans, PH.D (Johns Hopkins University), *Lecturer in Mathematics*

Susan J. Hilligoss, M.A. (University of Pennsylvania), *Part-time Lecturer in English*

Frances S. Hoekstra, PH.D. (Bryn Mawr College), *Part-time Lecturer in French*

Wendell P. Holbrook, A.B. (Morgan State College), *Lecturer in History*

Constance Jordan, PH.D. (Yale University), *Andrew W. Mellon Post-doctoral Fellow* and *Lecturer in English* and *French*

Ramona Livingston, A.B. (William Jewell College), *Advisor to International Students* and *Lecturer in English*

Ruth W. Mayden, M.S.S. (Bryn Mawr College), *Visiting Lecturer in Social Work and Social Research*

Jane R. McConnell, PH.D. (Bryn Mawr College), *Part-time Lecturer in Biology*

Laurie McNally, M.S.S. (Bryn Mawr College), *Part-time Lecturer in Social Work and Social Research*

Frank J. Miller, PH.D. (Indiana University), *Part-time Lecturer in Russian*

Braulio Montalvo, M.A. (Columbia University), *Caroline S. Rogers and Lucia Rogers Vorys Visiting Lecturer in Social Work and Social Research*

Kathryn G. Orkwiszewski, PH.D. (Bryn Mawr College), *Lecturer in Biology*

Aigli H. Papantonopoulou, PH.D. (University of California at Berkeley), *Lecturer in Mathematics*

Gloria F. Pinney, PH.D. (University of Cincinnati), *Lecturer in Classical and Near Eastern Archaeology*

Patricia Onderdonk Pruett, PH.D. (Bryn Mawr College), *Associate Dean of the Undergraduate College* and *Lecturer in Biology*

Jutta Ramin, PH.D. (Johns Hopkins University), *Lecturer in German*

Enrique Sacerio-Garí, M.PHIL. (Yale University), *Lecturer in Spanish*

Djordje Soc, M.S.W. (University of California), *Lecturer in Social Work and Social Research*

Larry Stein, PH.D. (University of Iowa), *Visiting Lecturer in Psychology*

Donald K. Swearer, PH.D. (Princeton University), *Visiting Lecturer in History of Religion*

George E. Thomas, PH.D. (University of Pennsylvania), *Lecturer in The Growth and Structure of Cities*

Stephen E. Toulmin, PH.D. (Cambridge University), *Mary Flexner Lecturer in History and Philosophy of Science*

Mona Wasow, M.S.W. (University of Wisconsin), *Visiting Lecturer in Social Work and Social Research*

Jacquelyn H. Wolf, M.A. (University of Pennsylvania), *Part-time Lecturer in Sociology*

Instructors

Robert G. Eby, B.S. (University of California, Davis), *Instructor in Geology*

Colette T. Hall, M.A. (Bryn Mawr College), *Instructor in French*

Laboratory Coordinators

Erika Rossman Behrend, PH.D. (University of Pennsylvania), *Part-time Laboratory Coordinator*

Chung Wha Lee Iyengar, PH.D. (Bryn Mawr College), *Part-time Laboratory Coordinator*

Josephine R. Landrey, A.B. (Radcliffe College), *Part-time Laboratory Coordinator*

Alice S. Powers, PH.D. (Bryn Mawr College), *Part-time Laboratory Coordinator*

Tamara Brooks, M.S. (Julliard School of Music), *Director of Chorus and Orchestra on joint appointment with Haverford College*

Carol W. Campbell, M.A. (University of Pennsylvania), *Curator of Slides and Photographs*

Assistants

Anne M. Belcher, B.A. (Oberlin College), *Assistant in Chemistry*

Janer D. Belson, M.A. (Bryn Mawr College), *Assistant in Classical and Near Eastern Archaeology*

Raymond N. D'Angelo, M.A. (New School for Social Research), *Assistant in Sociology*

Elizabeth A. DelPezzo, A.B. (College of Mount St. Vincent), *Assistant in Psychology*

Anna Dugan, M.S.N. (Yale University), *Assistant in Anthropology*

Mark Fullerton, M.A. (Bryn Mawr College), *Assistant in Classical and Near Eastern Archaeology*

Susan J. Gan, B.A. (LaSalle College), *Assistant in Biology*

Denise Gavula, B.A. (Rosemont College), *Assistant in Biology*

Michael G. Gonzales, B.A. (Beaver College), *Assistant in Mathematics*

Susan W. Groff, M.A. (Bryn Mawr College), *Assistant in German*

Mark K. Hamilton, B.S. (St. Joseph's College), *Assistant in Chemistry*
Susan Hardee, B.S. (Guilford College), *Assistant in Geology*
Darrell E. Jones, M.S. (Miami University), *Assistant in Chemistry*
Esther Kasangaki, B.A. (Makerere University), *Assistant in Anthropology*
Suzanne J. Kelly, B.A. (Rosemont College), *Assistant in Biology*
Walter Lammi, M.A. (Bryn Mawr College), *Assistant in Philosophy*
Paul A. LeBuffe, B.A. (St. Mary's College of Maryland), *Assistant in Psychology*
Sandra J. G. Linkletter, B.S. (University of Illinois), *Assistant in Chemistry*
Patricia Little, B.A. (Gettysburg College), *Assistant in Biology*
Michèle Mallet, M.A. (Aix-en-Provence), *Assistant in French*
Robert M. Purcell, B.S. (Slippery Rock State College), *Assistant in Physics*
Perri Lee Roberts, A.B. (Smith College), *Assistant in History of Art*
Janet Rodney, M.A. (Bryn Mawr College), *Assistant in Music*
Virginia M. Sague, B.A. (LaSalle College), *Assistant in Geology*
Cynthia H. Sarnoski, B.S. (Widener College), *Assistant in Chemistry*
Cheryl M. Schwamb, A.B. (Bryn Mawr College), *Assistant in Physics*
David Schwamb, B.S. (Widener College), *Assistant in Physics*
Bernadette Seredinski, B.S. (Gwynedd-Mercy College), *Assistant in Biology*
Christine Skarda, B.A. (University of Wisconsin), *Assistant in Philosophy*
Beverly Smith, B.A. (Chatham College), *Assistant in Psychology*
Therese D. Stamm, B.A. (Mundelein College), *Assistant in History of Art*
Roger Stoffregen, B.A. (Earlham College), *Assistant in Geology*
Noreen Tuross, B.S. (Trinity College), *Assistant in Chemistry*
Thomas R. Watters, B.S. (West Chester State College), *Assistant in Geology*
Howard Waxman, M.A. (University of Maine), *Assistant in Psychology*
Elna Yadin, M.A. (Bryn Mawr College), *Assistant in Psychology*
Sondra Zemansky, B.S. (Massachusetts Institute of Technology), *Assistant in Physics*

Librarians

James Tanis, TH.D. (University of Utrecht), *Director of Libraries*
Thomas Song, M.A., M.A.L.S. (University of Michigan), *Associate Director of Libraries*
Zoë M. Bemis, (Washington University, Yale University), *Reference Librarian*
Leo M. Dolenski, M.A. (Catholic University of America), M.L.S. (Drexel University), *Manuscripts Librarian*
John Dooley, M.L.S. (McGill University), *Bibliographer* and *Reference Librarian*
Florence D. Goff, M.A. (Villanova University), M.S.L.S. (Villanova University), *Cataloging Librarian*
Karen K. Helm, M.S.L.S. (Villanova University), *Rare Book Cataloguer*
John Jaffe, M.A., M.S.L.S. (Villanova University), *Acquisitions Librarian*
Mary S. Leahy, M.A. (Bryn Mawr College), *Rare Book Librarian*
Eileen Markson, M.A. (New York University), M.L.S. (Queens College of City University of New York), *Head, Art and Archaeology Library*

Catherine E. Pabst, M.A. (University of Wisconsin), M.S.L.S. (Drexel University), *Head, Acquisitions Department*

Gertrude Reed, M.S.L.S. (Rutgers University), *Head, Reference Division* and *Archivist*

Pamela G. Reilly, M.S.L.S. (Drexel University), *Head, Public Services Department*

Penelope Schwind, M.S.L.S. (Drexel University), *Head, Cataloging Department*

Barbara F. Siegel, M.S.L.S. (Drexel University), *Serials Librarian*

Arleen Speizman, M.S.L.S. (Drexel University), *Cataloging Librarian*

Ethel W. Whetstone, A.B.L.S. (University of North Carolina), *Head, Sciences and Social Sciences Libraries*

Administrative Officers

Jacqueline A. Akins, A.B. (Bryn Mawr College), *Associate Director of Admissions*

Alexandra Quandt Aldridge, A.B. (Bryn Mawr College), *Director of Resources*

Diane Balestri, PH.D. (Yale University), *Dean of the Class of 1981* and *Part-time Lecturer in English*

Judith Leopold Bardes, A.B. (Bryn Mawr College), *Director of Families and Friends*

Dolores E. Brien, PH.D. (Brown University), *Director of Career Planning*

Merle Broberg, PH.D. (The American University), *Associate Dean of The Graduate School of Social Work and Social Research*

Rita C. Grass, A.B. (University of California), *Associate Director of Public Information*

Tekla A. Harms, A.B. (Bryn Mawr College), *Assistant to the Director of Admissions*

Margaret M. Healy, PH.D. (Bryn Mawr College), *Executive Director of the Board of Trustees' Ad Hoc Committee on Financial Planning* and *Assistant Treasurer*

Joseph S. Johnston, Jr., M.A. (University of Chicago), *Assistant to the President*

Paul W. Klug, C.P.A., B.S. (Temple University), *Comptroller* and *Business Manager of the College*

Phyllis S. Lachs, PH.D. (Bryn Mawr College), *Associate Dean of The Graduate School of Arts and Sciences* and *Associate Professor of History*[1]

Rebecca Fox Leach, A.B. (Bryn Mawr College), *Dean of the Class of 1980*

Ramona L. Livingston, A.B. (William Jewell College), *Advisor to International Students* and *Lecturer in English*

Margaret G. McKenna, A.B. (Bryn Mawr College), *Personnel Administrator*

Samuel J. McNamee, B.S. (Temple University), *Assistant Comptroller*

Kathleen K. Mooney, M.A. (Syracuse University), *Assistant Director of Career Planning*

Caroline S. Moore, A.B. (Bryn Mawr College), *Admissions Counselor*

Julie E. Painter, A.B. (Bryn Mawr College), *Administrator of Records and Financial Aid*

Patricia Onderdonk Pruett, PH.D. (Bryn Mawr College), *Associate Dean of the Undergraduate College* and *Dean of the Class of 1978* and *Lecturer in Biology.*

Ellen Fernon Reisner, M.A. (Bryn Mawr College), *Assistant to the President, Alumna-in-Residence* and *Acting Director of Public Information*

Robb N. Russell, M.S. (University of Illinois), *Director of Computer Services*

Stefanie M. Tashjian, A.B. (Bryn Mawr College), *Admissions Counselor*

Thomas N. Trucks, B.S. (Villanova University), *Superintendent of Buildings and Grounds*

Jo-Anne Thomas Vanin, M.A.T. (Harvard University), *Dean of the Class of 1979*[4]

Christine Van Ness, M.A. (University of Pennsylvania), *Director of Foundation and Corporation Programs*

Deborah Wolk, A.B. (Smith College), *Acting Financial Aid Officer of the Undergraduate College*

Sarah E. Wright, *Director of Halls*

Health

Frieda W. Woodruff, M.D. (University of Pennsylvania School of Medicine), *College Physician*

Martina M. Martin, M.D. (Thomas Jefferson University Medical College), *Assistant College Physician*

Anne Lee Delano, M.A. (Columbia University), *Director of Physical Education*

Eileen A. Bazelon, M.D. (Medical College of Pennsylvania), *Consulting Psychiatrist*

Mary Geiger, M.D. (State University of New York at Albany), *Consulting Psychiatrist*

John F. Howkins, M.D. (Columbia University, College of Physicians and Surgeons), *Consulting Psychiatrist*

Lakshmi Nadgir, M.D. (Andhra University), *Consulting Gynecologist*

Margaret Temeles, M.D. (Tufts University, School of Medicine), *Consulting Psychiatrist*

Physical Education

Anne Lee Delano, M.A. (Columbia University), *Director of Physical Education*

Linda Fritsche Castner, M.S. (Smith College), *Instructor in Physical Education*

Elaine E. Johnson, M.S. (Indiana State University), *Instructor in Physical Education*

Barbara Lember, B.F.A. (Philadelphia College of Art), *Part-time Instructor in Dance*[5]

Paula Carter Mason, B.S. (University of Wisconsin), *Part-time Instructor in Dance*

Jenepher Shillingford, M.ED. (Temple University), *Instructor in Physical Education*

Alice E. Trexler, PH.D. (New York University), *Part-time Instructor in Dance*

Janet A. Yeager, *Instructor in Physical Education*

Halls of Residence

Jonita Carder, B.A. (Sweet Briar College), *Warden of Rockefeller*

Joan B. Connelly, A.B. (Princeton University), *Warden of Pembroke East*

Martine Feldmann, Licence (University of Paris) *Warden of French House in Haffner Hall*

Audrey Henry, A.B. (Princeton University) *Warden of Pembroke West*

Charles Heyduk, B.A. (La Salle College), *Warden of Radnor*

Katy H. Katrak, M.A. (Bryn Mawr College), *Warden of Denbigh*

Alice Pomponio Logan, M.A. (Bryn Mawr College), *Warden of Erdman*
Ilknur F. Ozgen, B.A. (Istanbul University), *Warden of Rhoads*
Brigitte Pieke, (Georg-August-University, Gottingen), *Warden of German House in Haffner Hall*
Jazmina Roman, B.A. (Temple University) *Warden of Spanish House in Haffner Hall*
Dessie Sangeloty, M.A. (Bryn Mawr College) *Senior Resident of the Graduate Center*
Wendy Weiss, M.A. (Bryn Mawr College) *Warden of Merion*

Child Study Institute

Janet L. Hoopes, PH.D. (Bryn Mawr College), *Director*[4]
Beatrice Schneider, M.S.S. (Bryn Mawr College), *Assistant to the Director*
Jean Ager, PH.D. (Bryn Mawr College), *Psychologist*
Beverly Alexandre, M.S.S. (Bryn Mawr College), *Counselor*
Shirley Alrich, M.A. (Bryn Mawr College), *Counselor*
Jean Astley, B.A. (University of Pennsylvania), *Reading Specialist*
Arlene Baggaley, M.A (Bryn Mawr College), *Part-time Counselor*
Eleanor Beatty, M.A. (George Washington University), *Psychologist*
Hannah Beiter, M.S. (University of Pennsylvania), *Reading Specialist*
Emma Dalsimer, PH.D. (Bryn Mawr College), *Counselor*
Charlotte Diamond, M.S.S. (Smith College), *Counselor*
Justine D'Zmura, PH.D. (Bryn Mawr College), *Counseling Psychologist*
Marjorie Edwards, M.S.S. (Bryn Mawr College), *Chief Counselor*
Anne D. Emmons, M.S. (University of Pennsylvania), *Reading Specialist*
Maxine Fields, M.S. (University of Pennsylvania), *Reading Specialist*
Kathleen Finnegan, M.A. (Temple University), *Psychologist*
Joel Goldstein, M.D. (Thomas Jefferson University Medical School), *Consulting Psychiatrist*
Anita Grinnell, M.S. (University of Pennsylvania), *Psychologist*
Ann Hamm, M.S.S. (Bryn Mawr College), *Social Caseworker*
Bernard Kanter, M.D. (Dalhousie University), *Consulting Psychiatrist*
Louella M. Kennedy, M.S.S. (Bryn Mawr College), *Part-time Social Caseworker*
Nina Korsh, PH.D. (Bryn Mawr College), *Part-time Counselor*
Frederic J. Kwapien, M.D. (Tufts University School of Medicine), *Consulting Psychiatrist*
Barbara J. Lorry, M.S. (University of Pennsylvania), *Reading Specialist*
Ann S. McIlvain, M.ED. (Boston University), *Reading Specialist*
Frances Rauch, M.S. (University of Pennsylvania), *Reading Specialist*
Suzanne Ross, M.S. (University of Pennsylvania), *Reading Specialist*
Herman Staples, M.D. (Hahnemann Medical College), *Consulting Psychiatrist*
Russell Sullivan, M.A. (Seton Hall University), *Counseling Psychologist*

Judith Vaden, M.S.S. (Bryn Mawr College), *Counselor*
Ann Van Arkel, M.S. (University of Pennsylvania), *Reading Specialist*
Isabel Westfried, M.A. (Bryn Mawr College), *Chief Psychologist*
Mary Lee Young, M.S. (University of Pennsylvania), *Reading Specialist*

Phebe Anna Thorne School

Susan E. Maxfield, M.S. (Syracuse University), *Director*
Sandra P. Juliani, M.ED. (Tufts University), *Assistant Teacher*
Karen Pendleton, B.A. (William Smith College), *Assistant Teacher*
Tess L. Schutte, M.A (Bryn Mawr College), *Teacher*

Introduction

Bryn Mawr effectively combines a small undergraduate college with two graduate schools. In both The Graduate School of Arts and Sciences and the Undergraduate College the study of the liberal arts and sciences is pursued with members of the faculty who normally teach on both levels. They find that the teaching of undergraduates and the direction of graduate student research complement each other, so that the stimulation of investigation in the various fields of graduate study is reflected in all departments of undergraduate work. The undergraduate program emphasizes both depth and breadth of knowledge and understanding. No field is so broad that it cannot take advantage of the specialist's deep understanding; no specialty is so narrow that it may not profit from a breadth of perception.

Bryn Mawr College is convinced that intellectual discipline and enrichment provide a sound foundation for living. It believes in the rights of the individual and thinks of the college community as a proving ground for the freedom of individuals to think and act as intelligent and responsible members of a democratic society.

In these beliefs Bryn Mawr has preserved the purpose and much of the tradition of its founders, a group of men and women belonging to the Society of Friends who were convinced that intelligent women deserve an education as rigorous and stimulating as that offered to men.

History of the College

This concern about the opportunity for women to study at the university level was felt strongly by Dr. Joseph Taylor, a New Jersey physician who decided to give his estate to provide the land, the first buildings and the endowment for the new college. With much care Dr. Taylor chose the site, thirty-nine acres of land on a hill in Bryn Mawr, eleven miles west of Philadelphia. He supervised the erection of the first building and took part in formulating the plans that led to a new educational venture. This was the opening in 1885 of the first college for women with undergraduate instruction for the A.B. and graduate instruction for the M.A. and PH.D. degrees in all departments.

As he planned the College Dr. Taylor thought first of the education of young Friends. As Dr. Taylor's trustees in the early years considered the policies of the College they found themselves bound to allow freedom of conscience to all students. By 1893 it is clear from their studies and reports that they were determined to maintain a non-denominational college while strongly supporting the Friends' position of freedom of conscience and providing for continued opportunity within the College and through the College to encourage the student to develop and strengthen her own religious faith.

The first president of Bryn Mawr College was James E. Rhoads, a physician and one of the trustees responsible for the initial plans. The first dean was M. Carey Thomas, who devoted her life to securing for women the opportunity for higher education and the right to share in all the privileges and responsibilities of American citizenship. Miss Thomas succeeded to the presidency in 1893, after the resignation of Dr. Rhoads. In 1922 she was followed by Marion Edwards Park, already distinguished in the academic world for her scholarship in the classics and her ability as a teacher and administrator. From 1942 to 1970 Katharine Elizabeth McBride presided over the College in a time of great change and tremendous growth. The fifth president, Harris Llewellyn Wofford, Jr., was elected in 1969.

Since the early years of Bryn Mawr, the campus has grown from 39 to about 112 acres; new buildings have been added as required by additional students and by new undertakings in teaching and research.

The College As Community

Bryn Mawr admits students of any race, color, national and ethnic origin, as well as the handicapped, to all the rights, privileges, programs and activities generally accorded or made available to students at the College. It does not discriminate on the basis of race, color, national or ethnic origin or handicap in administration of its educational policies, admissions policies, scholarship and loan programs, and athletic and other College-administered programs, or in its employment practices.

As required by Title IX of the 1972 Federal Education Amendments, it is also the policy of Bryn Mawr College not to discriminate on the basis of sex in its educational programs, activities, or employment practices. The admission of women in the Undergraduate College is in conformity with a provision of the Act. Inquiries regarding compliance with Title IX and other policies of non-discrimination may be directed to the Assistant to the President, Taylor Hall, or to the Director of the Office for Civil Rights, Department of Health, Education and Welfare, Washington, D.C.

Believing that a small college provides the most favorable opportunity for the students to participate in their own education, Bryn Mawr limits the number of undergraduates to approximately nine hundred and fifty. And since diversity in background and training serves not only to stimulate discussion but also to develop an intelligent understanding of such diversity, the undergraduate enrolment includes students from various types of schools, independent and public, foreign as well as American. The whole group, both graduate and undergraduate, is composed of students from all parts of the United States as well as from many foreign countries.

The resources of Bryn Mawr as a small residential college are augmented by its participation at the undergraduate level with Haverford College and Swarthmore College in an arrangement which coordinates the facilities of the three institutions while preserving the individual qualities and autonomy of each. Students may take courses at the other colleges, with credit and without additional fees. All three colleges share in some facilities and in various curricular and extra-curricular activities, but geographical proximity makes possible more regular and closer cooperation between Bryn Mawr and Haverford, which are only a mile apart. The calendars for the year are coordinated so that vacations and examination periods coincide.

During 1976-77 a two-college committee comprising members of the faculties, administrations and student bodies of Bryn Mawr and Haverford was charged with recommending to the faculties and Boards of the two colleges a new proposal for increased two-college cooperation. The two faculties voted in the spring to accept the committee's report and as a consequence students may take full advantage, starting in 1977-78, of the major offerings at both institutions. Departments will be meeting during 1977-78 to develop cooperative academic plans. The cooperation greatly augments and enriches the academic offerings of both colleges. Collections in the two libraries are cross-listed, and students may study in either library.

The cooperation between Bryn Mawr and Haverford naturally extends beyond the classroom. Student organizations on the two campuses work closely together in matters concerned with student government and in the whole range of activities. Cooperation in living arrangements was initiated in 1969-70, and several residence halls on the two campuses are assigned to students of both colleges.

Bryn Mawr itself sponsors a broad cultural program which supplements the curriculum and enriches its community life. Various lectureships bring scholars and other leaders in world affairs to the campus not only for public lectures but also for classes and conferences with the students. Such opportunities are provided by the Mary Flexner Lecturer in the humanities and by the Anna Howard Shaw Lectures in the social sciences, the visiting professors on the Katharine E. McBride Fund for faculty appointments and by various individual lecturers in many of the departments of the College. The President's Office sponsors seminars on current issues which bring together distinguished leaders from the worlds of business, politics, finance and scholarship. Several of the student organizations also arrange conferences and lectures both on current national and international problems and within particular fields of social and cultural interest. The musical, dramatic and dance programs of the College are under the direction of the faculty and staff of Bryn Mawr and Haverford colleges and are arranged by the appropriate student organizations of the two colleges. The Arnecliffe Studio has facilities for painting and sculpture, where guidance and criticism are provided by the artist-in-residence. There is a dance studio in Rockefeller Hall.

Student organizations have complete responsibility for the many aspects of student activity, and student representatives join with members of the faculty and administration in making and carrying out plans for the college community as a whole: The Student Self-Government Association, to which every student belongs, provides a framework in which individuals and smaller groups function. The Association both legislates and mediates in matters of social and personal conduct. Through their Government Association, the students share with the faculty the responsibility for the administration of the Academic Honor System. The Association also coordinates the activities of the many special interest clubs, open to all students; it serves as the liaison between students and College officers, faculty and alumnae. It has most recently been instrumental in perfecting a system of meal exchanges with Haverford, extending the shuttle bus service which the two colleges provide and introducing college transportation between the two colleges and Swarthmore.

The Association is aided by the Committee on Student Life of the Board of Trustees and by the staff of the College to bring students in touch with their churches, to sponsor lectures or discussions on religious subjects, to plan services for worship and to take responsibility for giving students an opportunity to pursue and extend their religious interests.

Other major student organizations are concerned with political affairs, community service, the arts and athletics. Student organizations sponsor speakers, organize discussions and provide outlets for active participation in contemporary political issues.

The Bryn Mawr-Haverford Arts Council, independently or with other groups (College Theater, Orchestra, Chorus, Little Theater) sponsors work and performances or exhibitions in the arts. Under the aegis of the Athletic

Association, the Dance Club choreographs its own productions. The Athletic Association also provides opportunities for all kinds of activities, from the Outing Club to organized intramural and varsity contests. *The Bryn Mawr-Haverford News,* published weekly, welcomes the participation of students interested in reporting and editing.

One of the most active of student organizations is the Curriculum Committee, which has worked out with the Faculty Curriculum Committee a system of self-scheduled examinations, currently in operation, as well as the possibility of receiving academic credit for "project" courses of a creative studio type or in social field work. Students participated in meetings of the Faculty Curriculum Committee for the first time in 1969-70 and continue to work with the faculty on an overall curriculum review which has to date resulted in a revision of the grading system, the initiation of five new interdepartmental majors and an interdepartmental area of concentration, and the opportunity to fulfill the divisional requirements at either Bryn Mawr or Haverford and to major in departments at Haverford College which have no counterpart department at Bryn Mawr.

Black students' organizations have also been active in arranging with members of the faculty and staff for visiting lecturers to teach new courses in the appropriate departments and in opening, in 1970-71, a Black Cultural Center which sponsors cultural programs open to the College community. It provides residence space for a few students. An active Women's Alliance has been working for several years with various departments on the establishment of appropriate courses on women. In 1971-72, in 1974-75 and again in 1975-76, a volunteer student group organized an all-College colloquium which involved discussion on the aims and direction of the College.

In 1970-71 for the first time the faculty voted to invite three seniors elected by the undergraduates to serve with faculty members on the College Admissions Committee. The Board of Directors requested the Undergraduate College and the student organizations from each of the graduate schools to elect representatives to sit with the Board in its stated meetings. Two undergraduate students began meeting with the Board in May 1971. Like the faculty representatives to the Board, the student members join in discussion but do not vote. In 1973 the faculty invited three students elected from the three upper classes to serve with alumnae and faculty on the Undergraduate Scholarship Committee.

Through their interest and participation in these many aspects of the College community the students exemplify the concern of Bryn Mawr's founders for intellectual development in a context of social commitment.

Admission

Bryn Mawr College is interested in candidates of character and ability who wish a liberal arts education and are prepared for college work by a sound education in school. The College has found highly successful candidates among students of varied interests and talents from a wide range of schools and regions in the United States and abroad.

In its consideration of candidates the College looks for evidence of ability in the student's high school record, her rank in class and her College Board tests, and asks her high school advisor and several teachers for an estimate of her character, maturity and readiness for college.

Program of Secondary School Studies

Candidates are expected to complete a four-year secondary school course. The program of studies providing the best background for college work includes English, languages and mathematics carried through most of the school years and, in addition, history and a laboratory science. A school program giving good preparation for study at Bryn Mawr would be as follows: English grammar, composition and literature throughout four years; at least three years of mathematics, with emphasis on basic algebraic, geometric and trigonometric concepts and deductive reasoning; four years of one modern or ancient language, or a good foundation in two languages; some work in history and at least one course in laboratory science, preferably biology, chemistry or physics. Elective subjects might be offered in, for example, history of art, history of music or biblical studies to make up the total of 16 or more credits recommended for admission to the College.

Since school curricula vary widely, the College is fully aware that many applicants for admission will offer programs that differ from the one described above. The College is glad to consider such applications provided students have maintained good records and continuity in the study of basic subjects.

Application for Admission

Students are advised to apply for admission to Bryn Mawr between the end of the junior year and January 15 of the senior year of high school. The College welcomes earlier consultation about school programs.

Only in exceptional circumstances will applications to the freshman class be accepted after January 15 of the student's senior year.

Application forms may be obtained from the Director of Admissions, Bryn Mawr College, Bryn Mawr, Pennsylvania 19010. A fee of $20 must accompany each application and is not refundable.

Candidates will be notified of the Committee on Admissions' action concerning their application in mid-April of the senior year.

Entrance Tests

The Scholastic Aptitude Test and three Achievement Tests of the College Entrance Examination Board are required of all candidates and should be taken by January of the senior year. If possible, Achievement Tests should be taken in current subjects. Students should offer three of the one-hour tests: one in English composition and two others. The College recommends but does not require that one of the three tests be taken in a foreign language, since a score of 650 or above satisfies an A.B. degree requirement (see page 48, III B. I, C for details on language exemption). No special preparation, other than work well done in a good school, is required for successful performance on these tests.

Candidates are responsible for registering with the College Entrance Examination Board for the tests. Information about the tests, test centers, fees and dates may be obtained by writing to College Entrance Examination Board, P.O. Box 592, Princeton, New Jersey 08540.

Interviews

All candidates are expected to have an interview, before January 15, either at the College or with an alumna area representative. Appointments for interviews and campus tours should be made in advance by writing or telephoning the Office of Admissions (215 LA5-1000). The Office of Admissions is open from nine to five on weekdays and, except during March, June, July and August, on Saturdays from nine to one. A student who is unable to visit the College should write to the Director of Admissions for the name and address of an alumna representative in her area.

Early Decision Plan

The Early Decision Plan is intended for promising students who have chosen Bryn Mawr as their first choice college by the fall of the senior year. Candidates under this plan may initiate applications at other colleges but they are expected to make only one Early Decision application. They agree;

if admitted to Bryn Mawr under Early Decision, to accept admission and to *withdraw all other applications.*

Applications must be completed by November 15. Decisions on admission and financial aid will be mailed no later than December 15, and all other applications must be withdrawn by January 1.

A student who is applying for Early Decision should:

1. Complete the Scholastic Aptitude Test (SAT) and three Achievement Tests (ATs) of the College Entrance Examination Board no later than November.
2. File the Preliminary Application (a set of four cards), including the Early Decision Agreement Card, together with the twenty dollar application fee, between late spring of the junior year and November 1 of the senior year.
3. See that all other application forms (a personal history form, a secondary school report, two teacher recommendation forms) are returned by November 15. These forms will be mailed only after the Preliminary Application has been received by Bryn Mawr.
4. Arrange to have the required interview either at the College or with an alumna area representative before November 15.

Each candidate who has completed the Early Decision Application by November 15 will be notified of the Committee on Admissions' decision no later than December 15. She will: (1) be informed that she has been admitted for the following academic year, or (2) be advised to transfer her application to the Regular Plan of admission, or (3) be refused admission.

A student who is admitted under Early Decision agrees to withdraw all other applications immediately, and she is asked to make a deposit of $100 by February 1, unless an extension is granted. The deposit will remain with the College while she is enrolled as an undergraduate and will be returned upon graduation or withdrawal from the College after one year of attendance.

Early Admission

Each year a few outstanding students are admitted after the junior year of high school. Students who wish to apply for Early Admission should plan to complete a senior English course before entrance to college and should write to the Director of Admissions about application procedures.

Deferred Entrance

A student admitted to the College may defer entrance to the freshman class for one year provided that she writes to the Director of Admissions requesting deferred entrance by May 1, the Candidate's Reply Date.

Advanced Placement

Students who have carried advanced work in school and who have honor grades (4 and 5) on the Advanced Placement Tests of the College Entrance Examination Board may, after consultation with the Dean and the departments concerned, be admitted to one or more advanced courses in the freshman year. Bryn Mawr accepts Advanced Placement Tests with honor grades in the relevant subjects as exempting the student from college requirements for the A.B. degree.[1] With the approval of the Dean and the departments concerned, one or more Advanced Placement Tests with honor grades may be presented for credit. Students who enter with three or more Advanced Placement Tests passed with honor grades may apply for sophomore standing.

The Advanced Placement Tests are given at College Board centers in May. Students may also consult the Dean or the Director of Admissions about the advisability of taking placement tests given by the College during Freshman Week.

Transfer Students

Each year a few students are admitted on transfer to the sophomore and junior classes. Successful transfer candidates have done excellent work at other colleges and universities and present strong high school records which compare favorably with those of entering Bryn Mawr freshmen.

Transfer candidates should file applications as early as possible and no later than March 15 for entrance in September, or no later than November 1 for the second semester of the year of entrance. Application forms and instructions may be requested from the Director of Admissions.

Transfer candidates will be asked to submit official test reports from the College Entrance Examination Board of the Scholastic Aptitude and Achievement Tests taken in high school. Those who have not previously taken these tests will be required to take only the Scholastic Aptitude Test. Test registration information may be obtained from the College Entrance Examination Board, Box 592, Princeton, New Jersey 08540.

To qualify for the A.B. degree transfer students must have completed a minimum of two years of full-time study at Bryn Mawr. No credit will be

---

[1] The grade of 5 is required in English and in History.
See also pages 47-48. sections II and III.

given for work done elsewhere until the student has successfully completed a year's work at the College. Students who have failed to meet the prescribed standards of academic work or who have been put on probation, suspended or excluded from other colleges and universities, will under no circumstances be admitted.

Candidates for transfer will be notified of the action taken on their applications by early June or, for the second semester, in December.

Foreign Students

Bryn Mawr welcomes applications from foreign citizens who have outstanding secondary school records and who meet university entrance requirements in their native countries.

Application forms and instructions are available from the Director of Admissions. Foreign applications should be filed early in the year preceding entrance and must be complete by February 15. No application fee is required.

Foreign applicants will be asked to take the Scholastic Aptitude Test of the College Entrance Examination Board. Achievement Tests are recommended but not required. Test registration information may be obtained from the College Entrance Examination Board, Box 592, Princeton, New Jersey 08540. Registration arrangements for students taking the tests abroad should be made at least two months prior to the scheduled testing date.

All foreign applicants whose native language is not English will be required to present credentials attesting to their proficiency in English. The Test of English as a Foreign Language (TOEFL) is recommended but not required for all non-native speakers of English unless they have a diploma from an institution in which English is the sole medium of instruction. TOEFL registration information can be obtained by writing to the Educational Testing Service, Princeton, New Jersey 08540.

Post-Baccalaureate Students in Premedical and Allied Health Fields

Men and women who hold an A.B. degree and need additional undergraduate training before making initial application to medical schools or graduate programs in allied health fields may apply as post-baccalaureate students. Applications are considered only for the fall semester. All forms and supporting credentials should be submitted as early as possible and no later than May 15. Application forms and instructions may be requested from the Director of Admissions.

Special Students

Highly qualified men and women who do not wish to undertake a full college program leading to a degree may apply for admission as special students to take courses on a fee basis prorated according to the tuition of the Undergraduate College, space and resources permitting and subject to the approval of the Committee on Admissions and the department concerned. Application forms and instructions may be requested from the Director of Admissions.

Withdrawal and Readmission

A student who has withdrawn from College is not automatically readmitted. She must request readmission and should consult her Dean and the Director of Admissions concerning the procedure to be followed. Evidence of the student's ability to resume work at Bryn Mawr may be requested in the form of records from another university or medical approval. Applications for readmission will be reviewed twice during the year, in late February and in June. Students who file an application by February 15 will be notified of the Committee's decision in early March. Those who file by June 1 will be notified late in June.

Leaves of Absence

A student whose status at the College is not in question may apply to her Dean for a leave of absence. A leave may be requested for one or two semesters and once approved, reinstatement will be granted. The estimated residential space available at the time a student wishes to return to the College will be a factor in the consideration of requests for leaves. Application must be made in writing by July 1 of the academic year preceding the requested leave (or November 1 for second semester leave). The deans and members of the student's major department will review any questions raised by the student or her Dean regarding the approval of the leave. In case of study at another institution, either foreign or domestic, the transfer of credits will be treated in the usual manner by the Committee on Transfer. A student should confirm her date of return, by letter to her Dean, by March 1 preceding return for the fall semester and by December 1 for return in the spring semester. (See page 39, Tuition.)

A student extending her leave beyond the approved period will have to apply for readmission.

Medical Leave of Absence

A student may, on the recommendation of the College Physician or her own doctor, at any time request a medical leave of absence for reasons of health (see page 39, Tuition). Re-entrance will be granted upon evidence of recovery.

Academic Facilities and Residence

Libraries

The new Mariam Coffin Canaday Library was officially opened in April 1970. As the center of the College's library system, it offers expanded facilities for study and research. The collections for the humanities and social sciences are largely in the Canaday Library, except for art and archaeology in the M. Carey Thomas Library, music in Goodhart Hall and psychology in Dalton Hall. In addition, there are libraries for the sciences and mathematics in the Science Center. The collections of the Haverford College Library, which complement and augment those of Bryn Mawr, are equally accessible to the students.

Bryn Mawr's libraries operate on the open-stack system, allowing students free access to the collections, which comprise over 450,000 volumes. A union catalogue for all the libraries of Bryn Mawr and Haverford is located in the Canaday Library, as are the basic reference and other service facilities of the system. Students are urged to familiarize themselves with the various aids provided for study and research. A series of pamphlets on library use is available for handy reference, and the staff of librarians may be consulted for further assistance.

In addition to the books, periodicals and microfilms basic to a college library, the Canaday Library offers students a small but distinguished collection of research materials among its rare books and manuscripts. The Marjorie Walter Goodhart Medieval Library, for example, provides the basic texts for probing the mind of the late Middle Ages and the thought of the emerging Renaissance. These treasures are supplemented by a growing collection of sixteenth-century texts. Another noteworthy resource is the Louise Bulkley Dillingham Collection of Spanish-American books, which range from sixteenth-century exploration and settlement to contemporary Spanish-American life and culture.

The Rare Book Room houses the Marjorie Walter Goodhart Medieval Library of incunabula and medieval manuscripts. Important and extensive collections of early material on Latin America, Africa and Asia are to be found in the Dillingham, McBride and Plass collections. The Castle and Adelman collections expand the opportunities for the study of the graphic arts in books. In addition to these special collections are numerous other rare books and manuscripts.

The M. Carey Thomas Library still houses in the West Wing the books and other study materials of the departments of Classical and Near Eastern Archaeology and History of Art. The study area in the stacks has been increased and the collections of slides and photographs have been made more accessible. Also in the West Wing is the Quita Woodward Memorial Room for recreational reading, with recent books on literature, art, religion and current affairs as well as many classics. The Record Club's collection is also housed and serviced there. The rest of the M. Carey Thomas Library provides offices for many of the faculty in the humanities and social sciences as well as the Great Hall, serving now as a Commons for the College community.

Haverford and Swarthmore Colleges and the libraries in Philadelphia are generous in making their resources available to students. The Union Library Catalogue of Philadelphia, situated at the University of Pennsylvania, enables students to locate easily the material in approximately one hundred seventy-five libraries in the Philadelphia metropolitan area.

Students wishing to use another library for material not available at Bryn Mawr must secure from the Head of the Public Services Department of the Library a letter of introduction stating the subject to be consulted.

Archaeology Collections

The Ella Riegel Museum of Classical Archaeology, housed on the third floor of the M. Carey Thomas Library, West Wing, contains a small study collection of Greek and Roman minor arts, especially vases, and a selection of pre-classical antiquities. The Museum was formed from private donations such as the Densmore Curtis Collection presented by Clarissa Dryden, the Elisabeth Washburn King Collection of classical Greek coins, and the Aline Abaecherli Boyce Collection of Roman Republican silver coins. The late Professor Hetty Goldman gave the Ella Riegel Museum an extensive series of pottery samples from the excavations at Tarsus in Cilicia. The collections are used for small research projects by undergraduate and graduate students.

Anthropology Museum and Laboratory

The Anthropology Laboratory in Dalton Hall houses several large collections of New World artifacts, including the W. S. Vaux Collection of archaeological and ethnological materials. This important collection, made during the last half of the nineteenth century, has as its main emphasis the artistic works of New World Indians. The Anne and George Vaux Collection represents a wide selection of American Indian basketry from the Southwest, California and the Pacific Northwest. The extensive Ward Canaday Collection contains outstanding examples of most of the ceramic and textile traditions for which Peru is known. Other comprehensive collections, given by faculty and friends of the College, represent the Old World Paleolithic and Neolithic, Paleo-Indian, Eastern Woodland, Southwestern, Middle Mississippian and Mexican antiquities. These collections have been enlarged by osteological materials and casts of fossil hominids. There is also a small but growing collection of ethnomusical recordings, representing the music of native peoples in all parts of the world. Students are expected to make use of these materials and laboratory facilities; there are limited display areas available for those interested in working on museum exhibits.

Laboratories

Laboratories, classrooms and libraries for Biology, Chemistry, Geology, Mathematics and Physics are located in the three buildings of the Science Center. Laboratories and classrooms for Psychology are in Dalton Hall.

In the Science Center the central building is the Marion Edwards Park Hall for Chemistry and Geology. Adjoining this building on the north is a building for Biology. South of Park Hall is the building for the physical sciences, which provides additional space for Chemistry and Geology, all the laboratories for Physics and classrooms and a library for Physics and Mathematics.

In all three buildings of the Science Center and in Dalton Hall there are large laboratories and lecture rooms for undergraduate students and smaller seminar rooms and laboratories for graduate students. In addition to the usual equipment, the science departments have special apparatus and instruments needed in particular research projects by faculty and graduate students and acquired, in part, through the Plan for the Coordination of the Sciences and through research grants from industry and other private sources and from government agencies.

In the Science Center there is an instrument shop with a staff of expert instrument makers to serve all the science departments, and several departments have smaller shops for the use of their own faculty and students. A glassblowing shop is manned by a part-time glassblower. There are rooms specially equipped for work with radioactive materials and for photographic work.

The Geology Department makes available for study and research several important collections. On deposit from the U. S. Geological Survey and the Defense Mapping Agency are 40,000 maps. The Department has extensive reference and working mineral collections, including the George Vaux, Jr., Collection and the Theodore D. Rand Collection, approximately 10,000 specimens each.

Through its membership in the Uni-Coll Corporation, a regional educational computer consortium, Bryn Mawr College has access to the resources and technical support of a major computing center. A high speed, remote batch terminal (printer at 600 lines per minute, card reader at 600 cards per minute) and nine teletypewriter terminals located on campus link the College with the Uni-Coll IBM 370, Model 168 computer. These facilities make available to faculty and students batch, remote job entry, and interactive computing supported by a large variety of programming systems.

Language Laboratory

The modern language departments jointly maintain a Language Laboratory. Its library of tapes contains recordings from the various literatures as well as material especially prepared for language drills. The simple but versatile equipment offers opportunities to improve both the speaking and comprehension proficiency of the student of foreign languages.

Halls of Residence

Nine halls of residence on campus each provide full living accommodations for from 50 to 142 students. Denbigh Hall, Merion Hall, Pembroke East, Pembroke West and Radnor Hall are named for counties in Wales, recalling the tradition of the early Welsh settlers of the area in which Bryn Mawr is situated. Rockefeller Hall is named for its donor John D. Rockefeller, and Rhoads North and South for the first president of the College, James E. Rhoads. Erdman Hall, first opened in 1965, was named in honor of Eleanor Donnelley Erdman, Class of 1921 and member of the Board of Directors. The Clarissa Donnelley Haffner Hall, which brings together into a "European village" three houses for students of French, German, Italian and Spanish, was opened in the fall of 1970. There is a Russian corridor in Erdman Hall.

In the year 1969-70 an experiment in coeducational living was tried: Radnor Hall housed students from both Bryn Mawr and Haverford; other Bryn Mawr students occupied suites in a Haverford residence hall. The success of the experiment and increased interest in these arrangements have resulted in an extension of coeducational living to Rhoads, Haffner and Erdman Halls at Bryn Mawr and to further units at Haverford.

College officers called wardens are in charge of the residence halls. They may be single women or married couples who are members of the Dean's staff but at the same time close to the undergraduates in age and engaged either in teaching or in studying for an advanced degree. They are interested in all aspects of each student's welfare and they work, as well, with the student officers in each hall.

The College offers a variety of living accommodations including a few suites and a number of double rooms. However, many students occupy single rooms. The College provides basic furniture, but students supply linen, bed pillows, desk lamps, rugs, curtains and any other accessories they may wish.

The maintenance of halls is the responsibility of the Director of Halls and a staff of managers. Food service is provided by a national food service organization. No special foods or diets can be obtained.

Rules for Residence

Residence in the college buildings is required of all undergraduates with these exceptions: those who live with their families in Philadelphia or the vicinity, and no more than fifty students who are permitted to live in houses or apartments of their own choosing after having received permission to do so from both the College and their parents. Married couples live off campus.

A student enrolled in the College who plans to be married must inform the Dean in advance and must make her own living arrangements.

The College maintains the halls of residence in order to provide simple, comfortable living for its students. It expects students to respect its property and the standards on which the halls are run. A printed statement of residence regulations is given each student. The College makes every effort to keep the residence charge low; the present rates are possible only because the students have agreed to assume the major responsibility for keeping their rooms clean and in order, thus permitting a reduction in service. Failure on the part of a student to meet the requisite standard in the care of her room may cause the College to refuse her residence the following year.

All the undergraduate halls are closed during the Christmas vacation. One hall is kept open during the spring vacation and here undergraduates may occupy rooms at $7.00 per day (including meals).

Non-Resident Students

For non-resident students, there is a suite of rooms in Erdman Hall containing study space, a kitchenette, dressing room and showers. College mail and campus notices will be sent there throughout the academic year. The warden of Erdman Hall is available for consultation.

Non-resident students are liable for all undergraduate fees except those for residence in a hall. A Dispensary fee of $50 entitles them to medical examination and consultation with the College Physician.

All foreign students will be automatically enrolled in the Student Health Service at a cost of $50 for non-residents.

Fees

Tuition

The tuition fee in 1977-78 for all undergraduate students, resident and non-resident, is $4625 a year.

The entire fee will be billed in July 1977 and due August 15, 1977. In the event of withdrawal from the College, refunds will be made according to the following schedule:

Withdrawals July 15 through September 7, 1977	100%
For new students only: withdrawals within the first two weeks of classes	100%
Withdrawals September 8 through October 31, 1977	75%
Withdrawals November 1 through January 15, 1978	50%
Withdrawals January 16, 1978 through March 10, 1978	25%
Withdrawals after March 10, 1978	0

The average cost of teaching each undergraduate is over $6700 a year. The difference over and above tuition must be met from private gifts and income from endowment. Contributions from parents able and willing to pay an additional sum are most welcome to help meet the expenses of instruction.

Residence

The charge for residence is $1990 a year and will be billed with tuition in full in July and be paid in two equal payments, that is, on August 15, 1977 and January 1, 1978. Refunds will be made according to the schedule above.

Students are permitted to reserve a room during the spring semester for the succeeding academic year, prior to payment of room and board fees, if they intend to be in residence during that year. Those students who have reserved a room, but decide later to withdraw from the College or take a leave of absence, will be charged a room change fee of $25.00. This charge will be deducted from the student's general deposit.

Procedure for Securing Refunds

Written notice must be received by the student's dean at least one week prior to the effective date of the withdrawal. Students who have received federally insured loans (loans guaranteed by state agencies-GSLP and National Direct Student loans-NDSL) to meet any educational expenses for the current academic year must make an appointment with the Comptroller of the College before leaving the campus to arrange for the appropriate refund of the loans in question.

General Deposit

All entering students are required to make a deposit of $100. This deposit will remain with the College while the student is enrolled as an undergraduate. After one year of attendance, the deposit will be returned thirty days after graduation or withdrawal from College. However, any unpaid bills and any expenses incurred as a result of destruction or negligence on the part of the student will be applied against the deposit.

Summary of Fees and Expenses for 1977-78

Tuition $4625
Residence 1990

Minor Fees

Laboratory fee per semester:
    One course of 2 hours or less a week $12.50
    One course of more than 2 hours a week 25.00
    Two or more courses of more than 2 hours a week 50.00

Health Insurance (Students' Health Care Plan) 59.50

(For foreign students) 67.20

Dispensary fee for non-resident students 50.00

Graduation fee (payable in the senior year) 25.00

Schedule of Payments

Tuition and residence fees will be billed in full and may be paid as follows:

For resident students

$5620 due not later than August 15

$ 995 due not later than January 1

For non-resident students

$4625 due not later than August 15

No student will be permitted to attend classes or to enter residence until payment of the College charges has been made. No student will be registered at the beginning of a semester, or be graduated, or receive a transcript until all accounts, including a single yearly activities fee of approximately $75.00, collected by the students, are paid. All resident students are required to participate in the College food plan.

An alternate payment plan is offered those who wish to pay tuition in two equal installments by August 15 and January 1. A service charge of $45.00 will be added to the second semester bill.

Faced with the rising costs affecting all parts of higher education, the College has had to raise tuition each of the last several years, and further increases may be expected.

Monthly Payment Plan

For parents who wish to pay college fees on a monthly basis the College offers the one year insured tuition plan in cooperation with the Provident National Bank. The College also offers a prepayment plan with monthly payments at no interest and a long-term repayment plan enabling parents to pay four years of College costs over six to eight years with monthly installments of principal and interest. Both plans are offered in cooperation with the Richard C. Knight Insurance Agency.

General Information

Student Advising

The deans are responsible for the general welfare of undergraduates, and students are free to call upon them for help and advice on academic or more general problems. Each class has its own Class Dean. In addition to their class deans, students may work with the Financial Aid Officer who administers the financial aid program, including grants and loans, and with the Director of Career Planning. The wardens of residence halls, who are members of the Dean's staff, also are ready to advise and assist students. The College Physician, the consulting psychiatrists and counselors are also available to all students. The deans and wardens will give students information about appointments with these specialists.

For freshmen, the Student Freshman Week Committee and the College provide a special period of orientation. Freshman are asked to come into residence before the College is opened to upperclassman. The wardens of the various halls and a committee of upperclassmen welcome them and are available to answer questions and give advice. Freshmen with their parents may meet at that time with the President. In addition, freshmen have individual appointments with the deans to plan their academic program for the year. New students also take placement tests and a physical examination. To acquaint them with the many other aspects of college life, activities are sponsored by the undergraduate organizations.

Academic Standards and Regulations

Faculty rules governing academic work and the conduct of courses are stated in "Academic Rules for Undergraduates," given to each freshman. All students are responsible for knowing the rules thoroughly. Rules concerning the Academic Honor System and student conduct are also stated in the Student Handbook.

Each student's academic work must be of sufficiently high quality to meet the academic standards set by the College. The Council of the Undergraduate College, composed of one faculty member from each department, reviews the records of those students whose work has fallen below the required standard. In such cases the Undergraduate Council may set specific requirements to be met by the student concerned and may also curtail privileges. In extreme cases the Undergraduate Council may exclude a student or require her to withdraw for a period of time from the College.

Integrity of all work is demanded of every student. Information about the Academic Honor System dealing with the conduct of examinations, written quizzes and other written work is given to all entering students. Any infraction of these regulations or any action contrary to their spirit constitutes an offense. Infractions are dealt with by an Administrative Board composed of faculty and students.

Attendance at Classes

Regular attendance at classes is expected. Responsibility for attendance rests solely with each student. In general no attendance records are kept. Each instructor will make clear his view concerning absence from class.

Students should note that instructors are not notified of absences because of illness unless a student has missed three days of classes.

Absences for health or other urgent reasons are excused by the Dean, but any work missed must be made up. After a brief absence the student should consult her instructors about making up the work. In the case of a prolonged absence the Dean must be consulted as well as the instructors. If it seems probable to the Dean that a student's work may be seriously handicapped by the length of her absence, she may be required to drop one or more courses. Any student absent for more than twenty-five consecutive class days will generally be required to drop a course.

Exclusion

The College reserves the right to exclude students whose academic standing is unsatisfactory or whose conduct renders them undesirable members of the college community. In such cases fees will not be refunded or remitted in whole or in part; fellowships and scholarships will be cancelled.

Family Educational Rights and Privacy Act of 1974

The Family Educational Rights and Privacy Act of 1974 was designed to protect the privacy of education records, to establish the right of students to inspect and review their education records, and to provide guidelines for the correction of inaccurate or misleading data through informal and formal hearings. Students have the right to file complaints with The Family Educational Rights and Privacy Act Office (FERPA), Department of Health, Education, and Welfare, 330 Independence Avenue, S.W., Washington, D.C. 20201, concerning alleged failures by the institution to comply with the Act.

Copies of Bryn Mawr's policy regarding the Act and procedures used by the College to comply with the Act can be found in the Office of the Undergraduate Dean. The policy is printed in the Bryn Mawr-Haverford Academic Regulations, which also list all education records maintained on students by this institution.

Questions concerning the Family Rights and Privacy Act may be referred to the Office of the Undergraduate Dean.

Designation of Directory Information

Bryn Mawr College hereby designates the following categories of student information as public or "Directory Information." Such information may be disclosed by the institution for any purpose, at its discretion.

Category I   Name, address, dates of attendance, class.

Category II   Previous institution(s) attended, major field of study, awards, honors, degree(s) conferred

Category III   Date of birth

Category IV   Telephone number

Category V   Marital status

Currently enrolled students may withhold disclosure of any category of information under the Family Educational Rights and Privacy Act of 1974 by written notification which must be in the Office of the Recorder, Taylor Hall, by 5 p.m. on Friday, September 30, 1977. Forms requesting the withholding of "Directory Information" are available in all Deans' Offices and in the Office of the Recorder.

Bryn Mawr College assumes that failure on the part of any student to specifically request the withholding of categories of "Directory Information" indicates individual approval for disclosure.

Health

Students receive clinic and hospital care in the College Dispensary and Infirmary, where a College Physician is in daily attendance. The 18-bed Infirmary is open when College is in session. Additional medical and surgical facilities are readily available at the Bryn Mawr Hospital and in nearby Philadelphia.

Students at Bryn Mawr and Haverford receive out-patient care in their respective College Dispensaries and in-patient care when necessary in the

Bryn Mawr College Infirmary. Medical and psychiatric consultations with the College staff are available by appointment.

The Counseling Service is staffed by a clinical psychologist and consulting psychiatrists who are employed by the Health Service on a part-time basis. This service is available to all students eligible for Dispensary care and is limited to discussion of acute problems, diagnosis and recommendations for further care. A charge is made for visits in excess of four.

Certain health regulations must be met by all entering students. A medical examination blank provided by the College must be filed before July 1. As part of this health report, certification of immunization against tetanus, diphtheria and poliomyelitis, an intradermal tuberculin test and ophthalmologist's certificate are required. If the intradermal tuberculin test is reported positive a chest x-ray is necessary. Students who have failed to hand in these reports will not be permitted to register until they have completed the necessary examinations and immunizations.

The residence fee paid by resident students entitles them to treatment in the College Dispensary and to care in the Infirmary for seven days, not necessarily consecutive, during the year, to attendance by the college physicians during this time and to general nursing. In cases requiring a special nurse, the expense incurred must be paid by the student. The fee for each day in the Infirmary after the seven-day period is $30. A nominal charge will be made for medicines and laboratory tests.

Non-resident students may pay a fee of $50, which entitles them to full use of the Student Health Service. Non-resident students need not pay the fee unless they desire Student Health Service privileges.

All communications from parents and guardians, outside physicians and others, concerning the health of a student should be addressed to the College Physician. Any student who becomes ill when absent from College must notify the Office of the Dean and present to the Infirmary when she returns a signed statement from her physician. If a student leaves the campus for reasons of health she should notify her Class Dean or the Infirmary.

The College reserves the right, if the parents or guardians of a student cannot be reached, to make decisions concerning operations or other matters of health.

Health insurance is required of all undergraduate students. If a student is not already covered, a student health care insurance plan is available through the Head Nurse at the Infirmary. The cost is $59.50 a year and includes coverage for one full calendar year. Foreign students must carry health insurance valid in the United States. The cost for such insurance taken out at Bryn Mawr is approximately $70 for a twelve-month period. Foreign students may obtain application forms for insurance from the Comptroller.

Insurance

The College is not responsible for loss due to fire, theft or any other cause. Students who wish to insure against these risks should do so individually or through their own family policies.

Curriculum

The present plan of study takes into account both the changes of recent years in secondary school education and the expectation of graduate school on the part of most students. It provides flexibility and makes it possible for students to include a wide range of fields of knowledge and to have great freedom to explore and elect. Some of the flexibility has been achieved by including all departments of the College in a divisional system, thus allowing both humanist and scientist a variety of ways in which to meet college requirements.

The Plan for the Curriculum

I. All candidates for the A.B. degree shall present 16 units[1] of work. In all cases one of these will be a unit of Senior Conference in the major subject.

II. Students must complete a full unit of work in one subject for each of the four following disciplinary groups (exception: Group III, see footnote 8) with courses that introduce students to these disciplines offered under departmental sponsorship at either Bryn Mawr or Haverford colleges. A student with suitable preparation may, in consultation with the appropriate faculty members and her Class Dean, elect a course at the intermediate or advanced level.

Group I	Group II[5]	Group III[8]	Group IV
History	Biology	English	History
Philosophy	Chemistry	Literature	Philosophy
Anthropology[2]	Geology	Modern	Archaeology
Economics	Physics	Literatures	History of Art
Education	Psychology 101[6]	Classical	History of Religion[9]
Political Science	[Mathematics][7]	Literatures	Music[10]
Psychology[3]			
Sociology[4]			

---

1. A unit of work is the equivalent of eight semester hours and is either a year course or, when appropriate, two one-semester courses.
2. Anthropology 101, if at Bryn Mawr.
3. Two semester courses chosen from: 206, 207, 208, 305; any Haverford courses numbered 111 and above, with the exception of 240b.
4. At least one semester of work at the 100-level is required.
5. A unit of work in laboratory science to meet the *Group II* requirement must include a laboratory that meets a minimum of three hours a week.
6. Or in special cases Psychology 201a and 302b.
7. Mathematics alone may not be used to fill any *group* requirement. See page 48, II, a & c; III, B, 2.

47

The following directions and qualifications are to be noted:

A. A student (not majoring in subjects under Group II) may elect a second course under Group II, including Mathematics, as an alternative to any one of her other divisional requirements.

B. No course may satisfy more than one divisional requirement. Students majoring in History or Philosophy may count courses in their major as satisfying the requirement in either Group I or Group IV, but not both. Students majoring in Psychology may count courses in their major as satisfying either Group I or Group II, but not both. Students majoring in History of Religion may count courses in their major as satisfying either Group III or Group IV, but not both.

C. Courses taken to satisfy the requirements in English and Mathematics described below do not count as fulfilling divisional requirements.

III. In addition to the divisional requirements, each student must:

A. Include in her program two semesters of English composition (English 015) unless by a score of 5 on the Advanced Placement Test she has shown evidence that she has attained proficiency at this level.

B. Achieve a certain level of proficiency in languages or in one language and Mathematics, the level to be demonstrated in one of the three following ways:

1. She may demonstrate a knowledge of two foreign languages by

a. passing an examination offered by the College every spring and fall, or

b. passing with a grade of at least 2.0 a College course (one full unit) above the elementary level, or

---

8. Any combination of courses at Bryn Mawr listed below will satisfy the requirement:
   English 101 and all 200 courses under "Literature"
   French 201,202,203 and all 300 courses
   German 202 and all 300 courses
   Greek 101, 201, 202b, 203 and 301
   Italian 201a, 204, 301 and 303
   Latin 101, 201, 202, 207, and all 300 courses
   Russian 203, 204, and all 300 courses with the exception of 305
   Spanish 201 and all 300 courses
   History of Religion 103, 104, 201b, 207a, 208b, 305b.

   at Haverford:
   Classics 201a, 202b, 203a, 204b, 301a, 302b, 303a, 304b
   English 101 and all advanced courses with the exception of 190a
   French 200 level and above
   German 202a & b and all 300 courses
   Spanish 200 level and above.
9. Or Religion at Haverford.
10. Music 101 or 102, if at Bryn Mawr.

c. attaining a score of at least 650 (in one language) on a College Board Achievement Test or by passing with an honor grade an Advanced Placement Test.

2. She may offer one language to be tested as described above and demonstrate proficiency in Mathematics by

a. attaining a grade of 4 or 5 on the Advanced Placement Test, or

b. passing an examination offered by the Department of Mathematics each spring and fall, or

c. achieving a grade of at least 2.0 in a course in Mathematics (one full unit, to include at least one half-unit of calculus).

3. She may offer one language to an advanced level of proficiency to be demonstrated by passing with a grade of at least 2.0 one course or two semester courses at the 300 level.

IV. At the end of the sophomore year each student must choose a major subject and in consultation with the departmental advisor plan an appropriate sequence of major and allied courses. Usually a major is made up of four courses, two courses of allied work and one unit of Senior Conference in the major subject. No student will be required to offer more than six courses in the major subject. Students invited to participate in the Honors program count the Honors project as one of the major subject units.

In brief outline, each student's program will include:

A. a unit of work in English, unless she is exempt

B. work to achieve the required level of proficiency in

one language, or

two languages, or

one language and mathematics

C. four units of work, one from each of the divisions I-IV

D. a major subject sequence of at least four units of work and two units of allied work and a Senior Conference

E. elective units of work to complete an undergraduate program of at least 16 units.

Each major department offers Honors work to a number of its senior students who have demonstrated unusual ability. Honors work is of more advanced character than that done in the regular courses and requires more initiative and power of organization than is usually expected of undergraduate students. Such work may be carried on in connection with an advanced course or may be planned especially for individual students. It usually includes independent work of a critical and analytical nature with source material, periodic reports and the preparation of an Honors paper.

A student with unusual interest or preparation in several areas could consider one of the interdepartmental majors, a double major, a major with a strong minor or a special program involving work in several departments built around one major as a core. Such programs can be arranged by consulting the Dean and members of the departments concerned.

A student who wishes to pursue the study of a special area, figure or problem within a given discipline, may, if she finds a faculty member willing and able to supervise such work, substitute a supervised unit of independent study for one semester or year course.

In 1974 the faculty voted to change from a grading system employing only the letters A, B, C, D and F to a numerical system consisting of a scale of 4.0 to 0.

Each student must attain a grade of 2.0 or above in at least half of her graded courses and a grade of at least 1.0 in the remainder. In all courses in her major subject, she must attain grades of 2.0 or above. Should she receive a grade below 2.0 in a second-year or advanced course in the major subject, she may be required to change her major.

The degree of Bachelor of Arts is conferred upon students who have completed the course of study described above. The degree may be awarded *cum laude, magna cum laude,* or *summa cum laude.* To students who have completed Honors work in their major subject and received a grade of at least 3.0 in the senior conference the degree is awarded with Honors in that subject.

Credit for work taken elsewhere is given as follows:

1. Transfer credits (see page 30)

2. Cooperation with neighboring institutions

Under the Three-College Plan for Cooperation, full-time students at Bryn Mawr may register for courses at Haverford College and Swarthmore College without payment of additional fees. Such registration must be approved by the Dean and, in the case of required or major and allied work, by the departments concerned. Credit toward the Bryn Mawr degree will be granted for such courses.

3. Summer School Work

Students desirous of supplementing their work at Bryn Mawr by taking courses in summer school are encouraged to do so after their freshman year. Students who wish to present summer school work for credit should first obtain approval of their plan from their Class Dean and from the department concerned. No credit will be given for work in which a student has received a grade below 2.0. Credit given will be calculated on an hour-for-hour basis.

Supplementary requirements for the Degree:

1. Physical Education—All students must meet the requirement in Physical Education (see page 163).

2. Residence—Every candidate for the degree of Bachelor of Arts unless she is a transfer student or is permitted to accelerate her program or to take a junior year away will normally attend Bryn Mawr College for a period of four years. Students admitted on transfer from other colleges must complete sixteen units, eight of which must be taken while enrolled as a degree candidate at Bryn Mawr College. At least four of these units must be completed at Bryn Mawr during the junior or senior year.

3. Full Program of Work—With few exceptions, all students carry a complete program and do not spend more than the equivalent of the four undergraduate years in completing the work for the A.B. degree.

Student Health Lecture Series

A series of lectures and discussion is presented each year by the College Health Service. Such topics as drug addiction, sex counseling, adolescent mental health and basic health care are discussed. All freshmen must attend the program which is given in the fall.

Premedical Preparation

Bryn Mawr, through the curriculum in liberal arts and sciences, provides the opportunity of meeting requirements for admission to the leading medical schools of the country, and each year a number of its graduates enters these schools. The minimal requirements for most medical schools are met by the following courses: Biology 101, Chemistry 101, Chemistry 202, Mathematics 101, Physics 101. A second course in biology is required for all students who plan to attend medical school in the midwest, southwest or west.

The requirements may be fulfilled by a major in biology, with the election of Mathematics 101 and Physics 101, or by a major in chemistry, with the election of Biology 101. They can also be met by a major in other subjects, such as literature or history, with careful planning of the student's courses during her four years at Bryn Mawr and some work in the summer at an institution giving summer courses acceptable either to Bryn Mawr in substitution for its regular course work or to the medical school of the student's choice. Students planning premedical work should consult early in their careers with the Associate Dean who is the premedical advisor for the College.

The College is able to award a number of scholarships for medical study from funds given for that purpose by friends interested in the advancement of women in medicine (see page 189). These may be applied for on admission to medical school and are awarded at the end of the senior year for use during the first year of medical study, with the prospect of renewal for later years if the student's need and her record in medical school warrant it.

Post-Baccalaureate Premedical Program

A post-baccalaureate premedical program is available to graduates of Bryn Mawr and other four-year accredited institutions. The program is designed to meet the needs of students who have not completed the premedical requirements during their undergraduate years and who have never applied for admission to a medical school. For details of the program, please write to the Premedical Advisor of the College, Taylor Hall, Bryn Mawr College, Bryn Mawr, Pennsylvania 19010.

Preparation to Teach

Students majoring in a liberal arts field which is taught in secondary school may, by appropriate planning early in the undergraduate career, prepare themselves to teach in the public junior and senior high schools of Pennsylvania. By reciprocal arrangement the Pennsylvania certificate is accepted by a number of other states. A student who wishes to teach should consult early in her college career with the chairman of the department concerned and of the Department of Education and Child Development so that appropriate curriculum plans may be made. (See page 76).

Coordination in the Sciences

In 1935 a grant from the Carnegie Corporation of New York enabled the College to put into operation a Plan for Coordination in the Sciences. Through the grant, the College is able to offer both undergraduate and graduate scholarships to students who wish to prepare themselves for future work in areas of interest to more than one natural science department. The chairmen of the departments included in this plan (Biology, Chemistry, Geology, Mathematics, Physics, Psychology) will be glad to see students interested in this program and to advise them about their course of study. Such students should consult with the chairmen of the departments as early as possible.

Interdepartmental Work

Interdepartmental majors are offered in Classical Languages, Classical Studies, French Studies, The Growth and Structure of Cities, and Russian Studies; an interdepartmental area of concentration in Hispanic and Hispanic-American Studies (see page 158) is also offered.

In addition, each year certain courses are offered which cut across well-defined areas of knowledge and emphasize relationships among them. The interdepartmental courses are usually offered at the advanced level since the material considered requires some background in at least two disciplines.

Credit for Creative Work in the Arts

Students may major in Fine Arts at Haverford College under the direction of Bryn Mawr's Professor of Fine Art (see Fine Art under History of Art). Serious students of music, creative writing and the dance may receive elective academic credit for work in these fields. For details see the Performing Arts, the Department of Music and the Department of English.

Language Houses

Haffner Hall, which opened in the fall of 1970, comprises three separate units for qualified students of French, Italian, German and Spanish. In 1972-73 a small group of students wishing to speak Italian was included in a section of Haffner Hall. Students from Bryn Mawr and Haverford interested in the study of Russian occupy a section of Erdman Hall.

Sophomores, juniors or seniors who wish to live in a language house should apply to the head of the appropriate department. Adequate preparation in the language is a prerequisite and those who are accepted agree not to speak English at any time. Residence in a language house provides an excellent opportunity to gain fluency in speaking a foreign language and is highly advisable for students planning to spend the junior year abroad.

Institut d'Etudes Françaises d'Avignon

Bryn Mawr College offers a summer program of intensive work in significant aspects of French culture. The program is open to men and women students from other colleges and from Bryn Mawr. Certain of the courses carry graduate credit. The *Institut* director and faculty members are French professors teaching in colleges and universities in the United States and France. Classes are held in the Palais du Roure and the facilities of the

Bibliothèque Calvet are available to the group. Students live with families in Avignon. Applicants for admission must have strong academic records and have completed a course in French at the third-year college level or the equivalent. For detailed information concerning admission, curriculum, fees, academic credit and scholarships, students should consult Dr. Michel Guggenheim of the Department of French.

Centro de Estudios Hispánicos en Madrid

Bryn Mawr also offers a summer program of intensive work held in Madrid, Spain. The program, under the direction of a member of the Department of Spanish, is open to men and women students from other colleges and from Bryn Mawr. The instructors are members of college and university staffs familiar with teaching standards and practices in this country.

Courses are offered both for the student whose interest is Spain and for the student who wishes to specialize in Latin American affairs. Students live with Spanish families. All participate in study trips and attend an excellent series of carefully planned lectures and cultural events. Applicants must have strong academic records and must have completed the equivalent of three years of college-level Spanish. For information students should consult Dr. Eleanor Paucker of the Department of Spanish. A small number of scholarships is available each year. The *Centro* was made possible by a grant from the Henry L. and Grace Doherty Charitable Foundation of New York.

The Junior Year Abroad

Qualified students may apply for admission to certain groups which offer a junior year in Europe. Bryn Mawr students may study in Paris under the junior year plans sponsored by Barnard, Columbia, Sarah Lawrence, Smith and Sweet Briar colleges or at *L'Académie;* in Geneva, Florence or Hamburg with groups organized by Smith College or in Munich or Freiburg with the group sponsored by Wayne State University. Students may apply for admission to other Junior Year Abroad programs which have the approval of their major department and the Curriculum Committee.

Applicants must have excellent academic records and must give evidence of competence in the language of the country in which they plan to study. In general, two years of study at the college level are necessary to provide adequate language preparation. The junior year groups are not limited to language majors; they often include majors in, for example, History of Art, History or the social sciences. All students who plan to study abroad should consult the chairmen of their major departments to be certain that the work done in Europe may be coordinated with the general plan for the major subject.

Intercollegiate Center for Classical Studies in Rome

The Center is maintained by a cooperating group of colleges and universities, of which Bryn Mawr is a member. Students majoring in Latin, Greek or Archaeology who meet the Center's entrance requirements may apply for admission for one or both semesters of the junior year. The Center's curriculum includes courses in Greek and Latin literature, ancient history and archaeology and provides for the study of Italian.

Guest Senior Year

A student, after consultation with her major department and her Dean, may apply for a guest senior year at another institution in the following circumstances: (a) if a program offered elsewhere will provide her with an opportunity of furthering her academic goals in a way not possible at Bryn Mawr (such cases to be submitted to the Curriculum Committee for approval), (b) for reasons of health or family emergency, (c) if she will be married and not remain in the Bryn Mawr area.

Scholarships and Other Student Aid

All students are, strictly speaking, on scholarship in the sense that their tuition fees cover only part of the costs of instruction. To those students well qualified for education in liberal arts and sciences but unable to meet the college fees, Bryn Mawr is able to offer further scholarship aid. Alumnae and friends of the College over many years have built up endowment for scholarships. Annual gifts from alumnae and alumnae clubs and from industrial and professional groups add to the amounts available each year. It is now possible to provide at least partial scholarships for approximately forty percent of the undergraduate students in the College. Full information about the scholarships available and other forms of help for meeting the expenses of college education will be found in the section, Financial Aid.

Child Care

Child care is available for Bryn Mawr and Haverford college families at the New Gulph Child Care Center, 1109 County Line Road, Rosemont, just five minutes from campus. Children 3 months through 5 years old are eligible. The center is open five days a week, 9 am-5 pm.

The center, conducted by a professional staff, incorporates appropriate age group developmental activities with high quality group care, plus a nursery school program. Flexible schedules can be arranged to accommodate the programs of students, staff, faculty and alumnae parents, based on the college calendar. A minimum of six hours regular use per week is required. Following Commencement, a summer program is conducted for approximately two months.

The fee scale is based on the age of the child and the number of hours in attendance at the center. Tuition for the semester is payable in advance. Financial assistance is available. Early registration for all programs is essential. For information contact the Director at 525-7649.

Career Planning

Students and alumnae are invited to make use of the services of the Career Planning Office which include: a) career and job counseling, b) group and private sessions on resume writing and job-hunting techniques, c) information on and referrals for on- and off-campus part-time jobs, and summer and permanent positions, d) maintaining and furnishing to employers, upon request, credentials files of alumnae containing biographical data and letters of recommendation.

During the academic year the Office sponsors career conferences to provide students with a broader knowledge of career options. These conferences, made possible by a grant from the William C. Whitney Foundation in memory of Alexandra Colt Werkman '60' have focused within recent years on careers for women in law, medicine, the arts and business and management.

In cooperation with the Alumnae Association, the office provides students with access to a network of alumnae who make themselves available to students for personal consultation on career-related questions and who in practical ways assist students in determining their career fields. Students interested in exploring specific career fields may participate during the spring vacation in the Extern program, working as "shadow colleagues" with alumnae and other sponsors who are specialists in these fields. In addition a number of competitive, paid, summer work-internships are made available to Bryn Mawr students by grants from business corporations.

Bryn Mawr participates in the Federal College Work-Study Program established by the Economic Opportunity Act of 1964. This program provides funds for on- and off-campus jobs for students who meet the federal eligibility requirements. Students interested in this program should consult the Director of Financial Aid. (See page 166.)

Courses of Study 1977-78

Key to Course Numbers and Symbols

001-099	indicate elementary and intermediate courses. *With the exception of Greek 001 and Russian 001 these courses are not part of the major work.*
100-199	indicate first-year courses in the major work.
200-299	indicate second-year courses in the major work.
300-398	indicate advanced courses in the major work; 399 is used for the Senior Conference.
400-499	indicate special categories of work (e.g., 401 for Honors, 403 for a supervised unit).
	indicates elective courses, open to all students without prerequisite unless a special prerequisite is stated.
a	the letter "a," following a number, indicates a half-course given in the first semester.
b	the letter "b," following a number, indicates a half-course given in the second semester.
	the letter "c," following a number, indicates a half-course given two hours a week throughout the year.
· d	the letter "d," following a number, indicates a course of six-weeks' duration to be followed by an additional six weeks of independent supervised work.
⌈ ⌉	square brackets enclosing the title of a course indicate that the course is not given in the current year.

In general, courses listed as full-year courses must be carried through two semesters. In some cases one semester of such a course may be taken with credit but only with permission of the student's Class Dean and the department concerned. One unit of work carried throughout the year is the equivalent of eight semester hours, or eleven quarter hours.

Selected Haverford and Swarthmore College courses are listed in this catalogue when applicable to Bryn Mawr programs. Consult the Haverford and Swarthmore College catalogues for full course descriptions.

Anthropology

Professor: Jane C. Goodale, PH.D.

Associate Professor: Philip L. Kilbride, PH.D.*Chairman*

Assistant Professors: Robert A. Braun, PH.D.
Richard H. Jordan, PH.D.
Judith R. Shapiro, PH.D.

Assistants: Anna Dugan, B.A.
Esther Kasangaki, B.A.

Associate Professor of Linguistics in Anthropology and German: Nancy C. Dorian PH.D.

The aim of the department is two-fold: (1) to introduce the liberal arts student to the discipline of anthropology: its aims, methods, theories and contributions to an understanding of the nature of human culture and society and (2) to provide for the major in anthropology, in addition to the above, a firm understanding of the basic concepts and history of the discipline through examination of theoretical works and intensive studies in the ethnography and prehistory of several world areas. Laboratory experience is provided in a number of courses.

Requirements in the Major Subject: 101, 203a, 320a and two additional half-units of intermediate (200) work chosen from 201a, 204a, 204b, 208a, 208b and 210a and one 300-level semester course in the area of ethnography, plus 399a and b (Senior Conferences). Two and one-half additional units of major or allied work are required, which may be taken at Bryn Mawr or Haverford, at least one-half unit at the 300-level.

Allied Subjects: Biology, The Growth and Structure of Cities Program, Classical and Near Eastern Archaeology, Economics, English Literature, Geology, History of Art, History of Religion, Linguistics, Philosophy, Political Science, Psychology, Sociology and interdepartmental "Culture and Civilization" courses (such as INT. 290 *"La Civilisation française,"* INT. 210a. "Hispanic Culture and Civilization," and INT. 307b. "Introduction to Celtic Civilization").

101. *Man, Culture and Society:* Members of the Department.
Man's place in nature, human evolution and the history of culture to the rise of early civilizations in the Old and New Worlds; forms of culture

and society among contemporary peoples. Because the subject matter is extensive and the basic concepts unfamiliar, a full year is needed to gain an adequate understanding of the subject; therefore, both semesters are required for credit.

Afro-American Heritage: Mr. Kilbride.]

American Indian Heritage.]

Introduction to Peoples and Cultures of the Middle East: Miss Witty.]

Archaeological Methods of Analysis: Mr. Jordan.

Lectures, laboratory and field experience will stress the methodological framework of archaeological investigation and interpretation. Prerequisites: 101, or equivalent introductory course in a related discipline, and permission of instructor.

Primitive Society: Miss Shapiro.

Social organization: an introduction to theory and methods and a study of significant contributions. Prerequisite: Anthropology 101.

South American Prehistory: Mr. Braun.

The cultural history of the Andes and Amazonia up to the Spanish conquest. Interrelationships with Mesoamerica, Africa and Asia are explored. Cultural dynamics and stylistic and iconographic analysis of art are stressed. Prerequisite: Anthropology 101 or permission of instructor.

North American Prehistory: Mr. Jordan.

A study of North American archaeology and cultural history. Introduction to methods and theory in archaeology and in the analysis of archaeological data. Prerequisite: Anthropology 101 or permission of instructor.

Old World Prehistory: Mr. Jordan, Mr. Braun.]

Human Evolution: Mr. Jordan.]

Community Politics: A Cross-Cultural Approach: Mrs. Ross, Mr. Ross.]
See Political Science 218b.

Marginal Religions in America: Miss Whitehead (at Haverford).

Religious innovation and sect formation in 19th and 20th century America, in sociological and anthropological perspectives, with reference also to psychotherapeutic doctrines and movements. Readings from Weber, Smelser, Bellah, Niebuhr, Geertz and Worsley.

255b. *Anthropology of Religion:* Mr. MacGaffey (at Haverford).

Contemporary ethnographic work in the field of religion considered in relation to the most important theoretical contributions, particularly those of French authors. A knowledge of French is helpful but not essential. Not open to freshmen.

256a. *Anthropology of Law:* Mr. MacGaffey (at Haverford).

The comparative study of simple and complex societies from a legal perspective; public rules, violations and sanctions in institutional and cultural context. Anthropological definitions of law compared: Gluckman, Bohannan, Pospisil, Smith and others. Strong emphasis on field studies of legal processes. Prerequisite: one other course in Sociology and Anthropology or Political Science.

302b. *Africa: Sub-Saharan Ethnology:* Mr. Kilbride.

A study of selected Sub-Saharan societies and cultures, illustrating problems in ethnography. Prerequisite: Anthropology 203a.

303b. *Oceania: Topics in Melanesian Ethnography:* Miss Goodale.

An intensive study of selected Melanesian cultures and societies with emphasis on such topics as politics, law, economics, sex roles and identities, magic, religion, cultural dynamics and political development. Prerequisite: Anthropology 203a.

[304a. *The American Indian.*]

[305a. *Latin America: Native Cultures of South America:* Miss Shapiro.]

[306b. *Peasants:* Mr. Kilbride.]

308. *Language in the Social Context:* Miss Dorian.
(INT.) See Interdepartmental course 308

[310a. *Introduction to Descriptive Linguistic Techniques:* Miss Dorian.]
(INT.)

[312b. *Field Methods in Linguistics:* Miss Dorian.]
(INT.)

[313b. *Linguistic Anthropology:* Miss Shapiro.]

314a. *Comparative Hunters and Gatherers:* Miss Goodale.

An intensive study of Australian Aboriginal peoples, Bushmen of the Kalahari of Southern Africa and other peoples who today subsist primarily by utilizing resources extracted from their environment through hunting and gathering technologies. Major topics to be examined will include:

man/land relationships (technological, legal, and religious), independence and interdependence of social groupings, ethno-epistemology, and the theoretical importance of hunters and gatherers to anthropological thought today. Prerequisite 203a or permission of instructor.

Cultural Theory: Miss Shapiro..

The relationship of anthropology to other social sciences and an examination of the important anthropological contributions to cultural theory. Prerequisite: a half-unit of advanced (300) work.

Culture and Personality: Mr. Kilbride.

Approaches to an understanding of culture through study of cultural factors in the development of human personalities, and individual experiences in different socio-cultural settings. Prerequisite: a half-unit of advanced (300) work.

Physical Anthropology.}

Cultural Ecology: Mr. Braun.

The interrelationships among cultural forms, adaptation, and natural and social environments. Examples are drawn from ethnography (nonwestern and complex societies), archaeology, and physical anthropology. Prerequisite: one half-unit of advanced (300) work.

Woman, Culture and Society: Miss Shapiro.}

Political Anthropology: Mr. MacGaffey (at Haverford).

Theory of corporations, social morphology, and social change; selected topics in the comparative study of government and law.

Senior Conferences:

The topic of each seminar is determined in advance in discussion with students. Sections will normally run through the entire year and have an emphasis on field research and analysis. Class discussions of work in progress, and oral and written presentations of the analysis and results of research will form the basis of evaluation for the year. Seminars for 1977-78 are:

Advanced Topics in the Social Anthroplogy of Modern Latin America: Mr. Braun.

Historic Archaeology: Mr. Jordan.

Cultural Deviance: Mr. Kilbride.

Sex Roles: Miss Shapiro.

401. *Honors Work:*

   Honors work will be offered to seniors who petition the department with a specific proposal and whose previous work shows sufficiently high level of accomplishment and marked ablity.

403. *Independent Work:*

   Independent work is open usually to junior and senior majors who wish to work in a special area under the supervision of a member of the faculty and subject to faculty time and interest.

Biology

Professor: Robert L. Conner, PH.D., *Chairman*

Associate Professors: Anthony R. Kaney, PH.D.
   David J. Prescott, PH.D.

Assistant Professors: Patricia J. Olds-Clarke, PH.D.‡
   Steven N. Treistman, PH.D.

Lecturers: Diana L. Cassel, PH.D.
   Jane R. McConnell, PH.D.
   Kathryn G. Orkwiszewski, PH.D.
   Patricia Onderdonk Pruett, PH.D., *Associate Dean of the Undergraduate College*

Assistants: Denise Gavula, B.A.
   Susan J. Gan, B.A.
   Suzanne J. Kelly, B.A.
   Patricia Little, B.A.
   Bernadette Seredinsky, A.B.

Laboratory Coordinators: Josephine R. Landrey, A.B.
   Chung Wha Lee Iyengar, PH.D.

Professor of History of Science: Jane M. Oppenheimer, PH.D.

Assistant Professor of Chemistry: Kenneth Strothkamp, PH.D.

---

‡On leave for the year 1977-78.

The courses offered are designed to present the principles underlying biological science to liberal arts students interested in understanding the biotic world in which man lives and his own position in it. Primary consideration is devoted, both in class and in the laboratory, to the interplay of development, structure and function in determining the unity and diversity which characterize the plant and animal kingdoms and to dynamic interrelationships of living organisms with each other and with their environment. Genetics, cell and molecular biology and biochemistry are emphasized as unifying disciplines.

Requirements in the Major Subject: Biology 101 (unless either or both semesters are exempted), 201a, 362a, and any two of the following three courses—309b, 310b, 364b, and at least one other unit (two semester-courses) of advanced work, the Senior Conference, and Chemistry 101 and 202. Physics 101 and Mathematics 101 are strongly recommended as additional courses. Students should note that the ability to read French or German is essential for graduate work.

Allied Subjects: Chemistry, Physics, History of Science.

General Biology: Mrs. McConnell, Mr. Treistman, Mrs. Orkwiszewski, Mr. Kaney.
Laboratory: Mrs. McConnell and assistants.
   A presentation of the fundamental principles of molecular, cellular and organismic biology. A selection of plants and animals is studied to illustrate problems and theories dealing with living systems and their interaction with the environment. Lecture three hours, laboratory three hours a week.

Genetics: Mr. Kaney.
   A study of heredity and gene action. Lecture three hours, laboratory four hours a week. Prerequisite: Biology 101 or permission of instructor.

Developmental Biology: Mrs. Olds-Clarke.]

Comparative and Systems Physiology: Mr. Treistman.
   A study of the strategies employed throughout the animal kingdom to ensure adaptive interaction of individuals with widely-differing environments.

History of Scientific Thought: Miss Oppenheimer.
)   See History 314.

350b. *Problems in Cellular Physiology:* Mr. Conner.

An inquiry into the recent literature about membrane phenomena, including the mechanisms for bulk transport, small molecule transport and chemical specificity. Lecture two hours a week. Prerequisites: Biology 362a and 364b or permission of instructor.

351a. *Problems in Genetics:* Mr. Kaney.

A seminar course emphasizing in depth analysis of current topics in modern genetics. Presentations from recent literature will be given and discussed. Two hours a week, no laboratory. Prerequisites: Biology 201a and Biology 362a, or permission of the instructor.

352a. *Problems in Molecular Biology:* Mrs. Cassel.

A course dealing with current topics of interest in the field of molecular biology. Class meeting two hours a week. Prerequisites: Biology 362a and 364b.

353a. *Biochemistry: Macromolecular Structure and Function:* Mr. Prescott, Mr.
(INT.) Strothkamp.

The structure, chemistry and function of proteins; nucleic acids and polysaccharides are discussed with special emphasis on their roles in living systems. Lecture three hours, laboratory six hours a week. Prerequisites: Chemistry 202 and Biology 362a or permission of instructors. Physics 101 and Mathematics 101 are recommended.

353b. *Biochemistry: Intermediary Metabolism:* Mr. Conner, Mr. Prescott.
(INT.) Metabolic relationships of carbohydrates, lipids and amino acids are discussed with emphasis on the control of various pathways. Lecture three hours, laboratory six hours a week. Prerequisite: Biology 353a.

{354a. *Recent Advances in Cell Biology*}

{355b. *Problems in Neurophysiology:* Mr. Treistman.}

{356. *Biophysics:* Miss Hoyt.}

357a. *Computer Usage in the Life Sciences:* Mrs. Pruett.
(INT.) Experiments in the life sciences will be analyzed using computer techniques. The Fortran IV language will be developed and used throughout the course. Limited to advanced students with research experience; no previous training in the use of the computer required. Lecture two hours, laboratory two hours a week.

358a. *Problems in Developmental Biology:* Mrs. Orkwiszewski.

A seminar course devoted to the study of the control of gene expression as it relates to the developmental process. Two hours a week, no laboratory. Prerequisites: Biology 201a, Biology 309b and Biology 362a, or permission of the instructor.

. *Cellular Physiology:* Mr. Conner.

A course devoted to a study of the activities of cells in terms of physical and chemical processes. Lecture three hours, laboratory four hours a week. Prerequisites: Biology 201a and Chemistry 202, which may be taken concurrently.

. *Cell and Molecular Biology:* Mrs. Cassel.

An examination of the ultra-structural organization, function and molecular development of selected eukaryotic organelles. Lecture three hours, laboratory four hours a week. Prerequisite: Biology 201a.

. *Senior Conference:*

During one semester, all seniors will write a comprehensive paper in a prescribed area of biology in conjunction with a faculty member. These papers serve to relate materials from various subdisciplines of biology to each other, to examine subjects of current biological interest and to relate the field to the larger aspects of society. In the other semester, students will take a seminar course chosen from the available offerings.

. *Honors Work:*

All qualified students are encouraged to do Honors work in one of the advanced fields. This entails one unit of laboratory work on an independent experimental research problem.

. *Supervised Research in Biology:* Members of the Department.

Laboratory research under the supervision of a member of the Department.

Teaching Certification: A sequence of work offered by the Department of Biology and the Department of Education of the College leads to a certificate to teach in the secondary schools of Pennsylvania.

COURSES AT HAVERFORD

. *Biochemistry of Membrane Transport:* Mr. Lowey.

. *Biosynthesis of Organelles:* Mr. Santer.

. *Molecular Virology:* Mr. Goff.

. *Cell Motility:* Mr. Kessler.

Chemistry

Professors: Jay Martin Anderson, PH.D.
　Ernst Berliner, PH.D.
　Frank B. Mallory, PH.D.‡
　George L. Zimmerman, PH.D., *Chairman*

Associate Professor: Joseph Varimbi, PH.D.

Assistant Professor: Kenneth G. Strothkamp, PH.D.

Lecturers: Frances Bondhus Berliner, PH.D.
　Cecile K. Dalton, PH.D.

Assistants: Anne Belcher, B.A.
　Mark K. Hamilton, B.S.
　Darrell E. Jones, M.S.
　Sandra J. G. Linkletter, B.S.
　Cynthia H. Sarnoski, B.S.
　Noreen Tuross, B.S.

Associate Professor of Biology: David J. Prescott, PH.D.

The major in chemistry is designed to give the student a sound background in the four major fields of chemistry: inorganic, analytical, organic and physical chemistry. The courses are arranged in such a sequence as to convey an insight into the development of chemical theories from basic scientific principles. In the advanced courses the student begins to be acquainted with current problems in special fields and with modern approaches to their solutions. The emphasis throughout is on the fundamental principles on which chemistry is based and which are exemplified and further clarified by laboratory work taken in conjunction with each course.

Requirements in the Major Subject: Chemistry 101, the three 200-level courses, one unit of advanced work and the Senior Conference. The required unit of advanced work shall consist of two semesters of courses selected from among 301b, 302a, 302b, 303a, 303b, 353, and 356b, with the provision that at least one of the semesters shall include laboratory work (i.e., 302a, 302b, 303b, 353). Physics 101 and Mathematics

---

‡On leave for the year 1977-78.

101 are also required. Students are encouraged to take additional mathematics. A reading knowledge of German is valuable for work in chemistry beyond the undergraduate level.

Allied Subjects: Biology, Geology, Mathematics, Physics.

General Chemistry: Mr. Zimmerman, Mrs. Berliner and assistants.

An introduction to the theories of chemistry and the study of the non-metals. Introductory quantitative techniques. No knowledge of chemistry is presupposed. Three lectures, three hours of laboratory a week.

General Chemistry: Mr. Berliner, Mrs. Berliner and assistants.

Ionic equilibria and the systematic qualitative analysis of inorganic substances. A study of the metallic elements. Three lectures, three hours of laboratory a week.

Inorganic Chemistry: Mr. Varimbi.

Correlations of chemical and physical properties based on the periodic table; structures of inorganic compounds; equilibria in acid-base and complex-ion systems. Laboratory work includes analytical techniques, synthesis, purification, and characterization of a variety of compounds by chemical and instrumental methods. Three lectures, five hours of laboratory a week.

Organic Chemistry: Mr. Berliner, Mrs. Dalton.

First semester: aliphatic chemistry; second semester: aromatic chemistry and natural products. Three lectures, five hours of laboratory a week.

Physical Chemistry: Mr. Anderson.

Structure and kinetic-molecular theory of matter, elementary thermodynamics and chemical kinetics. Two lectures and one conference, laboratory five hours a week. Prerequisites: Mathematics 101 and Physics 101. (The latter may be taken concurrently with Chemistry 203.)

Advanced Inorganic Chemistry: Mr. Varimbi.

Group theory and some of its applications to structural and spectroscopic problems of ligand field theory. Elements of solid state chemistry: metals, semiconductors and surface reactions. Three lectures a week.

Advanced Organic Chemistry: Mrs. Dalton, Mr. Berliner.

Lectures: theories and fundamental principles of organic chemistry. Laboratory: (first semester) organic qualitative analysis; (second semester) advanced synthesis and laboratory techniques. Two lectures, six hours of laboratory a week.

303a. *Quantum Mechanics of Atoms and Molecules:* Mr. Chesick (at Haverford 1977-78)
Prerequisites: Chemistry 203 and Mathematics 201 or its equivalent.

303b. *Atomic and Molecular Spectroscopy:* Mr. Zimmerman
Topics include absorption and emission spectroscopy in the vacuum ultraviolet, the ultraviolet-visible and the infrared regions, nuclear magnetic resonance spectroscopy and raman spectroscopy. Two lecture-discussions, five hours of laboratory a week and regular use of a computer. Prerequisites: Chemistry 303a and some elementary knowledge of Fortran programming.

[304b. *The Dynamics of Environmental Systems*]
(INT.)

313a. *Mathematical and Numerical Methods in Chemistry:* Mr. Anderson.
Selected topics from linear algebra, calculus, and differential equations as applied to problems in spectroscopy, thermodynamics, and kinetics. Three lectures per week and regular use of the computer. Prerequisites: Chemistry 203 and Mathematics 101 or equivalents; permission of the instructor.

353a. *Biochemistry: Macromolecular Structure and Function:* Mr. Prescott, Mr.
(INT.) Strothkamp.
See Biology 353a.

353b. *Biochemistry: Intermediary Metabolism:* Mr. Conner, Mr. Prescott,
(INT.) Mr. Strothkamp.
See Biology 353b.

356b. *Biochemical Mechanisms:* Mr. Lerman (at Haverford).
Prerequisite: Chemistry 202.

399. *Senior Conference:*
The Senior Conference consists of four half-semester special topic seminars. In each year, eight such seminars will be offered. Four of these will be given at Bryn Mawr and four at Haverford, and students are free to select the seminars at either institution according to their own interests and preparation. These special seminars will be in the broad areas of chemistry, for instance, biochemistry, inorganic, organic and physical chemistry, and will cover subject matter not usually taken up, or only briefly treated, in the regular courses. They will be on a level which has at least one semester of a 200-level course as a prerequisite. The topics will

vary from year to year, and a list of topics will be made available to students towards the end of their junior year.

01. *Honors Work:*

Honors work, consisting of individual research under the supervision of a member of the Department, may be undertaken in conjunction with any of the advanced courses by qualified students who are invited by the Department to participate in this program.

Teaching Certification:

A sequence of work offered by the Department of Chemistry and the Department of Education of the College leads to a certificate to teach in the secondary schools of Pennsylvania.

Supervised Units of Independent Study:

(See under *Curriculum,* The Plan for The Curriculum, IV).

Classical and Near Eastern Archaeology

Professors: Machteld J. Mellink, PH.D., *Chairman*
Kyle M. Phillips, Jr., PH.D., *Resident Director of Massenzia, Rome*
Brunilde S. Ridgway, PH.D.†

Professor of Classical and Near Eastern Archaeology and of *History of Art:*
Phyllis Pray Bober, PH.D., *Dean of The Graduate School of Arts and Sciences*

Associate Professor: Richard S. Ellis, PH.D.‡

Associate Professor of Latin: Russell T. Scott

Lecturers: Harrison Eiteljorg, II, PH.D.
Gloria F. Pinney, PH.D.
Maria deJ. Ellis, PH.D.

Assistants: Janer D. Belson, M.A.
Mark Fullerton, M.A.

---

†On leave, semester II.
‡On leave for the year 1977-78.

The major courses provide an extensive survey of the ancient Mediterranean and Near Eastern civilizations, with emphasis on Greek art and archaeology.

Requirements in the Major Subject: Archaeology 101, 201a (or another Near Eastern course), 203a and b, 205b, 301a and 302a or b and the Senior Conference. All majors are urged to take Greek and ancient history and to acquire a reading knowledge of French and German.

Allied Subjects: Ancient History, Anthropology, History of Art, Greek, Latin, Akkadian, Hebrew.

101. *An Introduction to Ancient Art:* Miss Mellink, Mr. Eiteljorg.
    An historical survey of the art of the ancient Near East, Greece and Rome. Three hours of classes, one hour of informal discussion a week.

{201a. *The Archaeology of Mesopotamia before 1600 B.C.:* Mr. Ellis.}

202a. *Ancient Greek Cities and Sanctuaries:* Mrs. Ridgway.
(INT.)   A study of the form and cultural importance of the major Greek centers.

203a. *Hellenistic and Roman Sculpture:* Mrs. Ridgway.
    From the Hellenistic period to the end of the Roman Empire.

{203b. *Greek Sculpture:* Mrs. Ridgway.}

{204a. *The Ancient City:* Mr. Scott.}
(INT.)

{204b. *Egypt and Mesopotamia from 1600-500 B.C.:* Mr. Ellis.}

205a. *The Ancient Near East:* Mrs. Ellis.
    See History 205a.

205b. *Aegean Archaeology:* Miss Mellink.
    The pre-Greek and early Greek cultures of the Aegean area: Minoan Crete, Troy, the Aegean Islands, Mycenaean Greece and their overseas connections.

{206b. *Ancient Near Eastern Architecture:* Mr. Ellis, Miss Mellink.}
(INT.)

{208a. *Medes and Persians*}

208b. *Texts as Sources for Near Eastern Archaeology:* Mrs. Ellis.
    The use of ancient documents for the reconstruction of material culture and society in the ancient Near East.

. *Greek Vase-Painting:* Mrs. Pinney.
Greek vase-painting as an original form of art, its relation to other arts, and its place in archaeological research.

. *Greek Architecture:* Mr. Eiteljorg.
.) The Greek architectural tradition in its historical development.

. *Roman Architecture:* Mr. Scott.
.) The architecture of the Republic and the early Roman Empire.

. *Etruscan Archaeology:* Mrs. Pinney.
An introduction to the sites and monuments of Etruria.

. *Monumental Painting:* Mrs. Pinney.
The arts of wall painting and mosaics in the Greek world and in Italy from the archaic period to the third century A.D.

. *The Bronze Age in Syria and Palestine:* Mr. Ellis.}

. *Senior Conference:*
Weekly two-hour seminars with assigned readings and reports. Semester I: Mr. Eiteljorg; semester II: Miss Mellink.

See also History 205a. *The Ancient Near East:* Mrs. Ellis.

. *Honors Work:*
A long written paper is submitted on a topic selected by the student and approved by the Department. In preparation, the student confers throughout the year with the member of the Department under whose direction the paper is prepared.

Interdepartmental Work:
The Department of Classical and Near Eastern Archaeology participates in the interdepartmental majors in Classical Studies and The Growth, and Structure of Cities. See pages 152 and 155.

Excavation:
The Department has two excavation projects. The excavation of Karatash-Semayük in Lycia (Turkey) is conducted as a field seminar in the fall, with full credit for graduate students and seniors by invitation. The second project, the excavation of an Etruscan archaic site at Murlo near Siena, takes place during the summer on a non-credit basis for graduate and undergraduate students of archaeology.

Economics

Professor: Richard B. Du Boff, PH.D., *Chairman*

Associate Professors: Noel J. J. Farley, PH.D.†
Helen Manning Hunter, PH.D.

Assistant Professor: Li Way Lee, PH.D.

At Haverford

Assistant Vice-President: Samuel Gubins, PH.D.

Professor: Holland Hunter, PH.D.

Associate Professor: Vernon J. Dixon, PH.D.

Instructor: Michael Weinstein, B.A.

The major in economics consists of courses given at Bryn Mawr and Haverford. It is designed to provide an understanding of economic processes and institutions and the interactions among the economic, political and social structures, to train students in the methods used to analyze those processes and institutions, and to enable them to make policy judgments.

Requirements in the Major Subject: Economics 111a and b and 112a and b, three units of intermediate and advanced work (including at least one unit of a 300-level course) and the Senior Conference. Courses 111a and b and 112a and b are designed to give the kind of informed perspective on economic principles and problems that is an integral part of a liberal education, as well as to provide a foundation for students to do further work in economics. The group of intermediate courses offers a full range of material on major topics in the discipline and is designed to meet a wide variety of student interests. The group of advanced courses supplies a methodological and theoretical foundation for those planning to make use of economics in their professional careers. In the selection of courses the student is urged to take three of the following courses: 203a or b, 303a, 304b, 310a. Students intending to do graduate work in economics should take 302b and Mathematics 101 and 201 and they should consult with members of the Department about their plans before selecting their courses.

---

†On leave, semester II

Prospective majors in economics are advised to take Economics 111a and b and 112a and b by the end of the first semester of the sophomore year. As a general rule, the prerequisites for intermediate and advanced-level work are Economics 111a and b and Economics 112a and b or permission of instructor.

Allied Subjects: Mathematics, Political Science, History, Philosophy, Psychology, Sociology, Anthropology.

111a. *Introduction to Macroeconomics:* Members of the Department.
& b. The analysis of national economic behavior including prosperity and depression. Theories of inflation and unemployment. The role of government in managing and mismanaging the economy by influencing total national expenditure and by regulating financial institutions. The international role of the United States. Focus is on Western mixed-capitalist economies.

112a. *Introduction to Microeconomics:* Members of the Department.
& b. Techniques of analysis which apply to all economic systems in general and modern mixed-capitalism in particular. Topics include: determination of costs and prices for goods and services; the functioning of the marketplace; causes of wealth, poverty and income inequality; environmental protection; public goods. The course is intended to provide a method of examining economic behavior which will continue to be useful in a changing economic world.

115a. *Economic Accounting:* Mr. Dixon (at Haverford).

201b. *American Economic Development:* Mr. Du Boff.
Long-term trends in output, resources and technology; structure of consumption, production and distribution; foreign trade and investment, and the role of the state. Quantitative findings provide the points of departure, and the framework is one of imbalances and disequilibria in an expanding capitalist economy. Prerequisites: Economics 111a or b and Economics 112a or b.

202b. *Latin American Economic Development.*]

203a. *Statistical Methods in Economics:* Members of the Department.
& b. Frequency distributions, probability and sampling theory, simple correlation and multiple regression and an introduction to econometric terminology and reasoning. The computer programming and other techniques required are developed as part of the course. Prerequisites: Economics 111a or b and Economics 112a or b.

[205a. *The Corporation and Public Policy:* Mr. Lee.]

206b. *International Economic Theory and Policy:* Instructor to be announced
   Current problems in international trade. The theory of trade. The balance of payments and theory of disturbances and adjustment in the international economy. Economic integration. The impact of growth in rich and poor countries on the development of the world economy. Prerequisite: Economics 111a or b and Economics 112a or b or permission of the instructor.

207b. *Money and Banking:* Mrs. Hunter.
   The development and present organization of the financial system of the United States; domestic and international problems of monetary theory and policy. Prerequisites: Economics 111a or b and Economics 112a or b.

208b. *Economics of the Public Sector:* Mr. Lee.
   The concept of public goods. Expenditure and financing decisions within the frameworks of efficiency and the distribution of benefits and costs. Case studies of particular government decisions with emphasis on education and housing. Prerequisites: Economics 111a or b, Economics 112a or b.

209a. *Urban Economics:* Mr. Dixon (at Haverford).
(INT.)

210a. *Developing Economies:* Mr. Hunter (at Haverford).
   Analysis of the structural transformation and developing economies. Causes and roles of saving, investment, skills, technological change and trade in the development process; strategies and methods of economic planning. Prerequisites: Economics 111a or b and Economics 112a or b.

[211a. *The Soviet System:* Mr. Hunter (at Haverford).]
(INT.)

[216a. *Economic History and Growth, 1750-1970:* Mr. Du Boff.]

[217a. *Topics in Cliometric History of the United States:* Mr. Weinstein (at Haverford).]

222b. *History of Economic Thought:* Mr. Du Boff.
   Examination of the Mercantilists, the Physiocrats, Smith, Malthus, Ricardo, Marx, Mill, Marshall, and Keynes. Emphasis on theories concerning economic growth and the stationary state, value and distribution, and the role of the state. Prerequisites: Economics 111a or b and 112a or b.

Labor History and Economics: Mr. Weinstein (at Haverford).

Topics in Economics: Mr. DuBoff.

The study of contemporary problems from the economist's viewpoint, selected from such areas as United States foreign economic policies, population studies, cross-cultural economics, minority economic development, radical political economy, planning in the United States economy, the economics of education. Topic in the fall 1977-78: radical political economy. Prerequisites: Economics 111a or b and Economics 112a or b or permission of the instructor.

Introduction to Econometrics: Mrs. Hunter.

The econometric theory presented in Economics 203a and b is further developed and its most important empirical economic applications are considered. Each student will do a six-week empirical research project using multiple regression and other statistical techniques. Prerequisites: Economics 203a or b and permission of instructor.

Macroeconomic Analysis: Mr. Dixon (at Haverford).

Microeconomic Analysis: Mr. Lee.

Systematic investigation of analytic relationships underlying consumer welfare, efficient resource allocation and ideal pricing. Introduction to operations research. Prerequisite: Economics 112a or b or permission of instructor.

Theory of Capital Markets: Mr. Lee.

Introduction to the theory of capital markets. Emphases on portfolio theory and applications to individual and firm decision making. Instruments, institutions and procedures of capital markets. Special attention to corporate mergers and failures. Prerequisites: Economics 112a or b and Economics 203a or b or consent of instructor.

Interindustry Economics: Mr. Hunter (at Haverford).

Economic Integration: Theory and Policy: Mr. Farley.

Models of economic integration in the world economy. Static and dynamic benefits and costs of increased trade in a customs union arrangement. Analysis of international factor mobility. The role of the multinationals. The Eurodollar market. Prerequisite: Economics 206b.

Advanced Economic Theory: Mr. Weinstein (at Haverford).

Quantitative Analysis of Economic Change: Mrs. Hunter.

Business cycles and economic growth: theory, measurement and forecasting. Prerequisite: Economics 203a or b.

399. *Senior Conference:*

Weekly two-hour seminars for which readings are assigned and reports are prepared. Semester I: economic theory; semester II: topic to be chosen by the students. Each student will have the option of writing a paper or taking an examination.

401. *Honors Work:*

One unit of Honors work may be taken by students recommended by the Department.

Interdepartmental Work:

The Department of Economics participates in the interdepartmental major in The Growth and Structure of Cities and in the interdepartmental concentration in Hispanic and Hispanic-American Studies. See pages 155 and 158.

Teahing Certification:

A sequence of work offered by the Department of Economics and the Department of Education of the College leads to a certificate to teach in the secondary schools of Pennsylvania.

Education and Child Development

Professors: Janet L. Hoopes, PH.D., *Director. Child Study Institute**
Ethel W. Maw, PH.D., *Chairman*

Associate Professors: Susan E. Maxfield, M.S., *Director, Thorne School*
Emmy A. Pepitone, PH.D.
Faye P. Soffen, ED.D.

Assistant Professors: Fred Rothbaum, PH.D.
Samuel S. Snyder, PH.D.

---

*On leave, semester I.

The work in education is designed for students preparing for teaching or for work with children in a variety of fields. The curriculum treats the nature and development of the child, the psychology of teaching and learning and principles of measurement. It deals with the history, philosophy and objectives of the school as a social institution.

Although there is no major in education, a sequence of courses in the department enables the student to prepare for teaching in the secondary school. Students expecting to teach are urged to confer with the Department during the freshman year.

For students preparing for teaching, the first semester of the senior year is an extremely busy one. During student teaching, the student must be prepared to be in the school throughout the school day, five days a week.

The Thorne School is maintained by the Department as a laboratory for child study where undergraduates have experience with young children. The pre-kindergarten program, in which advanced students assist, provides training for those planning to teach.

The Department also operates the Child Study Institute. This is a mental health service supported by the College, by the Lower Merion Township Schools and by fees. Problems of learning and behavior are studied; psychological testing, psychiatric treatment, remedial teaching and a program of counseling for children and parents are carried on. Graduate students participate in the work, and undergraduate and graduate students observe in the schools and at the Institute.

. *The Social Foundations of Education:* Mrs. Pepitone.

. *History and Philosophy of Education:* Mrs. Pepitone.]

. *Educational Psychology.* Mr. Snyder.

Topics in the psychology of human cognitive, social, and affective behavior are examined and related to educational practice. Laboratory work is required. Prerequisite: Psychology 101.

. *Developmental Psychology:* Mr. Snyder. (In alternate years, Psychology 206a: *Developmental Psychology:* Miss Wannemacher.)

The development of cognitive, social, and affective behavior with an emphasis on early and middle childhood. Laboratory work is required. Prerequisite: Psychology 101.

. *Adolescent Development:* Mr. Rothbaum.

Patterns and problems of development—physical, cognitive, emotional, and social—as they relate to the adolescent period. Theory and research focusing on adolescents in home, school and society. Three hours a week with laboratory or other independent work required. Prerequisite: Education 206a or permission of instructor.

301a. *Principles of Teaching in the Secondary School:* Mrs. Maw.

The objectives, curriculum and organization of the secondary school. The nature of the learner and his relation to the school program and aims. Two-hour seminar a week; student teaching in the junior or senior high school. A full unit of work. Prerequisite: permission of instructor.

[302a. *Principles of Teaching in the Elementary School:* Mrs. Maw.]

See also Psychology 63b. Perception, Psycholinguistics and Reading: Mr. Travers (at Swarthmore).

Selected Graduate Seminars:

For certain undergraduates who have taken developmental psychology or educational psychology the following graduate seminar is open upon the consent of the instructor with the permission of the student's Class Dean and the Dean of The Graduate School of Arts and Sciences:

Critical Issues in Human Development: Mr. Snyder.

Teaching Certification:

Requirements for the state certificate to teach in the public secondary schools can be met by the appropriate selection of courses in this Department and in the major field or fields. Though each state has its own requirements, most follow the same pattern, namely the Bachelor of Arts degree with emphasis upon a content area offered in the secondary school plus professional preparation for teaching. At Bryn Mawr the suggested sequence includes Psychology 101 followed by Education 101b, 201a and 102b or 206a or 206b. Required of all is Education 301a.

English

Professors: Robert B. Burlin, PH.D.
K. Laurence Stapleton, A.B.*

Professor of English and Performing Arts: Robert H. Butman, M.A.

Associate Professors: Carol L. Bernstein, PH.D.
Thomas H. Jackson, PH.D.
Joseph E. Kramer, PH.D., *Chairman*

Katharine E. McBride Visiting Associate Professor: Georgia Christopher, PH.D.

Assistant Professors: Sandra M. Berwind, PH.D.‡
Peter M. Briggs, PH.D.
Katrin Ristkok Burlin, PH.D.
Susan Dean, PH.D.
Stephen Goodwin, M.A.‡
E. Jane Hedley, PH.D.
Eileen Tess Johnston, PH.D.
Anne Kaier, PH.D.
Annette Niemtzow, PH.D.

Lecturers: Diane Balestri, PH.D., *Dean of Class of 1981*
Victory V. Chase, M.A.
Christina Gillis, PH.D.
Christopher Davis, A.B.
Susan J. Hilligoss, M.A.
Constance Jordan, PH.D., *Andrew W. Mellon Post-Doctoral Fellow*
Ramona T. Livingston, A.B.

The Department offers an opportunity to explore all periods of English literature. Through comprehensive reading as well as close analysis, the major in English seeks to develop an historical perspective, critical and writing abilities and an understanding of the imaginative process.

Requirements in the Major Subject: Prerequisite: English 101a and b (Bryn Mawr or Haverford) or its equivalent. Four second-year or advanced units in English literature. At least one full unit must be at an advanced (300) level.

---

*On leave, semester I.
‡On leave for the year 1977-78.

At least one half-unit must be in the literature of the Middle Ages. Students may in consultation with their departmental advisors offer no more than one half-unit of advanced fiction writing or verse composition toward fulfillment of the four-unit requirement. Students may in consultation with their departmental advisors take a portion of their work at Haverford. The Senior Conference.

Allied Subjects: Majors are urged to build a strong ally in classical or modern literature, History, Philosophy or History of Art. Other courses in Music, History of Religion, Political Science, Sociology and Linguistics may also be counted. A second-year writing course may be substituted for one unit of allied work.

Students contemplating graduate work in English are reminded that most graduate schools require a reading knowledge of French and German, and frequently Latin as well, for the Ph.D.

015. *English Composition and Reading:* Members of the Department.

Training in writing discursive prose, with emphasis on the critical analysis of a few works by selected authors. There will be weekly papers, two class meetings a week and regular conferences. Brief descriptions of the topics and reading lists for 1977-78 will be sent to each student in May, to allow her to indicate her preference. (Note: there is one division of this course, called "Readings in English Literature," which may be substituted for the prerequisite to the English major. In this division there will be three class meetings a week, as well as more reading. The paper requirements are the same as for the other divisions.)

WRITING COURSES

Weekly papers are required in the following courses. Students who cannot meet this requirement should not elect any of these courses.

190a. *Introduction to Creative Writing:* Mrs. Walker (at Haverford).
& b.

[191b. *Prose Writing:* Mr. Goodwin.]

192a. *Fiction Writing:* Mr. Davis.

Class discussion, reading and writing assignments are designed to introduce students to the techniques of prose fiction. Weekly papers are required.

193b. *Advanced Fiction Writing:* Mr. Davis.

The writing of at least two extended pieces of short fiction. Student writing and some assigned texts will be discussed in class. Prerequisites: English 190a and b, or 192a. All students must submit a portfolio of writing for admission to this course.

Verse Composition: Miss Stapleton.

Playwrighting and Production: Mr. Butman.
　Writing of two original one-act plays.

* *Advanced Playwrighting and Production:* Mr. Butman.
　Writing of a full-length play and preparation of its production-book. Prerequisite: permission of instructor.

Projects in Writing: Mr. Goodwin.]

LITERATURE

Major Works in English Literature: Members of the Bryn Mawr and Haverford Departments.
　This prerequisite to the English major, taught jointly at Haverford and Bryn Mawr, is the critical study, in chronological sequence, of major works by major authors, including Chaucer, Spenser, Shakespeare, Milton, Pope and Wordsworth, and one other major work. The emphasis will be on close reading and on the continuity of traditions and modes in English and American literature.

Chaucer and His Contemporaries: Mr. Burlin, Miss Malard (at Haverford).
　The first semester will be devoted to a close reading of the *Canterbury Tales.* Prerequisite: English 101a.
　The second semester will concentrate upon Chaucer's early poems and the *Troilus,* with supplementary readings from the Middle English period.

Medieval Narrative: From Beowulf to Malory: Mr. Burlin.]

Literature of the English Renaissance: Mr. Satterthwaite (at Haverford).

Renaissance Lyric Poetry: Mrs. Hedley.
　Close reading of individual poems and sonnet sequences will illuminate the development of lyric poetry through the Renaissance. Wyatt, Sidney, Shakespeare, and Donne will receive primary emphasis.

Shakespeare: Miss Malard (at Haverford), Mr. Kramer.
　The first semester will be devoted to the histories and comedies; the second semester to the tragedies and romances.

Modern Drama: Mr. Kramer.]

233a. *Age of Milton:* Mr. Rose (at Haverford).

240a. *Restoration and Early Eighteenth-Century Literature:* Mr. Briggs.

Developments to be examined in the first semester include the rise of new literary genres and the contemporary effort to find new definitions of heroism and wit, good taste and good manners, sin and salvation. Principal readings will be drawn from Dryden, the Restoration dramatists, Swift and Pope.

[247b. *Eighteenth-Century English Novel:* Mrs. Burlin.]

[250a. *Nineteenth-Century English Poetry:* Mrs. Johnston.]
& b.

252a. *The Romantic Movement:* Miss Kaier.

Studies in the poetry and prose of Byron, Shelley, Hazlitt, and Keats.

254a. *Victorian Period:* Mr. Lester (at Haverford).

256b. *Hopkins and Swinburne:* Mr. Satterthwaite (at Haverford).

258b. *Development of the Novel:* Mr. Lester (at Haverford).

259a. *Nineteenth-Century English Novel:* Mrs. Burlin.

The study of selected novels in the context of relevant nineteenth century intellectual trends and critical approaches: Austen, Dickens, Thackeray, Charlotte and Emily Brontë, Trollope, Eliot.

260a. *American Literature to 1915:* Mr. Ransom (at Haverford).
& b.

261a. *Black American Literature:* (at Haverford).
& b.

264b. *American Literature from 1915 to the Present:* Mrs. Dean

Selected writers of prose, drama, and poetry with attention to their development of new themes and techniques for the twentieth century. Authors will include S. Anderson, Fitzgerald, Hemingway, Faulkner, O'Neill, Pound, H. Crane, Stevens, Williams.

265a. *American Studies:* Mr. Ashmead (at Haverford).
& b.

267a. *Introduction to American Folklore:* Mr. Ashmead (at Haverford).

[268b. *Modern Short Fiction:* Mr. Goodwin.]

270a. *Twentieth-Century Literature:* Mr. Jackson.
& b. Twentieth-century literature in its relationship to earlier literary and

intellectual traditions, principal themes and technical achievements, seen through extensive study of selected major twentieth-century writers.

Post-Colonial Fiction in English: Mr. Jackson.]

Tragedy: Miss Malard (at Haverford).

Comedy: Mr. Rose (at Haverford).

The Lyric: Mrs. Johnston.

Instruction in the techniques (tropological, rhetorical, formal and prosodic) by which poetry expresses its meaning. There will be some discussion of critical theory, but most of the time will be devoted to practical analysis of short poems from different periods.

The Language of Drama: Mr. Burlin.

A look at dramatic language and plays "about" language. Readings from the English drama of the past four centuries.

The Nineteenth-Century Urban Novel: Mrs. Bernstein

A study of the novels of Victorian cities with attention to the themes, characters, symbols and plots which arise from the urban milieu. Authors will include Dickens, James, Gissing, Gaskell, Trollope, Conrad.

The following courses are open primarily to advanced students; enrollment will be restricted at the discretion of the instructor.

Old English Literature: Mr. Burlin.]

Readings in Middle English Literature: Mr. Burlin.

Medieval Topics: Miss Malard (at Haverford).

Renaissance Topics: Mr. Satterthwaite (at Haverford).

Sixteenth-Century Chivalric Romance: Mrs. Hedley.]

English Drama to 1642. Mr. Kramer.]

Renaissance English Tragedy: Mr. Kramer.

Specimen tragedies of Marlowe, Chapman, Jonson, Webster, Middleton, Tourneur, Ford, and Shirley will be read closely in the context of theatrical developments from 1560-1642.

Shakespearean Topics: Mr. Satterthwaite (at Haverford).

Theatre of Ben Jonson: Mr. Kramer.]

83

330a. *The Seventeenth Century:* Miss Christopher.

Cultural currents of the seventeenth century: Donne to Bunyan, with emphasis upon the poetry of the period.

352b. *Romantic Poetry and Prose:* Miss Kaier.

A study of major works by Coleridge, Wordsworth, Byron, Shelley, Hazlitt and Keats. The course will focus on several central Romantic concerns: the nature of the creative mind; poems about the poet and the factors which foster or impair the growth or exercise of poetic genius; aims for the social, moral and aesthetic effects of poetry on the reader. Prerequisite: permission of instructor.

[355b. *Major Victorian Poetry:* Mrs. Johnston.]

356a. *Victorian Literature and the Religious Experience:* Mrs. Johnston.

The course aims to study, in the context of cultural and literary history, the dialectic of faith and doubt in the minds of many Victorian writers. It will address the problems of how religious questions (both personal dilemmas and public controversies), ideas, values and paradigms of experience informed the authors' literary choices about genre, structure, point of view, characterization, imagery, and style. The primary readings will include crisis autobiographies, lyric poems, dramatic monologues, polemical and theoretical writings, and popular and serious novels.

358a. *Jane Austen:* Mrs. Burlin.

An examination of Jane Austen's development as a novelist and critic. Students will be expected to familiarize themselves with relevant earlier fiction. Some attention will be paid to Austen's influence on later fiction, particularly on that of women writers.

358b. *"Women of Talent":* Mrs. Burlin.

Selected novels of female writers from the eighteenth to the twentieth centuries.

364b. *T. S. Eliot:* Mr. Rose (at Haverford).

365a. *American Autobiography:* Miss Niemtzow.

A study of selected texts in the genre, from the Puritans to the present.

365b. *The American Dream:* Miss Niemtzow.

Political, social, and economic visions of America based on a selection of literature from the Puritans to the present.

366a. *American Poetry since 1945:* Mr. Ransom (at Haverford).

368a. *American Literary Utopias:* Mr. Ashmead (at Haverford).

The Development of Modern Poetry: Mr. Jackson.]

James Joyce: Mr. Lester (at Haverford).

William Butler Yeats: Mrs. Berwind.]

The Theory of Fiction: Mrs. Bernstein.

The study of several theories of fiction in historical, conceptual and systematic contexts. After an examination of ideas of fiction as they appear from the eighteenth century to the early modern period, there will be an intensive scrutiny of the meaning and function of such central conceptions as character, plot and style. The course will then focus on major theories ranging from the structural to the sociological. Three novels will be included in the readings.

Problems in Satire: Mr. Briggs.

A review of major developments in English satire since 1600 and simultaneously an exploration of traditional problem areas: the persona; social, moral and literary decorum; the limits of satiric metaphor and satire itself; form, mock-form and the tendency of satire to invade prevailing literary types. Major readings from Donne, Swift, Pope, Sterne, Blake, Byron and selected modern satirists.

Literary Theory and Criticism: Mr. Rose (at Haverford).

Modern Poetic Theory: Mr. Jackson.

Theories of poetry and criticism since Imagism and their background in the late nineteenth century. Pater, the Decadents, Pound, Hulme, and Eliot are among the writers to be covered; in addition, some coverage of more recent theories, e.g. structuralism.

Studies in Twentieth-Century Criticism: Mr. Jackson.]

The Realistic Mode: Miss Jordan.

See Interdepartmental Courses.

The Pastoral: Miss Jordan

See Interdepartmental Courses.

The Idea of Imitation in Renaissance Literature: Miss Jordan.

See Interdepartmental Courses.

Senior Conference:

a: Mr. Burlin, Mrs. Hedley; b: Mr. Briggs, Mr. Kramer.

The Senior Conference will continue for the entire year and will focus upon a core of reading, determined in advance by the two instructors for

85

each semester. The reading will consist of substantial and significant works drawn from all periods of English and American literature, ranging from the late medieval period to the modern.

Majors in English will be expected to know the works in advance—either through course work or summer reading. The conferences will consider kinds of critical approaches to these works and will demand of the students further reading, as well as responsible participation. A work may be considered in its historical context (political, philosophical, occasional background); in the context of other works by the author (for both thematic and formal comparison); in the context of other works of the same period and, for structural and generic studies, in the context of the entire spectrum of English and American literature. Concurrently the student will become acquainted with examples of practical and theoretical criticism which exemplify these various approaches.

At the end of the year the students will be examined by a committee of four members of the Department who are not involved in supervision of the conference. The student may elect either a four-hour written examination or a fifty-minute oral. The examination will allow for many kinds of exemplification as well as intelligent use of supplementary and secondary reading. The grade for the year will be determined by the Examination Committee in consultation with the conference instructors.

Honors Work:

In the senior year, Honors work, consisting of independent reading, reports and conferences, is offered to students of marked ability. Honors papers are due on the Friday two weeks before the end of classes.

Students wishing to continue work in English at Bryn Mawr in order to obtain a Master of Arts degree may, with the permission of the Department, begin research toward a Master's paper during the senior year in place of an honors unit. It is hoped that the paper can be completed, along with the required three graduate units and examination, during a year of graduate study, thereby making possible the conferral of the M.A. degree in the year following the B.A. In exceptional cases, students accelerating or transferring to Bryn Mawr who complete undergraduate requirements before the end of the senior year may petition to be admitted to graduate courses before the conferral of the B.A. degree.

Teaching Certification:

A sequence of work offered by the Department of English and the Department of Education of the College leads to a certificate to teach in the secondary schools of Pennsylvania.

French

Professors: Gérard Defaux, D. ès L., *Chairman*
Michel Guggenheim, PH.D.
Pauline Jones, PH.D.
Mario Maurin, PH.D.

Visiting Professors: Marcel Gutwirth, PH.D.
Madelyn Gutwirth, PH.D.

Associate Professor: Catherine Lafarge, PH.D.

Assistant Professors: Margaret Simpson Maurin, PH.D.
Grace Armstrong Savage, PH.D.‡

Lecturer: Frances Stokes Hoekstra, PH.D.

Instructor: Colette Hall, M.A.

Assistant: Michèle Mallet, M.A.

The major in French includes work in both literature and language. In the first year students are introduced to the study of French literature, and special attention is given to the speaking and writing of French. Second-year courses treat French literature from the beginning to the present day. In these courses, students whose command of written French is inadequate will be expected to attend regular sessions devoted to special training in writing French. A second-year half-course is devoted to advanced language training, with practice in spoken as well as in written French.

Advanced courses offer detailed study of individual authors, genres and movements. Students are admitted to advanced courses after satisfactory completion of two semesters of 200-level courses in French literature or by placement test and permission of Department.

Students in all courses are encouraged to make use of the Language Laboratory. In French 001, 002 and 205c, the use of the Laboratory and intensive oral practice in small groups directed by a Department assistant form an integral part of the course. French majors find it valuable to supplement the work done at Bryn Mawr by study abroad either during

---

‡On leave for the year 1977-78.

the summer at the *Institut* in Avignon or by study abroad during the sophomore or junior year. Residence in French House for at least one year is advisable.

Requirements in the Major Subject: French 101, French 205c, four semesters of 200-level literature courses, two semesters of advanced literature courses and the Senior Conference. Students whose preparation for college has included advanced work in language and literature may, with consent of the Department, substitute a more advanced course for French 101. Occasionally, students may be admitted to seminars in the Graduate School. Such arrangements are made at the suggestion of the Department, with the approval of the Dean of The Graduate School of Arts and Sciences.

All French majors are expected to have acquired fluency in the French language, both written and oral. Unless specifically exempted by the Department, they are required to take French 205c.

Allied Subjects: Any other language or literature, European History, History of Art, Music, Philosophy.

001. *Elementary French:* Members of the Department.

The speaking and understanding of French are emphasized, particularly during the first semester. The work includes regular use of the Language Laboratory and is supplemented by intensive oral practice sessions three or four times a week. The course meets five times a week.

002. *Intermediate French:* Members of the Department.

The emphasis on speaking and understanding French is continued, texts from French literature are read and short papers are written in French. Students are expected to use the Language Laboratory regularly and to attend supplementary oral practice sessions twice a week.

101. *Introduction to Literary Analysis:* Members of the Department.

Presentation of essential problems in literary analysis by close reading of works selected from various periods and genres (drama, poetry, novels and short stories.) Participation in discussion and practice in written and oral expression are emphasized.

201a. *French Literature of the Seventeenth Century:* Mr. Maurin.

The course will cover representative authors and literary movements. Special attention will be given to the concept of the Baroque, the development of Tragedy, and the Age of Classicism.

French Literature of the Eighteenth Century: Miss Lafarge.

The course will include texts representative of the Enlightenment and the Pre-Romantic movement, with emphasis upon the development of liberal thought as illustrated in the *Encyclopédie* and the works of Montesquieu, Voltaire, Diderot and Rousseau.

French Literature of the Nineteenth Century (Novel and Drama): Mr. Guggenheim.

From Chateaubriand and Romanticism to Zola and Naturalism: a study of selected novels and plays.

Nineteenth Century Lyric Poetry: Miss Jones (at Haverford).

· The lyrical rebirth of the nineteenth century: Vigny, Hugo, Baudelaire, Rimbaud, Verlaine, Mallarmé.

French Literature of the Twentieth Century: Mr. Guggenheim, Mr. Maurin.

A study of selected works illustrating the principal literary movements from the turn of the century to the present. Gide, Proust, Valéry, Claudel, Surrealism, Existentialism, the Theater of the Absurd, the New Novel.

French Literature of the Middle Ages: Mrs. Savage.]

French Literature of the Sixteenth Century: Mr. Defaux.]

Stylistique et traduction: Mr. Guggenheim, Miss Jones.

Intensive practice in speaking and writing. Conversation, discussion, advanced training in grammar and stylistics, translation of literary and non-literary texts and original composition. With the addition of a third hour each week, the course may be taken as either 205a or 205b.

La Civilisation française: Mr. Guggenheim, Mrs. Gutwirth.

See INT. 290 in the interdepartmental major in French Studies.

Paris in the Seventeenth and Eighteenth Centuries: Miss Lafarge.]

Littérature, histoire et société de la Renaissance à la Révolution: Mr. Guggenheim.]

Le Seizième Siècle à travers le roman historique: Mr. Salmon.]

French Lyric Poetry.]

Le Roman au XVIIIe siècle: Miss Lafarge.

An in-depth study of works representative of the eighteenth-century

French Novel. Special attention will be given to the memoir-novel (Marivaux and Prévost), the philosophical novel (Diderot and Voltaire) and the epistolary novel (Rousseau, Laclos and Restif de la Bretonne).

[303a. *La Vision de la femme dans la littérature française.*]

[304a. *Ecrivains engagés de Montaigne à Sartre.*]

[304b. *Le Théâtre de 1880 à 1939.*]

[305a. *Baudelaire.*]

[306a. *Le Roman du vingtième siècle.*]

306b: *La Démolition du héros au XVIIe siècle: Pascal, Molière, La Rochefoucauld:* Mr. Defaux.

A study of one of the three main philosophical and ethical currents of the *Grand Siècle* within the framework of the conflict between free will and predestination. Special attention will be given to the influence of the seventeenth-century concept of anti-heroism on such twentieth-century authors as Gide and Sartre.

309a. *Valéry et Sartre:* Mr. Maurin.

A survey of the diverse literary modes tried out by these two writers, with particular emphasis on their elaboration of a critical framework and a concept of literature.

311a. *Advanced Topics in French Literature:* Mr. Cook (at Haverford).

Topic for 1977-78: Gide, Mauriac, Bernanos. Catholic and Protestant views of personal religious crises and sainthood—a close study of selected novels of A. Gide, F. Mauriac and G. Bernanos.

311b. *Advanced Topics in French Literature:* Mr. Gutwirth.

Topic for 1977-78: To be announced.

399. *Senior Conference:* Mr. Gutwirth, Mr. Guggenheim.

A weekly seminar on representative works of French literature followed at the end of the year by an oral explication of a French literary text and a three-hour written examination.

401. *Honors Work:*

On the recommendation of the Department, students in their senior year will be admitted to Honors work consisting of independent reading, conferences and a long paper.

Interdepartmental Work:

The Department of French participates in the interdepartmental majors in French Studies and The Growth and Structure of Cities. See pages 153 and 155.

Junior Year Abroad:

Students majoring in French may, by a join recommendation of the Dean of the College and the Department of French, be allowed to spend their junior year in France under one of the junior year plans, such as those organized by Barnard and Columbia, Hamilton, Hood, Sarah Lawrence, Smith, Swarthmore and Sweet Briar Colleges, New York University, Vanderbilt University, University of Vermont or L'Académie.

Summer Study:

Students wishing to enroll in a summer program may apply for admission to the *Institut d'Etudes française d'Avignon,* held under the auspices of Bryn Mawr. The *Institut* is designed for selected undergraduates and graduate students with a serious interest in French culture, most particularly for those who anticipate professional careers requiring a knowledge of the language and civilization of France. The curriculum includes general and advanced courses in Frednch language, literature, social sciences, history and art. The program is open to students of high academic achievement who have completed a course in French at the third-year level, or the equivalent.

Teaching Certification:

A sequence of work offered by the Department of French and the Department of Education of the College leads to a certificate to teach in the secondary schools of Pennsylvania.

Geology

Associate Professors: Maria Luisa B. Crawford, PH.D, *Chairman*
William A. Crawford, PH.D.
Lucian B. Platt, PH.D.
William Bruce Saunders, PH.D.*

Assistant Professor: George C. Stephens, PH.D.

Instructor: Robert G. Eby B.S.

---

*On leave, semester I

Assistants: Susan Hardee, B.S.
Virginia M. Sague, B.A.
Roger Stoffregen, B.A.
Thomas R. Watters, B.S.

The Department seeks to make students more aware of the physical world around them. The subject includes a study of the materials of which the world is made, of the physical processes which have formed the earth, especially near the surface, of the history of the earth and its organisms and of the various techniques necessary to investigate earth processes and history. Geology borrows widely from its sister sciences, combining many disciplines into an attack on the problem of the earth itself. An essential part of any geologic training lies outside the classroom, in field work.

Requirements in the Major Subject: Geology 101a and b, 201a and b, 202a, 204b, one advanced unit, the Senior Conference, and one full-year course in two of the following departments: Chemistry, Mathematics, Physics. Students may meet some of the major and allied requirements by advanced standing or placement examinations. A student who wishes to follow a career in geology should plan to attend a summer field course, usually following the junior year. A third course from one of the allied subjects is also strongly recommended.

Allied Subjects: Biology, Chemistry, Physics, Mathematics, Statistics; Astronomy, Anthropology, Archaeology, or Economics are accepted in special cases.

101a. *Physical Geology:* Members of the Department.
A study of materials and structures of the earth; surface and near-surface processes such as the action of streams, glaciers and volcanoes and of the features to which they give rise. Three lectures, three hours of laboratory or field work a week, plus a one-day field trip on a Saturday.

101b. *Historical Geology:* Members of the Department.
The history of the earth from its beginning and the evolution of the living forms which have populated it. Three lectures, three hours of laboratory or field work a week. A three-day field trip is taken in the spring. Prerequisite: Geology 101a or its equivalent.

201a. *Crystallography and Mineralogy:* Mrs. Crawford.
The study of geometrical crystallography and crystal chemistry; de-

scriptive and determinative mineralogy. The emphasis is on the relation between the physical properties of crystalline substances and their structures and chemical constitution. Three lectures, four hours of laboratory a week. Prerequisite: Geology 101a and b or permission of instructor.

Optical Mineralogy and Mineral Paragenesis: Mrs. Crawford, Mr. Crawford.

Further work on determinative mineralogy, emphasizing the use of the petrographic microscope. The occurrence and typical associations of minerals. Three lectures, four hours of laboratory a week. Prerequisite: Geology 201a.

Invertebrate Paleontology: Mr. Eby.

A systematic survey of animal groups in geologic time, with emphasis on their morphology, ecology and evolution. Three lectures, three hours of laboratory a week. Prerequisite: Geology 101a and b or permission of instructor.

Structural Geology: Mr. Platt.

Recognition and description of deformed rocks; introduction to mechanics and patterns of deformation. Three lectures and three hours of laboratory or field work a week. Prerequisite: Geology 101a and b or permission of instructor.

Introduction to Geochemistry: Mr. Crawford.]

Stratigraphy: Mr. Platt.

Principles, theory, and criteria for recognition of processes of formation of sedimentary rocks. Environments of deposition, basic stratigraphic relations, and interpretations of specific lithotopes. Three lectures a week, field trips. Prerequisite: Geology 202a.

Oceanography: Mr. Eby.

A study of the geological, biological, chemical and physical characteristics of the oceans and how these characteristics interact. Three lectures a week. Prerequisites: Geology 101a and b or permission of the instructor.

Environmental Geology: Mr. Stephens.

Study and evaluation of geological processes as they relate to mineral resource use and conservation, land-use planning and urbanization. Three lectures, three hours of laboratory or field work a week. Prerequisite: Geology 101a or permission of instructor.

Advanced Paleontology: Mr. Saunders.

Principles, theory and application of various aspects of paleontology such as evolution of interest. Three lectures, three hours of laboratory a week (with occasional augmentation by field work). Prerequisite: Geology 202a or permission of instructor.

303a. *Thermodynamics for Geologists:* Mr. Crawford.

An elementary treatment of thermodynamics and phase diagrams as applied to geological systems. The laboratory consists of determination of thermodynamic properties, phase equilibria experiments and familiarization with basic electronics as applied to laboratory apparatus. Three lectures and three hours of laboratory a week. Prerequisites: Geology 101a and b, Geology 201a and b, Chemistry 101 or permission of instructor.

[303b. *Geochemistry:* Mr. Crawford.]

304. *Introduction to Petrology:* Mr. Crawford, Mrs. Crawford.

The origin, mode of occurrence and distribution of igneous, metamorphic and sedimentary rocks. The laboratory emphasizes hand-specimen and microscopic petrography and will include some field projects. Three lectures, three hours of laboratory a week. Prerequisites: Geology 101 and 201.

305b. *X-ray Crystallography:* Mrs. Crawford.

An introduction to the elements of x-ray crystallography including the geometry of crystals, the physics of x-rays and how x-rays interact with crystalline matter. The laboratory covers the study of powder and single crystal x-ray diffraction. Two lectures, four hours of laboratory a week. Prerequisite: any 101 science.

307a. *Principles of Economic Geology:* Mr. Stephens.

An introduction to the formation, localization and exploitation of metallic mineral deposits. Three lectures, three hours of laboratory a week. Prerequisite: Geology 101a and b, 201a or permission of instructor.

307b. *Introduction to Geophysics:* Mr. Stephens.

A survey of geophysical principles and techniques including magnetic, gravity, seismic and electrical methods. Three lectures and three hours of laboratory a week. Prerequisite: Geology 101a and b or permission of instructor.

399. *Senior Conference* shall consist of:

1. "Topics in Geology," led by members of the Department.

2. A written report on an independent project in the field, laboratory or library.

401. *Honors Work:*

Qualified students are admitted to Honors Work on the recommendation of the Department. This consists of one unit of field or laboratory work on a independent research problem.

Selected Graduate Courses:

Certain graduate courses are open to properly trained undergraduates with the approval of the student's Class Dean and the Dean of The Graduate School of Arts and Sciences.

German

Professor: Hans Bänziger, PH.D.*

Associate Professors: Nancy C. Dorian, PH.D., *Acting Chairman*
Gloria Flaherty, PH.D.‡
Stephen Jaeger, PH.D.

Lecturers: Susan Joan Erickson, M.A.
Jutta Ramin, PH.D.

Assistant: Susan W. Groff, M.A.

The purpose of the major in German is to lay the foundation for an understanding and appreciation of German culture through its literature and language. Students may elect to concentrate on the German language or on German literature during their major program. The former program includes an introduction to applied German linguistics, Middle High German and Germanic philology. The latter program concentrates on important epochs and genres of literature in the German-speaking lands. A broad base for students in both options is attained through a common core of courses. All German majors are expected to acquire fluency in the German language both written and oral. They are encour-

---

*On leave, semester I.
‡On leave for the year 1977-78.

aged to gain supplementary exposure to the German language through residence in the German House or by study abroad during the summer or the junior year or both.

The German departments of Bryn Mawr College and Haverford College cooperate to offer the widest possible range of courses to students of both colleges. Haverford German courses conducted in German are applicable to the Bryn Mawr German major.

Requirements in the Major Subject: The normal course sequence for the major is German 101, 201a or b, 202a and b and at least two other units at the 300-level. The Senior Conference is also required. Special consideration is given to students who have supplemented their linguistic training as outlined above.

Allied Subjects: Any language or literature, History, Political Science, Philosophy, Music, History of Art, History of Science. While undergraduate German majors are not required to learn a foreign language besides German, the German Department urges them to do so, particularly those students who plan to continue their studies at the graduate level.

001. *Elementary German:* Members of the Department.

The course offers the foundation of the language with emphasis on the four basic skills: reading, writing, listening and speaking. Increased importance is given to reading as the course progresses.

002. *Intermediate German:* Members of the Department.

Thorough review of grammar, exercises in composition, oral practice and specially selected readings for students who have had the equivalent of two years of high school German and for those who are not adequately prepared to take German 101.

101. *Readings in German Literature:* Members of the Department.

Thorough review of grammar with continued practice in speaking and writing. Reading and discussion of selected works of German literature, including poetry, *novellas* and drama.

201a. *Advanced Training in the German Language:* Mr. Cary (at Haverford)
& b. and Mr. Bänziger.

First semester at Haverford. Advanced training in grammar, speaking and writing; stylistic exercises; reading of non-fictional material; oral reports and discussions; compositions.

Goethe and Schiller: Miss Ramin.

Representative works will be read and examined closely. Special attention will be given to their historical and aesthetic backgrounds as well as to their position in the history of German literature.

Romanticism: Miss Ramin.

A study of works by Novalis, Tieck, Kleist, Hoffman, Brentano and Eichendorff with emphasis on their relationship to the major artistic, intellectual and social trends of the time.

Germanic Mythology: Mr. Jaeger.

The culture, religion and mythology of the Germanic peoples before and during the conversion to Christianity. Reading of the Eddas, some epics and historical sources. (In English.)

A Survey of German Literature: Mr. Bänziger.]

History of the German Language: Miss Dorian.

History of the German language from its Indo-European origin to its modern dialects.

Vernacular Literature in Medieval Germany: Mr. Jaeger.]

Modern German Prose: Mr. Bänziger.]

The German "Novelle": Miss Erickson.

The theory and practice of this literary genre and its relationship to 19th-century German culture.

Modern German Drama: Mr. Bänziger.

Trends in German drama from Hofmannsthal to Handke; discussion of the most important modern plays, among them those of Brecht and Dürrenmatt.

The Literature of Reformation: Mr. Jaeger.]

Introduction to Middle High German: Mr. Jaeger.

The language of the courtly literature of Germany in the high Middle Ages. Readings from *Das Nibelungenlied, Tristan und Isolde, Parzival,* the lyric of Minnesang.

Lessing and the Enlightenment: Miss Flaherty.]

German Lyric Poetry: Mr. Elmore (at Haverford).

Advanced Topics in German Literature: Mr. Cary (at Haverford).

399. *Senior Conference:* Members of the Department.

All senior majors are to participate in weekly conferences on selected works, topics and problems directly related to the study of German literature, language and culture. They will be required to submit papers or problem-sets to each of the instructors conducting each of the mini-mesters into which the two semesters will be divided. The material covered in Senior Conference will be tested either in individual units or with a comprehensive examination.

401. *Honors Work:*

On recommendation of the Department, students in the senior year will be admitted to Honors work consisting of independent reading, conferences and a substantial paper.

Teaching Certification:

A sequence of work offered by the Department of German and the Department of Education of the College leads to a certificate to teach in the secondary schools of Pennsylvania.

Greek

Professor: Mabel Louise Lang, PH.D., *Chairman*

Associate Professors: Gregory W. Dickerson, PH.D.
    Richard Hamilton, PH.D.

Lecturer: Neil Forsyth, PH.D., *Andrew W. Mellon Post-Doctoral Fellow*

The courses in language and literature are designed to acquaint the students with the various aspects of ancient Greek culture through a mastery of the Greek language and a comprehension of Greek mythology, religion and the other basic forms of expression through which that culture developed. The works of poets, philosophers and historians are studied both in their historical context and in relation to subsequent Western thought.

Requirements in the Major Subject: 001, 101a, 201a and b, 301a and b, one other half-unit course and the Senior Conference. Prospective majors in Greek are advised to take Greek 001 in the freshman year.

Allied Subjects: Ancient History, Classical Archaeology, History of Art, History of Religion, any language, Philosophy.

Elementary Greek: Miss Lang.

Semester I: elements of grammar, prose composition, readings from ancient authors and the *New Testament.* Semester II: Plato's *Apology* and *Crito*; sight readings in class from Euripides' *Cyclops.*

Herodotus: Mr. Dickerson.

After a review of Attic Greek with Lucian the reading is Book VI of Herodotus' *History*; prose composition is required.

Tragedy I: Mr. Hamilton.

Euripides' *Alcestis* and Sophocles' *Antigone*; a critical literary paper is required.

Plato and Thucydides: Mr. Hamilton.

The *Symposium* and an abridged version of the history of the Sicilian Expedition, with required prose composition.

Tragedy II: Mr. Dickerson.

Euripides' *Bacchae*, Sophocles' *Oedipus Rex* and Aristotle's *Poetics*; a critical literary essay is required.

Homer: Mr. Forsyth.

Several books of the *Odyssey* are read and verse composition is attempted. A short essay is required.

Greek Literature in Translation.}

Greek Literature in Translation.}

Myth in Practice and Theory: Miss Lang.

See Interdepartmental course 213a.

Development of Greek Tragedy: Mr. Hamilton.

Various approaches will be examined and major developments traced in the works of Aeschylus, Sophocles and Euripides (in translation).

Hesiod and the Lyric Poets: Mr. Hamilton.

The Works and Days, and early elegiac and lyric poetry, including the odes of Pindar.

301b.   *Aeschylus and Aristophanes:* Mr. Dickerson.
      Aeschylus' *Agamemnon* and Aristophanes' *Frogs.*

[303a.   *Advanced Prose Reading.*]

360a.*   *Forms of the Epic:* Mr. Forsyth.
(INT.)   See Interdepartmental course 360a.

399a.   *Senior Conference: Development of Attic Tragedy.* Mr. Dickerson.

399b.   *Iliad and Oral Epic:* Miss Lang.
      By the end of the year all seniors doing their major work in Greek will be required to have completed satisfactorily three examinations: sight translation from Greek to English; Greek Literature and History; and either of the two special fields covered by the Senior Conference.

For work in Greek History see History 205b.

401.   *Honors Work:*
      Honors may be taken by qualified seniors either in conjunction with the advanced course or after its completion.

Interdepartmental Work:
      The Department of Greek participates in the interdepartmental majors in Classical Languages and in Classical Studies. See page 152.

History

Professors: Charles M. Brand, PH.D.
    Arthur P. Dudden, PH.D., *Chairman*
    Mary Maples Dunn, PH.D.†
    Elizabeth Read Foster, PH.D.
    Barbara M. Lane, PH.D.‡
    Jane M. Oppenheimer, PH.D., *History of Science*
    J. H. M. Salmon, M.LITT., LIT.D.
    Alain Silvera, PH.D.‡
    James Tanis, TH.D., *Director of Libraries*

Associate Professor: Phyllis S. Lachs, PH.D., *Associate Dean
of The Graduate School of Arts and Sciences*‡

---

†On leave, semester II.
‡On leave for the year 1977-78.

Assistant Professor: Stephen Poppel, PH.D.

Lecturer: Wendell P. Holbrook, A.B.

Mary Flexner Lecturer in History and Philosophy of Science: Stephen E. Toulmin, PH.D.

Professor of Social Work and Social Research: Milton D. Speizman, PH.D.

Associate Professor of Greek: Gregory W. Dickerson, PH.D.

Associate Professor of Latin: Russell T. Scott, PH.D.

Lecturer in Classical and Near Eastern Archaeology: Maria deJ. Ellis, PH.D.

The history major is designed to enable the student to acquire historical perspective and historical method. Courses stress the development of ideas, cultures and institutions—political, social and economic—rather than the accumulation of data about particular events. Students study some topics and periods intensively in order to learn the use of documentary material and the evaluation of sources. Extensive reading is assigned in all courses to familiarize majors with varied kinds of historical writing and, in most courses, critical or narrative essays are required.

Requirements in the Major Subject: Students are expected to complete four units of history and two units of allied work meaningfully related to the discipline of history. The basic selection of courses is planned in the spring of the sophomore year and depends upon the special interests of each student together with the availability of courses. History 111 will ordinarily be required of all history majors, but it will not satisfy the departmental distribution requirements. A suitable distribution of work in history to be undertaken by history majors should include at least: (1) one European course, (2) one non-European course, (3) one ancient, medieval, or early modern course concentrated before 1789, (4) one modern course concentrated after 1789, (5) one and one-half 300-level courses with one half-unit at least to be taken during the senior year. A particular course may very well satisfy more than one of the above qualifications. History majors will, in addition to the foregoing requirements, participate in the History Senior Conference.

Allied Work: A wide choice is open to majors in history; in general those in modern fields will find courses in the social sciences most suitable, while those in earlier periods may select, with the permission of the department concerned, courses in classical studies, in philosophy and history of art.

Intermediate or advanced courses in literature and in language may also serve to enrich the major offering.

Cooperation with Haverford College: The History departments of Haverford College and Bryn Mawr College have coordinated their course offerings. History 111 is offered jointly by members of both departments; several intermediate courses are given at one College or the other in alternate years. All courses offered by both departments are open to students of both Colleges equally, subject only to the prerequisites stated by individual instructors. Both departments encourage students to avail themselves of the breadth of offerings this arrangement makes possible at both colleges.

111. *Western Civilization:* Members of the two departments.

A Bryn Mawr–Haverford combined course surveying Western European civilization from the fall of Rome to the present. The course deals with both institutional and intellectual currents in the Western tradition. Conferences, discussions and lectures deal with both primary materials and secondary historical accounts. The course is intended for freshmen and sophomores, but one section is designed for upperclassmen.

190. *The Form of the City:* Mr. Thomas.
(INT.)   See INT. 190 in the interdepartmental major in The Growth and Structure of Cities.

{200b. *Urban Society:* Mrs. Lane, Mr. Ross.}
(INT.)

201a. *Medieval England:* Mr. Beckerman (at Haverford).

202. *American History:* Mr. Lane (at Haverford).

203. *Medieval European Civilization:* Mr. Brand.
Western European development from the fall of Rome to about 1350. Economic, institutional and intellectual developments in the major kingdoms of the West and the history of the Latin Church will be included.

{204. *Europe, 1789-1848:* Mr. Silvera.}

205a. *The Ancient Near East:* Mrs. Ellis.
An introduction to the history of the ancient Near East from the beginning of the third millennium B.C. to the rise of the Persian Empire. The sources and nature of the earliest history of Egypt and Mesopotamia; the international developments in Western Asia and Egypt during the

second millennium B.C.; the Dark Ages and survival of traditions in the Near East at the beginning of Greek history.

Ancient Greece.]

Roman History: Mr. Scott.

A study of Rome from the Iron Age to the end of the Republic with special attention to the rise of Rome in Italy, the Hellenistic world and the evolution of the Roman state. Ancient sources, literary and archaeological, are emphasised.

The Roman Empire: Mr. Scott.

Imperial history from the Principate of Augustus to the House of Constantine with particular attention to the evolution of Roman culture as presented in the surviving ancient evidence, literary and archaeological.

Latin America: Colonies and Revolutions: Mrs. Dunn.

The conquest of South America, the transplantation and modification of European institutions, the colonial society, economy, and culture will be studied, followed by the revolutionary movements, and the establishment of new nations.

Byzantine History: Mr. Brand.]

Early American History: Mrs. Dunn.]

The Near East: Mr. Silvera.]

Medieval Mediterranean World: Mr. Brand.]

Renaissance and Reformation: Mr. Salmon.]

American Economic History: Mr. Weinstein (at Haverford).]

Europe since 1848: Mr. Poppel.

The history of Europe from mid-nineteenth century to the present, with special attention to comparative aspects. Topics to be covered include socialism, economic and cultural development, revolution, responses to modernization, war and peace, and fascism. Either semester may be taken for credit, with the approval of the instructor.

The Age of Absolutism: Mr. Spielman (at Haverford).

The Common Law: Mr. Beckerman (at Haverford).

A History of the Afro-American People: Mr. Holbrook.

Concentration is on the experiences, concepts, organizations and struggles of the Black people in the United States, from the commencing of the modern slave trade in the fifteenth century to the present era; attention will be given to the intertwining of this history with United States and world history.

240b. *History and Principles of Quakerism:* Mr. Bronner (at Haverford).

242a. *Early American Diplomatic History:* Mr. Gould (at Haverford).

242b. *American Diplomacy in the Twentieth Century:* Mr. Gould (at Haverford).

245. *Russia in the Twentieth Century:* Mrs. Gerstein (at Haverford).

261. *History of China:* Miss Mihelich (at Haverford).

272b. *Modern Jewish History:* Mr. Poppel.

The history of the Jews in Europe and America since the mid-eighteenth century. Topics to be covered include Hasidism, the Enlightenment, emancipation, assimilation, religious and intellectual modernization, anti-Semitism, migration, nationalism and Zionism.

290. *La Civilisation française:* Mr. Guggenheim, Mrs. Gutwirth.
(INT.) See INT. 290 in the interdepartmental major in French Studies.

300b. *The American City in the Twentieth Century:* Mr. Speizman.
(INT.) See INT. 300b in the interdepartmental major in The Growth and Structure of Cities.

[301a. *Europe in the Twentieth Century:* Mr. Poppel.]

302. *France, 1559-1661:* Mr. Salmon.

The period from the religious wars to the personal rule of Louis XIV is treated as a unity in which revolutionary changes occurred in the structure of French society. These changes are examined in the light of French literature and political thought in the period.

303a. *Topics in the Recent History of the United States:* Mr. Dudden.

Social developments since the late nineteenth century, with the problems peculiar to constructing the history of the recent past. The current focus is on the impact of the Indochina War.

[305a. *The Italian City-State in the Renaissance:* Mrs. Lane.]
(INT.)

[307b. *Medieval Cities: Islamic, Byzantine, and Western:* Mr. Brand.]
(INT.)

308a. *The Jews in the Middle Ages:* Mr. Brand.

The economic, social, and political position of the Jews in the Islamic world, the Byzantine Empire, and Western Europe, from the seventh to the thirteenth centuries. A reading knowledge of *one* foreign language is required.

History of Women in Colonial America: Mrs. Dunn.]

History of Scientific Thought: Miss Oppenheimer.
Changing relationships among developing scientific ideas and other intellectual, cultural and religious traditions.
Semester I: Classical and medieval natural history;
Semester II: The scientific renaissance and modern science.

Topics in Modern British History: Mrs. Lachs.]

Mexico: Independence to the Present: Mrs. Dunn.]

The Rise of the Dutch Republic: Mr. Tanis.
The emphasis will be on politics and religion, Christian divisions and national unity in the Netherlands in the sixteenth century, with attention given also to art, commerce, and culture. A reading knowledge of French or German or Latin is required.

Revolution within the Church: Mr. Tanis.]

Religious Forces in Colonial America: Mr. Tanis.]

Colonial Towns in North and South America: Mrs. Dunn.
A comparative examination of origins of selected towns.

France since 1870: Mr. Silvera.]

A History of Blacks in the American City: Mr. Holbrook.
The early nineteenth-century experiences of slaves and freemen in American cities. A study of successive waves of black migrations which have contributed much to the contemporary American urban demographic pattern. Students will have the opportunity to do research and to write on the history of the black experience in Philadelphia.

West African Leadership: Mr. Holbrook.
The course treats the themes of continuity and the patterns of change in West African leadership from the eleventh century to the present. After a study of leadership in both state and segmentary societies of pre-colonial West Africa, the course continues with readings and research focused upon: chiefs and other traditional leadership under colonialism, nationalists, parliamentary leaders, one-party systems, and military rule.

[339. *The Great Society:* Mr. Dudden.]

340b. *Topics in American History:* Mr. Lane (at Haverford).
Topic for 1977-78: History of the Family. Prerequisite: consent of the instructor.

347b. *Topics in Far Eastern History:* Miss Mihelich (at Haverford).

351a. *Topics in Regional History: The Westward Movement:* Mr. Bronner (at Haverford).

355a. *Topics in Early Modern European History: The Golden Age of Spain:* Mr. Spielman (at Haverford).
Prerequisite: reading knowledge of Spanish.

356b. *Topics in Modern European History:* Mrs. Gerstein (at Haverford).

359a. *Topics in Medieval Social History: The Hundred Years' War:* Mr. Beckerman (at Haverford).

360. *England under the Tudors and Stuarts:* Mrs. Foster.
A study of the life and institutions of the English people, 1509-1714. Students will make extensive use of primary source materials.

[370a. *The Great Powers and the Near East:* Mr. Silvera.]

[375b. *Topics in the Renaissance:* Mr. Salmon.]

380a. *Topics in the Enlightenment:* Miss Oppenheimer.
Scientific and philosophical ideas in the eighteenth century and their interplay with social and political thought. Each year a particular country (chosen by the students enrolled) will be treated in detail in reading and discussion; one long paper will be required.

393b. *Great Britain in the Sixteenth and Seventeenth Centuries:* Mrs. Foster.
(INT.)   Self-portrait of an age. A study of British history, descriptions of England and Englishmen, social criticism, and biographical sketches.

399. *Senior Conference:* Mr. Dudden, Mr. Salmon.
A required seminar for history majors on the History and Philosophy of History, with alternative choices between American and European topics.

401. *Honors Work:*
Honors work in any of the advanced fields is offered for the senior year to any history major who completes her third year with a record of distinction. An essay based on source material must be presented.

403. *Supervised Study:* Members of the Department.
Permission of instructor and Department chairman required.

Interdepartmental Work:

The Department of History participates in the interdepartmental majors in French Studies and The Growth and Structure of Cities and the concentration in Hispanic and Hispanic-American Studies. See pages 153 and 155 and 158.

Teaching Certification:

A sequence of work offered by the Department of History and the Department of Education of the College leads to a certificate to teach in the secondary schools of Pennsylvania. Current requirements call for two and one-half units of allied work in the social sciences.

History of Art

Professors: Charles G. Dempsey, M.F.A., PH.D., *Chairman*
Charles Mitchell, M.A., B.LITT., D.LITT.
James E. Snyder, M.F.A., PH.D.

Assistant Professors: Dale Kinney, PH.D.‡
Steven Z. Levine, PH.D.

Professor of Classical and Near Eastern Archaeology and *of History of Art:* Phyllis Pray Bober, PH.D., *Dean of the Graduate School of Arts and Sciences*

Professor of Fine Art: Fritz Janschka, *Akad. Maler*

Assistants: Perri Lee Roberts, B.A.
Therese Dolan Stamm, M.A

The Department regularly offers an introductory course, a series of general intermediate courses and more concentrated advanced half-courses and instruction on special topics to majors in their senior year. The program is open also to undergraduates of Haverford College.

---

‡On leave for the year 1977-78.

Requirements in the Major Subject: At least four units of course work in art history, normally including History of Art 101 and always one unit of advanced course work, together with the Senior Conference and two units of allied work. Intermediate courses with supplementary work may sometimes be counted as advanced at the discretion of the Department.

Students contemplating a major in History of Art are strongly advised to consult the Department as early as possible in their college careers, especially with regard to language preparation.

Allied Subjects: Archaeology, Greek, Latin, History, modern languages; others in consultation with the Department. Students are especially encouraged to undertake, in consultation with the Department, allied work in modern languages, which are essential for advanced work in History of Art.

101. *Introduction to Art History:* Members of the Department.

The course is designed as an introduction to the methods and scope of history in the field of Western art from medieval to modern times.

{210. *Early Medieval and Byzantine Art:* Mrs. Kinney.}

211. *Art of the Later Middle Ages:* Mr. Snyder.

212. *Renaissance Art:* Mr. Mitchell.

213. *Baroque Art:* Mr. Dempsey.

214. *Modern Art:* Mr. Levine.

321a. *Traditions in Dutch Painting, 1450-1650:* Mr. Snyder.

322b. *Donatello:* Mr. Mitchell.

323b. *Nicolas Poussin:* Mr. Dempsey.

324a. *Problems in Film Theory:* Mr. Levine.

399. *Senior Conference:*

Members of the Department hold regular conferences with senior majors on their special subjects. The evaluation is in three parts, each of three hours:

1. An examination to test knowledge of works of art,
2. A general examination on the history of art,
3. An examination on a special topic.

Honors Work:

Offered to students on invitation of the Department.

FINE ARTS MAJOR PROGRAM

Professor: Fritz Janschka, *Akad. Maler* (Vienna)

At Haverford:

Professor of Fine Arts: Charles Stegeman, *Académie Royale des Beaux-Arts* (Brussels)

Associate Professor of Fine Arts: R. Christopher Cairns, A.B., M.F.A.

The major program in fine art is coordinated with, and complementary to, the fine arts major program at Haverford College, courses on either campus being offered to students of either College with the approval of the respective instructors.

The program is under the direction of the Bryn Mawr Professor of Fine Art, with whom intending fine art majors should plan their major curricula.

Requirements in the Major Subject: At least four units in fine art, which must include Haverford 101, one 300-level course (or an approved Haverford equivalent) and the Senior Conference. Fine art majors must also success-fully take two units of allied work, of which a course in history of art must be one.

Allied Subjects: History of Art, History, classical and modern languages, Mathematics, Chemistry, Physics; others, by exception, in consultation with the Professor of Fine Art.

(For Haverford Fine Arts courses see the Haverford College Catalogue.)

225. *Graphic Arts:* Mr. Janschka.

Intaglio and relief printing; etching, aquatint and soft-ground; drypoint; woodcutting and combined use of various methods. Prerequis-ite: Haverford Fine Arts 101 or proof of adequate previous training in drawing.

335. *Color Lithography:* Mr. Janschka.

An advanced graphic arts course with emphasis on color printing by lithographic processes. Making of editions. Prerequisites: Fine Art 225 or Haverford Fine Arts 231 or 241.

345. *Advanced Drawing:* Mr. Janschka.

Drawing as an independent art form. Line as a dominant composition factor over color. All drawing media and watercolor, tempera and acrylic paints. Prerequisite: Haverford Fine Arts 231 or 241 or Fine Art 225.

399. *Senior Conference:*

Individual or joint approved projects pursued through the year under the direction of the Professor of Fine Art at Bryn Mawr.

401. *Honors Work:*

Suitable fine art majors may be invited by the Professor of Fine Art to present an Honors project. Honors work requires (a) a major project in fine art approved by the Professor of Fine Art, and (b) an extended paper discussing the theoretical, technical and other relevant problems involved in the achievement of the major project. Both the project and the paper will be evaluated by the Professor of Fine Art and a member of the History of Art Department, who may be joined, where it is judged appropriate, by a member of the Fine Arts faculty of Haverford College.

403. *Supervised Project:* Members of the Department.

Permission of instructor and Department chairman required.

Final Examination in the Major Subject: this is in three parts—
1. The presentation of one portfolio of work arising from courses taken in advanced drawing and a second portfolio resulting from work in advanced courses in painting or sculpture or graphics,
2. The formal exhibition of a small selection of advanced works,
3. The presentation of work done in the Senior Conference.

Work presented in the final examination will be judged and graded by a jury consisting of the Professor of Fine Art, members of the Haverford Fine Arts faculty and a member of the History of Art Department.

History of Religion

Professor: Samuel Tobias Lachs, PH.D., *Chairman*

Visiting Professor: Norman Gottwald, PH.D.

Assistant Professor: David Rabi, PH.D.

Visiting Lecturers: Nancy Bancroft, M.A.
  Donald K. Swearer, PH.D.

Roian Fleck Resident-in-Religion: John Drury, M.A.

Director of Libraries and *Professor of History:* James Tanis, TH.D.

The history of religion major concentrates on the historical study of the religious traditions which have contributed most to shaping the culture of the West: the religion of Israel, Rabbinic Judaism and Christianity. The student is expected to achieve facility in critical analysis of the primary sources of these traditions and in tracing their development against the background of the cultural situations in which they arose and matured.

Requirements in the Major Subject: Four full courses in history of religion, of which at least one must be in a tradition other than that of the student's concentration. The Senior Conference is also required.

The normal pattern for the major consists of one introductory course (100 level), two intermediate courses (200 level) and two advanced half-courses or a full-year course (300 level). Students in advanced courses who are majoring in history of religion are required to demonstrate a working knowledge of the language appropriate to their field of concentration: Hebrew for the religion of Israel or Rabbinic Judaism, Greek for New Testament or Early Christianity, Latin for medieval Christianity, German for the Reformed period.

Allied Subjects: Latin and Greek, Philosophy, History, Archaeology, Anthropology.

LANGUAGE COURSES

. *Elementary Hebrew:* Mr. Rabi.

Grammar, composition and conversation with primary emphasis on fluency in reading. Course designed for preparation in reading classical religious texts.

. *Readings in the Hebrew Bible:* Mr. Rabi.

Readings in prose of Genesis. Course will include Hebrew composition, grammar, and conversation based on the Hebrew text.

. *Readings in Rabbinic Literature:* Mr. Lachs.]

. *Readings in the Hebrew Bible:* Mr. Rabi.

The Book of Deuteronomy.

. *Readings in the Greek New Testament.*]

. *Tutorial in Semitic Languages:* Mr. Rabi.

HISTORY OF RELIGION COURSES

103a. *History and Literature of the Bible:* Mr. Gottwald.
& b.   a. A study of the history of Israel and its sacred literature against the background of the ancient Near East, the development of the legal, prophetic and wisdom traditions.
      b. The beginnings of Christianity, tracing the influences of Judaism and of Hellenistic culture and religion on the life and thought of the New Testament community.

104a. *History and Literature of Judaism:* Mr. Lachs.
& b.   a. Historical study of Judaism from the Exile through the Geonic period, with major focus on the literature.
      b. Modern movements from the French Revolution to the present.

[105b. *Introduction to Asian Religions:* Mr. Swearer (at Swarthmore).]

[106b. *Hinduism and Indian Culture.*]

107a. *Mysticism East and West:* Mr. Swearer.

201b. *Topics in Biblical Literature:* Mr. Gottwald
      1977-1978: Prophecy.

207a. *Jesus and the Gospel Tradition:* Mr. Gottwald.
      The social, cultural and conceptual background of the Gospels, their literary structure and genre.

208b. *Paul and the Rise of Gentile Christianity:* Mr. Gottwald.
      A study of the life and letters of Paul, of the cultural shift of Christianity into the Roman world and of the impact of Paul on the Early Church.

· 210a. *Rabbinic Ethics and Theology:* Mr. Lachs.
      A study of rabbinic concepts of God, Man, Society, and the Law.

213b. *Tradition and Design in Luke-Acts:* Mr. Drury.
      A study of Early Christian historiography.

220b. *Ethics and Society in Christian Perspective:* Miss Bancroft.
      A critical-historical review of changing Christian social thought in the 20th century, emphasizing the thought of Reinhold Niebuhr, Christian socialism, and current liberation theologies.

300a. *Studies in Early Rabbinic and Medieval Judaism:* Mr. Lachs.
& b.   Topic for 1977-78: Sects and Institutions of the Second Commonwealth. Among the subjects to be discussed are Pharisees, Sadducees, Essenes, Synagogue, School, Judicial System.

Religion and Politics in the Hellenistic World: Mr. Gottwald.

Religion and Politics in Judaism and Early Christianity, with special attention to the Maccabean Revolt, the political charges brought against Jesus, and the relation of Judaism and the Early Church to Roman authority down to the time of Constantine.

Myth and History in the Gospel of John.]

Studies in Early Christianity.]

Christianity and Marxism: Miss Bancroft.

An historical study of Marxist social thought and a comparative analysis of Marxist and Christian social thought in the U.S., Europe and Latin America.

Senior Conference:

Consists of a year-long seminar in which the students will be introduced to the major literary materials, secondary sources, reference works and critical issues in the literature of Judaism and Early Christianity during the period approximately 200 B.C. to 200 A.D. In the second semester the students will present to the seminar a report on some theme or problem on which they will have conducted research, based on their ability to handle one or many primary sources in the original language. Staff.

COURSES GIVEN IN THE HISTORY DEPARTMENT

Modern Jewish History: Mr. Poppel.

The Jews in the Middle Ages: Mr. Brand.

The Rise of the Dutch Republic: Mr. Tanis.

COURSES AT SWARTHMORE

Existentialism and Religious Belief: Mr. Urban.]

Religion and Ethics: Mr. Urban.]

Honors Work:

Qualified students are admitted to Honors work on the recommendation of the Department.

Italian

Assistant Professors: Nancy Dersofi, PH.D.
Nicholas Patruno, PH.D., *Director*

The aims of the major are to acquire a knowledge of the Italian language and literature and an understanding of Italian culture and its contribution to Western civilization. Majors in Italian are urged to spend the junior year in Italy or to study in an approved summer school in Italy or in the United States, and they are also encouraged to take advantage of the facilities offered by Italian House.

Requirements in the Major Subject: Italian 102a, 201b, 301, 303a and b and at least one other advanced course. For students who enter the College with Italian, proper substitutions will be made. In all courses students are urged to use tapes available in the Language Laboratory.

Allied Subjects: Any other language or literature, Archaeology, History, History of Art, Philosophy, Music, Political Science; with departmental approval, any other field allied to the student's special interests.

001. *Italian Language:* Mr. Patruno, Miss Dersofi.

A practical knowledge of the language is acquired through hearing, speaking, writing and reading, going from concrete situations to the expression of abstract ideas and with a gradual introduction to the reading of Italian literature.

101. *Intermediate Course in the Italian Language:* Miss Dersofi, Mr. Patruno.

Intensive grammar review, readings from selected Italian authors and topics assigned for composition and discussion. Conducted entirely in Italian.

102a. *Advanced Course in the Italian Language:* Mr. Patruno.

Advanced work in composition and critical examination of literary texts. Prerequisite: permission of the Department, sometimes determined by a brief written examination. This course is recommended for students who wish to continue work in Italian literature.

[201a. *Novel and Poetry of Modern Italy.*]

[204a. *Foscolo, Leopardi and Manzoni.*]

. *Literature of the Nineteenth Century:* Mr. Patruno.

A study of the literary currents following the Romantic movement. Special attention given to *Decadentismo* and *Verismo.*

. *Dante, Petrarch and Boccaccio in Translation.*]

. *Dante.*]

. *Petrarca, Boccaccio and the Early Humanists:* Mr. Patruno.

. *Literature of the Italian Renaissance:* Miss Dersofi.

Selected readings from the works of Poliziano, Lorenzo de'Medici, Castiglione, Machiavelli and Tasso. Special attention will be given to comedy and Ariosto's *Orlando furioso.*

. *Arcadia and Enlightenment:* Miss Dersofi.

An introduction to the *Scienza Nuova* of Vico and a study of plays by Metastasio, Goldoni, Gozzi and Alfieri, Patrini's *Giorno* and opera libretto in the context of eighteenth century social custom and theatrical tradition.

. *History of the Italian Theatre:* Miss Dersofi.]

. *Senior Conference:*

In the first semester weekly meetings devoted to the study of special topics in Italian literature chosen by the students, evaluated by an oral examination in January. In the second semester each senior will prepare under the direction of the instructor a paper on an author or a theme which she has chosen. At the end of the year students must demonstrate knowledge of the development of Italian literature by either an oral or written examination, according to their preference.

. *Honors Work:*

On the recommendation of the Department a student may undertake Honors work in Italian. Students work in a special field adapted to their interest under the direction of the Department.

Latin

Professor: Myra L. Uhlfelder, PH.D.

Associate Professors: Julia H. Gaisser, PH.D.
  Russell T. Scott, PH.D., *Chairman*

Lecturers: Neil Forsyth, PH.D., *Andrew W. Mellon Post-Doctoral Fellow*
  Gloria F. Pinney, PH.D.

The major in Latin is planned to acquaint the student with the world of the Romans and their contribution to the modern world.

Requirements in the Major Subject: Latin 101a and b, 201a and b, 301a and b or 302a and b and the Senior Conference. 203b is a prerequisite for Honors work and required for those who plan to teach.

Courses taken at the Intercollegiate Center for Classical Studies in Rome (see page 55) are accepted as part of the major. For non-majors, Latin 201a and b are prerequisites for 300-level courses.

Allied Subjects: Greek, Hebrew, History, Classical and Near Eastern Archaeology, History of Art, History of Religion, Linguistics, Philosophy, Anthropology, any modern language or literature.

001. *Elementary Latin:* Miss Uhlfelder, Mr. Scott.
      Basic grammar and composition, reading in classical prose and poetry.

002. *Intermediate Latin:* Mrs. Gaisser, Mrs. Pinney.
      Review of grammar with reading in prose and poetry for students who have had two years of Latin in school or do not feel adequately prepared to take Latin 101.

101a. *Latin Literature:* Miss Uhlfelder.
      Selections from Catullus' poems, Vergil's *Eclogues* and readings in prose. Prerequisite: more than two years of Latin in school, Latin 001 or Latin 002.

101b. *Latin Literature:* Mrs. Gaisser.
      Selections from Livy, Book I, and from Horace's *Odes*.

201a. *Horace and Satire:* Mrs. Gaisser.
      Selections from Horace's *Satires* and *Epistles,* the works of Petronius and Juvenal.

Latin Literature of the Silver Age: Mr. Scott.

Readings from major authors of the first and second centuries A.D.

Medieval Latin Literature: Miss Uhlfelder.

Latin Style: Members of the Department.

A study of Latin prose style, based on reading of prose authors and exercises in composition, and of Latin metrics with practice in reading aloud.

The Ancient City: Mr. Scott.]

Latin Literature of the High Middle Ages: Miss Uhlfelder.]

Latin Authors and English Literature: Members of the Department.]

Vergil's Aeneid: Miss Uhlfelder.]

Livy and Tacitus: Mr. Scott.]

Cicero and Caesar: Mr. Scott.

Lucretius: Mrs. Gaisser.

Forms of the Epic: Mr. Forsyth.

See Interdepartmental course 360a.

For Roman history, see History 206a and b.

Senior Conference:

Regular meetings with members of the Department to discuss reading in Latin literature are intended to supplement and synthesize work done in courses. The method of evaluating the work of the conference is determined each year. Majors must pass an examination in Latin sight translation which will be offered in September, February and May.

Honors Work:

Honors work is offered to qualified students in classical or Medieval Latin literature or in Roman history. The results will be presented in a paper directed by a member of the Department.

Interdepartmental Work:

The Department of Latin participates in the interdepartmental majors in Classical Languages, Classical Studies and The Growth and Structure of Cities. See pages 152 and 155.

Teaching Certification:

A sequence of work offered by the Department of Latin and the Department of Education of the College leads to a certificate to teach in the secondary schools of Pennsylvania.

Mathematics

Professors: Frederic Cunningham, Jr., PH.D., *Chairman*
John C. Oxtoby, M.A.

Assistant Professor: Françoise Schremmer, PH.D.‡

Lecturers: Nancy L. Hagelgans, PH.D.
Aigli Papantonopoulou, PH.D.

Assistant: Michael G. Gonzales, A.B.

The major in mathematics is designed to provide a balanced introduction to the subject, emphasizing its nature both as a deductive and as an applied science, at the same time providing the technical foundation for more advanced study.

Requirements in the Major Subject: at least four and one-half units including Mathematics 101, 201a or b, 202b, 301, 303a, or the equivalent. The Senior Conference is also required.

Allied Subjects: Chemistry, Economics, Philosophy, Physics, Psychology.

001a. *Basic Math Skills:* Mrs. Hagelgans and student assistants.
A remedial course designed to overcome deficiencies of background in preparation for college level mathematics courses.

{100a. *Introduction to Automatic Computation.*}

101. *Calculus, with Analytic Geometry:* Mr. Oxtoby, Mrs. Papantonopoulou, Mrs. Hagelgans.
Differentiation and integration of algebraic and elementary transcendental functions, with the necessary elements of analytic geometry and

---

‡On leave for the year 1977-78.

trigonometry; the fundamental theorem, its role in theory and applications.

Methods and Models: Mrs. Hagelgans.

Mathematical concepts, notations and methods commonly used in the social, behavioral and biological sciences, with emphasis on manipulative skills and real problem solving.

Intermediate Calculus and Linear Algebra: Mr. Cunningham.

Vectors, matrices and linear maps, functions of several variables, partial derivatives, multiple integrals.

Intermediate Calculus and Linear Algebra: Mr. Cunningham.

Line integrals, vector analysis, infinite series, Taylor's theorem, differential equations.

Advanced Calculus: Mr. Oxtoby.

The classical theory of real functions, based on a construction of the real number system; elements of set theory and topology; analysis of Riemann integral, power series, Fourier series and other limit processes. Prerequisite: Mathematics 202b.

Introduction to Abstract Algebra: Mrs. Papantonopoulou.

Groups, rings and fields and their morphisms. Prerequisite: Mathematics 201a or b.

Topics in Algebra: Mrs. Papantonopoulou.

Theory of Probability with Applications: Mrs. Hagelgans.

Game Theory.]

Introduction to Applied Mathematics: Mrs. Schremmer.]

Dynamical Systems: Mrs. Schremmer.]

Theory of Functions of a Complex Variable: Mr. Oxtoby.]

Differential Equations: Mrs. Schremmer.]

Topology.]

Real Analysis: Mr. Oxtoby.]

Senior Conference:

Selected topics from various branches of mathematics are studied by means of oral presentations and the solution and discussion of problems.

Honors Work:

Qualified students are admitted to Honors work on recommendation of the Department.

Teaching Certification:

A sequence of work offered by the Department of Mathematics and the Department of Education of the College leads to a certificate to teach in the secondary schools of Pennsylvania.

Music

Professors: Isabelle Cazeaux, PH.D.
  Robert L. Goodale, A.B., B.MUS., A.A.G.O., *Chairman*

Assistant Professor: Carl B. Schmidt, PH.D.

Lecturer: Courtney Adams, PH.D.

Assistant: Janet Balshaw Rodney, B.A.

Director of Chorus and Orchestra: Tamara Brooks, M.S.

The purpose of the music major is to enable the student to appreciate the significance of music from an historical and sociological as well as from an aesthetic point of view and to develop a technique of intelligent listening, a faculty of critical judgment and the ability to use the materials of music as a means of expression for creative talent.

Students in the courses in history and appreciation of music must devote two hours or more a week to listening to recordings.

Students who are sufficiently advanced and who have completed at least one year of voice or music lessons while at the College may, with the approval of the Department, offer for one unit of academic credit a year of voice or instrument lessons. The unit of credit will include the lessons and also a recital or proficiency test arranged by the Department. The unit of credit will count as elective work and will not be counted toward the major.

Requirements in the Major Subject: Music 101, 102, 103c and at least two and one-half units of additional work, at least one of which must be advanced, the selection of courses depending upon the student's desire to specialize in the history and literature of music or the technique of composition. The Senior Conference is also required. A student intending to major in music must have sufficient knowledge of pianoforte or organ playing to enable her to play music of the technical difficulty of a Bach figured chorale. She is strongly urged to be a member of the Chorus or the Orchestra or an ensemble group.

Allied Subjects: History, History of Art, modern languages, English, Greek, Latin, Philosophy, History of Religion.

An Introduction to the History and Appreciation of Music: Members of the Department.

A comprehensive survey, with special emphasis on the technique of intelligent listening.

Music Materials: Mr. Goodale.

A course in the elements of theory. The study of harmony and counterpoint, simple formal analysis and an introduction to orchestration.

Sight Singing and Dictation: Mr. Schmidt.

Prerequisite: The ability to read music and elementary ability at the piano. (Given alternate years.)

Romantic Music: Miss Cazeaux.

An historical treatment of the music of the age with particular attention to certain representative composers.

Advanced Theory and Analysis: Mr. Goodale.

A continuation of Music 102, with emphasis on analysis (harmonic, contrapuntal and formal) of larger forms. Prerequisite: Music 102 or its equivalent.

Studies in Vocal Music of the Nineteenth Century: Mr. Schmidt.]

The Music of Beethoven: Mr. Schmidt.

A survey of the symphonic, chamber, vocal and keyboard music of Beethoven with emphasis on the composer's stylistic growth. Prerequisites: Music 101 or permission of the instructor.

The Operas of Mozart: Mr. Schmidt.

An examination of the various types of opera written by Mozart including such works as *Don Giovanni, Idomeneo, The Magic Flute, The Marriage of Figaro* and *The Abduction from the Seraglio.* Prerequisite: Music 101 or permission of the instructor.

The Symphonic Music of Bruckner, Mahler and R. Strauss: Mr. Schmidt.]

211. *Symphonic Style:* Mrs. Adams.

First semester: A study of the symphonic concept from its origins in the pre-classic writing of Sammartini and K.P.E. Bach through the works of Schumann, Berlioz and Liszt.

Second semester: The development of the symphony from the second half of the 19th century to the present: the compositions of Bruckner, Mahler and others through Ives and Stravinsky. Prerequisite: Music 101 or permission of the instructor.

212a. *The Classic Period:* Mrs. Adams.

An investigation of the keyboard and orchestral styles of Mozart and Haydn in the sonatas, divertimentos, concertos, symphonies and sacred music. Prerequisite: Music 101 or permission of the instructor.

212b. *Studies in Renaissance Music:* Mrs. Adams.

The chanson, mass and motet before and during the period of Josquin des Prez. Earlier composers will include Dufay, Busnois and Ockeghem among others. Prerequisite: Music 101 or permission of the instructor.

301. *Music of the Twentieth Century:* Mr. Goodale.

302a. *Medieval and Early Renaissance Music:* Miss Cazeaux.

302b. *Late Renaissance and Baroque Music:* Miss Cazeaux.

303b. *Orchestration:* Mr. Goodale.

Prerequisites: Music 101, 102 and 202 or their equivalents. Music 202 may be taken concurrently with this course.

305. *Free Composition:* Mr. Goodale.

This course is designed for those students whose chief interest lies in the field of composition. Prerequisite: permission of instructor.

{306b. *Opera and Music Drama:* Miss Cazeaux.}

307a. *Musical Criticism:* Miss Cazeaux.

Prerequisite: Music 101 or its equivalent.

399. *Senior Conference:*

Three conferences dealing with some aspects of the theory and history of music. Students may substitute for one of these a conference in an allied subject. Candidates' understanding of the material may be tested by written assignments, oral reports or other appropriate means.

401. *Honors Work:*

Honors work is offered for students recommended by the Department.

Interdepartmental Work:

The Department of Music participates in the interdepartmental concentration in Hispanic and Hispanic-American Studies. See page 158.

The following organizations, carrying no academic credit, are sponsored by the Department:

The Bryn Mawr-Haverford Chorus. Director is Tamara Brooks. Several major choral works from different periods are offered in concerts during the course of the year.

The Renaissance Choir. Students (and faculty) who are confident sight-readers have the opportunity to perform a cappella music with one or two singers per voice part.

The Orchestra, whose Director is Tamara Brooks, is organized jointly with Haverford College. It plays concerts of its own and frequently joins the Chorus in the presentation of major works.

The ensemble groups are also organized jointly with Haverford College. Students in these groups are afforded the opportunity of studying chamber-music literature at first hand, as well as the experience of playing in public at student recitals.

Lessons in pianoforte, organ and voice may be taken at the student's expense. Lessons in other instruments may be arranged. The Department will be glad to assist in these arrangements.

Philosophy

Professors: José María Ferrater Mora, *Lic Fil*
George L. Kline, PH.D, *Chairman*
Jean A. Potter, PH.D.
Isabel Scribner Stearns, PH.D.

Associate Professors: Michael Krausz, PH.D.‡
Mary Patterson McPherson, PH.D., *Dean of the College*
George E. Weaver, Jr., PH.D.*

---

‡On leave for the year 1977-78.

*On leave, semester I.

Assistant Professors: Richard Gaskins, PH.D., J.D.
Tracy Marie Taft, PH.D.

Lecturer: Thomas Song, M.A., M.A.L.S., *Associate Director of Libraries*

Assistants: Walter Lammi, M.A.
Christine Skarda, B.A.

The philosophy curriculum is organized into four divisions: Core, Metaphysics–Epistemology, Value Theory, and Persons–Periods. Courses in the Core Division are intended to provide students with a common background in philosophical problems, concepts and argumentation. Broadly, the Metaphysics–Epistemology Division is concerned with what there is and the basis for our knowledge; the Value Theory Division is concerned with the nature of evaluative concepts such as Goodness and Beauty and the justification for claims involving these concepts; the Persons–Period Division is concerned with significant individual thinkers and traditions in the history of philosophy.

Intermediate-level courses in these divisions are intended to acquaint the student with the major areas of philosophical study both past and present and to provide a foundation for more advanced study. Advanced-level courses in these divisions are intended to provide the student with the means of integrating philosophy with her other studies and the opportunity for more intensive study in those areas of particular interest.

Both the division and level of a course can be determined from its three-digit course number. The first digit indicates level: 1 designates introductory; 2, intermediate and 3 advanced. The second digit indicates the division: 0 designates the Core Division; 1, the Metaphysics–Epistemology Division; 2, the Value Theory Division, and 3 the Persons–Periods Division.

Divison 0: (Core): Greek philosophy, problems in philosophy, logic, modern philosophy.

Division 1: (Epistemology–Metaphysics): epistemology, metaphysics, intermediate logic, philosophy of science, philosophy of religion, philosophy of history, analytic philosophy, existentialism, philosophy of time, history and philosophy of mathematics, philosophy of language, philosophy of social science, philosophy of creativity.

Division 2: (Value Theory): ethics, aesthetics.

Division 3: (Persons–Periods): Plato, Aristotle, medieval philosophy,

Kant, Hegel, texts in medieval philosophy, Russian philosophy, Marx and Russian Marxism, British Idealism.

Prerequisites: No introductory-level course carries a prerequisite. However, all courses on both the intermediate and advanced levels carry prerequisites. Unless stated otherwise in the course description, any introductory course satisfies the prerequisite for an intermediate-level course and any intermediate course satisfies the prerequisite for an advanced-level course.

Requirements in the Major Subject: Each student majoring in philosophy must take a minimum of four units of course work and the Senior Conference. The courses which the student must take are: (1) either Greek philosophy (101a or b) and modern philosophy (201b) or history of Western thought (100a and b); (2) logic (103a); (3) one half-unit of course work from each of divisions 1, 2 and 3; (4) one unit of advanced-level work. Any advanced-level course or courses may be taken to satisfy either requirement (3) or (4) above.

Courses in Philosophy at Haverford College: In any academic year, students may take for credit toward the major any course taught by members of the Haverford Philosophy Department not taught at Bryn Mawr in that year.

Allied Subjects: Biology, Chemistry, Economics, English, History, History of Art, Mathematics, Music, Physics, Political Science, Psychology, classical and modern literatures and certain courses in Anthropology, History of Religion and Sociology.

Introduction to Philosophy: History of Western Thought: Mr. Ferrater Mora.
   The continuity of the philosophical tradition from Ancient Greece to the Middle Ages, with emphasis on the relation between philosophy and its religious, political, and artistic backgrounds.

Introduction to Philosophy: History of Western Thought: Mr. Ferrater Mora.
   The continuity of the philosophical tradition from the end of the Middle Ages to the present time, with emphasis on the relation between philosophy and its scientific, religious, and political backgrounds.

Introduction to Philosophy: Greek Philosophy: Members of the Department.
   The origins and development of Greek philosophy, including the pre-Socratics, Plato, and Aristotle.

Repeat of course 101a.

102a. *Introduction to Problems in Philosophy:* Mr. Kline.
     A critical examination of such problems as the nature of knowledge; fact and value; freedom and determinism; rationality and irrationality; and the existence of God. Readings will be drawn from twentieth-century authors.

103b. *Logic:* Mr. Weaver.
     An introduction to the fundamentals of deductive reasoning.

201b. *Introduction to Philosophy: Modern Philosophy:* Members of the Department.
     The development of philosophic thought from Descartes to Kant.

211a. *Epistemology:* Mr. Gaskins.
     A study of modern theories of knowledge and its relation to belief, will, and action. Readings from Descartes, Hume, Kant, Schopenhauer, Hegel, and Dewey.

[212a. *Metaphysics:* Miss Potter.]

[213b. *Intermediate Logic:* Mr. Weaver.]

221b. *Ethics:* Mr. Kline.
     A close study of classical and contemporary texts, with attention to such problems as the nature of moral conflict, freedom, responsibility, obligation, and decision.

[222b. *Aesthetics:* Mr. Krausz.]

231a. *Plato: Early and Middle Dialogues:* Miss Taft.
     An examination of several dialogues, including *Lysis, Charmides, Meno, Protagoras, Phaedrus, Symposium* and the *Republic.* Special attention will be given to structural and dramatic elements in the dialogues.

[232b. *Aristotle:* Miss Taft.]

[234b. *History of Chinese Philosophy:* Mr. Song.]

[235b. *Medieval Philosophy:* Miss Potter.]

[310b. *Philosophy of Science:* Mr. Krausz.]

[311a. *Philosophy of Religion:* Miss Potter.]

312a. *Philosophy of History:* Mr. Kline.
     A critical study of both speculative and analytical philosophies of history, with attention to such questions as the pattern and meaning of historical change and the nature of historical explanation.

[313b. *Analytic Philosophy:* Mr. Ferrater Mora.]

Existentialism: Mr. Ferrater Mora.

A detailed analysis of the philosophies of Ortega y Gasset and Jean-Paul Sartre.

Concepts of Time: Mr. Kline.]

History and Philosophy of Mathematics: Mr. Weaver.

Philosophy of mathematics. An examination of the major schools in the philosophy of mathematics, with particular emphasis on structuralism.

Philosophy of Creativity: Mr. Krausz.]

Philosophy of Language: Formal Grammars: Mr. Weaver.]

Philosophy of the Social Sciences: Mr. Krausz.]

Philosophy of Anarchism: Mr. Kline.]

The Nature of Legal Reasoning: Mr. Gaskins].

The nature of the reasoning process in the field of law. No prerequisites.

Kant: Mr. Ferrater Mora.

An examination of the central themes of the *Critique of Pure Reason.*

Hegel: Mr. Gaskins.]

Texts in Medieval Philosophy: Miss Potter.]

Russian Philosophy: Mr. Kline.]

Marx and Russian Marxism: Mr. Kline.]

British Idealism: Miss McPherson.]

Plato: Late Dialogues: Miss Taft.]

Senior Conference:

The Senior Conference is designed as a seminar combined with tutorial sessions. The Conference emphasizes critical thinking and intensive writing on a central philosophic issue.

Honors Work:

Honors work consists of independent reading and conferences with the instructor, directed to the preparation of a paper on a subject dealing with the technical problems of philosophy or emphasizing the connection of philosophy with general literature, history, politics and science or with some special field in which the student is working.

Physics

Professors: Rosalie C. Hoyt, PH.D. ‡
John R. Pruett, PH.D., *Chairman*

Associate Professor: Alfonso M. Albano, PH.D.

Assistant Professors: Peter Beckmann, PH.D.
Stephen R. Smith, PH.D.

Assistants: Robert M. Purcell, B.S.
Cheryl Mills Schwamb, A.B.
David H. Schwamb, B.S.
Sondra Zemansky, B.S.

The courses in physics emphasize the concepts and techniques that have led to our present state of understanding of the material universe; they are designed to relate the individual parts of physics to the whole rather than to treat them as separate disciplines. In the advanced courses the student applies these concepts and techniques to increasingly independent studies of physical phenomena. Students are encouraged to supplement their courses in physics and mathematics with work in related sciences and by units of independent study or experimental work. Opportunities exist for interdisciplinary work, for participation by qualified majors in the research programs of the faculty and for training in machine shop, glass blowing, computer and electronic techniques. Special arrangements make advanced courses available to majors in other sciences.

Requirements in the Major Subject: Physics 101 or its equivalent, 201a, 202b, 306a, 307b and an additional half-unit of 300-level work in physics at Bryn Mawr or at Haverford, or in astronomy. (In special cases the Department will consider the substitution of other 300-level work for Physics 306a or 307b.) Two semesters of Senior Conferences, one year of college level chemistry or its equivalent, Mathematics 101 and 201 or Haverford Mathematics 113a/114b (or 119a) and either 221 or 220; additional mathematics is strongly recommended. Students are encouraged to meet some of the major and allied requirements by advanced standing or placement examinations.

---

‡On leave for the year 1977-78.

Allied Subjects: Astronomy (at Haverford), Biology, Chemistry, Geology, Mathematics, Philosophy, Psychology.

Introduction to Modern Physics: Mr. Pruett, Mr. Smith.

A study of the principal phenomena of classical and modern physics in the light of the developments of the past seventy years. Any mathematical methods needed beyond those of high school mathematics will be developed in the course. Three lectures and three hours of laboratory a week.

Electromagnetism: Mr. Smith

Electrostatics; electric currents and magnetic fields; electromagnetic induction; Maxwell's equations. The concepts of vector and scalar fields will be introduced and used throughout. Vector calculus will be introduced and developed as needed. Laboratory work will deal with direct and alternating current circuit theory, and with solid state electronic devices and circuits. Three lectures and four hours of laboratory a week. Prerequisites: Physics 101, or Haverford Physics 111a and 112b; Mathematics 201 (which may be taken concurrently), or Haverford Mathematics 113a and 114b, or 119a. With the permission of the instructor, Haverford Mathematics 119a may be taken concurrently.

Electromagnetic Waves and Optics: Mr. Albano.

Application of Maxwell's equations and electromagnetic wave phenomena, superposition, interference and diffraction. Geometrical optics. Polarization. Dispersion and scattering of electromagnetic radiation. Introduction to the quantum nature of light. Selected topics in laser physics and modern optics. Three lectures and four hours of laboratory a week. Prerequisites: Physics 201a and either Mathematics 201 (or Haverford Mathematics 114b) which may be taken concurrently, or Haverford Mathematics 119a.

Physical Basis of Computer Science: Mr. Pruett.]

‑Electronics: Mr. Pruett.

Band theory of conduction, principles of solid state electronic devices and circuits, with applications to digital and analog computers and other instruments. Computer interaction with measuring and control devices. Two hours of lecture and four hours of laboratory a week. Prerequisites: Physics 201a or Haverford Physics 213a. Interested students not satisfying these prerequisites see INT. 357b.

Classical and Quantum Mechanics I: Mr. Albano.

A unified treatment of the classical and quantum descriptions of physical phenomena. Intermediate classical mechanics through the Hamiltonian formulation. Coupled oscillations, normal modes and extension to continuous wave systems. Einstein and de Broglie relations, uncertainty and complementarity. Schrodinger's equation and elementary wave mechanics. Three lectures and four hours of laboratory a week. (With permission of the department, Haverford physics majors and majors in mathematics or chemistry may replace the laboratory by extra supervised work.) Prerequisites: Physics 202b, or Haverford Physics 213a, and Mathematics 201, or Haverford Mathematics 114b or 119a.

307b. *Classical and Quantum Mechanics II:* Mr. Beckmann.

Quantum-mechanical measurement theory, state functions and transition probabilities. Classical and quantum descriptions of angular momentum. Central-force motion. The harmonic oscillator and the structure of the hydrogen and helium atoms. Three lectures and four hours of laboratory a week. (With permission of the Department, Haverford physics majors and majors in mathematics or chemistry may replace the laboratory by extra supervised work.) Prerequisite: Physics 306a.

308a. *Advanced Mechanics of Discrete and Continuous Systems:* Mr. Davidon (at Haverford).

309. *Advanced Electromagnetic Theory:* Mr. Beckmann

Boundary value problems involving static electric and magnetic fields; electromagnetic waves and their applications. Mathematical methods will be introduced as needed. Four hours a week. Pre- or co-requisite: a 300-level physics course. (With permission of the instructor, advanced work in chemistry, astronomy, or mathematics may be substituted.)

{351b. *Applications of Physics to Biology:* Miss Hoyt.}

357a. *Computer Usage in the Life Sciences:* Mrs. Pruett.
(INT.)   See Biology 357a.

399. *Senior Conferences:*

The Senior Conferences consist of discussion meetings based on assigned readings and problem work. The students are examined at the end of each semester.

a. *Thermodynamics and Statistical Mechanics:* Mr. Smith.
b. *Contemporary Physics* (solids, nuclei, particles and other current research topics): Mr. Albano, Mr. Beckmann, Mr. Pruett.

401. *Honors Work:*

Honors work may be taken by seniors recommended by the Department. It consists of reading and original theoretical or experimental work on some problems of physics.

3a. *Supervised Units in Special Topics:* Members of the department.

b.   Open to qualified juniors or seniors who wish to supplement their work with independent study or laboratory work in a special area of physics, subject to faculty time and interest. A written paper will be required at the end of the semester or year.

Teaching Certification:

    A sequence of work offered by the Department of Physics and the Department of Education of the College leads to a certificate to teach in the secondary schools of Pennsylvania.

Political Science

The Caroline McCormick Slade Department of Political Science

President of the College: Harris L. Wofford, Jr., A.B., J.D.

Professors: Melville T. Kennedy, Jr. PH.D., *Acting Chairman*
    Gertrude C.K. Leighton, A.B., J.D.‡

Visiting Professor on the IBM Hispanic Studies Fund: Dorothy Nepper
    Marshall, PH.D.

Associate Professors: Charles E. Frye, PH.D.
    Marc Howard Ross, PH.D., *Chairman*‡
    Stephen Salkever, PH.D.‡

Lecturers: Alan Charles Emdin, PH.D.
    Elaine Friedrich, M.A.

The major in political science is concerned with the study of normative and empirical theories of government and with an analysis of the structures and processes of modern political communities.

---

‡On leave for the year 1977-78.

Requirements in the Major Subject: Students majoring in political science must take a minimum of four units of course work and the Senior Conference in the major and two units in allied work. At least one unit of major work must be taken in advanced courses. As a prerequisite to all other courses offered, majors must complete one unit of work chosen from among the following: 200b (INT.), 201a, 202, 203a, 204b, 205a, 206a, 207b, 208, 209, 210. Students who are not majors in the Department may meet this prerequisite in the same way or alternatively by completing one half-unit of allied work and one half-unit in political science chosen from the list of courses above.

The fields of the major, from which two must be selected for special concentration, are: political philosophy and theory, politics and law in American society, comparative politics, international politics and law. At least three courses (one and one-half units of work), including a minimum of one advanced course, must be taken in each of the fields selected. For courses arranged according to fields, see page 137. With the permission of the Department one of the fields may be taken in an allied subject.

Non-majors wishing to take a special field in political science must consult the chairman for approval of course plans in order to qualify for required Senior Conference program. See page 135.

With the permission of the Department, courses at Haverford, other than those listed below, may be taken for major or allied credit.

Allied Subjects: Anthropology, Economics, Education, History, Philosophy, Psychology and Sociology. With the permission of the department, certain courses offered by the modern language departments may be accepted as allied subjects.

{200b. *Urban Society:* Mrs. Lane, Mr. Ross.}
(INT.)

201a. *American Politics:* Mrs. Friedrich.

An examination of the forces shaping political behavior and values in the United States, with particular attention to the processes of political socialization, public opinion formation, agenda building, decision making and policy implementation.

202a. *American Political Institutions and Their Dynamics:* Mr. Waldman,
or b. Mr. Wilde (at Haverford).

203a. *Government and Politics in East Asia:* Mr. Kennedy.

An approach to modern Asian politics through a study of the major philosophic and institutional features of dynastic China and areas under Chinese cultural influence. India and Japan are considered for comparative purposes.

Twentieth-Century China and India: Mr. Kennedy.

A comparative examination of the politics of China and India in the twentieth century with special attention to the roles of nationalism and communism.

Government and Politics in Western Europe: Mr. Frye.

A comparative analysis of the contemporary political systems of Great Britain and France with special reference to factors making for stable and effective democracy.

Comparative Government and Politics: Mr. Glickman (at Haverford).

Government and Politics in Western Europe: Mr. Frye.

A comparative analysis of the contemporary political systems of Germany, Italy and the Soviet Union.

International Politics: Mr. Glickman (at Haverford).

Western Political Theory (Ancient and Early Modern):
(a) Miss Shumer (at Haverford), (b) Mr. Emdin.

A study of fundamental problems of Western political thought. The course is designed to introduce the student both to the careful and critical reading of philosophic texts and to some of the important ways of formulating and answering central questions in political theory. Readings will be drawn from both ancient and early modern sources such as Plato, Aristotle, Machiavelli, Hobbes, Locke and Rousseau. (Limit 20 at Haverford).

The Soviet System: Mr. Hunter (at Haverford).]

Western Political Thought: Ancient and Medieval.]

Law and Civil Disobedience: Mr. Wofford.

An exploration, through common seminar readings and discussion and through individual research papers, of the theory and practice of civil disobedience. Possible grounds for disobedience and forms of non-violent action will be examined, with historical examples from Socrates to Thoreau, Gandhi and King.

Community Politics: A Cross-Cultural Approach: Mrs. Ross, Mr. Ross.]

219a. *American Constitutional Law:* Mr. Emdin.

An analysis of some of the basic principles and processes of American public law. Attention will be centered on decisions and opinions of the Supreme Court as they relate to the formation of public policy and to the value patterns of American liberal democracy.

[221a. *International Law:* Miss Leighton.]

[230a. *Political Behavior:* Mr. Ross.]

231b. *Western Political Theory (Modern):* Mr. Emdin.

This course will focus on the same themes as Political Science 209, drawing on readings from a few of the following modern theorists: Rousseau, Burke, Kant, Hegel, Marx, Mill, Weber, Durkheim, Arendt, Marcuse. Prerequisite: Political Science 209a or b or permission of instructor.

[232b. *Law and Education:* Mr. Wofford.]

233b. *Elections and Political Change:* Mrs. Friedrich.

An examination of the forces affecting election outcomes in American politics. The course will consider current controversies surrounding electoral behavior such as the importance of issues to the electorate, the role of the media, and the transformation of the party system.

234b. *Urban Politics and Public Policy:* Mr. Emdin.
(INT.) A review of the major approaches to the study of public policy with cases drawn from urban America. Special attention will be given to the concept of power.

▪ [301a. *Law and Society:* Miss Leighton.]

[302b. *Law, Policy and Personality:* Miss Leighton.]

303a. *Problems in International Politics:* Mr. Kennedy.

A rapid review of major approaches to the field, both analytic and substantive, followed by intensive consideration of particular operational concepts in international politics and of related concrete problems selected by the seminar.

[305b. *European Fascism:* Mr. Frye.]

[307b. *Modern Germany:* Mr. Frye.]

[308a. *American Political Theory.*]

309b. *Topics in Modern Political Thought:* Mr. Frye.

Study of a medley of political problems (including alienation, freedom, political obedience) of modern societies from the perspective of different thinkers including Sartre, Marx and Marcuse.

Problems in Comparative Politics: Mr. Frye.}

Theory and Practice in Political Philosophy: Mr. Salkever.}

China, Japan, India: Problems in Modernization: Mr. Kennedy.

Intensive review of established assessments and definitions of modernization and political development followed by a study of examples of recent political change in these societies. The seminar will participate in determining the countries and central questions on which the study focuses.

Problems in Constitutional Law.}

American Bureaucracy.}

Ethnic Group Politics: Mr. Ross.}

Political Culture and Political Leadership: Mr. Frye.

A study of relations between political cultures and styles of political leadership in different Western countries.

Problems in Legal Theory: Mr. Salkever.}

The Nature of Legal Reasoning: Mr. Gaskins.}

Philosophical Basis of Social Science: Mr. Emdin.

This course will consider several philosophical and methodological problems which arise in the course of working social science with special attention to political science: the application to society of natural science concepts, the application of this perspective to the study of man as contrasted with empathic understanding, and the extension of empathic understanding to society in general.

Latin American Politics: Responses to Dependency: Mrs. Marshall.

A review of the theory of dependency as it has developed in recent years and an intensive examination of its applicability to three cases.

Senior Conference:

Each major is required to take at least one half-unit from the advanced research colloquia (399a at Bryn Mawr, 391-396 at Haverford) in the fall of her senior year and to write a senior research paper in the spring (399b). The colloquium will offer the student experience in conducting original research in political science. A student will normally take the colloquium in the fall of her senior year after having completed or while completing her other work in the appropriate area of concentration. The senior research paper will normally be in either of the student's two fields of concentration and will be supervised by a member of the Department whose specialty is in the same or related fields. The seniors will meet as a group towards the end of the second semester to share their research findings. A student may take more than one colloquium. Honors majors can fulfill their Senior Conference requirement in one of three ways: (1) they may take two colloquia in the first semester of their senior year, (2) they may take one colloquium in the fall and write their senior research project in the fall, or (3) they may take one colloquium in the fall and write their senior research paper in the spring.

Sections for 1977-78

1. *Political Socialization:* Mr. Frye.
   A cross-cultural examination of how people acquire characteristic patterns of political orientation and behavior.

2. *Topics in International Politics:* Mr. Kennedy.
   A focus on current forces and directions in Asian politics.

3. *Public Opinion in American Politics:* Mrs. Friedrich.
   What is the impact of public opinion on the actions of political elites? This colloquium will examine several alternative theoretical perspectives to this important question of political linkage in light of recent empirical research.

399b. *Senior Research:* Members of the Department.
   Students will conduct independent research under the direction of a member of the Department.

COURSES AT HAVERFORD

224b. *The American Presidency and the Bureaucracy:* Mr. Waldman.

227b. *American Political Theory:* Miss Shumer.

321a. *Problems in Public Management:* Mr. Fisher.

323a. *Congress:* Mr. Waldman.

324b. *Suburban Politics Workshop:* Mr. Glickman.

335a. *Politics of Modernization: Latin America:* Mr. Wilde.

356b. *Topics in Modern Political Theory:* Miss Shumer.

91a. *Research Seminar: The President, Congress, and Energy Policy:* Mr. Waldman.

94a. *Research Seminar in American Foreign Policy Towards Africa:* Mr. Glickman.

96a. *Research Seminar: Politics of Revolution:* Miss Shumer.

FIELDS OF CONCENTRATION

1. *Political Philosophy and Theory:* political analysis; Western political philosophy; recent political philosophy: sources and varieties; Western political thought: ancient and medieval; political behavior; theory and practice in political philosophy; selected topics in modern political thought; American political theory (at Haverford); problems in contemporary American political theory (at Haverford); philosophical basis of social science.

2. *Politics and Law in American Society:* American national politics; community politics; ethnic group politics; political behavior; constitutional law; law and education; law and society; law, policy and personality; the American political process: parties and the Congress (at Haverford); problems in contemporary American political theory (at Haverford); elections and political change; public opinion and public policy.

3. *Comparative Politics:* government and politics in East Asia; twentieth-Century China and India; government and politics in Western Europe; Western European integration; European Fascism; problems in comparative politics; China, Japan, and India: problems in modernization; the Soviet system (at Haverford); comparative politics: political development (at Haverford); community politics.

4. *International Politics and Law:* international law; problems in international politics; courses on Asia and Europe; international relations (at Haverford); international organization (at Haverford); politics and international relations in the Middle East and North Africa (at Haverford); international politics of Communism (at Haverford).

401. *Honors Work:*

Seniors admitted to Honors work prepare an independent research paper (one unit of credit) under the supervision of a member of the Department. Field work is encouraged.

Interdepartmental Work:

The Department of Political Science participates in the interdepartmental concentration in Hispanic and Hispanic-American Studies and in the interdepartmental major in The Growth and Structure of Cities. See pages 158 and 155.

Teaching Certification:

A sequence of work offered by the Department of Political Science and the Department of Education of the College leads to a certificate to teach in the secondary schools of Pennsylvania.

Psychology

Professors: Richard C. Gonzalez, PH.D., *Chairman*
Howard S. Hoffman, PH.D.*
Matthew Yarczower, PH.D.

Katharine E. McBride Visiting Professor: Nicholas J. Mackintosh, D. PHIL

Associate Professors: Clark McCauley Jr., PH.D.
Earl Thomas, PH.D.

Assistant Professor: Jill T. Wannemacher, PH.D.‡

Visiting Lecturer: Larry Stein, PH.D.

Laboratory Coordinators: Erika Rossman Behrend, PH.D.
Alice S. Powers, PH.D.

Assistants: Elizabeth DelPezzo, M.A.
Paul LeBuffe, B.A.
Beverly Smith, B.A.
Howard Waxman, M.A.
Elna Yadin, M.A.

---

*On leave, semester I.
‡On leave for the year 1977-78.

The department offers to the major student a representative account of methods, theory and findings in comparative, developmental, experimental, physiological and social psychology. The program of work is coordinated with that at Haverford College (which offers training in experimental, personality and social psychology). It is planned to encourage the student, in the first two years of study, to sample widely from among the course offerings in these areas and to permit her, in the final two years, to focus attention (by course work and research) on the one or two areas of her principal interest.

Requirements in the Major Subject: Psychology 101 and two courses from each of the following groupings of courses: (a) Psychology 201a, 202b, 203a, 204b (or Haverford course 240b), (b) Psychology 206a, 207b, 208b (or Haverford course 208a), Haverford courses 200a, 209a (or 210b), 238b, (c) Psychology 301b, 302b, 305b, Haverford courses 309a, 344b; one unit of allied work in either biology, chemistry, physics or mathematics. The Senior Conference is also required. Psychology 205a is strongly recommended to students preparing for graduate work. Psychology 101 is prerequisite to all other courses offered by the Department with the exception of Psychology 205a. Some second-semester courses at the 200 level, with permission of the Department, may be taken concurrently with Psychology 101.

Allied Subjects: Anthropology, Biology, Chemistry, Education, History of Science, Linguistics, Mathematics, Philosophy, Physics, Sociology. At least one unit must be taken from among Biology, Chemistry, Physics and Mathematics.

101. *Experimental Psychology:* Mr. Gonzalez, Mr. McCauley, Mr. Thomas, Mr. Yarczower.

A survey of methods, facts and principles relating to basic psychological processes, their evolution, development and neurophysiology. Three hours of lecture and four hours of laboratory a week.

The following courses include individual laboratory research projects:

201a. *Learning Theory and Behavior:* Mr. Gonzalez.

Comparative studies of conditioning and instrumental learning; theories of learning; the evolution of intelligence.

202b. *Comparative Psychology:* Mr. Yarczower.

Evolution and behavior. The phylogeny of learning, perception, language, aggression and social behavior. Prerequisite: Psychology 201a.

[203a. *Motivation:* Mr. Thomas.]

204b. *Sensory Processes:* Mr. Hoffman.

Peripheral and central mechanisms of sensory experience, with particular emphasis on analysis in the visual and auditory modalities. Classical psychophysics and modern signal detection theory.

205a. *Experimental Methods and Statistics:* Mr. McCauley.

Measurement, descriptive statistics, probability, association, testing of hypotheses, the design of experiments and associated problems.

206a. *Developmental Psychology:* Mr. Snyder.

Development and behavior. The ontogeny of attention, perception, learning, language, intelligence and social interaction.

[207b. *Language and Cognition:* Miss Wannemacher.]

208b. *Social Psychology:* Mr. McCauley.

Social influence and persuasion: audience and coaction effects; group dynamics; leadership, attitude change in relation to behavior change; stereotypes; social comparison theory; helping behavior.

301b. *Contemporary Issues in Behavior Theory:* Mr. Mackintosh.

Analysis of contemporary theory and research on: classical conditioning; attention, generalization and discrimination; punishment and avoidance; inhibition; biological constraints on learning. Prerequisite: Psychology 201a.

302b. *Physiological Psychology:* Mr. Thomas.

The physiological and anatomical bases of experience and behavior: sensory processes and perception, emotion, motivation, learning and cognition. Prerequisite: Psychology 201a.

305b. *Psychological Measurement:* Mr. McCauley.

Theory of testing and evaluation of representative psychological tests: reliability and validity; decisions using tests; IQ tests and the structure and inheritance of intelligence; selected aptitude and personality tests: SAT, GRE, MMPI, Rorschach.

311a. *Selected Problems in Comparative Psychology:* Mr. Yarczower.

Primarily a laboratory course concentrating on the comparative analysis of aggressive behavior in Siamese fighting fish, pigeons, and rats. Students will participate in the entire experimental process, beginning with the theoretical framework within which the research will be cast, the design of the experiments, the analysis of the results, and the writing of a paper. Prerequisite: Psychology 202b.

Selected Problems in Physiological Psychology: Members of the Department.

Selected Problems in Experimental Psychology: Members of the Department.

Selected Problems in Social Psychology: Mr. McCauley.

Process and effects of mass media communications: pornography; television violence; commercial advertising; political advertising, including the psychology of voting; the agenda of public issues.

Selected Problems in Developmental Psychology: Members of the Department.

Computer Usage in the Life Sciences: Mrs. Pruett.

Experiments in the life sciences will be analyzed using computer techniques. The Fortran IV language will be developed and used throughout the course. Limited to advanced students with research experience; no previous training in the use of the computer is required. Lecture two hours, laboratory two hours a week.

Senior Conference:

Seniors select four of the seven to ten mini-seminars offered by individual members of the faculty on topics announced late in the junior year. The topics vary from year to year, but each focuses on contemporary research in the faculty member's area of specialization. A paper is required in each seminar.

Honors Work:

One unit of Honors work may be taken by students nominated by the Department.

Supervised Research in Psychology: Members of the Department.

Laboratory or field research under the supervision of a member of the Department.

COURSES AT HAVERFORD

Human Learning and Memory: Miss Naus.

Social Psychology: Mr. Perloe.

Theories of Personality: Mr. Wagner.

Personality and Culture: Mr. Davis.

238b. *Psychology of Language:* Mr. D'Andrea.

[240b. *Perception:* Miss Naus.]

[306a. *Individual Differences:* Miss Naus.]

309a. *Psychology of the Abnormal Personality:* Mr. Davis.

[344b. *Development Through the Life Span:* Mr. Heath.]

Russian

Associate Professors: Dan Davidson, PH.D.
  Ruth L. Pearce, PH.D., *Chairman*

Assistant Professors: George S. Pahomov, PH.D.‡
  Lynn Visson, PH.D.

Lecturer: Frank J. Miller, PH.D.

Professor of Philosophy: George L. Kline, PH.D.

At Haverford:

Professor of Economics: Holland Hunter, PH.D.

Professor of History: Linda G. Gerstein, PH.D.

The Russian major is designed to offer the student the opportunity to learn to both read and speak Russian and to achieve an understanding of the literature, thought and culture of pre-revolutionary and contemporary Russia. The study of the Russian language is combined with a study in depth of one of the following areas of concentration: Russian literature, economics, Russian history or philosophy.

Students in all courses are encouraged to make use of tapes available in the Language Laboratory. Majors are encouraged to take advantage of various Russian language summer programs offered both here and in the Soviet Union and to compete for a place in a semester language program

---

‡On leave for the year 1977-78.

(senior year) in Leningrad or Moscow. Residence in the Russian House for at least one year is advisable.

Requirements in the Major Subjects: Three years (or the equivalent) of work in the Russian language, two years of work in the area of concentration (Russian literature, economics, history or philosophy) of which one must be at the advanced level, one year of work outside the area of concentration and Senior Conference. A paper based on sources in Russian is required for an advanced course in the area of concentration. A comprehensive examination in the Russian language and in the area of concentration is given.

Allied Subjects: Any language or literature, Economics, History, History of Art, Music and Philosophy.

001. *Elementary Russian:* Members of the Department.

The basic grammar is learned with enough vocabulary to enable the student to speak and understand simple Russian and to read simple texts. The course meets five times a week.

100. *Intensive Russian.*]

101. *Intermediate Russian:* Members of the Department.

Continuing grammar study, conversation and vocabulary building. Readings in Russian classics and contemporary materials. The course meets five times a week.

200. *Advanced Training in the Russian Language:* Members of the Department.

Intensive practice in oral and written expression based on literary and non-literary texts of Modern Standard Russian. Conducted in Russian.

201. *Readings in Russian:* Mrs. Pearce.

Reading of literary and non-literary texts, selected in accordance with the needs and interests of the students. Emphasis is placed on vocabulary building and exposure to varying styles to enable the student to read advanced texts in her own or related fields.

[203. *Russian Literature in Translation.*]

204a. *Tolstoy in Translation:* Mr. Davidson.

Readings of selected fictional and non-fictional works with emphasis on Tolstoy's struggle to adjust experiential and ideological perceptions of reality. Close analysis of texts and study of Tolstoy's Russian and European background.

204b. *Dostoevsky in Translation:* Mr. Davidson.

Extensive readings in the varieties of psychological narrative explored by Dostoevsky with emphasis on his studies of extremist mentalities, both criminal and saintly, and on the author's struggle to create a viable myth of salvation. Close study of the major works within Russian and European contexts.

[302. *Pushkin and His Time.*]

303a. *Twentieth-Century Russian Literature:* Miss Visson.
Close readings in Russian poetry from the Symbolists to the present day.

303b. *Twentieth-Century Russian Literature:* Miss Visson.
Close readings in Soviet prose from Gorky to the present.

305. *Advanced Russian Grammar:* Mrs. Pearce.
A systematic and comprehensive study of Russian grammar with emphasis on contrastive analysis and the mastery of complex grammatical points.

[306a. *Russian Prose and Poetry from Classicism to the Rise of Realism.*]

[306b. *Russian Literature of the Second Half of the Nineteenth Century.*]

399. *Senior Conference:* Members of the department.
The Senior Conference is intended to supplement course work. Form and topic vary from year to year according to the needs and interests of th students. The work of the conference will be evaluated by examination.

401. *Honors Work:*
Honors work is offered to students recommended by the Department.

SEE ALSO

Economics 206b. *International Economic Theory and Policy:* Mr. Farley.

Economics 210a. *Developing Economies:* Mr. Farley and Mr. Hunter.

hilosophy 333a. *Russian Philosophy.*]

hilosophy 333b. *Marx and Russian Marxism.*]

COURSES AT HAVERFORD

Economics 211a. *The Soviet System.*]

Economics 398a. *Research Seminar:* Mr. Weinstein.

[History 244. *Russian History.*]

History 245. *Russia in the Twentieth Century:* Mrs. Gerstein.

History 356b. *Fin de Siècle: Russia 1890-1914:* Mrs. Gerstein.

480. *Independent Study.*

Sociology

Professor: Eugene V. Schneider, PH.D., *Chairman*

Associate Professor: Judith R. Porter, PH.D.

Assistant Professors: Sheila Kishler Bennett, PH.D.
Robert Earl Washington, PH.D.

Lecturer: Jacquelyn H. Wolf, M.A.

Visiting Lecturer: Stanley S. Clawar, PH.D.

Assistants: Raymond D'Angelo, M.A.
Mary T. Robinson, B.A.

The aim of the major in sociology is to provide the student with a general understanding of the structure and functioning of modern society, its major institutions, groups and values, and of the interrelations of these with personality. Stress is also placed on the major strains and problems of modern society. Free elective work is offered to those who may be interested in applying their knowledge to the field of social work.

The work of this program is closely integrated with the work in sociology offered at Haverford College. Students should inquire about the possibilities of coordinated work with Haverford.

Requirements for the Major Subject: Sociology 102a and b, 302a and 305b and additional work to be chosen from courses offered at Bryn Mawr or at Haverford. A total of three and one-half units of course work is required in addition to the Senior Conference.

Allied Subjects: Anthropology, Economics, Social Psychology, Political Science, American and African History, Mathematics.

02a. *Introduction to Sociology:* Mrs. Porter.

Analysis of the basic sociological perspectives, methods and concepts used in studying society. Emphasis is placed on culture, social system, personality and their interrelations. Concrete applications of sociological analysis are examined.

02b. *American Social Structure:* Mr. Schneider.

Analysis of the structure and dynamics of complex, industrial societies. Examples will be drawn from several societies, but major emphasis is on the United States.

[202a. *Social Welfare and the Individual and His Environment.*]

[202b. *Social Problems and Social Work Practice.*]

[205b. *Social Stratification:* Mrs. Bennett.]

207a. *Intergroup Relations:* Mrs. Porter.
   An examination of cultural, structural and personality change with a focus on minority groups. Emphasis is on black-white and minority relations in the U.S.; there will be a cross-cultural comparison with race relations in South Africa.

209b. *Sociology of Religion:* Mrs. Porter.
   Analysis of the interrelations between religion and society, drawing upon the works of major social theorists. Emphasis is placed on the connection between religious systems and secular culture, social structure, social change, secular values and personality systems.

212b. *Sociology of Poverty:* Mrs. Porter.
   An analysis of the causes and effects of poverty in the United States. Issues covered will include the culture of poverty, the effects of poverty on institutions like the family, and the government poverty programs.

215a.* *Field Work in Urban Studies:* Mr. Clawar.
& b.   An approach to the urban situation by participation in educational settings. A few hours a week of field work in schools, alternative centers and clinics will be integrated with weekly seminars. Seminar topics include: *Semester* I—tutorial relationships, interaction skills, social aspects of cognitive development, education and opportunity structure, expectation theory, bilingual populations; *Semester* II—labeling theory and student performance, the ethnic family, bureaucracy, demographic shift patterns, sex roles and the schools and juvenile delinquency, decentralization, future trends.

217a. *Comparative Perspectives on Kinship:* Mrs. Bennett.
   Kinship and domestic groups in contexts of socioeconomic change. Among perspectives and problems developed: evolutionary perspectives on the family and kinship, the impact of industrialization and urbanization (including the colonial experience), the Black family, American kinship.

218a. *Modernization:* Mr. Washington.
   Sociological problems of development confronting third world societies. The following topics will be covered: theories of modernization;

146

the Western capitalist, the socialist and the Japanese patterns of modernization; the social problems created by colonialism, rapid population growth, social class exploitation, ethnic prejudice, urbanization, etc.; the problem of political priorities; democracy vs. political stability.

Marginal Communities: the Sociology of the Outsider: Mr. Washington.]

Women, Sex Roles and Socialization: Miss Wolf.

A critical analysis of the cultural, social, structural and personality theories of sex-role socialization. Students will have the opportunity to test the various theories in recent empirical data. Readings for the course will be selected from the areas of anthropology, sociology and child development, and an attempt will be made to construct a comprehensive interdisciplinary approach to sex-role socialization. The dynamics of social change with regard to the Women's Movement will also be investigated.

Women and the Social Structure: Miss Wolf.

The position of women in the economic, political and social systems of the United States. Emphasis will be placed on the economic system and the factors affecting women in the labor force. The aspirations and goals of various social categories of women will be investigated in depth in relation to the Women's Movement.

Urban Sociology: Mr. Washington.

An analysis of urban social structures. Topics considered are: the urban polity, the psychology of urban life, the economic function of cities and contemporary urban problems.

Social and Cultural Change: Mrs. Bennett.

Perspectives on social and cultural change examined with particular attention to underlying images of society and the individual, and the nature of social and cultural systems. Psychological modernity and diffusion theories of cultural change are dealt with as they relate to transformations of institutional structures and political and economic relations.

Social Problems: Mr. Washington.

A survey of major problems in American society as seen by sociologists and social critics. Topics considered: crime, education, drug addiction, the police, divorce, racial ghettos and violence.

The Sociology of Alienation: Mr. Washington.

An examination of a variety of theoretical approaches to the phenomena of powerlessness, loss of meaning, estrangement and inauthenticity and an analysis of the social conditions giving rise to and resulting from alienation.

[280b. *Industrial Sociology:* Mr. Schneider.]

302a. *Social Theory:* Mr. Schneider.

An examination of the extent to which the writings of classical and modern theorists throw light on wide-ranging social, cultural and historical processes.

305b. *Sociological Methods:* Mrs. Bennett.

An examination of various techniques for conducting empirical enquiry in research design, collection of data, methods of interviewing and analysis.

399. *Senior Conference:*

The form and evaluation of the conference will be determined in consultation with the senior majors.

401. *Honors Work:*

Honors work is offered to students who have demonstrated proficiency in their studies in the Department of Sociology and will consist of independent reading and research, conferences and the preparation of a written report.

Interdepartmental Work:

The Department of Sociology participates in the interdepartmental concentration in Hispanic and Hispanic-American Studies and in the interdepartmental major in The Growth and Structure of Cities. See pages 158, 155.

In general students may enroll for major credit in any course in the Department of Sociology at Haverford. Since alternative programs are possible, the student should consult the Department of Sociology at Bryn Mawr.

Spanish

Professors: Joaquín González-Muela, *D. en Fil.*
   Willard Fahrenkamp King, PH.D., *Chairman*

Associate Professor: Eleanor Krane Paucker, PH.D.

Lecturer: Enrique Sacerio-Garí, M.PHIL.

Professor of Philosophy: José María Ferrater Mora, *Lic. Fil.*

The major in Spanish offers work in both language and the literature of all centuries, with emphasis on those periods when Spain and Spanish America have made their maximum contributions to Western culture.

The introductory courses treat a selection of the outstanding works of Spanish and Spanish-American literature in various periods and genres. Advanced courses deal more intensively with individual authors or periods of special interest. Students are admitted to advanced courses after satisfactory completion of two semesters of 200-level courses in Spanish literature or by a placement test and permission of the instructor. In certain cases, with the approval of the Department and the Dean of The Graduate School of Arts and Sciences, advanced students may also take one graduate course.

One course is devoted to training in written and spoken Spanish. It is recommended that students supplement their course work by spending the junior year in Spain or Spanish America, studying in the summer at the *Centro* in Madrid or living in the Spanish House. It is strongly advised that all students make use of the tapes available in the Language Laboratory. In Spanish 001 the use of the Laboratory forms an integral part of the course.

Requirements in the Major Subject: The normal course sequence in the major is Spanish 101a and b, 201a or b, 202a or b, at least four semesters of advanced work and the Senior Conference. Students who spend the junior year in Spain may substitute an advanced literature course for Spanish 202a or 202b, and students whose pre-college training includes advanced work in literature may, with the permission of the Department, substitute a unit of more advanced work for 101a and b.

Allied Subjects: Any other language or literature, Anthropology, Economics, Hispanic Studies, History, History of Art, History of Religion, Linguistics, Music, Philosophy, Political Science and Sociology.

001. *Elementary Spanish:* Mrs. Paucker, Mr. Sacerio-Garí.

Grammar, composition, oral and aural training, readings ·on the Spanish and Spanish-American background.

003. *Intermediate Spanish:* Mr. González-Muela, Mr. Sacerio-Garí.

Intensive grammar reviews, exercises in composition and conversation, selected readings from modern Spanish texts.

101a. *Readings in Hispanic Literature:* Mr. García-Barrio, Mrs. Paucker (at
& b. Haverford).

A general view of Spanish history and culture as revealed in outstanding literary works of various periods and genres. Oral expression and practice in writing are emphasized.

[201a. *Hispanic Literature of the Nineteenth Century:* Mrs. Paucker.]

[201b. *The Generation of 1898 and Modernismo:* Mrs. Paucker.]

202a. *Advanced Language Training and Composition:* Mr. Sacerio-Garí.
& b. Training in phonetics and practice in conversation. Interpretation of texts, translation and original composition in Spanish. Assignments adapted to the needs and level of achievement of the individual student.

[204a. *Contemporary Spanish American Poetry.*]

206a. *Narrative Structure:* Mr. Sacerio-Garí.

Study of the elements of narrative—point of view, myth, metaphor, sequence, and simultaneity—in a selection of Pre-Columbian, Spanish, and Spanish American texts from the *Popol-Vuh* to Borges.

[208b. *The Mexican Novel since the Revolution of 1910:* Mrs. Paucker.]

210a. *Hispanic Culture and Civilization:* Mrs. King.
(INT.) See INT. 210a in the interdepartmental area of concentration in Hispanic and Hispanic-American Studies.

302a. *Medieval Spanish Literature:* Mrs. Paucker.

The Castilian epic, lyric poetry, and narrative prose from the *Poema del Cid* to Jorge Manrique, with special attention to the intermingling of Arabic, Jewish and Christian cultures.

303a. *Modern Poetry in Spain:* Mr. González-Muela.

Emphasis on the contemporary period. Texts by García Lorca, Hierro, Blas de Otero, and others.

The Modern Novel in Spain: Mrs. King.

Twentieth-century experiments in the form and language of fiction. Emphasis on the contemporary period. Texts by Unamuno, Valle Inclán, Cela, Delibes, J. Goytisolo, and others.

Cervantes: Mrs. King.]

Spanish Poetry and Drama of the Golden Age: Mrs. King.]

Senior Conference:

a. In the first semester a senior seminar is devoted to the study of a special topic in Spanish literature chosen by the students, to be evaluated by a written examination in January.

b. In the second semester individual conferences between each student and her instructor are designed to aid the student in the preparation of a paper on an author or theme as seen in the context of a whole period in Spanish literature and history. At the end of the semester each student has a brief oral examination in Spanish consisting of the explanation and interpretation of a Spanish text and serving, along with the papers, as the method of evaluation of this conference. (With the approval of the Department, the student may substitute the Hispanic Studies seminar for the second-semester Senior Conference, see page 158.)

Honors Work:

Honors work is offered to students recommended by the Department. This work consists of independent reading, conferences and a long paper.

Interdepartmental Work:

The Spanish Department participates in the interdepartmental area of concentration in Hispanic and Hispanic-American Studies. See page 158.

COURSES AT HAVERFORD

Caribbean Literature: Mr. García-Castro.

Theater of the Golden Age: Mr. García-Barrio.

Literature of the Present in Spanish America: Mr. García-Castro.

The Essay in Latin America: Mrs. Rooney.

Interdepartmental Work

As new fields of study open up and as old fields change, it becomes necessary for those interested in them to acquire the information and to learn the methods needed to understand them and to work in them, and these may sometimes be quite diverse. In order to provide an opportunity for students to work in these new areas, the faculty has approved the establishment of the following interdepartmental majors and interdepartmental area of concentration.

I. Interdepartmental Majors

Classical Languages

Major Advisors: Professor Lang (Greek)
  Professor Scott (Latin)

The major in classical languages is designed for the student who wishes to divide her time equally between the two languages and literatures.

Requirements: Six units of course work in Greek and Latin, normally three of each. At least one unit of advanced course work but no allied units. A special Senior Conference will be made up from the offerings of the two departments. See pages 98 and 116 for descriptions of courses and conferences.

Classical Studies

Major Advisors: Professor Lang (Greek)
  Professor Scott (Latin)
  Professor Ridgway (Classical and Near Eastern Archaeology)

The major in classical studies will provide a broad yet individually structured background for students whose interest in the ancient classical world is general, and who wish to lay the foundation for more specialized work in one particular area.

Requirements: Eight units of course work, at least one in each of the following: ancient history (History 205a and b, 206a and b), ancient philosophy (Philosophy 101a or b, 231a, 232b), classical archaeology

(Classical and Near Eastern Archaeology 101, 202a, 203a, 203b, 205b, 301a, 302a, 302b, 304a), Greek (all courses except 203a and b, 213a, 214b), Latin (all courses except 204a and 205a and b). At least one unit of advanced work is required, but no allied work. The Senior Conference will be in two parts: one in the field of the advanced unit and a special Classical Studies Conference on some topic to which all fields may contribute. (Two of the required eight units may be taken at Haverford College with the approval of the major advisors.)

French Studies

Major Advisors: Professors Salmon and Silvera (History)
   Professor Guggenheim (French)

The major in French studies, offered jointly by the French and History departments, is intended for students who wish to acquire in depth an understanding of French life and culture. The major concentrates on a sequence of French and history courses so that literary themes and their historical context may be studied in parallel. In addition to the introductory course and the conference, courses specially designed for the program will be offered from time to time. Relevant courses in allied fields, such as political science, philosophy and history of art or music will be made available where possible. A junior year in France under one of the plans recommended by the French Department or summer study at the *Institut d'Etudes françaises d'Avignon* (held under the auspices of Bryn Mawr) forms an integral part of the program. Where students intend to take the junior year in France, early election of the major and the taking of the introductory course at sophomore level are recommended. Alternatively, special arrangements may be made to take an equivalent course in French civilization at a French university during the junior year in France. A good command of French, both written and spoken, is required. At least a year of residence in the French House in Haffner is advisable.

Requirements: Students whose interests are literary will normally elect three units of French literature and two of French history, while those whose bent is historical will elect three units of history and two of literature. At least one of these units from either department will be at the advanced level. Interdepartmental 290. *La Civilisation française* serves as the introductory course. French 205c. *Stylistique et traduction,* or the equivalent, is a required course.

Allied Subjects: Economics, The Growth and Structure of Cities, History of Art, Music, Philosophy, Political Science, Sociology.

COURSES SPECIALLY DESIGNED FOR THE PROGRAM

290. *La Civilisation française:* Mr. Guggenheim, Mrs. Gutwirth.
(INT.)   The first part of this course studies French society from the Religious Wars to the Revolution as reflected in representative texts (letters, memoirs, plays, essays) with special emphasis on the historical background of French literature. In the second semester the course examines the arts and politics of France since 1789 in order to establish the ground of its present character and dilemmas. Texts will be drawn from history, fiction, letters, music, graphic art, film and periodical literature. Given in French, the course serves as an introduction for French Studies majors, but is open to other qualified students. Prerequisite: a good command of French.

[295b. *Littérature, histoire et société de la Renaissance à la Révolution:*
(INT.) Mr. Guggenheim.]

[297a. *Le Seizième Siècle à travers le roman historique:* Mr. Salmon.]
(INT.)

399. *Senior Conference:* Mr. Salmon.
       A series of weekly seminars examining the relationship between literature, political theory and historiography within a selected period.

FRENCH LITERATURE

   See course listings under the French Department.

FRENCH HISTORY

   For description of courses offered at Bryn Mawr in the current year, see listings under the History Department.

[204. *Europe, 1789-1848:* Mr. Silvera.]

[241a. *The Impressionist Era:* Mr. McCarthy (at Haverford).]

[243b. *Contemporary France:* Mr. McCarthy (at Haverford).]

[295a. *Paris in the Seventeenth and Eighteenth Centuries:* Miss Lafarge.]
(INT.)

302. *France, 1559-1661:* Mr. Salmon.
(INT.)   See History 302.

30. *France since 1870:* Mr. Silvera.}

5a. *Topics in Early Modern European History: The French Revolution:* Mr. Spiel-man (at Haverford).}

COURSES AT THE INSTITUT D'ETUDES FRANÇAISES D'AVIGNON

The following courses are given during the summer session:
Political Science s201. *La France d'aujourd'hui.*
Sociology s202. *La Vie quotidienne en France.*

01. *Honors Work:*

On the recommendation of the Major Advisors, qualified students in their senior year will be admitted to Honors work consisting of independent reading and a long research paper.

The Growth and Structure of Cities

Director of the Program: Professor Barbara Miller Lane‡

Major Advisor: Professor Catherine Lafarge

Lecturer: George Thomas

In this interdisciplinary major, the student will study the city from several points of view. City planning, art and architecture, history, political science, anthropology, archaeology, economics and sociology will contribute toward her understanding of the growth and structure of cities.

Requirements: All students must take Interdepartmental 190 and Interdepartmental 200b (one and one-half units). Each student should select, in addition to these courses, three units from among the other major courses listed below. Two additional units, above the introductory level, must be chosen from any one department listed under Allied Subjects. Each senior will prepare a paper or project embodying substantial research. The paper or project will be presented in written form to the Committee on The Growth and Structure of Cities and in oral or visual form to all seniors in the major, meeting as a group. These oral presentations and the resulting discussions will serve as the Senior Conference.

---

‡On leave for the year 1977-78.

Allied Subjects: Anthropology, Fine Art, Classical and Near Eastern Archaeology, Economics, Greek, History, History of Art, Latin, Political Science, Sociology. Occasionally, with the permission of the Dean of the Graduate School, courses in Social Work and Social Research.

190. *The Form of the City:* Mr. Thomas.
(INT.)   The physical character of historic and contemporary cities. A variety of factors—geography, economic and population structures, planning and aesthetics—will be considered as determinants of urban form.

[200b. *Urban Society:* Mrs. Lane, Mr. Ross.]
(INT.)

202a. *Ancient Greek Cities and Sanctuaries:* Mrs. Ridgway.
(INT.)   See Classical and Near Eastern Archaeology 202a.

[204a. *The Ancient City:* Mr. Scott.]
(INT.)

[206b. *Ancient Near Eastern Architecture:* Mr. Ellis, Miss Mellink.]
(INT.)

207a. *Latin America: Colonies and Revolutions:* Mrs. Dunn.
(INT.)   See History 207a.

209a. *Urban Economics:* Mr. Dixon (at Haverford).
(INT.)   See Economics 209a.

[218b. *Community Politics: A Cross-Cultural Approach:* Mrs. Ross, Mr. Ross.]
(INT.)

234b. *Urban Politics and Public Policy:* Mr. Emdin.
(INT.)   See Political Science 234b.

240b. *Urban Sociology:* Mr. Washington.
(INT.)   See Sociology 240b.

[295a. *Paris in the Seventeenth and Eighteenth Centuries:* Miss Lafarge.]
(INT.)

300b. *The American City in the Twentieth Century:* Mr. Speizman.
(INT.)   (Graduate School of Social Work and Social Research)
Social transformations under the impact of rapid urbanization. Includes some comparative study of urbanization in other societies.

302a. *Greek Architecture:* Mr. Eiteljorg.
(INT.)   See Classical and Near Eastern Archaeology 302a.

Roman Architecture: Mr. Scott.
   See Classical and Near Eastern Archaeology 302b.

The Dynamics of Environmental Systems: Mr. Anderson.}
)

The Italian City-State in the Renaissance: Mrs. Lane.]
)

Architecture in Philadelphia: Mr. Thomas
)   The course will survey the modern movement in architecture as it is
represented in the Quaker City, presenting styles and theory from the
Greek Revival of the early nineteenth century to the nationally recognized
"Philadelphia School" of the past decade. Special emphasis will be placed
on the relationship between the traditional historiography of contemporary architecture and the reality of the built city.

Medieval Cities: Islamic, Byzantine and Western: Mr. Brand.}
)

Ethnic Group Politics: Mr. Ross.}
)

Mexico: Independence to the Present: Mrs. Dunn.}
)

Colonial Towns in North and South America: Mrs. Dunn.
)   See History 328a.

A History of Blacks in the American City: Mr. Holbrook.
)   See History 335a.

Topics in the History of Modern Architecture: Mrs. Lane.]
)

Senior Conference: Mr. Thomas and members of the Committee on The
Growth and Structure of Cities.

II. Interdepartmental Area of Concentration

Hispanic and Hispanic-American Studies

Major Advisors: Professor Dunn (History)
Professor King (Spanish)

Visiting Professor on the IBM Hispanic Studies Fund:
Dorothy Nepper Marshall (Political Science)

The program is designed for students interested in a comprehensive study of the society and culture of Spanish America or Spain or both. Its aims are (1) to provide the student, through a formal major in anthropology, history, history of art, history of religion, economics, music, political science, sociology or Spanish, with a valid means for thorough study of one aspect of Hispanic or Hispanic-American culture, (2) to afford an introduction, through the study of allied courses dealing with Spain or Spanish America, to other aspects of the cultural complex, (3) to effect a synthesis of the student's studies through a Senior Conference, in which all students in the program participate, on a broad topic that cuts across all the major areas involved.

Requirements: Competence in Spanish; a major chosen from those listed above; Hispanic Studies 210a; at least two units of work chosen from courses listed below (or from approved courses taken in Spain or Spanish America); in the junior or senior year, a long paper or project dealing with Spain or Spanish America; the Senior Conference in Hispanic and Hispanic-American Studies. (In effect, the student supplements a major in one of the departments listed above with a concentration in Hispanic or Hispanic-American studies.)

210a. *Hispanic Culture and Civilization:* Mrs. King.
(INT.) A brief survey of the political, social and cultural history of Spain and Spanish America, concentrating on the emergence of specifically Hispanic values and modes of life. Major topics: spread of the Spanish Empire, Spanish-American Independence, racial and ethnic conflict, current social and economic problems, Spanish America's recent attempts to define its own identity.

399b. *Senior Conference:* Major Advisors.

Courses: Anthropology 101a, 204a, [305a], [306b], INT. 308, [INT. 312b], History 207a, [211b], [212], 308a, [INT. 317a], INT. 328a,

H355a, History of Art 213, History of Religion [300b], 328a, Philosophy 314b, Political Science H335a, 340b, Sociology 102a, Spanish: any course (including those given at the Centro de Estudios Hispánicos in Madrid) except 001, 003 and 202.

Interdepartmental Courses

Each year, certain courses are offered which cut across well-defined areas of knowledge and emphasize relationships among them. Such courses may be taught by two or more members of the faculty working in close cooperation. Since the material considered requires some background in at least two disciplines, the interdepartmental courses are usually offered at the advanced level. For students who have progressed to the more complex aspects of their major subjects, the interdepartmental courses provide an opportunity to apply their training to new and broader problems and to benefit from the experience of seeing their own subject from the points of view of several specialists. To facilitate free discussion, registration is generally restricted to a limited number of well-qualified students.

The Form of the City: Mr. Thomas.
    See INT. 190 in the interdepartmental major in The Growth and Structure of Cities.

Urban Society: Mrs. Lane, Mr. Ross.}

Ancient Greek Cities and Sanctuaries: Mrs. Ridgway.
See Archaeology 202a.

The Ancient City: Mr. Scott.}

Ancient Near Eastern Architecture: Mr. Ellis, Miss Mellink.}

Latin America: Colonies and Revolution: Mrs. Dunn.
See History 207a.

Urban Economics: Mr. Dixon (at Haverford).
See Economics 209a.

210a. *Hispanic Culture and Civilization:* Mrs. King.
(INT.)   See INT. 210a in the interdepartmental area of concentration in Hispanic and Hispanic-American Studies.

[211a. *The Soviet System:* Mr. Hunter (at Haverford).]
(INT.)

213a. *Myth in Practice and Theory:* Miss Lang.
(INT.)   Greek and other myths will be examined from two points of view: as a testing ground for various approaches to the study and interpretation of myths, both ancient and modern; as raw material for literary exploitation and development.

[218b. *Community Politics: A Cross-Cultural Approach:* Mrs. Ross, Mr. Ross.]
(INT.)

234b. *Urban Politics and Public Policy:* Mr. Emdin.
(INT.)   See Political Science 234b.

240b. *Urban Sociology:* Mr. Phillips.
(INT.)   See Sociology 240b.

250b. *Germanic Mythology:* Mr. Jaeger.
(INT.)   See German 250b.

290. *La Civilisation française:* Mr. Guggenheim, Mrs. Gutwirth.
(INT.)   See INT. 290 in the interdepartmental major in French Studies.

[295a. *Paris in the Seventeenth and Eighteenth Centuries:* Miss Lafarge.]
(INT.)

[295b. *Littérature, histoire et société de la Renaissance à la Révolution:* Mr.
(INT.) Guggenheim.]

[297a. *Le Seizième Siècle à travers le roman historique:* Mr. Salmon.]
(INT.)

300b. *The American City in the Twentieth Century:* Mr. Speizman.
(INT.)   See INT. 300b in the interdepartmental major in The Growth and Structure of Cities.

301b. *Europe in the Twentieth Century:* Mr. Poppel.
(INT.)   See History 301b.

302a. *Greek Architecture:* Mr. Eiteljorg.
(INT.)   See Classical and Near Eastern Archaeology 302a.

302b. *Roman Architecture:* Mr. Scott.
(INT.)   See Archaeology 302b.

The Dynamics of Environmental Systems: Mr. Anderson.]

The Italian City-State in the Renaissance: Mrs. Lane.]

Architecture in Philadelphia: Mr. Thomas.
See INT. 306b in the interdepartmental major in The Growth and Structure of Cities.

Introduction to Celtic Civilization: Miss Dorian.
The course will trace the thread of Celtic civilization from the emergence of the Celts in pre-history to their marginal survival in modern times, concentrating on the contributions of mythology, the bardic tradition and the legal system to the uniqueness of Celtic society, and on the ancient continuities to be found in surviving Celtic folk custom and tradition.

Medieval Cities: Islamic, Byzantine and Western: Mr. Brand.]

Language in the Social Context: Miss Dorian.
Language in the social context: human versus animal communication; childhood language acquisition; bilingualism; regional dialects; usage and the issue of "correctness"; social dialects; speech behavior in other cultures; linguistic relativity.

Introduction to Linguistic Techniques: Miss Dorian.]

Diachronic Linguistics: Miss Dorian.]

Field Methods in Linguistics: Miss Dorian.]

History of Scientific Thought: Miss Oppenheimer, Mrs. Reeds.
See History 314.

Ethnic Group Politics: Mr. Ross.]

Mexico: Independence to the Present: Mrs. Dunn.]

Colonial Towns in North and South America: Mrs. Dunn.
See History 328a.

A History of Blacks in the American City: Mr. Holbrook.
See History 335a.

Topics in the History of Modern Architecture: Mrs. Lane.]

353a. *Biochemistry: Macromolecular Structure and Function:* Mr. Prescott, Mr.
(INT.) Young.
   See Biology 353a.

353b. *Biochemistry: Intermediary Metabolism:* Mr. Conner, Mr. Prescott.
(INT.)   See Biology 353b.

357a. *Computer Usage in the Life Sciences:* Mrs. Pruett.
(INT.)   See Biology 357a.

360a. *Forms of the Epic:* Mr. Forsyth.
(INT.)   An exploration of the epic genre with special emphasis on the conventions which govern its composition and its reception by the audience. Readings will include Odyssey, Song of Roland, Beowulf, Vergil, Tasso and Milton.

390a. *The Realistic Mode:* Miss Jordan.

(INT.)   The course will explore the nature of realistic representation in selected works of literature and painting in 19th Century France and England; and examine relationships between painters and writers, photographic techniques in painting, caricature, optics, perspective and the psychology of visual perception.

390b. *The Pastoral:* Miss Jordan.
(INT.)

391b. *The Idea of Imitation in Renaissance Literature:* Miss Jordan.
(INT.)

393b. *Great Britain in the Sixteenth and Seventeenth Centuries:* Mrs. Foster.
(INT.)   See History 393b.

Performing Arts

. *Dance Composition:* Mrs. Mason.

.   Designed to teach modern dance technique in conjunction with choreographic theory. Assignments in composition are given to aid artistic awareness and the development of performing skills.

. *Modern Dance: Advanced Techniques and Choreography:* Mrs. Mason, Mrs. Lember.]

. *Voice* or *Instrument*

   Students who are sufficiently advanced and who have completed at least one year of voice or music lessons while at the College may with the approval of the Department of Music offer for one unit of academic credit a year of voice or instrument lessons. The unit will include the lessons and also a recital or proficiency test arranged by the Music Department.

Physical Education

Director: Anne Lee Delano, M.A.

Instructors: Linda Fritsche Castner, M.S.
     Elaine E. Johnson, M.S.
     Barbara Lember, B.F.A.‡
     Paula Carter Mason, B.S.
     Jenepher Shillingford, M.ED.
     Alice Trexler, PH.D.
     Janet A. Yeager

The Department of Physical Education has developed a program to:

   1. Recognize the student with a high degree of neuromuscular coordination and physical stamina and encourage her to maintain this status.

---

‡On leave for the year 1977-78.

163

2. Provide incentive for all students to find some form of activity in which they may find pleasure and show improvement.

3. Contribute to the total well-being of the student.

The program provides a Physical Education Profile Test optional for freshman and sophomores. Above-average performance releases the student from physical education for one year.

There is a two-year requirement to be completed preferably by the end of the sophomore year. In the freshman year each student will take three hours a week during the first semester: two hours in an activity of her choice and one hour in a specialized unit. The units are Dance Orientation, Relaxation and Sports Orientation. In the second semester and during the sophomore year each student will participate two hours a week in an activity of her choice. Each semester is divided into two terms in order that the student may participate in a variety of activities should she wish to do so.

All students must complete the freshman and sophomore requirements satisfactorily. Upperclassmen are invited to elect any of the activities offered. Transfer students will have their physical education requirement reviewed by the Director of Physical Education.

The Optional Test for Release

Areas contributing to a physical education profile to be determined by testing, using standardized tests and procedures adapted to college women:

1. Aptitude and Achievement Battery (performance skill)
   a. Standing long jump b. Sandbag throw c. Obstacle course
2. Fitness Battery (strength and endurance)
   a. Standing long jump c. Push-ups—modified
   b. Sit-ups   d. 12-minute run
3. Body weight control

The Swimming Test (for survival)

1. Jump into deep end of pool (feet first entry), demonstrate two strokes while swimming lengths of pool for ten minutes without stopping, resting or touching bottom or sides of pool, backfloat motionless for two minutes, tread water one minute.
2. The swimming test is administered to every new student at the beginning of the year unless she is excused by the College Physician.
3. Students unable to pass the test must register for beginning swimming.

Seasonal Offerings ·

Fall: archery, modern dance, golf, hockey, riding*, swimming, tennis, volleyball, Advanced Life Saving, jogging, and trampoline.

Winter: badminton, basketball, modern dance, ballroom dancing, fencing, gymnastics, riding*, swimming, volleyball and American Red Cross Water Safety Instructor Training Course.

Spring: archery, modern dance, golf, gymnastics, lacrosse, riding*, swimming, tennis, trampoline, Advanced Life Saving and jogging.

A Modern Dance Club and Varsity teams are open to students with special interests in those areas.

---

*with permission of the chairman of the Department

Financial Aid

The scholarships listed on the following pages have been made available to able and deserving students through the generosity of alumnae and friends of the College. Many of them represent the income on endowed funds which in some cases is supplemented by an additional grant, usually taken from expendable gifts from alumnae and parents. A student requesting aid does not apply to a particular fund but is considered for all awards administered by the College for which she is qualified.

The Alumnae Regional Scholarship program is the largest single contributor to Bryn Mawr's scholarship awards. Bryn Mawr is the only college with an alumnae-based scholarship program independent, yet coordinated with the College's own financial aid program. The Alumnae raise funds, interview candidates requesting and needing aid and choose their scholars. An Alumnae Regional Scholarship carries with it special significance as an award for excellence, academic and personal.

An outstanding scholarship program has been established by the National Merit Scholarship Corporation, and several large corporations sponsor scholarship programs for children of employees. In addition to the generous awards made by these companies there are many others made by foundations and by individual and professional groups. Some of these are regional in designation. Students are urged to consult their schools and community agencies for information in regard to such opportunities.

Bryn Mawr College participates as a sponsor in the National Achievement Scholarship program. As sponsor, the College awards several scholarships through the National Merit Corporation. National Achievement finalists who have indicated that Bryn Mawr is their first choice institution will be referred to the College for consideration for this award.

Financial aid is held each year by approximately forty percent of the undergraduate students. The value of the scholarships ranges widely, but the average grant is approximately $2500. Requests for financial aid are reviewed by the Scholarship Committee and judged on the basis of the student's academic promise and achievement, and on her financial situation and that of her family. Bryn Mawr College, as a member of the College Scholarship Service of the College Entrance Examination Board, subscribes to the principle that the amount of aid granted a student should be based upon financial need. There are no financial aid funds in the award of the College which are awarded solely on merit. The Service assists colleges and other agencies in determining the student's need for financial assistance. All applicants must submit in support of application for financial aid either the Parents' Confidential Statement (Early Decision Plan applicants) or the Financial Aid Form (Regular Plan applicants). When the total amount of aid needed has been determined, awards are made in the form of grants, loans and jobs.

Bryn Mawr College administers two kinds of loan programs. The first consists of funds established through the generosity of alumnae and friends of the College and the second is based on government funds made available through the National Direct Student Loan program. Full descriptions can be found on page 191.

Another federally funded program, the College Work-Study program, enables the College to expand job opportunities for qualified students with on- and off-campus jobs, summer and winter, with eligible employers, either locally or near the student's home.

Applications for Financial Aid at Entrance

Application forms for financial aid are included in application materials sent to applicants who have submitted the preliminary application for admission. Each candidate for aid must also file with the College Scholarship Service either the Parents' Confidential Statement or the Financial Aid Form. One of these forms must be filed with the College and with the College Scholarship Service *no later than January 15* of the student's final year in high school in the case of regular applicants and *no later than November 1* in the case of applicants under the Early Decision Plan. Applications for financial aid for transfer students are due *no later than March 1*.

As the cost of tuition continues to increase, the number of applicants requiring financial assistance also increases. The funds available for award, however, are not growing at the same rate and the competition for financial aid funds therefore increases. Each year the College is in the position of admitting some academically qualified applicants who need financial assistance but to whom no aid can be granted.

Since scholarship funds of the College are not sufficient to cover the needs of the many well-qualified applicants, students are urged to consult with their school counselors about national and local scholarships which may be available and to submit appropriate applications. Specific questions regarding aid at Bryn Mawr should be directed to the Financial Aid Officer.

Renewal of Undergraduate Financial Aid

Application for the renewal of financial aid must be made annually. The renewal of the award depends on the student's maintaining a good record and her continued need for assistance. Adjustments are made to reflect changes in the financial situation of the family. Marriage or reaching the age of 21, however, are not considered valid reasons for the withdrawal of parental support or for an increase in financial aid.

The necessary forms for renewal may be obtained in the Financial Aid Office and should be filed with the College Scholarship Service no later than January 31.

Scholarship Funds

The Mary L. Jobe Akeley Scholarship Fund was established by bequest of Mary L. Jobe Akeley. The income from this fund of $149,597 is to be used for undergraduate scholarships with preference being given to students from Ohio. (1968)

The Alumnae Bequest Scholarship Fund, now totaling $8,696, was established by bequests received for scholarships from alumnae of the College. (1965)

Alumnae Regional Scholarships are available to students in all parts of the United States and Canada. These scholarships, raised by alumnae, vary in amount and may be renewed each year. The awards are made by local alumnae committees. Holders of these scholarships who maintain a high standard of academic work and conduct, and who continue to need financial aid after the freshman year, are assured assistance either from alumnae committees in their districts or from the College. (1922)

The Marion Louise Ament Scholarship Fund, now totaling $81,989, was established by bequest of Berkley Neustadt in honor of his daughter Marion Louise Ament of the Class of 1944. The income is to be used for scholarships. (1967)

The Evangeline Walker Andrews May Day Scholarship was established by bequest of Evangeline Walker Andrews of the Class of 1893. The income from this fund of $10,000 is to be used for undergraduate scholarships in the Department of English. Mrs. Andrews originated the Bryn Mawr May Day which was first held in 1900. (1963)

Note: The dates in parentheses in the listings on this and the following pages indicate the year the scholarship was established.

The Edith Heyward Ashley and Mabel Pierce Ashley Scholarship Fund was founded by bequest of Mabel Pierce Ashley of the Class of 1910. In 1969 the fund was increased by $25,000 by bequest of Edith Heyward Ashley of the Class of 1905. The fund now totals $50,000, and the income is to be awarded as a scholarship or scholarships to undergraduate students majoring in History or English. (1963)

The Elizabeth Congdon Barron Scholarship Fund. In 1960, by Mrs. Barron's bequest of $2,500, the Elizabeth Congdon Barron Fund was established "for the general purposes of the College." Through gifts from her husband Alexander J. Barron the fund was increased to $25,000 and the Elizabeth Congdon Barron Scholarship Fund was established. Through further gifts from Mr. Barron, the endowment has been raised to $55,063. (1964)

The Elizabeth P. Bigelow Memorial Scholarship Fund was established by gifts now amounting to $50,209 from Mrs. Henry B. Bigelow in memory of her daughter, Elizabeth P. Bigelow, who was graduated *cum laude* in 1930. (1960)

The Star K. Bloom and Estan J. Bloom Scholarship Fund was established by a gift of $10,000 from Star K. Bloom of the Class of 1960 and her husband, Estan J. Bloom. The income is to be awarded to academically superior students from the southern part of the United States with first preference being given to residents of Alabama. (1976)

The Book Shop Scholarships are awarded annually from the income from the Book Shop Fund, which now amounts to $98,630. (1947)

The Bertha Norris Bowen and Mary Rachel Norris Memorial Scholarship Fund was established by bequest under the will of Mary Rachel Norris of the Class of 1905 in memory of Bertha Norris Bowen, who was for many years a teacher in Philadelphia. (1973)

The James W. Broughton and Emma Hendricks Broughton Scholarship Fund was established by a bequest from the estate of Mildred Hendricks Broughton of the Class of 1939 in honor of her parents. The income from this fund shall be used for the purpose of paying tuition and other necessary expenses of students attending Bryn Mawr College. The students selected for such financial aid shall be from the midwestern part of the United States. (1972)

The Hannah Brusstar Memorial Scholarship Fund was established by a bequest from the estate of Margaret E. Brusstar of the Class of 1903. The income from this fund is to be awarded annually to an undergraduate student who shows unusual ability in Mathematics. (1976)

The Bryn Mawr Alumnae Physicians Fund for Premedical Students was established under the sponsorship of two alumnae Directors of the College. The income from this fund is to provide a flexible source of financial help to women at Bryn Mawr who have decided to enter medicine, whether or not they choose to major in physical sciences. (1976)

Bryn Mawr at the Tenth Decade—Undergraduate Student Aid. A pooled fund was established in the course of the Tenth Decade Campaign for those who wish to contribute to endowment for undergraduate student aid, but who do not wish to designate their gift to a specific named fund.

The Mariam Coffin Canaday Scholarship Fund was established by a gift of $18,866 from the Ward M. and Mariam C. Canaday Educational and Charitable Trust. The income from this fund was capitalized until in 1969 the fund reached the amount of $25,150. The income henceforth is to provide scholarships with preference given to students from Toledo, Ohio, or from District VI of the Alumnae Association. (1962)

The Antoinette Cannon Memorial Scholarship Fund was established by a gift of $30,400 by Janet Thornton of the Class of 1905 in memory of her friend Antoinette Cannon of the Class of 1907. (1963)

The Jeannette Peabody Cannon Memorial Scholarship Fund, now totalling $13,441, was established in memory of Jeannette Peabody Cannon, Class of 1919, through the efforts of the New England Alumnae Regional Scholarship Committee, of which she was a member for twenty years. The scholarship is awarded every three years on the nomination of the Alumnae Scholarship Committee to a promising member of the freshman class, residing in New England, who needs financial assistance. The scholarship may be held during the remaining three years of her college course provided a high standard is maintained. In 1962 the fund was increased from $7,405 to $13,491 by a generous gift from Mrs. Donald Wing of New Haven. (1949)

The Susan Shober Carey Award was founded in memory of Susan Shober Carey by gifts now totalling $3,300 from the Class of 1925 and is awarded annually by the President. (1931)

The Florence and Dorothy Child Memorial Scholarship of Bryn Mawr College was founded by bequest of Florence C. Child of the Class of 1905. The income from this fund of $115,494 is to be used for the residence fees of students who without such assistance would be unable to live in the halls. Preference is to be given to graduates of the Agnes Irwin School and to members of the Society of Friends. If no suitable applicants are available in these two groups, the scholarship aid will then be assigned by the College to students who could not live in residence halls without such assistance and who are not holding other scholarships. (1957)

The Augusta D. Childs Scholarship Fund was established by bequest of $45,495 from the estate of Augusta D. Childs. The income is to be used for undergraduate scholarships. (1970)

The Jacob Orie and Elizabeth S. M. Clarke Memorial Scholarship was established by bequest of $5,075 from the estate of Elizabeth Clarke and is awarded annually to a student born in the United States or any of its territories. (1948)

The Class of 1903 Scholarship Fund was established by gift of $12,305 on the occasion of the fiftieth reunion of the Class. The income from this fund is to be awarded annually to a member of the freshman, sophomore or junior class for use in the sophomore, junior or senior years. (1953)

The Class of 1922 Memorial Scholarship Fund was established at the suggestion of members of the Class of 1922 as a perpetual class fund to which members of the Class can contribute during the Tenth Decade Campaign and beyond. (1973)

The Class of 1943 Scholarship Fund was established by gifts of $36,804 from the James H. and Alice I. Goulder Foundation Inc. of which Alice Ireman Goulder of the Class of 1943 and her husband are officers. Members of the Class of 1943 and others add to the fund which continues to grow, and it is hoped that eventually the yearly income will provide full scholarship aid for one or more students at Bryn Mawr. (1974)

The 1967 College Bowl Scholarship Fund of $16,000 was established by the Bryn Mawr College team from its winnings on the General Electric College Bowl television program. The scholarship grants were donated by the General Electric Company and by *Seventeen* magazine and supplemented by gifts from the Directors of the College. The members of the team were Ashley Doherty (Class of 1971), Ruth Gais (Class of 1968), Robin Johnson (Class of 1969) and Diane Ostheim (Class of 1969). Income from this fund will be awarded to an entering freshman in need of assistance. (1967)

The Julia Cope Collins Scholarship was established by bequest of $10,000 from the estate of Julia Cope Collins, Class of 1889. (1959)

The Alice Perkins Coville Scholarship Fund, now totalling $76,587, was established by Agnes Frances Perkins of the Class of 1898 in honor of her sister, Alice Perkins Coville. The income from this scholarship fund is used to aid a deserving student in need of financial assistance. (1948)

The Regina Katharine Crandall Scholarship was established by a group of her students as a tribute to Regina Katharine Crandall, Margaret Kingsland Haskell Professor of English Composition from 1918 to 1933. The income from this fund, which now amounts to $10,225, is awarded to a sophomore, junior or senior who in her written English has shown ability and promise and who needs assistance to continue her college work. (1950)

The Annie Lawrie Fabens Crozier Scholarship Fund was established by a gift of $61,933 from Mr. and Mrs. Abbott P. Usher in memory of Mrs. Usher's daughter, Annie Lawrie Fabens Crozier of the Class of 1951. The scholarship, in varying amounts up to full tuition, is to be awarded to a junior or senior of distinction who is majoring in English. (1960)

The Rebecca Taylor Mattson Darlington Memorial Scholarship Fund was established by members of her family in memory of Rebecca Taylor Mattson Darlington, Class of 1896. The income is to be used for undergraduate scholarships. (1967)

The E. Merrick Dodd and Winifred H. Dodd Scholarship Fund of $2,000 was established by bequest of Dr. and Mrs. Dodd. (1953)

The Abby Slade Brayton Durfee Scholarship Fund, which now amounts to $13,000, was founded in honor of his wife by bequest of Randall N. Durfee, Jr. and Mrs. Charles Bennett Brown of the Class of 1930. Preference is given to candidates of English or American descent and to descendants of the Class of 1894. (1924)

The Ida L. Edlin Scholarship Fund was established by a bequest from the estate of Ida H. Edlin. The income only is to be used for scholarships for deserving students in fine arts or humanities. (1977)

The Frances C. Ferris Scholarship Fund was established by a bequest of $8,000 from the estate of Frances C. Ferris. The income from this fund is to be used to assist Friends who would otherwise be unable to attend Bryn Mawr College. (1977)

The Susan Grimes Walker Fitzgerald Fund was established by a gift from Susan Fitzgerald of the Class of 1929 in honor of her mother Susan Grimes Walker Fitzgerald of the Class of 1893. It is to be used for foreign graduate and undergraduate students studying at Bryn Mawr or for Bryn Mawr students doing research abroad in the summer or during the academic year. (1976)

The Anne Long Flanagan Scholarship was established by a gift of $29,687 from Anne Long Flanagan of the Class of 1906 on the occasion of the 55th reunion of the Class. The income is to be used to provide scholarships for Protestant students. (1961)

The Cora B. Fohs and F. Julius Fohs Perpetual Scholarship Fund was established by a gift of $75,000 from the Fohs Foundation. The income only is to be used. (1965)

The Folly Ranch Fund was established by an anonymous gift of $100,000, the income from which is to be used for graduate and undergraduate scholarships in honor of Eleanor Donnelley Erdman, Class of 1921, Clarissa Donnelley Haffner, Class of 1921, Elizabeth P. Taylor, Class of 1921, and Jean T. Palmer, Class of 1924. (1974)

The Foundation Scholarships, varying in amount up to full tuition and tenable for four years, are made available by the Trustees of Bryn Mawr College. They are awarded to members of the Society of Friends who cannot meet the full expenses of tuition and residence. (1894)

The William Franklin Scholarship Fund was established by a bequest of $35,985 from Susan B. Franklin of the Class of 1889. The income from this fund is to be used for scholarships for deserving girls, preference being given whenever possible to girls from the Rogers High School, Newport, Rhode Island. (1957)

The Edgar M. Funkhouser Memorial Scholarship Fund of $30,000 was established from his estate by Anne Funkhouser Francis of the Class of 1933. Awards may vary in amount up to full tuition and be tenable for four years. Income from this fund may be awarded annually, first preference being given to residents of southwest Virginia; thereafter to students from District IV eligible for aid in any undergraduate year. (1964)

The Helen Hartman Gemmill Scholarship, value $500, first given for the year 1970-71, is awarded annually to a student majoring in English from funds provided by the Warwick Foundation. (1967)

The Edith Rockwell Hall Scholarship Fund was established by a bequest of $20,000 from the estate of Florence R. Hall in memory of her sister Edith Rockwell Hall of the Class of 1892. (1977)

The Anna Hallowell Memorial Scholarship was founded in memory of Anna Hallowell by her family. The income on a fund of $2,585 is awarded annually to the junior in need of aid who has the highest academic record. (1912)

The Alice Ferree Hayt Memorial Prize was established by a bequest of $5,000 from the estate of Effie Todd Hayt in memory of her daughter Alice Ferree Hayt. The income of the fund is to be awarded annually to one or more students of the College in need of financial assistance for their personal use. (1977)

The Katharine Hepburn Scholarship, value $1,000, first given for the year 1969-70, is awarded annually in honor of Katharine Hepburn to a student interested in the study of drama and motion picture and in the cultivation of English diction and literary appreciation. (1952)

The Katharine Houghton Hepburn Memorial Scholarship was given in memory of Katharine Houghton Hepburn of the Class of 1900. The income on this fund, now totalling $51,050, is awarded for the junior or senior year to a student or students who have demonstrated both ability in her or their chosen field and independence of mind and spirit. (1957)

The Jeanne Crawford Hislop Memorial Scholarship Fund of $5,000 was given in memory of Jeanne Crawford Hislop of the Class of 1940 by Mr. and Mrs. John H. Hislop and Mrs. Frederic W. Crawford. The income from this fund has been supplemented by gifts from Mrs. John H. Hislop. This scholarship, awarded to a junior, may be renewed for the senior year. (1939)

The George Bates Hopkins Memorial Scholarships were founded by a gift of $10,056 from Mrs. Elizabeth Hopkins Johnson in memory of her father. Preference is given to students of Music and, in default of these, to students majoring in History and thereafter to students in other departments. (1921)

The Maria Hopper Scholarships, two in number, were founded by bequest under the will of Maria Hopper of Philadelphia and are awarded annually. The income from this fund of $10,224 is used for aid to a sophomore. (1901)

The Leila Houghteling Memorial Scholarship Fund in the amount of $10,180 was founded in memory of Leila Houghteling of the Class of 1911 by members of her family and a group of her contemporaries. It is awarded every three years on the nomination of the Alumnae Scholarship and Loan Fund Committee to a member of the freshman class in need of financial assistance and is held during the remaining three years of her college course. (1929)

Huguenot Society of America Grant. On the recommendation of the College a student of Huguenot ancestry may be nominated for a grant up to $1,000 to be used for college expenses. (1962)

The Shippen Huidekoper Scholarship Fund of $5,000 was established by an anonymous gift. The income is awarded annually on the nomination of the President. (1936)

The Evelyn Hunt Scholarships, two in number, were founded in memory of Evelyn Hunt by bequest of $10,000 under the will of Evelyn Ramsey Hunt of the Class of 1898. (1931)

The Lillia Babbitt Hyde Scholarship Fund was established by gifts of $25,600 from the Lillia Babbitt Hyde Foundation to establish the Lillia Babbitt Hyde Scholarship for award in so far as possible to students whose major subject will lead to a medical education or a scientific education in chemistry. (1963)

The Jane Lilley Ireson Scholarship was established by a bequest of $246,776 under the will of Jennie E. Ireson, her daughter. The income on each $5,000 of this fund is to be awarded as a scholarship to a worthy student who may require financial assistance. (1959)

The Alice Day Jackson Scholarship Fund of $10,195 was given by the late Percy Jackson in memory of his wife, Alice Day Jackson. The income from this fund is awarded annually to an entering student. (1930)

The Elizabeth Bethune Higginson Jackson Scholarship Fund was established by gifts in memory of Elizabeth Bethune Higginson Jackson of the Class of 1897 by members of her family and friends. The income from the fund is to be used for scholarships for undergraduate students as determined by the College Scholarship Committee. (1974)

The Sue Mead Kaiser Scholarship Fund was established by the alumnae of the Bryn Mawr Club of Northern California and other individuals in memory of Sue Mead Kaiser of the Class of 1931. (1974)

The Kathryn M. Kalbfleisch and George C. Kalbfleisch Scholarship Fund was established under the will of Kathryn M. Kalbfleisch of the Class of 1924; the income from the fund of $220,833 is to be used for scholarships. (1972)

The Alice Lovell Kellogg Fund was founded by a bequest of $5,000 by Alice Lovell Kellogg of the Class of 1903. The income is to be used for undergraduate scholarships. (1967)

The Minnie Murdoch Kendrick Memorial Scholarship, tenable for four years, was founded by bequest under the will of George W. Kendrick, Jr., in memory of his wife. The income on this fund of $5,362 is awarded every four years to a candidate nominated by the Alumnae Association of the Philadelphia High School for Girls. (1916)

The Misses Kirk Scholarship Fund, now amounting to $1,401, was founded in honor of the Misses Kirk by the Alumnae Association of the Kirk School in Bryn Mawr. (1929)

The Elizabeth B. Kirkbride Scholarship Fund was established by a gift of $1,150 from Elizabeth B. Kirkbride of the Class of 1896. The income is to be used for undergraduate scholarships. (1964)

The Clara Bertram Little Memorial Scholarship was founded by Eleanor Little Aldrich, in memory of her mother. The income from a fund now totalling $11,000 is awarded to an entering student from New England on the basis of merit and financial need. (1947)

The Mary Anna Longstreth Memorial Scholarship, established by a gift of $5,000 and carrying free tuition, was given in memory of Mary Anna Longstreth by alumnae and children of alumnae of the Mary Anna Longstreth School and by a few of her friends. (1913)

The Lorenz-Showers Scholarship Fund now amounting to $5,000 was established by Justina Lorenz Showers of Dayton, Ohio, of the Class of 1907, in honor of her parents, Edmund S. Lorenz and Florence K. Lorenz, and of her husband, John Balmer Showers. (1943)

The Alice Low Lowry Memorial Scholarship Fund was established by gifts in memory of Alice Low Lowry of the Class of 1938 by members of her family and friends. The income from a fund now totaling $30,126 is to be used for scholarships for undergraduate and graduate students. (1968)

The Katharine E. McBride Undergraduate Scholarship Fund was established by a gift of $5,000 made by Gwenn Davis Mitchell, Class of 1954. This fund now amounts to $10,060. The income is to be used for scholarships. (1969)

The Gertrude Howard McCormick Scholarship Fund was established by gift of $25,000 by the late Gertrude Howard McCormick. The scholarship, value $1,000, is awarded to a student of excellent standing, preferably for her freshman year. If she maintains excellent work in college, she may continue to receive scholarship aid through her sophomore, junior and senior years. (1950)

The Mary McLean and Ellen A. Murter Memorial Fund, now amounting to $14,320, was founded in memory of her two aunts by bequest of Mary E. Stevens of Germantown, Philadelphia. By vote of the Board of Directors the income is used for an annual scholarship. (1933)

The Midwest Scholarship Endowment Fund was established by the Alumnae of District VII in order "to enlarge the benefits which can be provided for able students from the midwest." The income from this fund is to be awarded in the same manner as regional scholarships. (1974)

The Beatrice Miller Memorial Scholarship Fund was established by a bequest of $83,966 from the estate of Beatrice Miller Ullrich of the Class of 1913. The income only is to be used for scholarships. (1969)

The Constance Lewis and Martha Rockwell Moorhouse 1904 Memorial Scholarship Fund, now amounting to $17,930, was established by the Class of 1904 in memory of their classmates Constance Lewis and Martha Rockwell Moorhouse. (1920)

The Evelyn Flower Morris Cope and Jacqueline Pascal Morris Evans Scholarship Fund, amounting to $13,094, was established by members of their families in memory of Evelyn Flower Morris of the Class of 1903 and Jacqueline Pascal Morris of the Class of 1908. (1959)

The Jean Brunn Mungall 1944 Memorial Scholarship Fund, now amounting to $39,766, was established by the Class of 1944. The Class on its 25th reunion in 1969 increased the fund by $16,600. The income is to be used for scholarships. (1955)

The Frank L. Neall and Mina W. Neall Scholarship Fund was established by a legacy of $25,000 from the estate of Adelaide W. Neall of the Class of 1906 in memory of her parents. The income is to be used for scholarship purposes at the discretion of the Trustees of the College. (1957)

The New Hampshire Scholarship Fund of $15,000 was established in 1965 by the Spaulding-Potter Charitable Trust. A matching fund was raised by contributions from New Hampshire alumnae. Income from the two funds will be awarded each year to an undergraduate from New Hampshire on the recommendation of the New England Regional Scholarship Committee. (1965)

The Alice F. Newkirk Scholarship Fund was founded by a bequest of $2,500 by Alice F. Newkirk. The income is for scholarships. (1965)

The Mary Frances Nunns Scholarship was established by a bequest of $25,275 under the will of Mary Frances Nunns. The income only is to be used. (1960)

The Pacific Northwest Student Aid Endowment Fund was established by a gift from Natalie Bell Brown of the Class of 1943 for Bryn Mawr at the Tenth Decade. The fund is to be used for students needing financial aid, with preference given to students from the Pacific Northwest. (1977)

The Florence Morse Palmer Scholarship was founded in memory of Florence Morse Palmer by her daughter, Jean T. Palmer, of the Class of 1924, by gifts now totalling $10,000. (1954)

The Margaret Tyler Paul Scholarship was established by a 40th reunion gift of $30,000 from the Class of 1922. (1963)

The Fanny R. S. Peabody Scholarship Fund was established by bequest of $177,927 in the will of Fanny R. S. Peabody. The income from the Peabody Fund is awarded to students from the western states. (1943)

The Delia Avery Perkins Scholarship was established by bequest of $58,474 from Delia Avery Perkins of the Class of 1900. Mrs. Perkins was Chairman of the New Jersey Scholarship Committee for a number of years. The income on this fund is to be awarded to students entering from Northern New Jersey. (1965)

The Ethel C. Pfaff Scholarship Fund was established by a bequest of $295,616 from Ethel C. Pfaff of the Class of 1904. The income from this fund is to be awarded to entering freshmen. (1967)

The Philadelphia Board of Public Education Scholarships, tenable for four years, are awarded to graduates of Philadelphia high schools nominated by the Board of Public Education of Philadelphia. (1898)

The Louise Hyman Pollak Scholarship was founded by the Board of Trustees from a bequest of $5,061 by Louise Hyman Pollak of the Class of 1908.

The income from this fund, now totalling $6,681, which has been supplemented by gifts from the late Julian A. Pollak and his son, David Pollak, is awarded annually to an entering student from one of the central states, east of the Mississippi River. Preference is given to residents of Cincinnati. (1932)

The Anna M. Powers Memorial Scholarship was founded in memory of Anna M. Powers by a gift from her daughter, Mrs. J. Campbell Harris. The income on this fund of $5,542 is awarded annually to a senior. (1902)

The Anna and Ethel Powers Memorial Scholarship was established by a gift of $1,000 in memory of Anna Powers of the Class of 1890 by her sister, Mrs. Charles Merrill Hough. The fund is now re-established at $13,634 in memory of both Anna Powers and her sister, Mrs. Hough (Ethel Powers), by Nancy Hough Smith of the Class of 1925. (1919)

The Thomas H. Powers Memorial Scholarship was founded in memory of Thomas H. Powers by bequest under the will of his daughter, Mrs. J. Campbell Harris. The income on this fund of $4,598 is awarded annually to a senior. (1902)

The Princeton Book Sale Scholarship was established by the alumnae of the Bryn Mawr Club of Princeton. The income from the fund is to be used for scholarships for students chosen by the College Scholarship Committee. (1974)

The James E. Rhoads Memorial Scholarships were founded in memory of the first President of the College, Dr. James E. Rhoads, by the Alumnae Association of Bryn Mawr College. In 1958 and 1959 the Alumnae Association increased the fund to $27,010, the income from which is awarded annually to two students. The James E. Rhoads Memorial Junior Scholarship is awarded to a student who has attended Bryn Mawr College for at least three semesters, has done excellent work and expresses her intention of fulfilling the requirements for the degree of Bachelor of Arts at Bryn Mawr College. The James E. Rhoads Memorial Sophomore Scholarship is awarded to a student who has attended Bryn Mawr College for at least one semester and who also meets the above conditions. (1898)

The Amelia Richards Scholarship was founded in memory of Amelia Richards of the Class of 1918 by bequest of $11,033 under the will of her mother, Mrs. Frank P. Wilson. It is awarded annually by the Trustees on the nomination of the President. (1921)

The Ida E. Richardson, Alice H. Richardson and Edward P. Langley Scholarship Fund was established by bequest of $81,065 under the will of Edward P. Langley. The income is to be used for scholarships. (1970)

The Maximilian and Reba E. Richter Scholarship Fund was established by a bequest of $50,000 in the will of Max Richter, father of Helen Richter Elser of the Class of 1913. The income from this fund is to be used to provide assistance for one or more students in the obtaining of either an academic or professional degree. The fund shall be administered on a non-sectarian basis to such applicants as are deemed worthy by habits of character and scholarship. No promises of repayment shall be exacted but it is hoped that students so benefited will desire when possible to contribute to the fund in order that similar aid may be extended to others. Such students shall be selected from among the graduates of public high schools or public colleges in the City of New York. (1961)

The Nancy Perry Robinson Memorial Scholarship Fund was established by a gift of $15,000 from Mrs. Huston B. Almond, of Philadelphia, in memory of her godchild, Nancy Perry Robinson, of the Class of 1945. The income of the fund is to be awarded annually to an undergraduate student, with preference being given to a student majoring in the French language. (1973)

The Serena Hand Savage Memorial Scholarship was established in memory of Serena Hand Savage of the Class of 1922 by her friends. The income from a fund of $25,562 is awarded to a member of the junior class who shows great distinction of scholarship and character and who needs financial assistance. This scholarship may be renewed in the senior year. (1951)

The J. Henry Scattergood Scholarship Fund was established by a gift of $15,000 from the Friends' Freedmen's Association to be used for undergraduate scholarships for black students. (1975)

The Constance Schaar Scholarship Fund, now totalling $4,866, was established in 1964 by her parents and friends in memory of Constance Schaar of the Class of 1963. The Class of 1963 added their reunion gift in 1964 to this fund. (1964)

The Scholarship Endowment Fund was established by a gift of $4,300 from Constance E. Flint. The income only is to be used for scholarships. (1970)

The Judith Harris Selig Scholarship Fund was established in memory of Judith Harris Selig of the Class of 1957 by members of her family, classmates and friends. In 1970 the fund was increased by a further gift of

$18,000 from her parents, Dr. and Mrs. Herman S. Harris. The income from the fund, now totalling $43,674, is to be used for undergraduate scholarships. (1968)

The Mary Williams Sherman Memorial Scholarship Fund, now amounting to $4,150, was established by bequest of Bertha Williams of Princeton, New Jersey. (1942)

The Frances Marion Simpson Scholarships, carrying up to full tuition and tenable for four years, were founded in memory of Frances Simpson Pfahler of the Class of 1906 by Justice Alexander Simpson, Jr., by gifts amounting to $20,682. One scholarship is awarded each year to a member of the entering freshman class who cannot meet in full the fees of the College. In awarding these scholarships first preference is given to residents of Philadelphia and Montgomery Counties who have been prepared in the public schools of these counties; thereafter, under the same conditions, to residents of other counties of Pennsylvania, and, in special cases, to candidates from other localities. Holders of these scholarships are expected to repay the sums advanced to them. If they become able during their college course to pay the tuition fees in whole or in part, they are required to do so. (1912)

The Gertrude Slaughter Scholarship Fund was established by bequest of $19,909 by Gertrude Taylor Slaughter of the Class of 1893. The income on this fund is to be used for undergraduate scholarships, preferably to students of Greek or Latin. (1964)

The Anna Margaret Sloan and Mary Sloan Scholarships were founded by bequest of Mary Sloan of Pittsburgh. The income from this fund of $16,858 is awarded annually to students majoring in Philosophy or Psychology. (1942)

The Cordelia Clark Sowden Scholarship Fund was established by a bequest of $15,000 from the estate of Helen C. Sowden. The income from this fund is used for scholarships to be awarded by Bryn Mawr College under the rules in effect at the time of the award. (1957)

The Amy Sussman Steinhart Scholarship, carrying full tuition, was founded in memory of Amy Sussman Steinhart of the Class of 1902 by her family and friends. The income from gifts now totalling $33,652 is awarded annually to an entering student from one of the states on the west coast. (1932)

The Mary E. Stevens Scholarship Fund was given in memory of Mary E. Stevens by former pupils of The Stevens School in Germantown. The income on this fund of $3,188 is awarded annually to a junior. (1897)

The Anna Lord Strauss Scholarship and Fellowship Fund was established by a gift from Anna Lord Strauss to support graduate and undergraduate students in need of financial assistance who are interested in fields leading to public service or which involve education in the process of government. (1976)

The Summerfield Foundation Scholarship was established by a gift from the Solon E. Summerfield Foundation. The income from this fund, which now totals $19,000, is to be used to assist able students who need financial help to continue their studies. (1958)

The Mary Hamilton Swindler Scholarship was established in honor of Mary Hamilton Swindler, Professor of Classical Archaeology from 1931 to 1949, by a group of friends and former students, by gifts totalling $8,493. The income from this fund is used for a scholarship for the study of Archaeology. (1950)

The Elizabeth P. Taylor Scholarship Fund, now amounting to $20,771, was established by a bequest from Elizabeth P. Taylor of the Class of 1921. (1961)

The Ethel Vick Wallace Townsend Memorial Fund was established by Elbert S. Townsend in memory of his wife, Ethel Vick Wallace Townsend, of the Class of 1908. The income on this fund, held by the Buffalo Foundation, is to be used for undergraduate scholarships. (1967)

The Trustees' Scholarships, varying in amount up to full tuition and tenable for four years, are made available by the Trustees of Bryn Mawr College for students prepared in the high schools of Philadelphia and its suburbs. Two of these scholarships are awarded annually to candidates who have received all their preparation for entrance in Philadelphia high schools and are recommended by the Board of Public Education of Philadelphia; two are awarded annually to candidates who have received all their preparation for entrance in public schools in the suburbs of Philadelphia and are awarded by the College after consultation with the principals of the schools presenting candidates. The amount of the award varies according to the need of the applicant. (1895)

Two or sometimes three of these scholarships are supported by the income from *The Jacob Fussell Byrnes and Mary Byrnes Fund,* which was established in memory of her mother and father by a bequest of $51,513 under the will of Esther Fussell Byrnes. (1948)

The Mildred Clarke Pressinger von Kienbusch Scholarship Fund was established by C. Otto von Kienbusch in memory of his wife, Mildred Clarke Pressinger von Kienbusch, of the Class of 1909. The income from this fund of $30,000 will be awarded each year to a student in need of assistance. (1968)

The Mary E. G. Waddell Scholarship Fund was established by a bequest from the Estate of Mary E. G. Waddell. The income from this fund is to be used for scholarships for undergraduates and graduate students interested in the study of Mathematics who are daughters of American citizens of Canadian descent. (1971)

The Julia Ward Scholarship Fund was established by a gift of $7,075 for a scholarship in memory of Julia Ward of the Class of 1923 by one of her friends and by additional gifts from others. The income on this fund which now amounts to $35,146 is to be used for undergraduate scholarships. (1962)

The Eliza Jane Watson Scholarship Fund was established by gifts of $25,000 from the John Jay and Eliza Jane Watson Foundation. The income from this fund is to be used to assist one or more students as selected by the College to meet the cost of tuition. (1964)

The Elizabeth Wilson White Memorial Scholarship was founded in memory of Elizabeth Wilson White by a gift of $7,513 by Thomas Raeburn White. It is awarded annually by the President. (1923)

The Thomas Raeburn White Scholarships, established by a gift of $25,000, made by Amos and Dorothy Peaslee in 1964 in honor of Thomas Raeburn White, Trustee of the College from 1907 until his death in 1959, Counsel to the College throughout these years and President of the Trustees from 1956 to 1959. The income from this fund is to be used for prizes to undergraduate students who plan to study foreign languages abroad during the summer under the auspices of an approved program. (1964)

The Mary R. G. Williams Scholarship Fund was established from the Fund for Promoting College Education for Women established by bequest of Mary R. G. Williams. The income from this fund of $5,694 will be used for emergency grants for students who are paying their own way through college. (1957)

The Mary Peabody Williamson Scholarship was founded by bequest of $1,000 by Mary Peabody Williamson of the Class of 1903. (1939)

The Marion H. Curtin Winsor Memorial Scholarship was established by a bequest of $10,000 in the will of Mary Winsor, in memory of her mother. The income on this fund is to be awarded to a resident black student. (1960)

The Mary Winsor Scholarship in Archaeology was established by a bequest of $3,000 under the will of Mary Winsor. The income only is to be used. (1960)

The Ellen Winsor and Rebecca Winsor Evans Memorial Scholarship Fund was established by a bequest of $5,230 in the will of Rebecca Winsor Evans. The scholarship is to be awarded to a resident black student. (1962)

The Rebecca Winsor Evans and Ellen Winsor Memorial Scholarship Fund was established by a bequest of $5,230 in the will of Ellen Winsor. The scholarship is to be awarded to a resident black student. (1962)

The Gertrude Miller Wright Scholarships were established under the will of Dorothy M. Wright of the Class of 1931, for needy students of Bryn Mawr College. (1973)

The Lila M. Wright Memorial Scholarship was founded in memory of Lila M. Wright by gifts totalling $2,681 from the alumnae of Miss Wright's School of Bryn Mawr. (1934)

The Georgie W. Yeatman Scholarship was founded by bequest of $1,000 under the will of Georgie W. Yeatman of Philadelphia. (1941)

Scholarships for Foreign Students

The Bryn Mawr Canadian Scholarship will be raised and awarded each year by Bryn Mawr alumnae living in Canada. The scholarship, varying in amount, will be awarded to a Canadian student entering either the undergraduate or graduate school. (1965)

The Chinese Scholarship comes in part from the annual income of a fund now totalling $50,185 established by a group of alumnae and friends of the College in order to meet all or part of the expenses of a Chinese student during her four undergraduate years at Bryn Mawr College. (1917)

The Marguerite N. Farley Scholarships for foreign students were established by bequest of Marguerite N. Farley. The income from a fund of $331,425 will be used for scholarships for foreign graduate and undergraduate students covering part or all of their expenses for tuition and residence. (1956)

The Margaret Y. Kent Scholarship Fund, Class of 1908 was established by bequest of Margaret Y. Kent of the Class of 1908. The income from the fund of $7,000 is to be used to provide scholarship assistance to foreign students. (1967)

The Middle East Scholarship Fund was established by a gift from Elizabeth Cope Harrison of the Class of 1958. The purpose of the fund is to enable the College "to make scholarship awards to able students from a number of Middle Eastern Countries." (1975)

The Special Trustees' Scholarship is awarded every four years to a foreign student. It carries free tuition and is tenable for four years. The scholarship for students from foreign countries was first offered by the Trustees in 1940.

The Undergraduate Scholarship, raised by the Undergraduate Association and awarded by the Association in consultation with the Director of Admissions, is awarded each year to a foreign student entering Bryn Mawr. (1938)

Prizes and Academic Awards

The following awards, fellowships, scholarships and prizes are in the award of the faculty and are given solely on the basis of academic distinction and achievement.

The Bryn Mawr European Fellowship has been awarded each year, since the first class was graduated in 1889. It is given for merit to a member of the graduating class, to be applied toward the expenses of one year's study at some foreign university.

The Maria L. Eastman Brooke Hall Memorial Scholarship was founded in memory of Maria L. Eastman, Principal of Brooke Hall School for Girls, Media, Pennsylvania, by gifts totaling $3,310 from the alumnae and former pupils of the school. It is awarded annually to the member of the junior class with the highest general average and is held during the senior year. Transfer students who enter Bryn Mawr as members of the junior class are not eligible for this award. (1901)

The Elizabeth Duane Gillespie Fund for Scholarships in American History was founded by a gift from the National Society of Colonial Dames of

America in the Commonwealth of Pennsylvania in memory of Elizabeth Duane Gillespie. Two prizes are awarded annually on nomination by the Department of History, one to a member of the sophomore or junior class for work of distinction in American History, a second to a student doing advanced work in American History for an essay written in connection with that work. The income from this fund of $1,970 has been supplemented since 1955 by annual gifts from the Society. (1903)

The Elizabeth G. Shippen Scholarships were founded by two bequests of $5,000 each under the will of Elizabeth S. Shippen of Philadelphia. Three scholarships are awarded annually, one to the member of the senior class who receives The Bryn Mawr European Fellowship and two to members of the junior class, as follows: 1. *The Shippen Scholarship in Science* to a student whose major subject is Biology, Chemistry, Geology or Physics, 2. *The Shippen Scholarship in Foreign Languages* to a student whose major subject is French, German, Greek, Italian, Latin, Russian or Spanish. To be eligible for either of these two scholarships a student must have completed at least one semester of the second-year course in her major subject. Neither may be held by the winner of the Charles S. Hinchman Memorial Scholarship. Work in elementary courses will not be considered in awarding the scholarship in foreign languages, 3. *The Shippen Scholarship for Foreign Study* (See The Bryn Mawr European Fellowship, page 185). (1915)

The Charles S. Hinchman Memorial Scholarship was founded in the memory of the late Charles S. Hinchman of Philadelphia by a gift of $12,000 made by his family. It is awarded annually to a member of the junior class for work of special excellence in her major subjects and is held during the senior year. (1917)

The Sheelah Kilroy Memorial Scholarships in English were founded in memory of their daughter Sheelah, by Dr. and Mrs. Phillip Kilroy by a gift of $5,000. These scholarships are awarded annually on the recommendation of the Department of English as follows: to a student for excellence of work in second-year or advanced courses in English, and to the student in the first-year course in English Composition who writes the best essay during the year. (1919)

The Jeanne Quistgaard Memorial Prize was given by the Class of 1938 in memory of their classmate Jeanne Quistgaard. The income on this fund of $690 may be awarded every two years to a student in Economics. (1938)

The Esther Walker Award was founded by the bequest of $1,000 from William John Walker in memory of his sister, Esther Walker, of the Class of 1910. It may be given annually to a member of the senior class who in the judgment of the faculty shall have displayed the greatest proficiency in the study of living conditions of northern blacks. (1940)

The M. Carey Thomas Essay Prize is awarded annually to a member of the senior class for distinction in writing. The award is made by the Department of English for either creative or critical writing. It was established in memory of Miss Thomas by her niece, Millicent Carey McIntosh, of the Class of 1920. (1943)

The Katherine Fullerton Gerould Memorial Prize was founded in 1946 by a gift of $1,300 from a group of alumnae, many of whom were students of Mrs. Gerould when she taught at Bryn Mawr from 1901 to 1910. The fund was increased by a bequest of $2,400 by one of her former students. It is awarded by a special committee to a student who shows evidence of creative ability in the fields of informal essay, short story and longer narrative or verse. (1946)

The Hester Ann Corner Prize for distinction in literature was established in memory of Hester Ann Corner of the Class of 1942 by gifts totalling $2,625 from her classmates and friends. The award is made annually to a junior or senior on the recommendation of a committee composed of the chairmen of the departments of English and of classical and modern foreign languages. (1950)

The Academy of American Poets Prize of $100 has been recently awarded each year to the student who submits to the Department of English the best poem or group of poems. The award, given by the Academy of American Poets, was first made in 1957.

The Helen Taft Manning Essay Prize in History was established in honor of Helen Taft Manning, in the year of her retirement, by her class (1915). The income on a fund of $2,600 is to be awarded as the Department of History may determine. (1957)

The Bain-Swiggett Poetry Prize was established by a gift of $1,000 from Mr. and Mrs. Glen Levin Swiggett. This prize is to be awarded by a committee of the faculty on the basis of the work submitted. The income only is to be used. (1958)

The Charlotte Angas Scott Prize in Mathematics. A prize to be awarded annually to an undergraduate on the recommendation of the Department of Mathematics was established by an anonymous gift in memory of Charlotte Angas Scott, Professor of Mathematics and a member of the faculty of Bryn Mawr College from 1885 to 1924. The income only from this gift is to be used. (1961)

The Anna Pell Wheeler Prize in Mathematics. A prize to be awarded annually to an undergraduate on the recommendation of the Department of Mathematics was established by an anonymous gift in honor of Anna Pell Wheeler, Professor Emeritus of Mathematics and a member of the faculty of Bryn Mawr College from 1918 until her death in 1966. The income only from this gift is to be used. (1961)

The Emma Osborn Thompson Prize in Geology was founded by bequest of Emma Osborn Thompson of the Class of 1904. From the income on the bequest of $500 a prize is to be awarded from time to time to a student in Geology. (1963)

The Gertrude Slaughter Fellowship was established by a bequest of $50,000 in the will of Gertrude Taylor Slaughter of the Class of 1893. The Fellowship is to be awarded to a member of the graduating class for excellence in scholarship to be used for a year's study in the United States or abroad. (1964)

The Commonwealth Africa Scholarship was established by a grant of $50,000 from the Thorncroft Fund Inc. at the request of Helen and Geoffrey de Freitas. The income from this fund will be used to send, for at least six months, a graduate to a university or college in Commonwealth Africa, or former British colony in Africa, to teach or to study, with a view to contributing to mutual understanding and the furtherance of scholarship. (1965)

The Alexandra Peschka Prize was established in memory of Alexandra Peschka of the Class of 1964 by gifts from her family and friends. The prize of $100 is awarded annually to a member of the freshman or sophomore class for the best piece of imaginative writing in prose. The award will be made by a committee of the Department of English who will consult the terms stated in the deed of gift. (1968)

The Katherine Stains Prize Fund in Classical Literature was established by Katherine G. Stains in memory of her parents Arthur and Katheryn Stains, and in honor of two excellent twentieth-century scholars of classical literature, Richmond Lattimore and Moses Hadas. The income on the fund of $1,000 is to be awarded annually as a prize to an undergraduate student for excellence in Greek literature, either in the original or in translation. (1969)

The Horace Alwyne Prize was established by the Friends of Music of Bryn Mawr College in honor of Horace Alwyne, Professor Emeritus of Music. The award is presented annually to the student who has contributed the most to the musical life of the college. (1970)

The Hope Wearn Troxell Memorial Prize is awarded annually by the alumnae of Southern California to a student from Alumnae District IX, with first consideration to a student from Southern California. The prize is awarded in recognition of the student's responsible contribution to the life of the College community. (1973)

The Berle Memorial Prize Fund in German Literature was established by Lillian Berle Dare in memory of her parents, Adam and Katharina Berle. The income on the fund of $1,000 is awarded annually to an undergraduate for excellence in German literature. Preference is given to a senior who is majoring in German and who does not come from a German background. (1975)

Scholarships for Medical Study

The following scholarships may be awarded to seniors intending to study medicine, after their acceptance by a medical school, or to graduates of Bryn Mawr intending or continuing to pursue a medical education. Applications for the scholarships should be made to the Premedical Advisor before March 15 preceding the academic year in which the scholarship is to be held. Applications for renewal of scholarships must be accompanied by letters of recommendation from instructors in the medical school.

The Linda B. Lange Fund was founded by bequest of $30,000 under the will of Linda B. Lange of the Class of 1903. The income from this fund will provide the *Anna Howard Shaw Scholarship in Medicine and Public Health,* awarded on recommendation of the President and faculty to a member of the graduating class or a graduate of the College for the pursuit, during an uninterrupted succession of years, of studies leading to the degrees of M.D. and Doctor of Public Health. The award may be continued until the degrees are obtained. (1948)

The Hannah E. Longshore Memorial Medical Scholarship was founded by Mrs. Rudolf Blankenburg in memory of her mother by a gift of $10,000. The scholarship is awarded by a committee of the faculty to a student who has been accepted by a medical school. It may be renewed for each year of medical study. (1921)

The Jane V. Myers Medical Scholarship Fund of $10,000 was established by Mrs. Rudolf Blankenburg in memory of her aunt. The scholarship is awarded by a committee of the faculty to a student who has been accepted by a medical school. It may be renewed for each year of medical study. (1921)

The Harriet Judd Sartain Memorial Scholarship Fund was founded by bequest of $21,033 under the will of Paul J. Sartain. The income from this fund is to establish a scholarship which is awarded to a member of the graduating class who in the judgment of the faculty needs and is deserving of assistance for the study of medicine. This scholarship may be continued for the duration of her medical course. (1948)

Loan Funds

Bryn Mawr College administers two kinds of loan programs. The first consists of four funds established through the generosity of alumnae and friends of the College. Applications for loans must be accompanied by the Parents' Confidential Statement or the Financial Aid Form prepared by the College Scholarship Service of the College Entrance Examination Board.

The Students' Loan Fund of the Alumnae Association of Bryn Mawr College was founded by the Class of 1890 for the use of students who need to borrow money in order to continue their college work. The fund is managed by the Alumnae Scholarships and Loan Fund Committee.

Loans may be used for any purpose approved by the committee, but not more than $500 may be borrowed by a student in any one year. The total for four years must not exceed $1,500. Students who wish loans may obtain from the Financial Aid Office or the Alumnae Office the necessary blanks which must be accompanied by a letter of recommendation from the Financial Aid Officer.

While the student is in college no interest is charged, and she may reduce the principal of the loan if she so desires. The interest rate is three percent, to be paid after the student leaves the College. The entire principal must be repaid within five years of the time the student leaves college at the rate of twenty percent each year.

Contributions to the Loan Fund may be sent to the Chairman of Scholarships and Loan Fund, Bryn Mawr College Alumnae Association, Bryn Mawr, Pennsylvania 19010.

The Mary Hill Swope Loan Fund was established in 1945 by a gift of the late Mrs. Gerard Swope (Mary Hill, A.B. 1896) under the following conditions:

To assist in the education of young women irrespective of race, color or creed attending Bryn Mawr College, the income of the fund to be lent to students in the following manner:

a. The following order of preference shall be followed in awarding such loans—to students coming from New Jersey, to students coming from Missouri, to students coming from any other location who have had not less than one year of residence at the College.

b. The loans in the above order of preference, and in the following manner, shall be awarded by the President of Bryn Mawr College or by a committee appointed by him from time to time.

c. Applicants for loans shall be considered not only from the standpoint of academic attainment and financial need, but also from the standpoint of character and personal qualifications for deriving the greatest good from a continuation of their studies.

d. These loans shall be used primarily to enable the exceptional student to continue her studies, which otherwise would be prevented through lack of means.

e. Except under extraordinary circumstances, the maximum amount which may be borrowed annually is $500. No interest is charged while the student is in college. The interest rate is three percent, to be paid after the student leaves college. The principal is to is to be repaid within five years of the time the student graduates or leaves Bryn Mawr at the rate of twenty percent each year.

The Gerard and Mary Hill Swope Loan Fund was established in 1962 under the following conditions:

a. Non-scholarship students and graduate students are also eligible to apply for loans from this fund.

b. The maximum amount which can be borrowed for any given academic year is $500.

c. While the student is in college or graduate school no interest is charged, but she may reduce the principal of the loan if she so desires. The interest rate is three percent, to be paid after the student leaves college. The entire principal must be repaid within five years of the time the student leaves college at the rate of twenty percent each year.

d. Loans are awarded by the Scholarship Committees of the Undergraduate School, The Graduate School of Arts and Sciences and The Graduate School of Social Work and Social Research.

The Clareth Fund was established in 1971 by a bequest to the College from the estate of Ethel S. Weil. The income only is to be used for students "specializing in economics or business." There is no interest due but the student must begin to repay the loan within six years after graduation.

The second kind of loan program, administered by the College, is based on government funds made available through *The National Direct Student Loan Program*. Applications for loans must be accompanied by the Parents' Confidential Statement or the Financial Aid Form prepared by the College Entrance Examination Board. The three percent interest rate and repayment of the loan begin one year after the student has completed her education.

Students who, upon graduation, teach on a full-time basis in public or private non-profit elementary and secondary schools in an economically depressed area as defined by the H.E.W. National Register or who work with handicapped children are allowed cancellation of their debts at the rate of 15% per year for the first and second years, 20% per year for the third and fourth years and 30% for the fifth year or total cancellation over five years.

International Initiatives Loan Fund makes loan funds available to currently enrolled undergraduate and graduate students through a special donation for the purpose of supporting independent study or research projects abroad. It is not normally available to students in a regular junior year abroad program. Full information and applications are available in the Office of the Associate Dean.

The Federally Insured or *State Guaranteed Student Loan Programs* are government subsidized programs which were instituted to enable students to meet educational expenses. Application is made through the students' home banks. Each year the student may borrow from $1,000 to $2,500 depending on the State regulations in effect in her State. Repayment begins nine months after the student is no longer enrolled, at least half-time, at an accredited institution. The interest is seven percent. The government will pay this interest until the repayment period begins provided the financial situation of the family warrants it. The Parents' Confidential Statement or the Financial Aid Form must be submitted to the institution in order to determine whether or not the family qualifies for this interest subsidy. If the family does not wish to submit financial information, the student is still eligible for the loan but she is responsible for the interest payments while she is in school.

Alumnae Representatives

Officers of the Alumnae Association

President, Mrs. William S. Cashel, Jr., 1144 Norsam Road,
Gladwyne, Pennsylvania 19035

First Vice President, Mrs. David S. Cooper, 225 Kelburne Avenue,
N. Tarrytown, New York 10591

Second Vice President, Mrs. R. Thomas Unkefer, Jr.,
102 North Woodstock Street, Philadelphia, Pennsylvania 19103

Third Vice President, Mrs. Michael C. Mitchell, 1507 Mt. Pleasant Road,
Villanova, Pennsylvania 19085

Recording Secretary, Ms. Barbara Schieffelin Powell, 46 Sacramento Street,
Cambridge, Massachusetts 02138

Corresponding Secretary, Mrs. Josephine E. Case, 80 North Moore Street, Apt.
34J, New York, New York 10013

Treasurer, Mrs. Francis R. Manlove, 500 Williamson Road,
Gladwyne, Pennsylvania 19035

Chairman, Alumnae Fund, Mrs. Richard E. Fisher, 425 Glyn Wynne,
Haverford, Pennsylvania 19041

Chairman, Selection Committee, Mrs. Robert Cavanaugh,
912 W. Northern Parkway, Baltimore, Maryland 21210

Chairman, Scholarship & Loan Fund Committee, Mrs. Richard W. Day,
36 Lloyd Road, Montclair, New Jersey 07042

Chairman, Wyndham Committee, Mrs. Fred Alexander, 1400 Youngsford Road,
Gladwyne, Pennyslvania 19035

Executive Director, Mrs. Betsy F. Havens

Executive Secretary, Alumnae Fund, Mrs. Charles P. Dethier

Coordinator for Graduate Alumnae/i, Karla Klein Berger

The Editor, The Alumnae Bulletin, Mrs. Samuel Mason,
Wyndham, Bryn Mawr College 19010

Director, Oral History Project, Mrs James A. Rittenhouse

Alumnae Trustees of Bryn Mawr College

Ms. Gillian B. Anderson, 1320 North Carolina Avenue N.E.,
Washington, D.C. 20002

Mrs. Thomas Bates, 1312 Middle Road, Bettendorf, Iowa 52722

Mrs. John G. Laylin, 438 River Bend Road, Great Falls, Virginia 22066

Mrs. John E. Lippmann, 90 Riverside Drive, New York, New York 10024

Mrs. J. Peter Schmitz, 6401 Wydown Boulevard, Saint Louis, Missouri 63105

Mrs. Bernard L. Schwartz, 1020 Prospect Street, Suite 318, La
Jolla, California 92037

Mrs. William H. Taft III, 3101 35th Street, N.W.,
Washington, D. C. 20016

Officers of Alumnae Groups and College Representatives

District I: Maine, New Hampshire, Vermont, Massachusetts, Rhode Island, Connecticut (except Fairfield County)

Councillor, Mrs. George S. Reichenbach, 123 West Street, Carlisle, Massachusetts 01741

District Admissions Coordinator, Mrs. Martin A. Hitchcock, 29 Wildwood Street, Winchester, Massachusetts 01890

Club Presidents:

Boston . . . . Mrs. Carroll P. Griffith, Jr., 5 Fox Run Road, Bedford, Massachusetts 01730

Hartford . . . . Mrs. Thomas Groark, Jr., 45 Woodside Circle, Hartford, Connecticut 06105

New Haven . . . . Mrs. Charles Tu, 408 Curtis Hall, 350 Canner Street, New Haven, Connecticut 06511

Rhode Island . . . . . . Mrs. Nicholas Retsinas, 64 Blaisdell Avenue, Pawtucket, Rhode Island 02860

District II: New York, Fairfield County (Connecticut), Northern New Jersey

Councillor, Mrs. Joseph M. Schack, 127 West 12th Street, New York, New York 10011

District Admissions Coordinator, Mrs. George L. Curran, R. D. 2, Box 308A, Red Hook, New York 12571

Club Presidents:

Fairfield County . . . Mrs. Stanley B. Garrell, 310 Hillbrook Lane, Fairfield, Connecticut 06430

New York . . . . Julia L. Kagan, 377 Bleecker Street, 4-B, New York, New York 10014

Long Island . . . . Miss Natalie Naylor, 496 Clarendon Road, Uniondale, New York 11553

Westchester . . . . Mrs. Richard J. Miller, 62 Taconic Road., Box 386, Millwood, New York 10546

Albany, Troy,
Schenectady . . . . . Mrs. Arthur W. Wright, 642 Western Avenue, Albany, New York 12203

Buffalo . . . . Mrs. Marcella Brett, 20 Colonial Drive, Buffalo, New York 14226

Rochester . . . . Mrs. Thomas F. Griswold, Huntington Hills, Rochester, New York 14622

Princeton . . . . Miss Diana D. Lucas, 105 Mercer Street, Princeton, New Jersey 08540

Northern New Jersey Mrs. John F. Parell, 6 Jerome Place, Upper Montclair, New Jersey 07043

Candidates for admission who wish to talk with an alumna are invited to write to the District Admissions Coordinator in their area

District III: Pennsylvania, Southern New Jersey, Delaware
Councillor, Mrs. Frank M. Masters, Jr., R. D. 4, Box 848,
Harrisburg, Pennsylvania 17112
District Admissions Coordinator: Mrs. Samuel Diamond, 2021 Pine Street,
Philadelphia, Pennsylvania 19103
Club Presidents:
Philadelphia ...... Mrs. Charles H. Greenbaum, 1237 Imperial Road,
Rydal, Pennsylvania 19046
Central Pennsylvania Mrs. Richard Sasin, 1117 Amy Lane,
Lancaster, Pennsylvania 17601
Western
Pennsylvania .... Mrs. Irving Sikov, 1215 Minnesota Avenue, Natrona
Heights, Pennsylvania 15065
Delaware .... Mrs. Ernest H. Beck, 48 Paschall Road,
Wilmington, Delaware 19803

District IV: Maryland, Virginia, West Virginia, District of Columbia
Councillor, Ms. Joan T. Briccetti, 4506 Monument Avenue,
Richmond, Virginia 23230
District Admissions Coordinator: Mrs. Charles M. Boteler, Jr., 11921 Oden Court,
Old Farm, Rockville, Maryland 20852
Club Presidents:
Washington ...... Mrs. Norman Grossblatt, 6711 Georgia Street,
Chevy Chase, Maryland 20015
Baltimore .... Mrs. William R. Richardson, 1003 Wagner Road,
Ruxton, Maryland 21204
Richmond .... Mrs. Jacob Haun, Jr., 1408 Wilmington Avenue,
Richmond, Virginia 23227
Norfolk .... Mrs. Ralph W. Miner, Jr., 1006 Hanover Avenue,
Norfolk, Virginia 23508

District V: North Carolina, South Carolina, Georgia, Florida, Alabama,
Mississippi, Louisiana, Arkansas, Tennessee
Councillor, Mrs. Henry M. Farrell, 208 Park Shore East, Columbia, South
Carolina 29204
District Admissions Coordinator: Mrs. Thomas J. Davis, Jr., 825 Overton Lane,
Nashville, Tennessee 37220
Club Presidents:
Piedmont .... Miss Mary J. Wilson, 1413 Watts Street,
Durham, North Carolina 27701
Florida .... Mrs. David C. Aschman, 20 S. Prospect Drive,
Coral Gables, Florida 33133
Louisiana .... Maud M. Walsh, 4536 Folse Drive,
Metairie, Louisiana 70002
Georgia .... Gail McK. Beckman, 3200 Lenox Road, C-400,
Atlanta, Georgia 30324

District VI: Ohio, Indiana, Kentucky, Michigan
Councillor, To be appointed.
District Admissions Coordinator: Mrs. J. R. Taylor Bassett III,
  3356 Chalfant Road, Shaker Heights, Ohio 44120
Club Presidents:

Indiana .... Ms. Victoria Munn, 5830 N. Haverford, Indianapolis,
  Indiana 46220

Detroit .... Mrs. Bruce Steinhauer, 1304 Bishop Road,
  Grosse Pointe, Michigan 48230

Ann Arbor .... Mrs. Peter B. Davol, 2634 Devonshire Road,
  Ann Arbor, Michigan 48104

Cincinnati .... Mrs. Garven Dalglish, 3937 Beech Street,
  Mariemont, Ohio 45227

Cleveland .... Mrs. Edward J. Stevens III, 16106 Chadbourne Road,
  Cleveland, Ohio 44120

Columbus .... Mrs. Harold E. Coon, 1901 Coventry Road,
  Columbus, Ohio 43212

District VII: Illinois, Iowa, Wisconsin, Minnesota, North Dakota, South Dakota,
  Nebraska, Kansas, Missouri
Councillor, Mrs. Terence Lilly, 627 S. Oak Street, Hinsdale, Illinios 60521
District Admissions Coordinator: Mrs. John H. Morrison, 2717 Lincoln Street,
  Evanston, Illinois 60201
Club Presidents:

Chicago .... Mrs. John H. Morrison, 2717 Lincoln Street,
  Evanston, Illinois 60201

St. Louis .... Mrs. Richard Zacher, 6605 Waterman,
  St. Louis, Missouri 63130

Kansas City .... Mrs. Walter M. Dickey, 8133 Sagamore Road,
  Leawood, Kansas 66206

District VIII: Colorado, Arizona, New Mexico, Texas, Oklahoma
Councillor, Mrs. Donald H. Nelson, 4131 Oak Road, Tulsa, Oklahoma 74105
District Admissions Coordinator: Mrs. Irwin L. Bernstein,
  3526 West Northview Avenue, Phoenix, Arizona 85021
Club Presidents:

Colorado .... Mrs. George A. Lincoln, 32854 Upper Bear Creek Road,
  Evergreen, Colorado 80439

Tucson .... Mrs. Thacher Loring, 10858 East Tanque Verde Road,
  Tucson, Arizona 85715

Dallas .... Mrs. Robert L. Lichten, 6338 Aberdeen Avenue,
  Dallas, Texas 75230

Houston .... Ms. Margaret K. Klineberg, 2109 Goldsmith,
  Houston, Texas 77025

Austin .... Mrs. Benjamin D. Meritt 712 West 16th Street,
  Austin, Texas 78701

Greater Phoenix ... Lynn Badler, 8221 E. Garfield, L-17,
Scottsdale, Arizona 85257

District IX: California, Nevada, Utah, Hawaii

Councillor, Mrs. Pauline A. Adams, 1020 San Mateo Drive, Menlo Park,
California 94025

District Admissions Coordinator: Mrs. Richard C. Walker, 927 Candlelight Place,
La Jolla, California 92037

Club Presidents:

Northern California . (Acting) Rowena L. Korobkin, M.D., 1364 Filbert
Street, San Francisco, California 94109 .

Southern California .. Mrs. Dave Watson, 627 Seventh Street, Santa Monica,
California 90402

San Diego .... Mrs. Richard C. Walker, 927 Candlelight Place,
La Jolla, California 92037

District X: Washington, Oregon, Idaho, Montana, Wyoming, Alaska

Councillor, Mrs. Samuel H. Brown, 11604 Interlaaken Drive S.W. Tacoma,
Washington 98498

District Admissions Coordinator: Mrs. Robert Mazo, 2460 Charnelton Street,
Eugene, Oregon 97405

Club President:

Portland .... Mrs. Charles H. Geoffroy, 11511 Southwest Military
Lane, Portland, Oregon 97219

Seattle .... Mrs. John L. Eddy, Jr.. 2628 82nd Avenue N.E.,
Bellevue, Washington 98004

Foreign

Argentina: Miss Ana Maria Barrenechea, Coronel Diaz 1815,
80 "A", Buenos Aires

Canada: Mrs. I. Bernard Schacter, 411 Richview Avenue, Toronto, Ontario
Mrs. Helen H. Nixon, 150 McLeod Street, Ottawa, Ont. K2P, 0Z7
Mrs. David G. Carter, 49 Rosemount Avenue, Westmount, Montreal,
217 P.Q., H3Y 3G6

Denmark: Mrs. Harald Vestergaard, Hambros Alle 19, 2900 Hellerup

England: Mrs. Fortunato G. Castillo, 40 Brompton Square, London S.W. 3

France: Mme. Jean Maheu, 1 Rue Clovis, Paris V
Mme. Michel Worms de Romilly, 63, rue Notre-Dame-des-Champs 75006,
Paris
Mrs. Charles B. Wakeman, 9 Boulevard du Chateau, 92200 Neuilly-sur-Seine

Germany: Mrs. Hans Loening, 2802 Fischerhude,
In der Bredenau 81, West Germany

Greece: Miss Elizabeth Douli, Korae 18, Nea Smyrne, Athens

India: Miss Harsimran Malik, 7 Palam Marg, Vasant Vihar, New Delhi 57

Italy: Mrs. Enrico Berra, Piazzale Biancamano, 20121, Milano

Japan: Miss Taki Fujita, 20-4, 2-chome, Higashi-Nakana, Nakano-ku, Tokyo

Libya: Mrs. E. A. Eriksen, Esso Standard Libya Inc. Essofield P. O. Box 385,
Tripoli

Mexico: Mrs. Arturo Gomez, Liverpool 149-102, Mexico 6, D.F.

Norway: Mrs. Harald Sommerfeldt, Hoff Terrace 4, Skoyen, pr Oslo

Philippine Islands: Mrs. Ofelia Torres Reyes, 14 Ilagan Street,
San Francisco del Monte, Quezon City

Turkey: Dr. Suna Kili, Bogazici Universitesi, P.K. 2, Bebek-Istanbul

Venezuela: Mrs. Oscar deSchnell, Apartado 69, Caracas

Index

Absence
 from Classes, 43
 from College, 32
Academic Awards, 185
Academic Honors, 50
Academic Honor System, 42
Academic Schedule, 3-4
Academic Standards, 42
Administration, Officers of, 7, 18
Admission, 27
Advanced Placement, 30
Advising, 42
Alumnae Officers, 194
Alumnae Representatives, 194
Anthropology, 58
Anthropology Museum and
 Laboratory, 35
Application for Admission, 27
Archaeology, Classical and
 Near Eastern, 69
Archaeology Collections, 35
Arts Council, 25
Athletic Association, 25
Attendance at Classes, 43
Auxiliary Libraries, 34
Avignon, Summer Institute, 53, 91

Bachelor of Arts Degree,
 Requirements for, 47-51
Biology, 62
Biochemistry, 64
Black Cultural Center, 26
Board of Trustees, 5
Boyce Collection, 35

Canaday, Mariam Coffin,
 Library, 34
Canaday, Ward, Collection, 36
Career Planning Office, 56
Charges, Minor Fees, 40
Charges, Reduction of for
 Absence, 39
Chemistry, 66
Child Study Institute, 20, 77
Classical and Near Eastern
 Archaeology, 69
Classical Languages, 152
Classical Studies, 152
College Entrance
 Examination Board, 29
College History, 22
Computer Center, 37
Conduct, 43
Cooperation with Neighboring
 Institutions, 24, 35, 50

Coordination in the Sciences,
 Plan for, 52
Correspondence, Names for, 2
Council of the Undergraduate
 College, 42
Course Numbers, Key to, 57
Creative Work in the Arts, 53
Credit for Work at Other
 Institutions, 30, 50
Curriculum, 47-56
Curriculum Committee, 26
Curtis Collection, 35

Deans, 42
District Councilors, 195-199

Early Admission, 29
Early Decision Plan, 28
Economics, 72
Education, Department of, 76
Employment and Vocational
 Counseling, 56
English, 79
Entrance Requirements, 27
Entrance Tests, 28
European Fellowship, 185
Excavations, 71
Expenses, 39-41

Faculty, 7-16
Family Educational Rights and
 Privacy Act of 1974, 43
Fee, Residence and Tuition, 40
Financial Aid, 166
Fine Art, 109
Flexner Lectures, 24
Foreign Students, 31, 184
French, 87
French House, 53
French Studies, 153
Freshmen, Arrival of, 42

General Deposit, 40
Geology, 91
German, 95
German House, 53
Goldman, Hetty, Collection, 35
Goodhart, Medieval Library, 34
Government, Student, 25
Grades, 50
Graduate School, 22
Greek, 98
Growth and Structure of Cities, 155
Guidance
 Academic, 42
 Vocational, 56

Haverford College, Cooperation
 with, 24-26, 35, 50

Health, 44
Hebrew, 111
Hispanic and Hispanic-American
    Studies, 158
History, Department of, 100
History of Art, 107
History of Religion, 110
History of Science, 105
Honors, Degree with, 50
Honors Work, 49
Hygiene, 51

Infirmary, 44
Insurance
    Health, 45
    Personal Property, 46
Interdepartmental
    Courses, 53, 159
    Work, 152
Intercollegiate Center for
    Classical Studies in Rome, 55
Italian, 114

Junior Year Abroad, 54

King Collection, 35

Laboratories, 36
Language Examinations, 48
Language Houses, 53
Language Laboratory, 37
Language Requirement, 48
Latin, 116
Leaves of Absence, 32
Libraries, 34
Loan Funds, 191

Madrid, Summer Institute, 54
Major and Allied Work, 49
Mathematics, 118
Medical School Scholarships, 189
Music, 120

National Direct Student Loan
    Program, 192
Non-resident Students, 39

Officers
    Administration, 7, 18
    Alumnae Association, 194
    Board of Trustees, 5
Performing Arts, 163
Phebe Anna Thorne School, 21, 77
Philosophy, 123
Physical Education, 163
Physical Examination, 164
Physics, 128
Placement Tests, 30
Political Science, 131
Premedical Preparation, 31, 51

Presidents of the College, 23
Privacy Act, 43
Prizes, 185
Psychology, 138

Readmission, 32
Requirements for Admission, 27
Requirements for the
    A.B. Degree, 47-51
Residence, 38, 40
    During Vacations, 38
    Halls, 38
    Rules for, 38
Riegel Museum, 35
Russian, 142

Scholarships, 168
Science Center, 36
Sciences, Plan for
    Coordination in, 52
Secondary School Studies,
    Program of, 27
Senior Conference, 49
Shaw Lectures, 24
Sociology, 145
Spanish, 149
Spanish House, 53
Staff, 17-21
Student Organizations, 25-26
Students' Association for
    Self-Government, 25
Students' Loan Fund, 191
Summer Institutes Abroad, 53-54
Summer School Work, 50
Supplementary Requirements for
    the Degree, 51
Swarthmore College,
    Cooperation with, 24, 35, 50

Teaching, Preparation for, 52
Thomas, M. Carey, Library, 35
Transfer Students, 30
Trustees, 5
Tuition, 39

Undergraduate Association, 25
Union Library Catalogue, 35
U. S. Geological Survey
    Map Collection, 37

Vacations, Residence during, 38
Vaux Collections, 35-36
Vocational Guidance, 56

Werkman Fund, 56
Withdrawal from College, 32
Woodward, Quita,
    Memorial Library, 35
Work-Study Program, 56

Directions to Bryn Mawr College

By automobile from the East or Southeast take the Walt Whitman Bridge to I-676/Schuylkill Expressway and follow this north until it meets with I-76; or take the Benjamin Franklin Bridge to I-76/Vine Street until it meets with I-676. In either case, continue north on I-76 to Exit 41, "City Ave.—U.S. 1 South." Proceed south on City Ave./U.S. 1 for 1.1 miles from the exit ramp and then turn right on Conshohocken State Road (PA 23). (There is a shopping center on the right shortly before this turn.) After three-tenths of a mile, Conshohocken State Road makes a sharp turn to the left over a railroad overpass and comes to a traffic light. Continue straight through this intersection; you are now on Montgomery Avenue, which you follow for about five miles (bearing right at a fork at about the three mile point), to Morris Avenue in the town of Bryn Mawr. Harcum Junior College will be on the left shortly before Morris Avenue. Turn right onto Morris Avenue, proceed to the next traffic light and then turn left onto New Gulph Road for approximately 1½ blocks. Visitors may use the College parking lot, entering at Merion Gate, which is directly opposite 815 New Gulph Road. The parking lot on Morris Avenue also may be used by visitors.

By automobile from the South take I-95 through Wilmington, Delaware, to Chester, Pennsylvania, then take the exit marked "PA 352—Edgemont Ave." (It is also marked with a sign for "Chester Business District.") Immediately look for, and follow, signs for PA 320 North. Continue north on PA 320 for approximately 10.5 miles from the I-95 exit, until you come to Bryn Mawr Avenue. (This is about two miles after you cross PA 3, and has a traffic light.) Turn right, and follow Bryn Mawr Avenue for approximately two miles until you come to a traffic light at Haverford Road. Continue on Bryn Mawr Avenue, which bears slightly to the left, until you come to Lancaster Avenue in the town of Bryn Mawr. (This is the second traffic light after Haverford Road.) Turn right on Lancaster Avenue for one block, and then left at the first traffic light onto Morris Avenue. Follow the road, which will curve under the railroad tracks, until you come to the traffic light at Montgomery Avenue. Proceed across Montgomery Avenue to the next traffic light. Turn left on to New Gulph Road for approximately 1½ blocks. Visitors may use the College parking lot, entering at Merion Gate, which is directly opposite 815 New Gulph Road. The parking lot on Morris Avenue also may be used by visitors.

By automobile from the West, North or Northeast take the Pennsylvania Turnpike to the Valley Forge Exit (24). From the Valley Forge Exit of the Turnpike, take the Schuylkill Expressway (I-76) east, turning off at Exit 36, "PA 320, Gulph Mills," which is 3.5 miles from the toll gate. Follow PA 320 south for approximately four-tenths of a mile and turn left at the first traffic light onto Old Gulph Road. Proceed on this for approximately three miles, and the College will be on your right. The College parking lot is the third entrance on the right after Roberts Road.

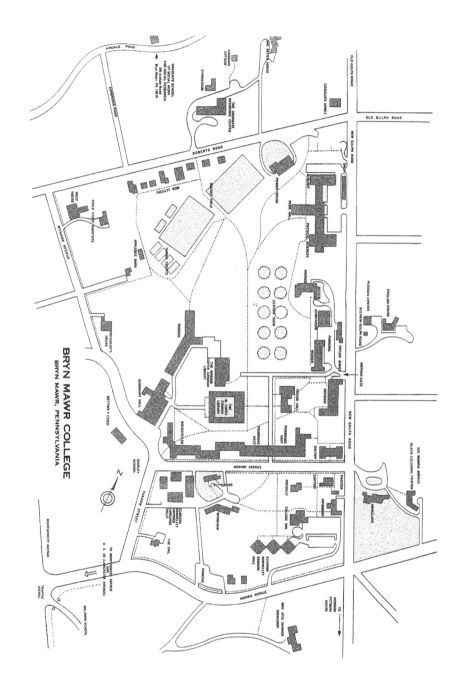

BRYN MAWR COLLEGE
BRYN MAWR, PENNSYLVANIA

ADUATE SCHOOL

SOCIAL WORK &

CIAL RESEARCH

1977-78

Bryn Mawr College Calendar
The Graduate School
of Social Work and Social Research

Issue for the Session 1977-78
September 1977 *Volume LXX Number 4*

The Graduate School of Social Work and Social Research of Bry Mawr College offers a basic two-year program leading to th degree of Master of Social Service, a one-year post-Master's pr(gram leading to the degree of Master of Law and Social Policy, an an advanced program leading to the degree of Doctor of Philosoph}

The Master of Social Service degree program is based upon th premise that preparation for social work practice and researc requires a core of knowledge as well as skill in the application of th knowledge. A curriculum of concurrent course work and practicu is provided.

The Law and Social Policy program is a new curriculum designe for persons presenting a Master's degree in Social Work or kindre professional area. It offers a full year of instruction in basic leg processes and legal problems, with special effort to relate leg perspectives to major problems in social work practice. The pr(gram is open to students who are enrolled concurrently for th M.S.S. degree at Bryn Mawr and to persons who already hold th M.S.S. or its equivalent.

The Doctor of Philosophy program is planned to broaden th student's knowledge of social welfare in general and, through inte sive research, to deepen his or her knowledge in one field in partic lar. The curriculum is intended for full-time study; however, st dents who have been admitted to the doctoral program may arran to begin on a part-time basis.

The degree of Master of Social Service is accredited by t Council on Social Work Education.

CORRESPONDENCE regarding admission to The Graduate School of Social Work Social Research should be addressed to:

Office of Admissions
The Graduate School of Social Work and Social Research
Bryn Mawr College
300 Airdale Road
Bryn Mawr, Pennsylvania 19010

BRYN MAWR COLLEGE CALENDAR published December, July, August September by Bryn Mawr College, Bryn Mawr, Pennsylvania 19010. *Second cl postage paid at Bryn Mawr, Pennsylvania.*

Contents

Academic Calendar 7

Admission to The Graduate School of Social Work
    and Social Research 9
    Foreign Applicants 9
    Financial Aid 10
    Occupational Outlook 10
    Endowed Funds 10
    Prizes 12
    Transfer Credit 12
    Residence Requirements 12
    Registration 14
    Grading 14
    Mutual Accountability 14
    The Master's Student Adviser 15
    The Doctoral Student Adviser 16

Graduate Program for the Master of Social Service 18

Graduate Program for the Master of Law and
    Social Policy 37

Graduate Program for the Doctor of Philosophy 42

Fees 55

Resources for Graduate Work at Bryn Mawr 58

History of the School 59

Graduate Student Housing 62

Health 63
    Medical Services 63
    Medical Requirements 63
    Insurance 64

Child Care Center 64

Career Planning Office 65

Student and Alumni Associations 66
    Recruitment of Minority Group Students 66

College Facilities 67

Trustees of Bryn Mawr College 68

Officers of the College 69

Officers of Administration of the College 70

Advisory Board of the School 71

Faculty of the School 72

Administration of the School 73

Standing Committees of the Faculty 74

Frontispiece–
The Graduate School of Social Work and Social Research

Ethnic Minority Content in the Curriculum

Because racism constitutes a profound problem in this country, The Graduate School of Social Work and Social Research seeks to mitigate the effects of racism among its students and faculty through its educational program. In addition, the School hopes to develop and make available reports and curriculum material which will combat racism among administrators, alumni, and all social welfare professionals.

The School accepts the responsibility for educating social workers prepared to serve all persons within the social welfare system and will strive to change those economic, political and social structures which constrain the opportunities and potential of minority groups.

The School is undertaking to incorporate appropriate content on ethnic minority groups in courses throughout the curriculum. By accepting this task as a central and continuing concern the School intends to foster self-awareness, clearer perspectives and more sensitivity toward all people on the part of both minority and non-minority students and faculty.

Academic Calendar 1977-78
The Graduate School of
Social Work and Social Research

First Semester—1977

Sept. 6   *Graduate residences open. Orientation programs begin.*

Sept. 7   *Registration of all social work students.*

Sept. 8   *Convocation. First semester seminars begin.*

Sept. 15   *First day of practicum in first semester.*

Oct. 7   *Ph.D Foreign Language Examinations.*

Oct. 21   *Fall vacation begins at 5:00 p.m. (Practicum continues on regularly scheduled days.)*

Oct. 21-28   *Ph.D Preliminary Examinations.*

Oct. 26   *Fall vacation ends at 9:00 a.m.*

Nov. 23   *Thanksgiving holiday begins after last seminar. (No practicum.)*

Nov. 28   *Thanksgiving holiday ends at 9:00 a.m.*

Dec. 13   *Last day of seminars for first semester. (Practicum continues on regularly scheduled days.)*

Dec. 19-21   *Examinations.*

Dec. 21   *Winter vacation begins at 6:00 p.m.*

1978

Jan. 5   *Practicum resumes on regularly scheduled days.*

Jan. 13   *Last day of practicum in first semester.*

Second Semester—1978

Jan. 16   *Convocation. Second semester seminars begin. (Practicum resumes on regularly scheduled days.)*

Feb. 1   *Ph.D. dissertations must be submitted to the Office of The Graduate School of Social Work and Social Research for Oral Examination prior to April 1. (See March 29 below for Oral Examination after April 30.)*

Feb. 3   *Ph.D. Foreign Language Examinations.*

Mar. 10   *Spring vacation begins at 5:00 p.m. (Practicum continues on regularly scheduled days.)*

Mar. 10-17   *Ph.D. Preliminary Examinations.*

Mar. 20   *Spring vacation ends at 9:00 a.m.*

Mar. 29   *Final Date for submission of Ph.D. dissertations to the Office of The Graduate School of Social Work and Social Research for Commencement, 1978. (Oral examination will be scheduled after April 30.)*

Apr. 7   *Ph.D Foreign Language Examinations.*

Apr. 27   *Last day of seminars and practicum.*

May 1   *Master's Papers due.*

May 3-5   *Examinations.*

May 15   *Conferring of degrees and close of 93rd academic year of the College and the 62nd year of the School. Graduate residences close.*

The information in this Calendar is the best available at the time of publication. The contents are subject to change and are not binding on the College.

Admission to The Graduate School of Social Work and Social Research

The Graduate School of Social Work and Social Research is open to qualified graduates from colleges or universities of recognized standing. Both men and women are admitted to the School and are accepted as candidates for the degrees of Master of Social Service, Master of Law and Social Policy, and Doctor of Philosophy.

Application for admission, to be made to the Office of Admissions of the School, must be supported by official transcripts of the applicant's academic record, both graduate and undergraduate. The Miller Analogies Test is required. (Information concerning locations for taking the MAT is available upon request.) A letter from the dean of each college or university attended and letters from two or more professors with whom the applicant did his or her preparation are required.

An application fee of $25 must accompany the application. This fee is not refunded or credited toward tuition. The closing date of applications is February 1.

A personal interview is not required but may be arranged with the Coordinator of Admissions of the School. If the applicant lives a considerable distance from Bryn Mawr, an interview can usually be arranged with an appropriate person in the area.

Within ten days after official notice of admission to The Graduate School of Social Work and Social Research, an enrollment fee of $100 is to be paid to the Comptroller of Bryn Mawr College. This fee is credited to the tuition for the first semester. It is not refunded if the student fails to register.

The principal practice focus for the first year in the Master of Social Service program is either Social Casework or Community Social Work. Students are admitted into one or the other of these categories, and their academic course flows from this initial choice. Permission to transfer from one practice focus to another in the first year is rarely granted.

Foreign Applicants

The closing date for applications is February 1 for admission the following September. Applications must include the scores of the Test of English as a Foreign Language (TOEFL). For information concerning the TOEFL write to: TOEFL, Educational Testing Service, Princeton, New Jersey 08540.

A very limited amount of financial support is available for foreign students.

9

Financial Aid

A limited amount of financial aid is available for full-time students in The Graduate School of Social Work and Social Research. Some fellowships and scholarships are provided from the general funds of the College, the Alumnae Association, from the gifts of alumni and other generous donors, and from government agencies and private foundations.

Bryn Mawr also participates in the National Direct Student Loan Program and the College Work-Study Program.

The terms of the various awards and loans differ and will be discussed with the applicant at the time of the admission interview. Both merit and need are factors to which consideration is given in making certain awards. Requests for financial assistance are considered after the application process is completed and applicants have been admitted into The Graduate School of Social Work and Social Research. *The School requires that students seeking financial aid file an application for financial aid with the Graduate and Professional School Financial Aid Service.* This form will be sent upon request after a student is admitted.

Students are urged to explore loans which are made available through the state in which they have established residence, such as the Pennsylvania Higher Education Assistance Authority loan in Pennsylvania.

Occupational Outlook

The following information refers to 1976 Master of Social Service degree graduates:

Option	Total	Seeking Work in U.S.	Number Reporting Salaries	Salary Range	Median
Clinical Social Work	35	34	30	$ 9,900-14,000	$12,000
Social Service Management	8	6	6	10,600-15,500	12,000
Program Planning and Administration	17	17	12	10,400-13,500	12,500
Policy Research and Development	9	5	5	10,500-14,097	13,250

Endowed Funds

Emily Greene Balch Lecture Fund for Social Work and Social Research. Inspired by the alumna niece of Emily Greene Balch, A.B. '89, this permanent lecture fund honors one of the two American women ever to receive the Nobel Peace Prize.

Agnes M.H. Byrnes Memorial for Social Work and Social Research. Established for The Graduate School of Social Work and Social Research by the bequest of Miss Byrnes, who received her Ph.D. in Social Work in 1920.

The Fanny Travis Cochran Scholarship Fund. Established in 1936 on the occasion of the 50th Anniversary of the College. Miss Cochran was a member of the Class of 1902.

Alfred and Mary Douty Student Loan Fund. A gift from the Alfred and Mary Douty Foundation established this self-perpetuating student loan fund.

Marguerite N. Farley Scholarship Fund. Established in 1956 to provide scholarships for foreign students.

Anita D. Lichtenstein Memorial Fund. Established in memory of Anita Lichtenstein, M.S.S. 1966 and a candidate for the Ph.D. when she died. The fund, established by her husband, friends, and colleagues, is used to provide an annual colloquium in which a family theorist or therapist lectures and conducts workshops for social work professionals and students.

Margaret Friend Low Fund for General Purposes–School of Social Work and Social Research. Established by an alumna of the Class of 1911 impressed by the work of graduate students in Social Work and Social Research.

Lillian and Jack Poses Scholarship Fund. Established by Lillian Shapiro Poses, a former student in Social Work and Social Research, and her husband, for student aid in The Graduate School of Social Work and Social Research.

Joan Sall Rivitz Memorial Scholarship Fund for Social Work and Social Research. This scholarship fund was established as a memorial by the father of an alumna of the Bryn Mawr Graduate School of Social Work and Social Research. Mrs. Rivitz received her M.S.S. in 1963 and her Ph.D. in 1972.

J. Henry Scattergood Scholarship. Established by a grant of the Friends Freedmen's Association to scholarship endowment for the support of black students at Bryn Mawr. The fund is named in memory of a former Trustee who served as Treasurer of the College for 26 years.

Lelia Woodruff Stokes Fund for Faculty Support in The Graduate School of Social Work and Social Research. This fund was created by an alumna of the Class of 1907 shortly before her death. Lelia Woodruff Stokes was a friend and classmate of Carola Woerishoffer, whose legacy was the impetus for establishing The Graduate School of Social Work and Social Research.

11

Chair in Social Work and Social Research Fund. A $10,000 gift from an anonymous donor established this fund as a nucleus to attract further donations.

Prizes

The Susan B. Anthony Memorial Prize, value $500, commemorating the great work of Susan B. Anthony for women, was founded by her friend Anna Howard Shaw and her niece Lucy E. Anthony. It is offered every two years to a graduate student at Bryn Mawr College who has published or submitted in final form for publication the best study dealing with the industrial, social, economic or political position of women. The award is made by a committee of which the President of the College is chairperson.

The Susan M. Kingsbury Grant in Social Research, value $300, is awarded every third year on the recommendation of the Dean of The Graduate School of Social Work and Social Research to advanced students, men and women, preferably candidates for the degree of Doctor of Philosophy.

Transfer Credit

Transfer credit in an amount up to the equivalent of one year of the program for the M.S.S. may be allowed for work done at other accredited schools of social work. Such transfer credit will not be given until the candidate has completed a semester's work at Bry Mawr. In each case transfer credit must be recommended by the Dean.

Ph.D. students may petition for transfer of credits to the Ph.D. program, and decisions are made on an individual basis after one semester's work is completed at Bryn Mawr.

Residence Requirements

For both the Ph.D. and Master's degrees one year in full-time residence is required. Two sequential semesters in one academic year meet this requirement.

Persons registering for full-time programs should consult wit advisers before undertaking employment concurrent with a full time academic program because of the demands upon time for th expected high-quality performance of students. It is expected tha full-time students will give priority to academic commitments.

Persons registered as full-time students who are provided fellow ship or scholarship support through Bryn Mawr College may be employed up to eight hours per week during the academic year a long as satisfactory academic performance is maintained. In principle, this amount of time for employment beyond the full-time curriculum is reasonable.

University of Pennsylvania Reciprocal Plan

Under the Reciprocal Plan, courses at the University of Pennsylvania Graduate School of Arts and Sciences are available during the academic year to Bryn Mawr graduate students. All full-time students and such part-time students as intend to become candidates for degrees are eligible. The number of courses which may be taken at the University is limited to one per semester. The procedure for registration and payment of tuition fees is the same as for students enrolled wholly at Bryn Mawr, with the exception that the student will present a letter of introduction to the Dean of The Graduate School of Arts and Sciences of the University of Pennsylvania when registering there. The University charges a small general fee for the use of the library, a library deposit, which is refundable, and fees for late registration. Ordinarily students are not advised to undertake such work during their first year at Bryn Mawr.

Degree Candidacy

Students become candidates for advanced degrees only after they have met the School's requirements and, in the case of the Ph.D. degree, made formal application which has been approved by the members of the faculty on the Doctoral Committee of The Graduate School of Social Work and Social Research.

Continuing Enrollment

Students who have completed the required course work for the Ph.D. degree and are continuing independent work on their dissertations must retain their enrollment and degree candidacy by registering for one or more seminars each semester or must register under the Continuing Enrollment Plan. Such students will be billed under the Continuing Enrollment Plan unless they have asked for a leave of absence in writing and a leave has been granted.

In addition, students who are not planning to register for academic seminars but who are planning (1) to present themselves for College examinations, (2) to use the College libraries, or (3) to consult members of the Faculty must register under the Continuing Enrollment Plan. Such enrollment does not carry academic credit.

13

Summer Work

In special cases arrangements may be made for doctoral students to continue research during the summer or to enroll for tutorials or independent study. Such requests should be discussed with the student's adviser and the Dean before the end of the second semester.

Registration

Every student in The Graduate School of Social Work and Social Research must register for courses during the registration period. Permission to make any change in registration must be received from the Dean of the School. Students who do not complete their registration during the registration period or who change their selections after the close of the registration period are subject to the Late Registration Fee, and after a specified date, the Add-Drop Fee.

Only courses given in The Graduate School of Social Work and Social Research are described in this Calendar. Unless otherwise noted, these are for one semester. Descriptions of other graduate courses given at Bryn Mawr may be found in the Calendar of The Graduate School of Arts and Sciences.

Grading

Two grades are given for graduate work, *Satisfactory* and *Unsatisfactory*. Ph.D. students may be given extensions to November 1 if there are extenuating circumstances. However, there will be no extension beyond November 1 of the academic year following that in which the work was due. After November 1 the work will be graded *Unsatisfactory* or the term *Incomplete* will remain permanently on the record.

First-year Master's students must complete all work by July 31 in order to move into the second year. Extensions beyond the date the Grade Sheets are due in the Dean's Office are only given when there are extenuating circumstances.

Mutual Accountability

The essential educational relationships in the School are based upon the principle that members of the faculty and students are accountable to each other on an equitable basis. Procedures to implement this principle which have been developed through joint effort of members of the faculty and members of the Student Association are given below.

14

It is the instructor's responsibility to provide the student with an evaluation (i.e., Satisfactory, Unsatisfactory, or Incomplete grade) for the course or seminar on the provided Grade Sheet. A qualitative analysis of oral or written presentations, examinations, or other educational performances is required. In addition, the instructor may choose to provide a written analysis of the student's performance, which is a private communication between the instructor and the student.

The student's responsibility, as a condition of receiving a grade, is to (a) participate in either an oral or written mid-term analysis of the quality of the course or seminar, and (b) prepare and sign for the instructor and the Dean an end-of-semester evaluation of faculty performance. These evaluations make systematic the student contribution to the development of the School, particularly with regard to questions of faculty reappointment, promotion, and tenure. Completion and signing of an additional end-of-semester analysis of the instructor's performance, which is a confidential communication between the instructor and the student, is optional.

The Master's Student Adviser

At the beginning of each academic year a member of the faculty is assigned to serve as adviser to each student. Responsibilities of the adviser include: providing educational guidance in selection of a student's course of study; registering the student; orienting the student to the School, its curriculum, and its policies; identifying and consulting with the student on problems which may be interfering with the student's educational progress; informing the Dean when a student's performance places him or her in academic jeopardy and presenting to the Committee on the Evaluation of the Educational Performance of Master's Students a summary of the student's performance in each course; and representing the student's interests when necessary.

The faculty adviser is expected to schedule three conferences each semester, one of which may be the course registration conference. Additional conferences may be initiated by the student or scheduled by the adviser.

In the M.S.S. program the adviser consults with first-year students about choice of second-year practice options and the option of the Master's Paper.

15

The Doctoral Student Adviser

The primary role of the adviser is to serve as: an educational counselor; an interpreter of procedure and policy; a source of information on such matters as courses available in other settings, and research and funding opportunities; and as a consultant on course selection. The adviser also has an educational and evaluative role in recommending the student for candidacy.

Exclusion

The College reserves the right to exclude at any time any student whose academic standing is unsatisfactory or whose conduct renders him or her an undesirable member of the College community. In such cases fees will not be remitted or refunded in whole or in part; fellowships and scholarships will be cancelled.

Withdrawal and Readmission

A student who has withdrawn from the School is not automatically readmitted. After a year's absence he or she may request readmission and should consult the Dean and the Chairperson of Admissions concerning the procedure to be followed.

Leaves of Absence

A student whose academic work is in good standing may apply to the Dean for a leave of absence. A leave is generally requested for an academic year. If the student wishes to return to the program at the end of that year, he or she should write to the Dean requesting reinstatement. Available space in the program and length of time the student has been away from the School will be factors affecting reinstatement. A student extending leave beyond the approved period will need to reapply for admission to the School.

Medical Leave of Absence

The student may, on the recommendation of a physician, request a medical leave of absence for reasons of health at any time. Readmission may be granted upon recommendation of the Dean based upon evidence of the student's capacity to meet the demands of his or her program.

Membership in Professional Organizations

We strongly recommend that students join one or more related professional organizations, such as the National Association of Social Workers, the Council on Social Work Education, American Public Welfare Association, Child Welfare League of America, the Association for Clinical Social Work, the Gerontological Society and the Alliance of Black Social Workers. These organizations offer reduced rates for students and provide a number of benefits, including publications and insurance programs. The National Association of Social Workers, particularly through its state chapters and local divisions, gives students an immediate opportunity to participate in professional activities with leaders in the field.

Cancellation of Courses

The School reserves the right to cancel scheduled courses on the basis of size of enrollment or availability of instructors.

Programs and Degrees

Bryn Mawr College awards the degrees of Master of Social Service, Master of Law and Social Policy, and Doctor of Philosophy in The Graduate School of Social Work and Social Research.

Graduate Program for the Master of Social Service

The program for the M.S.S. degree is designed to prepare graduates for Clinical Social Work, Social Service Management, Policy Research and Development, or Program Planning and Administration. Two academic years of full-time study are required. The degree represents the completion of a concurrent program of course work and practicum. Provision is made for field instruction in a range of public and voluntary agencies and organizations with programs in such fields and settings as: aging, child welfare, community mental health, consumer organizations, corrections, day care, drug and alcohol dependency and abuse, family services, housing, intergroup relations, legal services, legislative offices, maternal and child health, mental retardation, neighborhood organization, physical rehabilitation, psychiatric services, public assistance, public education, public health, public welfare administration, school social work, social planning, social welfare research, teaching undergraduate programs, women's issues, and youth services.

Prerequisites. The prerequisite for the M.S.S. degree is a Bachelor's degree or its equivalent from a college or university of recognized standing in the United States, or a degree or certificate of the same standard from a foreign university.

REQUIREMENTS FOR THE MSS DEGREE

Candidates for the M.S.S. degree must complete a minimum of eighteen semester courses, including a practicum. Each student's program of study consists of a combination of required and elective courses. One course credit may be an acceptable Master's Paper in an area of social work or social welfare.

ELECTIVES

Electives are offered in this School and in The Graduate School of Arts and Sciences at Bryn Mawr. With permission of the Dean of The Graduate School of Social Work and Social Research, students in the School may elect courses in The Graduate School of Arts and Sciences of the University of Pennsylvania under the Reciprocal Plan.

The reduction of required courses and the increase in electives is one principle which has guided the development of the curriculum. Another principle provides the opportunity for each student who demonstrates competence in a required course, excluding the practicum and practice seminars, to request a waiver of this required course in favor of an additional elective.

SPECIAL PART-TIME PROGRAM

It is possible for a small number of students for the Master's degree to extend the two-year program to three years. The pattern is to complete the first graduate year's requirements over a period of two years on a part-time basis, and to complete the second year's requirements during the third year on a full-time basis. Further information about the part-time program is available upon request.

Bryn Mawr only enrolls students registered for degree programs.

PROGRAM OF WORK

The first-year program is similar for all students except that the student selects either Social Casework or Community Social Work as his or her principal focus in social work practice. The first-year required courses are:

> Social Casework *or* Community Social Work (two semesters)
> Field Instruction—coordinated with one of the above
>   (two semesters)
> Social Statistics (one semester) and Research Design
>   (one semester)
> Personality Theory *or* Normal Growth and Behavior:
>   Childhood, Adolescence, and Early Maturity *or* Normal
>   Growth and Behavior: From the Age of Thirty Onwards
> Social Theory and Social Work
> Social Welfare Policy and Services: Historical Perspectives,
>   *or* Social Welfare Policy and Services: Social Policy
>   Analysis

In addition, the student is expected to select one elective during the first year. Thus, the usual first-year program is composed of ten semester courses.

It is possible for students to waive by written examination to be given at the beginning of fall and spring semesters any required course with the exception of the practicum and practice seminars. This does not reduce the number of courses required for the M.S.S. degree, but the student may take an elective in place of the waived course.

The courses required in the second year are in part determined by the student's area of concentration in social work practice. The second-year options are: Policy Research and Development, Program Planning and Administration, Clinical Social Work, or Social Service Management. Field Instruction is coordinated with one of these choices. Normally, the first-year preparation for Policy Research and Development or Program Planning and Administration is Community Social Work; the preparation for Clinical Social Work or Social Service Management is Social Casework. In addition, the student is expected to enroll in four electives, two each semester. A Master's Paper in an area of social work or social welfare may be undertaken for credit as one elective. Thus, the usual second-year program is comprised of eight semester courses or seven semester courses plus a Master's Paper.

Students in Clinical Social Work are required to take any three of the following course offerings:

Comparative Personality Theory

Normal Growth and Behavior: Childhood, Adolescence, and Early Maturity

Normal Growth and Behavior: From the Age of Thirty Onwards

Personality Theory

Psychopathology

M.S.S. degree students are required to take at least one course designated as particularly relevant to minority concerns. Courses which meet this requirement vary from semester to semester and are designated prior to pre-registration by the Curriculum Committee Task Force on Incorporating Content on Minorities into the curriculum. Examples of such courses include: Culture, Poverty and Human Development; Social Work and Ethnic Minorities; and Contemporary Black Life: Implications for Social Services.

REQUIRED COURSES

Community Social Work I

Community Social Work is based on the assumption that many crucial human problems, such as poverty, racism, and the oppression of groups because of age, class, and sex, derive largely from the structure of institutions, communities, and from the larger social-economic order. Consequently, philosophies and strategies for change at the institutional, community, and societal level have been developed. The aim of this seminar is to introduce students to a broad range of community social work philosophies and strategies, and to assist each student in clarifying his or her own approach. Specific emphasis is placed on increasing skills in the analysis of communities, organizations, and social policies and on increasing basic practice skills in community work.

Community Social Work II

The second semester seminar places special emphasis on: understanding the economic context of community practice; increasing awareness of political structures and processes; expanding awareness of "third world"-"first world" relationships in such issue areas as world hunger, the energy crisis, etc.; and, finally, improving skills in direct organizing of disenfranchised groups.

Social Casework I

The function of social casework in social work as related to the problems of individuals and primary groups is considered. Theory and application of the technical processes of psychosocial study, diagnosis and casework services are examined. Attention is given to understanding the person and the dynamic relationship with his or her social-cultural environment and to the conflicts and issues in social work practice.

Social Casework II

Understanding the basic processes applied to casework practice in varying age groups, areas of problem and agency settings is deepened. Increasing use is made of students' case materials. The seminar studies the relationships among purpose, skill, social resources, social systems and human needs.

Field Instruction I and II

A practicum in basic social work principles and concepts in a field setting is provided. Field instructors carry responsibility for facilitating students' learning in relation to all areas of the curriculum. Field Instruction I and II are taken collaterally with Social Casework I and II or Community Social Work I and II. Students in the first year spend two days a week in the field.

Personality Theory

Fundamental ideas in personality theory are presented which are considered to be especially pertinent to the various practices of social workers. Presentation leans heavily upon psychoanalytic theory, but students are encouraged to study in several theories of personality of their own choosing. Emphasis is upon general principles connected with the determination of the shape and content of an individual's personal-social functioning.

21

Normal Growth and Behavior: Childhood, Adolescence, and Early Maturity

This seminar considers major biological, psychological, social, and cultural determinants of normal human growth and behavior through early maturity. Cross-cultural perspectives are emphasized. Stress is placed on the individual's continuing adaptation to change within himself or herself and in the world. Discussion includes optimal life experiences which promote healthy growth.

Normal Growth and Behavior: From the Age of Thirty Onwards

In keeping with the growing body of knowledge which examines the human life cycle from the age of thirty until death, this seminar concentrates on the psychological, social, and cultural determinants of normal adult behavior. It examines the psychological and social dilemmas and tasks confronted by individuals at different developmental stages of adult life. These are explored with sensitivity to specific personal and societal issues, such as selection of life style, selection of profession, and changes in the individual's stance towards societal institutions, and with sensitivity to cultural variation.

Social Theory and Social Work

Starting with a general consideration of theory and its relevance to social practice, this course provides a working acquaintance with major contemporary sociological models which have special bearing upon social work. The course emphasizes analyses of the family, the community, social deviance, conflict management, power, professions, bureaucracy, and social movements.

Social Welfare Policy and Services: Historical Perspectives

The organization and growth of social welfare and social work as major social institutions are examined from historical and philosophical viewpoints. The evolution of social welfare attitudes and services in Great Britain and the United States is studied with attention given to the philosophical systems within which developments have taken place. Particular attention is given to the establishment of the current social welfare system in the United States and proposals to reform or change it. The role of social work within that system is described, and its future role discussed.

Social Welfare Policy and Services: Social Policy Analysis

This course begins with a discussion of some of the leading theoretical statements on contemporary social policy and social services, then moves to a case study approach in different policy areas. Child care and health care services receive special emphases.

SOCIAL RESEARCH AND STATISTICS AREA

Social Statistics (one semester) and *Research Design* (one semester) are required of all students. If students pass the written waiver examination in either or both, they may select an elective in place of the waived course. Additional offerings in the Social Research and Statistics Area are coordinated with practice areas of the curriculum.

Social Statistics

The goal of this seminar is functional knowledge of the basic statistical techniques. Emphasis is on the organization of data, extraction of information from data and interpretation of information contained in formal presentation of data. Classroom time is divided between lectures and discussion of assigned problems. This seminar does not meet the Bryn Mawr College statistics requirement for the Ph.D. degree.

Research Design

This course is intended as an introduction to formulating research questions and methodologies around social work related issues. Students will develop the skill of critique and evaluation of published research designs, as well as understanding of the skills necessary to successfully design and implement a research project of their own. Methodologies to be discussed are sampling, questionnaires, interviewing techniques, participant observation, and historical and bureaucratic record use. Analytical skills of interpreting data and the ethics of research will also be discussed.

Clinical Research

This seminar focuses on intensive research as an adjunct to clinical treatment in social casework, and mental health. Bodies of technique, such as case study, experiments, use of personal documents, participant observation, and content analysis of interviews are considered. Current clinical research in social work is reviewed, and attention is also given to professional and ethical issues.

Evaluative Research

Various modes of evaluation—process, goal achievement, impact—are viewed in the context of public and agency programming. Related matters, such as responses to requests for proposals, design of evaluation, administration of evaluative components as well as the relationship of evaluation to budgeting, cost/benefit analysis, policy formation, and information system development are considered.

Institutional and Community Research

Bodies of technique for analyzing larger social units, such as organizations, communities, urban areas, are stressed. The relationship of this mode of analysis to policy formation, social planning, and the legislative process is reviewed. Utilization of existing data series as well as gathering primary data is a keynote.

Statistics and Computing

The practical application of statistical methods to answer research questions is the central focus of this seminar. Computing is taught as a body of skills and as a means of overcoming computational hurdles. Use of SPSS is taught.

Second Year of the MSS Program

The second-year options are Policy Research and Development, Program Planning or Administration, Clinical Social Work, and Social Service Management. Field Instruction III and IV are coordinated with these choices.

Normally, the first-year preparation for Policy Research and Development or Program Planning and Administration is Community Social Work; for Clinical Social Work or Social Service Management the preparation is Social Casework.

Clinical Social Work (two semesters)

Clinical Social Work is concerned primarily with direct service to individuals, families, and small groups. A related concern is improvement of the structure and functioning of social services. Content of the course emphasizes critical analysis of theories of practice and the interventions arising from these, the development of knowledge and skills in the assessment of psychosocial problems and of ways of effecting constructive change.

Social Service Management (two semesters)

Social Service Management has as its central goal the improvement of the structure and quality of social services. Social Service Management prepares students to assume the responsibility for organizing and marshalling the delivery of services; identifying and translating client needs into appropriate agency programs; training and supervision of other categories of social welfare personnel; manpower development and examination and evaluation of policies; and developing the monitoring of organizational structure and procedures in relation to delivery of services.

Policy Research and Development (two semesters)

During the two semesters significant literature from a combination of academic disciplines is examined for the purpose of providing students with understanding and analytic skills in the following areas: policy definition, specifically in social welfare issues; an understanding of the policy-making process and the identification of key elements in policy formulation; the construction of analytic frameworks for policy analysis and policy research; an examination of the processes of policy implementation; identification of the administrative issues implicit in policy formulation and implementation; examination of the issues and techniques for policy research and evaluation; and the formulation of research designs for the analysis of policy development, implementation, and evaluation in specific social problem areas. The course is conducted in seminar style, with shared faculty-student responsibility for the learning process.

Program Planning and Administration (two semesters)

This practice concentration provides knowledge and skills required for administering, planning, implementing, and evaluating human service programs. Areas of consideration include planning and control, community analysis, program and budget development, consumer participation, social policy intervention, leadership, staff relations, and a range of issues in administration. Knowledge in depth of at least one substantive field of human services is encouraged.

Field Instruction III and IV

A practicum is taken collaterally with Clinical Social Work, Social Service Management, Policy Research and Development, and Program Planning and Administration. For all second-year students the practicum ordinarily consists of three days per week for each of the two semesters. Students who elect two days per week in the field will be required to carry an additional course.

25

ELECTIVES

American City in the Twentieth Century

This course deals primarily with social transformations in the cities under the impact of rapid urbanization. It also considers political, aesthetic, and cultural changes in American cities. (Offered in conjunction with the inter-departmental program, The Growth and Structure of Cities.)

Contemporary Black Life: Implications for Social Services

An historical perspective and analysis of social services, their policies, planning, and implementation will be examined in the context of contemporary Black America.

Change and Resistance to Change in Social Work

This course examines social work in general as the expression of liberalism and the consequent problems that attend it. The welfare state, modes of treatment, professionalism, and social change perspectives in the light of a liberal-radical differentiation are analyzed. Some alternate expressions of social work are developed. Students are expected to participate in the development and management of the seminar within the constraints of the topic.

Community Organizing

Community Organizing stresses the strategies, tactics, and value-issues involved in direct work with groups mobilizing against major social problems, such as poverty, racism, and sexism. Direct community and workplace organizing within the social service sector is emphasized. Urban community development, neighborhood and workplace-based social action, and social movement organizing are three types of organizing explored in this elective course.

Comparative Personality Theory

This seminar systematically examines and compares some of the major personality theories as well as newer theories. There is an attempt to apply the theories critically to a range of social work situations and concerns, and evaluate their use to social workers.

Culture, Poverty, and Human Development

The course reviews concepts utilized for describing poverty, its causes, "cultures," and some of the attempts employed to abolish it. The course relies on the students' effort to detect relationships between the phenomena of racism and the maintenance of poverty.

Lectures and videotapes are used occasionally as a basis for discussion.

Family Therapy

The purpose of this seminar is to provide a framework within which students can understand the philosophy and different schools of family therapy. The focus is on family systems and the changes which can be made within these systems. Healthy and maladaptive family interaction patterns from the current and intergenerational view are examined, as are problem areas and basic principles. Various schools of thought on working with couples and families are considered. Attention is given to areas of student interest.

Gerontology: Theory and Research

The origins and boundaries of gerontology are examined. Roles and role-expectations of the elderly in different cultures are compared. The demographic characteristics of the elderly and the physiological and psychological changes associated with aging are identified. Changes in the nature of human productivity in later life and the potential of the elderly as a political bloc are considered. Readings and discussion focus on findings and problems of research in each area.

Group Process

This seminar undertakes to study characteristics of the group process and content of understanding individual and group behavior. Typical problems include basic issues in working with groups; interaction patterns; practical applications of group theory; effective ways of working with committees, citizen-community groups, therapy groups, agency personnel, boards, clients; tools and techniques in working with groups; moving toward problem-solving and change through groups.

Juvenile Offender Treatment and Delinquency Prevention

Issues and practices in the delivery of human services to the juvenile and his family, the community, and the justice system and ancillary agencies are examined in the areas of prevention and treatment of delinquency. Developing roles for social work in keeping pace with emerging patterns in prevention, programs, and treatment practices, including de-institutionalization, are studied. Visits to selected institutions and agencies in this field, for direct exposure to such settings and discussion with their staffs, may be planned.

27

Marriage Counseling

This seminar examines theories of marital interaction, theories of therapy, and value systems of the marital counselor. Specific topics are chosen by participants who carry responsibility for presentation of materials and class discussion.

Master's Paper

A Master's Paper may be undertaken with the permission of two faculty persons who would serve as Readers, or as the result of a research project in a particular interest area with one instructor and a second Reader. Whether students are enrolled in such research projects or whether students are developing a Master's Paper independently with first and second Readers, one course credit will be given after satisfactory completion of the Master's Paper.

The Ombudsman and Other Advocacy Systems

Institutional arrangements for communication, redress, and advocacy for citizens in their dealings with various levels of government are reviewed. Emphasis is given to the development and application of a classification scheme for such organizations and to the consideration of such models as the classical ombudsman and the decentralized agency. Comparative material is used from various American schemes and such foreign experience as that in Scandinavia, Great Britain and New Zealand.

Organizations and Social Welfare

Major theoretical developments in the field of formal organizations are considered with special emphasis on their application to social welfare, including such matters as the structure and processes of public welfare bureaucracies, organizations as instruments of policy, relationships with professions and the role of informal organization.

Problems and Treatment of Alcoholism and Drug Abuse

Therapeutic techniques and program planning for alcohol and drug abusers are examined. Focus includes: causation theories, institutional and community programs, abuse and enforcement, the concept of "the addictive personality," prevention, and public education. Special attention is given to the processes of interviewing and counseling drug abusers, as well as the steps involved in the planning, implementation, development, and evaluation of a drug treatment program. Staff members and clients of treatment and planning agencies may be involved as guest lecturers and seminar leaders.

Psychopathology

The symptomatic pictures seen in adults in the major clinical diagnoses of the psychoses, psychosomatic disorders, character disorders, addictions and the neuroses are covered. Genetic, dynamic, and structural aspects of these illnesses are examined with discussion of implications for prevention and treatment.

Social and Cultural Aspects of Health, Illness and Treatment

Starting with the assumption that social and cultural influences shape definitions and expectations concerning health, illness, and treatment, this seminar identifies instances and implications of such influences. More specifically, attention is given to areas of information essential for understanding common acute and chronic diseases and health issues, and their associated social and psychic problems. The possible roles of the social worker as contributing agent for change are examined. Specific content may include information re: normal body functions and changes, birth control and obstetrics, childhood diseases, common diseases (e.g., circulatory, gastrointestinal, venereal, arthritic, sensory, neurological); doctor, patient, and social worker relations; epidemiology; systems of health care delivery, as well as when and how to use them; and economics and medical care. A brief overview will be included of planning in preventive and remedial health care, as well as community systems of resources and how to use them effectively. (This course is open to both Master's and doctoral students. If a Master's student taking this course enters the doctoral program at a later date, however, the student may not count this course for doctoral credit.)

Social Welfare Policy and Issues: Specific Areas

The following courses are open to both Master's and doctoral students. If Master's students taking these courses enter the doctoral program at a later date, however, they may not count these courses for doctoral credit.

Child Welfare

Current issues and questions in the field of child welfare and their meaning for practitioners are considered. Content is drawn from areas such as child abuse and neglect (both institutional and parental), child care, health, adoptions, placement, and advocacy. Attention is paid to programs currently existing, their rationale and impact, and the gaps that persist.

Community Mental Health

This seminar examines the theoretical roots of the present community mental health system. Community mental health concepts of comprehensiveness, prevention, community participation, and continuity of care are analyzed in relation to policies governing the design and operation of Community Mental Health Centers. Students participate in the criticism and design of mental health service delivery policies.

Gerontology

Focused readings and discussions by students alternate with guest lectures by specialists in gerontology. Policies and issues in legislation, health, mental health, income maintenance, social service programs, research, housing, and nursing home care are considered.

Health

This course deals with a range of issues in the delivery of health care services. Among the topics discussed are national health insurance, community mental health, the division of labor among health professionals, and movements of health consumers.

Women's Issues

This course explores various aspects of the situation of women in contemporary American society. Social policies with particular relevance for women are examined, and women are discussed as both consumers and providers of social services. Among the specific areas covered in the course are AFDC and other income maintenance strategies, the women's health movement, family planning policies, child care and other policies affecting working women. Particular attention is paid in this course to the situation of minority women.

Social Work and Ethnic Minorities

This course considers some of the special social welfare problems of ethnic minorities in American society, particularly blacks, Puerto Ricans, Mexican Americans, and native Americans. The course undertakes to help students cope realistically with problems of culture, prejudice and ethnic difference. Special attention is given to increasing understanding of the underlying causes of prejudice and sterotyping, and to developing ways of dealing with these problems in direct practice and policy planning.

Staff Supervision in Social Service

This seminar is designed for those Master's students who will be expected to assume supervisory and/or staff development responsibilities. The seminar takes its direction from the function of supervision which is seen as primarily twofold: 1) the provision of more effective delivery of service to the consumer; and 2) the education and professional development of staff.

Treatment of Children in Families

An overview of treatment of children from a range of social and economic backgrounds. The seminar examines approaches to the understanding and modification of problems by intervention through the family. Emphasis is placed on careful examination of interactional patterns rather than systematic study of the total treatment process. The development of theory very closely related to the happenings in the family is attempted. Video tapes are used, along with readings and other sources of information.

Treatments of the Criminal: History, Myths, Current Trends, Clinical Methods, and Radical Approaches

A working knowledge of institutional and community-based corrections is provided. The concept of "the criminal personality," societal trends in correctional reform, current thinking on the treatment of the female offender, and the evolving role of the social worker in adult corrections are discussed. Current psychotherapeutic approaches (reality therapy, TA, behavior therapy, guided group interaction. . .), the politics of corrections, and issues in radical criminology are also examined. Ex-offenders and staff members from correctional agencies may be involved as guest lecturers or seminar leaders.

Urban Economics

The purpose of the course is to introduce the student to the tools of economic analysis that apply to urban problems and the techniques of benefit-cost analysis as applied to social welfare programs.

Students may also elect courses from the program in Law and Social Policy. See course descriptions on pages 37-41.

CERTIFICATION FOR SOCIAL WORK IN THE SCHOOLS

If a student is interested in social work in the schools in Pennsylvania, certification may be acquired through the Department of Education and Child Development.

The choice of certain electives both in The School of Social Work and Social Research and in the Department of Education, and a practicum in a school setting will prepare a student for such certification as part of the MSS program. Students interested in such an option should confer with the appropriate faculty person in the Department of Education and Child Development.

NON-CREDIT SEMINAR

Supervision in Social Work

Emphasis in this seminar is placed on identifying learning patterns of the student or staff member, the appropriate use of the supervisory method, and selection of educational experiences related to varying patterns. It is given on an audit basis for those with limited field instruction or supervisory experience. There is no fee for persons who are serving as field instructors for students in the practicum.

PRACTICUM

The practicum is an integral part of the curriculum for the Master of Social Service degree. A placement is arranged for each student: in both semesters of the first year in Social Casework and in Community Social Work; in the second year in Clinical Social Work, Social Service Management, Policy Research and Development, and Program Planning and Administration. The purpose of the practicum is to provide the opportunity for the student to apply theory in order to deepen knowledge and develop skill in its use. Students' assignments are goal-oriented and are planned to give content, sequence, and progression in learning. Practicum experience in an agency or in a field laboratory runs concurrently with the practice seminar in order to maximize opportunity for the student to integrate the content of the two. Each student's practicum is usually arranged in a different setting for each year of the program. Most practicums are in the five-county Philadelphia metropolitan area. Placements are made regularly, however, in Harrisburg, in the State of Delaware, and in the national capital area. The practicum for M.S.S. students has been provided in field placements concerned with the following topics, among others:

Aging
Child welfare
Community mental health
Consumer organizations

Corrections

Day care

Drug and alcohol dependency and abuse

Family services

Health services

Housing

Intergroup relations

Legal services

Legislative offices

Maternal and child health

Mental retardation

Neighborhood organization

Physical rehabilitation

Psychiatric services

Public assistance

Public education

Public health

Public welfare administration

School social work

Social planning

Social welfare research

Teaching—undergraduate programs

Women's issues

Youth services

FIELD INSTRUCTION SETTINGS

Students were placed during 1976-77 in the following agencies a
organizations:

Albert Einstein Medical Center, Community Mental Health/Men
Retardation Center

Albert Einstein Medical Center, Social Service Department

American Friends Service Committee, Inc.

American Oncologic Hospital

Berks County Intermediate Unit 14

Bryn Mawr Youth Psychotherapy Center

Bucks County Opportunity Council, Inc.

Catholic Social Services

Center for Rape Concern

Central Montgomery Mental Health/Mental Retardation Center

Chester County Children's Services

Child Care Service of Delaware County
    Media Office
    Eastern Community Office, Upper Darby

Child Study Institute of Bryn Mawr College

Children's Aid Society of Pennsylvania

Children's Hospital of Philadelphia

Citizens Committee on Public Education in Philadelphia

Community College of Philadelphia, Division of Social and
    Behavioral Sciences and Human Service Careers

Community Education Center, Inc.

Community Legal Services, Inc.

Community Life Services, Inc., of Delaware County

Crozer-Chester Medical Center
    Adult Outpatient Unit
    Emergency Room
    Maternal and Infant Care
    Research and Evaluation Service Unit

Delaware County Juvenile Court, Probation Department

Delaware County Legal Assistance Association, Inc.

Delaware County Mental Health/Mental Retardation Board

Delaware County Services for the Aging

Delaware Guidance Services for Children and Youth

Delaware, State of
    Division of Aging
    Division of Social Services

Diagnostic and Rehabilitation Center, Inc.

Drenk Memorial Guidance Center

Episcopal Community Services of the Diocese of Pennsylvania

Eromin Center, Inc.

Family Service of Montgomery County

Family Service of Philadelphia
    North District Office
    Northeast District Office

Family Service Mental Health Centers of Chester County

Germantown Settlement House

Girls' Clubs of Philadelphia

Green Tree School

Hahnemann Medical College and Hospital
Franklin Institute
Van Hammitt Clinic

Health and Welfare Council, Inc., Delaware County Area Office

International Alcohol and Mental Health Associates, Inc.

Irving Schwartz Institute for Children and Youth

Jewish Family Service of Philadelphia

Jewish Y's and Centers of Greater Philadelphia

Life Guidance Services, Inc.

Lower Merion Counseling Services

Lower Merion School District

Medical College of Pennsylvania, Division of Social Science

Montgomery County Mental Health/Mental Retardation Program
Drug and Alcohol Program
Mental Health Program

Montgomery County Office on Older Adults

National Association of Social Workers

National 4-H Foundation

National Urban League

National Women's Health Network

New World Consulting

Northeast Community Mental Health

Northwest Center for Mental Health/Mental Retardation Programs

Olde Kensington Redevelopment Corporation, Senior Wheels East

Opportunity Board of Montgomery County

Parents Union for Public Schools

Parkway Day School

Pennsylvania, Commonwealth of
Department of Health
Department of Public Welfare, SERO, Medical Assistance Operations
Department of Public Welfare, Office for the Aging
Eastern Pennsylvania Psychiatric Institute, Children's Unit

Haverford State Hospital
State Senator Louis G. Hill
Southeastern Regional Office, Office of Planning

Pennsylvania Hospital, Hall/Mercer Child and Family Mental Health Service

Pennsylvania Prison Society

Philadelphia Child Guidance Clinic

Philadelphia, City of
Court of Common Pleas, Adult Probation Department
Court of Quarter Sessions, Special Services
Special Services Office, Counseling and Referral Service

Philadelphia Geriatric Center

Philadelphia Psychiatric Center
Adult Inpatient Unit
Drug Unit

Planned Parenthood Association of Southeastern Pennsylvania

St. Christopher's Hospital for Children
Psychiatric Center
Fourth Street Academy

School District of Philadelphia, District V

Sleighton Farm School

South Philadelphia Community Center, Youth Services

Teen-Aid, Inc.

Thomas Jefferson University Medical Center

United States Department of Health, Education, and Welfare
Office of the Deputy for State Programs, Office of Child Support Enforcement
Office of Regional Director, Region III, Office of Long-Term Care
Office of Regional Director, Region III, Regional Equal Opportunity Employment Office

United States District Court, Eastern District of Pennsylvania

United Way of Southeastern Pennsylvania

Veterans Administration Hospital

West Philadelphia Community Mental Health Consortium, Consultation and Education Department

William Penn School District

Graduate Program for the Master of Law and Social Policy

The Degree of Master of Law and Social Policy

The Law and Social Policy program is a new curriculum designed for students of social service. It offers a full year of instruction in basic legal processes and legal problems, with a special effort to relate legal perspectives to major problems in social work practice. The program makes no pretense of surveying all fields of law as one finds them in law school, nor does it try to teach legal doctrine or paralegal skills. The aims rather are to prepare social service professionals to analyze legal problems relevant to their work, to enable them to work productively and critically with lawyers, and to help them become effective agents for social change through law.

The program is open to students who are enrolled concurrently for the M.S.S. degree at Bryn Mawr. Such students may begin the sequence of law courses in their second year and will continue in full-time study for a third year, during which they will complete all requirements for the M.S.S. and the M.L.S.P.

In addition, beginning in 1977-78, persons who already hold the M.S.S. or its equivalent will be able to enroll for the entire program of law courses in a single year of full-time study. They will receive the M.L.S.P. degree at the end of that year.

The courses in this program are also available on an individual basis to students in the regular M.S.S. program, students in the Ph.D. program, holders of the M.S.S. or its equivalent, and other interested persons. Students who are enrolled for the M.S.S. degree may count a limited number of these courses as electives. However, classes will be kept small, and first priority for enrollment will go to students who choose the program as a whole.

Part-time study in this program may be allowed under special circumstances.

The curriculum has been carefully planned to provide a thorough grounding in legal methods, a balanced treatment of the entire legal system, and an integration of the legal perspective with the problems of social service and social policy. The courses to be offered are as follows:

Foundation Courses:

Judicial Process
Legislative and Administrative Processes

Legal Research and Reform

Seminars:

The Adjudicatory Mode of Dispute Resolution
Equality and the Law
The Right of Individual Self-Determination
Law and Social Policy (a course with varying themes, for
1977-78 the topic will be Income Maintenance)
Practice Skills: Advocacy and Negotiation

Practicum

All of these courses will be offered each academic year. All are required for students who expect to receive the M.L.S.P. degree.

Candidates for this new degree will be strongly urged to take the three foundation courses in the same semester. These courses are designed to give an intensive orientation in basic skills of legal analysis as well as an introduction to the legal problems dealt with in later courses. The seminars will provide varied settings for the integration of law and social service concerns. Some will concentrate on policy analysis and reform, others will emphasize personal interactions with lawyers and social welfare clients. All of them, it is hoped, will offer insights into substantive rights and normative judgments in areas of urgent social problems.

Every effort will be made to design field instruction in settings where legal and social service interests converge. Individual placements will depend on particular interests and backgrounds.

The Law and Social Policy program is a new type of program with unique possibilities. It differs from a number of joint-degree programs with law schools in that it does not require students to complete a conventional J.D. program alongside course work in another professional school. The concepts and materials of legal study have here been reorganized for the benefit of professionals who do not intend to become practicing members of the bar. While lawyers have participated in planning the new program and will be among those teaching, a significant effort has been made to create new courses which analyze law as part of a larger social process and which draw on social science and normative methods to supplement legal analysis.

As the program grows, these goals may lead to the sponsoring of special summer institutes devoted to specific issues in law and social policy.

Foundation Courses

Judicial Process

This is a study of how courts interpret, apply, and, in an important sense, make the law. It probes the judicial method of argument—mastery of which is sometimes called "thinking like a lawyer"—as it is used by judges and advocates. Students will learn how to read a court opinion and how to frame an argument in legal terms. Consideration will be given to variations on the method as it occurs in common law, statutory interpretation, and constitutional law. In each area judicial action will be analyzed not only in logical terms but also from behavioral and political perspectives. Such study poses the question of the competence of courts to deal with complex social problems, such as the enforcement of school desegregation orders or the supervision of public institutions.

Legislative and Administrative Processes

In contrast to the preceding course, this one will concentrate on the more consciously political, less formal and legalistic branches of the legal system: the legislative process with its broad scope for deliberation over the ends of public policy, and administrative bodies, whose role in modern society has increased enormously. This course will be built around a series of problems or case studies designed to illustrate the variety of influences on legislative and administrative action, influences in addition to the formal and legal restraints which are built into each process. Specific case studies will explore the varieties of legislative regulatory devices, delegation of authority and oversight, the scope of administrative discretion, and at least one complex problem involving the interaction of state and federal agencies, courts, and legislatures.

Legal Research and Reform

This course introduces students to the basic techniques of legal research and asks them to apply those techniques in formulating proposals for legal reform. Lectures and library exercises will be used to communicate essential research skills, including use of court opinions, statutes, regulations, legal scholarship, and the wealth of legal finding aids. Short individual research problems will then be assigned, and midway through the semester students will cooperate in a common research effort in a selected area of statutory activity, such as Freedom of Information laws. Working either individually or in small groups, students will prepare a research report on a particular part but will also become familiar with the whole of the overall effort. These reports will then be used as the basis for drafting model statutes or for proposing changes in existing laws.

Seminars

The Adjudicatory Mode of Dispute Resolution

This course will examine the trial process as a method of resolving disputes and will compare this process to such alternative forms as administrative hearings, arbitration, and informal tribunals. The effectiveness of these processes in a variety of contexts will be assessed—custody disputes, welfare hearings, criminal cases. A central purpose will be to define the procedures necessary for a fair hearing in these different settings. An attempt will be made to relate the structure of a case—its procedural context—to the justice of the outcome. In this connection rules of evidence will be discussed, the role of judge and jury, and the techniques of judicial enforcement.

Equality and the Law

Equality is central to the legal process as a public policy goal, as a constitutional value, and as the formal ideal of all adjudication. There is, however, an important tension between the material or substantive notions of equality found in policy planning and the more formalistic sense of equality developed in the judicial process. This conflict will be explored in depth in at least four areas: racial segregation, public education, poverty, and sex discrimination. An examination will be made of some of the landmark constitutional cases which have led the law toward more substantive interpretations of equality. The seminar will also see how the abstractness of the standards and imperfections of legal enforcement with respect to the Constitution have shifted the conflict between substance and formalism more into the legislative arena. Recent sociological and economic literature on race, education, and poverty will also be discussed.

The Right of Individual Self-Determination

This course will explore the legal and social consequences of marking off a private sphere of action free from public control. At least two distinct traditions have encouraged this concern for individual rights: the classical liberal objections to state interference in autonomous social and economic areas, and more recent arguments for protecting the individual personality from encroachments by either the state or civil society. Both of these trends will be assessed in a variety of substantive areas: sexual privacy and abortion, the right to treatment, the right to refuse treatment, and family law. A search will be made for the legal substance behind these and other purported rights—in recent constitutional theory, in the state action doctrine extending the powers of the federal government, and in the procedural safeguards that have accompanied governmental power in its modern expansion.

Law and Social Policy: Income Maintenance

This course will look at the major cash programs—old-age insurance, unemployment insurance, and public assistance—as well as related "in-kind" assistance programs which together constitute public law of income maintenance. The social policies and values behind these programs will be discussed in the context of their historical development, their contemporary legislative and administrative support, and their judicial clarification in court challenges to welfare administration. The effect of judicial review on state compliance with federal law and on evolving standards of fair procedure will be examined in detail. In addition to its central importance for social service, this field of social policy also raises important issues of federal-state interaction, public administration, public finance, and fiscal policy—all of which need to be accounted for in planning a policy of income maintenance.

This is the first course to be offered under the general title of Law and Social Policy. Other topics may be examined as the program develops.

Practice Skills: Advocacy and Negotiation

This course will emphasize the informal techniques and interpersonal skills of successful practice in the border areas between law and social service. A series of problems will be presented which encourage role-playing and critical analysis in various settings: client interviews, negotiating sessions, administrative hearings, formal testimony of experts in court. Themes will be selected from family law, mental health, corrections and rehabilitation, community action, and contacts with bureaucracy. The course will be taught by a team of lawyers and social workers, and the workshop format is designed to encourage students to see and sense the reactions of both professions to the same set of problems. Social work students will experience some of the conflicts of working alongside lawyers, but they will also discover the rich possibilities in successful collaboration.

PRACTICUM I and II

The Law and Social Policy program continues the tradition of the School that classroom instruction should be supplemented by work in the field. Students in this program will be assigned placements that emphasize the interaction of law and social service. Ordinarily, the placement requires two days per week during the academic year.

41

Graduate Program for the Doctor of Philosophy

The curriculum for the Ph.D. provides a program of study from which a person may enter one of many careers, depending upon the changing needs and opportunities in social welfare and the interests and capabilities of the individual. Preparation for research and teaching is central to the goals of the program. Development of a variety of research competencies is encouraged; preparation for teaching in all areas of the social work curriculum, graduate and undergraduate, is also provided. The study of social work practice emphasizes theoretical work. Social policy development and analysis is given special attention.

The Ph.D. program in social work and social research prepares the student for understanding the nature and interdependence of individual and societal needs, and developing and promoting means by which these needs can be met most fully. Successful completion of the Ph.D. degree presumes demonstration of the scholarly pursuit of knowledge characterized by abstract logical thinking, critical evaluation, ability to reach new integration, and capacity to disseminate appropriately what one knows.

The candidate for the Ph.D. degree should have ability of a high order, intellectual curiosity, critical judgment, independence, a broad general education, and a Master's degree, usually in social work. Some experience in social welfare is desirable.

The program is planned to broaden the student's knowledge of social welfare in general and, through intensive study and research, to deepen his or her knowledge in one field in particular. The curriculum includes the following areas:

Social Work and Social Welfare: Past and Present

Social and Behavioral Sciences

Social Research

Social Work Practice: Theories, Research, and Issues
   1. Societal Focus
   2. Community/Institutional Focus
   3. Individual/Family/Group Focus

A student's course of study and Preliminary Examination are organized around a Major Area. The Major Area may be either Social Work and Social Welfare: Past and Present, or Social and Behavioral Sciences.

Minimum requirements include four courses in the Major Area, and two courses in each of the other areas. In Social Work and Social Welfare at least one course shall be taken in the Social Policy area and one in the History area. In Social Work Practice the two required courses must be taken in the same practice area. In the Social and Behavioral Sciences at least one course should be taken in the Social area and one in the Behavioral area.

In general, a minimum of twelve semester seminars plus two courses focusing on the dissertation is completed in preparation for the Ph.D. degree. Beyond the required seminars, doctoral students may elect courses in this School, The Graduate School of Arts and Sciences at Bryn Mawr, or The Graduate School of Arts and Sciences at the University of Pennsylvania under the Reciprocal Plan.

The requirements for the Ph.D. degree in The Graduate School of Social Work and Social Research are listed below.

1.   An acceptable baccalaureate degree and undergraduate preparation satisfactory to the School.

2.   In general, a Master's degree from an accredited school of social work or social welfare and preparation satisfactory to the School. Exceptions may be made for a student who has completed a Master's degree and satisfactory preparation in an allied field and presents significant experience in social work or social welfare or for a student in the M.S.S. program whose competence and qualifications as demonstrated in performance in this program promise that he or she can meet the demands of the Ph.D. program without first completing the M.S.S. degree.

3.   Completion of a minimum of one academic year in full-time residence in The Graduate School of Social Work and Social Research. The residence requirement is met by two consecutive semesters of study from September through May; three or four courses are to be taken in each of these semesters.

4.   Satisfactory completion of a course of study consisting of a minimum of twelve semester courses or seminars, including both those which are required and those which are elective. In addition, two tutorials in supervised work on the dissertation are required.

5.   A reading knowledge of a modern foreign language tested by a written examination. In certain circumstances students whose native language is not English may offer English as a foreign language.

6.   The acceptance of the student into candidacy for the Ph.D. degree. Application for candidacy may be made only after successful completion of the residence requirement.

7.   Satisfactory completion of the Preliminary Examination consisting of written examinations in four areas and an oral examination

43

by the candidate's Supervising Committee. The examinations are intended to test the candidate's general knowledge in his or her areas and fields rather than familiarity with particular courses. They are organized around the student's Major Area. One of the written examinations may be a take-home examination arranged between the student and the supervising committee. Preliminary Examinations are scheduled in October and March.

8. The preparation of a dissertation judged to be worthy of publication. The dissertation must represent independent investigation and writing and must contain new material, results, or interpretations.

9. A satisfactory Final Oral Examination in the special area in which the dissertation has been written.

10. The publication of the dissertation in whole or in part. Microfilming is accepted as a method of publication.

Social Work and Social Welfare: Past and Present

American Postwar Social Thought

This course is a careful examination of the books, chiefly outside of social work, which have been instrumental in the development of social and political movements since World War II. Selections range through philosophy, theology, psychiatry, economics, and sociology. They are works which have been widely read by the educated public and policy makers. Some of the authors represented in past terms are Reinhold Niebuhr, Robert Nisbet, John Dewey, Milton Friedman, Daniel Bell, David Riesman, J.K. Galbraith, and Victor Frankl. The list changes every time the course is offered. (Not offered 1977-78.)

Comparative Social Welfare: Social Service Programs

Social welfare programs in various societies other than the United States are studied. Among those to be examined are the systems in Sweden and the United Kingdom.

The Contribution of Social Science to Social Policy and Practice

This seminar examines how policy-related social science is organized and financed in the United States, then questions usefulness of such research and strategies which might make such research more purposeful for social policy and social practice. (Not offered 1977-78.)

Introduction to English and American Social Welfare History and Thought

Social welfare is examined as an historical institution. The development of a succession of philosophical systems within which this institution evolved is considered, and the influence upon both philosophy and welfare of social and economic changes is studied. Stress is placed upon historical and contemporary literature, which is examined for the light it casts upon the field of study. Anglo-American experience until 1930 is emphasized in this course.

Introduction to Social Policy

Different concepts of social policy are examined with special attention to issues in a number of different fields, such as: income transfers, medical care, social services, manpower training, education and housing. Attention is given to problems of implementation, practice, and the role of social science.

45

New Deal, Fair Deal, New Frontier, and Great Society: American Social Welfare 1930-69

The past half-century is studied intensively as the seminal period for contemporary social welfare programs. The collapse of traditional relief measures before the onslaught of the Great Depression, the ameliorative and reform measures of the Roosevelt administrations, and efforts to expand and correct these and other programs in the ensuing twenty-five years are examined, all with a view to understanding the weight of the past upon the present, and to judge the directions in which further change is most likely.

Personality Issues in Social Policies and Programs

This seminar is concerned with personality and policy; the assumptions about personality functioning in social policies; the impact of public social policy on personality; the impact of personality factors on policies; personalities in policy-making positions; personality theories as origins for the development of social policy; and social equality and personality.

Policy Analysis of Service Systems

The seminar will focus on policy analysis of social service systems. Attention will be given to three major themes: the service markets—consumers and potential consumers of social service programs; the suppliers—agencies and organizations, public and private, which make up the social service system; and efforts at reorganization of service functions and the redesign of their interrelationships.

Social Policy and the Family

The main theme of this course is the relationship between the state and the family. Various social policies regulating family life are examined from a historical and contemporary perspective. Among the specific issues discussed are the recent rise of single-parent families, child care policies, juvenile justice policies, and current developments in marriage and divorce laws. (Not offered 1977-78.)

Social Policy and Social Services

This course begins with a consideration of leading theoretical statements on social policy by British and American writers. It proceeds to a more concrete discussion of dilemmas in the organization of human services. Among these are public sector vs. private sector, accountability of service professionals, and the emergent roles of service consumers. (Not offered 1977-78.)

Social Welfare Policy and Issues: Specific Areas

The following courses are open to both Master's and doctoral students. If Master's students taking these courses enter the doctoral program at a later date, however, they may not count these courses for doctoral credit.

Child Welfare

Current issues and questions in the field of child welfare and their meaning for practitioners are considered. Content is drawn from areas such as child abuse and neglect (both institutional and parental), child care, health, adoptions, placement, and advocacy. Attention is paid to programs currently existing, their rationale and impact, and the gaps that persist.

Community Mental Health

This seminar examines the theoretical roots of the present community mental health system. Community mental health concepts of comprehensiveness, prevention, community participation, and continuity of care are analyzed in relation to policies governing the design and operation of Community Mental Health Centers. Students participate in the criticism and design of mental health service delivery policies.

Gerontology

Focused readings and discussions by students alternate with guest lectures by specialists in gerontology. Policies and issues in legislation, health, mental health, income maintenance, social service programs, research, housing, and nursing home care are considered.

Health

This course deals with a range of issues in the delivery of health care services. Among the topics discussed are national health insurance, community mental health, the division of labor among health professionals, and movements of health consumers.

Women's Issues

This course explores various aspects of the situation of women in contemporary American society. Social policies with particular relevance for women are examined, and women are discussed as both consumers and providers of social services. Among the specific areas covered in the course are AFDC and other income maintenance strategies, the women's health movement, family

47

planning policies, child care and other policies affecting working women. Particular attention is paid in this course to the situation of minority women.

Social and Behavioral Sciences

Comparative Personality Theories

Some of the more well known dynamics of personality theories are examined in relation to the development of the human personality. An attempt is made to understand the similarities and differences of the theories and to relate the theories to the development of the total person.

Fact and Value in Recent Social Theory

A study of reasons for and reactions to the methodological division between fact and value and the related separation of theory and practice in social policy. Positions surveyed will include the positivistic and phenomenological residues of Weber's theories, neo-Marxism, ethno-methodology, and structuralist models.

Freud's Psychoanalytic Theory

Examination is made of psychoanalysis as a personality theory. Special attention is paid to metapsychology in psychoanalytic theory and to psychoanalysis as social theory. Intensive analysis of basic writings by Freud and his collaborators forms the focus of the seminar. (Not offered 1977-78.)

Formal Organizations

This seminar considers structure and process in large-scale organizations. Starting from major theories of social organization, the course focuses upon those organizations which are planned to coordinate the efforts of large numbers of persons to accomplish specific goals. Leadership, organizational pathologies and the role of the individual are considered.

Group Theory

This seminar undertakes an investigation of group process characteristics. Individual and group behavior are studied, using significant group theorists, such as Homans, Lewin, Festinger, Goffman, Yalom, Blau, Kelman, and Bales. Theory will be related to the basic issues involved in research on interaction and leadership patterns in a variety of work-oriented and therapy groups.

Human Development in the First Third of Life

This course examines human development as a total system physically, socially, emotionally, and cognitively, from prenatal development through young adulthood. Major human development theorists, such as Erikson, Piaget, and others are reviewed. Implications for social policies that will contribute to maximum potential human development are explored. (Not offered 1977-78.)

Occupations and Professions

This course reviews classic and contemporary sociological approaches to the study of occupations and professions. The focus is on the dynamics of professionalization, the bureaucratization of professional work, professional/client relations, and related issues. Particular attention is paid to human service professions. (Not offered 1977-78.)

Psychoanalysis after Freud

Psychoanalytic writings from the 1930s to the present are studied. Emphasis varies with class selection among the array of theorists and directions that have developed in psychoanalytic theory. (Not offered 1977-78.)

Race and Ethnic Relations

This seminar critically examines the theoretical concepts of prejudice, institutional racism, and cultural racism. Concepts of ethnicity, and ethnic movements and relations are also reviewed. Problems of social policy, social services, and social work practice are then studied in the light of ethnic and race relations concepts. (Not offered 1977-78.)

Social and Cultural Aspects of Health, Illness and Treatment

Starting with the assumption that social and cultural influences shape definitions and expectations concerning health, illness, and treatment, this seminar identifies instances and implications of such influences. More specifically, attention will be given to areas of information essential for understanding common acute and chronic diseases and health issues, and their associated social and psychic problems. The possible role of the social worker as contributing agent for change will be examined. Specific content may include information re: normal body functions and changes, birth control and obstetrics, childhood diseases, common diseases (e.g. circulatory, gastrointestinal, venereal, arthritic, sensory, neurological); doctor, patient, and social worker relations; epidemiology; systems of health care delivery, as well as when and how to use them; and

49

economics and medical care. A brief overview will be included of planning in preventive and remedial health care, as well as community systems of resources and how to use them effectively. (This course is open to both Master's and doctoral students. If a Master's student taking this course enters the doctoral program at a later date, however, the student may not count this course for doctoral credit.)

Social Change

This seminar engages in an active search for an adequate abstract model of social change. Special attention is directed to modern systems theory. Major social theories are examined for relevant contributions to an understanding of social change; contemporary patterns of change in society are documented; and limitations in attempts to guide change at different levels of social organization are noted.

Social Philosophy and the Problem of Ideology

The problem of ideology consists of clarifying the standpoint of the observer (or agent) who wishes to understand (or change) society. It forces us to ask what kind of value structure we impose on our social environment and what the consequences are for social theory and public policy planning. The course begins with a careful reading of two classic sources on the nature of ideology (Marx and Mannheim) and then turns to consider the positivistic challenge to ideological thinking posed by natural scientific method. Particular attention will be given to modern critiques of science and technology which find elements of relativism and ideology hidden behind the pretense of objectivity (Kuhn, members of the Frankfurt School). Finally, the problem of ideology in the area of public policy will be discussed, particularly as it affects the choice between legal and political methods of social control. (Not offered 1977-78.)

Social Research

Data Analysis I

Data analysis is seen as one step in the research process. Statistical methods of analysis include descriptive and inferential statistics with major emphasis on partial and multiple correlation and regression, and analysis of variance and co-variance. Knowledge of the assumptions and conditions under which statistical methods are valid, and discrimination in the selection, application and interpretation of statistical tests is developed. Use of the computer in analysis is also taught.

Data Analysis II

Special attention is given to recent innovations, persistent problems and current issues in multivariate data analysis. Among the topics covered in this seminar are multiple factor analysis, step-wise regression analysis, path analysis, problems of handling cross-cultural data, and techniques for developing data to test social policy.

Historical Methodology in Social Welfare

The use of historical research in social welfare is studied and applied. Selection of possible topics for study, uncovering of sources, methods of research are among the topics covered. The literature of historical methodology is examined and its lessons applied to social welfare. Development of skills in preparation and writing of research papers is stressed. (Not offered 1977-78.)

Qualitative Data Collection: Theory and Method

This course introduces students to the basic techniques of participant observation through involvement in a group research project in an institutional setting. The class also reads and discusses major works in the participant observation tradition. (Not offered 1977-78.)

Research Methodology

In this seminar a study is made of contemporary methodological approaches to problems in social and behavioral research with application for social welfare. There is intensive coverage of survey research design, case study and clinical method, design of social experiments, and evaluation of social work programs.

Social Work Practice:
Theories, Research, and Issues

SOCIETAL FOCUS

Intervention in Governmental Processes

This course cuts across the several levels of American Government in identifying those points in the legislative process and the implementation of government programs where influence by professionals or client and citizen groups may be applied. Mechanisms, organizational vehicles, and strategies for exerting such influence are inventoried.

Politics and Practice of Contemporary Social Policy Development

The course will develop and apply a variety of analytic tools for the examination of a range of social policies. It will apply these frameworks with a concern for distinguishing the different governmental levels of policy formulation and implementation as well as the different stages in the process of policy development. The student is expected to develop in-depth knowledge of one substantive field through his/her analysis of a contemporary issue at the federal level.

Program Development

This seminar examines the process of developing programs in response to federal and state legislation, regulations, and guidelines. Students participate in developing a framework for the comparative analysis of practice in this process. (Not offered 1977-78.)

COMMUNITY/INSTITUTIONAL FOCUS

Community Organization and Community Development

This seminar focuses on several distinct philosophies and theories of community organization in the advanced industrial nations, and of community development in developing nations. Issues of social change vs. social service, participation vs. cooptation, ideology and values, and the role of the community worker are examined in the light of current theory and research. The experiences of international social agencies in community development are also explored.

Program and Agency Evaluation

This seminar focuses on appropriate processes and systems for evaluating human service organizations and their individual programs. Various approaches to evaluating effectiveness and efficiency are carefully examined. Practical problems of implementation are discussed. Students create an evaluation design, have it criticized, and criticize other designs. Skills in evaluative research are sharpened. (Not offered 1977-78.)

Program Development and Agency Administration

This seminar engages a series of alternative theories and concepts of organizations, administration, decision-making, program planning and community structures. Theoretical material is related to specific administrative issues, such as establishing a concrete planning process, establishing policies and procedures, evaluating agency efficiency and impact, and mobilizing community resources.

Social Movements

This seminar examines major theories of social movements with an emphasis on movements for social and economic change in the advanced industrial nations. Such theories are then applied to problems of social work practice and social policy. Specific emphasis is given to research on the role of the organizer within social movements. (Not offered 1977-78.)

INDIVIDUAL/FAMILY/GROUP FOCUS

Critical Appraisal of Strategies of Intervention

The essence of this seminar is the linking of practice research to practice. While the emphasis is on effectiveness of intervention strategies, other related areas are also examined, such as characteristics of the problem population and those of the helpers. (Not offered 1977-78.)

Descriptive Analysis of a Range of Interventive Strategies

A broad range of interventive strategies on the individual and small group level is studied. Emphasis is placed upon comparative examination of many perspectives. Choice of particular strategies is worked out with the class.

Problem Definition, Practices, Strategies and Related Issues

This seminar focuses on social casework (individual, group, and family treatment) in the perspective of social problems, strategies, issues of practice, education, and professional leadership. These areas are examined in the light of the history of clinical social work and the developing trends within the context of societal factors and the state of knowledge.

Specific Intervention Strategies: Family Therapies

This seminar analyzes various approaches in family therapy in relation to theory, research, population needs, and issues of training. (Not offered 1977-78.)

Law and Social Policy

Doctoral students may also enroll in courses from the program in Law and Social Policy as electives. See course descriptions on page 37-41.

Other Courses

Courses in the Bryn Mawr Graduate School of Arts and Sciences may be elected as part of the student's program with the permission of the Dean of The Graduate School of Social Work and Social Research and the instructor of the course to be taken.

Graduate courses in The Graduate School of Arts and Sciences of the University of Pennsylvania are also available during the academic year for doctoral students of Bryn Mawr College. For information regarding the reciprocal arrangement with the University, see the section under Admissions (page 13).

Fees

Application: $25 (non-refundable).

Tuition

Full-time Students: $3,925 a year (1977-78).*

Part-time Students: $675 a semester for each course or seminar.

Auditors: Fees for auditors are the same as those for students registered in courses for credit.

All students enrolled in three or more courses are charged a general materials fee of $20 per semester.

Students enrolled in the practicum are charged a practicum materials fee of $30 a semester. In addition, students are required to meet traveling and other expenses incurred in relation to the practicum.

Continuing enrollment for Ph.D. candidates: Candidates who have completed the required academic courses including two tutorials in dissertation research and who are continuing independent work on their dissertations either in the vicinity of Bryn Mawr or in other places must retain their enrollment and degree candidacy by registering for one or more courses each semester or by paying a continuing enrollment fee of $150 each semester.

Students who wish to present themselves for examinations must be enrolled.

Doctoral students who are not working on dissertations and not consulting with the faculty or using the library may apply to the Dean of The Graduate School of Social Work and Social Research for a leave of absence for one or more semesters. No fee is required while on leave of absence. Students will be expected to be enrolled in courses or on the Continuing Enrollment Program unless granted a leave of absence.

---

*Faced with the rising costs of higher education, the College has had to raise tuition each of the last seven years. Further increases may be expected.

Payment of Fees

The tuition fee will be billed by semester. In the event of withdrawal from The Graduate School of Social Work and Social Research, refunds will be made according to the following schedule.

For Semester I
    Withdrawals prior to September 7   100%
    Withdrawals September 7 through October 31   50%
    Withdrawals November 1 to end of semester   0%
For Semester II
    Withdrawals prior to January 16   100%
    Withdrawals January 16 through March 10   50%
    Withdrawals March 11 to end of semester   0%

For those students living at the Graduate Residence Center, the charge for residence is $1990 in 1977-78. In accordance with the above schedule, if a student withdraws from graduate study a refund will be made of that portion of the fee which represents room, with the proviso that the College is able to reassign the student's space to some other student not previously in residence. The student is not entitled to dispose of the room he or she leaves vacant.

Appropriate reduction or remission will also be made for that portion of the residence fee which represents the cost of food.

Procedure for securing refunds: Written notice must be received by the Dean of The Graduate School of Social Work and Social Research at least one week prior to the effective date of the withdrawal. Students who have received federally insured loans (loans guaranteed by state agencies—Guaranteed Student Loan Program - GSLP and National Direct Student Loans - NDSL) to meet any educational expenses for the current academic year must make an appointment with the Comptroller of the College before leaving the School to arrange for the appropriate refund of the loans in question.

Tuition is due at registration or upon receipt of bill. Students whose fees are not paid within 10 days of receipt of bill in each semester will not be permitted to continue in residence or to attend classes. Degrees will not be awarded to any student owing money to the College or any College facility, nor will any transcripts be issued.

Summary of Expenses for the Academic Year 1977-1978

Regular

Tuition Fee	$3,925
One Semester Course or Seminar	675
Residence in graduate student housing	1,990

Contingent

Application Fee	$ 25
Charge for microfilming Ph.D. Dissertation	40
Continuing Enrollment Fee	300
Dispensary Fee	50
Graduation Fee for all Graduate Degrees	25
Health Insurance (United States citizens)	60
Health Insurance (foreign students)	70
Late Registration Fee[1]	10
General Materials Fee	40
Practicum Materials Fee (Master's Students only)	60
Add-Drop Fee[2]	10

Effective after September 13, semester I, and January 24, semester II.
The period for adding and dropping courses or seminars without fee will end September 27, semester I, and February 7, semester II.

Resources for Graduate Work at Bryn Mawr

Library

The Mariam Coffin Canaday Library, and the eight auxiliary libraries of Bryn Mawr College, including the Art and Archaeology collection in the M. Carey Thomas Library, contain over 450,000 books and regularly receive more than 2000 periodicals as well as many scholarly series. The Library is open throughout the year with a liberal schedule of hours. Books are readily accessible on open stacks and in study rooms; individual carrels are available for advanced students.

The John D. Gordan Reference Center provides a focus for reference books and services in the library. In its card catalog, the main entry cards of the Haverford College Library join those of the Bryn Mawr Library, thus bringing more than 685,000 entries into one file. In addition, the Library is a member of the Union Catalogue of Pennsylvania, which locates approximately 7,200,000 volumes in the Philadelphia area and throughout the state, including the libraries of the American Philosophical Society, the Library Company of Philadelphia, the Historical Society of Pennsylvania, the Academy of Natural Sciences, the Free Library of Philadelphia, the Franklin Institute, the College of Physicians, the Rosenbach Foundation, the University of Pennsylvania and Temple University.

Computer Center

Through its membership in the Uni-Coll Corporation, a regional educational computer consortium, Bryn Mawr College has access to the resources and technical support of a major computing center. A high speed, remote batch terminal (printer at 600 lines per minute, card reader at 600 cards per minute) and nine teletypewriter terminals located on campus link the College with the Uni-Coll IBM 370, Model 168 computer. These facilities make available to faculty and students batch, remote job entry, and interactive computing supported by a large variety of programming systems.

History of the School

The Graduate School of Social Work and Social Research was opened at Bryn Mawr College in the fall of 1915 as the Carola Woerishoffer Graduate Department of Social Economy and Social Research. It was established as a tribute to Carola Woerishoffer, a Bryn Mawr graduate of the class of 1907, and was the first graduate program of social work education to be offered by a college or university. Subsequently the name was modified from Social Economy and Social Research to Social Work and Social Research. In August 1970, it became one of the three Schools which comprise Bryn Mawr College.

The School opened with eight graduate students; no undergraduates were admitted. Under the initial plan, two-thirds of the student's time was given to the study of theory and statistics, the remaining third to "practical investigation," with a half year spent in "field work" in a social service institution or a social welfare organization in Philadelphia or New York.

The course of study was planned for one, two, or three years, with three years required for the Ph.D. degree and one and two years for a certificate. The Master of Social Service degree replaced the two-year certificate in 1947. Its plan of "field work" and its inclusion of work in labor and industrial relations and in community organization made it somewhat different from the other early schools of social work. Under its first director, Dr. Susan M. Kingsbury, four fields of study were offered: Community Organization, Social Casework, Industrial Relations, and Social and Industrial Investigation. Included among the organizations offering field work for students in these early days were: The Family Society of Philadelphia, The Children's Aid Society, the White Williams Foundation, the Big Sister Association, the Young Women's Christian Association, the Criminal Division of the Municipal Court of Philadelphia, the Social Services Department of the University of Pennsylvania Hospital, and various social settlements.

In 1919, Bryn Mawr became one of the six charter members of the American Association of Schools of Social Work. In this period following World War I, social work education was rapidly changing in response to the continuous expansion of social work into new settings. The curricula of the schools responded to these changes in a variety of ways. At Bryn Mawr, preparation for social casework was expanded and additional courses in public welfare and social

59

legislation were offered. However, the emphasis on research and social investigation which was central to the early curriculum of the School continued.

Bryn Mawr had the first doctoral program in social work education and awarded the first Ph.D. in 1920. The doctoral program at the School of Social Service Administration at the University of Chicago followed later in the 1920s. Today thirty-one schools in the United States offer doctoral programs.

By 1935 Bryn Mawr was one of twenty-nine schools belonging to the American Association of Schools of Social Work. Twenty-five were in colleges or universities and only four were independent schools. Bryn Mawr is currently a member of the Council on Social Work Education, successor to the American Association of Schools of Social Work and the accrediting body for social work education.

The Graduate School of Social Work and Social Research currently has approximately one hundred seventy-five full-time students. A number of factors have contributed to this expansion: the acquisition in 1958 of a separate building at 815 New Gulph Road and increased Federal support for education for social work, especially scholarship aid in the form of traineeships.

There are more than eighty graduate schools of social work accredited by the Council on Social Work Education in the United States and Canada. Although many changes have taken place both at Bryn Mawr and in social work education, the vision of those responsible for the design of the School at its founding has been proven by experience to have been remarkably correct.

The School now has approximately 1,100 living graduates. Since its inception it has granted awards to more than 1,250 persons; this includes awards of professional certificates and M.A. degrees, neither of which has been offered since 1947. The School has granted 75 Ph.D. degrees and, since 1947, more than 1,000 M.S.S. degrees.

At the time of its founding, the School admitted only women; since the late 1930s both men and women have been admitted and during the last ten years men have constituted about one third of the student body..

Graduates of the School are located in all regions of the United States and many foreign countries. Their present positions range within a wide spectrum of governmental and voluntary organizations and agencies. They are widely represented in child and family welfare, community mental health, corrections, gerontology, health, housing, intergroup relations, legal services, mental retardation, prevention and treatment of alcohol addiction and drug abuse,

neighborhood organization, public education, public welfare a
ministration, social planning, social rehabilitation, and social w
fare research. Approximately half are executives, supervisors
administrators, or consultants. Recipients of the doctoral degree a
chiefly in teaching and research positions.

In the fall of 1975 the School celebrated its sixtieth anniversai
At the same time it moved to a new building at 300 Airdale Road.
the academic year 1976-77 a new degree of Master of Law and Soc
Policy was established. Over the course of its sixty-two years, t
School's graduates have contributed substantially to leadership
both public and voluntary social welfare.

Graduate Student Housing

Housing on campus is provided for about sixty-five graduate students in the Graduate Residence Center, Batten House, and the Annex. There is a separate bedroom for each student. No housing on campus is available for married students. Rooms are furnished except for rugs and curtains. Students should bring towels and bed linen. (Local rental services will supply sheets and pillowcases for a modest fee. Arrangements can be made on arrival.) Because of College fire regulations, smoking is not permitted in the bedrooms. There are smokers on certain floors. The dining room, available to all resident students, is located in the Center.

Application for a room should be made as early as possible. A room contract, which will be sent upon request, must be signed and returned to the Office of The Graduate School of Arts and Sciences with a deposit of ten dollars. The deposit will be deducted from the residence fee; it will be refunded only if the student cannot be accommodated.

A student who has reserved a room will be held responsible for the residence charge unless notice of withdrawal is sent in writing to the Dean of The Graduate School of Arts and Sciences before August 15.

The regular charge for residence (room, board and health service) for graduate students is $1,990 a year, payable one half early in the first semester and the other half early in the second. Although one or more housing units may be closed during Christmas and spring vacations, when food and health services are not provided, residence on campus covers the period from the opening of College in the fall until Commencement Day.

Baggage will be accepted at the College after August 20. It should be sent prepaid, addressed to the Graduate Center and marked with the owner's name.

Health

Medical Services

The College maintains an 18-bed infirmary with a staff of physicians and nurses. The infirmary is open when College is in session. The college physicians may be consulted without charge by students residing in campus housing and by students living off campus who have paid the dispensary fee. Specialists practicing in Bryn Mawr and Philadelphia serve as consulting physicians to the College. If consultation is necessary, the student must meet the expense.

The residence charge paid by graduate students living in campus housing entitles them to treatment in the College dispensary, and to care in the Infirmary for seven days (not necessarily consecutive) during the year, and to attendance by the college physicians during this time. After the seven-day period, the fee is $30.00 for each day in the Infirmary.

Graduate students who do not live in campus housing may pay a $50.00 fee which entitles them to full use of the Student Health Service. The fee is not billed automatically and is not covered by scholarship or other grants. The dispensary fee is to be paid in the Comptroller's Office where a dispensary card is issued.

The College maintains a counseling and diagnostic service staffed by clinical social workers and consulting psychiatrists. They are at the Infirmary on a part-time basis. All students eligible for dispensary care may use this service. The counseling service offers confidential consultation and discussion of personal and emotional problems. Definitive and long-range psychotherapy is not available. A charge is made for visits in excess of four.

Medical Requirements

All graduate students, after admission but before registration, must file a medical history and health evaluation form with the Infirmary. There are no exceptions to this rule.

In addition to a statement of health, signed by a physician, the following are required: tetanus and polio immunizations; proof of freedom from active tuberculosis based on either a negative skin test to tuberculosis or, in the presence of a positive test, a normal chest x-ray within six months of admission.

Insurance

All graduate students are urged to carry health insurance. Students are entitled to the Bryn Mawr College Student Health care insurance at a cost of about $59.50 per year. Those wishing more complete coverage may purchase Blue Cross and Blue Shield insurance on an individual basis, subject to screening by the insurance company. Application for College health insurance should be made through the Head Nurse in the Infirmary.

Foreign Students. The College also makes available a policy which provides fuller coverage of medical, surgical, and hospital costs. This insurance is required of all students whose permanent residence is not in the United States unless they have equally complete protection of another kind effective in the United States. The cost for students under age thirty is about $70.00 for a twelve-month period, starting in September.

All foreign students will be automatically enrolled in the Student Health Service at a cost of $50 for non-residents.

Child Care Center

Child care is available for Bryn Mawr and Haverford college families at the New Gulph Child Care Center, 1109 County Line Road, Rosemont, just five minutes from campus. Children 3 months through 5 years are eligible. The center is open five days a week, 9 a.m.-5 p.m.

The center, conducted by a professional staff, incorporates appropriate age group developmental activities with high quality group care, plus a nursery school program. Flexible schedules can be arranged to accommodate the programs of students, staff, faculty, and alumnae parents based on the college calendar. A minimum of six hours regular use per week is required. Following Commencement a summer program is conducted for approximately two months.

The fee scale is based on the age of the child and the number of hours in attendance at the center. Tuition for the semester is payable in advance. Financial assistance is available. Early registration for all programs is essential. For information contact the Director at 525-7649.

Career Planning Office

Graduate students are invited to make use of the services of the Career Planning Office. These services include counseling on career interests and concerns; information on specific openings for summer, temporary and permanent, full- and part-time positions; consultation on job-hunting methods. Upon request the Career Planning Office also collects, maintains and makes available to prospecive employers the credentials of graduate students and alumnae/i. The credentials include biographical data and faculty and employer references.

Equality of Opportunity

Bryn Mawr College admits students of any race, color, national and ethnic origin to all the rights, privileges, programs and activites generally accorded or made available to students at the College. It does not discriminate on the basis of race, color, or national or ethnic origin in administration of its educational policies, admissions policies, scholarship and loan programs, and athletic and other College-administered programs.

As required by Title IX of the 1972 Federal Education Amendments, it is also the policy of Bryn Mawr College not to discriminate on the basis of sex in its educational programs, activities, or employment practices. Inquiries regarding compliance with Title IX and other policies on non-discrimination may be directed to the Assistant to the President, Taylor Hall, extension 381, or to the Director of the Office for Civil Rights, Department of Health, Education and Welfare, Washington, DC.

Bryn Mawr College is an equal opportunity employer.

Student and Alumni Associations

Student Associations of The Graduate School of Social Work and Social Research

All Master's students in The Graduate School of Social Work and Social Research are eligible for membership in the Student Association. The Student Association, faculty and administration work together to promote the objectives of the School.

The Doctoral Student Association is open to all full- and part-time doctoral students. It provides an open forum for discussion of common concerns with reference to the advanced program as well as broader professional interests.

Alumni Association of The Graduate School of Social Work and Social Research

The Alumni Association of the School was organized to further the interests of the School and its alumni. This Association is part of the larger Alumnae Association of Bryn Mawr College.

Recruitment of Minority Group Students

A Student-Faculty-Alumni Committee is active in recruitment of interested and qualified minority group students.

The Graduate School of Social Work and Social Research is especially interested in having minority group students explore graduate social work education at Bryn Mawr. Inquiries may be directed to the Office of Admissions, 300 Airdale Road, Bryn Mawr, Pa. 19010.

College Facilities

Student-Faculty Lounge

There is a Student-Faculty Lounge at The Graduate School of Social Work and Social Research for the use of Social Work faculty and students.

Parking

Parking for Social Work students is available at The Graduate School of Social Work and Social Research. Regular bus service is available from The Graduate School of Social Work and Social Research to Canaday Library.

Mailboxes

There are student mailboxes at The Graduate School of Social Work and Social Research. Mail addressed to students in the School should include 300 Airdale Road, Bryn Mawr, Pennsylvania 19010.

Wyndham

Wyndham is the College Alumnae House where the headquarters of the Bryn Mawr College Alumnae Association is located. Graduate students are invited to use the dining and other facilities.

Officers of the College

Harris L. Wofford, Jr. AB (University of Chicago) JD (Howard University and Yale University) *President of the College*

Bernard Ross PH D (University of Michigan) *Dean of The Graduate School of Social Work and Social Research*

Merle Broberg PH D (The American University) *Associate Dean of The Graduate School of Social Work and Social Research* and *Acting Dean Semester II*

Phyllis Pray Bober PH D (New York University) *Dean of The Graduate School of Arts and Sciences*

Mary Patterson McPherson PH D (Bryn Mawr College) *Dean of the Undergraduate College*

Gertrude C. K. Leighton AB (Bryn Mawr College) JD (Yale University) *Secretary of the General Faculty*‡

Willard F. King PH D (Brown University) *Acting Secretary of the General Faculty*

Milton D. Speizman PH D (Tulane University) *Secretary of the Faculty of The Graduate School of Social Work and Social Research*

James Tanis TH D (University of Utrecht) *Director of Libraries*

Frieda W. Woodruff MD (University of Pennsylvania) *College Physician*

---

‡On leave 1977-78.

69

Officers of Administration of the College

Dolores E. Brien PH D (Brown University) *Director of Career Planning*

Margaret M. Healy PH D (Bryn Mawr College) *Executive Director of the Board of Trustees' Ad Hoc Committee on Financial Planning*

Joseph S. Johnston, Jr. MA (University of Chicago) *Assistant to the President*

Paul W. Klug CPA BS (Temple University) *Comptroller* and *Business Manager of the College*

Ramona L. Livingston AB (William Jewell College) *Adviser to Foreign Students* and *Lecturer in English*

Margaret G. McKenna AB (Bryn Mawr College) *Personnel Administrator*

Samuel J. McNamee BS (Temple University) *Assistant Comptroller*

Julie E. Painter AB (Bryn Mawr College) *Administrator of Records and Financial Aid*

Alexandra Quandt Aldridge AB (Bryn Mawr College) *Director of Resources*

Patricia Onderdonk Pruett PH D (Bryn Mawr College) *Associate Dean of the Undergraduate College*

Ellen Fernon Reisner MA (Bryn Mawr College) *Assistant to the President* and *Acting Director of Public Information*

Thomas N. Trucks BS (Villanova University) *Superintendent of Buildings and Grounds*

Sarah E. Wright *Director of Halls*

The Advisory Board of
The Graduate School of
Social Work and Social Research

The Honorable Arlin M. Adams
Chairman

Mrs. Charles R. Bardes
Mrs. Thomas Bates
Mr. David B. Bernhardt
Mr. Curtis Clapham
Mrs. William T. Coleman
Mr. Edward H. Da Costa
Mrs. Carl Goldmark, Jr.
Mr. Shelton B. Granger
Mr. Thomas B. Harvey, Jr.
Mrs. A. G. Hawkins
Mr. Wilbur E. Hobbs
Mr. Hobart Jackson
Mr. Norman V. Lourie
The Rev. Msgr.
  James T. McDonough
Mr. William L. Rafsky
Mr. Sidney Repplier
Mr. Henry Scattergood
Mr. Isadore Scott
Mrs. Elias Wolf

Faculty Members:

Joyce Lewis
Miss Greta Zybon

Alumni Members:

Mrs. Edward B. McDaid
Ms. Rhonda Weiss

Student Members:

Ms. Helen Plotkin
Mr. Nathaniel Worley

Ex Officio:

Mr. Harris L. Wofford, Jr.
Mr. Bernard Ross

Faculty of The Graduate School of Social Work and Social Research for the Academic Year 1977-78

Leslie B. Alexander PHD (Bryn Mawr College) *Assistant Professor*

John Archibald MSS (Bryn Mawr College) *Lecturer*

Charles C. Bray PHD (University of Pittsburgh) *Associate Professor*

Merle Broberg PHD (The American University) *Associate Dean of The Graduate School of Social Work and Social Research, Acting Dean Semester II,* and *Associate Professor*

Dennis Brunn PHD (Washington University) *Assistant Professor*

Sandra S. Cornelius PHD (Bryn Mawr College) *Assistant Professor* and *Coordinator of Field Instruction*

Richard H. Gaskins JD, PHD (Yale University) *Assistant Professor* and *Coordinator of the Law and Social Policy Program*

Samuel Gubins PHD (The Johns Hopkins University) *Visiting Lecturer*

Stephen Holden PHD (Bryn Mawr College) *Assistant Professor*

Isaac C. Hunt JD (University of Virginia) *Visiting Lecturer*

Carole Joffe PHD (University of California, Berkeley) *Assistant Professor*‡

Toba S. Kerson DSW (University of Pennsylvania) *Assistant Professor*

Jane C. Kronick PHD (Yale University) *Associate Professor*

Howard Lesnick LLB (Columbia Law School) *Visiting Professor in the Law and Social Policy Program*

Joyce Lewis MSS (Bryn Mawr College) *Assistant Professor*

Philip Lichtenberg PHD (Western Reserve University) *Professor*

Katherine D.K. Lower PHD (University of Wisconsin) *Professor Emeritus*

Ruth W. Mayden MSS (Bryn Mawr College) *Visiting Lecturer*

Laurie N. McNally MSS (Bryn Mawr College) *Lecturer* and *Coordinator of Admissions*

Braulio Montalvo MA (Columbia University) *Caroline S. Rogers and Lucia Rogers Vorys Visiting Lecturer*

Martin Rein PHD (Brandeis University) *Visiting Professor*

Bernard Ross PHD (University of Michigan) *Dean of The Graduate School of Social Work and Social Research* and *Professor*

---

‡On leave 1977-78.

Djordje Soc MSW (University of California, Berkeley) *Lecturer*

Milton D. Speizman PH D (Tulane University) *Professor* and *Secretary of the Faculty of The Graduate School of Social Work and Social Research*

Ruth O. Stallfort MSS (Simmons College) Third-Year Certificate (Columbia University) *Associate Professor*

James Tanis TH D (University of Utrecht) *Director of Libraries*

William W. Vosburgh PH D (Yale University) *Associate Professor*

Mona Wasow MSW (University of Wisconsin) *Visiting Lecturer*

Tawana Ford Whaley MSS (Bryn Mawr College) *Lecturer*

Robert J. Wicks PSY D (Hahnemann Medical College) *Assistant Professor*

Cathie J. Witty PH D (University of California, Berkeley) MPA (Harvard University) *Assistant Professor*

Harris L. Wofford, Jr. JD (Howard University and Yale University) *President of the College*

Greta Zybon DSW (Western Reserve University) *Associate Professor*

Administration of The Graduate School of Social Work and Social Research

Bernard Ross PH D (University of Michigan) *Dean*

Merle Broberg PH D (The American University) *Associate Dean* and *Acting Dean Semester II*

Milton D. Speizman PH D (Tulane University) *Secretary of the Faculty*

Sandra S. Cornelius PH D (Bryn Mawr College) *Coordinator of Field Instruction*

Laurie N. McNally MSS (Bryn Mawr College) *Coordinator of Admissions*

Grace M. Irish AB (Vassar College) *Administrative Assistant*

Standing Committees of the Faculty of The Graduate School of Social Work and Social Research for 1977-78

Secretary of the Faculty
Mr. Speizman 1976-79

Committee on Nominations
Mr. Soc 1975-78
Mrs. Kerson 1977-78
Mr. Gaskins 1977-80

Committee on Policy
Dean Ross *Chair*
Mr. Speizman *ex officio*
Miss Zybon 1975-78
Mr. Gaskins 1976-79
Mr. Brunn 1977-80

*Committee on Admissions and
Financial Awards*
Mr. Broberg *Chair*
Dean Ross *ex officio*
Ms. McNally *ex officio*
Mrs. Whaley *ex officio*
Mr. Soc 1976-78
Mr. Bray 1976-78

Committee on Master's Curriculum
Dean Ross *ex officio*
Mrs. Cornelius 1976-78
Mr. Vosburgh 1976-78
Mr. Lichtenberg 1977-79
Mrs. Stallfort 1977-79

*Committee on Evaluation of
Educational Performance of
Master's Students*
Dean Ross *Chair*
Mrs. Cornelius *ex officio*
Mrs. Alexander 1977-78
Ms. Witty 1977-78

*Committee on Field Instruc
and Placement*
Mrs. Cornelius *Chair*
Mr. Broberg *Vice Chair*
Dean Ross *ex officio*
Mrs. Kerson 1977-78
Ms. McNally 1977-79

*Committee on Initial
Appointments*
Dean Ross *Chair*
Mr. Holden
Mrs. Kronick
Miss Zybon

Doctoral Committee
Mr. Vosburgh *Chair*
Dean Ross *ex officio*
Mrs. Alexander
Mr. Bray
Mr. Broberg
Mr. Brunn
Mrs. Cornelius
Mr. Gaskins
Mr. Holden
Ms. Joffe‡
Mrs. Kerson
Mrs. Kronick
Mr. Lichtenberg
Mr. Speizman
Mr. Wicks
Ms. Witty
Miss Zybon
and
All students enrolled in the
Doctoral Program

---

‡On leave 1977-78.

Representatives to the Advisory Board

Joyce Lewis 1977-78
Miss Zybon 1977-78

Representatives to Committee on Computer Facilities

Mr. Brunn 1976-78
Mr. Broberg 1976-78

Representative to the Committee to Supervise the Degree of Doctor of Philosophy

Mr. Bray 1975-78

Directions to Bryn Mawr

Bryn Mawr College is located approximately eleven miles west of Philadelphia and nine miles east of Paoli.

By air: From the Philadelphia International Airport take the airport limousine or SEPTA bus to 30th Street Station in Philadelphia and from there the Paoli Local to Bryn Mawr, or take a taxi or the Bennett Limousine Service directly to 300 Airdale Road from the airport, a distance of 14 miles.

By automobile: From the east or west take U.S. 30 or the Pennsylvania Turnpike. From the Valley Forge Exit of the Turnpike, take the Schuylkill Expressway (Pa. #43—Interstate #76), turning right at exit number 36, Pa. #320, Gulph Mills, which is 3.5 miles east of the toll gate; continue into Montgomery Avenue to the town of Bryn Mawr, a distance of 4 miles from the Expressway. Turn left at the traffic light at the intersection of Airdale Road and Montgomery Avenue. School is located at 300 Airdale Road.

Parking is available at The Graduate School of Social Work and Social Research.

By bus: All Greyhound buses arrive at the Philadelphia terminal at 17th and Market Streets, adjoining Suburban Station. Trailways buses arrive at 13th and Arch Streets, three blocks from Suburban Station. Take the Paoli Local from Suburban Station to Rosemont Station.

By railroad: Connections from the east, north and south are best made from 30th Street Station, Philadelphia, on the Paoli Local of the Penn Central Railroad, which leaves the station every thirty minutes. Those coming by rail from the west are advised to leave the train at Paoli (rather than North Philadelphia) and take the Local from Paoli to Rosemont Station.

To walk to the main campus from the Bryn Mawr Station, go one block to the traffic light at the intersection of Morris and Montgomery Avenues, cross Montgomery onto Morris and take the next left onto Yarrow Street, which leads directly to the campus.

To walk to The Graduate School of Social Work and Social Research, use the Rosemont Station, one stop beyond Bryn Mawr coming from the East and one stop beyond Villanova coming from the West. Cross Montgomery Avenue and continue on Airdale Road. School is on the left.

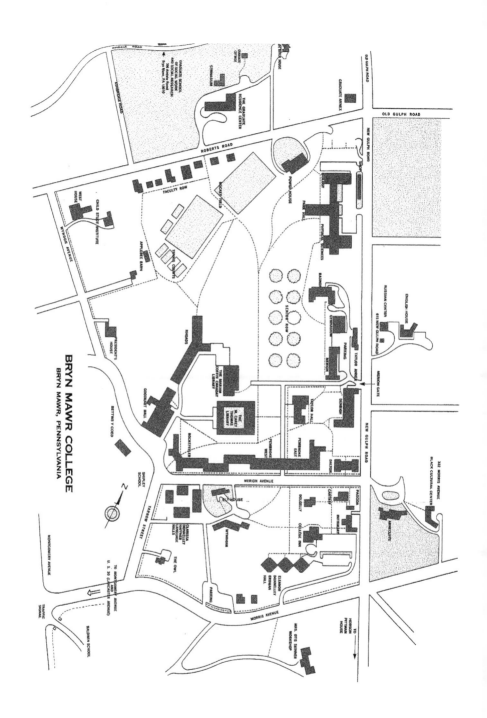

BRYN MAWR COLLEGE
BRYN MAWR, PENNSYLVANIA

Bryn Mawr
College Calendar

Bryn Mawr College Calendar
The Graduate School
of Arts and Sciences

Issue for the Session of 1977-78

July 1977 *Volume LXX Number 2*

BRYN MAWR COLLEGE CALENDAR published December, July, August, and S by Bryn Mawr College, Bryn Mawr, Pennsylvania 19010. *Second class pos at Bryn Mawr, Pennsylvania.*

Graduate Work at Bryn Mawr

Graduate education at Bryn Mawr is built upon a close working relationship between students and mature scholars. Each student begins training on the level appropriate for his individual experience and pursues a flexible program designed for his special requirements. Small seminars provide an opportunity to share research projects and to work under the direct supervision of the faculty.

Founded in 1885, the Bryn Mawr Graduate School was the first graduate school for women in the United States. Since 1931 both men and women have been admitted, but only after 1965 were adequate funds obtained to offer support for men comparable to that offered to women. Always small in relation to other graduate schools, Bryn Mawr has expanded gradually in response to the need for men and women well prepared for teaching and research. In 1970 The Graduate School of Arts and Sciences and The Graduate School of Social Work and Social Research were organized as two distinct schools. Today, the student enrollment in The Graduate School of Arts and Sciences is about four hundred fifty.

Graduate work leading to the degrees of Master of Arts and Doctor of Philosophy is available in:

Anthropology

Biochemistry

Biology

Chemistry

*Classical and Near
   Eastern Archaeology*

Economics

*Education and
   Child Development*

English

French

Geology

German

Greek

History

*History and Philosophy
   of Science*

History of Art

Latin

Mathematics

Mediaeval Studies

Music

Philosophy

Physics

Political Science

Psychology

Russian

Sociology

Spanish

· Work leading to the degrees of Master of Social Service and Doctor of Philosophy is available in The Graduate School of Social Work and Social Research.

College Calendar 1977-78
The Graduate School
of Arts and Sciences

First Semester—1977

Aug. 1   *Applications for loans due*

Aug. 20   *Final date for filing completed applications for admission for 1977-78*

Sept. 1, 2, 6, 7, 8, 9, 12, 13   *Registration period for semester I*

Sept. 6   *Graduate residences open*

Sept. 8   *Convocation*
Work of the 93rd academic year begins at 9 A.M.

Oct. 8   *German examinations for M.A. and Ph.D. candidates*

Oct. 21   *Fall vacation begins after last seminar*

Oct. 26   *Fall vacation ends at 9 A.M.*

Oct. 29   *Spanish, Italian, Russian, Latin, statistics examinations for M.A. and Ph.D. candidates*

Nov. 5   *French examinations for M.A. and Ph.D. candidates*

Nov. 23   *Thanksgiving holiday begins after last seminar*

Nov. 28   *Thanksgiving holiday ends at 9 A.M.*

Dec. 1   *Final date for filing completed applications for admission for semester II*

Dec. 5-14   *Registration period for semester II*

Dec. 21   *Winter vacation begins*

Seco
Jan.
Jan.
Jan. 2
Feb. 1
Feb. 18
Feb. 25
Mar. 4
Mar. 10
Mar. 20
Mar. 29
Apr. 5-7
Apr. 10
Apr. 19
Apr. 28   L
May 15

Convocation
Work of semester II begins at 9 A.M.

Applications for M.A. candidacy due in the Office of The Graduate School of Arts and Sciences

Final date for filing completed applications for scholarships (foreign students) for 1978-79

Final date for filing completed applications for fellowships, scholarships, and grants (citizens of the United States and Canada) for 1978-79

French examinations for M.A. and Ph.D. candidates

Spanish, Italian, Russian, Latin, statistics examinations for M.A. and Ph.D. candidates

German examinations for M.A. and Ph.D. candidates

Spring vacation begins after last seminar

Spring vacation ends at 9 A.M.

Ph.D. dissertations in all fields except natural sciences and Mathematics must be submitted to the Office of The Graduate School of Arts and Sciences

Spring registration period for semester I, 1978-79

M.A. papers due for candidates away from Bryn Mawr

Ph.D. dissertations in the natural sciences and Mathematics must be submitted to the Office of The Graduate School of Arts and Sciences

Last day of seminars

Conferring of degrees and close of 93rd academic year
Graduate residences close

Admission to The Graduate School of Arts and Sciences

Requirements

Students must be graduates of colleges or universities of acknowledged standing. For special requirements set by individual departments, see the departmental listings beginning on page 16.

Procedure

The applicant should write to the Dean of The Graduate School of Arts and Sciences, Bryn Mawr College, Bryn Mawr, Pennsylvania 19010, for application forms, indicating the field of special interest. The application must be supported by official transcripts of the student's complete academic record and by letters from the dean and two or more professors with whom he has done his major work. Although an interview is not required, candidates who wish to come in person to discuss their plans or the Bryn Mawr program are welcome. The applicant should write directly to the chairman of the department to arrange a meeting. No application will be considered until all the necessary documents have been received. Students are accepted for either full-time or part-time work. For citizens of the United States and Canada and for foreign students living in the United States, there is an application fee of $20.00 which is not refundable.

Graduate Record Examinations and Graduate School Foreign Language Tests

Applicants are advised to take the Graduate Record Examination Aptitude Test as well as the Advanced Tests in their fields of special interest. In certain departments these examinations are required, as indicated in the departmental listings. Inquiries concerning the Graduate Record Examinations should be addressed to Graduate Record Examination, Educational Testing Service, Box 955, Princeton, New Jersey 08540 or to Graduate Record Examination, Educational Testing Service, 1947 Center Street, Berkeley, California 94704.

Satisfactory scores in the Graduate School Foreign Language Test are accepted by some departments in fulfillment of the language requirement for higher degrees. Students should consult the departmental listings and make arrangements to take these tests at any Test Center. Applicants are encouraged to take the test within one year prior to the date they wish to enter. Interested students should write to Graduate School Foreign Language Test, Educational Testing Service, at the address listed above.

Dates

1. *Citizens of the United States and Canada:*
Applications for admission in all departments except Education and Child Development must be complete by August 20. Applications for admission to the Department of Education and Child Development must be complete by February 1. Graduate Record Examinations: October 15, December 10, 1977; January 14, February 25, April 22, and June 10, 1978. Graduate School Foreign Language Tests: October 8, 1977; February 4, April 8, and June 24, 1978.

2. *Foreign applicants:*
The closing date for admission is August 20, except for the Department of Education and Child Development, for which the closing date is February 1. Applications must include the scores of the Test of English as a Foreign Language (TOEFL), the Examination of the English Language Institute of the University of Michigan, or another approved language test. Since applications from students who desire financial aid must be completed by January 25, applicants must arrange to take language tests well before that date.

For information concerning the TOEFL write to: TOEFL, Educational Testing Service, Princeton, New Jersey 08540. Tests are given on September 24 and December 3, 1977; February 11, April 15, and June 7, 1978. Students in departments requiring the Graduate Record Examination should also arrange to take these tests not later than October.

3. *Applicants for financial aid:*
Students wishing to apply for fellowships, scholarships, assistantships, tuition grants, or other forms of financial aid must present complete applications by the following dates:

For United States and Canadian citizens:
    Applicants for fellowships, scholarships, assistantships, full-time and part-time tuition grants .... February 1
    Applicants for loans .... August 1

For foreign citizens:
    Applicants for scholarships .... January 25

GAPSFAS forms must be submitted to the Educational Testing Service, Princeton, New Jersey 08540 by January 15 (see page 84).

Admission to Graduate Seminars and Courses

Admission to graduate seminars and courses is under the jurisdiction of the various departments. Students whose preparation is inadequate may be required to complete appropriate undergraduate courses before being enrolled in a full graduate program.

Registration

All graduate students, after consultation with the chairmen of their departments, must register at the Office of The Graduate School of Arts and Sciences in the M. Carey Thomas Library each semester during the registration period listed in the College Calendar. Changes in registration require the approval of the department chairman and the Dean.

Personal registration is an important obligation of the graduate student. Those who fail to register in the stated period will be charged a late registration fee.

Students wishing certification to outside agencies must complete a form to be signed also by the department chairman and deposited in the Office of The Graduate School of Arts and Sciences.

Continuing enrollment
Students who have completed the required academic units for the Ph.D. degree and are continuing independent work on their dissertations must retain their enrollment and degree candidacy by registering for one or more units each semester or under the continuing enrollment plan.

In addition, students who are not planning to register for academic units but who are planning (1) to present themselves for College examinations, (2) to use the College libraries or laboratories, or (3) to consult members of the faculty must register under the continuing enrollment plan. Such enrollment does not carry academic credit.

Degree Candidacy

Students become candidates for advanced degrees only after they have met departmental requirements and made formal application which has been approved by the Council of The Graduate School of Arts and Sciences.

Resources for Graduate Work at Bryn Mawr

The Mariam Coffin Canaday Library and the eight auxiliary libraries of Bryn Mawr College, including the Art and Archaeology Library in the M. Carey Thomas Library, contain over 450,000 books and regularly receive more than 2000 periodicals as well as many scholarly series. The Library is open throughout the year with a liberal schedule of hours. Books are readily accessible on open stacks and in study rooms; individual carrels are available for advanced students.

The John D. Gordan Reference Center provides a focus for reference books and services in the library. In its card catalog, the main entry cards of the Haverford College Library join those of the Bryn Mawr Library, thus bringing more than 685,000 entries into one file. In addition, the Library is a member of the Union Catalogue of Pennsylvania, which locates approximately 7,200,000 volumes in the Philadelphia area and throughout the state, including the libraries of the American Philosophical Society, the Library Company of Philadelphia, the Historical Society of Pennsylvania, the Academy of Natural Sciences, the Free Library of Philadelphia, the Franklin Institute, the College of Physicians, the Rosenbach Foundation, the University of Pennsylvania, and Temple University.

The Rare Book Room houses the Marjorie Walter Goodhart Mediaeval Library of incunabula and mediaeval manuscripts. Important and extensive collections of early material on Latin America, Africa, and Asia are to be found in the Dillingham, McBride, and Plass collections. The Castle and Adelman collections expand the opportunities for the study of the graphic book-arts. The Adelman Collection also substantially increases the Library's holdings of literary and related manuscripts. In addition to these special collections are numerous other rare books and manuscripts.

Bryn Mawr has a study collection of archaeological and ethnological materials which is used for research by graduate and undergraduate students. The Ella Riegel Museum of Classical Archaeology contains examples of the Greek and Roman arts, especially vases, and a small group of pre-classical antiquities. It includes the classical Greek coins assembled by Elisabeth Washburn King and the Aline Abaecherli Boyce Collection of Roman Republican silver coins, as well as the Densmore Curtis Collection presented by Clarissa Dryden. Professor Hetty Goldman donated an extensive series of pottery samples from the excavations at Tarsus in Cilicia. Old World Paleolithic, Neolithic, Paleo-Indian, Eastern Woodland, Southwestern, Middle Mississippian, and Mexican antiquities are also represented at Bryn Mawr in addition to the Ward Canaday Collection of outstanding examples of most of the known ceramic and textile traditions of Peru.

The Geology Department has valuable materials for research, including the extensive working and reference mineral collections of Theodore D. Rand and George Vaux, Jr. The Department is also a map repository for the U.S. Geological Survey and the Defense Mapping Agency.

In addition, students use the resources of the Philadelphia area: the Philadelphia Museum of Art, the Pennsylvania Academy of the Fine Arts, the Barnes Foundation, the Rodin Museum, the Rosenbach Museum, and the University Museum of the University of Pennsylvania. They take advantage of the musical life of the city by attending the Philadelphia Orchestra and by playing or singing with local groups.

Laboratories, classrooms, and libraries for Biochemistry, Biology, Chemistry, Geology, Mathematics, and Physics are located in the three buildings of the Science Center. At the Center are rooms designed for work with radioactive materials, for photomicrography and for glassblowing; there is a machine shop with expert instrument makers in charge and a workshop available to graduate students. Laboratories and classrooms for Anthropology and Psychology are in Dalton Hall. In addition to the usual equipment, apparatus and instruments for particular research projects by faculty and graduate students have been acquired, in part, through the Plan for the Coordination of the Sciences (see page 87), through research grants from industry and other private sources, and from government agencies.

Through its membership in the Uni-Coll Corporation, a regional educational computer consortium, Bryn Mawr College has access to the resources and technical support of a major computing center. A high speed, remote batch terminal (printer at 600 lines per minute, card reader at 600 cards per minute) and nine teletypewriter terminals located on campus link the College with the Uni-Coll IBM 370, Model 168 computer. These facilities make available to faculty and students batch, remote job entry, and interactive computing supported by a large variety of programming systems.

Program of Study

The program of study consists of selected seminars, courses, or individual work under the close direction of members of the faculty. For the sake of convenience, this program is divided into academic units which are to be completed at Bryn Mawr College. Three academic units constitute a full year's program. An academic unit may be a year's seminar or two semester seminars, one or more undergraduate courses for graduate credit, independent study in preparation for the Preliminary Examinations, or supervised units of work.

A minimum of three academic units at Bryn Mawr is required for the degree of Master of Arts. Candidates for the degree of Doctor of Philosophy generally complete three full years of graduate work which must, with certain exceptions, include a minimum of six academic units at Bryn Mawr. Of these units at least one must be a unit of supervised work on the dissertation. The dissertation units, undertaken after a student has been admitted to candidacy, may be part of the residence requirement or in addition to it.

The number of units required for the Doctor of Philosophy may be reduced to no less than four for those who have held academic appointments at Bryn Mawr College for two or more years. Students holding the A.B. degree from Bryn Mawr College shall offer a minimum of three units. The Council of The Graduate School of Arts and Sciences may, on recommendation of the departments, reduce the requirements for other students.

For the list of advanced undergraduate courses which with additional work may be accepted as graduate units subject to the approval of department chairmen and the Dean of The Graduate School of Arts and Sciences, see the departmental offerings beginning on page 16.

In many departments, members of the faculty and graduate students meet from time to time in Journal Clubs or Colloquia to discuss current research or to review recent publications in their field of study.

Under the Reciprocal Plan, courses at the University of Pennsylvania Graduate School of Arts and Sciences are available to Bryn Mawr graduate students. All full-time students and such part-time students as intend to become candidates for degrees are eligible. The number of courses which may be taken at the University is limited to the equivalent of one unit per year. The procedure for registration and payment of tuition fees is the same as for students enrolled wholly at Bryn Mawr, with the exception that the student must present a letter of introduction to the Dean of The Graduate School of Arts and Sciences of the University of Pennsylvania when registering there. The University charges a small general fee for the use of the library, a library deposit, which is refundable, and fees for late registration. Ordinarily students are not advised to undertake such work during their first year at Bryn Mawr.

Students enrolled in the program in the History and Philosophy of Science attend seminars at the American Philosophical Society and at the University of Pennsylvania and register for these seminars at Bryn Mawr.

Equality of Opportunity

Bryn Mawr College admits students of any race, color, national and ethnic origin as well as the handicapped, to all the rights, privileges, programs and activities generally accorded or made available to students at the College. It does not discriminate on the basis of race, color, or national or ethnic origin or handicap in administration of its educational policies, admissions policies, scholarship and loan programs, and athletic and other College-administered programs or in its employment practices.

As required by Title IX of the 1972 Federal Education Amendments, it is also the policy of Bryn Mawr College not to discriminate on the basis of sex in its educational programs, activities, or employment practices. The admission of women in the Undergraduate College is in conformity with a provision of the Act. Inquiries regarding compliance with Title IX and other policies of non-discrimination may be directed to the Assistant to the President, Taylor Hall, or the Director of the Office for Civil Rights, Department of Health, Education and Welfare, Washington, D.C.

Summer Work

Bryn Mawr has no regular summer session on campus. Occasionally, at the invitation of members of the faculty, arrangements can be made for graduate students to continue research during the summer. The amount of credit for the work and the tuition fee to be charged depend upon the particular circumstances. Students should register for such work at the Office of the Dean of The Graduate School of Arts and Sciences early in June.

Summer Institutes in France and Spain

Bryn Mawr College offers a summer program of intensive work in significant aspects of French culture at the *Institut d'Etudes Françaises d'Avignon*. Certain courses carry graduate credit. For information write to Dr. Michel Guggenheim, Department of French, Bryn Mawr College.

For a similar summer program in aspects of Hispanic culture at the *Centro de Estudios Hispánicos* in Madrid, write to Dr. Eleanor K. Paucker, Department of Spanish, Bryn Mawr College.

12

Degree Requirements

The Graduate School of Arts and Sciences offers programs leading to the degrees of Doctor of Philosophy and Master of Arts.

The Degree of Doctor of Philosophy

The course of study is designed to prepare students for professional careers as scholars and teachers. Candidates should have ability of high order, intellectual curiosity, critical judgment, independence, a broad general education, fundamental training in the major and allied fields, and the determination needed to carry through an exacting program.

The general requirements, to which should be added those of the various departments, are as follows:

1. Undergraduate preparation in major and allied fields which is satisfactory to the departments concerned and to the Council of The Graduate School of Arts and Sciences.

2. A minimum of three full years of work beyond the A.B. degree in major and allied fields. Graduates of other colleges must complete at least six academic units at The Graduate School of Arts and Sciences of Bryn Mawr College. Of these units, at least one must be a unit of supervised work on the dissertation. The dissertation units may be part of the residence requirement or in addition to it. The residence requirement may be reduced by the Council of The Graduate School of Arts and Sciences for candidates who have held academic appointments for two or more years at Bryn Mawr College and occasionally for others. Students who hold the A.B. degree from Bryn Mawr College must complete a minimum of three academic units at Bryn Mawr.

3. The recommendation of the student as a candidate by the director of the dissertation and the major department and the acceptance of the recommendation by the Council of The Graduate School of Arts and Sciences. Application for candidacy, on a form to be obtained at the Office of the Dean of The Graduate School of Arts and Sciences, may be made as early as the spring of the student's first year, provided that the student has been registered for two units of graduate work at Bryn Mawr.

4. Knowledge of the foreign languages, computer languages (such as FORTRAN, ALGOL, PL/I, etc.), and special techniques (such as statistics) required by the individual departments. In certain circumstances, students whose native language is not English may offer English for one of the languages. These requirements must be fulfilled before the student takes the Preliminary Examinations.

13

5. Satisfactory Preliminary Examinations in the fields established for the candidate. These examinations are intended to test the candidate's knowledge of the principles of the subject, exemplified by the command of several fields or areas, the ability to apply knowledge to new problems, and power of organization.

6. The preparation of a dissertation worthy of publication, which presents the results of independent investigation in the fields of the major subject and contains original material, results, or interpretations.

7. A satisfactory Final Oral Examination in the special fields in which the dissertation has been written.

8. The publication of the dissertation in whole or in part. Microfilming is accepted as a method of publication.

A special pamphlet describing regulations for the Ph.D. degree will be issued to students applying for candidacy.

The Degree of Master of Arts

The general requirements for the M.A. degree are as follows:

1. Undergraduate preparation in major and allied fields which is satisfactory to the departments concerned.

2. A knowledge of one modern foreign language and such additional foreign languages or special techniques as the individual departments may require. Students whose native language is not English, except for those majoring in the language and literature of their native tongue, are not required to present an additional language.

3. The completion of a satisfactory program of work endorsed by the department and accepted by the Council of The Graduate School of Arts and Sciences. Application for such endorsement must be submitted on appropriate forms to the Dean of The Graduate School of Arts and Sciences not later than one week after the beginning of the second semester of the academic year in which the candidate wishes to take the degree. The program of study must include three units of work: (1) one seminar or graduate course, (2) a second seminar or supervised unit of graduate work, (3) a third seminar or an undergraduate course recommended by the major department. If undergraduate courses are included in this last unit, they must be supplemented by additional individual work. Only one such course may be offered for the M.A. degree. Under certain circumstances advanced undergraduate courses in science can be counted as seminars, subject to the approval of the department and the Dean of The Graduate School of Arts and Sciences. Candidates whose major department conducts a Journal Club or Colloquium are expected to include it in their program.

4. The preparation of a paper in a special field normally related to one of the seminars or units of graduate work in the candidate's program. Candidates currently at Bryn Mawr College shall submit this paper by the date set by the department. Candidates not currently on campus must submit the paper 30 days before Commencement of the academic year of the degree.

5. Each candidate, after all other requirements have been completed, must pass a Final Examination.

6. Work for the degree may be spread over several years which need not be in succession but must be included in a five-year period (60 months).

Graduate Program in Arts and Sciences 1977-78

Graduate Seminars and Courses

Graduate seminars and courses vary from year to year. Parentheses designate courses or seminars not given in the current year. Undergraduate courses which may with additional work be offered for graduate credit are listed by number. The letter "a" following a number indicates a half-course given in the first semester; the letter "b" following a number indicates a half-course given in the second semester; the letter "c" following a number indicates a half-course given two hours a week throughout the year.

Special graduate requirements are listed under each department. For the general degree requirements for the M.A. and the Ph.D., see pages 13-15.

Anthropology

Professor: Jane C. Goodale PHD

Associate Professor: Philip L. Kilbride PHD *Chairman*

Assistant Professors: Robert A. Braun PHD
Richard H. Jordan PHD
Judith R. Shapiro PHD

Associate Professor of Linguistics in Anthropology and German:
Nancy C. Dorian PHD

Prerequisites. A good undergraduate preparation in Anthropology or a closely related discipline is desirable. Students whose undergraduate training is not entirely adequate will be required to take such undergraduate courses as may seem necessary.

Language Requirements. Candidates for the M.A. or Ph.D. must offer one of the following two options: (1) two modern languages (French, German, Russian, Spanish) or (2) one modern language (French, German, Russian, Spanish) and statistics or computer science. Language skills may be tested by either the Graduate School Foreign Language Test (GSFLT) of the Educational Testing Service or examinations administered by Bryn Mawr College. Entering students may offer scores of the GSFLT taken within twelve months of the date on which they begin graduate work at Bryn Mawr. Competence in statistics and computer science will be acknowledged when the student satisfactorily passes an approved graduate course in statistics or computer science. The statistics requirement may also be fulfilled by passing an examination administered by the Department.

Program and Examination for the M.A. For students with an excellent undergraduate preparation, the program may consist of a minimum of three units of work in seminars or advanced undergraduate courses arranged for graduate credit, one of which may be in an allied subject. The program usually takes two years. The M.A. paper may be based on an essay offered in a seminar. The Final Examination consists of one four-hour written examination, but the Ph.D. Preliminary Examinations may be substituted for the M.A. Examination. All graduate students are expected to take the M.A. before proceeding to the Ph.D. Those who enter Bryn Mawr College with an M.A. in Anthropology may petition the Department to proceed directly to the Ph.D. program.

Program and Examinations for the Ph.D. The Department emphasizes the holistic nature of the anthropological discipline and will expect each student to become familiar with various cultural, social, and archaeological approaches and the anthropology of at least two geographical regions, in addition to areas and topics of professional specialization.

The Preliminary Examinations for candidates for the Ph.D. (usually taken near the end of the third year of graduate work) will consist of four three-hour written examinations and an oral examination of one hour. One of these examinations may be in an allied field.

Since the dissertation is usually based upon field work, it is difficult for a student to obtain the degree in less than five years.

General Degree Requirements for the M.A. and the Ph.D. See pages 13-15.

SEMINARS AND GRADUATE COURSES

Four or five seminars are offered each semester. Rarely is the same seminar offered in consecutive years in order to allow the greatest possible choice and variety to each student over a two to three-year period. For advanced students units of supervised readings are sometimes substituted for seminars. Topics listed below indicate the areas in which seminars will be offered according to the needs of students.

Mr. Braun
  Neolithic and the Rise of Civilization
  Complex Societies

Miss Dorian
  Linguistic Techniques and Field Methods
  Socio-Linguistics

Miss Goodale
  Topics in Oceanic Ethnography (Australia, Melanesia, Polynesia and Micronesia)
  Methods in Ethnographic Research
  Social Organization

Mr. Jordan
  Arctic Archaeology
  Environmental Archaeology
  History of Archaeological Theory
  Human Evolution and Old World Prehistory

Mr. Kilbride
  Topics in African Ethnography
  Psychological Anthropology
  Cultural Dynamics and Modernization
  Quantitative Methods of Analysis

Miss Shapiro
  Topics in Lowland South American Ethnography
  Sex Roles
  Linguistic Anthropology
  Topics in Social and Cultural Theory

SELECTED UNDERGRADUATE COURSES

308 *Language in the Social Context*: Miss Dorian
314 *Comparative Hunters and Gatherers*: Miss Goodale
320 *Cultural Theory*: Miss Shapiro
321 *Culture and Personality*: Mr. Kilbride
324 *Cultural Ecology*: Mr. Braun
325 *Woman, Culture and Society*: Miss Shapiro

In addition, courses at the University of Pennsylvania are available under the terms of the Reciprocal Plan (see page 11).

Biochemistry

Committee on Biochemistry:

Professor of Biology: Robert L. Conner PHD

Professor of Chemistry: George L. Zimmerman PHD

Associate Professor of Biology: David J. Prescott PHD *Chairman*

Assistant Professor of Chemistry: Kenneth G. Strothkamp PHD

This interdisciplinary program offers work within the Departments of Biology and Chemistry and leads to the M.A. or Ph.D. degree. It is administered by the Committee on Biochemistry, which consists of members of the two departments. Depending on their backgrounds and interests, students may enter the program either through the Department of Biology or the Department of Chemistry.

Prerequisites. Undergraduate training consisting of a major or its equivalent in either Biology or Chemistry, one-year courses or their equivalents in organic chemistry and physical chemistry, and one year of work in physiology, cell biology, genetics, or developmental biology. Students lacking any one of these specific courses should make up this deficiency during their first year in the Biochemistry program.

Major and Allied Subjects. Students will receive their advanced degrees in either Biology or Chemistry with a major in Biochemistry. The allied field will usually be a branch of Biology or Chemistry different from Biochemistry. It may also be selected from fields in Biophysics, Physics, Mathematics, or Psychology. Other combinations may be accepted with the approval of the Committee and the Council of The Graduate School of Arts and Sciences.

Language Requirements. See the requirements set by each department.

Program and Examination for the M.A. Students who are candidates for the M.A. will usually offer one graduate course or seminar in Biochemistry, another seminar or advanced undergraduate course arranged for seminar credit, and a unit of research. This unit consists of an experimental investigation carried out under the direction of a member of either department. The results of this unit must be made the subject of a written paper. The Final Examination consists of a four-hour written examination or a three-hour written and one-hour oral examination.

Program and Examinations for the Ph.D. All students must take the core curriculum in Biochemistry, which includes Biochemistry 353, or its equivalent if taken elsewhere, and a series of graduate courses

19

and seminars in Biochemistry. In addition, students will usually take other graduate courses or seminars, depending on their interests, in either department in order to acquire a broad general background for research or teaching in Biochemistry. They will usually devote a large portion of their time to research carried out under the direction of one member of either department. The Preliminary and Final Examinations are taken in accordance with the regulations set by the department in which the student is enrolled.

General Degree Requirements for the M.A. and Ph.D. See pages 13-15.

SEMINARS AND GRADUATE COURSES

See listings under the Departments of Biology and Chemistry.

SELECTED UNDERGRADUATE COURSES

See listings under the Departments of Biology and Chemistry.

Biology

Professor: Robert L. Conner PHD *Chairman*

Associate Professors: Anthony R. Kaney PHD
David J. Prescott PHD

Assistant Professors: Patricia J. Olds-Clarke PHD‡
Steven N. Treistman PHD

Lecturers: Dianna L. Cassel PHD
Kathryn Z. Orkwiszewski PHD
Patricia Onderdonk Pruett PHD *Associate Dean of the Undergraduate College*

Professor of History of Science: Jane M. Oppenheimer PHD

Assistant Professor of Chemistry: Kenneth Strothkamp PHD

Prerequisites. An undergraduate major in Biology, Zoology, o Botany, including courses in general and organic chemistry. Som college-level preparation in Mathematics and Physics is desirable Students with majors in other subjects may be admitted but will b

---

‡On leave 1977-78

required to make up any deficiencies in their preparation in Biology before being admitted to graduate courses. All applicants should submit scores from the Graduate Record Examination Aptitude Test and the Advanced Test in Biology.

Major and Allied Subjects. Candidates for the M.A. and Ph.D. degrees may specialize in biochemistry, cell biology, cellular physiology, developmental biology, genetics, molecular biology, microbiology, or neurophysiology, but must take work also from areas not chosen for specialization. Allied subjects may be selected from fields in Chemistry, Physics, and Psychology, and in special cases from other related fields, with the approval of the Council of The Graduate School of Arts and Sciences.

Language Requirements. Candidates for the M.A. degree should offer French, German, or statistics. Candidates for the Ph.D. degree must offer two foreign languages: French and German (or some other language by special permission of the Department and the Council of The Graduate School of Arts and Sciences), or one foreign language and statistics. The statistics requirement may be satisfied by passing a graduate course in statistics at Bryn Mawr or by examination administered by the Biology Department. Language skills will be tested by the examinations administered by Bryn Mawr College.

Program and Examination for the M.A. One full year, or its equivalent, of course work in seminars and advanced undergraduate courses arranged for seminar credit and a written report on a piece of experimental work carried out under the direction of a member of the Department. Qualified students may substitute a unit of supervised research for formal course work. The Final Examination consists of a three-hour written examination covering the areas of study and a one-hour oral examination concentrating particularly on the interpretation and significance of the experimental problem and its relation to Biology more generally.

Program and Examinations for the Ph.D. The Preliminary Examinations for the Ph.D. consist of three written examinations, each of four hours' duration, and an oral examination of one to two hours. These examinations will cover the areas included in the course work in the major and allied fields. After the subject of the dissertation has been decided, the student will meet with the faculty of the Department to outline and discuss the subject and the proposed plan of research. The Final Examination is oral, covering the subject of the dissertation in relation to the general field of Biology.

General Degree Requirements for the M.A. and Ph.D. The Department expects all graduate students to become biologists who are professionals both in research and in education. It is anticipated that all graduate students will gain experience in teaching, usually in the capacity of a teaching assistant. See also pages 13-15.

21

Mr. Prescott
Advanced Biochemistry—semester I
A detailed examination of the structure and function of selected proteins. Physical and chemical means of determining the structure of macromolecules will be emphasized. Two hours' lecture. Prerequisites: Biology 353, Chemistry 203.

Mr. Strothkamp
Advanced Biochemistry—semester II
The kinetics and mechanisms of several enzyme systems will be examined in detail. Metalloenzymes will be emphasized. Two hours' lecture.

For Statistics: See offerings in The Graduate School of Social Work and Social Research and the Department of Psychology.

Journal Club: All faculty members and graduate students meet each week for presentation of current research in Biology. Graduate students, faculty, and outside speakers will participate.

SEMINARS

All seminars and advanced undergraduate courses arranged for seminar credit are offered for one semester each year. Four seminars are offered each year, with each area being offered in alternate years. The topics considered in any semester are selected in accordance with the needs and desires of the students enrolled. A list of seminar topics offered by each instructor in recent years is given below:

Mr. Conner
Cellular Physiology
  Membrane Structure and Function
  Regulation of Lipid Metabolism
  Molecular Endocrinology

Mr. Kaney
Genetics
  Somatic Cell Genetics
  Genetics of Ciliated Protozoans
  Structure and Function of the Chromosome

Mrs. Olds-Clarke
Developmental Biology
  Gametogenesis and Development
  Fertilization
  Sex Differentiation

Mr. Prescott
Biochemistry
Neurochemistry
Protein Structure and Chemistry
Peptide Hormones

Mr. Treistman
Neurophysiology
Organization of Motor Systems
Cyclic Nucleotide Involvement in Neural Functioning

SELECTED UNDERGRADUATE COURSES

The following advanced undergraduate courses with supplemental work may be taken for graduate credit:

350b *Problems in Cell Physiology*: Mr. Conner
351a *Problems in Genetics*: Mr. Kaney
352a *Problems in Molecular Biology*: Mrs. Cassel
353 *Biochemistry*: Mr. Conner, Mr. Prescott, Mr. Strothkamp
(355b *Problems in Neurophysiology*: Mr. Treistman)
(356 *Biophysics*: Miss Hoyt)
358a *Analysis of Development*: Mrs. Orkwiszewski
362a *Cellular Physiology*: Mr. Conner
364b *Cell and Molecular Biology*: Mrs. Cassel
Int. 357a *Computer Usage in the Life Sciences*: Mrs. Pruett

Chemistry

Professors: Jay Martin Anderson PHD
Ernst Berliner PHD
Frank B. Mallory PHD‡
George L. Zimmerman PHD *Chairman*

Associate Professor: Joseph Varimbi PHD

Assistant Professor: Kenneth G. Strothkamp PHD

Lecturers: Frances Bondhus Berliner PHD
Cecile K. Dalton PHD

Associate Professor of Biology: David J. Prescott PHD

---

‡On leave 1977-78

Fields of Study and Research. The primary aim of the instruction of graduate students in the Department of Chemistry is to provide a sound background in modern chemistry and to prepare men and women for a professional career in productive scholarship, research, and teaching in chemistry. Courses and seminars are offered to enable the students to acquire a command of their chosen fields, in addition to a sufficiently broad general background so that they will be prepared for the variety of assignments in chemistry teaching or research which they may later encounter. Thesis research is the major part of the training. Research training is centered on a variety of investigations carried out by the members of the faculty. Currently there are active research programs involving both faculty and students in the following areas of organic, inorganic, physical, and theoretical chemistry, and of Biochemistry: kinetics of electrophilic substitution and addition, relative reactivities of polynuclear aromatic systems, isotope effects, organic photochemistry, nuclear magnetic resonance as applied to substituent effects and through-space nuclear coupling, reactions in liquid ammonia and other non-aqueous solvents, photochemical cis-trans isomerizations, ultraviolet and vacuum ultraviolet absorption studies of inorganic ions, nuclear magnetic resonance as applied to nuclear relaxation, molecular collision dynamics, structure and function of copper proteins, evolution of metalloproteins, and binding of metal ions to nucleic acids.

Under the Plan for the Coordination of the Sciences there are special opportunities for research and training in such interrelated areas as geochemistry, chemical physics, etc. See page 87.

Prerequisites. An undergraduate preparation in Chemistry including courses in inorganic, analytical, organic, and physical chemistry, college Physics, and Mathematics (calculus). All applicants should submit scores on the Aptitude Test and the Advanced Test in Chemistry of the Graduate Record Examinations. Applicants lacking some of these prerequisites may be considered for admission under special circumstances in consultation with the Department.

Major and Allied Subjects. Students may specialize in Biochemistry, organic, inorganic, or physical chemistry. The allied subject for the Ph.D. may be chosen from the fields of Mathematics, Physics, inorganic geology, Biology and a branch of Chemistry different from that of the major subject. Other combinations may be accepted with the approval of the Council of The Graduate School of Arts and Sciences and on the recommendation of the Department. The typical work for the allied subject would be a year's course or seminar on an approved level.

Language Requirements. Candidates for the M.A. must offer German, French, or Russian. Candidates for the Ph.D. may offer German and either French, Russian, or demonstrated skill in digital computation, numerical analysis, and the theory of error. This skill may be demonstrated by an examination consisting of two parts, a practical part requiring the successful execution of a FORTRAN (or other equivalent language) program and a written examination on numerical analysis and error theory, or by a satisfactory grade in an appropriate course.

Language skills may be tested by either the Graduate School Foreign Language Test (GSFLT) of the Educational Testing Service or the examinations administered by Bryn Mawr College. Entering students may offer scores of the GSFLT taken within twelve months of the date on which they begin graduate work at Bryn Mawr.

Program and Examination for the M.A. Students who are candidates for the M.A. will usually offer one seminar in their special field, another seminar or advanced undergraduate course in Chemistry or an allied field, and one unit of research. This unit consists of an experimental investigation carried out under the direction of a member of the Department. The Final Examination consists of a four-hour written examination or a three-hour written and one-hour oral examination.

Program and Examinations for the Ph.D. Ph.D. students will normally be expected to devote a large portion of their time to experimental or theoretical research carried out under the direction of a member of the Department. They will usually take all seminars offered in their special fields during their stay at Bryn Mawr, in addition to such courses as will give them a broad background in Chemistry. The Preliminary Examinations will normally be taken in the student's third year of graduate study. They consist of two four-hour written examinations and two oral examinations, each one or two hours in duration. The two written examinations will be from the candidate's major field. One will be a broad examination in the general aspects of that field. The second will be in the special field of the candidate's research and will include questions designed to test familiarity with, and ability to interpret, material from the recent chemical literature. One of the oral examinations will be held soon after the written examinations have been completed and will be for the purpose of clarifying and augmenting the candidate's responses on the two written examinations. The three examinations described so far must be completed within a period of five weeks. The other oral examination will involve the defense of two original chemical research proposals previously submitted by the candidate. No more than one of these proposals may deal with work related to the special field of the student's research. All four of the examinations must be completed within a period of one year. The Final Examination is oral and is devoted to the subject matter of the student's dissertation.

General Degree Requirements for the M.A. and the Ph.D. See pages 13-15.

Colloquium. All members of the Department and the graduate students meet every week for a presentation of current research in Chemistry, usually by outside speakers.

SEMINARS AND GRADUATE COURSES

In order to meet the needs of the students and to offer them as wide a selection of topics as possible, the seminars are arranged in such a way that each one is usually given at least once within a three-year period. The topics listed below are given in one-semester seminars, counting one-half unit of credit each. Ordinarily four seminars are offered each year. Individual programs are flexible, and the contents of the seminars are likely to vary with the research interests of the students and the current research activities of the faculty.

The seminars listed below are illustrative of those that have been offered in recent years.

Mr. Anderson
Intermediate Quantum Mechanics
Non-equilibrium Thermodynamics
Nuclear Magnetic Resonance

Mr. Berliner
Physical Organic Aspects of Aromatic Chemistry
Physical Organic Chemistry
Structure and Physical Properties of Organic Compounds

Mrs. Berliner
Natural Products
Chemistry of Heterocyclic Compounds

Mr. Mallory
Organic Photochemistry
Recent Methods in Organic Synthesis
Spectral Applications in Current Organic Chemistry

Mr. Varimbi
Inorganic Chemistry
Statistical Thermodynamics
Theory of Electrolytic Solutions

Mr. Strothkamp
Topics in Biochemistry

Mr. Zimmerman
Surface Chemistry
Theory of Radiative and Non-radiative Transitions
Photochemistry

For additional seminars in Biochemistry, see the Department of Biology.

26

The following advanced undergraduate courses may be taken for graduate credit:

301b *Advanced Inorganic Chemistry*: Mr. Varimbi
302 *Advanced Organic Chemistry*: Mr. Berliner, Mrs. Dalton
303a *Quantum Mechanics of Atoms and Molecules*:
    Mr. Anderson and Mr. Chesick
303b *Atomic and Molecular Spectroscopy*:
    Mr. Zimmerman and Mr. Gavin
353 *Biochemistry*: Mr. Conner, Mr. Prescott, Mr. Strothkamp

Classical and Near Eastern Archaeology

Professors: Machteld J. Mellink PHD *Chairman*
    Kyle M. Phillips, Jr. PHD *Resident Director*
    of Massenzia, Rome
    Brunilde S. Ridgway PHD†

Associate Professor: Richard S. Ellis PHD‡

Lecturers: Harrison Eiteljorg, II PHD
    Maria deJ. Ellis PHD
    Gloria F. Pinney PHD

Dean of The Graduate School of Arts and Sciences and *Professor of Classical and Near Eastern Archaeology* and *of History of Art*:
    Phyllis Pray Bober PHD

Prerequisites: An undergraduate major in Archaeology or at least two courses in Archaeology combined with a major in Greek, Latin, ancient history,or History of Art. It is expected that students of Classical and Near Eastern Archaeology will have a basic knowledge of Greek, Latin, and ancient history. Students with incomplete preparation in Archaeology will be advised to take selected undergraduate courses during their first year in graduate school.

Allied Subjects. Greek, Linear B, Latin, Akkadian, Hebrew, Hittite, Egyptian, History of Art, ancient history, Anthropology, a science related to the archaeological program of the candidate.

---

†On leave semester II
‡On leave 1977-78

27

Language Requirements: For the M.A. and Ph.D., a good reading knowledge of German and French. For the Ph.D., a reading knowledge of Greek or a Near Eastern ancient language. Language skills may be tested by either the Graduate School Foreign Language Test (GSFLT) of the Educational Testing Service or the examinations administered by Bryn Mawr College.

Program and Examination for the M.A. Three units of work in Archaeology or in Archaeology and an allied field. The Final Examination is written (three hours) and oral (one hour).

Program and Examinations for the Ph.D. The students spend the first two years in residence, participating in seminars and preparing for the Preliminary Examinations. The third year is usually spent at the American School of Classical Studies in Athens or at another archaeological research center abroad. Bryn Mawr College is now opening a graduate study center in Rome, Massenzia. Museums in Europe and the Near East are visited during this year, and participation in excavations is arranged when possible (see below).

The Preliminary Examinations, normally taken at the end of three years of graduate work, consist of four four-hour papers in selected fields such as Greek and Roman sculpture, architecture, monumental painting, Greek vase-painting, numismatics, Aegean prehistory, prehistory of Western Asia, Mesopotamian art and archaeology, or the archaeology of Anatolia, Syria, Palestine, or Cyprus. One of the papers may be written in an allied field. The Final Examination covers the field of the dissertation.

General Degree Requirements for the M.A. and the Ph.D. See pages 13-15.

Excavations. The Department currently sponsors two excavation projects:
I. An investigation of the Bronze Age habitation of ancient Lycia in progress since 1963 at the third millennium B.C. site of Karatash near Elmali.[1] The final publication is being prepared on the basis of the joint field reports of the participants.
II. The Etruscan project, started in 1966, is the excavation of the archaic site of Murlo near Siena, organized in cooperation with the Archaeological Museum in Florence. The work takes place during the summer and offers qualified graduate and undergraduate students training in excavation techniques while participating in the study of a townsite and necropolis of the sixth century B.C.[2]

---

[1] cf. *American Journal of Archaeology* 68 (1964) 269-278; 69 (1965) 241-251; 70 (1966) 245-257; 71 (1967) 251-267; 72 (1968) 243-263; 73 (1969) 319-331; 74 (1970) 245-259; 75 (1971) 257-261; 76 (1972) 257-269; 77 (1973) 293-307; 78 (1974) 351-360; 79 (1975) 349-355; 80 (1976) 377-391.

Cooperation with the University of Pennsylvania. Attention is drawn to the courses offered by the Departments of Classical Archaeology, Anthropology, History of Art, Oriental Studies, and Biblical Archaeology at the University of Pennsylvania. Under the Reciprocal Plan, (see page 11), students may register for a unit of work at the University or pursue research at the University Museum.

SEMINARS AND GRADUATE COURSES

Seminar topics are determined for each semester in consultation with the graduate students. Some of the recent seminar topics are listed below.

Mrs. Bober
Antiquity in the Renaissance
(Roman Sarcophagi, Problems in Style and Iconography)

Mr. Eiteljorg
Greek Architecture of the Fifth Century B.C.
(The Dark Ages of Greece)
(The Problem of the Greek Architect)

Mr. Ellis
(Early Mesopotamian Archaeology)
(The Royal Cemetery of Ur)
(Mesopotamian and Syrian Sculpture)
(Syro-Phoenician Metalwork and Ivories)
(Problems of Ancient Technology)

Miss Mellink
· *Aegean Archaeology*
(Anatolian Architecture)
(The Early Bronze Age in Anatolia)
(Field Seminar in Anatolia)
(The Orientalizing Period of Greece)

Mr. Phillips
(Greek Vase Painting)
(Corinthian Pottery)
(The Western Greeks)
(Ancient Monumental Painting)
(Etruscan Archaeology)

Mrs. Pinney
Greek Vase Painting
Etruria in the Sixth Century B.C.

---

[2]cf. *American Journal of Archaeology* 71 (1967) 133-139; 72 (1968) 121-124; 73 (1969) 333-339; 74 (1970) 241-244; 75 (1971) 245-255; 76 (1972) 249-255; 77 (1973) 319-326; 78 (1974) 265-278; 79 (1975) 357-366; 81 (1977) 85-100.

Mrs. Ridgway
   Greek Sculpture of the Fifth Century B.C.
   (Hellenistic Sculpture)
   (Architectural Sculpture)
   (Greek Funerary Monuments)
   (Architecture of Magna Graecia)
   (The Parthenon)

SELECTED UNDERGRADUATE COURSES

202a *Ancient Greek Cities and Sanctuaries*: Mrs. Ridgway
203a *Hellenistic and Roman Sculpture*: Mrs. Ridgway
205b *Aegean Archaeology*: Miss Mellink
208b *Texts as Sources for Near Eastern Archaeology*: Mrs. Ellis
301a *Greek Vase-Painting*: Mrs. Pinney
302a *Greek Architecture*: Mr. Eiteljorg
302b *Roman Architecture*: Mr. Scott
303b *Etruscan Archaeology*: Mrs. Pinney
304a *Monumental Painting*: Mrs. Pinney
History 205a *The Ancient Near East*: Mrs. Ellis

Economics

Professor: Richard B. Du Boff PHD *Chairman*

Associate Professors: Noel J. J. Farley PHD†
                        Helen Manning Hunter PHD

Assistant Professor: Li Way Lee PHD

Prerequisites. An undergraduate major in Economics, with work in such related fields as History and Political Science. Superior applicants with majors in other disciplines may be admitted. Applicants must submit scores on the Aptitude Test and Advanced Tests of the Graduate Record Examinations. Students whose undergraduate training in Economics is incomplete may be required to take such undergraduate courses as the Department thinks necessary.

Allied Subjects. Most subjects in the other social sciences and in History and Philosophy are acceptable. Mathematics and statistics are necessary to advanced work in Economics.

---

†On leave semester II

Language Requirements. Candidates for the M.A. and Ph.D. must show reading proficiency in one modern foreign language. Candidates for the Ph.D. must in addition show either reading proficiency in a second modern foreign language or proficiency in Mathematics beyond the level required for admission to graduate seminars in Economics (i.e., beyond the level of first-year college calculus and basic linear algebra). Mathematical skills will be tested by an examination to be set by the Department. The topics to be covered will be agreed upon in advance and may vary according to the student's particular field of interest in Economics.

Language skills will be tested by the Graduate School Foreign Language Test (GSFLT) of the Educational Testing Service. Entering students may offer scores of the GSFLT taken within twelve months of the date on which they begin graduate work at Bryn Mawr.

Program and Examination for the M.A. It is expected that the work for the M.A. degree will require not less than one calendar year of graduate study. All candidates for the M.A. degree must complete three units of formal course work (seminars, courses, and supervised units) prior to submitting the M.A. research paper. One of these units must be in economic theory, one in statistics and econometrics, and one in the student's special field of interest. Course examinations in each of these three fields must be passed before the candidate presents the research paper. After acceptance of the paper a Final Examination must be passed.

Program and Examinations for the Ph.D. Candidates for the Ph.D. will take as much formal course work as is necessary to prepare them for the Ph.D. examinations. The Preliminary Examinations will consist of four three-hour written papers and an oral examination; one of the written papers will be in microeconomic analysis and one in macroeconomic analysis; the other two papers will be in fields related to the candidate's major interest. The Final Oral, taken after the dissertation has been accepted, will be devoted to the subject matter of the dissertation.

General Degree Requirements for the M.A. and the Ph.D. See pages 13-15.

General Degree Requirements for the M.A. and the Ph.D. See pages 13-15.

SEMINARS

Seminars are chosen each year from the following topics:

Mr. Du Boff
American Economic Development
Economic History and Growth 1750-1970

Mr. Farley
International Economic Development
International Trade Policy
International Trade Theory

Mrs. Hunter
Econometrics
Macroeconomic Analysis
Monetary Theory and Institutions

Mr. Lee
Corporate Financial Theory
Industrial Organization
Microeconomic Analysis
Public Finance

SELECTED UNDERGRADUATE COURSES

203a *Statistical Methods in Economics*: Mrs. Hunter
222b *History of Economic Thought*: Mr. Du Boff
302b *Introduction to Econometrics*: Mrs. Hunter
304b *Microeconomic Analysis*: Mr. Lee

Education and Child Development

Professors: Janet L. Hoopes PHD *Director**
Child Study Institute
Ethel W. Maw PHD *Chairman*

Associate Professors: Susan E. Maxfield MS *Director*
Phebe Anna Thorne School
Emmy A. Pepitone PHD
Faye P. Soffen EDD

Assistant Professors: Fred Rothbaum PHD
Samuel S. Snyder PHD

The program prepares students for college teaching and research in educational psychology and child development, for child guidance, for school psychology, school counseling, for teaching in the schools and for early childhood education. The program is carried on in a setting of service to public and laboratory schools and to the community at large. Classes, seminars, and staff conferences provide opportunity for students from several related disciplines to develop

---

*On leave semester I

competence in the team approach to the children's specialties in education, psychology, and guidance agencies. Trends in physical, intellectual, and emotional growth from infancy to maturity are stressed.

Bryn Mawr has program approval from the Pennsylvania Department of Education for several curriculum sequences which prepare candidates for public school professions. These courses of study include teacher education in ten liberal arts fields, school psychology, and school counseling, both elementary and secondary. Students who satisfactorily complete an approved program will, on the recommendation of this Department, receive the state certificate in the appropriate field.

Prerequisites: An undergraduate preparation in the liberal arts which must include work in general Psychology and statistics. Students whose undergraduate training in Psychology is not adequate will be required to take such undergraduate courses as seem necessary. Applicants for admission are asked to submit scores of the Graduate Record Examination Aptitude Test and a statement of their academic plans and goals. Undergraduate grades of at least B level are necessary.

Major and Allied Subjects: Candidates for advanced degrees are expected to become competent in several different areas: child and adolescent development, clinical evaluation, counseling and guidance, history and philosophy of education, educational psychology, social psychology and sociology of education, secondary education, elementary education, early childhood education, and psychological disorders of children. For the M.A., two fields are required. For the Ph.D., four fields must be presented. One field may be an allied field and is individually arranged. Field examinations are given once each semester.

Language and Statistics Requirements: For the M.A., students are required to pass an examination in one modern foreign language and demonstrate a working knowledge of descriptive and inferential statistics. For the Ph.D., students are required to pass an examination demonstrating reading knowledge of one modern foreign language and competence in statistics. The statistics requirement for both degrees may be satisfied by passing the course *Foundations of Research* at a satisfactory level or by demonstrating equivalent competencies. Language skills may be tested by either the Graduate School Foreign Language Test (GSFLT) of the Educational Testing Service or the examinations administered by Bryn Mawr College. Entering students may offer scores of the GSFLT taken within twelve months of the date on which they begin graduate work at Bryn Mawr.

Program and Examination for the M.A. Candidates will normally offer three units of graduate work in Education, although one of the

33

three may be taken in an allied field. A paper embodying the results of independent research is required. The Final Examination consists of two three-hour written examinations, one in each field offered, and a one-hour oral examination on the M.A. paper.

Examinations for the Ph.D. The Preliminary Examinations consist of four-hour written examinations in each of the fields offered and an oral examination. The Final Examination is an oral examination in the field of the Ph.D. dissertation.

General Degree Requirements for the M.A. and the Ph.D. See pages 13-15.

The Phebe Anna Thorne School and the Child Study Institute. The Phebe Anna Thorne School is maintained by the Department as a laboratory nursery school for normal children where students may observe and assist in the program for three- and four-year-olds. For those preparing for teaching, medical work with children, child welfare or guidance, the school provides opportunity for direct experience with early childhood development. Students preparing for early childhood education spend substantial blocks of time in the Thorne School.

The Department also operates at the College the Child Study Institute, a mental health center where problems of learning and behavior are studied and remedial measures planned and carried out with parents and children. The service is given by a staff of qualified specialists in child psychiatry, psychology, school counseling, and remedial teaching. Advanced students participate at various levels of responsibility. Referrals from the schools, from physicians, social agencies, and families give students the opportunity for acquaintance with a diversity of clinical material.

A separate building on the college grounds houses the Department, the Thorne School, and the Institute, with rooms equipped for nursery school teaching and for individual examination of pupils, remedial teaching, individual and group therapy, and student observation.

SEMINARS

The seminars offered are selected from the following. (In most cases, laboratory practice is required.) All seminars run throughout the academic year unless otherwise indicated. Some seminars are offered in alternate years.

Miss Hoopes
Clinical Evaluation
Advanced Theory and Practice in Clinical Evaluation
Assessment in Early Childhood

Mrs. Maw
Educational Psychology
Curriculum of the Elementary School—semester II

Miss Maxfield
Developmental Psychology
Early Childhood Education
Theory and Practice in Early Childhood Education

Mrs. Pepitone
History and Philosophy of Education—semester I
The Social Psychology of the School
The American School—semester II
Research in Children's Cooperation and Competition

Mr. Rothbaum
Psychological Disorders of Children
Advanced Topics in Social Development and Disorders

Mr. Snyder
Critical Issues in Human Development
Topics in Developmental Psychology—semester II

Mrs. Soffen
Principles and Organization of the Guidance Program
The Counseling Process: Theory and Practice
The Group Process in Counseling and Guidance
The Psychology of Occupations
Advanced Theory and Practice in Counseling and Guidance

Members of the Department
Foundations of Research

SELECTED UNDERGRADUATE COURSES

206a *Developmental Psychology*: Mr. Snyder
206b *Adolescent Development*: Mr. Rothbaum
301a *Principles of Teaching in the Secondary School*:
    Mrs. Maw
(302a *Principles of Teaching in the Elementary School*:
    Mrs. Maw)

Courses 301a and 302a satisfy the student-teaching requirement
most states. Plans for registration should be made with Mrs. Maw i
the spring before the student expects to take the course in the fal

English

Professors: Robert B. Burlin PHD
K. Laurence Stapleton AB*

Associate Professors: Carol L. Bernstein PHD
Thomas H. Jackson PHD
Joseph E. Kramer PHD *Chairman*

Katharine E. McBride Visiting Professor: Georgia Christopher PHD

Assistant Professors: Sandra M. Berwind PHD‡
Peter M. Briggs PHD
Katrin Ristkok Burlin PHD
E. Jane Hedley PHD
Eileen T. Johnston PHD
Anne Kaier PHD
Annette Niemtzow PHD

Andrew W. Mellon Post-Doctoral Fellow: Constance Jordan PHD

Prerequisites. An undergraduate major in English or its equivalent. Students should have had some training in at least one other field of the humanities: a classical or a modern foreign literature, History, the History of Art, or Philosophy. All applicants should submit scores in the Aptitude Test of the Graduate Record Examination.

Language Requirements. For the M.A. degree, a knowledge of either French or German adequate to the reading of basic scholarly and literary texts. For the Ph.D., the student must either pass examinations in both French and German or demonstrate superior competence in one by satisfactorily completing one unit of graduate work in that language or its literature at Bryn Mawr. (In special cases, with the approval of the appropriate language department and of the Department of English, equivalent work at another university may be accepted.) With the approval of the Department, another modern language may be substituted for French or German when it can be shown to be particularly pertinent to a projected dissertation. Students working toward the doctorate are also required to show evidence of an adequate knowledge of Latin or Greek. It is expected that the doctoral candidate will satisfy these requirements at the beginning of the second year of graduate study; they must be completely satisfied before the doctoral candidate takes the Preliminary Examinations.

Language skills may be tested by either the Graduate School Foreign Language Test (GSFLT) of the Educational Testing Service

---

*On leave semester I
‡On leave 1977-78

or the examinations administered by Bryn Mawr College. Entering students may offer scores of the GSFLT taken within twelve months of the date on which they begin graduate work at Bryn Mawr.

Program and Examination for the M.A. Three units of work in English or two in English and one in an allied field. The M.A. paper is due on April 21. The Final Examination is written, four hours in length, and on the general field of the M.A. paper. (If the M.A. courses are completed in one year, the paper and the Final Examination are frequently deferred through the following summer.)

Program and Examinations for the Ph.D. Work of the Department is carried on through small seminars and supervised units of independent study. Six units of graduate work are required, one of which may be in an allied field. Candidates will be expected to spend at least one year in full-time graduate work. The program must include some training in Old or Middle English or in the history of the English language.

After being accepted for doctoral candidacy, the student will take Preliminary Examinations in five parts: four written (four hours each) and one oral (one or two hours). One written examination may be in an allied field. The choice of the four fields will be determined by the student in consultation with the graduate adviser and the departmental examiners who will form the Supervising Committee. The candidate is expected to demonstrate a balanced knowledge of different periods.

Before proceeding with the dissertation, it is expected that the doctoral candidate will submit a prospectus to be discussed with the departmental members of the Supervising Committee. The Final Examination is in the field of the dissertation.

General Degree Requirements for the M.A. and the Ph.D. See pages 13-15.

SEMINARS

Seminars run for one semester and subjects are chosen from the following areas.

Mrs. Bernstein
Romantic Poetry—semester I
(Victorian Poetry and Prose)
(Nineteenth Century English Novel)

Mrs. Berwind
(James and Joyce)

Mr. Briggs
(Swift and Pope)

Mrs. Burlin
(Jane Austen, the Brontës, and George Eliot)

Mr. Burlin
  Chaucer—semester I
  (Medieval Drama)

Miss Christopher
  Milton—semester I

Mr. Jackson
  Twentieth Century Literature—semester II

Mrs. Johnston
  Victorian Literature—semester II

Mr. Kramer
  Shakespeare—semester II
  (Renaissance Drama)

Miss Stapleton
  Studies in Poetry or Prose—semester II
  (Milton)
  Studies in Poetry or Prose—semester II

SELECTED UNDERGRADUATE COURSES

301b *Readings in Middle English Literature*: Mr. Burlin
323a *Renaissance Tragedy*: Mr. Kramer
330a *Seventeenth Century Literature*: Miss Christopher
352b *Romantic Poetry and Prose*: Miss Kaier
356a *Victorian Literature and the Religious Experience*:
  Mrs. Johnston
358a *Jane Austen*: Mrs. Burlin
358b *Women of Talents*: Mrs. Burlin
365a *American Autobiography*: Miss Niemtzow
365b *The American Dream*: Miss Niemtzow
384b *Theory of Fiction*: Mrs. Bernstein
385b *Problems in Satire*: Mr. Briggs
388a *Poetic Theory*: Mr. Jackson
Int. 390a *The Realistic Mode*: Miss Jordan
Int. 390b *The Pastoral*: Miss Jordan
Int. 391b *The Idea of Imitation in Renaissance Literature*:
  Miss Jordan

French

Professors: Gérard Defaux *D ès L, Chairman*
Michel Guggenheim PHD
Pauline Jones PHD
Mario Maurin PHD

Associate Professor: Catherine Lafarge PHD

Assistant Professor: Grace Armstrong Savage PHD‡

Prerequisites. An undergraduate major in French, based on study in school and at least three years of college French, including some advanced work in literature, with evidence of ability to present reports and carry on discussion in French. Training in Latin corresponding to at least two years' study in school is advisable.

Applicants should submit scores in the Aptitude Test and Advanced Test of the Graduate Record Examinations taken within two years of the date on which they wish to begin graduate studies at Bryn Mawr. Candidates are required to support their application by at least one essay written in French for an advanced undergraduate course or graduate seminar previously taken, as well as by an essay written in English. They are strongly urged to arrange for a personal interview with a member of the Department.

Major and Allied Subjects. Students specialize in French literature from the Middle Ages to the present. Successful completion of a course in Old French philology and Mediaeval French literature is required of Ph.D. candidates. In special cases and with the consent of the Department, one of the following may be accepted as an allied subject: any literature, ancient or modern; comparative philology; European history; Philosophy; History of Art.

Language Requirements. For the M.A. degree, one Romance language other than French, *or* German, *or* evidence of extensive training in Mediaeval or advanced Latin. For the Ph.D. degree, *either* a reading knowledge of two modern languages (including one Romance language other than French) *or* superior competence in one. Students may satisfy the latter requirement by completing satisfactorily at least one unit of graduate work at Bryn Mawr in a Romance literature other than French, or in German literature. Language requirements must be fulfilled before the doctoral candidate takes the Preliminary Examinations.

Language skills may be tested by either the Graduate School Foreign Language Test (GSFLT) of the Educational Testing Service or the examinations administered by Bryn Mawr College. Entering

---

‡On leave 1977-78

students may offer scores of the GSFLT taken within twelve months of the date on which they begin graduate work at Bryn Mawr.

Program and Examination for the M.A. Candidates will offer two units of graduate work in French and a third unit in either French or an allied field. An M.A. paper on a topic related to the work in one of the seminars is required. The Final Examination consists of a three-hour written examination and a one-hour oral examination, both in French.

Admission to Candidacy for the Ph.D. After completing three full units of graduate work at Bryn Mawr, students are required to pass a qualifying examination before admission to doctoral candidacy. The paper and Final Examination required for the completion of the Bryn Mawr M.A. program may be substituted for the qualifying examination.

Program and Examinations for the Ph.D. Candidates will offer six units of graduate work, one of which may be in an allied field. Suitable related fields should be discussed with the department concerned and with the Department of French.

Students are encouraged to study and do research abroad whenever appropriate and feasible. Opportunities for summer study are provided by the graduate courses given at the Bryn Mawr *Institut d'Etudes Françaises d'Avignon.* Under the terms of an exchange agreement between Bryn Mawr College and *L'Ecole Normale Supérieure de Fontenay-aux-Roses,* a *poste de répétitrice* is available at Fontenay each year for an advanced doctoral candidate recommended by the Bryn Mawr Department of French.

The Preliminary Examinations consist of four papers written in French and an oral examination. The Final Examination is oral and covers the field in which the dissertation has been written.

General Degree Requirements for the M.A and the Ph. D. See pages 13-15.

SEMINARS AND GRADUATE COURSES

An introductory course in Old French philology and Mediaeval French literature is offered every two years. Students wishing further work in this field may register for a unit of supervised work at Bryn Mawr or attend graduate courses at the University of Pennsylvania. Graduate seminars in selected fields of French literature are given each year, so arranged that the same one will not be given in successive years. The seminars, conducted in French, are selected from the following:

Mr. Defaux
  (Villon, Charles d'Orléans, Marot)
  (Poètes du XVIe siècle)
  (Conteurs des XVe-XVIe siècles, Montaigne)
  Rabelais—semester I

40

Mr. Guggenheim
(Rousseau et le préromantisme)
(Précieux, mondains et moralistes du XVIIe siècle)
(Voltaire)

Miss Jones
(Verlaine et Rimbaud, Mallarmé, Laforgue)
(Vigny et Camus)
Baudelaire—semester I

Miss Lafarge
(Stendhal et Flaubert)
(Le Thème de la prison au XIXe siècle)
(Marivaux, Giraudoux)
Diderot—semester II

Mr. Maurin
(Essayistes du XXe siècle)
(Le Théâtre de 1940 à 1960)
(L'Autobiographie de Chateaubriand à Sartre)
(Réalisme et naturalisme)
(Valéry, Claudel, Proust, Gide)
(Travaux pratiques sur la littérature moderne)
Romancières du XXe siècle—semester II

Mrs. Savage
(L'Art du conte et de la nouvelle des Cent Nouvelles Nouvelle
à Flaubert)
(Philologie et littérature médiévales)·

SELECTED UNDERGRADUATE COURSES

(301 *French Lyric Poetry*)
302a *Valéry et Sartre*: Mr. Maurin
(303a *French Novel*)
(303b *La Vision de la femme dans la littérature française*)
(304a *Ecrivains engagés de Montaigne à Sartre*)
(304b *Le Théâtre de 1880 à 1939*)
306b *La démolition du héros: Pascal, Molière, La Rochefoucaul*
    Mr. Defaux
309a *Le Roman du XVIIIe siècle*: Miss Lafarge

Courses offered at the *Institut d'Etudes Françaises d'Avignon:*
    Molière or *Racine*
    Les Fleurs du mal or *Rimbaud*
    Le Surréalisme
    Travaux de traduction et de stylistique

Preparatory course for degree candidates in other departments:
    Reading French. This course, which does not carry academi

4

credit, is designed to assist students in meeting the language requirements for advanced degrees in fields other than French. An extra charge will be made. Specific information may be obtained from The Graduate School of Arts and Sciences during registration.

Geology

Associate Professors: Maria Luisa B. Crawford PHD *Chairman*
William A. Crawford PHD
Lucian B. Platt PHD
W. Bruce Saunders PHD*

Assistant Professor: George C. Stephens PHD

Prerequisites. A bachelor's degree in a natural science or Mathematics. Students who have not majored in Geology will be expected to make up deficiencies in their preparation during their first years of graduate study. Applicants must submit scores in the Aptitude Test of the Graduate Record Examinations.

Major and Allied Subjects. Students may specialize in economic geology, geochemistry, mineralogy–petrology, paleontology–stratigraphy, or regional and structural geology. The allied subject for the Ph.D. may be either another field of Geology or any one of the other natural sciences or Mathematics; other subjects may be accepted in special cases.

Language Requirements. For the M.A. degree, one of the following: Russian, German, or French. Candidates for the Ph.D. degree may offer two foreign languages from the following: Russian, German, or French; or one language from this list and proficiency in digital computation or statistics. This proficiency will be tested by the Department or may be demonstrated by the satisfactory completion of an appropriate course.

Language skills may be tested by either the Graduate School Foreign Language Test (GSFLT) of the Educational Testing Service or the examinations administered by Bryn Mawr College. Entering students may offer scores of the GSFLT taken within twelve months of the date on which they begin graduate work at Bryn Mawr.

Program and Examination for the M.A. At least three units of work are required, one of which will consist of a field or laboratory

---

*On leave semester I

research project under the direction of a member of the faculty. The results of the research project must be reported in a Master's thesis. The student must also pass a Final Examination consisting of a four-hour written and a one-hour oral test.

Program and Examinations for the Ph.D. Candidates will spend a major portion of their time on a research problem; ordinarily, this will involve field mapping and collecting, together with laboratory study. The number of units of course work to be taken will depend on the student's preparation. A set of Preliminary Examinations which test general knowledge in Geology, knowledge in the candidate's special field, and either an allied subject or an additional field in Geology must be passed before the student becomes deeply involved in the research project. A Final Examination follows the completion of the Ph.D. dissertation. This examination covers the field of the dissertation.

Every graduate student in the Department is expected to assist in the ongoing work of the Department.

General Degree Requirements for the M.A. and the Ph.D. See pages 13-15.

SEMINARS AND GRADUATE COURSES

Two or three courses or seminars are offered each semester. These are usually chosen so that each is offered once every other year. The specific content of the seminars is determined by the current interests of faculty and students. Students wishing to do so may also attend graduate courses at the University of Pennsylvania under the Reciprocal Plan (see page 11).

Mr. Crawford

Geochemistry and Analytical Techniques
Selected topics in the geochemistry of the earth combined with instruction in wet chemical and instrumental means of silicate analysis. Mechanical separations and experimental petrology.

Igneous Petrology
Selected subjects in the structure, physical chemistry, and origin of igneous rocks. Prerequisite: Geology 303a, *Thermodynamics for Geologists*, or its equivalent.

Mrs. Crawford

Metamorphism
The physical and chemical processes of metamorphism, accompanied by regional studies. Prerequisite: Geology 303a, *Thermodynamics for Geologists*, or its equivalent.

Advanced Mineralogy
The study of selected rock-forming mineral groups accompanied by instruction in optical, chemical, and x-ray techniques.

Mr. Platt
Structural Geology
Modern concepts in structural geology and theories of deformation.
Tectonics
Stratigraphic and structural relations of mountain ranges leading to analysis of their origin.

Mr. Saunders
Paleontology
Study of selected animal groups in geologic time.
Sedimentary Petrology
The constitution and the origin of sedimentary rocks; their source, transportation, and deposition.

Mr. Stephens
Ore Deposits
Nature and occurence of metallic ores and their depositing solutions. Introduction to ore microscopy.
Exploration Geophysics
Gravity and magnetics in the regional and local search for mineral deposits.

SELECTED UNDERGRADUATE COURSES

302b *Advanced Paleontology*: Mr. Saunders
303a *Thermodynamics for Geologists*: Mr. Crawford
304 *Petrology*: Mr. Crawford, Mrs. Crawford, Mr. Saunders
305b *X-Ray Crystallography*: Mrs. Crawford
307a *Principles of Economic Geology*: Mr. Stephens
307b *Introduction to Geophysics*: Mr. Stephens

German

Professor: Hans Bänziger PHD*

Associate Professors: Nancy C. Dorian PHD *Acting Chairman*
Gloria Flaherty PHD‡
C. Stephen Jaeger PHD

Lecturers: Susan Joan Erickson MA
Jutta Ramin PHD

---

*On leave semester I
‡On leave 1977-78

Prerequisites. An undergraduate major or minor in German or an equivalent preparation. All applicants are requested to submit scores in the Aptitude Test and Advanced German Test of the Graduate Record Examinations. They are also encouraged to write to the Chairman and seek a personal interview with the members of the Department, whenever possible.

Major and Allied Subjects. Students may specialize in either German literature or German philology. One of these two fields or an area in the humanities, especially the literatures, may serve as the allied subject. Graduate students are encouraged to acquaint themselves with the theory and practice of teaching German.

Language Requirements. Normally French for the M.A.; French and another language, preferably Latin, for the Ph.D. With the approval of the Department, the satisfactory completion of a graduate seminar at Bryn Mawr in a foreign literature other than German may be offered for one language requirement. In special cases, with the approval of the appropriate language department and of the Department of German, equivalent work at another university may be accepted.

Language skills are tested by the Graduate School Foreign Language Test (GSFLT) of the Educational Testing Service; should there be no GSFLT for a student's specialty, she or he should apply to the Department for examinations administered by Bryn Mawr College. Entering students may offer scores of the GSFLT taken within twelve months of the date on which they begin graduate work at Bryn Mawr.

All graduate students are required to complete the Bryn Mawr M.A. Should a student have an M.A. in German from another institution, she or he will be expected to take a four-hour qualifying examination in German literature or Germanic philology or both after one full year of study and before proceeding to do the remaining units in preparation for the Ph.D. Preliminary Examinations.

Program and Examination for the M.A. The program consists of three units in German literature and/or philology, or in German literature and philology and an allied field. In addition to providing familiarity with the field in general, the M.A. program is designed to introduce the student to various historical and critical approaches to the study of literature and language. Each student must demonstrate competence in spoken and written German. After completion of course work, each student must submit a Master's paper to the department clearly demonstrating independent research. The final examination, covering the student's general knowledge of the history of German literature, consists of a three-hour written examination and an oral examination of one hour.

Program and Examinations for the Ph.D. Every candidate must fulfill certain requirements in German literature and Germanic philology. Those majoring in Germanic philology take a minimum of one unit in German literature and will select the following courses: history of the German language, Gothic, Old High German, Middle High German, structural linguistics, and either Old English or Old Norse. Those majoring in German literature will take a minimum of one unit in Germanic philology and will normally take one unit each in the mediaeval, classical, and modern periods, as well as at least one genre course. The German Department encourages its students to participate in seminars given by other departments. It also encourages its students to study abroad and draws attention to the Anna Ottendorfer Memorial Research Fellowship for study at a German university. The Preliminary Examinations consist of four written tests, one of which must be taken in an allied field, and an oral examination. The Final Examination covers the field of the dissertation.

General Degree Requirements for the M.A. and the Ph.D. See pages 13-15.

SEMINARS

Mr. Bänziger
  (Brecht and Dürrenmatt)
  Franz Kafka—semester II
  (Gottfried Keller and German Realism)
  (Hofmannsthal and Rilke)
  (Thomas Mann and Max Frisch)

Miss Dorian
  (Comparative Germanic Grammar)
  (Old High German)
  (The Structure of German)

Miss Erickson
  (German Realism)

Miss Flaherty
  (Bibliography and Methods in Criticism)
  (German Baroque Literature)
  (Goethe and Schiller)
  (Romanticism)

Mr. Jaeger
  (German Renaissance Literature)
  (Middle High German Literature)

SELECTED UNDERGRADUATE COURSES

(300b *A Survey of German Literature*: Mr. Bänziger)
  301a *History of the German Language*: Miss Dorian
  (302a *Vernacular Literature in Mediaeval Germany*: Mr. Jaeger)

(303a *Modern German Prose*: Mr. Bänziger)
304b *The German "Novelle"*: Miss Erickson
305b *The Modern German Drama*: Mr. Bänziger
(307b *The Literature of the Renaissance and the Reformation*:
    Mr. Jaeger)
308a *Introduction to Middle High German*: Mr. Jaeger
(310b *Lessing and the Enlightenment: Miss Flaherty*)

Preparatory courses for degree candidates in other departments:
Reading German. This course, which does not carry academic credit, is designed to assist students in meeting the language requirements for advanced degrees in fields other than German. An extra charge will be made. Specific information may be obtained from The Graduate School of Arts and Sciences during registration.

Greek

Professor: Mabel L. Lang PHD *Chairman*

Associate Professors: Gregory W. Dickerson PHD
                  Richard Hamilton PHD

Andrew W. Mellon Post-Doctoral Fellow: Neil Forsyth PHD

Prerequisites. An undergraduate major or minor in Greek, based on at least four years of college Greek, or the equivalent, with representative reading from Greek literature and history which, in the opinion of the Department, provides an adequate basis for graduate work. It is expected that all graduate students in Greek will have some knowledge of Latin.

Allied Subjects. Any literature, ancient or modern, ancient history, ancient philosophy, Classical Archaeology, linguistics.

Language Requirements. Latin, French and German for both the M.A. and the Ph.D. Language skills may be tested by either examinations administered by Bryn Mawr College or the Graduate School Foreign Language Test (GSFLT) of the Educational Testing Service. Entering students may offer scores of the GSFLT taken within twelve months of the date on which they begin graduate work at Bryn Mawr.

Program and Examination for the M.A. The program consists of two units of graduate work in Greek and a third unit in an allied field.

47

Before admission to the Final Examination candidates must pass an examination in Greek sight translation. The Final Examination consists of a three-hour written examination and an oral examination of one hour.

Program and Examinations for the Ph.D. Before admission to the Preliminary Examinations candidates must pass a rigorous examination in Greek sight translation. The Preliminary Examinations consist of four written papers, one of which shall be in an allied subject, and an oral examination. The fields from which the three major papers may be selected include: epic poetry (with emphasis on Homer), lyric poetry (with emphasis on Pindar), tragedy, comedy, the orators, the historians, the Pre-Socratics, Plato, Hellenistic poetry, and various periods of Greek history. The Final Examination covers the field of the dissertation.

General Degree Requirements for the M.A. and the Ph.D. See pages 13-15.

SEMINARS AND GRADUATE COURSES

Mr. Dickerson
Sophocles—semester II

Mr. Hamilton
Pindar—semester I

Miss Lang
Archidamian War—semester I
Sicilian Expedition—semester II

In conjunction with other departments:
Mr. Forsyth
Myth, Folklore, and Literature—semester II

SELECTED UNDERGRADUATE COURSES

The following undergraduate courses are open to graduate students in other fields.

101 *Herodotus and Tragedy*: Mr. Dickerson, Mr. Hamilton
201 *Plato and Thucydides; Tragedy*:
    Mr. Hamilton, Mr. Dickerson
202b *Homer*: Mr. Forsyth
301 *Lyric Poetry; Aeschylus and Aristophanes*:
    Mr. Hamilton, Mr. Dickerson
Int. 360a *Forms of the Epic*: Mr. Forsyth

History

Professors: Charles M. Brand PHD
Arthur P. Dudden PHD *Chairman*
Mary Maples Dunn PHD†
Elizabeth Read Foster PHD
Barbara M. Lane PHD‡
Jane M. Oppenheimer PHD
J.H.M. Salmon LITD
Alain Silvera PHD‡
James Tanis THD *Director of Libraries*

Associate Professor: Phyllis S. Lachs PHD *Associate Dean
The Graduate School of Arts and Sciences*‡

Assistant Professor: Stephen Poppel PHD

Fields of Study. Master's and doctoral programs should be developed from seminars and courses available. Research for these and dissertations should grow out of seminars and units offered by the History Department and those allied with it.

Prerequisites. A thorough undergraduate preparation in History, the humanities, and the social sciences. Students who wish to work in ancient or mediaeval fields must be able to read the essential ancient languages. Those planning work in modern European history or American history must have a reading knowledge of one modern language, preferably French or German, upon entrance. Those planning doctoral programs should have two languages upon entrance or acquire the second language at once. Applicants are urged to take the Graduate School Foreign Language Test (GSFLT) of the Educational Testing Service before beginning their graduate studies.

Language Requirements. Entering students may offer scores of the GSFLT taken within twelve months of the date on which they begin graduate work at Bryn Mawr.

At least one modern foreign language, to be approved by the Department, is required of M.A. degree candidates. Either the College language examination or the GSFLT must be attempted before the end of the first semester's work; the examination must be passed before the end of the following summer or before candidacy for the degree is requested, whichever is earlier.

At least two modern foreign languages, the choice of which must be approved by the Department during the student's first academic

---

†On leave semester II
‡On leave 1977-78

year, are required of the Ph.D. candidates. Students entering with an A.B. must attempt either a College language examination or the GSFLT before the end of the first semester's work and must pass the examination in one language before they may enter upon a third semester of work. They must attempt an examination in the second language no later than their third semester of work and must pass an examination on this second language before they may enter upon a fifth semester of work. Students entering with an M.A. must attempt examinations in both languages before the end of their first semester and must pass examinations in both before they may enter upon a third semester of work. The time limit for part-time students is determined by the academic year, not by the number of units completed. Candidates for the Ph.D. in ancient or mediaeval history must also demonstrate ability to read one classical language. Directors of research may also require demonstration of ability in special techniques.

In practice, since not all languages are tested by GSFLT and since the College language examinations are scheduled toward the beginning of the second semester, proof of language facility must often be established early in the second semester of work to enable the student to enter upon a third semester of work. In addition, since financial aid decisions are made early in semester II, often before semester II language examinations are completed, students applying for financial aid for the succeeding academic year should demonstrate language competence before the end of semester I.

Program and Examination for the M.A. The program consists of three units of work in History or in History and an allied field, together with a paper and a final examination. The Final Examination is written and is usually four hours in length.

Program and Examinations for the Ph.D. All students are expected at some time to take a seminar or course in which aspects of historiography and historical method are studied. The Preliminary Examinations test the student's competence in four fields of History or in three fields of History and one field in an allied subject. For example, allied work in mediaeval literature, art, or philosophy is usually recommended to students of mediaeval history, and one of these may be offered in the Preliminary Examinations. Students whose dissertations are in American history will be required to take at least two fields in modern European history. Students specializing in English history must offer at least two fields of mediaeval or modern European history for examination. The field of the projected dissertation will be included in the Preliminary Examinations.

The purpose of the Final Examination is to test the candidate's knowledge of the special field or fields in which the dissertation has been written and to evaluate plans for publication.

The department reviews each student's progress and plans for work at all stages.

General Degree Requirements for the M.A. and the Ph.D. See pages 13-15.

The seminars are arranged to allow the fullest possible choice for students over a two- or three-year period of study. Normally the same seminar will not meet two years in succession. Topics listed below indicate the area in which seminars will be offered according to the needs of students and the current research interests of the faculty.

Ancient History

Students should consult pages 47 and 58 where the offerings of the Departments of Greek and Latin are listed.

Mediaeval and Renaissance History

Mr. Brand
Topics in Mediaeval History
The Fifth and Sixth Centuries
The Twelfth Century
Venice from the Tenth through the Thirteenth Centuries

Early Modern European History

Mr. Salmon
French Political Ideas from the Wars of Religion to the Enlightenment

Mr. Tanis
The Reformed Reformation in Northern Europe
Selected Topics in Sixteenth Century Religious Turmoil

Modern European History

Mrs. Lane
Modern Germany: National Socialism, Bauhaus
Topics in the History of Twentieth Century Europe

Mr. Poppel
Topics in the History of Nineteenth and Twentieth Century Europe

Mr. Silvera
The French Third Republic
Europe and the Near East

American and British History

Mr. Dudden
The Progressive Era
The New Deal

The United States in the Second World War
Topics in Recent American History

Mrs. Dunn
Seventeenth Century America
Eighteenth Century America
Social History of Colonial America

Mrs. Foster
Parliament in the Early Stuart Period
Social and Economic History of the Early Stuart Period

Mr. Tanis
Puritanism and the Great Awakening

Methodology and Historiography

Mr. Krausz
Philosophy of History—offered in the Department of
Philosophy

Mr. Salmon
Readings in Eighteenth Century Historiography

Mr. Tanis
Historiography of the Reformation

African and Afro-American History

Topic to be announced.

History of Science

Miss Oppenheimer
Embryology and Evolution

SELECTED UNDERGRADUATE COURSES

300-level courses may, with additional work, be offered for graduate credit.

300b *The American City in the Twentieth Century*: Mr. Spiezman
302 *France, 1559-1661*: Mr. Salmon
303a *Recent U.S.A.: The Indochina War*: Mr. Dudden
308a *The Jews in the Middle Ages*: Mr. Brand
314 *History of Scientific Thought*: Miss Oppenheimer
320a *The Rise of the Dutch Republic*: Mr. Tanis
328a *Colonial Towns*: Mrs. Dunn
360 *Tudors and Stuarts*: Mrs. Foster
380a *Topics in the Enlightenment*: Miss Oppenheimer
393b *Great Britain in the 16th & 17th Centuries*: Mrs. Foster

History and Philosophy of Science

Committee on History and Philosophy of Science:

Professor of Chemistry: Ernst Berliner PHD

Professor of History: Mary Maples Dunn PHD *Director*†

Professor of History of Science: Jane M. Oppenheimer PHD

Professor of Philosophy: José María Ferrater Mora *Lic Fil*

Mary Flexner Lecturer: Stephen E. Toulmin PHD

Associate Professors of Philosophy: Michael Krausz PHD‡
George Weaver PHD

At the University of Pennsylvania:

Professors: Thomas Park Hughes PHD *Chairman*
Alexander Vucinich PHD

Associate Professor: Diana Crane PHD

Assistant Professors: Mark Adams PHD
Robert E. Kohler, Jr. PHD
Russell Maulitz PHD

At the American Philosophical Society:
Whitfield J. Bell, Jr. PHD

This program within the Department of History has been developed in collaboration with the American Philosophical Society and the Department of the History and Sociology of Science at the University of Pennsylvania. Courses taken at any of the participating institutions may be credited toward an advanced degree.

Prerequisites. Undergraduate preparation in science, Philosophy, and History.

Major and Allied Subjects. The student's major subject will be History of Science, to be supported by intensive work in the field of History related to his special area of interest. Allied subjects may be Philosophy and other areas in science and History.

Language Requirements. Students must offer at least one modern foreign language, to be determined by the Department, for the Master's degree. Students who wish to continue work toward the Ph.D. must have completed the examinations in two modern foreign languages, to be determined by the Department, before taking the Preliminary Examinations.

---

†On leave semester II
‡On leave 1977-78

Language skills may be tested by either the Graduate School Foreign Language Test (GSFLT) of the Educational Testing Service or the examinations administered by Bryn Mawr College. Entering students may offer scores of the GSFLT taken within twelve months of the date on which they begin graduate work at Bryn Mawr.

Program and Examination for the M.A. The program consists of at least two units of work in the History of Science and one unit of work in a related field of History or Philosophy. The Final Examination is written and is usually four hours in length.

Program and Examinations for the Ph.D. The Preliminary Examinations test the student's competence in four general fields, three in the History of Science and one in a related field of History or Philosophy. The Final Examination covers the field of the dissertation which must be in History of Science.

General Degree Requirements for the M.A. and the Ph.D. See pages 13-15.

SEMINARS AND GRADUATE COURSES

Miss Oppenheimer, Mr. Toulmin
  Problems in the History and Philosophy of Science

At the University of Pennsylvania:

Mr. Adams
  Eugenics and Related Movements, 1860-1930

Mr. Bell
  Bibliography and Sources for the History of Science

Miss Crane
  Sociology of Science

Mr. Hughes
  Seminar in the Social History of Technology
  Technology in Industrial America, 1880-1950

Mr. Kohler
  Seminar in American Science
  History of the Bio-Medical Sciences

Mr. Vucinich
  Seminar in the Social History of Science
  Science and the Industrial Revolution

UNDERGRADUATE COURSES

314 *History of Scientific Thought*: Miss Oppenheimer

History of Art

Professors: Charles G. Dempsey MFA PHD *Chairman*
Charles Mitchell B LITT LITT D
James E. Snyder MFA PHD

Assistant Professors: Dale Kinney PHD‡
Steven Z. Levine PHD

Dean of The Graduate School of Arts and Sciences and *Professor of Classical and Near Eastern Archaeology* and *of History of Art*:
Phyllis Pray Bober PHD

Museum Assistant: Ian J. Lochhead MA

Field of Study. The history of Western art from early Christian to modern times.

Prerequisites. The normal prerequisite for admission is undergraduate training in art history, but students with special abilities or sound training in cognate disciplines are occasionally admitted. All applicants must submit scores in the Aptitude Test of the Graduate Record Examinations.

Allied Subjects. History, Archaeology, classics, modern languages; others, exceptionally, by arrangement.

Language Requirements. Students are expected to read or to be learning the languages necessary for their special fields of study and not to delay their research by lack of linguistic competence. Advanced study of Western art history normally involves a working knowledge of Latin, French, German, and Italian. Both M.A. and Ph.D. candidates are required to prove by examination their knowledge of two languages other than their own, to be approved by the Department.

Language skills will be tested by the examinations administered by Bryn Mawr College. Entering students may offer scores of the Graduate School Foreign Language Test (GSFLT) of the Educational Testing Service taken within twelve months of the date on which they begin graduate work at Bryn Mawr.

Program and Examination for the M.A. (a) Three units of graduate work, one of which may be in an allied field, (b) an extended paper on an approved topic, (c) a written (or written and oral) examination to test the candidate's ability to place this topic in its art-historical context.

Program and Examinations for the Ph.D. Prime emphasis is placed on a program of study and research leading to the dissertation, and

---

‡On leave 1977-78

students normally begin to work under a personal supervisor soon after entry. The Preliminary Examinations consist of four written papers and an oral examination on four areas of art history (or on three of these and one allied subject). After two or three years at Bryn Mawr, students normally go abroad for a period of research on their dissertations.

General Degree Requirements for the M.A. and the Ph.D. See pages 13-15.

Kress Program. The Department participates in the Samuel H. Kress Foundation Fellowship Program.

SEMINARS AND GRADUATE COURSES

Five one-term seminars on widely spaced topics that change from year to year are given annually, in addition to individual units of supervised work. Among those recently offered are the following:

Liturgy and Architecture
Early Christian and Byzantine Syria
The Art and Influence of Montecassino
Illustrated Psalters
Early Dutch Painting
Dutch Paintings from Geertgen to Heemskerck
Carel van Mander's Het Schilder-boeck
Mediaeval and Renaissance Drawing
The Patronage of Julius II
Leon Battista Alberti
Michelangelo
Problems in the Reform of Italian Art, 1550-1600
Selected Topics in Baroque Painting
Venetian Eighteenth Century Art
French Eighteenth Century Painting
Monet and Impressionism
Cézanne
Contemporary Spanish Painting
Picasso

Topics for 1977-78:

Mrs. Bober
Antiquity in the Renaissance (topic to be arranged)—semester II

Mr. Dempsey
Formal Traditions in Renaissance Iconography—semester I

Mr. Levine
Realism in 19th Century Art—semester II

Mr. Mitchell
Mantegna—semester I

Mr. Snyder
Van Eyck—semester II

Graduate students are sometimes advised to register for selected undergraduate courses which with additional work may be accepted for graduate credit.

SELECTED UNDERGRADUATE COURSES

321a *Traditions in Dutch Painting, 1450-1650*: Mr. Snyder
322b *Donatello*: Mr. Mitchell
323b *Nicholas Poussin*: Mr. Dempsey
324a *Problems in Film Theory*: Mr. Levine

History of Religion

Professor: Samuel Tobias Lachs PHD *Chairman*†
Visiting Professor: Norman Gottwald PHD
Professor of History: James Tanis THD *Director of Libraries*
Roian Fleck Resident in Religion: John Drury MA
Visiting Lecturer: Nancy Bancroft MA

A degree program at the graduate level is not offered in History of Religion. For work in this area, students should consult the offerings of the Department of History. The courses listed below are open to graduate students and, with additional work, may be taken for graduate credit with permission of the major department.

210a *Rabbinic Ethics and Theology*: Mr. Lachs
213b *Tradition and Design in Luke–Acts*: Mr. Drury
220b *Ethics and Society in Christian Perspective*:
    Miss Bancroft
300 *Studies in Early Rabbinic and Mediaeval Judaism*:
    Mr. Lachs
303a *Religion and Politics in the Hellenistic World*:
    Mr. Gottwald
316b *Christianity and Marxism*: Miss Bancroft

†On leave semester II

57

Italian

Assistant Professors: Nancy Dersofi PHD
                     Nicholas Patruno PHD *Director*

No graduate program is offered in Italian. The courses listed below are open to graduate students and may be taken for graduate credit with the permission of the major department.

(301   *Dante*)
303a *Petrarch, Boccaccio, and the Early Humanists*: Mr. Patruno
303b *Literature of the Italian Renaissance*: Miss Dersofi
305a *Arcadia and Enlightenment*: Miss Dersofi
(305b *History of the Italian Theater*: Miss Dersofi)

Latin

Professor: Myra L. Uhlfelder PHD

Associate Professors: Julia H. Gaisser PHD
                       Russell T. Scott PHD *Chairman*

Andrew W. Mellon Post-Doctoral Fellow: Neil Forsyth PHD

Prerequisites. An undergraduate major or minor consisting of at least three years of Latin in college. All graduate students in Latin are expected to have begun the study of Greek. Scores in the Aptitude Test of the Graduate Record Examination should be submitted.

Allied Subjects. The Department recommends as allied subjects: Greek, Classical Archaeology, ancient history, linguistics, or, for students whose special interest is in the mediaeval period, mediaeval history or a vernacular literature.

Language Requirements. French and German are required for both the M.A. and Ph.D. Language skills may be tested by either the Graduate School Foreign Language Test (GSFLT) of the Educational Testing Service or the examinations administered by Bryn Mawr College.

Program and Examination for the M.A. Candidates will normally offer two units of work in Latin and one unit in an allied field. Students will normally complete the work for the degree in one year, but, in cases in which it seems advisable to supplement the student's undergraduate preparation, a second year may be necessary. Candidates must pass a test in Latin sight translation before being admitted to the Final Examination, which consists of a three-hour written and a one-hour oral examination.

Program and Examinations for the Ph.D. Candidates will normally complete a two-year program of four units of work in Latin and two in an allied field. Three of these units may be those offered for the M.A. degree, which usually forms part of the doctoral program. Candidates should then undertake a program of independent reading planned to enable them to pass the Preliminary Examinations as soon as possible, after which they will concentrate on the dissertation. In some cases it may be advisable to carry one or two more units of work in the third year. The Preliminary Examinations consist of two four-hour written papers on Latin literature; one four-hour written paper on a special field such as a particular period of Roman history, the works of a special author, Mediaeval Latin literature, epigraphy, palaeography, or the history of classical scholarship; one four-hour written paper in the field of the allied subject, and a general oral examination. Students whose major interest is in the mediaeval period will take the two examinations in Latin literature, one in Mediaeval Latin literature, and a fourth in a field related to the Middle Ages or to the transmission of the classics. Before admission to the Preliminary Examinations, all students must pass tests in sight translation of Latin and Greek. The Final Examination will be oral and on the field of the dissertation.

General Degree Requirements for the M.A. and the Ph.D. See pages 13-15.

SEMINARS AND GRADUATE COURSES

Over a period of a few years, seminars will afford the student opportunity to work in specific areas of classical (Republican and Imperial) and mediaeval literature and civilization. Authors, genres, periods, or special topics dealt with in the seminars will vary according to the needs and desires of graduate students. A balance of prose and poetry, of literature and history, and of earlier and later periods is kept in mind in the establishment of the program.

The following seminars are offered in 1977-78:

Mr. Forsyth
Myth, Folklore, and Literature—semester II

Mrs. Gaisser
Lucretius—semester I

Mr. Scott
  Tacitus—semesters I and II

Miss Uhlfelder
  Boethius—semester II

SELECTED UNDERGRADUATE COURSES

202a,b *Mediaeval Latin Literature*: Miss Uhlfelder
(301a *Livy and Tacitus*: Mr. Scott)
(301b *Vergil's* Aeneid: Mrs. Gaisser)
302a *Cicero and Caesar*: Mr. Scott
302b *Lucretius*: Miss Uhlfelder

Mathematics

Professors: Frederic Cunningham, Jr. PH D *Chairman*
    John C. Oxtoby MA

Assistant Professor: Françoise Schremmer PH D‡

Lecturers: Nancy L. Hagelgans PH D
    Aigli Papantonopoulou PH D

Prerequisites. A good undergraduate preparation in Mathematics or in Mathematics and Physics.

Major and Allied Subjects. Students may specialize in any of the broad divisions of Mathematics: algebra, analysis, geometry, or applied mathematics but are expected also to acquire a well-rounded knowledge of the subject as a whole. Certain courses in Physics, Chemistry, or Philosophy (logic) are accepted as allied work.

Language Requirements. Candidates for the M.A. must have a reading knowledge of French, German, or Russian. Candidates for the Ph.D. must pass examinations in two of the three: French, German, Russian.

Language skills will be tested by either the Graduate School Foreign Language Test (GSFLT) of the Educational Testing Service or the examinations administered by Bryn Mawr College. Entering students may offer scores of the GSFLT taken within twenty-four months of the date on which they begin graduate work at Bryn Mawr.

---

‡On leave 1977-78

Program and Examination for the M.A. The program consists of three units of work in Mathematics, or in Mathematics and an allied field, and an M.A. paper. Advanced undergraduate courses which supplement the student's preparation may under certain conditions be taken for graduate credit. The Final Examination is usually oral and one hour in length.

Program and Examinations for the Ph.D. Candidates will take such courses and seminars as are needed to provide a sufficiently broad foundation. As they progress they will devote an increasing portion of their time to individual study and research under the direction of a member of the Department. The Preliminary Examinations are taken after the student is well advanced and usually consist of three or four written examinations intended to test the candidate's breadth of knowledge and understanding of the structure of Mathematics as a whole. An oral examination is usually included. The Final Examination is oral and is devoted to the candidate's special field and the subject of the dissertation.

General Degree Requirements for the M.A. and Ph.D. See pages 13-15.

Journal Club. A Mathematical Colloquium at the University of Pennsylvania meets approximately every two weeks. Lectures by visiting mathematicians are also frequently presented at Haverford and Swarthmore Colleges.

SEMINARS AND GRADUATE COURSES

At least three graduate courses or seminars are offered each year. Additional courses or directed reading and research can be arranged. The seminars offered in any year are selected to meet the needs of the individual students. Some may be offered for one semester only.

Mr. Cunningham
Functional Analysis
General Topology
Linear Spaces
Theory of Functions

Mr. Oxtoby
Measure Theory
Ergodic Theory
Point Set Topology
Theory of Functions

Mrs. Papantonopoulou
Algebra
Algebraic Geometry

Mrs. Schremmer
Partial Differential Equations
Applied Mathematics
Fluid Mechanics

SELECTED UNDERGRADUATE COURSES

301   *Advanced Calculus*: Mr. Oxtoby
303a *Introduction to Abstract Algebra*: Mrs. Papantonopoulou
303b *Topics in Algebra*: Mrs. Papantonopoulou
(308 *Introduction to Applied Mathematics*: Mrs. Schremmer)
(309b *Dynamical Systems*: Mrs. Schremmer)
(310a *Theory of Functions of a Complex Variable*:
       Mr. Oxtoby)   .
(311 *Differential Equations*: Mrs. Schremmer)

Mediaeval Studies

Committee on Mediaeval Studies:

Professor of English: Robert B. Burlin PHD

Professor of History: Charles M. Brand PHD *Chairman*

Professors of History of Art: Charles Mitchell B LITT LITT D
                               James E. Snyder MFA PHD

Professor of Latin: Myra L. Uhlfelder PHD

Professor of Music: Isabelle Cazeaux PHD

Professor of Philosophy: Jean A. Potter PHD

Professor of Spanish: Joaquín González-Muela D en Fil

Associate Professor of German: C. Stephen Jaeger PHD

Assistant Professor of French: Grace Armstrong Savage PHD‡

Assistant Professor of History of Art: Dale Kinney PHD‡

Graduate work for the M.A. in the mediaeval field may be done
either under a particular department or under the Mediaeval Studies
Committee. Doctoral studies in the mediaeval period will usually
come under the supervision of a particular department; in exceptional cases students with outstanding preparation will be permitted
to take the Ph.D. in Mediaeval Studies.

‡On leave 1977-78

Students applying for admission to the Mediaeval Studies program must submit: (1) a statement of their purpose in undertaking a degree in Mediaeval Studies, their plan of study, and their previous preparation in relevant fields; (2) a sample of their written work.

Mediaeval work in a particular department will fall under the regulations of that department. For work under the Mediaeval Studies Committee the regulations are as follows:

Prerequisites. The Committee must be satisfied that all candidates for admission have done sufficient undergraduate work to undertake graduate studies in the mediaeval field and have a reading knowledge of Latin and two modern languages.

Major and Allied Subjects. Any literature, ancient, mediaeval or modern, History, Philosophy, Classical Archaeology, History of Art, and History of Music.

Language Requirements. For the M.A. and Ph.D., Latin and two modern languages. Other languages may be substituted by permission of the Committee according to the candidate's special program. Language skills may be tested by either the Graduate School Foreign Language Test (GSFLT) of the Educational Testing Service or the examinations administered by Bryn Mawr College. Entering students may offer scores of the GSFLT taken within twelve months of the date on which they begin graduate work at Bryn Mawr.

Program and Examination for the M.A. Candidates will normally work in two departments and will offer at least two units of graduate work in any of the mediaeval fields and a third unit in any of the fields listed as allied. An extended paper, usually growing out of the work of one of the seminars, will be required in addition to an examination. The Final Examination may either be written (four hours) or written and oral (three hours—one hour).

Program and Examinations for the Ph.D. The course of study will normally be under the guidance of one professor. Prime emphasis will be placed on a program of research leading to the dissertation. The candidate will take Preliminary Examinations, written and oral, in three fields representing at least two departments. The three fields may all be mediaeval, or two may be mediaeval (in two different departments) and one an allied field (in a department represented on the Committee, or in a third department). The allied field should pertain either chronologically or topically to the Middle Ages; what constitutes a "field" should be worked out between the candidate and the faculty member concerned, with ultimate consent of the candidate's Supervising Committee. The Final Examination will cover the field of the candidate's dissertation.

General Degree Requirements for the M.A. and the Ph.D. See pages 13-15.

Music

Professors: Isabelle Cazeaux PHD
      Robert L. Goodale ABBMUS AAGO *Chairman*

Assistant Professor: Carl B. Schmidt PHD

Lecturer: Courtney Adams PHD

Prerequisites. Two years of harmony, counterpoint, and analysis, three years of history and appreciation of music, of which at least one should be in an advanced course, and a reading knowledge of one modern language, preferably German. Candidates must have a sufficient knowledge of pianoforte or organ playing to be able to play music of the technical difficulty of a Bach figured chorale.

Allied Subjects. Any modern language or literature, History, History of Art, History of Religion, Philosophy.

Language Requirements. Two modern languages are required for the M.A. degree, preference being given to German and French. For candidates for the Ph.D. degree two languages are required, one of which must be German. Language skills will be tested by the examinations administered by Bryn Mawr College.

Program and Examination for the M.A. The program consists of three units of work in Music or in Music and an allied field. The Final Examination is written and four hours in length.

Examinations for the Ph.D. The Preliminary Examinations consist of four papers in the major field or three papers in the major field and one in an allied field, and an oral examination. The Final Examination covers the subject matter of the dissertation.

General Degree Requirements for the M.A. and the Ph.D. See pages 13-15.

Practice rooms with pianos will be available for a fee of $10 per semester. Students permitted to play the organ in the Music Room will be charged $20 per semester.

SEMINARS AND GRADUATE COURSES

SEMINARS AND GRADUATE COURSES

Mrs. Adams
Bach—semester I
The String Quartets of Haydn and Mozart—semester II

Miss Cazeaux
Musicology

Mr. Goodale
Studies in Music of the Twentieth Century

Mr. Schmidt
Studies in Italian and French Opera of the Seventeenth Century

SELECTED UNDERGRADUATE COURSES

Undergraduate courses taken for graduate credit require additional work.

202 *Advanced Theory and Analysis*: Mr. Goodale
205a *Music Criticism*: Miss Cazeaux
305 *Free Composition*: Mr. Goodale
306b *Opera and Music Drama*: Miss Cazeaux

Philosophy

Professors: José María Ferrater Mora *Lic Fil*
George L. Kline PHD *Chairman*
Jean A. Potter PHD
Isabel Scribner Stearns PHD

Associate Professors: Michael Krausz PHD‡
Mary Patterson McPherson PHD *Dean
The Undergraduate College*
George E. Weaver, Jr. PHD*

Assistant Professors: Richard H. Gaskins PHD JD
Tracy M. Taft PHD

Lecturer: Thomas Song MA MALS *Associate Director of Libraries*

Prerequisites. In general, an undergraduate major in Philosophy. Students whose undergraduate training does not include a major in Philosophy may be required to take such undergraduate courses as

---

‡On leave 1977-78
*On leave semester I

the Department considers necessary. All applicants are requested to submit scores in the Aptitude Test of the Graduate Record Examinations.

Allied Subjects. Subjects in most fields of the humanities, Mathematics, and natural and social sciences.

Language Requirements. One modern language for the M.A., French and German for the Ph.D. At the discretion of the Department, another language may be substituted for French or German when the student's research requires it.

Language proficiency will be tested by either the Graduate School Foreign Language Test (GSFLT) of the Educational Testing Service or examinations administered by Bryn Mawr College. Entering students may offer scores of the GSFLT taken within twelve months of the date on which they begin graduate work at Bryn Mawr.

Program and Examination for the M.A. Three units of work in Philosophy or in Philosophy and an allied field. The Final Examination is usually written and four hours in length.

Program and Examinations for the Ph.D. All students must demonstrate competence in logic before receiving the Ph.D. This requirement may be met in several ways: by successful completion, before admission to candidacy, of an intermediate course or graduate seminar in logic; or by special examination before admission to candidacy; or by passing a preliminary examination in the systematic field of logic. The Preliminary Examination will consist of four written papers, two of which are to be in systematic fields and two in authors or periods.

General Degree Requirements for the M.A. and the Ph.D. See pages 13-15.

Graduate Philosophy Colloquium: Graduate students are encouraged to participate in the monthly meetings of the Graduate Philosophy Colloquium. Papers are read by faculty and students of Bryn Mawr as well as visiting lecturers. In addition, both the Fullerton Club and the Philadelphia Logic Colloquium hold their monthly meetings at Bryn Mawr and the graduate students are invited to attend.

SEMINARS

Mr. Ferrater Mora
  (Methods of Research in the History of Philosophy)
  (History of Philosophic Concepts)
  (Kant: Epistemology and Metaphysics)
   Phenomenology: Husserl and Heidegger

66

Mr. Kline
(*Ethics*)
Hegel: Phenomenology of spirit—semester I
(*Whitehead*)

Mr. Krausz
(*Aesthetics*)
(*Philosophy of Science*)
(*Theory of Inquiry*)

Miss Potter
Mediaeval Philosophy
(*Continental Rationalism*)
(*Philosophy of Religion*)

Miss Stearns
(*Epistemology*)
Metaphysics
(*American Philosophy*)

Miss Taft
(*Aristotle*)
Plato

Mr. Weaver
Intensional Logics—semester II
(*Logic: The Expressive Power of First Order Sentences*)
(*Completeness and Decidability*)
(*Introduction to Set Theory and Logic*)

SELECTED UNDERGRADUATE COURSES

312a *Philosophy of History*: Mr. Kline
314b *Existentialism*: Mr. Ferrater Mora
316b *History and Philosophy of Mathematics*: Mr. Weaver

Physics

Professors: Rosalie C. Hoyt PHD‡
John R. Pruett PHD *Chairman*

Associate Professor: Alfonso M. Albano PHD

Assistant Professors: Peter Beckmann PHD
Stephen R. Smith PHD

---

‡On leave 1977-78

Prerequisites. An undergraduate major in Physics or in a field of study closely allied to Physics (e.g., Mathematics, Chemistry, Engineering). Students who have not majored in Physics will usually find it necessary to take some undergraduate courses before entering graduate seminars. All applicants for admission to graduate work in Physics are requested to submit scores in the Aptitude Test and Advanced Test of the Graduate Record Examinations.

Allied Subjects. With permission of the Department, candidates for the Ph.D. degree may offer as an allied subject Mathematics, Biology, Chemistry, or Geology, provided they have taken advanced work in one of these fields.

Language Requirements. For the M.A. and the Ph.D. degrees, two languages are required: one, French, German, or Russian; the second, a computer language approved by the Department. Language skills will be tested by the examinations administered by Bryn Mawr College.

Program and Examination for the M.A. An oral qualifying examination must be passed before the student is admitted to candidacy. The subject matter of the examination will include only material ordinarily covered in undergraduate college Physics courses, but the student will be expected to handle this material on a reasonably mature level. The three units of work offered for the degree will ordinarily include one unit of experimental physics and at least one graduate seminar in theoretical physics. The paper will usually consist of a report on a special field related to one of the seminars or · units of graduate work offered for the M.A. The M.A. Examination is a one-hour oral examination.

Program and Examinations for the Ph.D. Each student is normally expected to have completed seminars in Quantum Mechanics and Electromagnetic Theory, or their equivalents, must have a mathematical preparation acceptable as adequate for the Ph.D. degree, and must have passed the oral qualifying examination described above before being recommended for candidacy.

The Preliminary Examinations are intended to test the candidate's general background and to determine whether it is broad and deep enough to serve as a preparation for original research work in a specialized field. In general, two years of full- or part-time graduate work should prepare the student for these examinations, and candidates for the Ph.D. are urged to submit themselves for examination at this stage of their work. The examinations will consist of three four-hour written examinations, one problem set, and an oral examination lasting approximately one hour. Each of the three four-hour examinations will cover one of the following fields of Physics, to be chosen by the Department: (1) classical mechanics, including relativity theory, vibrations, and wave motion; (2) electricity and magnetism, including field problems and electromagnetic waves, the latter with particular reference to optical phenomena; (3) quantum mechanics, with applications to atomic and nuclear structure; (4) thermodynamics and statistical mechanics, including both classical and quantum statistics. The student devotes approximately twelve hours to direct work on the problem set over a three-day period. Any books, periodicals, notes, etc. may be used in connection with the problem set. The oral examination is devoted to general Physics.

Unless the candidate has demonstrated adequate acquaintance with experimental physics in other ways, either the research leading to the dissertation must be, at least in part, experimental or the candidate must take a seminar in experimental physics. The Final Examination will cover the field of the dissertation.

General Degree Requirements for the M.A. and Ph.D. See pages 13-15.

Colloquium. All members of the Department and all graduate students meet weekly for the discussion of current problems.

See pages 13-15. See page 11.

SEMINARS

Three or more graduate seminars in theoretical physics are offered each year. In addition, a seminar in experimental physics is arranged individually for students so desiring; it generally serves as an introduction to a research problem. Students wishing to do so may also attend graduate courses at the University of Pennsylvania under the Reciprocal Plan. See page 11.

Experimental Physics

Mr. Beckmann, Miss Hoyt, Mr. Pruett, Mr. Smith

Theoretical Physics

Quantum Mechanics
Necessity for the quantum hypothesis. The Schroedinger and Heisenberg formulations with applications to atomic structure. The Dirac approach with applications to relativistic electron theory and the quantum theory of radiation. Prerequisite: an advanced undergraduate course in mechanics or in theoretical physics.

Electromagnetic Theory
Potential theory, Maxwell's Equations, applications to waves subject to various boundary conditions, transmission lines, wave guides, radiating systems. Prerequisite: an advanced undergraduate course in electricity and magnetism or in theoretical physics.

Statistical Mechanics

Classical kinetic theory and transport phenomena. Ensembles in classical and quantum statistical mechanics. Selected applications. Prerequisite: *Quantum Mechanics*.

At least one of the following advanced seminars in theoretical physics is given each year:

Mr. Albano

Non-Equilibrium Thermodynamics

Phenomenological theories of irreversible processes. Statistical foundations of non-equilibrium thermodynamics. Onsager-Casimir relations. The fluctuation-dissipation theorem. Interfaces and the non-equilibrium thermodynamics of boundary conditions. Prerequisite: *Statistical Mechanics* or consent of the instructor.

Advanced Quantum Mechanics

Symmetries and invariance principles, many-body techniques relativistic electron theory, introduction to relativistic quantum field theory.

Mr. Beckmann

Physics of the Solid State

Classification and characteristics of solids, theory of mechanical, electrical, thermal, and magnetic properties. Prerequisite: *Quantum Mechanics* and *Electromagnetic Theory*. Either may be taken concurrently.

Miss Hoyt

Chemical Physics and Biophysics

Interatomic and intermolecular forces, vibrational and rotational states of molecules. Dynamical properties of biological membranes, the biophysics of photosynthesis and photo-sensitive receptors. Prerequisite: *Quantum Mechanics*.

Mr. Pruett

Nuclear Physics

An introductory study of classical nuclear physics followed by applications of quantum mechanics to nuclear problems and associated high-energy phenomena. Some quantum electrodynamics and meson theory will be included. Prerequisite: *Quantum Mechanics* or its equivalent.

Mr. Smith

Quantum Optics

Interaction of the radiation field with quantum-mechanical systems. Quantization of radiation. Spontaneous and stimulated emission. Semi-classical and quantum theories of lasers and laser amplifiers. Operating characteristics of gas lasers. Optical coherence and statistical characteristics of various radiation fields. Prerequisites: *Quantum Mechanics* and *Electromagnetic Theory*.

306a Classical and Quantum Mechanics
307b Classical and Quantum Mechanics
308b Advanced Mechanics of Discrete and Continuous Systems
309a Advanced Electromagnetic Theory

Political Science

The Caroline McCormick Slade Department of Political Science

President of the College: Harris L. Wofford, Jr. AB JD

Professors: Melville T. Kennedy, Jr. PHD *Acting Chairman*
    Gertrude C. K. Leighton AB JD‡

Associate Professors: Charles E. Frye PHD
               Marc Howard Ross PHD *Chairman‡*
               Stephen G. Salkever PHD‡

Visiting Lecturers: Alan Charles Emdin PHD
             Elaine Friedrich MA

Prerequisites. A good undergraduate training in Political Science and related subjects. Scores of the Graduate Record Examination Aptitude Test and Advanced Test are required in applications for admission.

Major and Allied Subjects. The major fields offered in Political Science are political philosophy and theory, Western comparative politics, non-Western comparative politics, American political process, political behavior, American constitutional law, and international politics and law. Allied fields may be chosen in the other social sciences, in History and Philosophy, and, with the special permission of the Department, in certain subjects in literature. Candidates for the Ph.D. are expected to prepare themselves in four fields, one of which may be allied.

Language Requirements. One modern foreign language for the M.A. Two foreign languages (only one need be modern) or one modern language and statistics for the Ph.D. Language skills may be tested by either the Graduate School Foreign Language Test (GSFLT) of the Educational Testing Service or the examinations administered by Bryn Mawr College. The statistics requirement may be satisfied by passing an approved course in statistics.

---

‡On leave 1977-78

71

Program and Examination for the M.A. The program consists of three units of work in Political Science, but a unit from an allied field may be substituted for one of these. The Final Examination will be written or oral or both.

Program and Examinations for the Ph.D. Candidates are expected to offer four fields, one of them being the field in which the dissertation is written. These fields are tested by written and oral Preliminary Examinations. An oral Final Examination will cover fields related to the dissertation.

General Degree Requirements for the M.A. and the Ph.D. See pages 13-15.

SEMESTER SEMINARS

Mr. Emdin
Political Philosophy: Selected Topics

Mrs. Friedrich
(American Politics: Political Behavior)

Mr. Frye
European Comparative Politics
Intellectuals in Comparative Perspective

Mr. Kennedy
International Politics
Topics in Politics of China, Japan, India

Miss Leighton
(Aspects of Political Behavior)
(International Law)
(Jurisprudence)

Mr. Ross
(American Politics: Political Behavior)
(Community Politics)

Mr. Salkever
(Aristotle)
(Constitutional Law)

SELECTED UNDERGRADUATE COURSES

218b *Community Politics*: Mr. Ross
219a *Constitutional Law*: Mr. Emdin
230b *Political Behavior*: Mr. Ross
301b *Law and Society*: Miss Leighton
302b *Law, Policy, and Personality*: Miss Leighton
303a *Problems in International Politics*: Mr. Kennedy
305b *European Fascism*: Mr. Frye
311b *Theory and Practice in Political Philosophy*: Mr. Salkever

313b *Problems in Constitutional Law*: Mr. Salkever
316b *Ethnic Group Politics: Concepts and Process*: Mr. Ross
317a *Political Culture and Political Leadership*: Mr. Frye
319a *Problems in Legal Theory*: Mr. Salkever
320b *Philosophy of the Social Sciences*: Mr. Emdin

Psychology

Professors: Richard C. Gonzalez PHD *Chairman*
    Howard S. Hoffman PHD*
    Matthew Yarczower PHD

Katharine E. McBride Visiting Professor:
    Nicholas J. Mackintosh DPHIL

Associate Professors: Clark McCauley, Jr. PHD
    Earl Thomas PHD

Assistant Professor: Jill T. Wannemacher PHD‡

Lecturers: Alice S. Powers PHD
    Larry Stein PHD

Prerequisites. Undergraduate training in Psychology is recommended, but outstanding applicants with training only in related fields may be accepted. Students who have not majored in Psychology as undergraduates may find it necessary to devote a substantial portion of the first year to undergraduate courses. All applicants residing in the United States at the time of the application must submit scores on the Aptitude Test and Advanced Test of the Graduate Record Examinations.

Major and Allied Subjects. The orientation in the various fields is experimental, and there are no facilities for clinical training. Work in Psychology may be coordinated with work in one of the following allied areas: Anthropology, Biology, Chemistry, Mathematics, Philosophy, and Physics.

Language Requirements. Candidates for the M.A. must pass an examination in one of the following languages: French, German, Russian. Candidates for the Ph.D. must offer two foreign languages:

---

*On leave semester I
‡On leave 1977-78

French and German (or some other foreign language with permission of the Department) or one foreign language and statistics. The statistics requirement will be tested by the Department. Language skills will be tested by the examinations administered by Bryn Mawr College.

Program and Examination for the M.A. The program of work must include three units (six one-semester seminars or courses) which usually will be chosen from the group of seminars and courses listed below. Before final approval of the Master's paper, each candidate must pass a written examination in statistics. The Final Oral Examination, one hour in length, deals with the Master's paper and related topics.

Program and Examinations for the Ph.D. Ph.D. candidates are expected to devote a large portion of their time to supervised research. In the first year, the research is done under the close supervision of the candidate's faculty advisor; a written report of the year's research activities (the form and content of which are determined by the candidate and his advisor) is submitted to the Department, and an oral presentation based on the report is made to the faculty and graduate student members of the Department. In addition to research, candidates, in their first two years of residence, take the six one-semester graduate courses listed below (or, if they elect to do so, a written examination in the subject matter instead of any one or all of the courses). The Preliminary Examinations, which should be taken early in the third year, consist of three written examinations of four hours each and an oral examination of one to two hours. The written examinations are in the following areas: learning and motivation, physiological psychology, social psychology, developmental psychology, or, with approval of the Department, in two of these areas and in one of the allied subjects listed above. (The area of comparative psychology as such is not represented in a separate examination; comparative issues are treated in each of the other area-examinations.) The oral examination deals with the areas of the written examinations. Work beyond the Preliminary Examinations consists of seminars in selected topics and of dissertation research. The Final Oral Examination deals with the dissertation and the field in which it was written.

General Degree Requirements for the M.A. and the Ph.D. See pages 13-15.

GRADUATE COURSES

Mr. Gonzalez
  Learning Theory

Mr. Hoffman
  Statistics

74

Mr. McCauley
Experimental-Social Psychology

Mr. Thomas
Physiological Psychology

Miss Wannemacher
Developmental Psychology

Mr. Yarczower
Comparative Psychology

SEMINARS

Seminars are offered on specialized topics in the areas of experimental, comparative, developmental, physiological, and social psychology. Among those offered most recently are the following: *Communication Theory, Experimental Design, Parameters of Reinforcement, Physiological Techniques and Instrumentation, Psychopharmacology, Stimulus Control of Behavior, Aversive Control, Neurophysiology of Reward and Punishment, Comparative Neuroanatomy.*

SELECTED UNDERGRADUATE COURSES

201a *Learning Theory and Behavior*: Mr. Gonzalez
202b *Comparative Psychology*: Mr. Yarczower
203a *Motivation*: Mr. Thomas
204a *Sensory Processes*: Mr. Hoffman
(207b *Language and Cognition*: Miss Wannemacher)
302b *Physiological Psychology*: Mr. Thomas

Russian

Associate Professors: Dan E. Davidson PH D
Ruth L. Pearce PH D *Chairman*

Assistant Professors: George S. Pahomov PHD‡
Lynn Visson PH D

Professor of Philosophy: George L. Kline PH D

Prerequisites. An undergraduate major in Russian or an equivalent preparation with some work in literature. Applicants should submit

‡On leave 1977-78

scores in the Aptitude Test of the Graduate Record Examination, a brief biography written in Russian, and at least one essay written in English on a literary topic. The English essay may have been written for an advanced undergraduate course or graduate seminar previously taken.

Allied Subjects. Any language or literature, economics, Russian history, Political Science, Russian philosophy.

Language Requirements. For the M.A., French or German. For the Ph.D., French, German, and one Slavic language other than Russian. Language skills may be tested by either the Graduate School Foreign Language Test (GSFLT) of the Educational Testing Service or the examinations administered by Bryn Mawr College. Entering students may offer scores of the GSFLT taken within twelve months of the date on which they begin graduate work at Bryn Mawr.

Program and Examination for the M.A. Three units of work in Russian or in Russian and an allied field. The Final Examination consists of a three-hour written examination and an oral examination of one hour.

Examinations for the Ph.D. The Preliminary Examinations consist of four written papers, one of which must be taken in an allied field, and an oral examination. The Final Examination will cover the field of the dissertation.

General Degree Requirements for the M.A. and the Ph.D. See pages 13-15.

SEMINARS AND GRADUATE COURSES

Seminars offered each year are selected in accordance with the needs and interests of the students enrolled. Normally the same seminar is not given in two successive years. In cooperation with the Department of Slavic Languages of the University of Pennsylvania, the student may also register at that institution under the Reciprocal Plan (see page 11) for a unit of work chosen from the graduate courses offered in Slavic. Undergraduate 300-level courses, with additional work, may also be offered for graduate credit.

Mr. Davidson
Karamzin and Early Romanticism
Old Russian Literature
Russian Prose of the Early Modern Period
Versification

Mr. Pahomov
Chekhov
Classics of Russian Drama from Fonvizin to Chekhov
Russian Romanticism
The Russian Short Story: Karamzin to Chekhov
Turgenev and Goncharov

76

Mrs. Pearce
History of the Development of the Russian Literary Language
History of the Russian Language: Phonology and Morphology
Old Church Slavic: Phonology and Morphology
Readings in Old Church Slavic
Studies in the Structure of Russian

Miss Visson
Pushkin
The Russian Short Story: Chekhov to Solzhenitsyn

Mr. Kline
Theory and Practice of Literary Translation

SELECTED UNDERGRADUATE COURSES

303 *Twentieth-Century Russian Literature*
305 *Advanced Russian Grammar*
306 *Russian Prose and Poetry of the Nineteenth Century*
Philosophy 333a *Russian Philosophy*
Philosophy 333b *Marx and Russian Marxism*

Cooperation with the University of Pennsylvania. Attention is drawn to the graduate courses offered by the Department of Slavic Languages at the University of Pennsylvania. Students wishing to do so may register for a unit of work at the University under the Reciprocal Plan (see page 11).

Sociology

Professor: Eugene V. Schneider PHD *Chairman*

Associate Professor: Judith R. Porter PHD

Assistant Professors: Sheila Kishler Bennett PHD
Robert E. Washington PHD

Prerequisites. An undergraduate preparation in Sociology or some closely related social science is desirable. Students whose undergraduate training is not entirely adequate may be required to take certain undergraduate courses.

77

Major and Allied Subjects. Students may wish to take some work in related fields: Anthropology, Economics, Psychology, Political Science, History, and statistics. In addition, courses in Sociology and allied subjects may be taken at the University of Pennsylvania under the terms of the Reciprocal Plan (see pages 11-12).

Language and Statistics Requirements. Candidates for the M.A. must offer one modern foreign language and statistics. Candidates for the Ph.D. degree must offer two modern foreign languages (usually French and German) or one modern foreign language and statistics. The statistics requirement will be tested by the Department or may be met by passing a graduate course in statistics.

Language skills will be tested by the examinations administered by Bryn Mawr College. Entering students may offer scores of the Graduate School Foreign Language Test (GSFLT) of the Educational Testing Service taken within twelve months of the date on which they begin graduate work at Bryn Mawr College.

Program and Examination for the M.A. The program consists of three units of work. The Final Examination may consist of one four-hour written paper, or one three-hour written paper and an oral examination of one hour.

Program and Examinations for the Ph.D. The Preliminary Examinations for candidates for the Ph.D. will consist of four three-hour written papers and an oral examination of one hour. These examinations will be in general sociology, sociological theory, and two special fields, one of which may be an allied field. The Final Examination will cover the field of the dissertation.

General Degree Requirements for the M.A. and the Ph.D. See pages 13-15.

SEMINARS

Seminars will be given in special branches of Sociology, such as:

Sociological Theory	*Race Relations*
Social Stratification	*Sociology of Poverty*
Sociology of Religion	*Political Sociology*
Personality and	*Sociology of Developing*
Social Structure	*Countries*
Sociology of Knowledge	*Sociology of the Family*
Sociological Methods	*Social Change*
Industrial Sociology	

UNDERGRADUATE COURSES

Under exceptional circumstances a student may be registered for an advanced undergraduate course which with additional work may be accepted for graduate credit.

Spanish

Professors: Joaquín González-Muela *D en Fil*
Willard F. King PH D *Chairman*

Associate Professor: Eleanor K. Paucker PH D

Lecturer: Enrique Sacerio-Garí M PHIL

Professor of Philosophy: José María Ferrater Mora *Lic Fil*

Prerequisites. An undergraduate major in Spanish; representative reading from Spanish literature of the Middle Ages, Golden Age, and contemporary period. Spanish-American literature may be offered in addition. Applicants for admission in Spanish are asked to submit scores on the Aptitude Test and Advanced Test of the Graduate Record Examinations. Candidates are urged to arrange for a personal interview with a member of the Department whenever possible.

Allied Subjects. Any literature, ancient or modern, including Mediaeval Latin literature; European or Spanish-American history; classical or Romance philology; Spanish-American literature.

Language Requirements. For the M.A., either German or one Romance language other than Spanish. For the Ph.D., German and French; in special cases the Department may accept other languages. The Ph.D. candidate's preparation must give evidence of adequate knowledge of Latin; if it does not, Latin must be included ·in the graduate program.

Language skills may be tested by either the Graduate School Foreign Language Test (GSFLT) of the Educational Testing Service or the examinations administered by Bryn Mawr College. Entering students may offer scores of the GSFLT taken within twelve months of the date on which they begin graduate work at Bryn Mawr.

Program and Examination for the M.A. The program consists of three units of graduate work in Spanish or two units of graduate work in Spanish and one other in an allied field. An M.A. paper on a topic related to the work in one of the seminars is required. The Final Examination consists of a three-hour written section and an oral of one hour, both in Spanish.

Examinations for the Ph.D. The Preliminary Examinations consist of four written papers, one of which must be taken in an allied field, and an oral examination. Suitable related fields should be discussed with the member of the Department with whom the candidate plans to work on the dissertation. The Final Examination will cover the field of the dissertation.

General Degree Requirements for the M.A. and the Ph.D. See pages 13-15.

SEMINARS

The seminars are arranged to allow the widest possible choice for students over a two- or three-year period of study. Normally the same seminar will not be given two years in succession.

Mr. González-Muela
The History of the Spanish Language—semester I
(*The Mediaeval Castilian Epic and Lyric*)
(*Mediaeval Prose from Alfonso el Sabio to the Corbacho*)
(*Popular and Elite Styles in Golden Age Poetry*)
(*The Language of Poetry since 1950*)
Stylistics and Advanced Syntactic Analysis—semester II

Mrs. King
(*Ideological Currents in Renaissance Spain*)
(*Cervantes*)
The Spanish Novel of the 16th and 17th Centuries—semester II
(*Golden Age Drama*)
(*Modern Drama*)
Critical Approaches to Literature—semester I

Mrs. Paucker
(*Romanticism and Naturalism*)
(*The Urban Novel in Spain*)
Unamuno and Machado—semester II
(*The Novel of the Mexican Revolution*)
Gaucho Literature—semester I

Mr. Sacerio-Garí
(*Chroniclers of the New World*)
(*The Argentine Narrative since Independence*)
(*The Novel of the Caribbean*)
(*Borges and Cortázar*)

SELECTED UNDERGRADUATE COURSES

302a *Mediaeval Spanish Literature*: Mrs. Paucker
303a *Modern Poetry in Spain*: Mr. González-Muela
303b *The Modern Novel in Spain*: Mrs. King
(304a *Cervantes*: Mrs. King)
(304b *Poetry and Drama of the Golden Age*: Mrs. King)

Appropriate graduate seminars at the *Centro de Estudios Hispánicos en Madrid* may be included in the program for the M.A. or the Ph.D. (see page 12).

Fees

Application (payable by citizens of the United States and Canada and foreign students living in the United States): $20.

Tuition
    Full-time students:
      $3850 a year (or $1925 for a semester)
    Part-time students:
      2 academic units $2500 a year (or $1250 a semester)
      1 academic unit $1450 a year (or $725 a semester)
    Auditors:
      Fees for auditors are the same as those for students registered in courses for credit.

Continuing enrollment (see page 8): $200 a semester, except for students using Bryn Mawr College laboratories for dissertation research. In these cases fees will be determined in consultation with the major department.

Payment of Fees

Both tuition and residence fees will be billed by semester. The Education Plan of monthly payment in cooperation with the Provident National Bank is available for those who prefer to pay fees in monthly installments. Direct correspondence to the Comptroller of the College.

Students whose fees are not paid within ten days of receipt of bill in each semester will not be permitted to continue in residence or to attend classes. Degrees will not be awarded to any student owing money to any College facility, nor will any transcripts be issued.

Refund Policy

In the event of withdrawal from The Graduate School of Arts and Sciences, refunds will be made according to the following schedule:

For Semester I	
Withdrawals prior to Sept. 8	100%
Withdrawals Sept. 8 through Oct. 30	50%
Withdrawals through Jan. 15	0%
For Semester II	
Withdrawals prior to Jan. 16	100%
Withdrawals Jan. 16 through March 10	50%
Withdrawals March 11 to end of semester	0%

For those students living at the Graduate Residence Center, the charge for residence is $1990 in 1977-78. In accordance with the above schedule, if a student withdraws from graduate study a refund will be made of that portion of the fee which represents room, with the proviso that the College is able to reassign the student's space to some other student not previously in residence. The student is not entitled to dispose of the room he or she leaves vacant.

Appropriate reduction or remission will also be made for that portion of the residence fee which represents the cost of food.

Medical Leave

In case of absence from the College extending six weeks or more because of illness, there will be a proportionate reduction or remission in the charge for the cost of food.

Procedure for Securing Refunds

Written notice must be received by the Dean at least one week prior to the effective date of withdrawal. Students who have received loans under NDSL or GSL to meet any educational expenses for the current academic year must make an appointment with the Associate Dean before leaving the campus to arrange for appropriate repayment of the loans in question.

Summary of Expenses for the Academic Year

Regular

Tuition Fee (full time)	$3850
Residence in graduate student housing	1990

Contingent

Application Fee	$ 20
Continuing Enrollment Fee	400
Course in Reading German or French	100
(flat fee from September to February)	
Dispensary Fee.....................................	50
Health Insurance (United States citizens)	60
Health Insurance (foreign students)	70
Graduation Fee for all Graduate Degrees	25
Charge for Microfilming Ph.D. Dissertation	37
Late Registration Fee	10
Add and Drop Fee	10
(after the first week of a new semester)	

Faced with the rising costs of higher education, the College has had to raise tuition each of the last several years. Further increases may be expected.

Exclusion

The College reserves the right to exclude at any time students whose academic standing is unsatisfactory or whose conduct renders them undesirable members of the college community. In such cases fees will not be refunded or remitted in whole or in part; fellowships and scholarships will be cancelled.

Family Educational Rights and Privacy Act of 1974

The Family Educational Rights and Privacy Act of 1974 was designed to protect the privacy of education records, to establish the right of students to inspect and review their education records, and to provide guidelines for the correction of inaccurate or misleading data through informal and formal hearings. Students have the right to file complaints with The Family Educational Rights and Privacy Act Office (FERPA), Department of Health, Education, and Welfare, 330 Independence Avenue, SW, Washington, D.C. 20201, concerning alleged failures by the institution to comply with the Act.

Copies of Bryn Mawr's policy regarding the Act and procedures used by the College to comply with the Act can be found in the Office of the Dean. The policy is printed in the Bryn Mawr-Haverford Academic Regulations, which also list all education records maintained on students by this institution.

Questions concerning the Family Educational Rights and Privacy Act may be referred to the Office of the Graduate Dean.

Designation of Directory Information

Bryn Mawr College hereby designates the following categories of student information as public or "Directory Information." Such information may be disclosed by the institution for any purpose, at its discretion.

Category I   Name, address, dates of attendance, class

Category II   Previous institution(s) attended, major field of study, awards, honors, degree(s) conferred

Category III   Date of birth

Category IV   Telephone number

Category V   Marital Status

Currently enrolled students may withhold disclosure of any category of information under the Family Educational Rights and Privacy Act of 1974 by written notification which must be in the Office of the Records, Taylor Hall, by 5 p.m. on Friday, September 30, 1977. Forms requesting the withholding of "Directory Information" are available in all Dean's Offices and in the Office of the Recorder.

Bryn Mawr College assumes that failure on the part of any student to specifically request the withholding of categories of "Directory Information" indicates individual approval for disclosure.

83

Fellowships and Graduate Scholarships

Fellowships and graduate scholarships are provided from the general funds of the College, from the gifts of alumnae and other generous donors, and from government agencies and private foundations. The majority of these awards are made on the basis of an annual competition. Fellowships carry a stipend of $2300 in addition to tuition and are available only to students who have completed one full year of graduate work. Graduate scholarships have a value of $1800 in addition to tuition and may be held by citizens and noncitizens and by students at all levels of graduate work leading to the M.A. or Ph.D. degree. Other awards vary in value.

Application

Application from citizens of the United States and Canada should be made to the Dean of The Graduate School of Arts and Sciences and must be filed complete not later than February 1. In writing for forms applicants should state their fields of concentration. Applications from foreign students must be received not later than January 25. Scores of the Test of English as a Foreign Language (TOEFL) or the examination of the English Language Institute of the University of Michigan must be included.

Graduate and Professional School Financial Aid Service

The Graduate School of Arts and Sciences is a participant in the Graduate and Professional School Financial Aid Service (GAPSFAS), Educational Testing Service, Princeton, New Jersey 08540. All applicants for financial aid must file a GAPSFAS form entitled "Application for Financial Aid for the Academic Year 1978-79." Copies of the form are available locally in most colleges and universities; they may also be obtained by writing directly to Princeton. The completed form must be returned to the Graduate and Professional School Financial Aid Service by January 15.

The GAPSFAS form contains three sections: Part I for the applicant, Part II for the applicant's spouse or spouse to be, and Part III for the applicant's parents. Part I and, when applicable, Part II, must be completed as part of the application for financial aid at Bryn Mawr. Part III is not required for Bryn Mawr College aid. (See page 91 for loan requirements.)

84

Fellowship in the Award or Nomination of the College

Bryn Mawr College Fellowships of $2300 in addition to tuition are offered annually in Anthropology, Biochemistry, Biology, Chemistry, Classical and Near Eastern Archaeology, Economics, Education and Child Development, English, French, Geology, German, Greek, History, History and Philosophy of Science, History of Art, Latin, Mathematics, Music, Philosophy, Physics, Political Science, Psychology, Russian, Sociology, and Spanish.

Alumnae Association Fellowships are provided from the contributions of former graduate students to the Alumnae Fund; from the Alumnae Regional Scholarship Committees of Eastern Pennsylvania, Southern New Jersey, and Delaware and of New York and Southern Connecticut, and from the Alumnae Association of Cambridge and of New Haven.

Marion Louise Ament Fellowship. Graduate fellowships in Spanish are occasionally awarded from the fund established in 1966 in honor of Marion Neustadt, Class of 1944.

The Henry Joel Cadbury Fellowship Fund in the Humanities was established in 1973 by the Board of Bryn Mawr College in honor of Henry Joel Cadbury, Trustee Emeritus. The fund was made possible by donations from current and former trustees and directors of the College and friends of Dr. Cadbury in order to provide annual support for graduate students in the Humanities who have reached an advanced stage of their graduate work.

The Theodore N. Ely Fund. A fellowship or scholarship in Art or Archaeology is awarded to a graduate student from the interest on this fund, which was established in 1959 by bequest of Katrina Ely Tiffany, Class of 1897.

The Folly Ranch Fund was established by an anonymous gift in 1974. The income is used for graduate and undergraduate scholarships in honor of Eleanor Donnelley Erdman, Clarissa Donnelley Haffner, and Elizabeth P. Taylor, Class of 1921, and Jean T. Palmer, Class of 1924.

The Margaret Gilman Fund. A fellowship or scholarship in French is awarded from the interest on this fund, which was established in 1958 by bequest of the late Margaret Gilman, Professor of French at Bryn Mawr College.

The Howard Lehman Goodhart Fellowship is awarded to an advanced student in Mediaeval Studies.

The Helen Schaeffer Huff Memorial Research Fellowship is awarded| for a year of research work in Physics or Chemistry at Bryn Mawr College. Candidates must be students who have demonstrated their ability for research. If other qualifications are equal among a number of candidates, preference will be given to a student whose field of research overlaps the fields of Chemistry and Physics. This fellowship is normally awarded to a post-doctoral candidate to enable her to continue her research program. In such cases the stipend will be $6500. In exceptional cases, candidates engaged in important research who have not completed the work for the doctorate will be considered. For such students the stipend will be less, the amount to be determined on the basis of the candidate's qualifications.

The Helen Schaeffer Huff Memorial Research Fellow has no duties except those connected with her own research, but she may arrange with the department in which she is working to do a small amount of teaching if she so desires.

The S. Maude Kaemmerling Scholarship was established in 1959 by the estate of S. Maude Kaemmerling and increased by a gift in 1965. The income on the fund is to be used for graduate scholarships and fellowships.

The Melodee Siegel Kornacker Fellowship in Science was established in 1976 by Melodee Siegel Kornacker, Class of 1960. The income is used for a graduate fellowship in Biology, Chemistry, Geology, Physics, or Psychology.

The Samuel H. Kress Foundation Fellowships in varying amounts are awarded to advanced graduate students in History of Art.

The Katharine Elizabeth McBride Fellowship. In the 75th Anniversary Year a fund for a graduate fellowship in honor of Katharine McBride was established by certain alumnae. The endowment of this fellowship was increased by a gift from the Class of 1925 on its 40th reunion. The fellowship is awarded in any department to a candidate for the Ph.D. degree who is about to complete two years or more of graduate work.

The Emmy Noether Fellowship was founded by gifts from many donors in memory of Emmy Noether who came to Bryn Mawr College from Germany in 1933 and who died April 14, 1935. It is open to students in the United States and in foreign countries who are advanced graduate students of Mathematics. It is awarded by the Department of Mathematics of Bryn Mawr College and may be used, subject to the approval of the Department, at any institution in the United States or in a foreign country.

The Ida H. Ogilvie Fellowships in Geology are awarded each year from part of the income of the Ida H. Ogilvie Fund, which was established in 1965 through the bequest of Dr. Ogilvie, a member of the Class of 1896.

The Max Richter Fellowship Fund was established in 1962 and increased in 1965 by gifts from the Trustees of the Richter Memorial

Foundation. Income from the endowment provides fellowships to advanced students interested in public affairs.

The Mildred Clarke Pressinger von Kienbusch Fellowship was established in 1964 by a gift in honor of Mildred Clarke Pressinger von Kienbusch of the Class of 1909. The income on this fund is to be used for a graduate student working toward the doctorate. This award may be made to a beginning graduate student.

Scholarships and Fellowships under the Plan for the Coordination of the Sciences. The departments of the natural sciences and Mathematics administer a fund for the Coordination of the Sciences, given to the College in 1935 by the Carnegie Corporation of New York. Its purpose is to encourage and facilitate teaching and research in fields such as biochemistry, biophysics, geochemistry, geophysics, and psychophysics.

From this fund, the Committee for the Coordination of the Sciences awards fellowships, scholarships, assistantships, postdoctoral research fellowships, or other grants as seem appropriate.

The Mary Waddell Fellowship Fund provides grants of $1000 each for the study of Mathematics to daughters of American citizens of Canadian descent.

Whiting Fellowships in the Humanities are awarded to students in their final dissertation year. Each fellowship carries a stipend of $400 per month, plus tuition, together with a modest allowance for research expenses and a family allowance if needed. These fellowships are available in the Departments of Classical and Near Eastern Archaeology, English, French, German, Greek, History, History of Art, Latin, Mediaeval Studies, Music, Philosophy, Russian, and Spanish.

Fellows by Courtesy. Fellows who continue their studies at the College after the expiration of their fellowships may, by a vote of the Directors, receive the rank of Fellow by Courtesy.

Travelling Fellowships

The Fanny Bullock Workman Travelling Fellowship for a year of study or research abroad was established in 1927 by bequest of Fanny Bullock Workman and by gift of her husband, Dr. W. Hunter Workman. It is awarded to a candidate for the degree of Doctor of Philosophy at Bryn Mawr College who could not have the advantages of such a year without assistance. At the discretion of the faculty, the fellowship for any one year may be divided between two students, or the same student may hold the fellowship for more than one year.

The Anna Ottendorfer Memorial Research Fellowship in Teutonic philology and German language and literature, founded in 1907 by

87

Mrs. Anna Woerishoffer in memory of her mother, is to be applied to the expense of study and residence for one year at a German university. It is awarded to a student who has completed at least one year of graduate study at Bryn Mawr College and who shows ability to conduct independent investigations in the fields of Teutonic philology or German literature. The choice of a university is determined by the holder's preference, subject to the approval of the faculty.

The Ella Riegel Fellowship or Scholarship in Classical Archaeology was founded in 1937 by bequest of Ella Riegel. It is awarded on the recommendation of the Department of Classical and Near Eastern Archaeology to advanced students in this subject. It is given for study abroad but may, at the discretion of the Department, be used at Bryn Mawr College.

Graduate Scholarships

Bryn Mawr College Graduate Scholarships of $1800 each in addition to tuition are offered annually to students for work in any department of The Graduate School of Arts and Sciences.

Scholarships for Foreign Students. These scholarships are designated for foreign students who have excelled in their university studies. Applicants must have had three or four years of university training. Each scholarship carries a stipend which covers full tuition and residence in graduate student housing during the academic year. (Meals during vacations are not included and students will need to provide their own funds for these and other expenses.) Scholarship holders are expected to carry a full program of graduate work and to attend regularly the courses for which they are registered. Work is given in seminars or small discussion groups in which the students, as well as the instructor, actively participate. It is essential, therefore, that the student be able not only to read and write English, but to understand it and speak it fluently.

The Marguerite N. Farley Scholarships for Foreign Students, which provide tuition and a stipend to cover room and board on campus, are offered to students from any country outside the United States and Canada. Occasionally a fellowship is awarded from this fund to a foreign student who has completed at least one year at Bryn Mawr.

A special British Scholarship, which provides tuition and a stipend to cover room and board on campus, is awarded to students from the United Kingdom who are sponsored by The English-Speaking Union.

Special Foreign Scholarships for French, German, Hebrew, Italian, and Spanish, which provide tuition and a stipend to cover room and board on campus plus $200, have been established for students whose languages form a part of the Bryn Mawr curriculum. Holders of these scholarships are asked to devote four or five hours a week to supervised teaching or other assistance in the appropriate language department. The Special Scholarship for French has been named in memory of Marcelle Pardé who was a member of the French Department of Bryn Mawr College between 1919 and 1929. The Special Scholarship for Spanish has been named in memory of Miguel Catalan, distinguished Spanish physicist and friend of Bryn Mawr.

Duties of Fellows and Scholars

Fellows and Graduate Scholars are required to carry a full academic program at Bryn Mawr College. They are expected to attend official functions. Fellows are not permitted to accept other appointments. Scholars, with the permission of the Dean of The Graduate School of Arts and Sciences, may undertake a limited amount of paid work. Each Travelling Fellow is asked to present a written report of the work done during the fellowship year. This report should be sent about the first of March to the Dean of The Graduate School of Arts and Sciences for transmittal to the student's department.

Assistantships

Teaching Assistantships are available in some departments. These positions carry salaries of $2900-3100 for half-time work, $1950-2050 for one-third-time work, and include tuition without fee. The duties differ with departments. In departments of science, assistantships provide teaching and laboratory experience.

Graduate Assistantships are available in some departments. These positions provide full-time tuition and wages according to the hours of work given to the department.

Research Assistantships are available in the Departments of Biology, Chemistry, Geology, Physics, and Psychology.

Internships and Field Work Placements. The Department of Education and Child Development offers each year one internship, with stipend, in school psychology. The intern is placed in the Child Study Institute and receives individual supervision there. Supervised practicum experience at the Institute is also available, usually without stipend.

Supervised field work placements, with stipend, are available in school counseling. These are open to advanced, highly qualified candidates in the school counseling program sequence. Supervised practicum experience in counseling is also available, usually without stipend.

Tuition Grants

Tuition grants are available for full-time and part-time students. Gifts from the Alumnae Fund have increased the number of these grants.

Graduate Prize

The Susan B. Anthony Memorial Prize, commemorating the great work of Susan B. Anthony for women, was founded by her friend, Anna Howard Shaw, and her niece, Lucy E. Anthony. It is offered from time to time to a graduate student at Bryn Mawr College who has published or submitted in final form for publication the best study dealing with the industrial, social, economic, or political position of women. The award is made by a committee of which the President of the College is chairman.

Loan Funds

National Direct Student Loan Program. These loans are available to students who are United States citizens and who are registered for at least two units of graduate work. Application is made on a special form which is obtained from the Office of Admissions and Awards after a student has been admitted to The Graduate School of Arts and Sciences. The application and a GAPSFAS form (see page 84) must be filed by August 1. Allocation of loan funds is made early in September.

Guaranteed State Loan Program. Students are encouraged to apply for Guaranteed State Loans, available to United States citizens who are studying at least half-time, through their local banks. Part of the application is completed by The Graduate School of Arts and Sciences. A GAPSFAS form is required.

All students who are applying for National Direct Student Loans and Guaranteed State Loans are advised that GAPSFAS PART III *is required from those who do not meet the governmental definition of independent student.* Therefore, if you expect to apply for either a federal or state loan, complete Part III if, during the last twelve months, you a) resided with, or b) have been claimed as a federal income tax deduction by, or c) been the recipient of an amount in excess of $600 by one (or both) of your parents.

The Students' Loan Fund of the Alumnae Association of Bryn Mawr College was established by the Class of 1890 for the use of students who need to borrow money in order to continue their college work and for the purpose of receiving contributions, no matter how small, from those who are interested in helping students obtain an education. The fund is managed by the Alumnae Scholarships and Loan Fund Committee.

Loans may be used for purposes approved by the Committee, who try to provide small loans to meet special emergencies. As a rule, money is not lent students in their first semester of graduate work nor are these loans intended to meet the expenses of tuition. Not more than $500 may be borrowed by a student in any one year. The total for four years must not exceed $1500.

While the student is in college no interest is charged; after the student leaves college the interest rate is three percent. The entire principal must be repaid within five years from the time the student leaves college at the rate of twenty percent each year. Students who wish to borrow from the Loan Fund may obtain application blanks for this purpose from the Office of Admissions and Awards of The Graduate School of Arts and Sciences.

Career Planning Office

Graduate students are invited to make use of the services of the Career Planning Office. These services include counseling on career interests and concerns; information on specific openings for summer, temporary and permanent, full- and part-time positions; consultation on job-hunting methods. Upon request the Career Planning Office also collects, maintains, and makes available to prospective employers the credentials of graduate students and alumnae. The credentials include biographical data and faculty and employer references.

Graduate Student Council

The Graduate Student Council, composed of one representative elected annually from each department offering a graduate program, serves as a vehicle through which graduate students may voice their concerns and needs to the faculty and administration. When appropriate, the Council also initiates and carries out specific programs to meet these needs.

Graduate students work primarily in one department, so that the Council provides a means of communicating with students in all departments. Council meetings are held at least once a month in the Graduate Lounge located in the M. Carey Thomas Library. Graduate student opinion is sometimes solicited through questionnaires, so that the Council may best represent various opinions.

Representatives of the Council sit on various College committees such as those concerned with the Library and computer services. In addition, the Council is represented at meetings of the Board of Directors.

The Council also plays a major role in devising policies and procedures for on-campus graduate housing and supports a Housing Service to coordinate summer and off-campus housing opportunities.

Graduate Student Housing

Housing on campus is provided for about sixty graduate students in the Graduate Residence Center and Batten House. There is a separate bedroom for each student. Rooms are furnished except for rugs and curtains. Students should bring towels and bed linen. (Local rental services will supply sheets, blankets, and pillowcases for a modest fee. Arrangements may be made on arrival.) Because of college fire regulations, smoking is not permitted in the bedrooms. There are smokers on certain floors. The dining room, available to all resident students, is located in the Center.

Application for a room should be made as early as possible. A room contract, which will be sent upon request, must be signed and returned to the Office of The Graduate School of Arts and Sciences with a deposit of ten dollars. The deposit will be deducted from the residence fee; it will be refunded only if the student cannot be accommodated.

A student who has reserved a room will be held responsible for the residence charge unless notice of withdrawal is sent in writing to the Dean of The Graduate School of Arts and Sciences by August 15.

The regular charge for residence (room and board) for graduate students is $1990 a year, payable one half early in the first semester and the other half early in the second. Although one or more housing units may be closed during Christmas and spring vacations, when food and health service are not provided, residence on campus covers the period from the opening of College in the fall until Commencement Day. Baggage will be accepted at the College after August 20. It should be sent prepaid, addressed to the proper residence hall, and marked with the owner's name.

Health

Medical Services

The College maintains an 18-bed Infirmary with a staff of physicians and nurses. The Infirmary is open when College is in session. The college physicians may be consulted without charge by students residing in campus housing and by students living off campus who have paid the dispensary fee. Specialists practicing in Bryn Mawr and Philadelphia serve as consulting physicians to the College. If consultation is necessary, the student must meet the expense.

The residence charge paid by graduate students living in campus housing entitles them to treatment in the College dispensary, to care in the Infirmary for seven days (not necessarily consecutive) during the year, and to attendance by the college physicians during this time. After the seven-day period, the fee is $30.00 for each day in the Infirmary.

Graduate students who do not live in campus housing may pay a $50.00 fee which entitles them to full use of the Student Health Service. The fee is not billed automatically and is not covered by scholarship or other grants. The dispensary fee is to be paid in the Comptroller's Office where a dispensary card is issued.

The College maintains a counseling and diagnostic service staffed by clinical social workers and consulting psychiatrists. They are at the Infirmary on a part-time basis. All students eligible for dispensary care may use this service. The counseling service offers confidential consultation and discussion of personal and emotional problems. Definitive and long-range psychotherapy is not available. A charge is made for visits in excess of four.

Medical Requirements

All graduate students, after admission but before registration, must file a medical history and health evaluation form with the Infirmary. There are no exceptions to this rule.

In addition to a statement of health, signed by a physician, the following are required: tetanus and polio immunizations; proof of freedom from active tuberculosis based on either a negative skin test, or in the presence of a positive test, a normal chest x-ray within six months of admission.

Insurance

All graduate students are urged to carry health insurance. Students are entitled to the Bryn Mawr College Student Health care insurance at a cost of about $59.50 per year. Those wishing more complete coverage may purchase Blue Cross and Blue Shield insurance on an individual basis, subject to screening by the insurance company. Application for College health insurance should be made through the Head Nurse in the Infirmary.

Foreign Students. The College makes available a policy which provides fuller coverage of medical, surgical, and hospital costs. This insurance is required of all students whose permanent residence is not in the United States unless they have equally complete protection of another kind effective in the United States. The cost for students under age thirty is about $70.00 for a twelve-month period, starting in September.

All foreign students will be automatically enrolled in the Student Health Service at a cost of $50 for non-residents.

Child Care Center

Child care is available for Bryn Mawr and Haverford college families at the New Gulph Child Care Center, 1109 County Line Road, Rosemont, just five minutes from campus. Children 3 months through 5 years old are eligible. The center is open five days a week, 9am-5pm.

The center, conducted by professional staff, incorporates appropriate age group developmental activities with high quality group care, plus a nursery school program. Flexible schedules can be arranged to accommodate the programs of students, staff, faculty and alumnae parents, based on the college calendar. A minimum of six hours regular use per week is required. Following Commencement, a summer program is conducted for approximately two months.

The fee scale is based on the age of the child and the number of hours in attendance at the center. Tuition for the semester is payable in advance. Financial assistance is available. Early registration for all programs is essential. For information contact the Director at 525-7649.

96

; of the

Library Committee
Phyllis Goodhart Gordan, *Chairman*
Edmund B. Spaeth, Jr., *ex officio*
Harris L. Wofford, Jr., *ex officio*
Diana Morgan Laylin
Judith Zinsser Lippmann
Dorothy Nepper Marshall
Barbara Cooley McNamee
Barbara Bradfield Taft
Allen McKay Terrell

Committee on Student Life
Lovida Hardin Coleman, *Chairman*
Edmund B. Spaeth, Jr., *ex officio*
Phyllis Goodhart Gordan, *ex officio*
Harris L. Wofford, Jr., *ex officio*
Vera French Bates
Diana Morgan Laylin
Judith Zinsser Lippmann
Donald W. Macpherson
Millicent Carey McIntosh
Jonathan E. Rhoads
Elsie Kemp Schmitz

Academic Affairs Committee
Barbara Bradfield Taft, *Chairman*
Edmund B. Spaeth, Jr., *ex officio*
Phyllis Goodhart Gordan, *ex officio*
Harris L. Wofford, Jr., *ex officio*
Margaret Bell Cameron
Jonathan E. Rhoads
Henry Scattergood
J. Tyson Stokes
Barbara Auchincloss Thacher

Grounds Committee
Judith Zinsser Lippmann
Alison Stokes MacLean
Elsie Kemp Schmitz
Rosalyn Ravitch Schwartz

97

Faculty and Staff of The Graduate School of Arts and Sciences

for the Academic Year 1977-78

Harris L. Wofford, Jr., AB (University of Chicago) JD (Howard University and Yale University) *President of the College*

Phyllis Pray Bober PH D (New York University) *Dean of The Graduate School of Arts and Sciences*

Mary Patterson McPherson PH D (Bryn Mawr College) *Dean of the Undergraduate College*

Bernard Ross PH D (University of Michigan) *Dean of The Graduate School of Social Work and Social Research*

Willard F. King PHD (Brown University) *Acting Secretary of the General Faculty*

Phyllis S. Lachs PH D (Bryn Mawr College) *Associate Dean of The Graduate School of Arts and Sciences*‡

Gertrude C. K. Leighton AB (Bryn Mawr College) JD (Yale University) *Secretary of the General Faculty*‡

Joseph Varimbi PH D (University of Pennsylvania) *Secretary of the Faculty of Arts and Sciences*

Courtney Adams PH D (University of Pennsylvania) *Lecturer in Music*

Alfonso M. Albano PH D (State University of New York at Stony Brook) *Associate Professor of Physics*

Steven Alpern PH D (New York University) *Lecturer in Mathematics*

Jay Martin Anderson PH D (Harvard University) *Professor of Chemistry*

Nancy Bancroft MA (Columbia University-Union Theological Seminary) *Lecturer in History of Religion*

Hans Bänziger PH D (University of Zürich) *Professor of German**

Peter Beckmann PHD (University of British Columbia) *Assistant Professor of Physics*

Sheila Kishler Bennett PHD (University of North Carolina) *Assistant Professor of Sociology*

The notations throughout this section
refer to the following footnotes:
*On leave semester I
†On leave semester II
‡On leave 1977-78

Ernst Berliner PH D (Harvard University) *W. Alton Jones Professor of Chemistry*

Frances Bondhus Berliner PH D (Bryn Mawr College) *Lecturer in Chemistry*

Carol L. Bernstein PH D (Yale University) *Associate Professor of English*

Sandra M. Berwind PH D (Bryn Mawr College) *Assistant Professor of English‡*

Eleanor A. Bliss SCD (Johns Hopkins University) *Dean Emeritus*

Phyllis Pray Bober PH D (New York University) *Dean of The Graduate School of Arts and Sciences* and *Professor of Classical and Near Eastern Archaeology* and *of History of Art*

Charles M. Brand PH D (Harvard University) *Professor of History*

Robert A. Braun PH D (University of Illinois) *Assistant Professor of Anthropology*

Peter M. Briggs PH D (Yale University) *Assistant Professor of English*

Katrin Ristkok Burlin PH D (Princeton University) *Assistant Professor of English*

Robert B. Burlin PH D (Yale University) *Professor of English*

Rhys Carpenter PH D (Columbia University) LITT D *Professor Emeritus of Classical Archaeology*

Diana L. Cassel PH D (Bryn Mawr College) *Lecturer in Biology*

Isabelle Cazeaux PH D (Columbia University) *Professor of Music*

Georgia Christopher PH D (Yale University) *Katharine E. McBride Visiting Professor of English*

Robert L. Conner PH D (Indiana University) *Professor of Biology*

Rachel Dunaway Cox PH D (University of Pennsylvania) *Professor Emeritus of Education and Child Development* and *of Psychology*

Maria Luisa B. Crawford PH D (University of California) *Associate Professor of Geology*

William A. Crawford PH D (University of California) *Associate Professor of Geology*

Frederic Cunningham, Jr. PH D (Harvard University) *Professor of Mathematics*

Cecile K. Dalton PH D (University of California) *Lecturer in Chemistry*

Dan E. Davidson PH D (Harvard University) *Associate Professor of Russian*

Gérard Defaux *D ès L* (Sorbonne) *Professor of* French

Frances de Graaff PH D (University of Leyden) *Professor Emeritus of Russian*

Frederica de Laguna PH D (Columbia University) *Professor Emeritus of Anthropology*

Grace Mead Andrus de Laguna PH D (Cornell University) *Professor Emeritus of Philosophy*

Charles G. Dempsey MFA PH D (Princeton University) *Professor of History of Art*

Nancy Dersofi PHD (Harvard University) *Assistant Professor of Italian*

Gregory W. Dickerson PH D (Princeton University) *Associate Professor of Greek*

Max Diez PH D (University of Texas) *Professor Emeritus of German Literature*

Nancy C. Dorian PH D (University of Michigan) *Associate Professor of German*

John Drury MA (Cambridge University) *Roian Fleck Resident in Religion* and *Visiting Lecturer in History of Religion*

Richard B. Du Boff PH D (University of Pennsylvania) *Professor of Economics*

Arthur P. Dudden PH D (University of Michigan) *Professor of History*

Mary Maples Dunn PH D (Bryn Mawr College) *Professor of History* †

Harrison Eiteljorg II PH D (University of Pennsylvania) *Lecturer in Classical and Near Eastern Archaeology*

Richard S. Ellis PH D (University of Chicago) *Associate Professor of Classical and Near Eastern Archaeology*‡

Maria deJ. Ellis PHD (Yale University) *Lecturer in Classical and Near Eastern Archaeology*

Alan Charles Emdin PH D (University of Chicago) *Visiting Lecturer in Political Science*

Susan Joan Erickson MA (Yale University) *Lecturer in German*

Noel J. J. Farley PH D (Yale University) *Associate Professor of Economics*†

José María Ferrater Mora *Licenciado en Filosofía* (University of Barcelona) *Professor of Philosophy* and *Fairbank Professor in the Humanities*

Gloria Flaherty PH D (Johns Hopkins University) *Associate Professor of German*‡

Neil Forsyth PHD (University of California) *Andrew W. Mellon Post-Doctoral Fellow* and *Lecturer in Greek* and *in Comparative Literature*

Elizabeth Read Foster PHD (Yale University) *Professor of History*

Grace Frank AB (University of Chicago) *Professor Emeritus of Old French*

Elaine Friedrich MA (University of Michigan) *Visiting Lecturer in Political Science*

Charles E. Frye PH D (Princeton University) *Associate Professor of Political Science*

Julia H. Gaisser PH D (University of Edinburgh) *Associate Professor of Latin*

Mary Summerfield Gardiner PH D (Bryn Mawr College) *Professor Emeritus of Biology*

Richard H. Gaskins PH D JD (Yale University) *Assistant Professor of Philosophy*

Richard C. Gonzalez PH D (University of Maryland) *Professor of Psychology*

Joaquín González-Muela *D en Fil* (University of Madrid) *Professor of Spanish*

Jane C. Goodale PH D (University of Pennsylvania) *Professor of Anthropology*

Robert L. Goodale AB BMUS (Yale University) AA GO *Alice Carter Dickerman Professor of Music*

Norman K. Gottwald PH D (Columbia University) *Visiting Professor of the History of Religion*

Michel Guggenheim PH D (Yale University) *Professor of* French

Nancy L. Hagelgans PH D (Johns Hopkins University) *Lecturer in Mathematics*

Richard Hamilton PH D (University of Michigan) *Associate Professor of Greek* and *of Latin*

E. Jane Hedley PH D (Bryn Mawr College) *Assistant Professor of English*

Howard S. Hoffman PH D (University of Connecticut) *Professor of Psychology**

Wendell P. Holbrook A B (Morgan State College) *Lecturer in History*

Janet L. Hoopes PH D (Bryn Mawr College) *Professor of Education and Child Development* and *Director of the Child Study Institute**

Rosalie C. Hoyt PH D (Bryn Mawr College) *Marion Reilly Professor of Physics‡*

Joshua C. Hubbard PH D (Harvard University) *Professor Emeritus of Economics*

Helen Manning Hunter PH D (Radcliffe College) *Associate Professor of Economics*

Thomas H. Jackson PH D (Yale University) *Associate Professor of English*

C. Stephen Jaeger PH D (University of California) *Associate Professor of German*

Agi Jambor MA (Royal Academy of Budapest) *Professor Emeritus of Music*

Myra Richards Jessen PH D (Bryn Mawr College) *Professor Emeritus of German*

Eileen T. Johnston PH D (University of Chicago) *Assistant Professor of English*

Pauline Jones PH D (Bryn Mawr College) *Professor of* French

Constance Jordan PH D (Yale University) *Andrew W. Mellon Post-Doctoral Fellow* and *Lecturer in English* and *in Comparative Literature*

Richard H. Jordan PH D (University of Minnesota) *Assistant Professor of Anthropology*

Anne Kaier PH D (Harvard University) *Assistant Professor of English*

Anthony R. Kaney PH D (University of Illinois) *Associate Professor of Biology*

Melville T. Kennedy, Jr. PH D (Harvard University) *Professor of Political Science*

Philip L. Kilbride PH D (University of Missouri) *Associate Professor of Anthropology*

Willard F. King PH D (Brown University) *Acting Secretary of the* General *Faculty* and *Dorothy Nepper Marshall Professor of Spanish*

Dale Kinney PH D (New York University) *Assistant Professor of History of Art*‡

George L. Kline PH D (Columbia University) *Professor of Philosophy*

Joseph E. Kramer PH D (Princeton University) *Associate Professor of English*

Michael Krausz PH D (University of Toronto) *Associate Professor of Philosophy*‡

Phyllis S. Lachs PH D (Bryn Mawr College) *Associate Dean of The Graduate School of Arts and Sciences* and *Associate Professor of History*‡

Samuel Tobias Lachs PH D (Dropsie University) *Professor of History of Religion*†

Catherine Lafarge PH D (Yale University) *Associate Professor of French*

Barbara M. Lane PH D (Harvard University) *Professor of History*‡

Mabel L. Lang PH D (Bryn Mawr College) *Paul Shorey Professor of Greek*

Richmond Lattimore PH D (University of Illinois) LITT D *Professor Emeritus of Greek*

Li Way Lee PH D (Columbia University) *Assistant Professor of Economics*

Marguerite Lehr PH D (Bryn Mawr College) *Professor Emeritus of Mathematics*

Gertrude C. K. Leighton AB (Bryn Mawr College) JD (Yale University) *Secretary of the General Faculty* and *Professor of Political Science*‡

Steven Z. Levine PHD (Harvard University) *Assistant Professor of History of Art*

Angeline H. Lograsso PHD (Radcliffe College) *Professor Emeritus of Italian*

Nicholas J. Mackintosh DPHIL (Oxford University) *Katharine E. McBride Visiting Professor of Psychology*

Frank B. Mallory PHD (California Institute of Technology) *Professor of Chemistry*‡

Helen Taft Manning PHD (Yale University) *Professor Emeritus of History*

Mario Maurin PHD (Yale University) *Professor of* French

Ethel W. Maw PHD (University of Pennsylvania) *Professor of Education and Child Development*

Susan E. Maxfield MS (Syracuse University) *Associate Professor of Education and Child Development* and *Director of the Phebe Anna Thorne School*

Clark McCauley, Jr. PHD (University of Pennsylvania) *Associate Professor of Psychology*

Mary Patterson McPherson PHD (Bryn Mawr College) *Dean of the Undergraduate College* and *Associate Professor of Philosophy*

Machteld J. Mellink PHD (University of Utrecht) *Leslie Clark Professor of Classical and Near Eastern Archaeology*

Fritz Mezger PHD (University of Berlin) *Professor Emeritus of Germanic Philology*

Agnes Kirsopp Michels PHD (Bryn Mawr College) *Professor Emeritus of Latin*

Charles Mitchell BLITT (Oxford University) LITTD *Professor of History of Art* and *Andrew W. Mellon Professor of Humanities*

Milton Charles Nahm BLITT (Oxford University) PHD (University of Pennsylvania) *Professor Emeritus of Philosophy*

Annette Niemtzow PHD (Harvard University) *Assistant Professor of English*

Patricia J. Olds-Clarke PHD (Washington University) *Assistant Professor of Biology*‡

Jane M. Oppenheimer PHD (Yale University) *William R. Kenan, Jr. Professor of History of Science*

Kathryn Z. Orkwiszewski PHD (Bryn Mawr College) *Lecturer in Biology*

John C. Oxtoby MA (University of California) *Class of 1897 Professor of Mathematics*

George S. Pahomov PH D (New York University) *Assistant Professor of Russian‡*

Aigli Papantonopoulou PHD (University of California) *Lecturer in Mathematics*

Nicholas Patruno PH D (Rutgers University) *Assistant Professor of Italian*

Eleanor K. Paucker PH D (University of Pennsylvania) *Associate Professor of Spanish*

Ruth L. Pearce PH D (University of Pennsylvania) *Associate Professor of Russian*

Emmy A. Pepitone PH D (University of Michigan) *Associate Professor of Education and Child Development*

Kyle M. Phillips, Jr. PH D (Princeton University) *Professor of Classical and Near Eastern Archaeology* and *Resident Director of Massenzia, Rome*

Gloria F. Pinney PHD (University of Cincinnati) *Lecturer in Classical and Near Eastern Archaeology*

Lucian B. Platt PH D (Yale University) *Associate Professor of Geology*

Stephen Poppel PH D (Harvard University) *Assistant Professor of History*

Judith R. Porter PH D (Harvard University) *Associate Professor of Sociology*

Jean A. Potter PH D (Yale University) *Professor of Philosophy*

Alice S. Powers PH D (Bryn Mawr College) *Lecturer in Psychology*

David J. Prescott PH D (University of Pennsylvania) *Associate Professor of Biology*

John R. Pruett PH D (Indiana University) *Professor of Physics*

Patricia Onderdonk Pruett PH D (Bryn Mawr College) *Associate Dean of the Undergraduate College* and *Lecturer in Biology*

Brunilde S. Ridgway PH D (Bryn Mawr College) *Professor of Classical and Near Eastern Archaeology†*

Caroline Robbins PH D (University of London) LITT D LLD *Professor Emeritus of History*

Marc H. Ross PH D (Northwestern University) *Associate Professor of Political Science‡*

Fred Rothbaum PH D (Yale University) *Assistant Professor of Education and Child Development*

Enrique Sacerio-Garí MPHIL (Yale University) *Lecturer in Spanish*

Stephen Salkever PH D (University of Chicago) *Associate Professor of Political Science‡*

J. H. M. Salmon LITT D (Victoria University) *Marjorie Walter Goodhart Professor of History*

W. Bruce Saunders PH D (University of Iowa) *Associate Professor of Geology**

Grace Armstrong Savage PH D (Princeton University) *Assistant Professor of French‡*

Carl B. Schmidt PH D (Harvard University) *Assistant Professor of Music*

Eugene V. Schneider PH D (Harvard University) *Professor of Sociology*

Françoise Schremmer PH D (University of Pennsylvania) *Assistant Professor of Mathematics‡*

Russell T. Scott PH D (Yale University) *Associate Professor of Latin*

Judith R. Shapiro PH D (Columbia University) *Assistant Professor of Anthropology*

Alain Silvera PH D (Harvard University) *Professor of History‡*

Stephen R. Smith PH D (Massachusetts Institute of Technology) *Assistant Professor of Physics*

James E. Snyder MFA PH D (Princeton University) *Professor of History of Art*

Samuel S. Snyder PH D (Yale University) *Assistant Professor of Education and Child Development*

Faye P. Soffen ED D (University of Pennsylvania) *Associate Professor of Education and Child Development*

Thomas Song MA MALS (University of Michigan) *Associate Director of Libraries* and *Lecturer in Philosophy*

Arthur Colby Sprague PH D (Harvard University) *Professor Emeritus of English Literature*

K. Laurence Stapleton AB (Smith College) *Mary E. Garrett Alumnae Professor of English Literature**

Kenneth G. Strothkamp PH D (Columbia University) *Assistant Professor of Chemistry*

Isabel Scribner Stearns PH D (Bryn Mawr College) *Professor of Philosophy*

Larry Stein PH D (University of Iowa) *Lecturer in Psychology*

George C. Stephens PH D (Lehigh University) *Assistant Professor of Geology*

Tracy M. Taft PH D (State University of New York at Buffalo) *Assistant Professor of Philosophy*

James Tanis TH D (University of Utrecht) *Director of Libraries* and *Professor of History*

Earl Thomas PH D (Yale University) *Associate Professor of Psychology*

Stephen E. Toulmin PH D (Cambridge University) *Mary Flexner Lecturer in History and Philosophy of Science*

Steven N. Treistman PH D (University of North Carolina) *Assistant Professor of Biology*

Myra L. Uhlfelder PH D (Bryn Mawr College) *Professor of Latin*

Joseph Varimbi PH D (University of Pennsylvania) *Secretary of the Faculty of Arts and Sciences* and *Associate Professor of Chemistry*

Lynn Visson PH D (Harvard University) *Assistant Professor of Russian*

Jill T. Wannemacher PH D (Brown University) *Assistant Professor of Psychology on the Rosalyn R. Schwartz Lectureship*‡

Robert E. Washington PH D (University of Chicago) *Assistant Professor of Sociology*

George E. Weaver, Jr. PH D (University of Pennsylvania) *Associate Professor of Philosophy**

Roger Hewes Wells PH D (Harvard University) *Professor Emeritus of Political Science*

Harris L. Wofford, Jr. AB (University of Chicago) J D (Howard University and Yale University) *President of the College*

Mary Katharine Woodworth PH D (Bryn Mawr College) *Professor Emeritus of English*

Dorothy Wyckoff PH D (Bryn Mawr College) *Professor Emeritus of Geology*

Matthew Yarczower PH D (University of Maryland) *Professor of Psychology*

George L. Zimmerman PH D (University of Chicago) *Professor of Chemistry*

Officers of Administration

Dolores E. Brien PH D (Brown University) *Director of Career Planning*

Merle Broberg PH D (The American University) *Associate Dean of The Graduate School of Social Work and Social Research*

Margaret M. Healy PHD (Bryn Mawr College) *Director of the Ad Hoc Committee of the Board on the Financing of the College*

Joseph S. Johnston, Jr. MA (University of Chicago) *Assistant to the President*

Paul W. Klug CPA BS (Temple University) *Comptroller* and *Business Manager of the College*

Ramona L. Livingston AB (William Jewell College) *Advisor to Foreign Students* and *Lecturer in English*

Margaret G. McKenna AB (Bryn Mawr College) *Personnel Administrator*

Samuel J. McNamee BS (Temple University) *Assistant Comptroller*

Julie E. Painter AB (Bryn Mawr College) *Administrator of Records and Financial Aid*

Martha Stokes Price AB (Bryn Mawr College) *Director of Resources*

Patricia Onderdonk Pruett PH D (Bryn Mawr College) *Associate Dean of the Undergraduate College*

Ellen Fernon Reisner MA (Bryn Mawr College) *Assistant to the President* and *Acting Director of Public Information*

Thomas N. Trucks BS (Villanova University) *Superintendent of Buildings and Grounds*

Sarah E. Wright *Director of Halls*

Health

Frieda W. Woodruff M D (University of Pennsylvania) *College Physician*

Eileen A. Bazelon MD (Medical College of Pennsylvania) *Consulting Psychiatrist*

Anne Lee Delano MA (Columbia University) *Director of Physical Education*

Mary Geiger MD (State University of New York at Albany) *Consulting Psychiatrist*

John F. Howkins MD (Columbia University, College of Physicians and Surgeons) *Consulting Psychiatrist*

Howard B. Smith MD (Jefferson Medical College) *Consulting Psychiatrist*

Margaret S. Temeles MD (Tufts University School of Medicine) *Consulting Psychiatrist*

Librarians

James Tanis THD (University of Utrecht) *Director of Libraries*

Thomas Song MA MALS (University of Michigan) *Associate Direc-tor of Libraries*

Zoe M. Bemis (Washington University, Yale University) *Reference Librarian*

Leo M. Dolenski MA (Catholic University of America) MLS (Drexel University) *Manuscripts Librarian*

John Dooley MLS (McGill University) *Bibliographer and Reference Librarian*

Florence D. Goff MA MSLS (Villanova University) *Cataloging Librarian*

Karen K. Helm M.S.L.S. (Villanova University) *Rare Book Cataloger*

John Jaffe MA MSLS (Villanova University) *Acquisitions Librarian*

Mary S. Leahy MA (Bryn Mawr College) *Rare Book Librarian*

Eileen Markson MA (New York University) MLS (Queens College of City University of New York) *Head, Art and Archaeology Library*

Catherine E. Pabst MA (University of Wisconsin) MSLS (Drexel University) *Head, Acquisitions Department*

Gertrude Reed MSLS (Rutgers University) *Head, Reference Division and Archivist*

Pamela G. Reilly MSLS (Drexel University) *Head, Public Services Department*

Penelope Schwind MSLS (Drexel University) *Head, Cataloging Department*

Barbara F. Siegel MSLS (Drexel University) *Serials Librarian*

Arleen Speizman MSLS (Drexel University) *Cataloging Librarian*

Ethel W. Whetstone ABLS (University of North Carolina) *Head, Sciences and Social Sciences Libraries*

Child Study Institute

Janet L. Hoopes PH D (Bryn Mawr College) *Director*

Anne D. Emmons MS (University of Pennsylvania) *Director, Remedial Reading Service*

Beatrice Schneider MSW (Western Reserve University) *Administrative Assistant*

Isabel Westfried MA (Bryn Mawr College) *Chief Psychologist*

Phebe Anna Thorne School

Susan E. Maxfield MS (Syracuse University) *Director*

The Council of The Graduate School of Arts and Sciences

Dean Bober, *Chairman*
President Wofford *ex officio*
Mr. Berliner
Mr. Burlin
Mr. Conner
Mr. Dempsey
Mrs. Foster
Mr. Kennedy
Mrs. King
Dean Lachs
Mrs. Pepitone
Mr. Scott

Committee on Graduate Awards

Dean Lachs, *Chairman*
President Wofford *ex officio*
Dean Bober
Mrs. Crawford
Mr. Kramer
Miss Lafarge

Index

Academic Departments	3
Adelman Collection	9
Administrative Officers	107
Admission, to The Graduate	
School of Arts and Sciences	6
to Graduate Courses	8
Anthropology	16
Application for Admission	6
for Financial Aid	7
for Residence	93
Archaeology, Classical and	
Near Eastern	27
Art, History of	55
Assistantships	89
Avignon, Summer Institute	12
Awards, Academic	85
Awards, Graduate,	
Committee on	109
Biochemistry	19
Biology	20
Board of Trustees	96
Boyce Collection, Aline A.	9
Calendar for the	
Academic Year	4-5
Canaday Collection, Ward M.	10
Career Planning Office	92
Castle Collection	9
Centro de Estudios	
Hispánicos	12
Chemistry	23
Child Care Center	95
Child Study Institute	34
Child Study Institute Staff	109
Classical and Near Eastern	
Archaeology	27
Committees of Board of	
Trustees	97
Computer Center	10
Continuing Enrollment	8
Council of The Graduate	
School of Arts and Sciences	109
Courses	16-80
Curtis Collection, Densmore	9
Defense Mapping Agency Maps	10
Degree Candidacy	8
Degree Requirements	13-15
Dillingham Collection	9
Directions to the College	112
Doctor of Philosophy, Degree	13
Duties of Fellows and Scholars	89
Economics	30
Education and Child	
Development	32
Employment	92
English	36
Equality of Opportunity	12

Excavations	
Exclusion from the College	
Expenses	
Faculty	
Family Educational Rights	
and Privacy Act of 1974	
Fees	
Fellowships	
Financial Aid	
Foreign Students, Application	
Financial Aid	
Scholarships	
French	
Geology	
German	
Goldman Collection, Hetty	
Goodhart, Marjorie Walter,	
Mediaeval Library	
Gordan, John D., Reference	
Center	
Graduate Prizes	
Graduate Record Examinations	
Graduate Residence Center	
Graduate Student Council	
Greek	
Health	
Health Staff	
History	
History and Philosophy of	
Science	
History of Art	
History of Religion	
Housing	
Infirmary	
Institut d' Etudes Françaises	
d' Avignon	
Insurance, Health	
Italian	
King Collection, Elisabeth W.	
Laboratories	
Language Requirements	
Latin	
Libraries	
Library Staff	
Loan Funds	
Madrid, Summer Institute	
Master of Arts, Degree	
Mathematics	
Mediaeval Studies	
Music	
Officers	
Administrative	

Board of Trustees 96
Opportunity, Equality of 12

Phebe Anna Thorne School 33
Philosophy 65
Philosophy of Science 53
Physical Examination 94
Physics 67
Plan for Coordination in
  the Sciences 10, 87
Political Science 71
Program of Study 11, 16
Psychology 73

Rand Collection, Theodore 10
Rare Book Room 9
Reciprocal Plan, University
  of Pennsylvania 11
Registration 8
Riegel Museum, Ella 9
Religion, History of 57
Requirements for Admission 6
  for Degrees 13-15
Residence Center 93
Resources for Graduate Work 9
Russian 75

Scholarships 84, 88
Science Center 10
Sciences, Plan for
  Coordination in 10, 87
Seminars and Courses 16
Social Work and Social Research,
  Graduate School of 3, 22
Sociology 77
Spanish 79
Staff, Academic and
  Administrative 98
Student Employment 92
Summer Work 12

Teaching Certification 33
Trustees 96
Tuition 81
Tuition Grants 90
Tuition Scholarships 84, 88

University of Pennsylvania,
  Reciprocal Plan 11
U.S. Geological Survey Maps 10

Vaux Collection, George Jr. 10

111

Directions to Bryn Mawr College

By automobile from the East or Southeast take the Walt Whitman Bridge to I-676/Schuylkill Expressway and follow this north until it meets with I-76; *or* take the Benjamin Franklin Bridge to I-76/Vine Street until it meets with I-676. In either case, continue north on I-76 to Exit 41, "City Ave.—U.S. 1 South." Proceed south on City Ave./U.S. 1 for 1.1 miles from the exit ramp and then turn right on Conshohocken State Road (PA 23). (There is a shopping center on the right shortly before this turn.) After three-tenths of a mile, Conshohocken State Road makes a sharp turn to the left over a railroad overpass and comes to a traffic light. Continue straight through this intersection; you are now on Montgomery Avenue, which you follow for about five miles (bearing right at a fork at about the three mile point), to Morris Avenue in the town of Bryn Mawr. Harcum Junior College will be on the left shortly before Morris Avenue. Turn right onto Morris Avenue, proceed to the next traffic light and then turn left onto New Gulph Road for approximately 1½ blocks. Visitors may use the College parking lot, entering at Merion Gate, which is directly opposite 815 New Gulph Road. The parking lot on Morris Avenue also may be used by visitors.

By automobile from the South take I-95 through Wilmington, Delaware, to Chester, Pennsylvania, then take the exit marked "PA 352—Edgemont Ave." (It is also marked with a sign for "Chester Business District.") Immediately look for, and follow, signs for PA 320 North. Continue north on PA 320 for approximately 10.5 miles from the I-95 exit, until you come to Bryn Mawr Avenue. (This is about two miles after you cross PA 3, and has a traffic light.) Turn right, and follow Bryn Mawr Avenue for approximately two miles until you come to a traffic light at Haverford Road. Continue on Bryn Mawr Avenue, which bears slightly to the left, until you come to Lancaster Avenue in the town of Bryn Mawr. (This is the second traffic light after Haverford Road.) Turn right on Lancaster Avenue for one block, and then left at the first traffic light onto Morris Avenue. Follow the road, which will curve under the railroad tracks, until you come to the traffic light at Montgomery Avenue. Proceed across Montgomery Avenue to the next traffic light. Turn left on to New Gulph Road for approximately 1½ blocks. Visitors may use the College parking lot, entering at Merion Gate, which is directly opposite 815 New Gulph Road. The parking lot on Morris Avenue also may be used by visitors.

By automobile from the West, North or Northeast take the Pennsylvania Turnpike to the Valley Forge Exit (24). From the Valley Forge Exit of the Turnpike, take the Schuylkill Expressway (I-76) east, turning off at Exit 36, "PA 320, Gulph Mills," which is 3.5 miles from the toll gate. Follow PA 320 south for approximately four-tenths of a mile and turn left at the first traffic light onto Old Gulph Road. Proceed on this for approximately three miles, and the College will be on your right. The College parking lot is the third entrance on the right after Roberts Road.

Lightning Source UK Ltd.
Milton Keynes UK
UKHW011235310119
336488UK00006B/444/P